enigma
books

Also published by Enigma Books

---

*Hitler's Table Talk 1941-1944*
Hugh Trevor-Roper, ed.

*In Stalin's Secret Service*
W. G. Krivitsky

*Hitler and Mussolini: The Secret Meetings*
Santi Corvaja

*The Jews in Fascist Italy: A History*
Renzo De Felice

*The Man Behind the Rosenbergs*
Alexander Feklisov and Sergei Kostin

*Roosevelt and Hopkins: An Intimate History*
Robert E. Sherwood

*Diary 1937-1943*
Galeazzo Ciano

*The Battle of the Casbah:*
*Terrorism and Counter-Terrorism in Algeria 1955-1957*
General Paul Aussaresses

*Secret Affairs:*
*FDR, Cordell Hull, and Sumner Welles*
Irwin F. Gellman

*Hitler and His Generals:*
*Military Conferences 1942-1945*
Helmut Heiber & David M. Glantz, Eds.

*The Secret Front:*
*Nazi Political Espionage 1938-1945*
Wilhelm Höttl

Arno Lustiger

# Stalin and the Jews

## The Red Book

**The Tragedy of the Jewish Anti-Fascist Committee
and the Soviet Jews**

**Introduction by Roman Brackman
Foreword by Yefim Etkind**

enigma books

## enigma Books

580 Eighth Avenue, New York, NY 10018
www.enigmabooks.com

Published by arrangement with
Aufbau Verlag GmbH - All rights reserved.
©1999 Aufbau

First English-language Edition
First Printing
Printed in the United States of America
Translated by Mary Beth Friedrich and Todd Bludeau

ISBN 1-929631-10-3

Library of Congress Cataloging-in-Publication Data

Lustiger, Arno.
[Rotbuch.]
Stalin and the Jews : the red book : the tragedy of the Jewish Anti-Fascist
Committee and the Soviet Jews / Arno Lustiger ; translated by Mary
Beth Friedrich and Todd Bludeau ; [foreword by Yefim Etkind].—— 1st
English-language ed.

p. : ill. ; cm.

Includes bibliographical references and index.

ISBN: 1-929631-10-3

1. Evreiskii antifashistskii komitet v SSSR—History. 2. Jews—Soviet
Union—History. 3. Jews—Persecutions—Soviet Union. 4. Jews—
Soviet Union—Biography. 5. Soviet Union—Ethnic relations.
I. Friedrich, Mary Beth. II. Bludeau, Todd. III. Etkind, Yefim. IV. Title.
V. Title: Rotbuch. VI. Title: Stalin & the Jews VII. Title: Red book

DS135.R92 L87 2003
947/.004924

# Stalin and the Jews

# CONTENTS

Part II
JANUS-FACED LIBERATION:
THE JEWISH ASCENT AFTER THE OCTOBER REVOLUTION

Part III
PREHISTORY AND FOUNDATION OF THE JAFC

# Stalin and the Jews

Part VI

OPEN WAR AGAINST THE JEWS—
THE LAST YEARS OF STALIN'S DICTATORSHIP

Part VII
THE TRIAL

## Part IX

## THE PEOPLE

# INTRODUCTION

*by Roman Brackman*

Arno Lustiger has done more than offer the most exhaustive, indeed encyclopedic account of the monumental tragedy that befell the Soviet Jews during the rule of Joseph Stalin. He saved them from a second death and destruction through the failure of posterity to honor their memory. Arno Lustiger's book is the most valuable depository of facts ensuring that this memory will not vanish.

The book presents a panoramic view of Jewish history during the Tsarist and Soviet period. Arno Lustiger brings to light the role played by many Jewish leaders in the revolutionary movement before the Bolshevik "October Revolution" and the enthusiastic support given by Jewish communists to what they viewed as Soviet support for the advancement of Jewish culture. The author painstakingly follows the expressions of anti-Semitic tendencies throughout Soviet policies as steadily carried out during Stalin's rule of terror, most prominently during the 1930s.

The book sheds light on Stalin's two major provocations—the scheme of the Crimean Jewish Autonomous Republic, or as the author put it, "The Crimea—A Soviet Palestine?" and the Jewish Autonomous Region in Birobidzhan. The fate of the Jews following the German-Soviet Pact of 1939, the partition of Poland and the start of the Second World War is carefully described. The author, a survivor of several German concentration camps, recounts the mass deportations of Jews and others from Soviet occupied Poland, from Lithuania, Latvia, Estonia, and the elimination of Jewish culture in the occupied countries. For the first time Arno Lustiger writes that among the Polish prisoners of war murdered by the Soviets at the Katyn forest and other execution grounds there were many Jewish officers.

The author reconstructs in great detail the tragic history of the Jewish Anti-Fascist Committee, the arrests and interrogations of the original founders of the JAFC, Henryk Erlich and Victor Alter, and their eventual murders. He details the role of the JAFC in the war against Nazi Germany, the fund-raising trips of Mikhoels and Fefer to the United States, the murder of Solomon Mikhoels, as well as the tragic trial of the JAFC. The author examines the "Crimean case" and the execution of Jewish defendants in August 1952 and the "The Kremlin doctors conspiracy case" in 1953 as the major provocations of the last years of Stalin's life. An important part of the book is devoted to the persecution and trials of Jews in Eastern Europe—the Slansky Trial, and the planned trials in Poland and East Berlin.

Arno Lustiger's very important contribution to the search for historical truth is his account of the last days of Stalin's life when the dictator allegedly planned the extermination of Soviet Jews through a mass exile to Siberia and to their death. Prof. Benjamin Pincus writes in his book, *The Jews of the Soviet Union* (New York 1988) that "Stalin saw in the Jewish doctors' trial a way to prepare the ground for exiling the Jewish population from the center of the Soviet Union."

Stalin intended to have this mass murder begin during the Jewish holy day of Purim, which in 1953 began on the night of February 28. But on that night Stalin had a stroke, which paralyzed him. He died, or was poisoned, on March 5, 1953. His death allowed Lavrenti Beria to put an end to the plan for the exile of the Jews and release the Kremlin doctors from Lubyanka prison. This "Averted Catastrophe" has been consistently denied by all of Stalin's heirs. The Soviet leaders, including Gorbachev, always denied the existence of anti-Semitism in the Soviet Union.

Gennadi V. Kostyrchenko, the Russian author of the recently published and very informative book about Stalin's anti-Semitism, denied the existence of Stalin's plan to exile the Jews to Siberia. He blamed the "widely circulated propaganda myth about the purported deportation of the Jews about to take place at the end of Stalin's life" for the mass exodus of Soviet Jews. To substantiate his denial Kostyrchenko states, "even such a furious critic of Stalin as Khrushchev did no mention this plan in his memoirs." He also writes:

The fear of an unpredictable future, the total crisis of the Gorbachev regime that developed parallel to the spontaneous liberalization, led to the "explosion" of Jewish emigration from the USSR. In only one year, 1990, 186,000 Jews left the country. This was indeed a mass flight of people from the country, which was disintegrating before their eyes. The impressive exodus was also due to the fact that the World Zionist organization and the State of Israel then viewed as their main goal the radical liberation of all of Soviet Jewry from the "captivity of the Red Pharaoh" and assisted it with all their power. It was not by accident that precisely at that time began the widely circulated propaganda myth about a purported deportation of the Jews about to take place at the end of Stalin's life.

Stalin's plan to deport the Jews has been denied by Soviet leaders who for decades after Stalin's death covered it up and destroyed much of the related documents. Despite the persistent denial of the Stalin deportation plan of Soviet Jews by Soviet and Russian leaders, the visceral knowledge of the plan's existence was a factor in the mass exodus of Soviet Jews that started in the late 1960s and early 1970s.

Since the collapse of the Soviet Union, Soviet and then Russian leaders toned down their anti-Zionist and anti-Israeli rhetoric while disguising their anti-Semitism by championing the "Palestinian rights." They compensate their denial of Stalin's planned atrocity by allowing some measure of revival of Jewish cultural life in Russia and a few authors even published some books in Yiddish. For instance the book by the late author Nathan Zabara, who had been persecuted during Stalin's rule and whose manuscript had been confiscated at that time, was published in Yiddish, but by now there are fewer Jews remaining in Russia and many of them could not read Yiddish. It was reported that President Vladimir Putin went so far as to treat the visiting Israeli president to a dinner prepared in the "Kremlin's kosher kitchen." This particular report might have made the previous Kremlin masters, especially Tsar Ivan the Terrible and Stalin himself, to roll over in their graves in anguish and disgust.

----

ROMAN BRACKMAN obtained his Ph.D. from New York University. A native of Moscow, he grew up during the Great Purges. As a 19-year-old student at the Moscow Oriental Institute, he was arrested and imprisoned for "anti-Soviet activities," and for his attempt to escape from the Soviet Union across the Soviet-Turkish border. He survived Stalin's Special Regime Norilsk Prison Camps in Siberia, where he took an active part in the prisoners' uprising in the summer of 1953. Indeed, his research into Stalin's career started in the gulag, where he gathered the recollections and insights of fellow prisoners. After being released in the first post-Stalin amnesty, he left Russia in 1959 and went to live in the United States. For many years he maintained contacts with dissidents in the former Soviet Union, many of whom were his prison camp friends. Throughout all those years he continued to work on the research for his book, *The Secret File of Joseph Stalin. A Hidden Life* (London 2001).

# FOREWORD

*by Yefim Etkind*

## "It really was like this."

This is the title of a book that tells the fate of the Jews in Soviet Russia.[1] I find it highly emotional and, at the same time, extremely accurate. "It really was like this," I repeat with astonishment horror, disgust, and terror when I recall what Arno Lustiger recounts in such a detailed and epic way. I experienced some of these events myself. I mean that the author of the *Red Book* makes a heroic attempt to tell the impossible, the unspeakable, and the heartwrenching.

It is not easy to take the role of the historian and examine events with overwhelming calmness. It is even harder to find the necessary words, when instead one really wants to scream, to curse, to cry, to moan.

Arno Lustiger, who appears in the role of historian with this book about the Jews and Stalin, is both a contemporary and a witness. He knows the story of the Polish, Russian and German "Brider un Shvester" (brothers and sisters) first-hand. To him Auschwitz and Buchenwald are neither abstract concepts nor Holocaust museums. He spent his youth there. It is a miracle he lived through them.

A few years ago, Itzhak Katsenelson's splendid poem *Dos lied vunem oysgehargetn yidishn folk—Grosser Gesang vom ausgerotteten jüdischen Volk* was published. Arno Lustiger inspired Wolf Biermann to write a German version of this poem and created the phonetic transcript from the Yiddish original. The poem came into being in the concentration camp between the end of 1943 and the beginning of 1944. The poet was executed on May 1, 1944 in Auschwitz. In the thirteenth canto of the poem, in which Katsenelson reports on the revolt in the Warsaw ghetto, he reveals that one of the leaders of the uprising, Itzhak Zuckermann, urges him, the poet, to survive, so that he can report the truth to later generations:

He shouts to one of the fighters: "Go immediately and find a bunker in the yard and bring them there!" *Them* refers to Katsenelson and his son Zvi.)

The poet managed to stay alive a few more months, during which time he created his *Grosser Gesang* (Great Canto). Arno Lustiger did not share the fate of his favorite poet but survived the Shoah and has since then repeatedly told the story of the tragedy of the Jews, the resistance against the war and fascism. Lustiger dedicated his life, which was saved, to refuting the lie that the Jews went passively like helpless calves to their deaths in the gas chambers. Itzhak Katsenelson echoes the mourning lament of a few Polish Jews:

What a people! Allowing itself to be led like a herd of calves/To the slaughter block, what a people! The heads shook:/Pain to such a folk, it must be removed from this earth/be destroyed, because it cannot save itself...![2]

Possibly Katsenelson knew the "Hitler chorales" of Brecht, in which the same is said ironically:

Order you your ways
O calf, so often injured
The most sincere care
From the one who sharpens the knife!
From those who skin them
Thought out a new cross
This one will also find ways
How he can slaughter you.

No, it was never like that, says Arno Lustiger: "To us, the survivors of the Holocaust, the accusations of passivity are especially painful. For those who tried to protect their moral independence and assert themselves throughout all the darkness of a life in the underground and the concentration camp, and by doing so, shorten their potential life expectancy dramatically, such accusations are deeply insulting. ...Besides the armed resistance, which could be practiced on rare occasions only, numerous Jews constantly performed civil, passive and mental resistance. Every survivor is a witness to this resistance..."[3]

Lustiger quotes from the hymn of the Jewish partisans, which was written by the Yiddish poet Glik, who died in 1944 in Estonia, "with his weapon in his hands":

> Wherever a drop of blood falls from us
> There grows our strength and courage

The fate of the Jews in Russia and of the other republics of the former USSR is tragic in a different way than that of the victims of the Nazis (many of whom naturally existed in the USSR). Arno Lustiger shows in his *Red Book*, that the Jews did not act according to the words of the biblical prophet: "And I was like an innocent lamb that was led to the slaughter block and had not noticed what they planned against me." (Jeremiah 11:19.) Lustiger mentions with pride the large number of Jews who fought in the Second World War on the side of the Red Army (over 500,000) and who were decorated for their bravery: "The accomplishments of the Jews in the war were far greater than their numerical lot asserts. Jewish soldiers received 160,772 medals and tokens of distinction between 1941 and 1945, ranking them fourth among all the Soviet nationalities." During the war the outstanding military service of the Jews was valued, but at the war's conclusion the leaders of the party and state tried in every way possible to keep this heroism secret. They wanted it to be forgotten that many generals and "Heroes of the Soviet Union" (the absolute highest award of the Red Army) were of Jewish origin, and that the two journalists and writers whose articles and even novels had a very special meaning for the fighting troops, Ilya Ehrenburg and Vassily Grossman (both were on active duty during the war and their lives were in constant danger), were Jews. I personally served as lieutenant in Karelia, in the north. Our army commander (26th Army) was General Lev Skvirsky, a Jew, whom all soldiers and officers honored because of his determination, helpfulness, and bravery.

The anti-Semitism of the communist leadership in the postwar years—mainly in the last years of Stalin's reign (1948-1953)—was especially malevolent. In the mid-1930s and before the beginning of the terror of 1937-38, we Russian-Jewish intellectuals were passionate supporters of the communist regime. Today most representatives of the new generation cannot grasp this: why did you not see the bloody crimes of the Soviets? To understand the view of my contemporaries, we try to remember the position of the Jews in 1935, both in Soviet Russia and in Nazi Germany.

In 1935 many Jewish schools and publishers existed in the Soviet Union, as did numerous Yiddish-language newspapers and magazines, and there were good Jewish theaters in Moscow, Baku, Kiev, and Minsk. The Moscow theater GOSSET was especially famous, led by the exceptionally great actor, Solomon Mikhoels, who had already achieved worldwide acclaim for his interpretation of Benjamin (*The Journey of Benjamin III*, by Mendele Moikher Sforim) and Tevje (*Tevje the Milkman*, by Sholem Aleichem). The culture of the Russian Jews blossomed in all fields, supported by the Soviet state, which claimed internationalism as its ideological foundation. In the same year the Jewish Autonomous Region in Birobidzan was established. The propaganda praised "life there as a harmonious symbiosis of all nationalities…The Birobidzan Jews were shown to be a part of the Soviet people's family that, under the protection of their father Stalin, could not know any more discrimination."[4]

This is how things were in the USSR. In the same year, 1935, a totally different drama took place in Nazi Germany. The citizens of Soviet Russia did not know much about it, but enough to be able to imagine the German nightmare. In order to understand the situation of the Jews in 1935, here are a few notes from the diary of Victor Klemperer, a German professor of Jewish origin. Klemperer writes about the vote in the Saarland, where more than 90 percent voted in favor of Germany: "In the Reich too 90 percent want the Führer, and servitude and the death of scholarship, of thought, of the spirit of the Jews" (January 16, p. 109). "The Jew-baiting and the pogrom atmosphere grow day by day (…) Goebbels' speeches ("Exterminate like fleas and bedbugs!")…" (July 21, p. 128). "The Jew-baiting has become so extreme, far worse than during the first boycott, there are beginnings of a pogrom exist here and there and we expect to be beaten to death at any moment." (August 11, p. 130). "The Jew-baiting gets even worse (…) even crazier." (September 15, p. 131). "I have the impression that an explosion is imminent, I am reckoning on a pogrom, the ghetto, money and house to be taken away, anything. (…) I wait gloomy and helpless" (September 29, p. 134). In September 1935, the laws "on German blood and German honor": Prison for marriage and extramarital intercourse between Jews and "Germans," prohibition on "German" maids under 45 years of age (...) Withdrawal of civil rights. (...) Disgust makes one ill" (September 17, p. 133).[5]

In the same year, 1935, right at the time that in Germany "the harassment of the Jews became excessive," King Lear was performed at the GOSSET. All of Moscow, later all of Leningrad and all of Europe, admired the performance. Yiddish became the language of Shakespeare.

But first I should digress. I was thirteen years old when my father took me with him from Leningrad to Moscow and brought me to one of his friends, who had the very curious name of Mikhoels, Solomon Mikhoels. I only knew that Solomon was a distant relative and a man of the theater. When I saw him I was astonished—how could such an ape be an actor? All well-known actors, or so I thought, must be handsome men. Solomon was short with an ugly hanging lower lip, and he spoke loudly and carelessly. He hardly noticed me. A while later I saw him as King Lear, and I was shocked to see this peculiar and ugly face able to express the strongest passions and deepest emotions. His hoarse voice sounded tragic and soft, angry and severe. This short man was majestic, and the Yiddish that I sometimes had heard spoken at home, and that seemed to be only a parody of the German language, was the poetic, lofty language of Shakespeare. Suddenly I saw Solomon Mikhoels in a different light: he was a genius as a tragic actor. His constant companion, the fool, acted by Benjamin Zuskin, was a grotesque but also a tragic figure. The jokes of the fool evoked loud laughter, but this laughter could change easily into sobs. Both were unforgettable and in their polarity insepa-rable. Since then I have seen several Shakespearean tragedies in many countries, but nothing impressed me more than the Jewish Lear and his pendant, the Jewish fool.

> Master, anyone who serves you for property and money
> and only obeys for appearance
> packs it in as soon as rain falls,
> leaves you alone in the storm...(II, 4)

So sang the fool. His gestures were comical, but expressed love and sorrow. I still hear the last words of the dying king:

And dead, you poor little fool? — No? No life? —
A dog, a horse, a mouse should have life,
And you not one breath? — O, you will
not return ever, ever, ever, ever, ever...never again.

Much later I found out how both had died. Mikhoels was murdered
on Stalin's orders in Minsk in 1948; Zuskin was shot in Moscow a few
years later, after suffering long interrogations and inhuman torture. Both
were accused of Jewish nationalism: They spoke Yiddish and they performed Shakespeare's and Sholem Aleichem's plays in Yiddish. Was that
not reason enough to be sentenced to death by a socialist tribunal?

Is this fundamental change not incredible? Jewish publishing houses,
schools, theaters, and newspapers in Yiddish received applause on all levels in 1935; in 1948-1952, poets writing in Yiddish, Yiddish-speaking actors, and professors lecturing in Yiddish were being arrested and executed.
How was this reversal, this transition from "internationalism" to the
bloodiest persecution of Jews, from a seemingly humane patronage by
the socialist state to wild Nazism, possible? The state, the party—everything—stayed the same; nothing had changed. What had been encouraged and praised a few years ago had now become a great crime. Not so
long ago the poets Markish, Bergelson, Kvitko, and Fefer, and the actors
Mikhoels, Zuskin and many more, had been decorated with the highest
honors of the state; now they were "discovered" to be traitors. Mikhoels
was murdered, the others tortured and shot.

Arno Lustiger's book attempts to answer these questions. Lustiger did
everything conceivable to solve this puzzle. Numerous documents have
recently been published. Stalin's daughter, Svetlana, reported on some of
the things which before we could only conjecture. About her father she
wrote, "His anti-Semitism surely originated from the long years of struggle
with Trotsky and his supporters. What was originally political hate gradually became a feeling of racial hatred against all Jews, without exception."[6]
Racial hatred, said the daughter. This evidence is extremely important and
today there exist numerous scholarly documents concerning this subject.[7]

Yet the instruments of the totalitarian regime, not the personal opinion of the tyrants, are decisive. For both dictators, Stalin and Hitler, only
one thing was of any importance: to maintain absolute power.

Until the war's outbreak Stalin was sure that communist slogans would
be enough to keep him in control. He acted the role of Hitler's adversary
(even though he secretly admired him), the role of adherent to the ideals

of internationalism, and the role of leader of all anti-fascists and anti-racists in the world. Yet, by the beginning of the war, it had already become clear that German fanaticism was stronger than communist rhetoric. Nationalism had a deeper impact on the masses than the Soviet propaganda of the so-called people's friendship. As a result, Stalin changed his political tactics. In wartime the newspapers no longer mentioned socialist accomplishments but instead praised the merits of the Russian nation and glorified the work of the Orthodox Church, which until then had been condemned. It was during this period that the first restrictions and prohibitions on Jews were imposed. Jews were not allowed to hold any position in the diplomatic corps; subsequently they were prohibited from holding any important political offices at all.

Little by little these prohibitions covered all areas of social life. Outwardly, though, everything still appeared socialist, which is why the term "Jew prohibition" was never used publicly. The Jews were expelled from all universities and scientific institutes, not as Jews but as "cosmopolitans" and "rootless anti-patriots," and later as "Zionists" and "bourgeois nationalists." This insanity reached its apogee in 1948, when the entire leadership of the Jewish Anti-Fascist Committee was arrested. Three years later they were shot. Finally, the only accusation left was Yiddish, the "language of nationalists." The famous lyrical writer, Leib Kvitko, was beaten and tortured in the basements of the secret police, until he confessed and gave a declaration during his trial (1952), in which he denied his whole life and work as a writer. "The use of a language that the masses had given up," said Kvitko, "that had already left its history behind, that not only isolates us from life in the Soviet Union but also isolates the larger number of Jews outside, who already have been assimilated, is in my opinion a special form of nationalism. As for the rest, I have no feeling of guilt."

It was an absurd confession, but it was enough to have him shot on August 12, 1952, along with the twelve other members of the Jewish Anti-Fascist Committee.

What did Stalin want? What did the Communist Party of the Soviet Union want to accomplish with these senseless murders? Did they want the whole Jewish population of the USSR to be deported or maybe even exterminated, just like the title of the French translation from Aleksandr Borshchagovsky's book (*The Blood Will Be Accused*) suggests: "L'Holocauste inachevé"—"The Unfinished Holocaust." Two million Volga Germans, hundreds of thousands of Crimean Tatars, Chechen and Ingush, had already been transported to Siberia. Why should not the same be done with the Jews? The conspiracy of the Jewish doctors—fabricated by the secret police—who supposedly wanted to poison the leadership of the party and of the whole state government, could have delivered a beautiful excuse to effect the Soviet variation of the Final Solution.

But Stalin died on March 5. The Jews of the Soviet Union were temporarily saved.

Many articles and books have already been published on the history of the Jews in Russia and the USSR, mainly in America but lately in Russia too. Yet Arno Lustiger's book cannot be compared to any other of its kind. He knows everything that has been published until now, and from this he creates a synthesis. It is especially important that he has mastered all the languages that are necessary for reading the documents: Polish, Russian, English, Yiddish, Hebrew, French, and German. His book may finally force the reader in the West to understand that the crimes of Soviet communism committed against the Jews represented a different kind of Shoah. That is why I want to quote a sentence from the epilogue to Arno Lustiger's book about the Jewish resistance: "The myth about the Jews, that they had let themselves be led like sheep to the slaughter, belongs to the last of the historical lies. Lies that outlasted all phases of 'dismay' and 'consolidation' of newer German history."[8] Lustiger meant here the resistance that the Jews offered against the Nazi regime. In the *Red Book* he clearly shows how the Jews of the Soviet Union defended themselves. Despite the inhuman torture and dangers that threatened the families of the imprisoned, almost all of the accused, during the course of the trials of 1952, retracted their admission of guilt and declared the truth. They could hardly imagine that half a century later their words would be published. Most of the Jews of the Soviet Union spoke with dignity and pride to the judges, probably knowing that those men had been given the order to sentence them to death. This last act of dignity was the only possibility of moral resistance against the omnipotent party and its police.

Arno Lustiger's great contribution is that he found and published Albert Einstein's foreword to the *Schwarzbuch*. Einstein already had insight fifty years ago into what would be meaningful and important to the world of today and tomorrow. These few lines should end my foreword and at the same time form the theme of Lustiger's book. Albert Einstein wrote his words for the *Schwarzbuch* of 1946, but they are still valid for the *Red Book* of 1998.

This publication should convince the reader that an international organization for the protection of one's existence can only serve its purpose, when it is not limited to protecting states against military raids. It also has to protect national minorities within a state. Finally, it is the individual that should be protected from destruction and inhuman treatment.

It is true that this goal can only be reached if the principle of "non-involvement," which played such a disastrous role during the last few decades, is thrown overboard. Nobody can doubt today the necessity of this momentous step. It must be clear, even for someone whose only concern is to achieve a shield against military raids, that the catastrophes of war are prepared by certain developments inside individual countries, and not at all only by military and military-technical preparations.

Not until all countries, states, and people recognize and feel the same obligation—that the establishment and the guarantee of safety and humane conditions of existence for all mankind should be the most important obligation—does one have the right to speak about a civilized humanity.

## NOTES

1.  The book of the poet and journalist Maria Shkapskaia-Andreeva was published in 1942 under the title *Eto deistvitel'no sluchilos'*.
2.  Itzhak Katsenelson: *Dos lied vunem ojsgehargetn jidischn volk (Grosser Gesang vom ausgerotteten jüdischen Volk)*—Cologne 1994, p. 198; *'Skazanie ob istreblennom yevreiskim narode*, translated by Yefim Etkind, Moscow 2000.
3.  Arno Lustiger: *Zum Kampf auf Leben und Tod! Vom Widerstand der Juden 1933-1945*/Cologne 1994, p. 18.
4.  See Matthias Vetter: *Antisemitismus und Bolschewiki. Zum Verhältnis von Sowjetsystem Judenfeindschaft 1917-1939* Berlin 1995.
5.  Victor Klemperer: *I Shall Bear Witness. Diary 1933-1941*. New York 1999.
6.  Svetlana Allilueva: *Das erste Jahr/The First Year.* Vienna 1969, p. 141.
7.  Roman Brackman: *Anti-Semitism of Joseph Stalin. PhD. Diss.* New York University 1980. Here it is claimed, for example, that Stalin was a spy of the tsarist secret police and that Jewish officials played an important role in finding that file. See M. Vetter, *Anti-Semitism and the Bolsheviks, p. 288.*
8.  Arno Lustiger: *Zum Kampf auf Leben und Tod!/To the Life and Death Struggle!,* p. 592.

## Arno Lustiger

YEFIM ETKIND (1918-1999) studied German and Romance languages and literature. After 1952 he taught at the Herzen Institute in Leningrad. In the spring of 1974, shortly before the expulsion of Solzhenitsyn, he lost his membership in the Writers' Union as well as his professorship and job. Having no possibility of teaching or publishing, he left the Soviet Union that same year and accepted a professorship, from 1974 to 1986, in Russian and comparative literature, poetics and stylistics at the University of Paris X Nanterre. He was a corresponding member of the academies of Darmstadt, Mainz, and Munich, as well as a member of the Academy of Arts and Sciences in St. Petersburg.

Etkind has published numerous anthologies of Russian lyrical poetry, and studies of reproductions of German lyrics. *Der innere Mensch und die äussere Rede: Psychopoetik der russischen Literatur des 18. und 19. Jahrhunderts* (Moscow) was honored as best literary scholarly book of the year in 1997. In Germany he has published *Unblutige Hinrichtung, Warum ich die Sowjetunion verlassen musste* (Munich 1981), the anthology *Russische Lyrik* (18th-20th Centuries), (Munich 1981) and *Russische Lyrik von der Oktoberrevolution bis zur Gegenwart: Versuch einer Darstellung* (Munich 1984).

# THE EVENTS

At the second plenary session of the Jewish Anti-Fascist Committee held in the Soviet Union on February 20, 1943, Ilya Ehrenburg proposed the idea of publishing a *Red Book* about the battles of the Jewish soldiers, officers, and partisans in the war against Germany. Ehrenburg's project never came to pass. This *Red Book* is dedicated to the Jewish war heroes and to the victims of Stalinist persecution of all nationalities.

# Part I

# HISTORY OF THE RUSSIAN JEWS

## 1. THE JEWS UNDER THE TSARS

On August 12, 1952, leading representatives of the Yiddish culture were executed in the Soviet Union. This state-sponsored murder ended a tragic chapter in the history of the Jewish national culture in Russia and the Soviet Union. The roots of Jewish culture in Russia, of which Yiddish, spoken daily and used in literature, was the backbone, reached far into the Soviet Union's temporal and geographic borders.

In the following brief overview, some of the stages of the history of the Russian Jews will be examined. This is important for an understanding of the prehistory of the struggle of the Jewish Anti-Fascist Committee (JAFC) against Hitler and the destruction of the committee during Stalin's time.

During the time of the Romans, Jewish communities already existed in Central Europe. Records of the 6th century have been preserved that show Jews were allowed to buy property and that they were peasants, customs collectors, mint masters, or merchants. They were not subject to specific work restrictions far into the High Middle Ages. It was the Roman Catholic Church however that tried to isolate the Jews, who by then were legally free. The Church forbade by edict the sharing of meals between Christians and Jews, and mixed marriages carried the death sentence.

The principle of "protection of the Jews" during the reign of Charlemagne brought an economic and social revival for the Jews over a short period of time. These principles were ineffective during the Crusades (more than 10,000 Jews were murdered during the First Crusade in Central Europe (1096-1099)).

In the Middle Ages the most important representatives of Jewish religion on Russian territory were the descendants of the Khazars, a Turkic tribe from Central Asia, which already ruled the steppes of the Black Sea region in the 7th century. At the end of the 8th century the empire of this clan reached from the Crimean peninsula to the Caspian Sea and in the north to the Volga River. The Khazars were not exclusively nomadic; they also pursued agriculture and the trading of domestic animals. Colonists probably converted their ruling elite to Judaism. Slavic clans, immigrating in the 8th and 9th centuries, were under the protection of the Khazars and had to pay them tribute. The existence of Jewish merchants in Kiev is also documented.

It was not until the 18th and 19th centuries that the Russian empire confiscated the main settlement of the Mesopotamian Jews, who had immigrated through Persia into the Caucasus and Middle Asia, and the Jewish settlements on the northern coast of the Black Sea and on the Crimean peninsula, which had existed since ancient times.

The invasion by Mongolian clans in the 13th century destroyed the few early existing Jewish settlements in Russia. After the defeat of Mongolian rule under the leadership of Ivan III, also known as Ivan the Great (1462-1505), the grand dukes gradually developed a hostile position against re-immigrating Jews. The initial reason for it was the activity of a sect of Orthodox Christians, the *Zhidovstvuiushchie* (people who favor Judaism), which had many followers, especially in Novgorod. Tsar Ivan IV—Ivan the Terrible (1533-1584)—a fanatically religious man who felt the need to use his reign of terror to protect the Orthodox Church, did not tolerate either the *Zhidovstvuiushchie* or the Jews themselves in Russia. The Tsarinas Catherine I (1725-1727) and Elizabeth (1741-1762), the daughters of Tsar Peter the Great, extended the rigid policy of deportation during their reign, so that by the middle of the 18th century the number of Jews was insignificant in Russia.

### The Jews in Poland—The Cradle of Russian Judaism

In the kingdom of Poland-Lithuania, Jews from all over Europe had found a place of refuge from the pogroms of the Crusaders and the horrors of the plague. In Germany, the Jews were forced out of trades, or they were not allowed in certain occupations. Even the church in Poland had initiated decrees against Jews, but the kings made the Jews their direct subjects and basically guaranteed them the same rights as they guaranteed the Christians.

The Jews maintained their own identity toward the Polish-speaking population that harbored religious prejudice. Since the 16th century a "Vaad" (Council) controlled the right of internal Jewish self-administration. Proof of the identity of the Polish Jews was the obvious use of Yiddish, which had developed from "imported" Middle High German into an original literary language. The last great poets and millions of "ordinary speakers" of this language were brutally murdered during the 20th century.

The kingdom of Poland-Lithuania also included large portions of present day Ukraine and Belorussia. The aristocracy owned vast amounts of property in the eastern part of the country. They owned serfs, who were Orthodox and spoke east Slavic dialects, insofar as they were "Ukrainians." The landowners often employed the Jews as administrators. They also worked as innkeepers, merchants, and moneylenders. Many Ukrainian farmers hated the Jews because of these special positions.

When the leader of the Cossacks, Bogdan Khmelnitsky, led a rebellion in 1648-49 against the Polish aristocracy, he combined this rebellion with a massacre of the Ukrainian Jews: 100,000 were brutally murdered and 300 Jewish congregations were destroyed. That pogrom signaled the economic downfall and the poverty of the Polish Jew. Yet, barely 300 years later, Stalin awarded the Khmelnitsky medal to high-ranking military people, including Jews!

## Discrimination Under the Tsars

In the wake of Poland's division in 1772 and the complete destruction of the Polish aristocratic republic in 1793 and 1795, Russia was again confronted with the "Jewish question." The tsarist empire annexed territory in which was concentrated the largest Jewish minority in the world in the late 18th century. Therefore, the history of the Russian Jews, strictly speaking, is a continuation of the history of the Polish Jews and, by historical extension, even of the German Jews, which can be identified through many family names. In 1772 approximately 100,000 Jews became Russian subjects. After the third division their number climbed to 500,000.[1] In the beginning, they were granted more rights than the Jews in the states of Western and Central Europe.

Catherine II (Catherine the Great) and her successors tried to regulate the cohabitation of Christians and non-Christians through so-called enlightened absolutism. Their politics aimed at "utilization" of the Jews through "education" and adaptation. The new structural arrangement, the enlarged state territory, needed comprehensive administrative reform. In 1775 the constitution of governors (*namestnichestvo*) was established. The fifty new governments (*gubernii*) were presided over by the dukes of the provinces, who only needed to account to their empress and were able, endowed with the power and tools of the police, and with judicial and administrative means, to rule despotically over 300,000 to 400,000 subjects.

In the course of these structural reforms, individual groups of the population, or of different social classes, were assigned fields of activity and fixed living quarters. The Jews were classified in the social structure as urban craftsmen and merchants, even though in the former Polish regions only one-third of the Jews lived in cities while the majority lived in towns or small market towns. It is true that the authorities rejected displacement, but every Jew who made money in his trade in the country or pursued agriculture committed a criminal offense. Only a few model agricultural colonies were permitted to do this. The requirement of "residence at the place of registration," imposed on all social classes, meant ruin for many Jews. With the elimination of traditional structures, the authorities of the self-administration (Kahals) were reduced.

A charter easing restrictions gave all members of the merchants' guild and traders more mobility in 1785. Merchants in Moscow soon complained about growing competition. By decree, Catherine II restricted the mobility of the Jews drastically in 1791. In the future, Jews were only allowed to settle in regions specially designated for them, the so-called "Jewish Pale of Settlement" (*Cherta postoiannoi Evreiskoi osedlosti*). The territory of almost one million square kilometers covered an area from the Baltic Sea to the Black Sea and encompassed 25 governments (*gubernii*) in Belorussia, the Ukraine, Poland-Lithuania, the Baltic and the Caucasus Mountains. More than half the Jews of the world and 94 percent of the Russian Jews lived in this restricted area. The Russian Jews made up 11 percent of the entire population and they were often a majority in small towns (shtetls). Many of them barely survived, impoverished as "Luftmenschen"—traveling merchants—or craftsmen in small family businesses without any other employees or in small manufacturing. Before 1917, only 300,000 Jews were allowed to leave their region. Some of them were able to have social and economic success in the large central Russian towns.

Almost one-quarter of all merchants in the Pale were Jews. The economic duties imposed upon them led to an increase in the usual hostile Jewish clichés among the Russians. The typical accusations were profiteering, exploitation, cheating, defrauding of the Christians and desecration of hosts. The Jews were looked upon as members of a conspiratorial religion, opposed to Christianity. Collectively, they were made responsible for the crucifixion of Christ, and, absurd as it seems, they were accused of spilling the blood of Christian children in secret rituals. In 1869 the convert Jakob Brafman published *Book of the Kahal.* This tendentious work contained translations of the minutes of meetings of the Jewish congregation in Minsk at the end of the 18th century and at the beginning of the 19th century. In his introduction, Brafman accused the Jews of planning to create a "state within a state." Supposedly this secret government also reigned over naïve Christians.

All these fictions and delusions—which survived in their characteristic mutation during the Soviet period—unfortunately still enjoy undiminished vitality at the end of the 20th century. They gained more and more influence within official politics in the 19th century.

## Assimilation and "Utilization"

The commission to settle the "Jewish question" created by Aleksandr I (1801-1825) was misguided by the enlightened idea that the formal integration of the Jews would speed up cultural assimilation. In the statute for the Jews that had been made a law in 1804, it was stated that the peculiarity of the Jewish population "is caused by their abnormal legal situation and therefore can be corrected."[2] It guaranteed the Jews the right to education and access to state-owned schools, as well as the right to practice any religion. The borders of the Pale of Settlement were not lifted, but a few Jews were now able to work in agriculture as long as they possessed a special permit and were registered. However, the lucrative trade with spirits was still closed to them. The "unproductive profiteers" were to become useful producers who stabilized the agrarian state, which suffered repeated crises.

All subjects suffered under the repressive and authoritarian politics during the reign of Nicholas I (1825-1855). The tsar enacted approximately six hundred decrees against the Jews. In 1827 the order to serve in the military was introduced. Up to this time they were able to pay a fee instead of having to perform military service. Russia had a standing army, with the usual time of service being 25 years. In the "Cantonist decrees" the age of the Jews recruited was reduced from 18 to 12 years of age. Sometimes eight-year-olds were even drafted. Civil servants speculated that those uprooted boys would lose their Jewish beliefs and become Russified. The 40,000 Cantonists were prepared in special schools by brutal noncommissioned officers for military service and for quick conversion to Christianity. Baptism was forced upon entire units. Mass suicides were often committed during these ceremonies for the sake of "the sanctification of the holy name" (Kiddush Hashem).[3]

The Canton decrees, in force until 1865, increased the hatred of the Jewish population against the tsar's regime and aggravated the tensions in the communities that had come up with a contingent of recruits themselves. Often the Kahals handed over members that would not adapt or "khapper" (kidnap) children on the street or from the houses of poor people and widows. Corruption was a daily routine, because the rich wanted to avoid having their sons join the army. A Yiddish folk song described this tragedy and the suffering of the unhappy children and their families:

> Teardrops are falling down in little alleys,
> in children's blood one can wash oneself.
> Little birds one tears out of Sunday school (Bible lesson),
> they will be put in ordinary (heathen) clothes.

In 1826 the ministerial councilor ordered censorship of all Hebrew publications, and in 1836 all Jewish printing shops were closed—only one each was tolerated in Kiev and Vilna—and in 1835 the statute of 1804 was modified. Jews were not allowed to settle in Riga, Kiev, Sevastopol or Nikolaev—the largest towns of the region—or in a strip 50 versts wide along the western border, in order to prevent border violations. The government reformed the Jewish educational system in order to free the schools of the "Talmudist spirit" and convince more Jews to change their religion.

In 1844 a clothing tax was imposed, followed six years later by restrictions against wearing special Jewish dress. In 1865 the restriction was lifted again, and Jewish women were allowed to shave their hair; men were allowed to wear sideburns. In the same year the tsar ordered the dissolution of the Kahals. The Jews were under the authority of the general administration for all matters and were provided with just a few of their own resources, because the communal tax, which the Kahals as well as every community was allowed to collect, was converted into a state tax.

Jews had to obtain documents proving that they belonged to one of five categories: peasants, farmers, merchants (considered to be "useful"); permanent urban citizens (rabbis, owners of capital); and citizens "without permanent residence" (among others, coachmen, goldsmiths, and apprentices) who were considered to be "useless." Their rights were to be even more restricted and, among other things, it was planned to triple their drafting contingent. After the death of Nicholas I, the "classification program" was abandoned.

The reforms during the reign of Aleksandr II (1856-1881), at the height of the enlightenment and mainly carried out by the Russian bureaucracy, improved the lot of a small group within the Jewish population. Military service for the Jews was adjusted to be the same as for all other citizens. The settlement decree remained mainly unchanged. Only those who belonged to a "useful" working group were allowed to settle outside the Pale. Initially it applied to merchants of "the first guild" (who were paying the highest tax) and university graduates. Later, craftsmen and soldiers, who had served in the army of Nicholas I, were also included. The masses still had to live packed together in the colonization settlements, without enough opportunities for work in order to support themselves. The reservations that Aleksandr II had against the Jews, as well as the increasing power of the Slavophiles and the Ukrainian nationalists in the early 1860s, prevented serious reforms in the policies concerning the Jews. The publicly declared participation of the Jews in the Polish revolt of 1863, and during the attempted assassinations of the tsar in 1866, strengthened the position of those who demanded a tough approach against the national minorities within the tsar's empire.

## Anti-Semitism and Pogroms

With the murder of Aleksandr II (1881), a phase of limited inner liberalization ended for the Russian Jews. Populist anti-Jewish agitation, prompted by a circle of government loyalists, held the Jews responsible for the assassination and provoked a wave of pogroms that same year.

This caused the death of thousands, especially in the Ukraine. Jews who were living in the capitals of Moscow and St. Petersburg were transported back to the Pale. At the institutes of higher education a Jewish quota was established. These measures, caused by a fear of too much Jewish "power," pushed the Jewish intellectuals straight into the role that those who feared the Jews had warned about. In other words, it was not the existence of radical, rebellious Jewish intellectuals that was the reason for denying them the opportunity of a civil service career, but the opposite—their radicalization was the logical result of growing discrimination.[4]

The rulers of Russia had always tried to assimilate non-Russian subjects. The price they had to pay to integrate was high: they had to renounce their religions, customs and cultures. In 1881 Russian was declared the only official language. In the last two decades of the 19th century, when in the German Reich, and in Austria as well, legal restrictions against Jews were eased, the Jews of Russia suffered more than ever. they were looked upon as representatives of modern society, as pioneers of a capitalist economy. They presented a danger for the agriculturally based feudal Russian society, and, in connection with that, they also endangered the privileges of the aristocracy. The aggressive anti-Semitism of the bureaucracy became more popular than ever among Russian conservatives, who were mainly landowners, and it was these landowners who wanted to perpetuate the system of serfdom and felt threatened by modernization of any kind. They used their power to influence public opinion with the help of certain newspapers. They dominated several government departments (e.g., the Ministry of the Interior). The *Chornye Sotni*, the "Black Hundred," were the origin of many different radical parties, which mainly represented the interests of the landowners. This contingent approved and arranged violent activities against the Jews among the most impoverished people and thus channeled the anger and frustration of their subjects. The anti-Semitic propaganda of the "Black Hundred" tried to blame the Jews for all existing attempts to change society.

In contrast to Germany, the "Jew-phobia" of Russia had little to do with racial theories. For German anti-Semites, the Jews were the eternal destroyers pitted against the Germanic race, the race that was destined to rule mankind. For Russian "Jew-phobes," the Jews appeared to be intellectually superior members of a foreign religion. Baptism ended all discrimination for the Russian Jews, but it did not end all the prejudices of the conservatives. This became obvious in their envious aversion to those

Jews who were willing to "improve" themselves and assimilate into social life. It also showed how they rejected the backward Jewish poor from the western regions—Jews who continued to use their own language, peculiar culture and mysterious religion. The phobia toward assimilated Jews, as well as national Jews, became a typical code of Russian anti-Semitism; this also held true during the reign of the Soviets.

Alleged proof was often provided of the "Jewish danger." An anonymous forger in Paris, and a member of the Russian secret police, compiled from an old 1864 political pamphlet by Maurice Joly the so-called *Protocols of the Elders of Zion*—supposedly a plan by a group of Jewish rabbis seeking to rule the entire world. The complete text was published for the first time in 1905, the year of the revolution, as an appendix to the second edition of *The Great in the Small and the Antichrist as an Approaching Political Possibility* (*Velikoe v malom i Antikhrist kak bliskaia politicheskaia vozmozhnost'*), a work by Russian Synod official Sergei Nilus. The *Protocols* immediately became a welcome propaganda instrument and were distributed by the Black Hundred. They served as justification for the horrible pogroms. Aleksandra Fyodorovna, the wife of Nicholas II, is believed to have trusted the authenticity of these "documents."

After the revolution the *Protocols* was given worldwide distribution. Hundreds of thousands of copies appeared in Germany, the printing of which was financed by the German imperial government. The "Jewish world conspiracy" was willingly accepted as an explanation for the German defeat in World War I, and for the outcome of the disgraceful Treaty of Versailles. The National Socialists also used the conspiracy theory for their propaganda. Despite the fact that in several trials it was proved that the *Protocols* was a forgery[5] they are still being published and distributed in Russia today.

In 1992 a new edition of the *Protocols* was published in Moscow, with the original title *Velikoe v malom* by the long deceased "author" Nilus. Even on May 9, 1997, the official "Day of Victory" holiday, Russian anti-Semites sold this wretched piece of work on the streets of the capital. According to Mikhail Obshchugin in the magazine *Viasna* (No. 2/1998), a journal published in Minsk, the *Protocols* was introduced in a broadcast of the Belorussian State Broadcast Company on March 11, 1998, as a document of historic importance. In the program "Kulturreport" of the First German Television Station (ARD), on April 26, 1998, the Sheik (Rector) of the Al-Azhar University in Cairo, Abd al-Sabur Shehin, declared that the statements they contain are true.

Aleksandr III and Nicholas II, the two last tsars, really hated the Jews. They tried to arouse anti-Semitic sentiment among the population in order to use it as a political weapon. New research has proven that the government was not directly the moving force behind the campaigns and the six hundred pogroms against the Jews that cost the lives of thousands in the period between 1903 and 1906 in Kishinev, Gomel, Odessa, Moghilev, and Zhitomir. The government, as well as Nicholas II, described those excesses as acts of patriotism and loyalty.

The mix of religiously motivated anti-Judaism and political resistance to far-reaching social reforms could also be seen in the 1913 Beilis trial. In 1911 a Ukrainian boy disappeared. The rumor was spread that Jews had killed him for ritual purposes. Even though the real murderers—a well-known Ukrainian criminal gang—had been identified, the Jew Mendel Beilis was arrested and accused. His trial caused a stir almost as great as the Dreyfus affair in France. A jury cleared Beilis of all charges, but anti-Jewish harassment wouldn't end.[6]

The Jews reacted in different ways to legal discrimination, pogroms and accusations of ritual murder, poverty and difficult working conditions. Education and enlightenment seemed to be a way out of the misery. The Jewish enlightenment movement, the *Haskala*, which existed in Central Europe since the beginning of the 18th century, did not begin in Russia until the early 19th century. Because of the awful living conditions in the Pale of Settlement, only those economically and socially independent members of the communities supported the *Haskala*. An open confrontation took place between the majority of the Jews standing loyally by their traditions, and the *Maskilim*, who wanted to free the people from a life without dignity. The efforts to establish a Jewish educational system going beyond the traditional religious education were blocked by fights among Hebrew-speaking and Yiddish-speaking classes. Yiddish was the language of the masses, whereas Hebrew, in addition to Russian, was spoken in intellectual circles.

Other Jews decided to emigrate. Between 1880 and 1914, more than two million Jews left the Pale for North America; 200,000 went to Great Britain and 60,000 to Palestine. The United States became a center of Russian-Jewish culture. Newspapers in Yiddish were soon published, such as the social democratic and anticommunist-oriented *The Forward (Forverts)*.

The Jews had every reason in the world to participate in progressive and revolutionary movements.[7] Among the nationalities in the tsar's empire—including the Russians—the Jews were the best organized part of the population. They founded numerous political clubs and parties supporting their interests. The ideas of Jewish socialism were born in Russia and in the region of Poland belonging to Russia. The first Jewish socialist groups were formed in the surrounding area of the rabbinical seminar in Vilna. In 1877, Aron Liebermann (1845-1880) founded the first Jewish socialist newspaper, *The Truth* (*Ha'emet*). Like Liebermann, many Jews approached social-democratic ideology and the Jewish workers' movement via the populism of the *Narodniki*.[8]

## 2. THE JEWISH PARTIES

### The Bund

The cradle of the Jewish blue-collar workers' movement was in the annexed Polish provinces and in the six Belorussian provinces of the Russian empire, including the textile industry regions around Lodz and Bialystok and the intellectual center of Vilna. In 1864, more than 200 factories founded by Jews already existed in that region. Strikes were a common occurrence because of low wages and appalling working conditions. Night shifts for women and children were allowed until 1885, and the workday wasn't reduced to eleven and a half hours until 1897. Blue-collar workers organized themselves under the leadership of secular Jewish radicals. The work force demanded a ten-hour weekday, established strike funds and discussed its problems in socialist groups (*Krayslekh*). In addition to the newspapers *Yiddish Worker* (*Yidisher arbeter*) and *The Voice of the Worker* (*Die arbeter-stime*), numerous Yiddish pamphlets with socialist propaganda were published in Vilna. In 1895 more than 500 Jews celebrated May Day (May 1) in Vilna.

In June 1895 the Jewish workers' conference was held in Vilna and, at a conspiratorial meeting from October 7 to 9, The General Yiddish Workers' Union in Russia and Poland (the Bund) (*Algemeyner Yidisher Arbeter Bund in Lite, Poyln un Rusland*) was founded. At first it was not just a political party but also pursued union goals. Therefore it had no clear definition. The Bundists set up strike and health funds and considered themselves part of Russian social democracy, declaring the struggle against tsarist autocracy as their main political goal. The foreign office, located in Geneva since 1898, allowed the national sections to have far-reaching autonomy.[9] Even though the majority of the delegates of the Third Party Convention in Kovno still rejected the "Rights of Nationalities," the delegates to the Fourth Party Convention in Bialystok demanded that Russia change into a "federation of nationalities with complete national autonomy," independent of the territory where the people were living.

Some of the leaders of the Bund were Vladimir Kosovsky* (Nahum Mendl Levinsohn), Arkadi Kremer and Abraham Mutnik. When more than 20 Jewish workers were whipped on orders of the Russian governor of Vilna at the May 1902 demonstration, Hirsh Lekert, a young Bund member, attempted to assassination the governor. He was hanged six weeks later.

The Bund rejected individual acts of terror, but following the pogroms of 1903 self-defense units were organized, which caused a rapid increase of its influence among the workers. The Bund included 35,000 members in Russia in 1905, while the Social Democratic Workers' Party had only 8,400. The press department of the Bund, e.g., *The Worker* (*Der wecker*) and *People's Newspaper* (*Folkstsaytung*) were occasionally printed illegally in foreign countries.[10]

The Bund was an important and respected member of the Socialist International. In many countries, leaders of the workers' movement came from among Bundist ranks, for example in the United States and Poland, where the Bund existed as an independent but underground party until the 1940s.

In the course of the Bund's almost century-long existence, it fought for the interests of the Jewish workers, for the national and cultural autonomy of the Jews, and in favor of a secular democratic socialism. Ideologues like Kosovsky and Medem created the doctrine of *Being Here* (*Do'igkeyt*) in sharp contrast to the Zionist idea of statehood in Palestine. Militant opposition to Zionism remained a central part of the Bund's ideology and practice until World War II. The Bund founded a network of Yiddish-speaking schools and organizations to foster and cultivate the Yiddish culture, literature, and the language of the Jewish population.

## The Anthem of the Bund

"The Oath" ("Di shvue") was the most famous battle song of the Jewish workers in Eastern and Central Europe. The great Yiddish poet and author of the *Dybbuk*, Sch. An-Ski (Salomon Rappaport, 1863-1920),

---

* See the corresponding biography in the section "The People."

*14*

composed the anthem for the fifth anniversary of the foundation of the Union. G. Beck, who established Yiddish workmen's choirs in London, wrote the melody. It became the anthem of the Jewish proletariat and was heard all over the world during conferences, strikes, and demonstrations. Jewish revolutionaries sang it during the street fights of 1905 in Lodz, Bialystok, and other parts of the Russian empire, as well as in exile.[11]

## THE OATH

Brothers and sisters of work and poverty,
everything that is goes and falls apart
Together! Together! The flag is ready,
it flares with rage, from blood it is red!
An oath, an oath for life and death!

Heaven and earth will hear us,
Bright stars shall be witness.
An oath, an oath
with blood and with tears.
We swear! We swear! We swear!

We swear to fight for freedom and justice,
against all tyrants and their bondmen.
We swear to besiege the dark power
or die with heroic courage in the battle!
Heaven and earth ...

We swear to preserve a bloody hate
to the murderers and robbers of the working class,
the emperor, the ruler, the capitalists.
We swear to destroy them, devastate them
Heaven and earth...

We swear to lead a holy struggle
until the world will be renewed
No poor, no rich,
no master and no slave!
Equal shall be, who strong is and weak!
Heaven and earth...

We swear a loyalty without limit to the "Bund"
only it can free the slaves together

Its flag, the red is high and wide.
we swear it loyalty with life and death!
Heaven and earth…


## The Bund and the Establishment of the RSDRP

Many Jews became activists in Russian social democracy. Their umbrella organization, the Social Democratic Workers Party of Russia
(RSDRP), was founded in Minsk in 1898. That city was chosen because it
already had a strong Bund organization, which placed at its disposal an
illegal printing press. At the first party convention, four of the nine delegates were Jews (Edelman, Katz, Kremer, and Mutnik); Edelman and
Kremer were among the three members of the first central committee.
Almost all of the delegates were imprisoned shortly after its founding by
the tsar's secret police, the *Okhrana*.

As arranged at the party's founding convention, the Bund joined the
RSDRP as an autonomous organization and soon proved to be its strongest active union group. It became the sore spot not only of the anti-
Semites but also of the secret police. Even Plekhanov, the father of Russian Marxism, made sour comments about the Bund. He recognized its
importance as the vanguard of the workers' movement, but rejected their
demands for autonomy. Many non-Jewish Russian Marxists criticized the
fact that the Bund did not limit itself solely to class struggle (which they
saw as their priority), but that it demanded the status of a nation for the
Jewish proletariat, as well as the teaching of Jewish culture and language,
without a closed Jewish settlement area.

The Bundist Medem, who grew up in a family which converted to
Lutheranism, and whose native language was Russian and not Yiddish,
wrote in 1910:

> The organized Jewish proletariat is not only the backbone of the
> cultural movement, but also of the political movement. It combines
> the political struggle with the fight for the development of its demo-
> cratic culture. Free of any nationalistic demagogy the Jewish prole-
> tariat protects its social class interests and from there seeks national
> liberation.

Such a national concept, inspired by Austrian Marxists, was felt to be "divisive." In early Russian social democracy, the question concerning the nature of the party and the right to the self-determination of nations was strongly disputed. During party conventions, which had to be held in foreign countries because they were illegal in Russia, the party's structure, the internal party rules and the relation of the party to the proletariat were discussed. The group around Yuli Martov* and Pavel Axelrod, later referred to as the Mensheviks, pleaded for an open gathering of the workers movement without tight structures, while the group around Lenin aimed for a committed conspiratorial cadre of professional revolutionaries, as they were later represented by the Bolsheviks.

At the Second Party Convention of the RSDRP, which began on July 30, 1903 in Brussels and continued after 13 meetings on August 11 in London (24 meetings), the deep abyss between the totalitarian goals of Lenin's group and the free and democratically structured Bund and the group around Martov became obvious. Already during the preparation, Lenin revealed his mastery at manipulating the party the way he pleased. Forty-three delegates participated at the party convention, having 51 votes. Twenty of the delegates were Jews. Even though the Bund had more members than all Russian local groups together, only five delegates were granted to the Bund, three for all of Russia and Poland—that is, *one* mandate per 10,000 members and two for the foreign committee. The non-Jewish groups received each one or even two mandates. The outcome of this party convention was clear right from the start. With the help of his supporters, Lenin rejected the postulates of the Bund for the cultural and linguistic autonomy of the Jewish proletariat in the most acrimonious and tricky way.

In his speech during the sixth meeting, Mark Liber* said, among other things:

> I have never been at a meeting where the words "principles of revolutionary social democracy" were so often misused as at this conference. Not everybody who constantly shouts "God, my God" will go to heaven, and not everyone who speaks about principles of revolutionary social democracy is really defending them. Comrade Lenin often speaks about the necessity of destroying the Bund. Maybe he only leaves the Central Committee of the Bund alive, as an organization for smuggling illegal literature into Russia. But we need our CC [Central Committee] mainly to lead the Jewish proletariat... You forget that we, the representatives of the proletariat of Jewish na-

tionality, according to Kautsky's declaration, have transformed the Jews from being pariahs among the nations into a strong revolutionary force.

Vladimir Kosovsky stated at the same meeting:

> One asks, why is the Bund the only representative of the Jewish proletariat? Our answer is, because the Bund is the only organization that has gathered under its flags large masses of Jewish proletarians, and the Bund performs a special, systematic work among the Jewish proletariat…As for the question whether the Bund should continue to exist, we perceive the disappointment that the Bund has developed so quickly.[12]

The petition to recognize the Bund as the legitimate representation of the Jewish proletariat was rejected, as well as the demand for a federal structure for the RSDRP. Concerning this question, the main opponents were, among others, Martov and Trotsky,* who declared himself, at Lenin's behest, to be the representative of the Jewish proletariat—a *chutzpah* (Yiddish, meaning "impertinence") that had no equal. The Bund was forced to leave the RSDRP after five years of selfless revolutionary work.

The representatives of the Social Democracy of the Kingdom of Poland and Lithuania (SDKPiL) insisted in Brussels on total independence of the parties within the RSDRP and also demanded autonomy for Poland. Both demands were rejected. Rosa Luxemburg, who was one of the founders of the SDKPiL, argued intensely afterwards against Lenin's concept of a strictly centrally organized party, made up only of a small elite of professional revolutionaries. The SDKPiL did not join the RSDRP until the Fourth Party Convention, the unification convention in Stockholm in 1906.

The Bund's Central Committee refuted the accusations leveled against it at the party convention—that the organization was a historic anomaly, damaging, nationalistic, and bourgeois, with an appeal in December 1903:

> All this would be very laughable if it weren't so sad. What's sad is what became obvious at the party convention: the leaders of Russian social democracy knew nothing about the Bund. Total ignorance is evident concerning the character and content of its activities and there is no knowledge about the historical role the Bund has to play

because of the unique social-political circumstances determined by two thousand years of persecution of the Jews. Besides the economic and political repression, which the Bund, as well as the proletariat of other countries, are suffering, the Jewish proletarian has to live under a particular, horrible pressure: the disdain increasing through history, as a pariah among pariahs.

This appeal ends with the slogans: "Down with the civil war! Long live socialism!"

Because many Jews remained members of the RSDRP and both organizations acted parallel to one another, disputes occurred frequently when working for the party. In April 1903, a few months before the party convention, forty-five Jews were murdered within three days during a horrible pogrom in Kishinev; almost one hundred were injured, and seven hundred houses and six hundred shops were demolished. When a large number of Bundists were imprisoned in tsarist jails or exiled to Siberia, Lenin coldly attempted to take over or liquidate the Bund. To protect themselves they mourned their comrades killed in the pogroms. As a consequence of the failed revolution of 1905, in which many Jewish workers participated, Jews in Russia and Poland were harshly persecuted and pogroms were carried out in Lodz, Bialystok, Warsaw, Minsk, and many other centers of the Jewish workers' movement. A great number of Jewish revolutionaries were put in chains and sent into exile to Siberia.

In agreement with all left parties, the Bund boycotted the first Duma elections, to avoid democratically legitimizing the unjust tsarist regime. Before the revolution, Russian right-wing parties linked the anti-Semitic agitation against the Bund to anti-revolutionary propaganda slogans and declared that all Jews were revolutionaries—which was reason enough not to grant them any civil rights.

## The Zionists

Russian Jews were the first to struggle for a return to Palestine and the foundation of a Jewish state. During the second half of the 19th century several groups of the *Khoveve Zion* (Zion-loving movement) appeared. Russian author Peretz Smolenskin criticized Reform Judaism and demanded a Jewish state in Palestine. The Hebrew newspaper *Aurora* (*Ha-Shakhar*), which he founded in Vienna (1868-1884), became the leading instrument of the early Zionist movement. Leon Pinsker, a medical doctor and publicist from Odessa, also opposed assimilation. He published the paper *Auto-Emancipation, A Warning Call to His Clansmen by a Russian Jew* in 1882 in Berlin. In this paper he pleaded for "the establishment of a Jewish nationality, a people on its own land, the auto-emancipation of Jews, their equality as a nation among nations, by having their own home country." At the first convention of the *Khoveve Zion*, in November 1884 in Katowice, he mainly concentrated on the projects of the Maskilim—settlement in the countryside and work in agriculture—but later, influenced by the movement, he committed himself to Palestine as being the right territory for the Jewish state.

In 1887 the pre-Zionist Bilu movement was founded in Kharkov. The first colonists who emigrated to Palestine came from this organization. In August 1897, five weeks before the foundation of the Bund in Vilna, the Zionist World Organization was established at the First Zionist Congress in Basel. The chief organizer was Theodor Herzl. Of the 204 delegates, 85 were Russian Jews. The main slogan of the Basel program was, "Zionism strives for the establishment of a public, lawful, and secure homestead for the Jewish people."

For decades the Bundists and Zionists were the most important, competing revolutionary movements among the Jews worldwide. This applied of course especially to the Pale of Settlement and to Poland. At the Second Zionist Congress in 1898, the future leaders of Zionism—Weizman, Sokolov, and Lewin—participated as representatives of the Russian Jews. At that time it was decided to support the settlement in Palestine without waiting for political guarantees.

Along with the Bund, the Zionist organizations in Russia were the associations with the largest number of Jewish members. In 1898 there were 373 local groups; two years later 1,034 local groups existed. Those associates sent 200 delegates to the Fourth Zionist Congress. At the Second All-Russian Zionist Congress of 1902 in Minsk, five hundred delegates represented 75,000 members. The debates involving the character of cultural and educational activities, which had begun at a secret meeting in Warsaw, continued during that congress.

In 1903 the *Poale Zion, Ze'ire Zion, Bilu Hekhadosh* and other Zionist organizations were banned, but they were able to continue their work almost legally. These restrictions and the pogroms started a second *Aliyah*—a wave of immigration to Palestine—in which the future Israeli leaders, Ben Gurion, Sprinzak, and Ben Zvi participated.

At first Russian Zionists did not dispute that internal political development because most of the Jews declared emigration to Palestine to be their goal. In the revolutionary year of 1905, all non-socialist Jewish groups founded the "Union for the Establishment of Complete Rights for the Jewish People in Russia." The Zionists succeeded in including in the program the claim for Jewish national rights and national cultural self-determination. At the Third All-Russian Zionist Congress in Helsingfors in 1906, the "current work" in addition to the "Palestine work" were both stepped up. These new activities in the diaspora were meant to promote the democratization of the tsarist regime, autonomy for minorities, and the acknowledgement of Yiddish and Hebrew as national languages.

## Zion's Workers (*Poale Zion*) and Young Zionists (*Ze'ire Zion*)

Toward the end of the 19th century, socialist ideas gained acceptance in the Zionist movement in Western and Central Europe. Nachman Syrkin refined the idea of socialist Zionism in his book, *The Jewish Question and the Socialist Jewish State* (1898), which Moses Hess presented in his publication *Rome and Jerusalem* in 1862. They called themselves *Poale Zion* (*Zion's Workers*), but they possessed neither a party-like structure nor a consistent program up to that point. In 1901 various groups by this name operated in Russia, favoring a synthesis of Zionism and socialism. Many Jewish socialists became *Poale Zionists* when the Union stigmatized and branded Zionism as a "reaction of the bourgeois class against anti-Semitism, as a utopia" in 1901.

Ber Borokhov,* the most important thinker of workers' Zionism and one of the first Marxist theoreticians to analyze the national question of the Jewish people, founded a *Poale Zion* group in Yekaterinoslav in 1901. Under his leadership this group joined with other groups in Poltava in 1906 and became the Jewish Social Democratic Labor Party *Poale Zion*, which in 1907 joined other national associations to become the World Association *Poale Zion*. The party was banned in Russia in 1907 and its members were arrested and exiled. Of the 25,000 members, only a few hundred were able to continue working, albeit illegally.

The Young Zionists Party (*Tseire Zion*), established in 1903, was socialist but not Marxist. Many future kibbutz members in Palestine were recruited from this party, as well as a number of organizations that founded the United Zionist Workers' Party (*Hitakhdut*) in 1922.

## Zionists-Socialists (*Sionisty-Sozialisty*—S.-S.)

The workers' party, Zionists-Socialists, founded in 1904 by Jakob Leshchinski and others, was heavily attacked by the Bund because it was attracting the same potential socialist members. Like the Bund, the S.-S. also demanded a region for settlement in which the Jews would be able to develop their own economic structures. The S.-S. thought the prospects for Jewish settlers in Palestine were unrealistic.

When the plan to settle Jews in Uganda failed at the Seventh Zionist Congress in 1905, the S.-S. separated from the Zionist movement, but continued fighting side by side with other parties in the Revolution of 1905 and participated in the congress of the Second International in 1907 in Stuttgart. In 1917, the S.-S. and the Sejmists of the SERP joined forces and became the United Party (*Fareinikte*).

## Other Jewish Parties and Organizations

Simon Dubnov (1860-1941), one of the greatest historians of the Jewish people, founded the Yiddish People's Party (*Yidishe Folkspartei*), in 1906. This party demanded religious and cultural autonomy for the Jews and was supported by religious communities that were to form the core of the secular activities of the Jews in Eastern Europe. The party supported and worked for the foundation of Jewish schools, teacher and rabbinical seminaries, as well as other institutions. The plan was that the Jews should build up representation in every country, in order to defend their national interests.

Dubnov's destiny is revealing of the tragedy of the Russian Jews like no other: tsarist discriminations denied him an academic education and the Bolshevik dictatorship drove him into exile to Berlin, where his monumental ten-volume *World History of the Jewish People* (*Weltgeschichte des jüdischen Volkes*) was published. He fled to Riga, where, cruelly mocked by one of his former German students, the Germans murdered him in 1941.[13]

Chaim Shitlovski founded the Jewish Socialist Workers' Party (*Sotsialisticheskaia Evreiskaia rabochaia partiia*—SERP) in Kiev in 1906. Its program was based on a synthesis of Jewish-nationalist and socialist ideas, but was not Marxist. The party demanded national autonomy for minorities in multinational states like Russia. Every minority should have its own parliament (*Sejm* in Polish, origin of the label *Sejmists*). The party published the Yiddish paper *Voice of the People* (*Folksshtime*) and a Russian newspaper, *Serp*. It was in agreement with the social revolutionaries on the agrarian question and participated in the revolution of 1905. At the Second International, it demanded the establishment of a Jewish section together with other Jewish socialist parties.

In addition to the socialist-oriented parties, Jewish nationalist groups also existed in Russia, as in many other countries. One of these was the religious Zionists, organized into the national-religious *Mizrachi* party (*Merkas rukhani*—intellectual center) in Vilna in 1902. The goal of their founder, Rabbi Meir Berlin (Bar-Ilan), was that the land of Israel should be for the people of Israel, according to the laws of the Torah. In 1903, 210 local *Mizrachi* groups already existed in Russia. The anti-Zionist orthodox circles and their rabbis strongly fought the party.

## ORT

Institutions that coordinated the Jews' help for each other, in order to protect themselves from bankruptcy or confiscation, became especially important. The organization Association for the Support of Handicraft, Industry and Agriculture among the Jews (*Obshchestvo rasprostraneniia remeslennovo i zemledel'cheskovo truda sredi Evreiev*—ORT) played an important role in the vocational training in Russia in the 1880s. In 1917 the organization lost its founding capital, which by 1905 already amounted to one million rubles. After 1920 the organization was active again. The headquarters were in Berlin from 1921-1933; at present they are in Israel. The ORT supported agricultural projects in the Soviet Union in the 1920s and 1930s. Thus far the ORT union has given vocational training to more than 1 million people in more than 30 countries in Africa, Asia, and Latin America. Worldwide it is the largest nongovernmental organization in this field.

## OSE

In 1912 the Association for Jewish Healthcare (*Obshchestvo zdravookhraneniia Evreiev*—OSE) was founded in Russia. It supplied medical care for hundreds of thousands of victims of the war and the pogroms, refugees, and deported Jews. In 1917 the OSE operated 34 local organizations, 12 hospitals, 125 childcare centers, 40 school-meal centers, four sanatoriums for tuberculosis patients, and 60 emergency pharmacies. After the OSE was banned and dissolved in 1919 by the Soviet government, new national sections in many other European countries were rebuilt. The international central office was established in Berlin. The sister organization (TOZ) in Poland maintained 368 medical and sanitary facilities. Today there are national OSE centers in 10 European, 9 Latin American and 4 North African states, as well as in Israel, with facilities for medical treatment and childcare.


## EKOPO and YIDGEZKOM

In 1915 the Jews from the provinces (*gubernii*) of Kovno and the Kurland accused of befriending the German enemy were deported to Russia. This event created a wave of willingness to help and led to the foundation of the organization Jewish Aid Committee for War Victims (*Evreiski komitet pomoshchi zhertvam voiny*—EKOPO). Some of the founding members included the Jewish philanthropists and politicians M. Vinaver, L. Bramson, and H. Sliosberg. Because of foreign policy considerations and with regard to the Western allies the tsarist government allowed this organization to operate and supplied it with 16.5 million rubles (half the total budget). Petrograd Jews spent 2 million rubles, and the *Joint* (American-Jewish Joint Distribution Committee) transferred large amounts of money with the help of the U.S. embassy. Local EKOPO committees helped hundreds of thousands of Jews in Russian-occupied Galicia and in Bukovina. The organization was dissolved in 1920. Its work was handed over to the welfare organization YIDGEZKOM (Jewish Social Committee—*Yidisher gezelshaftlekher komitet*), which was founded by the *Yevsektsiia* and by the *Yevkom*. Jewish Bolsheviks hoped to increase the acceptance of the regime among the Jewish population and therefore claimed all the activities of the organization as their own, which were largely based on *Joint* donations. American Jews sent over 5,000 tons of clothing, food, and medicine to Russia. For that and for the rebuilding of destroyed Jewish settlements, American Jews donated $18 million between 1921 and 1924. YIDGEZKOM distributed the majority of the care packages, which were also intended for non-Jews.[14] In 1924 the organization was dissolved on the pretext that bourgeois elements wanted to convert it into Jewish congregations.

## Thriving Cultural Life Despite Repression

Despite the persecution and the awful poverty of large numbers of the population until 1917, Russian Jews developed a flourishing communal system with hundreds of cultural communities, numerous cultural facilities, clubs and parties—a cultural literary and newspaper infrastructure unparalleled at that time. Even for the poor Jews of the shtetls education was of paramount importance, and at least the male Jews learned how to read and to write. In 1897 only 21 percent of the population in Russia was able to read and write; by the beginning of World War I, 40 percent of the people were literate. The literacy rate was lowest among farmers.

More than 30 Jewish associations supported art, literature, music, education, higher education, and theater, archives, history, and religion as well as settlement projects. Bundists and Zionists especially established a tight network of clubs with pedagogical, cultural and scientific goals. Twenty synagogues, 25 schools, and many libraries and museums existed in St. Petersburg alone. In addition to the already mentioned welfare organizations, several welfare associations supported old people's homes, orphanages and hospitals.

Russia was also the cradle of the new Hebrew and Yiddish literature that spread across the whole Jewish world. More than a hundred Jewish newspapers and magazines were published. Ten Yiddish and two Hebrew daily newspapers, as well as numerous periodicals in Yiddish, Hebrew and Russian existed, such as the historical journals *Perezhitoe* and *Evreiskaia starina*.

### 3. JEWS IN RUSSIAN POLITICS
### BEFORE THE OCTOBER REVOLUTION

#### Cadets

At their first congress, on October 12-18, 1905, the Liberal Party of the Constitutional Democrats, commonly known as "Cadets," was founded in St. Petersburg. Their program called for a parliamentary constitutional form of government with a democratic right to vote, freedom and equal rights for all. These points appealed to the liberal and national aspirations of large circles of the Jewish bourgeoisie. Several leaders of the Cadets were Jews. Two hundred of the 486 representatives of the first Duma of 1906 were Cadets. Maxim Vinaver, vice chairman of the Cadets, the strongest faction of the Fourth Duma (1912-1917), was a judge at Russia's supreme court between the February Revolution and the October Revolution. The provisional government gave him the assignment to draft the constitution, which was to be passed by the legislative assembly, the Constituency. After the October Revolution, which he totally rejected, Vinaver temporarily held the post of foreign minister of the "white" opposition government in the Crimea. In 1919 he emigrated to France, where he died in 1926. M. Bomash, N. Friedman, Dr. I. Gurevich, Dr. S. Frenkel and four other Jewish Cadets were also representatives at the Fourth Duma. Three Jews, one of them Leonti Bramson, belonged to the faction of the social revolutionary *Trudoviki*. For many years Bramson was president of the world organization, ORT.

## Mensheviks

Despite many political differences, the Bolsheviks and the Mensheviks had worked hand in hand during the Revolution of 1905 and renewed their partnership at the Fourth Party Convention of the RSDRP in Stockholm in April 1906. At the Fifth Party Convention of the RSDRP, which took place in London in 1907, 342 delegates participated: 89 Bolsheviks, 88 Mensheviks, and 57 Bundists. The ideology and strategy of the Bolsheviks and Mensheviks was increasingly at odds. In 1912, at the Sixth All-Russian Conference of the RSDRP in Prague, after the resolution "about the liquidation and the liquidators" was accepted, they appeared as separate groups.

Marxism held a powerful attraction for the Russian intelligentsia. Jews also saw in Marxism "a way of reason" (Lydia Dan). The Mensheviks, who supported a socialist and democratic ideology, were the most powerful force in Russia after the revolution of 1905. They appealed to larger groups than did the Bolsheviks. Their program to create a post-revolutionary state, based on social democratic and humanistic principles with the obligation to provide for the welfare of the working population, appealed to many Jews. The democratic principles of the Mensheviks and their interpretation of Marxism corresponded much more closely to the Jewish tradition of free discourse than the Bolshevik's rigid practice of brutally suppressing diverging opinions. Beyond the strictly Jewish party spectrum, the Mensheviks had the largest number of Jewish members. Many of their leaders, who had built up social democracy at Lenin's side, were of Jewish origin, for example, B. Axelrod, Martov and Dan.*

The Bund and the Mensheviks shared common ground on many issues. Both were fundamentally reformist associations. Many of the most important functionaries of the Bund were also leaders of the Mensheviks. Stalin commented on how important Jews were among the Mensheviks:

> Statistics show that Jews are a majority within the Menshevik faction (naturally not including the Bundists), followed by the Georgians and then by the Russians. In contrast to the overpowering majority of Russians in the Bolshevik faction, followed by the Jews (of course not counting the Polish and Latvians), and then the Georgians, etc....To this, one of the Bolsheviks (I think it was Comrade Aleksinsky) remarked jokingly that the Mensheviks were a Jewish faction and the Bolsheviks a true Russian faction, and that it would not be bad if we, the Bolsheviks in the party, would start a pogrom.[15]

After the October Revolution the Mensheviks became fierce opponents of the Bolshevik dictatorship, even though they believed they had to protect "socialism" in Russia as a historic achievement. They condemned terror and the death penalty. Abramovich* and Martov dared to speak up against Stalin in a trial in 1918 and were therefore confronted with the vindictive feelings of the future dictator.[16] After the party was banned in 1921, the Mensheviks worked in the underground or went into exile. For the exiled leadership of the party, *Sotsialisticheskii vestnik*, became one of the most important platforms for well-founded criticism of the Soviet dictatorship from a leftist perspective. This journal, almost exclusively composed and edited by Jews, was published first in Berlin, then in Paris and finally in New York.

## Narodniki and Social Revolutionaries

The first revolutionaries of Jewish origin in the 19th century considered themselves to be Russians and were of the opinion that the emancipation of the Jews would depend on the liberation of the Russian people. They considered Jewish religion and culture to be obsolete. Some of them even converted to the Russian Orthodox faith and even dressed like peasants (*muzhiki*) in order to engage more effectively in revolutionary propaganda among the small farmers. A. Mikhailov and Mark Natanson founded the group Land and Freedom (*Zemlia i volia*), which in December 1876 organized the first demonstration in Russia. The program had four main demands: the handing over of land to the peasants, self-administration of the *Obshchina*, religious freedom, and the right to national self-determination.

*Zemlia i volia* spread the network of their organization across all of Russia. Their activities shifted, though, in the course of 1877 from the country to the city, because efforts at education and propaganda in the countryside were received indifferently or even with hostility. Vera Zasulich's attempt to assassinate the governor of St. Petersburg, in January of 1878, was the signal for a wave of terror. The idea was to undermine the tsarist regime. In the aftermath, violent actions by the police escalated, as well as revenge attacks by the Narodniki.

Mark Natanson, the popular, admired, and incorruptible patriarch of the social revolution and the son of a rich family, was born in 1850 near Vilna. As a nineteen-year-old medical student in St. Petersburg, he was arrested for his participation in the revolts. Further arrests followed and he was finally banished to Arkhangelsk where he was able to escape. After the *Zemlia i volia* was dissolved in August of 1879, he was arrested again, spending the next eleven years in exile in Siberia. Later he emigrated and became a CC member of the Social Revolutionaries, returning to Russia in 1917. He became one of the leaders of the Left Social Revolutionaries, who participated in the first Soviet government. Natanson died in Switzerland in 1919.

Joseph Aptekman, Aron Gobet, and Aron Sundelevich and other Jews were among the members and leaders of the revolutionary movement of the Nationalists (*Narodniki*). Even though the movement, which saw Russia's salvation in a kind of agrarian socialism based on old Russian traditions, partially welcomed the pogroms and spread anti-Semitic and anti-capitalist tendencies.

Jews also joined the terrorist movement; for example, Peoples' Will (*Narodnaia volia*), founded in 1879; Salomon Vitenberg, Meir Molodetskii, and Grigori Goldenberg, who at the age of 25 committed suicide in prison in 1880. Plekhanov convinced several prominent ex-Narodniki of Jewish origin to join the Black Redistribution (*Czorny peredel*—meaning: from the landowner to landless peasants), a more moderate successor group to *Zemlia i volia*—their leaders: Lev Deich (1855-1941), his lifetime companion Vera Zasulich (1849-1919), Pavel Axelrod (1850-1928) and O.V. Aptekman (1849-1926). Following the arrest of most of the group, including Aptekman, by the end of 1879, Deich, Plekhanov, Zasulich and other members temporarily lived abroad.

The successors of the Narodniki were the Social Revolutionaries (SR). This party resulted from the merger of several revolutionary groups in 1901-1902 and quickly became very popular. The leadership included, in addition to the founding members Viktor Chernov and Grigori Gershuni,* Mark Natanson, Mikhail, and Abram Gots,* Osip Minor,* who became mayor of Moscow in 1917, Ilya Rubanovich, as well as the infamous traitor Asev.[17]

The SR carried the main responsibility for the armed battle against the tsarist regime. In addition to political terror against the authorities, spreading revolutionary ideas among the farmers was an important point of their program. Kerensky, Chernov, and other members of the SR, as well as the closely connected *Trudoviki,* were part of the first government established after the February Revolution. The SR provided the strongest faction in the all-Russian executive committee of Soviet soldiers and Soviet workers.

The Leftist Socialist Revolutionaries, a radical socialist grouping within the SR, was excluded from the Third Congress of the party in June 1917. They constituted themselves as an independent party and demanded Russia's immediate withdrawal from World War I and socialization of the land. They had refused to collaborate with the provisional government. In March 1918 they withdrew their representatives from the council of the people's commissaries, in protest against the ratification of the treaty of Brest-Litovsk.

## Anarchists

Anarcho-syndicalism had many active followers among Jewish laborers in England and in the United States. In Russia this organization was one of the least organized revolutionary movements. After the revolution of 1917 the anarchists oscillated between opposition to the provisional government and temporary support for the Bolsheviks. Later they opposed the Soviet government and demanded a third, libertarian revolution, which proved to be reason enough for their brutal persecution and suppression by the regime. Three Jewish anarchists became legendary in Russia's history of anarchism and revolution: Vsevolod Volin,[*18] whose memoirs of revolution, civil war and the Makhno movement made him very well known, as well as the couple Emma Goldman and Aleksandr Berkman.

## Jewish Bolsheviks

Within the broad spectrum of Jewish organizations and the associated infrastructure, the number of Bolsheviks of Jewish origin was insignificant. They had almost no contact with the Jewish environment; they did not concern themselves with their own Judaism nor did they worry about the needs and problems of other Jews. Growing up between two cultures, they decided to become Russian. Only a few of them spoke Yiddish or Hebrew. Trotsky, a child of Jewish farmers living in one of the few tsarist settlement colonies in which Yiddish was not spoken, spoke the typical Russian-Ukrainian language mix. Kamenev* (actually Rosenfeld) was born in Moscow. He had a Russian mother and a Jewish father, who had let him be baptized. Yaroslavsky (actually Gubelman), the leader of the "Godless movement," was born in Chita, Siberia, as the child of Jewish farmers. He knew as little about the living conditions in the Pale as did Sverdlov,* who came from the central-Russian city of Nizhni Novgorod. Only Lazar Kaganovich,* whose native tongue was Yiddish, was generally identified as a Jew. This technocratic apparatchik, who for a long time was viewed as "number two" behind Stalin, came from a typical Ukrainian village.

Most Bolsheviks of Jewish origin did not have to suffer discrimination. Their families were often well off and economically independent. The fathers of Zinoviev* (actually Radomyselski) and of the agricultural commissar Yakovlev (Epstein) were teachers. Despite the Jewish quotas at universities and institutes of higher education, David Riazanov (later head of the Marx-Engels Institute) in Odessa and the financial commissar Sokolnikov (actually Brilliant) in Moscow, were able to receive a higher education. Radek,* the only leading "Jewish Bolshevik" who did not come from a Russian-speaking background, attended high school in Poland.

The tsarist society denied these men and women real possibilities for advancement. Their role as outsiders had somehow pushed them into embracing the "profession" of the revolutionary. Their personal decision to opt for Bolshevism, the most ruthless utopian direction, was shared only by a minority. A 1922 statistic shows that the party had only 964 Jewish members before the revolution (out of a total of 23,600 members, i.e., 4 percent). In 1917, 2,182 members joined, of whom some had previously been Mensheviks.[19] In other parties the number of Jewish members was higher before 1917. Thousands of Jews joined Jewish and general political parties after the February Revolution, where they filled important positions. Anti-Semites at that time coined the term "Judeo commune." The equation of Judaism and Bolshevism was at best a misunderstanding. In most cases, however, it was a calculated anti-Jewish rumor spread against better judgment. As well as the membership statistics, the attempted assassinations of major communist functionaries by two Jews also proved "Jewish Bolshevism" to be a lie.[20]

## Lenin and Stalin on the "Jewish Question"

In 1903 in several essays Lenin criticized the Bund: "Does the Jewish Proletariat Need an Independent Political Party?," "Assimilation or Dissimilation" and "The Last Word of Bundist Nationalism." Lenin had already presented in the party newspaper Spark (*Iskra*) his negative theses regarding Yiddish culture, which were erroneous and irrelevant, but which represented his opinion:

> The idea of a special Jewish people, totally untenable from a scientific perspective, is reactionary in its meaning. The latest history and political reality is proof, and delivers irrefutable evidence of this well-known fact. (...) The Jewish question is as follows and not anywhere else: Assimilation or dissimilation?—and the idea of the Jewish "nationality" openly carries its reactionary character, not only among their later followers (the Zionists), but also with those who try to combine this question with social democratic ideas (the Bundists). The idea of a Jewish nationality contradicts the interests of the Jewish proletariat because it creates a mood hostile to assimilation, a "ghetto" atmosphere.[21]

Lenin considered Yiddish to be a relic of the Middle Ages that would vanish with the assimilation of Jews. However, he had published his appeal, "To the Jewish workers," in Yiddish to attract their interest in Russian social democracy.

In 1913 the debates about the nationality question came to a head among the Bolsheviks. More than once in *Pravda*, the Bund was accused of having divisive intentions. The article "National Separatism," published on May 28, was followed by a contribution "About 'cultural national' autonomy." The Bund had rejected these attacks—which were also supported by Martov, the leader of the Mensheviks—in the organization's press and in other newspapers for many years.

Stalin had the final word concerning the rights of national minorities. Already in May 1913 he noted in his essay "Marxism and the National Question," the definition of "nation," which for the Jews was extremely important, and far-reaching:

> A nation is a historically justified stable community of people, born on the basis of the community of language, of territory, of economic life and of emotional characteristics identifying itself in the community of the culture.

Stalin stated that since the Jews were a non-nation, the only perspective for them was assimilation. He referred to Marx, Kautsky, and Otto Bauer, who was the "originator" of national-cultural autonomy and usually strongly attacked by the Bolsheviks. The Austrian social-democratic theoretician had described the Jews as a nation, but with the reservation that they did not have a common language.

In short, the Jewish nation ceases to exist—so for whom should one demand national autonomy? The Jews will be assimilated.[22]

Stalin reached this conclusion due to the absence of a closed Jewish settlement region and a Jewish peasant class. Since no "national market" of the Jews existed, but only services rendered for the nations in the majority, it would even lead to the disappearance of the Jewish language.

Massive attacks on the Bund followed, again using the famous accusation of "separatism": the organization would hinder the unity of the workers and would cause friction in the rank and file of the RSDRP. Stalin's attitude towards the Sabbath and the Yiddish language makes it obvious that for the Bolsheviks, who strived toward dictatorship, the Jews were an uncontrollable factor.

The Jews lived within the Pale regions and in the Polish and Baltic provinces, mostly scattered in towns and shtetls, but almost never in the surrounding rural country. There was no connected territory in which they were the majority of the population. The Pale existed until 1915. The tsarist government dissolved it during the war.

After the revolution Stalinist criteria still determined party doctrine. Even though the Bolsheviks, confronted by masses of settlers, acknowledged the Jews as a nationality in Russia after 1918, until the last days of the Soviet Union anyone claiming that the Jews were anything like a community beyond the borders of countries and indeed political systems, was guilty of "counterrevolutionary" heresy. This suspicion was explicitly directed at all former Bundists—a suspicion that brought persecution and death to countless politically active Jews. It made no difference if the person had changed and supported Lenin and Stalin and was ready to loyally defend that course. As early as 1913, Stalin had prepared the trap in which members of the JAFC were caught and mercilessly destroyed in 1952.

Like Stalin, Lenin wanted to use the politically active Yiddish-speaking working masses as a single combat unit without intending to give the several million Jews the rights of a nationality. In contrast to Stalin, who despised and mistrusted the Jews, Lenin appreciated the loyalty and idealism of assimilated Jewish comrades. He would have been willing to accept more followers into the Bolshevik sections, since they were the minority compared with the Mensheviks. In the "sealed railway compartment," which brought Lenin back from Switzerland to Russia in April 1917, there were several Jews traveling with him: Radek, Zinoviev, Sokolnikov, Rosenblum, Abramovich, Guberman, and Helene Kon.

Nobody suspected this trip to be part of the highly secretive and to this day almost unknown "Revolutionary and Insurgent Program," which had already been initiated in 1915 by the German government and the espionage service IIIb of the General Staff, with the authorization of the Kaiser. Its intent was to weaken the empire of the tsar and its armies from the inside out, in order to split off the western provinces from the Russian Empire. After the revolution succeeded, the plan was to impose a dictated peace on Russia, in order to achieve a "Siegfrieden" (peace through victory) on the Western Front. Russia's economic and mineral resources would in any case be exploited by German industry. Before and still long *after* the October Revolution, Lenin's Bolshevik party was financed by the German treasury for this purpose to the tune of many millions of Goldmarks.[23]

Lenin did not recognize the true nature of anti-Semitism, but he had also never used it. More than once he publicly spoke about the reasons for the tsarist pogroms, which he certainly deeply detested. In a speech on January 17, 1917 in Zurich he declared:

> Tsarism's hatred was directed especially toward the Jews. On the one hand, an extraordinarily high percentage (in relation to the total number of the Jewish population) of the leaders of the revolutionary movement were Jews. And even now, Jews incidentally have the merit of having an noticeably higher percentage of representatives of the internationalist movement than do other nations. On the other hand, tsarism knew very well how to take advantage of the worst prejudices of the most uneducated population against the Jews. That is how the pogroms could take place, most of the time supported, if not directed, by the police; a terrible slaughter of peaceful Jews, of women and children, which aroused the hatred of the whole civilized world against bloody tsarism. Naturally, I mean hatred of the truly democratic elements of the civilized world, and those are exclusively the socialist labor force, the proletarians. During this time, more than 4,000 dead were counted in 100 cities, and more than 10,000 were mutilated.[24]

The gifted analyst and prophet of the revolution did not sense that one month later the revolution in Russia would really break out.

## 4. FROM THE FEBRUARY REVOLUTION TO THE OCTOBER REVOLUTION

When the February Revolution swept the tsarist regime away in 1917, real prospects opened up to the Russian Jews for the first time in centuries, despite the misery and the war. Just a few days later Jewish parties and organizations were already continuing their legal activities. The provisional government ordered, by legal statute of March 20, 1917, the end to all discrimination against Jews. This was published in issue 15 of the official government paper *Vestnik vremennovo pravitel'stva*:

> Assuming that all citizens of a free country should be equal and that the conscience of each human being refuses the idea of restraint of citizens based on religion or origin, the provisional government determines: all restrictions of rights of Russian citizens by present

laws concerning their religion, their political views, or nationality are herewith abolished.[25]

All 150 abolished decrees were listed at the end of the text of the law. Suddenly the Jews were able to display their political opinions, as well as their social and cultural activities individually and as a national group. They were now able to determine their profession and decide where they wanted to live. The opportunity to create and mold their life according to their own standards suddenly freed previously repressed energy. In 1915 the courts had prohibited any kind of Jewish press, because of a lack of reliable censors who knew the language. Now, the Yiddish newspapers *Petrograd Daily* (*Petrograder togblatt*), *The Free Word* (*Dos freie wort*), *The Worker's Voice* (*Die arbeter-shtime*), *The Organ of the Bund*, as well as the Hebrew newspapers (*Haam* and *Hekhaver*) and the paper *Evreiskii student* in Russian, were published once again.

The Jews supported the new government with all their heart. Four Jewish politicians and lawyers became members of the senate: M. Vinaver, O. Gruzenberg, I. Gurevich, and G. Blumenfeld. Already on March 24 the chief of the provisional government, Duke Georgi Lvov, received the Jewish delegates of the Fourth Duma: M. Bomash, I. Gurevich, N. Friedman, and eleven members of the Jewish politburo, who expressed the gratitude of the Russian Jews for their liberation. On the same day this delegation visited the executive committee of the Council of Workers and Soldiers, where N. Cheidse, the committee's representative, welcomed them.

Until the October revolution the Cadet S. Lurye and the Mensheviks S. Schwarz and A. Ginzburg-Naumov served as deputy ministers of the provisional government. A. Halpern was the manager of the administration of the government. He was the first Jew ever to be a minister. Fyodor Dan, Menshevik, and Mark Liber, leader of the Bund, were members of the Central Executive Committee of the Soviets. Henryk Erlich* was, like Liber, a leading Bundist and was one of Petrograd's most important members of the workers council. The Bundists and Mensheviks also participated in the establishment of workers councils in the Russian provinces.

At a congress on March 15, 1917, the Zionist-Socialists and Sejmists of the SERP joined to form the United Party (*Fareinikte*). Its CC had its headquarters in Kiev. The Bund held its first legal conference in Petrograd from April 19-24 where the 88 delegates elected the first legal CC, which included Sch. Eisenstadt, Liber, Weinstein, Erlich, Rafes, and Abramovich.

Besides the left parties, new Jewish secular and religious groupings made their appearance: the Jewish National Union (*Netsakh Israel*), Tradition and Freedom (*Masores Veherus*) and Israel's Unity (*Ahdus Isroel*) and the anti-Zionist Orthodox party *Aguḍas Isroel*. The popular group founded by M. Vinaver strongly supported the cultural work in the communities, as well as Yiddish and Hebrew lessons in newly founded Jewish schools. Several Zionist organizations for school students, university students and in general for the youth were also established; for example, *Hekhaver*, *Histadrut*, *Kadima*, *Dror* and *Maccabi*.

Because of the new situation, the Russian Jews planned the unification of all associations and communities into a single main representative organization. The Zionists took the first step in this direction when they appointed the Seventh All-Russian Zionist Congress on May 24, 1917, in Petrograd (formerly St. Petersburg). Dr. Yekhiel Chlenov,* who led the congress, spoke in front of the 552 delegates and 1,500 guests representing 140,000 Zionists from 680 cities and towns in Russia. He conveyed greetings from the foreign secretary of the provisional government, M. Toroshchenko, and from the representative of the laborer council, N. Cheidse.

On July 16, 1917, preparations were made for the All-Russian Jewish Congress in Petrograd. The participants of the congress elected the official representatives of the Jews in Russia. Four delegates represented the Jews from each of the 13 cities that had more than 50,000 citizens: Berdytchev, Bobruisk, Kharkov, Gomel, Yekaterinoslav, Yelisavetgrad, Kiev, Kremenchug, Minsk, Moscow, Odessa, Petrograd, and Vitebsk.

In August 1917, the provisional government organized a state conference in Moscow, at which preparations were made for the formation of the government. The Jewish parties sent a socialist and a non-socialist: Rafael Abramovich (Bundist/Menshevik) and Oskar Gruzenberg (lawyer and civil rights activist). Both appealed, in the name of the Russian Jews, for the protection of the Russian fatherland against the German imperialists and their occupation forces. The text of their speeches was published in Yiddish in the *Workers' Voice* (*Arbetershtime*), the Union's mouthpiece, and in Russian in the *Evreiskaia nedelia*. Jewish parties listed a joint register at the elections to the constituent assembly. The Jewish delegates established their own faction, which was to follow the resolutions of the All-Russian conference.

This congress, planned for the end of 1917, did not take place because the Bolsheviks banned most Jewish organizations after the October Revolution. After the peace treaty of Brest-Litovsk the Germans occupied almost all the Jewish population centers. On March 24, 1918, the provisional Jewish national council was formed, with the most important representatives of the Russian Jews belonging to the presidium: Sch. Eisenstadt, M. Aleinikov, S. Dubnov, and H. Sliosberg. At the end of June 1918, the representatives of the Jewish cultural communities were called to Moscow to elect at least a chairmanship for their communities, even though the Ukraine had already separated and other regions were also unreachable. Among the 149 delegates from 40 communities, the Zionists were the strongest faction with 62 representatives. Only 21 delegates represented the Bund. This umbrella organization was also forbidden and abolished by a decree of Joseph Stalin, the commissar for nationalities, after June 19, 1919. The end of the organized Jewish community of the Soviet Union was thus decided.

After the elections of the town councilors, many Jews were involved in community politics. In July 1917, all leftist Jewish parties in Kiev joined to establish the "socialist bloc." The Zionist and Orthodox Jews formed the "democratic bloc." Together they obtained 15 seats in the town council. The Menshevik A. Ginzburg-Naumov became deputy mayor. In Minsk, 102 town councilors, including 28 Jews, elected the Bundist Weinstein as their chairman.

In Yekaterinoslav the Menshevik I. Polonsky was elected mayor. In Moscow the social revolutionaries represented the majority of the town Soviet.

## The Jews in Independent Ukraine 1917–1920

The Ukraine became famous as the setting of the cruelest Jewish persecution during the revolutionary years, even though the government had granted full national rights to the Jews—rights that were unthinkable during the reign of the tsars and under the Bolsheviks. The greatest paradox was the fact that many perpetrators of the pogroms were murdered in the name of the Ukrainian government (but not on its orders).

After the February Revolution, an institution by the name of *Rada*, the equivalent of the Russian Soviet, governed the Ukraine and it included mainly Ukrainian nationalists. Unlike other minorities, they had not been able to form legally under tsarism. The momentum of Ukrainians and Jews, as two nations that had both been repressed under tsarism, initially took an identical path after liberation.

The politicians of the *Rada*, who were always accused by the provisional government of breaking away, published their proclamation using the name Universal—hinting at Cossack tradition. At the first Universal in June 1917, the minorities were asked to participate equally in the establishment of a new state.

The Jews were skeptical about the Ukrainians' struggle for independence. The land had belonged to the Pale, the *Cherta osedlosti*. After the separation from Russia, the Jews that were living in those regions would again have been located beyond the borders of Moscow and Petrograd. At first the Jewish parties, especially the People's Party (*Folkspartei*) and the United Party, supported the politics of the *Rada*. The leftists—Bund and *Poale Zion*—agreed to the socialist direction they were taking; the Zionists, the strongest tendency in the Ukraine, also benefited from their concept of autonomy.

The draft of the constitution provided that all laws must be published not only in Ukrainian, but also in Russian, Polish, and Yiddish. These three main minorities obtained their own ministries, called vice-secretary offices. The first vice-secretary for Jewish affairs was Moshe Zilberfarb, a member of the United party. Zilberfarb wanted to call in a Jewish body of representatives. The experiment failed mainly because small groups like the people's party were supposed to have the same number of seats as the Zionists, who had many members and followers. In addition, the Zionists demanded that the Jews should form their own self-defense units. But this was something Zilberfarb rejected. The internal quarrel was particularly fateful, since the news about pogroms was spreading and an authorized Jewish group of representatives could have pressured the Ukrainian government to take on early preventive measures.

After the October Revolution the national vice-secretary offices were upgraded to secretary general offices and the "national personal autonomy" of the Jews, Poles, and Russians became law. Now everyone—no matter which part of the Ukraine he lived in—was able to register as a member of these minorities, and also had the right to elect national legislative institutions. The Ukrainian government guaranteed to the Jews whatever Lenin and Stalin had refused to give them, using the excuse that they did not have their own closed settlement regions.

When Red Army troops entered the Ukraine from the north, in January 1918, the *Rada* proclaimed the complete independence of the Ukraine. The Bund voted against this proclamation. The People's Party, United Party and *Poale Zion* abstained from voting and Zionists did not take part

in the vote. The fact that the Jewish parties did not support total separation from Russia without reservation, even though the constitution was
very favorable to them, was in part a result of the wish to not be completely separated from the Jews remaining, the Jewish workers' party and
the Zionist movement. More important was the rift between the concepts of the Ukrainian intellectuals who governed in Kiev and the reality
in the countryside. The Jews realized that the state was granting them
rights, but was unable—and apparently was also unwilling—to guarantee
them protection against marauding and pillaging bandits and from farmers' revolts.

Zilberfarb resigned by the end of January, along with all the ministers. He continued in his official functions in April, when the Bolsheviks,
who had conquered Kiev, were driven out and, with the help of the Germans, the *Rada* returned to power. After the Zionists gave up their boycott position, W. Latsky was elected as minister for Jewish affairs. In the
1952 trial against the JAFC leadership, Latsky was mentioned when the
poet David Bergelson* was forced to give a statement that he fled to
Germany because of Latsky's intervention. At that time Bergelson was
active in the Culture League. This organization, founded in Kiev, had
departments of literature, music, theater, painting and sculpture, as well
as schools for children and adults. By the end of 1918, they had at their
disposal more than 120·branch offices all over the Ukraine. Its members
came from the Bund, *Poale Zion*, and the United Party. The Culture League
founded its own university and in 1919 it was asked to take over the
Jewish educational system in the Ukraine.

At first the rights of the Jews were again reduced, when at the end of
April 1918 the Germans put Cossack General Skoropadsky, later a fol-
lower of the Nazis, in power. At the elections for community councilors
(only ten percent participated) the candidates of Zionist and religious
parties received approximately 60 percent and the candidates of the various leftist movements around 40 percent of the vote.

After the withdrawal of the Germans, the new government reinstalled the so-called "Directory," the "National Personal Autonomy"—
although only for Jews and not for Russians and Poles. The nationality
secretariat, which was dominated by Zionists, refused to support the new
minister for Jewish affairs, Abraham Revusky, a member of *Poale Zion*.
These quarrels happened at the same time as a wave of pogroms that
were much crueler than the previous ones. In 1919, in protest against
these mass murders, the Jewish deputy foreign minister, A. Margolin,

resigned. At this point many Ukrainian Jews permanently opposed independence for the Ukraine and had no choice but to look for protection from the Bolsheviks. Since the head of the Directory, the leftist nationalist Simon Petlyura, refused repeatedly to take action against the pogroms, the *Poale Zionists* also withdrew support and Revusky resigned. After Petlyura had publicly denounced the pogroms in April 1919, Pinchas Krasny took over the office, more or less on his own initiative. He managed to initiate aid for the victims of the pogroms and to extend the national autonomy rights. This, of course, was only a theoretical success, because the days of Jewish and Ukrainian autonomy were numbered, following the Bolshevik victory in November 1920.[26] When Revusky emigrated (in exile he wrote some very revealing memoirs), Krasny remained in the Ukraine and supported the new regime.

Part II

# Janus-Faced Liberation:
# The Jewish Ascent after the October
# Revolution

## 5. The Jews in Revolution and Civil War

The "dual reign" of the councils (Soviets) and the provisional government made it possible, in the short time between the February and October revolutions, for the Jews to engage in politics with the same rights as everyone else. Even though there were Bundists among the soviets, the leaders of the Jewish workers' movement, the leftist Zionists and other Jewish parties did not support these groups. Their justified concern was that the street riffraff, which sided with the Bolsheviks, would make no difference between "revolution" and pogroms of Jews, and in case of a suppression of the risky revolution, the Jews would become victims of the counterrevolution, as was the case in 1905. Gorky reported "how the soldiers, who so enthusiastically defended extremist slogans of the Leninists, were seduced by the Jew-baiting of certain people who made them believe that the Jewish influence in the worker's and soldier's council was too strong."[1]

It is true that men of Jewish origin had filled important positions in Bolshevik organizations. In many cases they were predominant. Three out of five members of the "committee of the revolutionary defense of Petrograd" were Jews: Moisei Uritzky, Goldstein, and Drabkin. After the

Tenth Party Congress of the Communist Party of Russia—the RSDRP (B) operated under this name since 1919—in April 1921 Lenin, Stalin, Trotsky, Zinoviev, and Kamenev were members of the Politburo. In the fall of 1917, Trotsky was elected chairman of the Soviet of Petrograd. He was also elected as one of fifteen members of the board of the people's commissars as commissar for foreign affairs; later he became commissar of the army and navy. Trotsky also took over the command of the Red Army and other party offices. Zinoviev, Kamenev, and Sverdlov were also among the core leaders. Yakov Sverdlov, often the representative of the party's central committee, was appointed as the first head of state of the Soviet Union. Those mentioned above, like other Jewish cadres, declared their nationality to be Russian.

The first Soviet government formed by a coalition of Bolsheviks and Left Social Revolutionaries was not supported by a majority of Russian Jews. Soon after the revolution it became clear that the politics of the Bolsheviks ran counter to the interests of the Jews.

The secret police (the Cheka), established by Felix Dzerzhinsky in December 1917, was given extraordinary authority "to fight against counterrevolution and sabotage." This organization mercilessly persecuted non-Bolshevik revolutionaries—Bundists, Anarchists, Mensheviks and Social Revolutionaries, among them many Jews—and consequently provoked counterattacks. In order to take revenge for his executed friend, in 1918 the young Jewish socialist Kannegisser shot Moisei Uritzky, who in the meantime had become head of the Moscow Cheka. The Jewish anarchist Fania Kaplan (born Feiga Roitblat) was involved in the attempted murder of Lenin. Documents that are now available show that she most probably was not the shooter, but covered the assassin. This attempt of August 30, 1918, gave the Bolsheviks the pretext for "an open and systematic mass terror against the bourgeoisie and their agents."

## The Pogroms

Between 1917 and 1921 there were 1,236 pogroms in 530 cities and shtetls. During this time 60,000 Jews were murdered. Half a million of them lost their home and property, and many would still suffer from the after-effects of their injuries for years.[2] Never before in the sorrowful history of the Russian Jews had there been a massacre of this size. The mercenaries' campaigns in the traditional settlement regions would begin the wave of murderous violence, for which the term "civil war" doesn't really apply.[3] On Ukrainian soil, Ukrainian units fought against the Bolsheviks. It was a war of independence. In Belorussia, the Polish conquerors advanced; in the Baltics the German free corps; in the south of Russia the "volunteer army" under the leadership of former tsarist generals. There were marauding troops everywhere: Cossack leaders (*Ataman*), rebellious farmers under the leadership of anarchists and criminal gangs, fortune seekers and deserters from the defeated tsarist army. The bulk of these troops—and most of the time their leaders as well—were united by their traditional Russian anti-Semitism.

The propagandists of the "Whites" and of the Ukrainian Ataman blamed the Jews for Bolshevism and its crimes. The old familiar battle cry "Kill the Jews and save Russia" became popular again. Leaflets were distributed during the pogroms, claiming to unmask the true rulers of the alleged Soviet Judea. Behind the party pseudonyms were placed not only real names—"Trotsky (Bronstein)"—but other names that were often invented.

The task forces that raged with fury across the Soviet Union against the Jews, starting in June 1941, with the support of the German armed forces, blamed every single Jew for Bolshevism, a fact that in their eyes justified the murder of the Jews. Both waves of murder cannot be put on one level, however, despite certain similarities. The National Socialists had ordered the total extermination of the Jews, while the pogroms after the October revolution remained localized. Neither Admiral Kolchak in Siberia, nor Ukrainian leader Petlyura nor Generals Denikin and Wrangel directly ordered the pogroms.

## Jews in the Red Units

Guchkov, the minister of war in the provisional government, ordered the democratization of the officer corps of the army right after the February Revolution in 1917. Appropriate candidates were assigned to take part in crash courses in hastily established officer candidate schools. Among these were also 2,600 Jewish soldiers, who had signed on because for the first time Jews were allowed to become officers. In the 19th century there had been only one Jewish officer in the Russian army. The former soldier, Herzl Tsam (1835-1915), hero of many battles, was promoted to staff captain only after forty years of service. Although Russian Jews lacked motivation and military traditions, many of them were decorated in the Russian-Japanese War; for example, Joseph Trumpeldor, the hero of the Battle of Port Arthur.

During the civil war, it became known very quickly that the Red Army also committed murders of Jews, but the Bolsheviks and their newly established dictatorship must have appeared to most Jews as the least of the competing evils. Any attempt to defend one's life was taken as evidence of a tendency to Bolshevism, and therefore, thousands of persecuted Jews were automatically candidates for execution. Many Jewish defense groups had no other choice but to actually join the Bolsheviks. Entire classes of the *yeshivas* were forced to give up their Torah and Talmud studies to take up weapons.

The victory of the White Guard Armies could have meant the complete annihilation of Russian Judaism. Thousands of volunteers flowed to the Red Army, many of whom were Bundists and Zionists. The Jewish parties had called their members to take this step, and cared for them in many different ways. Many newspapers on the front appeared in the Yiddish language. *The Yiddish Soldier (Der Yidisher Soldat),* mouthpiece of the military Zionist organization on the western front, reported about the organization of self-defense units of the Jews. The weekly newspaper, *The Free Soldier (Der freier Soldat)*, distributed by the executive committee of the Jewish soldiers of the 12th Army, published an obituary on December 20, 1917, of the classical author of Yiddish literature, Mendele Moikher Sforim, who had passed away shortly before at age 82. The *Red Army (Royte Armey)*, the newspaper of the central military section of the CC of the workers' party *Poale Zion*, was still being published for many years after the war ended. For their memorial book *Iskor*, the editorial office requested readers, in the issue of July 30, 1919, to write down memories of comrades who were killed in action and to send in their photos. At the end of a proclamation denouncing people who refused their duty or deserters, it said: "Down with the traitors of the working class and of the proletarian state." In February 1924 the *Royte Armey* printed an Agitprop text by Trotsky, ending with the words: "Our freedom, our country, our independence we will defend!"

## The End of the Bund

Pressed by the situation the Bund changed its position on Lenin's dictatorship and agreed to collaborate with the Soviets. The approach to the Bolsheviks led to the split within the organization. Despite their traditional enmity in the Ukraine, the communist group inside the Bund, the *Kombund*, joined with the pro-communist faction of the Zionist United Party, to become the *Komfarband*. The *Komfarband* then became affiliated with the communist party. A Jewish communist party was also formed in Belorussia. It entered into a union with the Lithuanian communists, which soon joined the communist party. In 1920 the rest of the Bund sections decided to join the Communist Party of Russia, at a time when the Bolsheviks were already acting under the party's name. As was the case before the revolution, the wish for some form of independence was denied. In 1921 the Bund had to announce its dissolution. Since the Bolsheviks, confronted with the masses of the Jewish labor movement, were unable to push through their one-party-state ideology with plain terror, they used methods of *divide et impera.** The old Bundist dream of national cultural autonomy without centralist patronage was over.

Similar to what happened with the JAFC later on, the Jewish communists continued to discuss whether the Soviet Union should act as the protector of all Jews—even though there was no unified Jewish nation, as Lenin and Stalin had "demonstrated." This clearly set them apart from those dogmatic Marxists to whom the protection of every pogrom victim—no matter whether they were workers or entrepreneurs—was considered to be equivalent to "bourgeois" treason to the cause of the proletariat.

## Lenin's Rhetoric Against the Pogrom Campaign

In order to get the pogroms of the Red Army under control, the council of the people's commissars sent a telegram with Lenin's signature to all government Soviets. The telegram ordered them to "take resolute measures in order to wipe out the anti-Semitic movement by the roots. It demanded that they take on the organizers of pogroms and those "who instigate outside the law." Since neither this edict nor the victories over

---

* Divide and conquer.

the counterrevolution nor the bravery of Jewish Red Army soldiers could erase this evil, Maxim Gorky decided to publish a pamphlet entitled "About the Jews" in 1919, in which he characterized the Jews as the "yeast of progress." Several Jewish communists interpreted these words as promoting "bourgeois nationalism." Lenin resisted their wish to confiscate this text and composed shortly afterward a proclamation to the soldiers, which was recorded on gramophone. The following words were broadcast to units of the Red Army:

Anti-Semitism is called the spreading of enmity against the Jews. When the damned tsarist monarchy lived through its last hours, it tried to goad the ignorant workers and farmers against the Jews. The tsarist police collaborated with the landowners and capitalists and organized the pogroms. They tried to turn the hatred of the impoverished workers and farmers away from the landowners and exploiters and toward the Jews. It is common in other countries as well that the capitalists stir up enmity against the Jews to blind the view of the workers and divert them from their real enemy, the capitalists. Only where landowners and capitalists have kept the workers and farmers in ignorance through serfdom can the enmity against the Jews endure. Only totally ignorant and repressed people would believe the lies and defamations that have been spread about the Jews. These are leftovers from the time of serfdom and slavery, when the popes had heretics burned on pyres, when the slavery of the farmers existed, when the nation was crushed and blind. But this old darkness of serfdom is vanishing. The people are beginning to see. The Jews are not the enemy of the working people. The enemies of the workers are the capitalists of all countries. Among the Jews there are workers, employees—and they are the majority. They are our brothers, our comrades in the fight for socialism, because they are being repressed by the capitalists. Among the Jews there are Kulaks, exploiters and capitalists, just as they exist among us. The capitalists are eager to introduce enmity among the workers of different religions, of different nations and of different races. Rich Jews, like rich Russians and the rich of all countries—all of them united—smash, repress and contaminate the laborers. Shame and disgrace on damned tsarism, which has harassed and persecuted the Jews. Shame and disgrace on the one who sows hate against other nations. Long live the brotherly trust and the unity of the working people of all nations for the downfall of capitalism![4]

Lenin condemned the pogroms more aggressively than either the anarchist Makhno or the nationalist Petlyura, but he remained true to the thesis that the "class question" was the only key to the solution of the problem: only the laborers are "our brothers, our comrades in the fight for socialism." Years later, when the members of the JAFC were looking for an alliance with the Jewish capitalists in the U.S., according to Leninist and Stalinist logic they betrayed the working class and the Soviet state. Only the highest center of power—the leader of the party—decided which alliances were necessary and which were to be rated as betrayal.

Documents that remained secret during the Soviet era reveal how strongly Lenin's relations to the Jews were determined by party doctrine. In a bill about the structure of the Soviet government that was to be established in the conquered Ukraine, he demanded the exclusion of the Jews in late 1919—the postscript read "somewhat more politely, the Jewish petty bourgeoisie."[5] However, one should not misinterpret the implied irony used by Lenin to speak about the Bolshevik ideology and acknowledge at the same time that among the leaders of the Bolsheviks were quite a number of Jews.

In 1920-21 he was informed of new pogroms with hundreds of casualties. The culprits were members of the Red cavalry, as well as marauding gangs. All Lenin did was to order this information filed "in the archive." It seems to be in contradiction with the flaming speeches he had recorded on gramophone, but Lenin—like Stalin after him—was mainly concerned with consolidating power and not with the (survival) interests of Jews. When it seemed opportune to attract the attention of the Jewish masses and to discipline his own party with appeals against anti-Semitism, the Bolshevik leader acted like a "philo-Semite," but when his proclamations would have harmed the victorious Budyonny Army, he ignored the bloody pogroms.

## 6. THE JEWISH COMMISSARIAT
### *YEVKOM* AND THE JEWISH PARTY SECTION *YEVSEKTSIIA*

After the revolution the Bolsheviks changed to a "Bundist" type policy and guaranteed the Jews as a "nationality" their own schools, administration units, territories, etc. In another basically similar paradoxical turn, the strong Zionist territorial demands from before the revolution reappeared. The discussion was about a Jewish republic, though naturally in the Far East—a republic that could have even become the establishment of a closed Jewish territory. Until the start of this pseudo-Zionism inside Soviet Russia in 1928, a small understated and isolated *Poale Zion* party existed as a "bloc party" that was tolerated at the fringes. The opposition to both the Jewish national movements, the Bund and Zionism, remained until the end of the Soviet Union as one of the few permanent characteristics of Bolshevik ideology and practice. A Jewish communist was also required to give up all national aspirations—except those specifically allowed by the CC.

The reason the rulers were willing to make concessions was obvious: the young Soviet state could not do without the Jewish cadres, because there was no replacement for them as yet. A forced Russification of the Jews would have been illusory. The October Revolution had to be brought into the "Yiddish street"—to mobilize the Jews for the party. This was the reason the Jewish commissariat, the *Yevkom*, was created in February 1918. The Jewish commissariat was under the control of the commissariat for nationalities under the leadership of Joseph Stalin, meaning that the Jewish commissariat came under the control of the strongest, hardest opponent of all national Jewish claims. The same applied to the Polish commissariat, which was founded a few weeks before the *Yevkom*. In both cases an organization was to be established for a nationality without its own territory. At first many non-Bolsheviks, like the *Poale Zionists*, left social revolutionaries and people who belonged to no party, worked at the *Yevkom*. Only a few Bolsheviks had connections or felt close to the Jewish milieu or spoke Yiddish. One of the few was Semyon Dimanstein,* the son of a plumber. In 1904 he already was one of Lenin's fighter comrades and was in Siberian exile for many years before the revolution. In 1918 he founded the official party newspaper, *Der Emes (The Truth)*. Until his arrest in 1938 he remained for all intents and purposes the absolute authority over Jewish problems in the Soviet Union—the real bosses sat in the Politburo, to which Dimanstein never belonged. The *Yevkom's* mission—besides the struggle against Zionists and Jewish parties—was to engage in propaganda for the new regime, provide support and help for returning refugees of the civil war, and the establishment of national Jewish institutions. The *Yevkom* and the entire nationality commissariat were liquidated in 1924. The representation of Jewish minorities in the government (and other nationalities without their own territory) was from then on the responsibility of the nationality council and the interior ministry of the individual Soviet republics.

The *Yevkom* was a government institution; while in the Soviet state party institutions were more important. The Communist Party's Jewish section was founded on October 20, 1918. Its designation was the Russian abbreviation *Yevsektsiia*.[6] As with the *Yevkom*, many competent and linguistically skilled cadres could not be found for the *Yevsektsiia*. Among the 64 founding members only 31 were Bolsheviks. Jewish sections (*Yevsektsii* in the Russian plural) existed in the communist parties of Russia, Belorussia, the Ukraine, and central Asian Turkestan. Some of their main objectives were to recruit Jewish members into the Communist party and undermine the influence of other parties. In the first three regions they published Yiddish party material and established Yiddish clubs.

The *Yevkom* was used, like the *Yevsektsii*, to eliminate any political competition for the Bolsheviks among the Jews. Initially, the members debated if the sections should be dissolved and changed into a propaganda section or set up as an independent Jewish communist organization. After many former Bundists were taken over by the CC, Tchemeriski, Mereshin, Vainstein, Litvakov,* and Esther Frumkin were elected to the central office. They were all murdered in the Great Terror of the 1930s.

A decision of the commissariat for national concerns, signed by Shmuel Agurski on June 19, 1919, and confirmed by Joseph Stalin, the commissar for nationalities, the all-Russian central office of the Jewish communities was abolished. Similar edicts soon followed, affecting all other Jewish organizations and parties. From then on they could exist only secretly or in a tolerated semi-legal situation.

## War against Zionism

After the regime stabilized at the end of the revolutionary turmoil, functionaries of the *Yevsektsii* were pejoratively called *Yevseki*. They now received instructions to brutally and thoroughly exterminate Russian Judaism's entire infrastructure. They had the monopoly of all the concerns and questions pertaining to the Jews. They eagerly fulfilled their task and with great thoroughness liquidated cultural communities, synagogues, Talmud schools, Hebrew libraries, publishing houses, printing shops, and newspapers; the writers and technical personnel were fired. Not only were traditional institutions destroyed, but also new establishments like the Culture League (*Kultur Lige*) in the Ukraine were, after being tolerated for a brief period, either repressed or allowed to continue under communist control. Yiddish culture and literature that conformed to the demands of the regime developed on top of the ruins of those institutions.

Initially the Soviet government mostly tolerated Zionism. Many members, such as the Bundists, saw the new regime as a lesser evil compared to the persecution under the tsars. Although the Zionists' central bureau had already been closed in September 1919, the parties could still hold congresses. At the third *Yevsektsiia* congress in July 1920, the order was issued for the total elimination of Zionism. Zionists were arrested straight out of their conferences, thrown into prisons, tortured and exiled to Siberia. The Soviet press ignored Zionism's multiple aspects and distorted "Zionism" as being a form of "Fascism," discussing a "soul relationship" between its followers and anti-Semitism.[7] This primitive argument was used mostly in the Soviet propaganda of the 1960s.

The Zionist-related pioneer movement *Hekhaluts*, founded in 1917 by Joseph Trumpeldor, the hero of Port Arthur, also fell victim to the *Yevsektsiia*. The *Hekhaluts* wanted to lead the Jews out of their confinement in the shtetls. In addition to land colonies, they also promoted cultural activities in the Hebrew language and made connections with Palestinian workers' parties. The *Khalutsim* and Zionists soon saw the coming danger, especially from the *Yevsektsii*, because the Jewish communists were very jealous of their political monopoly. In the mid-1920s as the arrests became more and more frequent, many members went into the underground. A few years later *Hekhaluts* land colonies no longer existed.

With the persecution of Zionism, attacks on the Hebrew language were common. The *Yevsektsii* activists were again much more intolerant than the government itself, which defined Yiddish as a national school language. Hebrew was not explicitly forbidden, but the Jewish sections repressed it whenever possible. In their publications they valued Yiddish as the language of the proletariat and Hebrew as the language of the petty bourgeoisie and "fascist" Zionists. Litvakov was especially hostile to this language. In the first half of the 1920s, only three Hebrew publications appeared in the Soviet Union.[8]

The *Yevsektsii's* harassing pressure to close down the Hebrew theater *Habimah*, established by Jewish actors, was not agreed to, even by nationalities commissar Stalin.[9] The support the theater received from non-Jewish and Soviet-Russian artists like, Gorky and Lunacharsky, could not change the fanatical persecution and terror of the *Yevsektsii*. In 1926 the actors did not return from a European tour; confronted by constant *Yevsektsii* terror they emigrated to Palestine.

In the early 1920s few Jews were able to leave Russia. The Zionists emigrated to Palestine; others went to Western Europe or America. In Berlin a Russian-Jewish diaspora established itself with its own Jewish newspapers and publishing houses.


## Persecution of the Jewish Religion

As with other religions, Judaism was also persecuted by the Soviet authorities. Jewish identity was affected more by state-sponsored atheism than, for example, the Russians, who were not burdened by pressure to assimilate. In losing the possibility of practicing their faith, they lost much more of their national and cultural independence than the majority nationalities. In 1921-22, the fight against the Jewish religion was one of the main activities of the Jewish party sections. The *Yevseki* confiscated and sometimes burned the Torah scrolls, desecrated synagogues and managed to convert them into clubs for workers or similar facilities, which, at first, they used for themselves. Twenty-three percent of all synagogues were closed in 1927 and almost all had been closed by 1939 (the *Yevseki* were not even necessary for this during the 1930s).

As the Soviet Union insisted upon a strict separation of church and state, the Kheyder schools, in which Jewish children studied the Torah, had to be changed into secular schools. Hebrew was forbidden as a school language and religious studies were generally prohibited in schools. Of course, an internal Jewish administration on the basis of religious regulations was unacceptable to the new state. Numerous central offices of the Jewish communities, the *Kehiles*, were closed, and their entire fortunes from the *Yerkoms* were confiscated. Individual communities remained in existence. More than 1,000 religious groups were registered in the Ukraine in 1926, but they no longer functioned as charitable organizations.

Religious traditions were not forbidden, but anyone who followed them was hindered and confronted with public mockery. The keeping of the Sabbath was seen more as a source of friction in the economic process than it had been in the time of the tsars. In the antireligious campaigns private matters, such as the laws for the preparation of kosher food, were strongly attacked. The officials placed slaughtering rituals and

*Mohelim* (circumcision beadles), under the pressure of hygiene regulations. Jewish Communists took donations from the Jewish-American
charities, especially the delivery of unleavened bread, as an opportunity
to chastise the reactionary character of the Jewish religion and the harmful influence of capitalism.[10]

During the first years after the revolution, numerous antireligious
plays appeared and street parades with antireligious tomfoolery were often organized. One of the most bizarre acts of the *Yevsekzi* was a trial in
1921 in Kiev against the Jewish religion and its rabbis that took place in
the same room that the anti-Semitic Beilis trial had been held ten years
earlier. It wasn't until 1924 that the *Yevsekzi* stopped such demonstrations, after the 13th party congress had decided to carry out antireligious
campaigns (as well as against Christianity and other religions). Through
methods of "agitation, propaganda and education" and turning them
into clubs for working people or similar institutions, which they then
used primarily themselves.

Defamation, restrictions and prohibitions, failed to produce the desired outcome. Therefore, as with Christianity, a pseudo-religious movement was established that was true to the system: the short-lived "living
synagogue" with "Red rabbis." Religious activities were taboo for party
members. Jews could be expelled from the party for circumcising their
male children.

The *Yevseki* never had real support from the Soviet Jews. Only five
percent of all members of Jewish descent were organized in the *Yevsektsii*.
One reason for this coolness toward the organization was that participation in the CP was always combined with the opportunity and desire for
possible advancement inside the system—and with that the pledge to use
the majority language, Russian. Lenin already considered Yiddish a "backward" language with no future. The Jewish sections now used newly established Yiddish periodicals to strengthen the Bolshevik influence in the
"Jewish street."

The *Yevseki* also fought against "Jewish nationalism," which encompassed any and every attempt to protect the Jewish lifestyle, even in defending itself against anti-Semitism. If Jews defended themselves against
anti-Semitism too strongly, it created the suspicion of "nationalism." These
arguments were used in the trial against the JAFC after World War II.

## 7. Jewish Life Under the Dictatorship

### The Jewish "Blossoming of Culture"

The destruction of the national Jewish and Hebrew culture and literature corresponded with a time when secular and communist-inspired Yiddish culture flourished. Because Jewish themes, motifs and subjects in literature, painting and music had played an important role, the impetus of Jewish culture from beginning of the century continued, at least partially, into the early 1920s. It became obvious that the Soviet state had set limits to it; for example, with Marc Chagall, who had worked for the Yiddish theater in the early Soviet Union. The constant "L'art pour l'art" (art for art's sake) accusation and the attempts to use the arts for official government political purposes drove him and others to emigrate.

The Jewish Academic Theater in Moscow became the Soviet Union's proof of its successful nationality policy and "liberation" of the Jews, and was used as a propaganda showpiece and was even sent on foreign tours. Actually it was true that the theater, with its director and star actor Solomon Mikhoels,* was an important factor in the Soviet Union's cultural life—and not only for Yiddish speakers.[11]

The Yiddish world of letters and literature blossomed for a time, despite the interference of the *Yevseki* and the party dictatorship. From 1928 to 1935, 2,460 Yiddish titles were published, in total 11.4 million copies. In 1928, 238 titles with a total of 870,000 copies were published. In 1932 it was 668 titles with total of 2,558,000 copies, but by 1939 the number of book titles declined by half.

Only one-tenth of the political literature was originally written in Yiddish. Most of the other nine-tenths was translated from Russian; 70 percent of the literary works, were Yiddish originals.[12] For the first time in history a state was promoting Yiddish language and literature. Many Yiddish authors and poets who had been forced to leave Russia shortly after the Russian Revolution returned during the 1920s. They were now convinced that the best conditions for their artistic productivity prevailed in the Soviet Union. The most famous and important ones were in the prisoners' dock during the trial against the JAFC in 1952.

Isaac Babel, Osip Mandelstam, Boris Pasternak, Eduard Bagritsky, Vassily Grossman,* Ilya Ilf; and the authors who emigrated temporarily, Ilya Ehrenburg,* Viktor Shklovsky* or Vladislav Khodasevich; the children's-book authors Lev Kassil' and Samuil Marshak; the lyricists

Svetlov, Samoilov, Slutsky, Kogan; and, last but not least, the Nobel prize winner Joseph Brodsky, enriched Russian literature of the 20th century with their great works.

## The Place of Jews in Soviet Society

Every Jew had the right to use Yiddish in schools, administration, and court and in all public institutions. Everywhere, when the number of citizens from a national minority reached a certain level, Soviets (local councils) had to be established in the minority's language. In the Soviet Union in 1927, 775 schools existed with Yiddish as the instructional language—including elementary schools, middle schools, vocational schools, technical colleges and teacher training colleges—with approximately 114,000 students. It is obvious that the equality of the Jewish population was taken seriously under the Bolshevik regime; for example, in the Bank forms of the Belorussian Soviet Republic with texts in Yiddish, Belorussian, Russian, and Polish.

After the elimination of all tsarist discrimination against the Jews after the February Revolution, however, the Jews were again discriminated against following the October Revolution—naturally this time not directly as Jews, but because of their social descent and much more often than the non-Jews around them. In a typical urban population, the Jews were represented in the professions to a higher degree than the rest of the population. Jewish participation in the Communist Party was also noticeably higher in the 1920s, with 5.2 percent compared to 1.8 percent of the total population. This resulted not from their political preference, but from their place of residence because townspeople were on the whole more strongly represented in the party than country people.

The high percentage of small merchants and artisans among the Jews' social structure stood first as a negative factor against them in view of the Soviet ideal of the worker's and farmer's state. In the dictatorship of the proletariat, only they had all rights as citizens. Those belonging to the non-proletarian classes were denied rights with the decree of July 10, 1918. According to the Soviet Constitution of 1922 and its associated state ideology, only the "working population" was allowed to participate in political life. This was denied to everyone who had served in the tsar's police force, and their children as well. The same applied to all clerics, and also to the people who lived off the exploitation and work of others.

This didn't mean the big capitalists, who no longer existed anyway, but mostly the small artisans and merchants whose family members had helped in the store or business—i.e., a great number of Jews who had tried to survive and keep their heads above water as self-employed people. In the mid-1920s in some shtetls, half of the Jews belonged to the so-called *lishentsy* (people without any rights). This deprivation (*lishenie* in Russian) of the most elementary human rights had serious consequences for those affected and their children. They couldn't join the unions, the cooperatives or collectives. They were denied higher education and certain professional qualifications. The worst was that they were not allowed to obtain groceries, products or other wares that were rationed or cheaper for the general population. In the Ukraine only 5.4 percent of the total population were Jews, but they made up 45 percent of all *lishentsy*.[13]

As the fight against private trade intensified, poverty in the shtetls increased. Before, marketplaces in Belorussia and the Ukraine were full of life and commerce, but now they were virtually dead. Few opportunities existed for the Jews to noticeably improve their lifestyle and circumstances, such as changing vocations like *korenizatsiia* (from the Russian word *koren'* = root). This word meant settling in the farmland in the countryside and working in agriculture or working in industry in factories.

The fight against private merchants, against the so-called *Nepman*—those successful in the "new economic policies" (NEP)—strengthened anti-Semitic prejudice among the population. The press stated in reports, for example, that the working comrades or fellow-lodgers in communal quarters mistreated Jewish workers. From 1927 to 1930 an extensive campaign against anti-Semitism was initiated as result of class antagonism. The newspaper *Pravda* wrote that kulaks and capitalists wanted to systematically destroy the unity of the working class using this weapon.

Trials of the perpetrators of anti-Semitic violence proved the negative influence of the tsarist military police, nuns and kulaks, on the proletariat. To inform the public about the disastrous results for socialist construction, the party's Agitprop section ordered the publication of many pamphlets and books that branded anti-Semitism as "poison." The combat against antagonism toward the Jews was not meant to educate the population to respect the Jews or to regard them as a nationality; rather, it was more about disciplining the workforce and the ideological monopoly of the party.[14]

In the 1920s the "organs" sent thousands of Bundists, Zionists and other political activists to Siberia. The *Hitakhdut*, one of many Zionist organizations founded by the legal agricultural colonies to ensure the survival of the Jews, was also terminated. It addressed a detailed 22-page report about the comrades' persecution and harassment to the Sixteenth Zionist Congress, which was held in July 1929 in Zurich. The German text contained several hundred names and more than 50 locations of exile in Siberia. In A. Rafaeli-Zenziper's great work there are group pho-tographs from several dozen places of exile in which new generations grew up.[15]

## The Shift in Professional Structures

Slightly more than 82 percent of the Jewish population lived in ur-ban settlements, while only 17.5 percent lived in the countryside in rural areas (these numbers cover the entire USSR). The ratio was exactly the opposite from the rest of the Soviet population.

To prevent and stop the economic ruin of the shtetl, the administra-tive authorities tried to resettle the Jews—with the help of major U.S. fi-nancial support—to agricultural colonies in Belorussia and the Ukraine as well as on the Crimean peninsula. In 1930, 11.1 percent of all Jews in the Soviet Union lived from agriculture; this figure was never to increase again. By the end of the 1930s the share had declined again to 5 percent because industrialization attracted much of the working force away from farming.

The Soviet press felt the fact that the Jewish share of those working in white-collar administration jobs was far above that of the total popu-lation, while the share of farmers and others doing physical work was far below was an "unhealthy social structure." On November 30, 1930 the *Komzet* introduced the "Five-year plan for the reconstruction of the USSR's Jewish population," whose number was announced as 2,853,000. Accord-ing to this directive, which belonged to the general *Piatiletka* (Five-Year Plan), by 1933, 50.7 percent of the Jews were supposed to be regrouped and incorporated into the economic labor process. The following identi-fication numbers were announced (the numbers in parentheses corre-spond to declarations from the year 1927): wage recipients: laborers 480,000 (153,000); employees 450,000 (241,000); self-employed (home industry) 2,000,000 (244,000); agriculture 170,000 (100,400); private trade 0 (96,300); pensioners 130,000, non-workers 15,000 (433,000); unemployed 0 (96,000). For the independent professions only 17,300 were declared for the year 1927.[16] Behind the term "non-workers" are hidden citizens of Soviet society without rights or work and thus without income—the unfortunate *lishentsy*.

In spite of the limitations, many Jews, thanks to their diligence and idealism, were able to obtain a position according to their qualifications in economics, administration, the military, science, and culture. In 1939 the Jewish workforce comprised 50 percent of specialized workers, 40 percent skilled workers, and only 10 percent non-skilled workers. Many Jews advanced in the 1930s into the intelligentsia, and in 1939 formed the largest professional group among the academics and those employed.

A large part of the professional reorganization project was supported and financed by charities from *Agrojoint* and other American welfare organizations. These were represented in the Soviet Union until the end of the 1930s. All these foreign support measures had a tragic echo after the Second World War, as contacts with the *Joint* were declared to be "espionage."[17]

## 8. PSEUDO-ZION

### "Productivity" and Survival of the Jewish Nation

The various projects to settle Jews in farmlands and thus to establish a closed territory were based in part on Zionist ideas that were in tune with Soviet demands. The main pragmatic reason for these efforts was to "place" somewhere the tens of thousands of Jews who had lost their livelihood after 1917: small merchants, self-employed artisans and others, who were viewed as unfit for Soviet society. Their method of earning a living, even considering certain liberalism during the NEP years, were not in tune with the monopolistic tendencies of the Soviet state. Through "productive pursuits" the Jews' social structure was to become "healthy," i.e., fit into the general population structure that showed an obvious overabundance of farmers during the late 1920s.

### The Crimea—A Soviet Palestine?

At that time, about 40,000 Jews lived in the Crimea, primarily in Simferopol, Sevastopol, Feodosia, Kerch, and Yevpatoriia. The former *Yevsektsiia* activist Lvavi explained that Stalin had agreed in the 1920s to plans to establish a Jewish territory, or even a republic, on the peninsula.[18] Moshe Litvakov, co-founder of the *Yevsektsiia* and editor in chief of the *Emes*, talked enthusiastically about the Crimea as the Soviet Palestine. In August 1924 the State Committee for Land Settlement of Working Jews (*Komitet far aynordnen arbetndike yidn oyf Komzet erd—Komerd*) was founded. *Komerd*, attempted and had planned to distribute land and state money for this colonization. Five months later the "voluntary" semi-official organization for land settlement of Jews—Agency for Incorporation of the Jews on the Land in FSSR (*Gezelshaft far aynondnen yidn oyf erd in FSSR—Gezerd*, in Russian *Ozet*) was formed. Both were to propagate and collect money for land settlement. The *Gezerd* had offices all over the world. Many *Gezerd* functionaries fought in 1936 as volunteers in the International Brigades in Spain. Almost without exception, Eastern Jewish laborers worked in Germany to promote Jewish settlement in the USSR and H. Gerson headed up the office in Frankfurt. In June 1932, 58 Jewish settlers emigrated from Germany to the Soviet Union. Two organizations with offices in New York, the American Association for Jewish Colonization in the Soviet Union (ICOR), which since 1927 had published the Yiddish journal *Neilebn*; and the American Committee for Settlement of Foreign Jews in Birobidzan (AMBIDZHAN), which especially promoted Birobidzan. The Argentine organization PROCOR also promoted and supported the "productivization" of impoverished and unfortunate Jews in the Soviet Union.

James Rosenberg,* the important Jewish-American philanthropist, lawyer, and publisher who founded the *Agrojoint* organization, had supported the voluntary resettlement of Jews and the construction of agricultural colonies in the Ukraine and the Crimea. For several decades this organization had worked and cooperated in close contact with Soviet officials. As early as 1921, Rosenberg traveled on behalf of the *Joint* to Russia. In the course of time, the *Joint* and *Agrojoint* transferred eight-figure dollar amounts to the Soviet Union.[19]

In the Crimea, 342,000 hectares of land were divided among the settlers. With the help of *Agrojoint* they built several villages in which only Jews lived and Yiddish was the administrative and judicial language. The village's names were consciously not based on Jewish traditions: Icor, Mershin, Roisenfeld, Ratndorf, Lenindorf, Stalinshtad, Roysndorf, Budianskov, Rykov, Maifeld, Pervomaisk, Oktiabr, Jungwald, Larindorf, and Kalinindorf, where Jews made up 84 percent of the population. From 1927 on, Jewish colonies and communities established their own administrative districts in the Crimea and the Ukraine; Fraydorf (Freetown) was named in 1938 as the fourth Jewish national district. As the 86 communal farms at the beginning of the 1930s were changed into kolkhozes (Yiddish, *Kolvirtshaftn*), the settlers were increasingly less able to maintain their particular lifestyle.

The Tatar, Russian, and Ukrainian population turned against these colonies in the Ukraine and the Crimea—ostensibly, they claimed, the Jews had received the most fruitful and best pieces of land. From a strategic viewpoint the peninsula was not an ideal region for a Jewish territory; moreover, there wasn't enough space. When Birobidzan was chosen as the new settlement region, subsidies for the Crimean projects ceased. After Yuri Larin's death in 1932, the settling of Jews on the peninsula was stopped.

Yuri Larin* (Mikhail Lurye), a Jewish high party functionary, was born in 1882 in Simferopol. He was Bukharin's father-in-law and Lenin's comrade in arms. He was also founder and first chairman of the *Ozet* and a leading member of the *Komzet*. Larindorf in the Crimea was named after him. In 1926 he had already privately called for the establishment of a Jewish territorial unit in the Crimea, but outwardly he rejected all "national" ambitions. His concern was not to give the *Yevseki* any cause for an evaluation of the colonies as a way to sustain the Jewish nation and in the fight against "bourgeois nationalism."

If the need to create a Jewish agriculture existed especially in the establishment of small national units and thereby to ensure the continued existence of the Jewish people, it would not be worth fighting for, considering the hopeless past history of the issue. The basic purpose and reason for this work was to uplift people out of poverty into socially useful work.[20]

In contrast to this—and to Lenin's and Stalin's analysis and intentions regarding Jewish assimilation—President M. Kalinin declared in 1926:

> The Jewish people are faced with the gigantic task of saving their nationality. For this purpose, a large part of the Jewish population has to change into settled peasants, into a compact rural country people of at least a hundred thousand. [...] As a counterweight to the assimilation and breaking down that threatens every small national group that is robbed of national development possibilities, the instinct of self-preservation and the fight for their own nationality have also developed in the Jewish people.[21]

He added that this was not to be a specific goal of the Soviet government; however, one would help the Jews if they really wanted to preserve their nationality. Stalin's point of view, that the Jews were above all not a nation because they had no farmer class, was carried through to its logical conclusion: become farmers, and thereby you will gain the right to be a nation. The Soviet state (and in this there was no disagreement between Stalin and Kalinin) "generously" offered the Jews a chance, whereby it was calculated from the beginning that the failure of agrarianization and victory of assimilation would discredit the "Zionist" aspirations once and for all.

## Birobidzan

In 1927 the Soviet leadership began to concentrate on a region far in the East at China's borders, where the rivers Bira and Bidshan flow into the Amur. It was annexed by Russia in the middle of the 19th century and was almost bare of settlements. Large numbers of the "white" emigrants gathered in northern China where the city of Harbin became a de facto Russian colony. Observing these developments, the Russian government was afraid that unrest would break out. The establishment of Jewish settlements promised to solve three problems all at once: (1) a border region was made more secure, (2) the Jews' goal for their "own" territory could come closer to reality without conflicting with the population living there, and (3) a failure of the project could serve as the final argument to refute all plans for colonization—such as in the Crimea, which still had many supporters in the *Gezerd*.

## Predictable Failure

From the beginning it was obvious that Birobidzan, some 9,000 km from the western Soviet Union, with a harsher continental climate and without any infrastructure, was an extremely unattractive territory. The most important leader in the resistance to Birobidzan was Yuri Larin. In 1929 he wrote about the utopian settlement plans:

> One thing already makes this program unrealistic (in contrast to the programs in the Crimea and the Ukraine, which were also spon-

sored with funds from foreign organizations). One cannot expect the state to make such funds available when better results can be attained in a nearby region where things cost less and conditions are more favorable to the long-term development of Jewish agriculture. Birobidzan's ground that is almost always frozen, swamp areas, a plague of insects and floods, long periods of frost with temperatures of -40 degrees Celsius, its cultural isolation, with a distance of more than 1,000 versts from the sea, an economy that can only function extensively, a short period of vegetation due to the unfavorable distribution of precipitation during the year, etc. This can hardly be an ideally suited location for such people, who are city folk entering country life for the first time.[22]

In 1927 a *Gezerd* expedition issued a relatively favorable report, although the measures required for development were not implemented. After the Soviet government had expelled everyone from the territory in March 1928, the first settlers arrived. They had to deal with a catastrophic situation. In the beginning, the returnees and newcomers kept things going. Many of them had already failed in the Ukraine. The *Gezerd* employees, who wanted to present much higher resettlement numbers, did not properly inform the Jews. Already in the second year, 1929, only 555 settlers came—the original plan was for 15,000—even though the new beginning was promoted and supported by favorable loan terms. In 1930 the number of Jews in the region was 8 percent, the majority being Russians, but many Koreans also lived there. In 1933, not more than 3,000 people resettled despite material incentives, while at first the goal had been to attract 25,000 for resettlement.

Surprisingly enough Birobidzan was named, on May 7, 1934, an Autonomous Jewish Region, even though the reaction within the Soviet Union and abroad was moderate if not rather indifferent. A political reevaluation without any obligation was attempted to counter all the fruitless efforts.

The Jewish share of the total population at that time was under 15 percent. An autonomous region as a substructure of the Russian Federation—and, like all other autonomous regions, managed by an executive committee—was in any case only the rudiment of a republic. To establish a true republic, according to a definition given by Stalin in 1936, more than a million people would have to live there and of these, as the name-giving nationality, a majority would have to be Jews.

At a reception for the Yiddish press in May 1934, President Kalinin again expressed himself favorably towards this project. His reasoning would also have put him in the prisoners' dock in the JAFC trials, charged with "Jewish nationalism" (Kalinin, who died in 1946, was not a Jew). He declared that the establishment of a Jewish region would be the only possibility for the Jewish nationality to develop normally. At a time in which Moscow's Jews became assimilated, Jewish national culture in Birobidzan was protected and anyone who wanted to save it would have to settle there. Kalinin's words made it clear that outside Birobidzan the preservation of the Jewish culture was not desired. After 1948 it was destroyed, even in that region.

Individual districts in Birobidzan had names of famous non-Jewish Soviet politicians. A national region must be developed, but "Jewish nationalism" must not be promoted. Jewish traditions based on religion were banned and the Soviet press commented with special pride on the creation of a pig farm. Numerous accounts described how the children of former *Luftmenshn* became useful working people in Birobidzan. The territorial project was also meant to create a counterweight to Zionism, which still had a large circle of followers among the Soviet Jews despite the various persecutions. Jewish communists and their sympathizers collected money for Birobidzan throughout the world. Convinced that they were building a proletarian homeland for the Jews, many Soviet Jews emigrated to Birobidzan, as did many Jews from the West and even from Palestine. Almost all were killed during the purges in 1937-1938. In 1940, 111 Jewish schools still existed with 17,000 students. Yiddish was the administrative language. The Yiddish newspaper *Birobidzan Star* (*Birobidzaner Stern*) was a copy of the official *Pravda*. In the 1980s around 5,000 Jews still lived in there.

The Jewish communist Otto Heller had enthusiastically promoted the Birobidzan project in Germany. He described his impressions in his book *The Downfall of Judaism* (*Der Untergang des Judentums*) and in many lectures. Heller died in 1945 in a concentration camp in Germany. Eli Strauss countered Heller's angry attacks against the Jewish colonization in Palestine on behalf of Austrian Zionists in his 1933 book *Is Judaism Perishing? (Geht das Judentum unter?)*, published in Vienna. In 1975 the Arab "Palestine Committee" in Bonn reprinted Heller's book without any changes.

## 9. UNDER STALIN'S REIGN OF TERROR

A telling signal for new directions in Stalin's nationality policy was the dissolution in 1930 of the *Yevsektsiia* and the party sections of other nationalities that didn't have their own territory. The *Yevsektsii* alone had engaged in many activities, some of them traditional, though considered suspect by the Stalinist leadership;[23] on the other hand, they also destroyed religious and cultural institutions. Although the Jews did not consider the *Yevsektsii* their representatives, the *Yevsektsii* at least kept the idea of a Jewish unity and the existence of a "Jewish problem" alive—both of which stood against the ideology of Stalin and Lenin in the end.

After the dissolution of the *Yevsektsii*, the Jews were viewed in the Soviet Union as an internal Soviet nation. It was considered sacrilege to cling to the idea of a nation spread over many countries; every Jew— whether he wanted it or not—had a national affiliation (Yevrei) that was recorded in his documents when national passes were introduced in 1932. Stalinism carried out a twofold attack on the Jews: those who wanted to assimilate and those who wanted to keep national Jewish identity. The former were branded with a permanent stigma and the goal of the latter was made impossible.

### The End of Yiddish Journalism

During the years between Kirov's murder in 1934 and the Great Terror with its show trials in 1937-38—the highlight of the *Yezhovshchina* (the period when Yezhov was the NKVD chief)—all the gains made during the cultural and social blossoming of the 1920s were wiped out. A significant example of this was the "mass elimination" of the press in the second half of the 1930s. Even newspapers and magazines established in part for the propagation of party politics among the Jews were decimated.

It should be noted that the "flowering" of Jewish publishing and literature after the October revolution was only a facade that sometimes hid the uniform content, but it was the expression nevertheless of a specific cultural life. The great bibliography of Khone Shmeruk lists more than four hundred Yiddish periodicals during this early and relatively liberal phase. Even after the regime's stabilization an impressive number were still being published. Only the *Birobidzan Star*, which had started publication in 1930, and the central newspapers in the Ukraine and

Belorussia, survived the elimination, only to then fall victims to the German invasion. The flagship of the Yiddish press, *Der Emes*, had to stop publication in 1938, even though hundreds of thousands spoke and read the language.

Step by step the party agencies liquidated the Jewish institutions, publishing houses and cultural associations. Often they were closed because the employees were arrested. Yiddish schools, except in Birobidzan and the Kiev Institute for Jewish Culture, were also affected by it and fell victim to the greater purge. Afterward it still became possible to establish a division for Jewish culture at the Ukrainian Academy of Sciences. Even this would also later be viewed as proof of "nationalistic" agitation. In 1952 such malignant reproaches were found in the indictment against the JAFC. In 1939 the idea of publishing Yiddish literature only in Russian or Ukrainian translation was not even discussed.

## Jews in the Grip of Terror

The persecution of the Jews at the end of the 1930s was not based on explicit anti-Semitic propaganda or agitation. Jewish communists also participated in the denunciations and public attacks on the "nationalistic deviants." They often became victims of the purges, even though they had been involved themselves; for example, Dimanstein, who had repeatedly taken part in the choir warning of the potential "Bundist counterrevolutionaries" and their influence in the *Gezerd*. In November 1937, attacks against him and the magazine *Tribuna*, the *Gezerd*'s official publication, appeared in *Emes* for the first time. In January 1938, Dimanstein was dismissed as the *Tribuna's* publisher and the magazine ceased publication because it did not represent "the view of the masses." Dimanstein was soon arrested and disappeared into a work camp where he probably died. The Jewish literature tsar and editor-in-chief of *Der Emes*, Moshe Litvakov, was soon the next victim.

What were those arrested being accused of? Even though there was no order to arrest targeted Jews at that time, the Stalinist terror before 1939 followed totally different rules than the Jews' persecution and harassment taking place in Germany. Hundreds of thousands of Soviet citizens were caught in the claws of the NKVD because their relatives lived abroad, because they had traveled to Western Europe in the 1920s, had fought in the Spanish Civil War, or had joined other parties (Bund or

Zionist) before the Revolution. In addition to other accusations, the latter affected the Jews more than other national minorities. Since Jews were over-represented in the CPSU (Communist Party of the Soviet Union) they were suspected of having at some time reflected the views of the "Trotskyite faction." Further Jewish deviations that were naturally only "typically Jewish" were "Bundism," "Jewish nationalism," and "Zionism."

Like all other *Yevsektsiia* activists, Samuel Agurski was also accused, based on the above excuses, and fell victim to the purges. Born in Grodno in 1884, he joined the Bund in 1902 and was forced to flee Russia. His first place of exile was Leeds in England. From 1906 on he lived in the United States, where he promoted anarchist ideas among Jewish workers. In 1917 he returned to Russia and with American journalist R. Williamson established the first international unit of the Red Army. As a Bolshevik he participated voluntarily in the Soviet Jews' estrangement from Judaism: he was one of the founders of *Yevsektsiia* and in 1919 signed, together with Stalin, the People's Commissar for Nationalities, the edicts shutting down the Kehiles, the Jewish religious communities. He was therefore the gravedigger of the Russian Jews' religious life. As the *Yevsektsiia's* leader in Belorussia, he fought angrily against leading Bolsheviks, who had formerly belonged to another party. Later he surveyed the history of the workers' movement and in the CPSU led the committee for the party's history. Agurski was unmasked in 1936–37 in the press as a Bundist and Trotskyite. He was arrested in Minsk and then exiled to Pavlodar in Kazakhstan, after 19 months in prison. During his illegal stay in Moscow in 1947, he met the JAFC members Bergelson, Kushnirov,* and Strongin.* He died that same year in exile.

In a letter to the future JAFC secretary Epstein—who had also lived as an emigrant in the United States—written probably at the end of 1940, Agurski described the reasons behind his arrest. In the letter he also exposed how Yiddish writer Isi Kharik and Moshe Kulbak were murdered:

> In the spring of 1937 in Minsk, the arrests of emigrants from Poland and Belorussia had started. Among those arrested was Damesek, who at that time was secretary of the publishing council for the magazine *Star* [*Stern*]. This creature confessed at the hearing that he was a member of a Nazi fascist organization that existed in Minsk under the cover name of *Star* magazine. Its publishers/editors Dunyets, Bronstein, Kharik, and Kulbak were also the leaders of the organization. Based on Damasek's fantastic proof, Bronstein was

immediately arrested and Dunyets was also brought back to Minsk from a distant prison camp where he had been deported. At a new trial Dunyets was asked: "Do you still want to hide your counter-revolutionary activities from the Soviet penal organs?" Dunyets replied that he had finally decided to capitulate, and to tell the truth in all earnestness and seriousness about his counterrevolutionary activities. He would also name all persons who had participated. [...] Dunyets divided the members of his fantasy organization into active and passive. The "active" ones were those who were to perform acts of terror. The passive ones knew about the organization but did not participate in the operations. He named Litvakov and Kulbak and some more so-called "horrible terrorists" as the most active members. These were already involved in preparations for terror acts. Dunyets included me among the passive members. This meant that I knew about the organization's existence. Based on Dunyets' lies and provocative fairytales, Kharik and Kulbak, the so-called "horrible terrorists," were immediately arrested (August 1937). Supported by the evidentiary material that was sent immediately to the CC secretary of the Belorussian CP, Sharangovich, this man ordered that I be exposed and expelled from the party.[24]

This letter to Epstein is not the only one providing evidence that the JAFC's activists knew very well what kind of regime they had to enter combat with against Hitler. Realizing what absurd results the witch-hunt and torture hearings of the Great Terror had produced, one admires even more the resistance of the JAFC members to this terror system when it turned against them in 1952 with these same methods.

### The Extermination of the Leaders in Birobidzan

The dream of Jewish autonomy was short lived under Soviet control. The autonomous region's entire leadership was murdered. The following 1939 article, written by Grigori Aronson and published in the Mensheviks' *Sotsialisticheskii vestnik* while he was in exile in Paris gives a feel for the downfall of the old guard Jewish communists:

August 1936—the days of the Zinoviev trial—took a fateful turn for the Jewish communists. The day on which Liberberg arrived in

Moscow [from Birobidzan], he was led straight away from the festive reception by Kalinin in the Kremlin to the GPU and there placed before a wall and shot—this day was the beginning of a newer kind persecution of the Jewish communists, that which was to lead to their final extermination. Of course, no one can say the exact number of Jewish communists who were crushed under Stalin's iron heel, but there is absolutely no doubt that thousands from the Jewish intelligentsia and semi-intelligentsia fell victim to the last lunatic bloodletting in the USSR. Who was shot or in some other way brought to their final rest, who still lives and remains in prison—one can only puzzle over these questions. We only found out about Mereshin's transformation from one of the most noticeable activists to a "public enemy" several years later from an article by Dimanstein in the *Emes* in 1937. We only learned of Esther Frumkin's liquidation because of A. Weinstein's irascible protest. Litvakov's dismissal as editor of the *Emes*, where he had worked for 16 years, only became well known when he was replaced by an anonymous editing staff. The *Emes* didn't report that Commissar Dimanstein had fallen out of favor until January 1938. The shooting of the leaders of Birobidzan only became public knowledge because they had been referred to as "Japanese spies," etc., so often. The Soviet readers could only read between the lines to find out about the fate of those who had been at the helm of the "Jewish work" for decades. Today, they still know nothing of Weinstein's suicide in prison, Esther Frumkin's and Litvakov's deaths, whose names are synonymous with the entire history of the Jewish Worker's Movement... Let's end this commentary with a list (of course, incomplete) of the most well-known Jewish communists who were liquidated: ...the leading team of Birobidzan: Liberberg, Khavkin, Katel, Gelder, Apshin, Riskin, Ia. Levin, Shvartsberg, Shvainstein, Furer, Guberman, Khasbiski, Lapitski, Idov." Liberberg, the chairman of the Birobidzan Soviet, was accused of working secretly as a counterrevolutionary nationalist for ten years. He supposedly wanted to invite the Jewish historian, Simon Dubnov, to the Institute of Jewish Culture of the Proletariat for these purposes. Seven months after Liberberg's murder, Khavkin, the first secretary for the Regional Committee of the Communist Party in Birobidzan, was accused of "Trotskyism" and arrested. He was also accused of favoritism, and all those who had any connection to him were also arrested. Out of the 51 members of the Regional Committee, only six managed to last through 1937. Strangely enough, the new political leadership was also made up of Jews. The number of Jews taking part in the Party Committee Meetings in Birobidzan did not noticeably decrease during the years of terror, although they by no means presented the majority in the regions also populated by Russians and Koreans. The accusation of "Jewish Nationalism" and similar offenses were not yet enough to reduce the representation of the Jews. Cleansing with a tendency to Russianize only appeared in the years after the war. This day was the beginning of this new Jewish communists' persecution that was to lead to their total elimination. Nobody can tell the exact number of Jewish communists who were trampled to death by Stalin's iron foot. There is no doubt, though, that thousands of the Jewish intelligentsia and semi-intelligentsia fell victim to the completely crazed bloodletting in the USSR. Some of them were shot or came to their end by other methods, some are still alive or sit in jail—about this, one can only wonder. We didn't hear about Mereshin's conversion from one of the most conspicuous activists into an "enemy of the people" until a few years later in an article by Dimanstein in *Emes*, from 1937. We didn't hear about Esther Frumkin's liquidation until the erupting protest of A. Vainstein. The removal of Litvakov, who had edited *Emes* for 15 years, became known because he was replaced in 1937; through an anonymous "editor's collegium." *Der Emes* did not report that Commissar Dimanstein had fallen into disgrace until January 1938. The shooting of the Birobidzan leaders became public only through various mentions of "Japanese spies," etc. The Soviet reader is only able to get information between the lines, regarding the fate of these persons who had been at the rudder of "Jewish work" for decades. The reader knows nothing about Vainstein's suicide in prison, the deaths of Esther Frumkin and Litvakov, whose names are connected with the overall history of the Jewish workers' movement. Let's end these notes with a list (naturally not a complete one) of the most famous liquidated communists—the leadership of Birobidzan: Liberberg, Khavkin, Katel, Gelder, Apshin, Riskin, Ia. Levin, Shvartsberg Shvainstein, Furer, Guberman, Khasbiski, Lapitski, and Idov.[25]

Liberberg,* the representative of the Birobidzan Soviet, was accused of having been working as a counterrevolutionary nationalist for ten years before that. This is why he wanted to invite the Jewish historian Simon

Dubnov to the Institute for Proletarian Jewish Culture.[26] Seven months after Liberberg's murder, under the accusation of "Trotskyism," the first secretary of the Birobidzan region's party committee was arrested. He was accused of favoritism, and everyone who had connections with him was arrested. Of the fifty-one regional committee members, only six survived the year 1937. The new cadres, though, were also Jews.

For decades, numerous journalists, writers and poets—also non-Jewish—had described with enthusiasm the fiction about Jewish Birobidzan. Faced with the horrible reality of poverty, they could only have done so against their better judgment and knowledge.

### Jewish Critics of the Soviet System

The slogan "Gotsliberdan," created by the communist Agitprop at the beginning of the 1920s as a synonym for treason and anti-communism, identified the main opponents of counterrevolutionary and anti-democratic Soviet communism, the social revolutionaries, Bundists and Mensheviks, by the names Abram Gots, Mark Liber and Fyodor Dan. All three men were Jews.

The saying that "the Trotskys made the revolution and the Bronsteins [Trotsky's birth name] paid the bill" holds a tragic resonance for the Soviet Jews to this day, since they are still accused and held responsible for the tragedy that Lenin and Stalin had brought upon the Soviet people. The Russian Jewess who continued to write the well-known Russian anti-Semitic phrases in a pamphlet entitled "The End of the Lies" ("Das Ende der Lügen"), in 1992 had undoubtedly overlooked this fact.[27]

On the one hand, the Jews were the earliest and most decisive critics of Soviet communism. Leading Jewish Bolsheviks were attacked especially sharply by them.[28] On the other hand, critical intellectuals like Lion Feuchtwanger fell for the propaganda. That writer, highly respected in the Soviet Union, had not only written with shocking naïveté in his travel report *Moscow 1937* about the cleansing actions, but had dreamily commented at the same time about the successful experiment of Birobidzan, in which he saw the utopia of a Jewish state come to life. While Manès Sperber broke with communism once and for all in 1937, Feuchtwanger would not or could not break away from this wishful thinking, on which many contemporaries placed great hopes. Joseph Roth had belonged to them as well. From August 1926 to February 1927 he stayed in Russia under contract to the *Frankfurter Zeitung*. The newspaper published eighteen reports. That same year, his book *Travels to Russia* was also published. Walter Benjamin met the writer in Russia and noted in his diary: "...he went as an (almost) convinced Bolshevik to Russia and left as a royalist." Roth also wrote on October 10, 1926, in Kiev, "If I were to write a book about Russia, it would have to describe the quenched revolution—a fire that is burning out, glowing embers and a lot of firemen." Even many historians did not come to this realization until half a century later.

# Part III

# PREHISTORY AND FOUNDING OF THE JAFC

## 10. ANTI-FASCISM, SOVIET PATRIOTISM AND DISGUISED ANTI-SEMITISM ON THE EVE OF WORLD WAR II

### A Land Without Anti-Semitism?

The Jews' proletarization and assimilation was not only furthered by the ideologically grounded and administratively brutal dissolution of Jewish national institutions and repression against national deviation. The instinct for self-preservation also drove the Jews ahead in the 1930s. In administration, government, economy, culture, and science the members of the second generation were strongly represented, and many of them held important positions. Medical doctors, intellectuals and artists belonged to the elite and were highly respected. The opinion also spread by Jews loyal to the regime, based on the Jewish people's renewal that a "Jewish problem" would no longer exist in the Soviet Union, turned out in a very short time to be a disastrous illusion. It was true—and the Soviet party members abroad referred to this—that anti-Semitism was officially still outlawed. Stalin had declared in 1931, in a written interview for the Jewish Telegraph Agency:

> National and racial chauvinism is a leftover of the misanthropic customs of the cannibalistic period. Anti-Semitism, as the most extreme racial form of chauvinism, is the most dangerous remnant of

cannibalism. Exploiters use anti-Semitism as a lightning rod to divert the workers' strikes away from capitalism. Anti-Semitism is a danger for the workers because it is a wrong path and leads them from the right path into the jungle. That is why the communists are consequently internationalists, irreconcilable and sworn enemies of anti-Semitism. In the USSR, anti-Semitism is severely punished as deeply hostile to the Soviet spirit of the law. Active anti-Semitism will, according to the law of the USSR, be punished with death.[1]

These statements were published for the first time in the Soviet press in 1936. Molotov, soldier of the Bolshevik revolution and chairman of the Council of the People's Commissars since 1930, quoted these in a speech about the constitution. The man who, until his death, thought the Great Terror as an absolutely necessary cleansing measure, who in a single night signed the death sentences for 3,187 humans (after which he watched wild west movies with Stalin), and who could not or did not want to protect even his own Jewish wife from the Gulag, condemned not only anti-Semitism but also joined in a song of praise for the Jews:

> It is unnecessary to spread the word that we act the same toward the capitalists and counterrevolutionaries of the Jewish nation as we do toward exploiters and enemies of our ideals. Whatever the present cannibals from among the fascist anti-Semites want to and could say, our brotherly feelings for the Jewish people are determined by the fact that they gave rise to the genius Karl Marx, creator of the idea of the communist liberation of humankind, who on a scientific basis had the greatest achievements of German culture and the culture of other nations at his disposal. Our feelings are determined by the fact that the Jewish people along with other highly developed nations, produced a great number of the most outstanding representatives in science, technology and art, glorious heroes of the revolutionary combat against oppression of the worker and, in our country repeatedly, new outstandingly talented leaders and organizers in all branches of our construction and protection of the concept of socialism. Our relations with the anti-Semites and the anti-Semitic monsters, wherever they came from, are influenced by all this.[2]

Those addressed by this pro-Jewish statement were not citizens of the Soviet Union nor specifically the Soviet Jews, but simply the Western countries that the Soviet Union itself wanted to involve as allies against fascism.

The statements are not, in content and tactics, in contradiction with traditional Bolshevik paradigms. Lenin had also often praised the progressive attitudes of the (assimilated) Jews. But in the same breath, though, he argued against Jewish national interests. While Lenin disliked provocative games with reactionary slogans, Stalin proved himself to be a brilliant, devilish master of that art.

## The Jews as the New "Judas"

In the hate campaigns against the "Trotskyite vermin," their origins were seldom singled out directly, but anti-Semitic allusions could not be avoided. The accusation that also became a stereotype; the "enemies of the people" were the "Judas," who bartered away the homeland and the blood of the working class, like the "Trotskyites" who had a secret pact with the Nazis.[3] Stalin himself called many Jewish victims of the terror "agents of the Gestapo." Trotsky remarked on more than one occasion that he was accused more or less openly of sending, together with the Gestapo, Jewish terrorists from Germany into the Soviet Union. Already during the 1920s, Stalin had used anti-Semitic resentment against the Trotskyites in the fight against the united opposition.[4] Later "anti-Zionist" campaigns, whose main purpose was to prove the Zionists' collaboration with the Nazis, followed that basic pattern.

The show trials were replete with latent anti-Semitism. Many old guard Bolsheviks who stood before the Court of Justice in 1936 and 1938, victims of the most obscure accusations, were of Jewish descent. In the trial against Zinoviev and Kamenev alone, eleven out of sixteen defendants were Jews. The list of the alleged "members of the illegal Trotskyite-Zinovievist terrorist organization" itself reads like a white guard pamphlet against "Jewish Bolshevism": Yefim Alexandrovich Dreytser; Isaak Reingold; David Pikel; Konon Berman-Yurin; Eduard Goltsman; Fritz David (alias Krugliansky); Moisei Lurye (alias Aleksandr Emel); Natan Lurye.[5]

*Arno Lustiger*

Russian Nationalism Rekindled

Not only did the show trials demonstrate that the era of internationalism and "national nihilism" embodied by the Jewish Bolsheviks had ended, but curricula, schoolbooks, literature, and films increasingly depicted Soviet power as the crowning of Russian history. In 1935 a leading article in *Pravda* praised "Soviet patriotism" as "the burning emotion of endless love, selfless devotion and loyalty toward the homeland, deepest responsibility for her fate and her defense" and the Soviet Union as "the spring of humanity." "The name of Moscow sounds for workers, farmers and all honest and cultured people around the world like a storm bell ringing, like hope for a light, a bright future and victory over fascistic barbarism!" Only two years later, the following triumphant Great Russian chauvinistic words were published by *Pravda*, when the friendship among different nations was usually celebrated: "In the brotherly cooperation of all the peoples of the USSR, as first among equals, the Russian people create their glamorous future." Among the Soviet nation there existed no more enmity, and above all no more skepticism, toward the Great Russians: "More importantly though, the feeling of friendship, of love and gratitude of the Soviet Union's nations toward the first among them—toward the Russian people—its language and its culture which has become tighter, yes, indissoluble and holy."[6] It was therefore absolutely logical that Yiddish culture and language had become "expendable," as well as the Jewish lifestyle and Yiddish Soviets, courts and schools. Almost all cultural institutions still existing were closed, including the more than 700 schools in which Yiddish was the language of instruction. The "successes" of the pathetically celebrated Russification strategy had immense consequences on other national minorities, especially since in 1938 Russian became obligatory in all schools in the USSR.

Peretz Markish's widow reported in her memoirs that the editors of *Komsomol'skaia Pravda* had suggested that he (Markish) and other Jewish authors in 1937 change their names, so that they would sound typically Russian: Rosenzweig was to became Borisov; Lasebnikov to Yefimov; and Markish* himself was to be named "Pyotr Markov."[7]

## The Diplomatic Service Becomes "Jew-Free"

The days of the Russian-assimilated Jewish intelligentsia, whose representatives had loyally served the Soviet state, were also numbered. In 1939 Stalin ordered that the percentage of individual nationalities in the upper echelons be checked. These measures led to the unofficial re-incorporation of the tsarist Jew quotas. In spite of all the cleansing, the Jews in many key positions were still represented more heavily in proportion to their share of the population.

The pro-Semitic statements by Stalin and Molotov were window dressing for new anti-Semitic initiatives. Stalin also used them at the same time to quiet down the Nazi regime. At the end of the 1930s he feared that Hitler could be plotting with the Western democracies against the Soviet Union. Molotov told the nationalist writer Felix Chuyev, who sympathized with him, at one of their many meetings in the 1970s:

> In 1939, as Litvinov was removed from office and I switched over to the foreign department, Stalin said to me, "Take the Jews out of the people's foreign department." Thank God he said this. The Jews made up the absolute majority in the leading positions, as in the diplomatic corps, and this is quite wrong, of course. The Latvians and the Jews...and each one pulls a string behind him. By the way, they also looked down their noses at me as I took my office; they made fun of the measures I began to implement... Of course, Stalin was aware of what the Jews were up to. Nevertheless, there was one who was most devoted to him: Kaganovich. Beria said behind Kaganovich's back, "Lasar, this Israel." – Stalin was not an anti-Semite, as some have suggested in the past. He acknowledged many characteristics to the Jewish people: efficiency, solidarity, political activity. They are most certainly more active than the average. That's why there are some who lean passionately in one direction and others who lean passionately in another. Under the conditions of the Khrushchev era, the latter raised their heads and hated Stalin intensely. But in the tsarist prisons and in exile, there were not really that many, and as we took power into our hands, many became Bolsheviks immediately, although the majority of them were Mensheviks.[8]

Molotov's statements indicate that the Stalinist leading guard automatically suspected even those Jews who took the right position politically (the party members), disguised as ex-Mensheviks, ex-Bundists or even Zionists. On the other side, they were not filled with stubborn and boundless hatred toward anything and everything Jewish. For example, they treasured the Jewish dynamic as a useful tool, if it could serve their own power. This aspect, though, leads back to the continuity since Lenin's time and not to a break between a "pro-Semitic" Lenin and an "anti-Semitic" Stalin.

The investigators of the People's Commissariat of Internal Affairs (NKVD) planned a great trial in which an "ambassador's plot" was to be uncovered. Litvinov's removal as foreign minister on May 5, 1939 was seen worldwide as an "anti-Jewish" gesture on the part of Stalin. Winston Churchill wrote in his *The Second World War:*

> The eminent Jew, the target of German antagonism, was flung aside for the time being like a broken tool, and, without being allowed a word of explanation, was bundled off the world stage to obscurity, a pittance, and police supervision. (…) The dismissal of Litvinov marked the end of an epoch. It registered the abandonment by the Kremlin of all faith in a security pact with the Western Powers and in the possibility of organizing an Eastern Front against Germany. (…) The Jew Litvinov was gone, and Hitler's dominant prejudice placated.[9]

After May 10, 1939, a new witch-hunt began against people belonging to the diplomatic service. Beria arranged the arrest of Litvinov's closest co-workers. Despite torture, they were unable to expose the dismissed foreign minister as a traitor. Litvinov's press chief, Yevgeni Gnedin, son of the famous Jewish revolutionary Parvus-Helphand, did not denounce him as an opponent of the Soviet government, who wanted to provoke a war[10] though he was denounced in turn by Mikhail Koltsov.

Based on the interrogation files, the list of the accused consisted of the following ambassadors: Maisky (who represented the Soviet Union in Great Britain), Surits (in Germany), Stein (Finland and Italy), Yurenyev (Japan, Italy, Austria), Rosenberg (Spain), Khinchuk (also Germany). They were all Jews. The only person who would have been included as a non-Jew was Alexandra Kollontai (Sweden). Arkadi Vaksberg rightly suspected that Stalin had interrupted the preparation of the trial to avoid creating the impression of an ideological rapprochement—including anti-Semitism—with Nazi Germany.

## First Investigations of a "Jewish Conspiracy"

The inquiry files evaluated by Vaksberg reveal very clearly that the NKVD had been gathering precise material for an "artists' trial" since 1937. The NKVD collected information since 1932 against and concerning Koltsov. His German wife, Maria Gresshörner, alias Maria Osten, a Prussian gentleman farmer's daughter, was accused of "Trotskyism." Special emphasis was naturally placed on the fact that the well-known journalist had, during the Spanish Civil War where he was a reporter, contacts with persons considered by the Soviet leadership as enemies: anarchists, Trotskyites, and all kinds of leftists who were unreachable for Moscow.[11] "Contamination" in Spain was reactivated after the war as an accusation—especially during the anti-Semitic show trials in 1952 in Czechoslovakia.

Koltsov was accused of having contacts with a "Zionists' nest." He "confessed" that he had been recruited by Karl Radek to become a counterrevolutionary. After long grinding interrogations and torture he accused the well-known theater director Vsevolod Meyerhold of having worked as an agent of the Japanese. The background was that Meyerhold had once employed a Japanese graduate student. This confession made it possible for the inquisitors to continue to uncover and neutralize this imaginary network of conspirators and plotters with the cultural milieu, which was established mostly by Jews.

Their concentration was directed especially toward Vsevolod Meyerhold. Critics had opened the campaign against him with the accusation that he was "defaming" and "disfiguring" Pushkin in his theater stagings. In January 1938 the government demanded that the theater be closed. Meyerhold was arrested at the beginning of the summer. His wife, Zinaida Reich, a celebrated actress, was murdered a few days later in her apartment. Meyerhold was a totally assimilated Jew, who, until his execution in February 1940, did not recognize—or even want to recognize—Stalin's role in the terror apparatus. In November 1939 he withdrew former accusations against persons accused earlier (not only Jewish) as "members" of an alleged cultural conspiracy: Boris Pasternak, Yun Oleshka, Konstantin Fedin, Vsevolod Ivanov,* Dmitri Shostakovich, and Sergei Eisenstein, among others.[12]

The same names are found in the files of Isaac Babel, who was considered to be one of the great Russian writers. He was accused of, among other things, describing in *Red Army* too many horrible and gruesome cruelties in the cavalry units during the civil war pogroms, and not emphasizing enough the leading role played by the party. This novella of genius is one of the few Soviet works in which the Reds' participation in the pogroms was not alluded to. The government interrogation officials tried to force a confession out of Babel. He supposedly led and maintained a conspiracy organ in the regional branch of literature; Sergei Eisenstein was supposedly supervising the conspiracy within the film department and Solomon Mikhoels was the chief plotter in the theater.[13] Meyerhold and Koltsov were both executed on February 2, 1940. Babel had been shot one week before.

Thus, already very early the first shadows fell over the future leaders of the JAFC. In 1952, during the trials against the JAFC, Peretz Markish pointed out that, starting in 1938, Mikhoels had especially aroused the interest of the power-struck and power-hungry leaders. The famous actor had been one of the four speakers at the Moscow Conservatory. He publicly expressed himself at that time against the November 1938 pogroms [Kristallnacht*] in Germany. That performance of the Soviet intelligentsia was broadcast throughout the world.

A few days after this event the party office secretary of the Soviet Writers' Association asked Markish by telephone who this Mikhoels was. This meant that at that time the wheels had already started turning, a certain attention and interest was directed at Mikhoels. It was no secret that there was talk about Mikhoels' colossal success and that his name was very well known at the CC." When the JAFC was established, Mikhoels was not at all an unknown "nationalist" but already a suspect to the secret police. Perhaps what saved Mikhoels' life in 1940 was that the interrogators could not force a confession out of everyone.

## 11. PERSECUTION AND DELIVERANCE—THE JEWS AT THE TIME OF THE GERMAN-SOVIET PACT

The news about the signing of the Nazi-Soviet Non-Aggression Pact in August 1939 had traumatized the three million Soviet Jews more than any other Soviet citizens. At the outbreak of the war, Mark Gallai flew the bombers he had helped develop. During a mission the 27-year-old pilot was shot down. After running and hiding for three weeks, he

---

* "Night of Broken Glass": November 8-9, 1938.

was able to reach his own lines. Later he became a test pilot of the first Soviet air force jet—the Mig-9. He was honored and promoted to colonel and became a "Hero of the Soviet Union." Twenty-five years after the German invasion, he spoke about his feelings in a magazine—feelings he shared with most Jewish Soviet citizens:

> For my generation, the twenty-two months between the non-aggression pact with Hitler and the war's outbreak were strange and incomprehensible ... The fascists were not called fascists anymore. That word couldn't be found in the press anymore nor in half of the official speeches...Most of us took the pact like medicine; uncomfortable but necessary. The developments following the pact's signature, though, were also incomprehensible. It was very hard to understand what was happening.[14]

Many historians marked the signing of the Nazi-Soviet Non-Aggression Pact, on August 23, 1939, as the beginning of the Second World War. The "non-aggression pact" between Germany and the Soviet Union was de facto an aggression pact against Poland, a land destined to be split again for the fourth time in its history. The Soviet Union openly told her German ally that she would not invade until Poland was conquered, in order—as the official reasoning went—to help the endangered Ukrainians and Belorussians. Not one word was mentioned or even offered to help the Jews. Of the total 3.3 million Jews in Poland, 2.1 million lived in the regions conquered and occupied by Germany and 1.2 million in the regions annexed by the Soviet Union.

### Eastern Poland Under Soviet Rule

The Red Army occupied a region of 200,000 square km. In this region lived 13 million people, the majority of whom were Ukrainians and Belorussians. The Poles made up one-third of the population and the Jews about one-tenth. Two hundred thirty thousand Polish soldiers were taken into captivity, including 25,000 Jews. All war-imprisoned officers were brought into prison camps at Kozielsk, Starobielsk, and Ostashkov. The civilian population to some degree welcomed the invasion of the Red Army on September 17, 1939, which was thought of as being directed against Germany. Soviet propaganda justified the annexation of

the Ukrainian and Belorussian population as national and social liberation from the Polish masters, the Pany. Among the minorities—also among
many Jews—the argument fell on fertile ground. In the first days it seemed
the Red Army would offer real protection, especially since in eastern Poland Ukrainian nationalists had committed pogroms against the Jews and
Poles and massive German bombing cost many lives to the civilian population in western and central Poland.

The Soviet leadership expected more loyalty from the Jews than from
the Ukrainians, who were suspected of nationalism, or from the Poles,
who were suspected of being loyal to the vanished republic. The occupiers at first fostered Jewish self-defense units. Jewish communists and other
left-oriented persons could play an important part in the "Revolutionary
Committee." They were also able to take over public positions from officials of the conquered Polish state. In the eyes of many Poles, the Jews
were profiteers of the new regime. Many Jews considered themselves
quite privileged, but the sympathy for the new rulers disappeared very
quickly. Communists from the old regions relieved the local functionaries
after only a few weeks. In October 1939, during the elections, the population was put under strong pressure. The new national conferences gathered at the end of October in Lvov and Bialystok proposed annexation
to the Soviet Union.[15]

Many Jews, especially small traders, merchants, and artisans, were
viewed as "capitalists" and were suspected by NKVD officials of being
"class enemies." The acquisition by the state of banks, shopping centers,
shops, artisan shops, and workplaces hit the Jewish upper bourgeoisie
especially hard. Small merchants were bankrupted through very high taxes
and had to make room for state-run trading organizations leading to the
economy's sudden downfall, and the Jews had the most to suffer. Grotesque as it may seem, Jews tried to get out of the Soviet zone and reach
the German zone. These, though, were few compared with the Jewish
masses that fled to the east across the German-Soviet demarcation line
and who were now suspected of being spies. Of the 600,000 persons
who fled to the east, 350,000 were Jews.[16] A large portion of these were
deported to the east, especially during the third deportation wave which
was known to have been particularly horrible, since everyone who did
not have papers accepted by the Soviet government was deported. This
naturally applied to many refugees.

Some of the refugees were exposed to aggressive anti-Semitic insults. Moshe Grossman reported that a Soviet interrogator had asked

him why he had fled the Soviet Union. To the answer, "Because we are Jews," the official countered, "They kill Jews? You call that murder? I could show you how you all should be murdered—damned race! You are all scoundrels and criminals. You came to the Soviet Union to destroy our development work, our socialist property, and our power! You should be shot like dogs, down to the last one."[17] Before the end of 1939, the borders were closed and refugees were sometimes sent back into the German regions. In the exchange of national groups (Ukrainians to the east, Germans to the west) Soviet agencies accepted only "pure Ukrainians" and no Jews.[18]

In 1940 the secret messenger of the Polish underground Jan Karski, who later smuggled the first reports about German extermination camps out of Poland,[19] wrote in a secret report, and with some resentment, to the Polish exile government:

> The Jews' attitude toward the Bolsheviks was very much noticed by the Polish population. In general, it is believed that the Jews betrayed the Poles and the Polish nation. They were basically communists, and went over to the Bolsheviks enthusiastically.
>
> It is true that in most cities the Jews greeted the Bolsheviks with baskets full of roses, with promises of devoted loyalty and speeches, etc. We must make some distinctions however. It is certainly correct that some Jewish communists welcomed the Bolsheviks with enthusiasm, regardless of their cultural or social class. The Jewish proletariat, small merchants, artisans, and all those whose position had improved structurally during the present time, and those who were first exposed to suppression, degradation and assaults from Polish elements—all reacted positively, if not even enthusiastically, to the new regime.
>
> I can understand their attitude. Certainly there were some bad cases, in which (the Jews) denounced the Poles, Polish nationalist students and politicians, if they work for the Bolshevik police from their offices or even if they are part of the police or if they poison the relations between (Poles and Jews) with false statements in the former Poland. Unfortunately, one must acknowledge that such incidents have been widely spread—much more widely than incidents demonstrating loyalty or a positive inclination toward Poland.
>
> On the other hand, I have the impression that the intelligentsia, the wealthy Jews and those with the highest cultural level (naturally

with some exceptions and not including the hypocrites), think about Poland more often with some kind of loyalty. They would be happy to welcome an independent Poland in the present situation. Naturally this has to do also with personal interest. At the moment they must also suffer many hardships, if not even collective extermination—their houses are confiscated, their shops, businesses and factories are taken away under the claim of so-called "socialization" and changed into a so-called cooperative (where the state's share and the fulfillment of state contracts play a very big role). This makes it impossible for them to support themselves or even to secure just the barest means of existence.[20]

## Mass Deportations

Between the two world wars there existed in Poland, despite unquestioned anti-Semitic government policies, a Jewish public with active communities, cultural and educational institutions and political parties. Bund and Zionism which, because they were considered as hostile trends, had been suppressed in the Soviet Union, found great acceptance operating along side conservative, religiously oriented parties. No one, not the schools, the press, publishing houses or writers suffered from the suppression of Hebrew or under one-party control. This rich national culture was to a certain extent destroyed as quickly as possible despite the fact that it had been used by the Soviet Union with its successfully tested methods of repression and partial integration in the early 1920s.

The Soviet authorities lifted all discriminatory measures against national minorities. Their new dictatorship had left the total population almost without any legal support. Examples included executions of many imprisoned Polish officers in Katyn. Numerous arrests and mass deportations were further evidence. From 1939 until 1941 it is highly probable that in eastern Poland more people were victims of repression than during the period of German occupation in western and central Poland. Fifty percent of the victims in the annexed Soviet regions were Poles, 30 percent Jews and 20 percent Ukrainians and Belorussians. Thousands of Jews, mostly Zionists, Bundists, and bourgeois "elements," were labeled class enemies, "national Jewish counterrevolutionaries," or "cosmopolitan elements," arrested and deported to Siberia. This actually ended up saving many of their lives. Anyone deported by the NKVD to Siberia could not be exterminated by troops from June 1941 on. It is estimated that about 30,000 Jews lost their lives due to these deportations, but almost another 100,000 were saved this way.[21]

In August 1943 the Polish ambassador to the USSR wrote a memorandum stating that the first wave of deportation, begun in February 1940, mainly removed civil officials, government judges and members of the police department from the cities. In the countryside, forestry workers, settlers and small farmers—almost all Poles, Ukrainians and Belorussians—were mostly deported. Several towns and communities were robbed of their entire population. In the second wave, April 1940, the deportees were the relatives and associates of those already arrested, those who fled to foreign countries or who were considered missing. These included merchants and traders, mostly Jews, agricultural workers on state-confiscated large farms or small farmers with very little land. During the third wave, June 1940, practically all Polish citizens who had fled before the German occupation in September 1939 were deported. Most of them were Jews. The NKVD also deported small merchants, medical doctors, engineers, lawyers, journalists, artists, university professors, teachers and persons related to Polish intelligentsia. In the fourth and last wave, shortly before the German attack in 1941, anyone the persecutors missed was arrested. This included children in summer camps and orphanages. The greatest number of Jews was deported to the USSR's hinterlands in June 1940.[22]

## Murder of Polish-Jewish Officers in Katyn

The Red Army's defeat outside the gates of Warsaw in August 1920 hindered the spread of Soviet communism in Western Europe. The loss revived the traditional enmity between Poles and Russians. In 1940 this hatred reached a climax in the Soviet Union when 14,552 Polish officers and 7,305 other prisoners of war were shot.

On July 30, 1941 the Polish government-in-exile, led by General Sikorski, and the Soviet Union agreed to a friendship pact. Inspired by Churchill, this pact had the Soviet Union acknowledge the Polish government-in-exile in London. It also obliged the Soviets to release all Polish civilian and war prisoners from camps and Gulags. During the rebuilding of the Polish army, which had fought on the side of the Allies, thousands of officers were found missing. What happened was not known until April 1943 when the German military allowed the existence of mass graves at Katyn to be publicly known. On April 25, 1943, the Soviet Union broke off diplomatic relations with the Polish government because of this alleged malicious defamation.

Even though they knew better, the Kremlin's rulers claimed for 50 years that Germans had committed these crimes. It wasn't until April 13, 1990, that they admitted their responsibility. In October 1992 Russia's representatives gave the Polish government the complete documentation and a list of the victims.

Among the victims at Katyn were 700 to 800 Jewish officers who had served in the Polish army.[23] These included the Polish army's highest-ranked chaplain, Rabbi Major Baruch Steinberg, born in 1897. Several Polish Legion veterans of World War I, including colonels Fabian Landau and Wladyslaw Nelken, were also discovered. In October and November 1940 the Red Army told the allied German army there were 42,000 war prisoners coming from western Poland. Without any remorse from the Soviet Union, thousands of Jewish prisoners remained under German control. They died later in German POW camps. Of the 60,000 Polish-Jewish soldiers who were taken into German war imprisonment, only a few hundred survived.[24]

### Destruction of Jewish Culture in Poland and the Baltic Provinces

Moshe Kleinbaum described in a report of 1940 to Nahum Goldmann the situation in Poland, in the spirit of the traditional reservations against the Bund:

> The liquidation campaign is directed above all against the Bund and Zionism. The GPU uses different tactics against both groups. The GPU assumes that the Bundists are trade union members and could be easily integrated under the Soviet Union's banner. Only the leaders, the secretary and functionary apparatus need to be removed. This calculation was correct. Erlich and Alter, the Bund's Central Committee leaders, were arrested, offices of the local Union committee taken over and employees and Unionist leaders imprisoned. The party apparatus was handed over to loyal communists

or, as usual under such circumstances, to fanatical new converts. That was how the Bund was liquidated. Its surviving "inventory" was transferred to Soviet property—as a communist leader in Lvov clumsily told me. The Bund's educational network, the Central Yiddish School Organization, was also completely taken over by the Soviet educational system without much trouble. The instructional language remained and most teaching institutions remained intact as well. Even pictures of Marx and Engels were not removed. In spite of an ideological revolution, symbols of continuity continued to exist.

The GPU proceeded differently against the Zionists. Unlike the Bundists, the Zionists did not have tight internal or external connections to communism. Also, psychological opposition to the Soviet regime was more deeply rooted in Jews with Zionist tendencies than among Bund members. Therefore, Zionists were systematically persecuted by the GPU. The persecution and agitation increased and affected broader Zionist circles in contradiction to the sudden disbandment of the Bund. The number of arrests of Zionists and Hebrew adherents increased daily. Hebrew schools were closed or changed into Soviet Yiddish schools.[25]

From 1939 until the German army's invasion the number of Jews living under the Soviet regime grew from three to about five million—some were also deported from other annexed countries, while others had fled from eastern Central Europe.

After the Soviet government opened military bases in the three Baltic republics in 1939 the Red Army marched in during the summer of 1940. These states had rejected ultimatums demanding a pro-Soviet government and free passage for the Red Army. Of course, elections were staged according to Soviet plans and thousands of the elite and its relatives were deported deep into the Soviet Union. This was done to destroy any potential resistance against the Soviet regime, a resistance that originated primarily in the bourgeois classes and included many Jews. Deportations began at the end of 1940 and climaxed in June 1941, with the removal of 11,000 persons from Estonia, 16,000 from Latvia, and 21,000 from Lithuania. Jews from these countries escaped with the help of the Germans and their allies.

*Arno Lustiger*

## Deliberate Overlooking of German Crimes

On June 17, 1940, when Molotov informed the representatives of the German Reich about the Baltic occupation, he congratulated them on the "marvelous success" of the war campaign in France. Two months later he declared the connection to Germany to be long term. When the pact was signed in the Kremlin in swastika-decorated Moscow, the German foreign minister felt himself "as among old [Nazi] party comrades." The Soviet press did not portray Germany as an aggressor until 1941, but instead labeled France and Great Britain imperialist warmongers. Even studies about Germany's earlier war of aggression were withdrawn from circulation.

All things German, especially culture and art, were given unimaginable prestige. In 1940 Sergei Eisenstein staged a Wagner opera at the Bolshoi Theater, but his own film *Aleksandr Nevsky*, which had a strong anti-German slant, was not shown. The films by Friedrich Wolf, *Professor Mamlock*, and Lion Feuchtwanger, *Oppermann Brothers*, were also removed from movie houses, because both films dealt with National Socialist anti-Semitism. The anti-Semitic theme wasn't allowed in fiction and serious literature either. Anything critical of National Socialism was confiscated. New works had to be rewritten in order to receive permission to be published—"reactionary racism" was used instead of "fascist racism." Examples were not Jews in Germany but blacks in the United States.

Crimes in German-occupied Poland and the pacts made with the German Reich regarding the resettlement of ethnic Germans from the Soviet Union's annexed regions were not mentioned. On the other hand, *Pravda* published an article on October 17, 1939, written by David Zaslavsky, one of the least principled journalists of Jewish descent during the Stalin era. Zaslavsky wrote profusely and in great detail about the connections between the Polish government in exile and Jewish bankers in Paris—as if during this time the Polish government in exile was murdering Poland's Jews. Official Soviet agencies were informed about and acknowledged the "German deportation projects," but kept the news to themselves. As a result, many Soviet Jews were unsure about Germany's plans in June 1941. Only in August 1941 did a pamphlet about "Hitler's massacres in Poland" appear, stating "immediately upon the occupation of Poland, German troops began a bloody, horrible massacre of innocent civilians, including helpless old men, women and children. Jews were deported with extreme brutality. They are not just removed from the western regions of Poland but exterminated."[26] During the first eight weeks of war, the mobile commandos had already shot about 50,000 Soviet Jews.

## 12. Henryk Erlich and Viktor Alter and the Creation of a Jewish Anti-Hitler Committee

Even after Leopold Trepper's "Red Orchestra" and the spy ring established in Switzerland by the Jewish spy Aleksandr Rado, and Richard Sorge from Tokyo had all informed Stalin about the planned German invasion, Soviet leaders had taken no precautions or made any defense preparations.

The Red Army could not withstand the German military and its 5.5 million soldiers, 47,000 cannon, 3,700 tanks, 5,000 airplanes and the support of the allied Italian, Finnish, Hungarian, Slovakian, and Romanian armies. Molotov, who had negotiated the Soviet Union's entry into the "Tripartite Pact" with Hitler in 1940 and who had not believed his country would be attacked, was the first to address the nation. Stalin did not interrupt his vacation and had supposedly refused to take any telephone calls. On June 30, the Defense Committee of the Soviet Union was established and the CPSU made the first proclamation, appealing to people to fight in the "Great Patriotic War." Not until July 3, when the German army had already advanced into the Kiev region and Minsk, did Stalin address the "comrades, citizens, brothers and sisters, soldiers of our army and navy." "Brothers and sisters"—this speech was totally incompatible with the class-conflict rhetoric before the war. It echoed Mikhoels's "Brider un shvester" speech made at the first JAFC meeting in August. The appeal was also directed to Britain and the United States and had great resonance at the Jewish meeting. Stalin declared, "In this war of liberation we will be not alone; in this war we will have loyal allies among the nations of Europe and America."[27] On July 31, 1941, Stalin issued the famous decree, ordering all Soviet citizens in occupied regions to engage in partisan warfare. Thousands of Jewish partisans followed this order.

After the Nazi assault on the Soviet Union in June 1941, Henryk Ehrlich and Victor Alter, prominent Jewish socialist labor union leaders of the Polish Bund, proposed creating an international Jewish anti-fascist organization. These famous journalists and authors were two of the most important Polish Jews and were also members of the Socialist International's executive committee.

Shortly before Poland's capitulation, the Bund's CC decided that party leaders should leave German-occupied regions in separate groups to avoid being captured by the Nazis. Victor Alter traveled with other comrades to Lublin. From there he went east to Kovel. While the German army marched into Lublin, the Gestapo searched Warsaw, Lodz, and other cities for Erlich and Alter. Several Jews with the same name were arrested as a precaution. In Kovel, Alter met his friends, the leaders of the Polish Railway Workers' Union, who had also fled.

In a combined resolution they expressed the hope that Soviet power would help Polish workers in the underground fight against the German occupation. The Soviet commanding officer of the town took the papers and promised a quick response. It came at dawn the next day, on September 29, 1939, when Alter was arrested.


## Erlich and Alter in the Clutches of the NKVD

After an adventurous flight lasting several weeks, Henryk Erlich arrived in Brest-Litovsk on October 1, 1939. On the same day, General Guderian, commander of the XIX Armored Corps of the Wehrmacht, and Soviet Armored Brigade General Semyon Krivoshein, a Jew, paraded the troops to the sound of the Soviet and German national anthems,[28] before the German armed forces turned the stronghold over to the Red Army.

Erlich knew that the NKVD was looking for him. He refused to use a disguise or to shave his beard. He was recognized by a Jewish communist at the Brest-Litovsk train station on October 5, arrested shortly thereafter and taken to the Butyrki jail in Moscow. Numerous Polish CP members incriminated him.

Through the recollections of other Bundists, some of whom were in contact with Erlich and Alter during their escape, while in jail, or during periods of occasional release between arrests, we are very well informed about their fate.[29] Victoria Dubnova, Henryk Erlich's niece in Moscow, was not allowed access to their files until 1992, after a long battle with the Russian bureaucracy. These six files provided more detailed information about the Bund leaders' martyrdom during their Soviet imprisonment. Gertrud Pickham from the German Historical Institute in Warsaw studied these files in Moscow.[30] Her conclusions supported the statements made by Bund members who met with Erlich and Alter in prison. The two men were forced to confess to the alleged crimes after being deprived of sleep, starved, isolated, and subjected to long hours of interrogation, usually at night. Beria himself participated in one of these interrogations.[31] Erlich and Alter were accused of using the Bund's CC commission to organize espionage and sabotage against the Soviet Union. They supposedly worked with Polish secret police to persecute communists and also agitated against the Stalin-Hitler Pact. The latter accusation was not completely unfounded. In August 1939 Bundists immediately recognized the monstrosity of this turn of events. Erlich tried to convince NKVD officers, via the Bund, of the invalidity of the accusations. Alter also strictly denied those fantastic accusations. In November 1939 he twice went on a hunger strike in order to remove from the executioners the death-penalty threat. A confession could not be forced out of him, even in Lefortovo Prison.

In July 1941, during the Red Army's great defeats, Alter and Erlich were taken to Saratov. They were sentenced to death in Moscow at a secret trial by a military commission of the Soviet Union's Supreme Court. Alter was full of contempt for the verdict and said not one word in his own defense. A few days later, the punishment was changed to ten years in a labor camp. The order could have only come from the highest office, probably from Stalin himself.

During his imprisonment, Erlich wrote—it is assumed he was ordered to do so by the NKVD (which was very interested in the relations of the Bund to Poland's CP and the Soviet Union)—about the history of the Bund in a 252-page essay. His work contains many details that are missing in the other few books published about the Bund and also cancels any suspicions against himself or the Bund. In a "Criticism of the Comintern's Measures and the Soviet Government," Erlich courageously criticized the splitting of the labor movement instigated by the Bolsheviks and the social fascist slogans used by the Comintern: "Would Fascism's victory in Germany have been possible, or at least could Hitler have achieved it so easily if the German working class had not been so hopelessly split into two nearly equally strong (and therefore also powerless) groups?"[32] Erlich also discussed the Bund militia, which had protected members from assault by Polish fascists, as well as the youth organization "Future" and the "Socialist Children's Union" (*Sotsialistisher Kinder Farband*—SKIF), to which this writer belonged for a time.

## Free Again—The Struggle for an Anti-Hitler Initiative

On August 12, 1941, by decree of the Supreme Soviet, almost all Polish citizens received amnesty and were released from Gulags and prisons. These included many high-ranking politicians and officers. Initiatives by union leaders of the still neutral United States and other union leaders of the free world with the Soviet government and the new Polish ambassador in Moscow, Professor Kot, also saved Alter and Erlich. On September 12, 1941, Erlich was released, as was Alter the following day. They received money for new clothes and the "privilege" of living in the Hotel Metropol, which was reserved for prominent citizens. It was a bad omen however that, unlike all the other freed prisoners, they did not receive passports from the Polish embassy. In Moscow they met Solomon Mikhoels and Peretz Markish, the founder of the JAFC. Shortly thereafter Aron Volkovysky, a Jewish NKVD colonel and a colleague of Beria, visited them. He told them their imprisonment and death sentence was an "error" and asked them in the name of the Soviet Union to forgive this injustice. It was time to fight against the common enemy, and the unpleasant past was to be forgotten. Volkovysky knew exactly how much the two Bund leaders were respected, especially by the powerful unions in England and America.

On October 15, 1941, with the German army outside Moscow, the Soviet government and diplomatic corps were evacuated to Kuibyshev on the Volga in a state of panic. Stalin however remained in the capital. Erlich and Alter also went to Kuibyshev, where they were put up in the Grand Hotel, normally reserved for prominent diplomats and the foreign press. It was astounding how they could find the strength to be involved in so many activities after two years in prison. They wrote a proclamation and presented it to the Polish ambassador, Professor Kot. Consisting of several pages, this document was a five-point program for the establishment of a free and democratic Poland in a post-war Europe. They addressed the now freed Jews, who had fled or been deported to the Soviet Union, and asked them to join the new Polish army. Thousands of Jewish volunteers showed up at the II Army Corps, under the command of General Wladyslaw Anders in Busuluk, Siberia. Many of these volunteers were not accepted and they protested to the Polish leadership. Alter and Erlich were also probably involved in the search for the Polish officers who were supposedly held in camps.

In addition, Erlich and Alter organized measures to help Polish Jews in the Soviet Union and contacted the embassies of Western countries. They used their influence to free Bundist comrades and to gain amnesty for Russian socialists still starving in the Gulags. But above all they were busy with the establishment of an International Jewish Anti-Hitler Committee. They were encouraged by Beria and by Volkovysky and Khazanovich, two Jewish NKVD officers, who visited them almost daily. In October 1941 Erlich and Alter drew up an extensive memorandum for Stalin with a cover letter to Beria (a copy of which was also sent to the Polish ambassador, Kot.) The text of the memorandum and the planned committee's personnel placement was discussed with the NKVD. The letter to Stalin began: "Never before has civilized humankind been faced with such danger as at the present time. Hitler and Hitlerism have become a deadly threat for all human culture, for the independence of all countries, for the freedom of all peoples."[33]

The preamble of the clearly structured memorandum demanded national liberation and social justice for all nations in all of occupied Europe. In various letters sent by Erlich and Alter, their wish for a postwar Europe led and managed by democrats and socialists was clear. A detailed seven-point program explained the tasks and structure of the Jewish Anti-Hitler Committee, including the participation of foreign, mainly American, Jews. The CC was to consist of ten persons: seven representatives from the Jewish population in the Nazi-occupied countries, and one Jewish representative each from the Soviet Union, England, and America. The presidium, consisting of three persons, was to be led by Erlich; Alter would be the secretary and another representative would still need to be elected but would probably be Mikhoels. Erlich would fly to London and Alter to New York to organize work in foreign countries. A Polish Jew would parachute into Poland. Honorary members of the presidium would include representatives from the Soviet government, the American, English, and Polish ambassadors to the Soviet Union, as well as prominent economists, artists and scientists from the Soviet Union and other countries.[34]

There was still no answer from Stalin at the end of November. Beria's officers repeatedly consoled the memorandum's authors. Erlich and Alter overestimated the dictator's goodwill, thinking that he would allow a permanent Jewish representation with representatives from the Allies and Jews from German-occupied regions and the Soviet Union who were totally isolated from foreign countries could come together. Based on the enormous amount of attention they received, Erlich and Alter also totally misjudged their own importance during this time of Moscow's siege. Because Moscow and Leningrad did not fall, the German blitzkrieg ran aground in December 1941. America's entry into the war that same month and the possibility of massive American military support enormously reduced the significance of a Jewish Support Committee.

## New Arrests and Murders

On December 3, 1941, General Sikorski flew to Moscow for a meeting with Stalin. They also discussed forming a legion of Polish refugees. Neither the Polish diplomats waiting in Kuibyshev nor Erlich sensed that, during this discussion, Stalin characterized the Jews as "bad and miserable soldiers."[35] They believed the Polish president wanted to meet his prominent Jewish compatriots in the city. But around midnight Erlich and Alter received a telephone call, asking them to come to the NKVD office. An orderly from Moscow was waiting for them and they were never seen again after that.

The Polish embassy in Moscow wanted to intervene while Sikorski was still there, but their telephone calls were probably intentionally interrupted. Anyone who later asked about Erlich and Alter was unable to get a clear answer. For example, the general prosecutor, Andrei Vyshinsky, explained that since the men were Soviet citizens, intervention on their behalf meant intervention in the Soviet Union's internal matters. Because they had participated in the February Revolution and Erlich was a member of the Worker's and Soldier's Council, they were now suddenly Soviet citizens. Their imprisonment was kept exceptionally secret, even by Soviet standards. No one in the jail in Kuibyshev was allowed to know their names, write about them or to even mention them. They were listed by the numbers of their cells.

On May 14, 1942, Prisoner No. 42, Henryk Erlich, hanged himself in his cell. Prisoner No. 41, Viktor Alter, threatened to commit suicide; he was shot on February 17, 1943 in Kuibyshev. The reports on these murders were stamped "Top Secret. Personal."[36] According to Leon Leneman, Stalin had personally written "shoot both" (*rasstreliat' oboikh*)[37] on the letter from Erlich and Alter. A document dated February 1943, from Molotov to Beria actually does exist with a statement mentioning that the military tribunal of the Supreme Court of the Soviet Union had sentenced Erlich and Alter to death. Probably the verdict is a backdated document to justify—with the remark about the first death penalty during the summer of 1941—the execution by shooting in 1943 with an internal document. The reason for the alleged verdict was that Erlich and Alter would have systematically appealed to the Soviet troops to ask for an immediate peace with Germany.[38] In December 1941 Soviet officials had already told the Polish ambassador that both had been arrested because of their "contacts with the Nazis."

## Interventions on behalf of Erlich and Alter

After their disappearance and because it was not known that they were dead, many organizations, parties, labor unions and press organs throughout the world asked for the release of those prominent union leaders. The intervention of President Roosevelt's personal representative, Wendell Wilkie, with Maxim Litvinov, the Soviet ambassador to the United States, was just as unsuccessful, as Jan Masaryk's request to Ambassador Maisky in London and the Polish government's approaches to Stafford Cripps. Albert Einstein also appealed to the Soviet government to release Alter and Erlich. On February 23, 1943, William Green, president of the powerful American Federation of Labor, received information that Erlich and Alter had been executed shortly after their arrest because of their "hostile activities, including appealing to Soviet troops to stop the bloodshed and make immediate peace with Germany." Despite the wave of worldwide protest, Alter had been shot just a few days earlier.

News about Erlich's and Alter's murders created a storm of protest from the Bund's members and their friends. The Jewish underground in Warsaw used a courier to inform the allies about their protest. The text of their statement was published in New York in March 1943. The Polish underground even allowed that a statement be issued in London. The Austrian Labor Committee in New York protested very harshly, as did almost every American labor union. One hundred representatives of Jewish literature and press in the United States signed a resolution. In leading newspapers and magazines like *The New Republic, The Nation, The New York Post,* and *Free World,* the murders were harshly criticized. Innumerable articles and obituaries were published about Erlich and Alter in the Jewish press. In the United States, a press war started between the pro-Bundist Yiddish newspaper *Forward (Forwerts)* and the Yiddish communist newspaper *A Free Tomorrow (Morgn Freiheit),* which was constantly defending the Soviet lies, also claimed that the Jews' future was in Europe and even that Palestine's existence depended upon Stalin.[39]

How could Erlich and Alter have possibly believed in the success of their initiatives? These men had already suffered as a result of the Bolsheviks during Russia's revolution in 1917; they had publicized Stalin's murderous policies in innumerable essays; and they were sentenced to death; they stayed alive only because the Soviet Union was attacked. How could they even think that Stalin would agree to their plans, which contrasted starkly with many basic principles of Soviet internal and foreign policy, including the way the government dealt with Jews, Social Democrats and especially the Bundists? Did they really believe Stalin would change his tactics and policies because horrible mistakes had already been made? Was this purely wishful thinking on the part of the Jewish socialists who thought that because there were a million Jewish victims that Soviet policy would change direction once again? Was their self-assurance and their positive outlook based on the contacts they had with western diplomats and visitors to the Soviet Union who promised them support and solidarity with their plans? The encouraging attitude of secret service chief Lavrenti Beria, who suggested that Stalin viewed the Jewish Anti-Hitler Committee's plans benevolently, obviously played an important part. Stalin, however—and Beria did nothing without his knowledge—had used Erlich and Alter in his own power game: they were arrested and sentenced to death only because the government wanted an advantage over the powerful Bundist movement in the annexed part of Poland. They were amnestied only because, faced with the deadly threat in 1941, the government was willing to "talk business" with Poland's government in exile. They were allowed to plot and make plans for a committee as long as the German army had Moscow almost within its reach. They were again sentenced once the danger receded, and another committee was formed by supposedly loyal—and their "own" Soviet—elements. They didn't have, as it was known in Stalinism, the destructive "mark of Cain" (something that despite Beria's help Erlich and Alter did have) as an independent initiative coming from the ranks. It was to be controlled from above from the very start.

While committee activities were underway, the two Bundists were kept alive as "safety factors." After the turning point of the war at Stalingrad, the political leadership was convinced that Alter, who was still alive, was no longer needed. According to Stalinist logic, both were principally safety risks, potential instigators of "Bundist" claims and probably defenders of "Polish interests." It took almost fifty years, until September 1992, for the KGB to publish information about the murders of Erlich and Alter in its paper, *Shield and Sword* (*Shchit i mech*).[40]

## 13. EARLY JEWISH ANTI-HITLER
### INITIATIVES AND THE FOUNDING OF THE JAFC

Soviet Jewish leaders knew that they had to take the initiative in defending vital Jewish interests in the country and in organizing foreign support measures. They also tried to establish appropriate forums and institutions. On July 18, well-known Yiddish writers turned to the Soviet Information Bureau (*Sovinformburo*), which had been established on June 21, 1941 under the supervision of the ministry of foreign affairs, and published an article that included information specifically aimed at foreign journalists. In this article they requested that the bureau allow the Yiddish party newspaper *The Truth* (*Der Emes*), to begin publishing again. The paper had been shut down in 1938, and its reopening would provide Soviet Jews, who had been evacuated inside the country or had fled, with war propaganda and encourage pro-Soviet leanings among Jews in the West.

The *Sovinformburo*'s chief, Aleksandr Shcherbakov (1901-1945), was a Stalin protégé and a pure anti-Semite. Because of his ignorance of foreign countries and his power-hungry chauvinism he sidestepped the new struggle for openness and tolerance in Soviet information policy suggested by the bureau and its representative, the worldly Jew Solomon Lozovsky. Shcherbakov denied the petition, with the "recommendation" that Jewish writers should write for Russian newspapers. The petition was resubmitted in September. This time, Mikhoels, Epstein, Zuskin, Orshansky and Strongin were among the signatories, in addition to Markish, Kvitko, Halkin, Bergelson, Nussinov, and Fininberg. The CC and Agitprop section agreed but, because of the situation at the front, the planned new issue for mid-October could not be published.

The above-mentioned personalities proposed that Solomon Lozovsky call a mass meeting to mobilize Jews at home and abroad, especially in the United States and Great Britain, to call for help and practical solidarity with the oppressed and endangered Soviet Union. The appeal included a list of speakers and a draft of the keynote speech. Lozovsky and Shcherbakov agreed.

## The First Meeting

On the evening of August 24, 1941, just two months after the Soviet Union was attacked, more than a thousand people gathered in the Central Park for Culture and Recreation, the largest such hall in Moscow, for a "public meeting of Jewish people's representatives." Press coverage of this event signaled that Stalin and his colleagues basically agreed with the plan of Henryk Erlich and Viktor Alter but to install not an International but a Jewish Soviet Committee.

Many of the most important people from the party, government, culture, science and the army attended the meeting, including the writers and poets: Ilya Ehrenburg, David Bergelson, Shmuel Halkin, Peretz Markish, Samuil Marshak, theater director Solomon Mikhoels, chief conductor Samuel Samosud of the Bolshoi Orchestra, Generals Kreizer and Katz, music virtuoso David Oistrakh, Jakob Sak, Emil Gilels, Jakob Flier, nuclear physicist Piotr Kapitsa, movie director Sergei Eisenstein, Friedrich Ermler, Aleksei Kapler, screenwriter of the famous films *Lenin in October* and *Lenin 1918*, baritone Mark Reisen, architect Boris Yofan (who designed a megalomaniacal palace for the Soviets), and author Theodor Plievier.

The first words of the message to the Jews were "Brothers and sisters, Jews of the whole world" ("Brider un shvester, yidn fun der gantser velt")—a community that was not supposed to exist, according to Stalin's definition dating back to 1913. The actor Solomon Mikhoels, who was chosen to be the meeting's leader, made a passionate appeal to Jews around the world:

> Brothers, Jews of England! Your great democratic country battles together with the Soviet Union for the destruction of Fascism. I believe that you will find yourselves in the front line of combat. Brothers, Jews of the United States and of the Americas! I am sure that you will be among the first to work to speed up American help and support measures. Jewish mothers! Give your son your blessing and send him into battle against Fascism, even if he is your only son.[41]

Peretz Markish:

> In the country of the Soviets, the Jews have found, after a thousand-year odyssey and persecution, a home and a homeland that is a

mother who has healed the wounds of the past. Here in the Soviet Union Jewish people are equal among equals. Here the Jewish mother tongue is spoken anew, here its culture has blossomed anew. In less than 25 years the Jewish people have developed, thanks to the fatherly welfare of our Soviet State, an extensive literature. Its art, its theater, its stages are among the best in the country. Do you know that in international music competitions the sons and daughters of our people, whose homeland has cared for and raised them like a mother, have won first prizes? The Soviet Union turned Jews into engineers, inventors, physicians, scholars and artists. On the chest of many Jews gleam the medals of the Soviet Union. Jewish brothers, the time when we surrendered fatefully to the executioner is the most disgraceful page in the history of our old people! None of us will again allow our great historical past to be stained by waiting passively for death. Death, though, is hovering at our doorstep. Jewish brothers, the seas and oceans have lost their magic meaning as unconquerable obstacles in our day. Every nation and every human is now mobilized for the stubborn and decisive battle. You are selected and called upon, everywhere in the world, using guns as soldiers bringing death or using words coming from your lips, in this holy war, the war against Fascism! You must do anything and everything in your power to make the enemy of the Jewish people drown in his own blood! You shall do this as we do here in the fire of the front lines! We are a united people and now also a united army!

Sergei Eisenstein:

At present there is a battle between life and death. There is Fascism, bearer of an animalistic ideology, and the Soviet Union bearer of human ideals, with its powerful allies in this fight, Great Britain and America. There should not be a single Jew on this earth who has not taken his oath to fight in this holy war with all the means and power available.

Ilya Ehrenburg:

I grew up in a Russian city. My mother tongue is Russian. I am a Russian writer. Like all Russians, I will defend my fatherland. The Nazis forced me to remember that my mother's name was Hanna. I am a Jew. I say that full of pride. Fascism hates us more than anybody or anything, and this is a badge of honor for us.

The fewer words the better. Words are not necessary, but bullets! My country, the Russian people, the people of Pushkin and Tolstoy, has stood up to fight before all others. I now turn to the Jews of America as a Russian writer and as a Jew. No ocean exists that can save you. Listen to the sounds of the guns at Gomel!

Jews, our place is in the front lines. We will not forgive those who are indifferent. We will condemn those who have washed their hands in innocence. Help all those who fight against the grim enemy. Hurry to help England! To help the Soviet Union! Let everyone do all that he can. Soon the time will come when one must answer for oneself, and what have you done? He has to speak for himself and is also responsible to the dead and living. He will also have to answer to himself!

The Yiddish author David Bergelson, who returned to the Soviet Union in 1933, also made a passionate speech. The original text was published on August 27 in *Our Word* (*Unzer vort*), a Yiddish underground newspaper, published by the Jewish resistance in Paris. The article was entitled: "For the national existence of the Jewish people. Unity of all Jews in the battle against Hitlerism. Historical meeting of the most respected personalities and heroes of the Red Army on Radio Moscow." Here is an excerpt from his appeal:

Bloodthirsty Hitler wants to exterminate anyone refusing to bow to his regime of slavery. More than anything he wants to destroy our race. For all people of occupied countries, Hitlerism means slavery, persecution and torture; for us Jews, though, it means total extermination and the end. The question of survival becomes absolutely clear. It concerns life or death for our people... Vandalizing Fascism still rages. It destroys everything, and we Jews will be the first to be thrown into the fire. Our people, though, will not perish, the people of Maimonides, Spinoza, Mendelsohn, Heine, Einstein; the people who, thousands of years ago, proudly told their tormentors, "*Lo amut ki ekhye*" "I will not die but live." [Hebrew quotation previously not used in proletarian Yiddish literature, A.L.] ... Beloved brothers and sisters, Jews of the whole world! None of you can forget for even a moment that the situation of Jews has never been as tragic and desperate... The obligation of every Jew is to join the ranks of the international anti-fascist front as quickly as possible. The place of every Jew is in the armies of the democratic coalition, with the partisans, in sabotage actions... Help mobilize the world to assist the Soviet Union in its holy war against the fascist beasts... In the course of our history we have already survived many attacks. We will survive this one as well. We will not perish. We will live.

Shakhne Epstein, a representative of the Jews in America, said:

Friends, brothers and sisters, Jews of Great Britain, the United States of America and all other countries! An immense and holy task is before you—with everything in your power, with relentless words and actions, you must contribute and courageously help completely exterminate the Fascist monster. There is no task more important and more holy for every Jew than the total elimination of the Fascists. Jewish brothers of the whole world! The voice of spilled blood does not want prayer and fasting, it demands vengeance. Not death or funeral candles but fire in which the executioners of humankind will be eliminated. Not tears but hate and resistance against the monsters and the cannibals! Not with words but with actions! Now or never!

All of these speeches were broadcast in several languages by Radio Moscow. Many participants signed a festive ceremonial declaration in the station's studio. This performance signaled a radical change of the previous policy, which had denied Jews recognition as a people. For the first time since the revolution, Jews were allowed contact with their sisters and brothers in the West—though Shcherbakov and Lozovsky reviewed every speech beforehand. Lozovsky explained, as a defendant during the trial against the JAFC, "I organized a meeting on behalf of the party. Every speaker was instructed by the CC. Every speech was read by me, Aleksandrov and Shcherbakov beforehand."[42]

## The Founding of the JAFC

Exactly when the Jewish Anti-Fascist Committee was founded still remains unclear. The committee was not mentioned during the August 1941 meeting. Years later members named different dates. The 1992 edition of the *Great Soviet Encyclopedia* listed 1941 as the year the committee was founded. When the committee was on trial in 1952, Lozovsky stated that he and Shcherbakov had discussed establishing it at the end of 1941. Archival documents show that it was already engaged in activity at that time and Mikhoels was asked to be a representative in mid-December 1941.

Approximately seven months passed from the time of the attack until the JAFC was organized. Why this delay? In January 1941 the front around Moscow had stabilized. When the United States entered the war after the Pearl Harbor attack on December 7, 1941, Stalin hoped the United States would be willing to deliver weapons and intervene in Europe, even without the appeal of a Jewish lobby. In addition, many of the future members of the committee had been evacuated to very distant regions in the Soviet Union and were still to be reached.

In mid-December 1941 the first organizational steps were taken under the supervision of Shcherbakov, who received his instructions directly from the Kremlin. The committee's true chief would be Solomon Lozovsky, who was a member of the CC and of the Supreme Soviet.

He was also a deputy to the Soviet foreign minister and deputy head of the *Sovinformburo*, making him part of the party and government elite of the Soviet Union. Shakhne Epstein a journalist writing in Yiddish and an NKVD agent was chosen as secretary general. Under these two people, the Kremlin, the party, government leaders, as well as the Lubyanka and the secret services, had the newly established JAFC firmly under control.

In February 1942 a program for the committee was agreed to and drafted. Lozovsky announced the establishment of the JAFC at a press conference of the *Sovinformburo* in Kuibyshev for the first time on April 23, 1942. He communicated the JAFC's goals with the following answer to a written inquiry from a foreign correspondent:

> The JAFC's main goal is to enlist Jewish people in all countries for the active fight against Fascism and to stage a campaign for maximum help for the Soviet Union and the Red Army, which is carrying the main burden in the combat against Fascism. There are two main tasks stemming from this goal. First, to make Jews of the entire world understand the unbelievably criminal essence of Fascism and the absolute gruesomeness of its bestialities, especially toward the Jewish population in the temporarily occupied Soviet regions and the occupied countries. Second, to make Jewish people aware of examples of courage, bravery and heroism of the Soviet nations, including

Soviet Jews, and to show how one can fight against Fascism directly at the front, through selfless and creative work inside the country.[43]

The committee had 70 members, 19 of them constituted the presidium. Solomon Mikhoels was appointed its chairman. He was an actor and director of the Jewish State Theater and a Lenin prizewinner. The secretary general was Shakhne Epstein and members included Dr. Boris Shimeliovich, General Katz, and Lina Stern, who was the only female member of the Academy of Sciences and a well-known biologist. All activities, especially concerning personnel questions, had to be agreed to and approved by the NKVD.

The committee's membership list reads like a *Who's Who* of Jews in the Soviet Union. Between 1942 and 1948 there were 44 writers and journalists, 12 connected to theater and film, 16 soldiers, officers and partisans. They included "Heroes of the Soviet Union" Buber, Fissanovich, and Milner. Generals Katz and Kreizer, as well as 15 artists, 18 state officials, party functionaries, and 14 scientists were also members.

## 14. The Strategy of Silence—The Holocaust in the Soviet Information and Propaganda Policies

The assault against the Soviet Union in June 1941 was a direct attack on the Jews living there. In the "Western Campaign" against France, the Benelux countries and Great Britain; in the attack on Denmark and Norway; and during the invasion of the Balkan states, the extermination of the Jews was not a pre-planned goal.

After occupying the Polish areas, the Germans instigated pogroms immediately and began setting up ghettos for Polish Jews. Measures for the extermination of the Jews were not systematically planned and carried out until 1941. From the beginning, the war against the Soviet Union was motivated by the "Final Solution" to the Jewish question and by the conquest of "Lebensraum" for "Germanic" settlers. The latter plan also included the extermination of the Slavic population that constituted the majority. Götz Aly analyzed and documented the "reciprocal action" (Eichmann) between the policy of ethnic cleansing on the one hand and the "Jewish question," on the other, in his study, "The 'Final Solution,' about the displacement and murder of the European Jews."[44] The Reich's task forces (*Einsatzgruppen*) began immediately to fulfill the order to murder along with local Ukrainian, Belorussian, and Lithuanian militia who joined them. During the attack on the Soviet Union, the absolute priority of the SS and National Socialists was the final elimination of the Jews, while the German military was more oriented toward anti-Bolshevism than anti-Semitism.

## The War Against the Jews

In mid-May 1941 a "Guideline for the Behavior of the Troops in Russia" included the following instructions: "The battle against Bolshevism, the deadly enemy, demands vigorous and ruthless action against bolshevist agitators, insurgents, saboteurs, Jews, and the total uprooting of any active or passive resistance."[45] This vocabulary ("ruthless and vigorous action") concealed the fact that Jews—regardless of age, sex, personal behavior, etc.—were declared to be an enemy and subjected to extermination.

Even though the Jews were to be "punished" for their alleged responsibility for Bolshevism, the Jews' extermination and the "anti-Bolshevist crusades" were not the same for the Nazi leaders. After Litvinov's release and "cleansing actions" in the Soviet Union, Hitler decided that Stalin was an anti-Semite and had created a "pan-Slavic" regime. In July 1942, during one of his "table talks," the Führer announced: "Stalin, while speaking to Ribbentrop, made no effort to disguise the fact that he was only waiting for the development of his own *inteligensiia* in the USSR to wipe out the Jewish leadership class, which he still needed."[46] That meant that Jews were to be exterminated for reasons more deeply rooted than their alleged connection to Bolshevism. The murder of Jews was not an "answer" to Bolshevism's "class murder," as Ernst Nolte had declared a few years before in the "Historians' Quarrel" in Germany.

On July 2, 1941, Reinhard Heydrich—who was given responsibility for the "overall solution of the Jewish question"—ordered his task forces (*Einsatzgruppen*) to liquidate all Jews in government and party positions in the Soviet Union.[47] This order to murder was very quickly spread to include "all" Jewish men, then "all" Jews, and finally the children. The task forces—at first a 3,000-man-strong special unit of the SS and the police—murdered half a million Jews through mass executions in the first five months of German occupation, mostly in the Baltic area and Bessarabia. They acted with the support of 170 mobile police battalions consisting mostly of local volunteers—Balts, Ukrainians, Russians, Cossacks, Belorussians, Tatars, and other local nationalities.

Since there was no formal plan for the evacuation of Jews from the Soviet Union's western regions[48] and since any public criticism of Germany was forbidden from September 1939 until July 2, 1941 these extermination proceedings caught many victims by surprise. Nazi anti-Semitism had only been mentioned in the Soviet press in 1938 in regard to "Kristallnacht." Anti-Semitism played no part in Soviet fascism, which was based on Italian fascism, which itself had practically no grievances against the Jews. The assessment of Mussolini's regime was more or less applied to Hitler's Germany.[49] When Nazi anti-Semitism was even mentioned, it was thought to be a deception: by assaulting Jews, Hitler wanted to present himself to the worker as "anti-capitalist," but behind the scenes he was financed and supported with capital from the Jewish bourgeosie.[50]

Ukrainian Jews remembered that, at the end of World War I, German occupation troops offered them relative security compared to the marauding gangs under the Ukrainian flags. This explains why in September 1941, Jews from Kiev who were asked to report to the Germans—by posters for "resettlement"—came forward in much greater numbers than their murderers had expected. These Jews still believed "in their resettlement until just before their execution, due to very clever organization," as could be read in the report of the taskforces. On September 29 and 30, in the ravine of Babi Yar, 33,771 Jews were executed. In the weeks that followed the number of those murdered grew by tens of thousands.[51]

## Collaboration and Anti-Semitic Agitation

Since the German army attacked the Soviet Union, the Wehrmacht became an accomplice in these mass murders with individual units also participating in the executions; many others supported the death units with logistical and organizational help. As in Minsk, ghettos were established by the German military alone.[52]

On February 21, 1941, the German army was already advised to design its own pamphlets for the troops as well as for the Russian population. The "Generalreferat Ostraum" in Goebbels' ministry produced radio shows, posters, pamphlets, movies, news reports and records in 18 languages of the Soviet nations after April 1941. Russian newspapers praised the German liberator's destruction of "Yiddish communism."

Political schooling was done in which thousands of themes like Judaism, "Question of race," and fabricated anti-Semitic works like *Protocols of the Elders of Zion*, were brought up for closer inspection.[53] On June 4, 1941, Goebbels decreed that the division of the Soviet Union into nationalities should not be publicly discussed. Propaganda was to be directed against Stalin himself and his "Jewish supporters." Mikhoels was one of the most hated and despised figures singled out for blame in the propaganda. Altogether, the German military produced over one billion propaganda pamphlets. By the end of 1941, 500 million were published and distributed. This was in contrast to the campaign against France, where only 12 million had been produced.

Even though the German military initiated pogroms in the regions annexed by the Soviet Union in 1939 (Lithuania, Galicia, etc.) the non-Jewish population in the core areas did not participate voluntarily in those actions.

German propaganda against the Jews worked especially well in the Ukraine and the Baltic countries. The Ukrainians greeted German troops enthusiastically. At the end of July 1941, on Himmler's orders, the Ukrainian Volunteer Police was established, which was placed under the Order Police (*Ordnungspolizei*). SD offices were located within the Ukrainian detective and protection forces. These killer commandos were armed and wore black uniforms; they were involved in all actions, including mass shootings and pogroms against Jews. They guarded the ghettos and extermination camps and in 1943 they became part of the Fourteenth Waffen SS Division *Galizien*.

Reports about the crimes committed by these volunteer units were suppressed in the Soviet Union. The passages relating to these activities were removed from the *Black Book* by the Soviet censors and were not included in any save the German edition of 1994, printed under my editorship.

In Polish Galicia and in Lithuania, members of the anti-Soviet underground accused Jews of being sympathizers, "exploiters," and helpers of the Soviet occupiers. Meanwhile, Jewish deportations by the Soviets were deliberately ignored. The commander of the Seventeenth Army, General Stülpnagel, complained in 1941 that murdering the Jews awakened "pity and sympathy" among the rest of the population and demanded the Ukrainians be enlightened about the Jews.[54] In reality, Soviet citizens identified with the Jews only as far as they believed that they would be next in line to be shot after the Jews.[55] The Germans equated the liberation of the Jews with communism, and most people had forced themselves to come to terms with the idea. This was the reason why they thought that what was happening to the Jews today could happen to the Russians as "low humans" and "communists" tomorrow.

In the Soviet regions under German rule, anti-Semitic agitation was part of the daily work of German military propaganda companies and their mobile printing presses. A pamphlet, distributed in September 1941, with an almost unimaginable print run of 160 million copies, urged: "Beat the Yid, the politruk; his snout longs for a brick! The commissars and politruks force you into pointless resistance. Chase away the commissars and come running over to the Germans." Of course the commissar was sketched to look like a "Jewish" type.

## Silence About the Slaughter of the Jews

If there were complaints during the plenary sessions of the JAFC, the response was that the war brought fascist anti-Semitic ideology into the attention of Soviet citizens. Beyond the committee there were no appropriate Soviet public reactions to the Germans' assault about an anti-Jewish extermination campaign. Reports from the front received most of the press and radio coverage, and almost nothing was reported about the suffering of the civilian population. The mass murders committed by task forces were not mentioned at the beginning or in the later weeks of the campaign.

The Polish government-in-exile had already received information about the murder of Jews, but only very limited news reached the West. The first report, in November 1941, appeared in the Jewish Telegraph Agency because it worked with independent correspondents. This report spoke of 52,000 people murdered in Kiev (Babi Yar); the same number was also mentioned in official Soviet announcements in January 1942. In March it was denied and the number was amended to only 1,000 Jews. Reports that were closer to reality still came only from exiled Polish or Scandinavian sources. Finally, on January 6, 1942, a note signed by Molotov confirmed that 52,000 Jews had been murdered in Kiev. However, the memorandum stated that the total number of victims was only 90,000, when in reality the number was already 500,000. This was a scandalous understatement. On April 27, the next memorandum from Molotov was published about the gruesome work of German occupation forces but it didn't even mention the crimes against the Jews.

On December 18, 1942, however, *Pravda* published a combined explanation from eleven Allied governments and governments-in-exile, including the Soviet Union, entitled "Regarding the Extermination of the Jewish Population of Europe by Nazi Officials." In this declaration the Allies pledged to punish those responsible for these crimes. On the following day, December 19, 1942, a multi-page memorandum appeared in the press. The author, Solomon Lozovsky, reported in detail for the first time about the extermination of the Jews; he named places and the number murdered; he also described the Nazi plan to carry out the murder of the Jews by driving them like cattle to the East.[56]

## A Few Exceptions

The general silence was seldom broken. Only Yiddish broadcasts by the JAFC and articles in *Eynikeyt* provided rare bits of information. One of these exceptions was a small pamphlet published in 1941 by the political administration of the Leningrad Front. The pamphlet declared that the occupation forces were proceeding with particularly gruesome brutality against Jews because they represented the source of all evil to Hitler.

The authors countered this analysis with Gorky's characterization of the Jews as the "old strong yeast of humanity"—a quotation that had been taboo during the twenty years of Soviet dictatorship—and Molotov's 1936 eulogy to the Jews. In that pamphlet Jews were described as working people and heroic members of the Red Army. Anti-Semitism was called the "greatest stupidity and greatest infamy of humankind and of the human race" (Mommsen). The pamphlet ended with a quote from Stalin—words of his that were taboo from 1931 to 1936—saying that communists were by nature enemies of anti-Semitism and that anti-Semitism would be persecuted in the Soviet Union as a particularly hostile activity.[57]

V. Struve quoted Stalin's definition of anti-Semitism as "leftover cannibalism" in the title of his pamphlet, which was also published in 1941.[58] The author, a member of the Academy of Sciences, described Nazi Germany as the antithesis of the Soviet Union where all nationalities were equal. He drew, referring to Gorky, a positive picture of the Jews who were persecuted and labeled the lowest race in Fascist Germany, describing how all Jews without exception fell victim to German anti-Semitism. The lie of Soviet propaganda from the 1930s, that the "Jewish bourgeoisie" supported Hitler, was therefore refuted. German crimes were objectively conveyed despite the use of typical phrases found in Soviet instructional material—this was not done as accurately again until the publication of the *Black Book*, which was also forbidden. Struve even quoted Nietzsche as a witness and came to terms with the *Protocols of the Elders of Zion*, which instigated anti-Semitism.

Only the JAFC's work interrupted the taboo surrounding the Holocaust. Official propaganda neither commented on the forced deportations, ordered by Stalin, of Volga Germans, Crimean Tatars, Siberian, and Caucasian peoples, nor did it talk about Jewish genocide. Instead, the victims were characterized as "peaceful Soviet citizens." The murder of Jews was reported only in publications that were not available to most of the Soviet public. Ehrenburg's reports about the murders were published in April 1944 in Yiddish translation in a 63-page booklet entitled, *Murder of a People* (*Merder fun felker*). One Russian magazine, however, published only a few excerpts of the original text.

### No Attempt to Save the Jews

What was the reason for the Soviet leadership's policy of silence? A quotation transmitted by Lev Kopelev offers an explanation. In 1943, a member of the Military Council of the front where Kopelev fought publicly read this supposed quote from Stalin:

> Some comrades still fail to understand that the important strength in our country is the Great Russian nation (…) some comrades of Jewish descent believe that this war is being fought to save the Jewish nation. These Jews are mistaken. We fight the Great Patriotic War for the salvation, the freedom and the independence of our homeland led by the Great Russian people.[59]

After that, according to Kopelev, Jews were relieved from certain positions so as not to offer Nazi propaganda an opening for an attack. In reality, the Soviet leadership had decided to "sacrifice" the Jews to a certain extent, at least in the eyes of the Soviet population and the fighting troops. Faced with latent anti-Semitism in Soviet society and persecution by the occupation force, the general propaganda was to avoid the impression that it was the Red Army's responsibility to save the Jews. These views could only be published in the Yiddish circles, which were limited to the JAFC.

Not only the memory of the victims and of those who participated in the resistance, but especially the crimes of the perpetrators would be suppressed. By the end of the war, while the victorious Soviet army freed its own territory and conquered large parts of Eastern and Southeastern Europe and Germany, the situation had completely changed. The Soviet leadership then had almost no interest in publicizing the realities of the Holocaust inside the Soviet Union.

The government commission, established on November 2, 1942, to research the crimes of the Nazis and their collaborators, was already dissolved by the end of 1945. The material presented to the military court in Nuremberg and later used in the *Black Book* did not explicitly state that Jews were the main victims.[60] During preliminary inquiries against the JAFC after 1949, the number of Jews murdered by the Germans was called a "military and state secret." During peacetime, this number was still kept hidden. Even accusations against former German occupation troops and their collaborators, as well as publications chronicling the suffering and torment of the Jews were soon stopped because those accusations didn't fit in with Soviet policy in the Soviet Occupation Zone and later the GDR. Stalin felt it more important to have fraternal relations with the Germans because he thought that the Germans had a strategic part to play in the expansion of Soviet influence in Western Europe. They would work with strong East German, French, and Italian communist parties. Stalin even declared that the *Soviet* and *German* people had been the two main victims of the Second World War—there was no more room or time to mention Jewish victims.

# Part IV

# JAFC Activities Inside and Outside the Soviet Union

## 15. The JAFC and Soviet War Propaganda

### Propaganda and Nationalism

The JAFC was, on the one hand, obliged to provide the usual indoctrination, and its members' views had to be in step with war propaganda as well as to Stalin's plans; on the other hand, the committee was in obvious contradiction with Soviet "Jewish" policy.

Stalin mistrusted the army and the people after the collapse of the country's defenses in June 1941. This is why he ordered the Party to control the military by appointing the top political commissars of the Red Army. General Lev Mekhlis of the NKVD, a former Bundist who joined the Bolsheviks after the October 1917 coup d'état, was relieved of his leadership of the main administration after repeated criticism in June 1942 and replaced by Aleksandr Shcherbakov.

After the Soviet Union was attacked, people who were part of the nation's cultural life now had to work for her defense. Nine hundred forty-three writers joined the army[1] and 275 of them died in battle. Out of 100 Jewish authors, 62 served as volunteers in the war. Innumerable poems were written on heroic themes, and published in large editions; literature referring to and describing the war comprised 40 percent of all book production.

The war theme also dominated music, film and painting. During this period works were created extending far beyond the propaganda purposes of the time. Poster creation and design must be mentioned as especially extraordinary. Works that became classics in this genre included those made by Deni, Dolgorukov, Yefimov (brother of Mikhail Koltsov, who was executed), and the Kukriniksy (Kupyanov, Krylov, and Sokolov, who always worked in a team of three). German crimes against Jews were not their themes.

Right after the attack the deputy patriarch of the Orthodox Church appealed to the people to defend their land. Officials quickly stopped publishing *The Godless (Bezbozhnik)*, which was aggressively atheist, and all other atheist propaganda. They wanted to show the world that official anti-religious measures were a thing of the past. Because churches and synagogues were no longer closed, Jews could celebrate important religious high holidays for the first time in decades, in the fall of 1941. In September 1943 Stalin received representatives of the Orthodox Church and, in recognition of their support of the war effort, allowed them to establish seminaries for priests. Moscow's chief rabbi, Shliffer, became a member of the JAFC in 1944.

The army and navy published and distributed more than 3,300 propaganda publications of more than two billion copies. In addition, there were the pamphlets from the combat troops' political divisions. According to German army figures, a total of 6,000 different pamphlets was issued by February 1944. Soviet radio broadcast 14 transmissions for the troops daily. War propaganda content was controlled by the Seventh Division of the Red Army's Political Head Administration. During the war, the *Sovinformburo* published 135,000 articles to serve as informational material[2] for foreign journalists.

The Soviets had already begun to place a high value on "fatherland" and the "homeland" since the mid-1930s. After the attack this belief grew and an appeal went out to all the Soviet Union's historians and history teachers. They were asked to participate in the destruction of the Soviet Union's "worst enemy and of all progressive humankind." They created many pamphlets to do exactly that—to agitate and to instill hatred. These pamphlets were distributed and became knapsack literature for the Red Army. The most popular themes included the Russian victory over the German knights in the 13th century, victory over the Tatars in the 14th century, and the defense of Moscow against the Poles in the 17th century. The defeat of Napoleon's army in Russia was another favorite theme. The basic tenor of all propaganda was the Soviet power's identification with Russian history. Stalin and his loyal comrades were the incarnation of Aleksandr Nevsky, Dmitri Donskoy, or General Suvorov. The title "Great Fatherland War," first used by the CC after the attack, recalls the defense used against Napoleon. Based on this, members of the JAFC decided that they had the right to identify themselves with heroic figures in Jewish history.

Soviet agitators used German nationalist themes in the battle against Hitler. This is why they dug deep into the arsenal of pre-republican tradition with appeals to capitulation, with the "National Committee for a Free Germany" and the "Union of the Officers" which were established in July or September 1943. The enemy was encouraged to desert and join the other side, where he would be converted to communist ideology. Military traditions were revived even in the Red Army along with traditional ideas and privileges.

In 1944 the words of the Soviet national anthem, the *International*, were changed. Until the downfall of the Soviet Union, "Great Russian" (a historical term for the predecessor of Russia) was sung, which was supposed to create an inseparable Union "forever." After Khrushchev began the process of de-Stalinization in 1956, the hymn glorifying Stalin was no longer sung, but the melody remained the same. After September 1, 1977, a new form was used with several political corrections, created under Mikhail Suslov, the Brezhnev era's chief ideologue. Lenin then replaced Stalin. The constant increase of the Russian leader's part during the 1940s endangered the context of the Stalinist nationality policy. The loyalty of the Oriental Soviet nations was particularly in danger of being undermined. Therefore international and Marxist propaganda was enforced and strengthened once again. The soldiers were to be immunized against influences in the conquered countries and territories through increased communist teaching.[3]

## Additional Anti-Fascist Committees

On April 24, 1942, writing in *Pravda* on behalf of the *Sovinformburo*, Solomon Lozovsky reported the activities of four more anti-Fascist Committees: the Pan-Slavic Committee, the Soviet Women's Committee, the Committee of Youth and the Scientists Committee. The Pan-Slavic Committee was to mobilize millions of Americans of Polish, Russian, and Ukrainian descent for the Soviet Union and foster identification with Slavism and the people's common past. Slavism was now included in schools' curriculum. In August 1941 the first pan-Slavic meeting was held. The concept of this meeting was much like the Jewish meetings. Out of all the committees, the JAFC had developed the greatest number of activities concerned with the Soviet Union's survival.

## The Second Meeting

On May 24, 1942, in Moscow, in the auditorium of the Broadcasting Committee, the second meeting of representatives of the Yiddish people (*Tsveyter miting fun forshteyer funem yidishn folk*) was held. This was the first public presentation made by the JAFC. Via Radio Moscow, its president, Mikhoels, addressed Jews in England, United States, Palestine, South America, South Africa, and Australia with an appeal to help the Soviet Union. The following is an excerpt of his opening speech:

> Our anti-fascist committee must become a constituent part of the battle and be part of the broad context of the fight. We cannot fight only using the weapons of the spoken and printed word. The watchword of the second meeting, money for 1,000 tanks and 500 bombers for the Red Army alone, is an enormous goal. This task is, without a doubt, unbelievably important and honorable and demanding of every ounce of our strength. If, however, we were to concentrate our activities only on these numbers, we would not completely fulfill our duties and obligations. We must show how the nations of our country have stood up to defend the Soviet fatherland, how they fight against the defenders of racial theory, of racial hate, against Hitler's fascism and against all those who openly or secretly assist him, and against those who do not understand that the dangerous poison of fascism is smuggled in along with anti-Semitism. The central task of the committee is to procure 1,000 tanks and 500 bombers for the Red Army. And, besides this honorable task, the committee must gather material to share about the participation of Jewish people and their heroic courage in the Great Fatherland War.

But already with the first words of his speech, whose text had been censored beforehand and approved by the Kremlin (by Shcherbakov and Lozovsky), Mikhoels defined the limits of this involvement:

> I am a representative of that part of the Jewish people, that no-where in the world can freely and with such conviction articulate the wonderful and meaningful word, the unbelievably dear, very much needed word, that is as important as the words *Tate un Mame,* Dad and Mom, the word, that is the source of courage and wonderful heroism, the word *Heymland* (homeland). Our Soviet country is the homeland. Though gigantic oceans separate us, we are unified by oceans of blood; the blood of our mothers and sisters, of our sons and brothers, that have been poured out by the fascists.

The Jews were to help balance the colossal loss at the front through contributions, and to call upon the Western governments for support. It was Bergelson, who again conjured up images from Jewish history:

> All the suffering that our already long-suffering people have en-dured—be it in antiquity, when Nero herded the Jews into circus arenas to be torn to pieces by the lions, or in the Middle Ages, when Jews clothed in shrouds climbed into the pyres or cut their children's throats to save them from an even more horrible fate—all this suffer-ing becomes nothing when compared to Hitler's inhuman cruelty[4]

The appeal of May 24, 1942, struck a chord in the Jewish world. It was published by the Jewish press in several languages and was in some cases the headline.

## The First Plenum of the JAFC

Speakers at the JAFC's plenary session on May 28, 1942, included the journalist David Zaslavsky, the writer David Bergelson, the physician Boris Shimeliovich, the poets Leib Kvitko, David Hofstein and Aron Kushnirov, a representative of the Jewish kolkhoz *Nei lebn,* D. Shchupak, the journal-ist Riklin, the sculptor Sabsai, and the writer Persov.* The literary critic Isaak Nussinov declared that the committee must document the heroic participation of the Jewish masses in the Fatherland War and in the build-up of the military. Pertinent material should be made available to reduce the general public's reservations against the Jews who had fled inside the country. He criticized the fact that Jews were not readily accepted into the Red Army, especially if they came from the Baltic countries or Poland. Lina Stern, a member of the Academy of Sciences and the Academy of Medicine, pleaded for the establishment of constant contact between the committee and social organizations in foreign countries, as well as for the establishment of Jewish Volunteer Legions.[5] Yekheskel Dobrushin* listed the work of the commission established by the committee. His suggestions included organizing Jews who lived in large cities, worked in culture and took part in the war to collect money for the Red Army.

Itsik Fefer, a poet, demanded that "Jewish friends" in foreign countries "replace" their support and sympathy with tanks and airplanes for the Red Army as quickly as possible. He closed with the words: "Let us do everything possible, so that heroic men and women partisans, sons and daughters of the Jewish people, can be forever glorified. We must not rest until the enemy is exterminated from the planet."

Like Epstein, he warned against engaging beyond clearly defined war propaganda or starting to mobilize without support for the Red Army. From the beginning, their attitude was clearly different from Nussinov's concerns and demands, to include the fight against anti-Semitism in their actions.

At the conference, the JAFC formed commissions to collect information from Jews about combat during the Great Fatherland War or about Hitler's crimes against the Jewish population. Commissions for editorial work, finance and military medical help were also established.

The Oath of the Jewish People

On June 22, 1942, the first anniversary of the German attack, the first plenum of the JAFC sent an appeal to all Jews, urging them to use all their power and energy to shatter fascism once and for all.

To Jews in all Countries:
    The existence of Jewish people is in danger: *Lekhaim o lemavet*—to survive or to die! Jews should be wiped off this planet!—says

Hitler. We say—the Jewish people will live! Hitler has already killed millions of our brothers; his murderous hand is raised against everyone of us, down to the last Jew. It doesn't matter where he is on this planet. In times of lesser peril, Jews have already united against their destroyer. *Lo amut ki ekhye*—We will not perish, but we will live—sounded the battle cry!

Responsibility for the very existence of Jewish people rests on all Jews together and on every single one of us. Together with all nations, Jews from the Soviet Union swear to sacrifice everything they possess, their body and life in the battle against murderous fascism. We have signed this oath with our blood, with the blood of our children and our brothers and sisters.

Fathers and sons, mothers and daughters, fight on all fronts—from the east to the west, from the north to the south. With airplanes and ships and tanks and submarines, and with cannons and machine guns, in the cavalry and in partisan divisions, in armaments factories, on collective farms under the hail of bombs—everywhere they carry the oath and fulfill it, as loyal sons of our Soviet fatherland, as loyal sons of Jewish people.

To you, Jews of the world, we, your Soviet brothers, send out the appeal:

Let us all work together to realize the Second Moscow conference's goals. Let us buy 1,000 tanks and 500 airplanes for the Red Army. Let us give tank columns and airplane squadrons the names of great Jewish fighters, the names of genius who created Jewish culture—Bar Kokhba, Yehuda Halevi, Baruch Spinoza, Heinrich Heine, Sholem Aleichem, Yitskhak Leib Peretz, Mendele Mojcher Sforim, Morris Vintschevski, Yulius Shimeliovich, Asher Schvartsman and Naftali Botwin. Let us use the names of Jewish heroes of the Fatherland War, including Shloyme Gorelik, Israel Fissanovich, General Yakov Kreizer, etc.

We appeal to you:

Declare July 22, 1942, to be the day when the hearts of all Jews beat in unison, throughout the whole world.

This shall be the day of mobilization of all powers and means for the final destruction of fascism in 1942!

This shall be the day of mobilization of all powers and means for the deliverance of human civilization.

This shall be the day of mobilization of all powers and means for the protection of the existence of Jewish people.

This shall be the day on which all Jews in the world, wherever and however many they be, stand up to the determined oath, the oath of obligation and duty, the oath to sacrifice everything in the holy war against the enemy. Every Jew shall take this holy oath:

"I, a child of the Jewish people, swear not to rest or leave my fighting brother until Hitler and his executioners, this blood enemy of all nations and people, this blood enemy of my people, is eliminated from the earth.

"I swear revenge for my brothers and sisters—tortured, burned alive, and buried alive in all the destroyed cities and villages, wherever the arm of the enemy could reach.

"For the death of women and children, for the torment and rape of my people, I swear revenge until my last breath!

"Blood for blood! Death for death!

"I swear with all my strength, without regard for my belongings or my life, to help my blood brothers and all freedom-loving nations in the battle against fascism. Nothing shall be too hard or too dear to save my people from destruction and elimination.

"Cursed and damned should be the ones who will remain idle during this battle; mockery and disgrace shall come upon their names from all generations.

"I swear that I will be among those who will fulfill their obligation, their holy duty in the battle for the life and honor of Jewish people.

"I swear it!'"

You—Jews in the United States of America, in England, Canada, Cuba, Mexico, Palestine, Argentina, Brazil, Uruguay, Chile, South Africa, Australia and all other nations—consider and remember that by taking this holy oath and by contributing tanks and airplanes for the glorious Red Army, you secure your own existence and the existence of your families. By rescuing the Jewish people, you help free the world of Hitler's executioners. Do your holy duty, so your conscience remains clean and you can face your children and your children's children!

Solidarity meetings were held in the United States, England, Palestine, and in other countries. It was decided that the Soviet Union should be given tangible support. As Lozovsky[6] wrote in one of his articles, "Even newspapers of other political views, like the pro-fascist (sic!) *The Forward* (*Forverts*) in New York, could not silently overlook the Red Army's role in "liberating nations from fascism, thus saving Jewish people." Yiddish papers representing social democratic workers of America had aroused the anger of Jews working for the Kremlin, because these American publications frequently reminded the world of what happened to Erlich and Alter. It wasn't even allowed to mention these men in the communist world and in circles friendly to the Soviets for many decades.

The JAFC supported the Soviet leadership's mobilization measures. A few days after the attack, production shifted to meet military needs. The Supreme Soviet issued a decree that made overtime mandatory and cancelled any vacation time. Those who worked in war-related production had to remain at their workplaces and positions. At first, industrial production decreased but by 1944, the 1940s level was passed. This growth was mainly due to the manufacture of weapons and war materiel and by 1942 the Soviet Union already produced more than Germany. The Soviet Union's war expenditures were more than 550 billion rubles. Very large sums were raised through lotteries, war credits, donations and contributions from the population. At massive meetings in several cities more than three million rubles were collected for the Red Army. On April 19, 1943, Stalin sent the following telegram to the JAFC:

> I ask to convey my brotherly greetings and the thanks of the Red Army to the working Jews of the Soviet Union, who donated an additional 3,294,823 rubles for the building of an air squadron, "Stalinist Friendship of Nations," and an armored brigade, "Soviet Birobidzan."[7]

## The Second Plenum

The JAFC's second plenum met in Moscow from February 18-20, 1943. It convened shortly after the Red Army's great victories, including the conquest of Stalingrad on January 31, 1943. Many members who were not part of Lozovsky's and Epstein's group finally realized that the committee's leaders intended them to be part of a propaganda agency, a tool that could be used if needed and disposed of when no longer necessary. Any public statement made by Lozovsky had to approved by Shcherbakov, chief of the *Sovinformburo*, and by the Soviet Army's Main Political Administration. There were heated debates about the JAFC's goals; many members did not want to just be a mouthpiece for government propaganda. They wanted to be understood and respected as official representatives of Soviet Jews. Numerous participants wanted the committee to increase the scope of its activity and thereby create more respect for the Jews.

In addition to other taboo themes, the now publicly known anti-Semitic excesses, including the collaboration and cooperation of Soviet citizens in the genocide of Jews, were discussed. Ehrenburg, Markish, Hofstein, and Nussinov spoke in favor and helped the committee create pro-Jewish activities, such as organizing help for the few survivors in the liberated regions. Many JAFC members were shocked by the level of virulent and widespread anti-Semitism in large parts of the population in the liberated regions. They had thought this anti-Semitism was just a holdover from the period of occupation. Shchupak, the representative of the Jewish kolkhoz *New Life* (*Nei lebn*), requested a plan for reconstruction of the Jewish kholkhozes in the Ukraine and the Crimea. Mikhoels recommended that every committee member help out in person as well as in his work surroundings as a publicly well-known personality but not in the name of the JAFC.[8]

The plenum's final resolution addressed the future of all Jews:

> The day is not far when Hitler and his gang will have to stand and face justice from all the nations in the world. All nations will demand what is due, but the greatest will be from the Jewish nation. Together with other peace-loving nations, the Jewish nation will appear as his accuser.

The concept of a Jewish nation had not been used previously in Soviet propaganda. Its use aroused the fury of the Comintern's Executive Committee press chief, Friedrich. In a secret report he denounced "the unacceptable vanity and arrogance of participants pertaining to the role of Jews in the war" and criticized the remarkable political errors during the meeting and in the newspaper *Unity* (*Eynikeyt*). In his opinion, even Ilya Ehrenburg had no right to publicly demand that people fight against anti-Semitism in the Soviet Union.[9]

## 16. THE ORGAN OF THE JAFC—THE YIDDISH NEWSPAPER *UNIFICATION (EYNIKEYT)*

The JAFC became the information center of Yiddish culture and literature. It published sixty-five books, many essays, documents and pamphlets about the persecution of Jews and their resistance in occupied European countries. Revolts and uprisings in the ghettos of Warsaw and Bialystok, in the camps of Auschwitz, Treblinka, and Sobibor, were characterized as glorious examples of self-denial in the history of Jewish people.[10] But what was most important was that an all-Soviet Yiddish newspaper appearing after *Emes* had been shut down. Those appealing for *Emes* to reopen, pointed out that the annexations of 1939 and 1940 and the flight of Jews to the Soviet Union had caused the Yiddish-speaking population to grow enormously. Up to 1944, there was only a single publication, the weekly newspaper *Birobidzaner Stern,* for this group of several million people. After repeated interventions by Yiddish writers, Georgi Aleksandrov, the chief of the CC's propaganda branch, finally allowed a new Yiddish newspaper. *Eynikeyt,* a publication of the committee, was to be printed three times a month, with an edition of 10,000 copies. Chief editor Shakhne had to make sure that the paper remained absolute loyal to the state. After Epstein's death in 1945, Grigori Shits became the new editor in chief. Mikhoels, Bergelson, Fefer, Kvitko, Kushnirov, Dobrushin, Halkin, and Strongin made up the editorial staff.

In Kuibyshev, seat of the Soviet government, a first four-page edition was published on June 7, 1942. At first the newspaper was distributed three times a month, then weekly, then three times per week from 1945 on. Since there were hundreds of thousands of Yiddish readers, the ridiculously small print run always sold out immediately. Even in 1943, only 2,000 copies were sold within the Soviet Union and 8,000—according to the propaganda commission of the JAFC—were sent to foreign countries.[11]

### A Few Examples

Since *Eynikeyt* was only available in a few libraries[12] and Hebrew script understood by very few people, I will describe the first editions of *Eynikeyt* in detail. The lead article of the first edition was entitled

"Unity in Battle." The next article had the headline "1,000 tanks, 500 bombers." This article was an appeal by Mikhoels, the president, for contributions, and contained his proclamation "To the Jews of the Whole World" (*"Tsu di yidn fun der gorer velt"*). A "letter" took up the largest amount of space to "dearest comrade Stalin" (*"Teirer khaver Stalin"*). In addition, speeches given at the "Second meeting of the Jewish people's representatives" were reprinted. The second edition contained Itsik Fefer's poem, "The Oath:"

The Oath

I swear by the bright sun, by the gleaming stars,
I swear today by all that a totally responsible human can still swear by,
I swear by the families that the enemy has broken,
I swear by the willows that stand, bending, by the Dnieper
I swear by the blood, by the light and sight in my two eyes:
My hate will not disappear, my rage will not be cooled by time,
Until the blood of the enemy is no more.

As was common in Soviet newspapers, the title page consisted of slogans in large script:

> The treaty between the Soviet Union and Great Britain and the agreement with the United States of America will be greeted with joy by large masses of people in these three great nations. Together with the brotherly Soviet nations, Jews acknowledge this great historic moment with joy and excitement.
> For a quicker victory!
> Let's hasten Hitler's defeat!
> Jewish brothers, let's buy 1,000 tanks and 500 airplanes for the heroic Red Army!

This appeal was followed by the text of the oath, signed by forty-seven members of the JAFC. Their names, titles, honors and medals were then listed on thirty-two double lines.

In the article "Fascist Hell in Lithuania," G. Erman described how Jews were persecuted in the Baltic ghettos. V. Lidin* detailed the suffering of Jewish refugees. That issue also contained poems by Leizer Wolf and A. Gontar, a story by David Bergelson and letters from the front.

Foreign countries' reaction to this appeal was reported in the minutes of the May 24, 1942 JAFC meeting. This report was written by Shakhne Epstein, secretary general of the JAFC, and quoted below:

> Jewish societies, unions and communities in many cities in England, Palestine and other countries have made large solidarity arrangements. Through the initiative of Jewish Communities in London and Jerusalem, the United "Committee to Help Russian Judaism" was established.
>
> In Buenos Aires a large solidarity meeting for the Soviet Union was held in October 1941. A proclamation from this meeting has been signed by prominent social representatives of Argentina including Erik and Max Dikman, delegates to the parliament, poets Samuel Eichnbojm and Cesar Tiempo, Professor Georgia Erman, etc. Similar meetings were also held in Mexico and Cuba, where, in addition to greetings to the Soviet Union and the Red Army, a resolution to help the Soviet Union through every possible effort was also delivered.
>
> The appeal had a special resonance in the United States of America. The "American Jewish Congress," headed by Rabbi Dr. Stephen Wise, delivered the warmest greetings to the JAFC and, in a separate resolution, promised a great deal of help for the Red Army.
>
> In response to the Soviet Jews' appeal, a committee was established in New York, made up of well-known writers, artists and scientists from America. The chairman of the committee was the well-known Jewish cultural figure Dr. Chaim Shitlovski. Branches of this committee were also established in other American cities.
>
> On October 26, 1941, the committee proclaimed solidarity with the Soviet Union in a national radio broadcast. Participants included well-known American actors Morris Carnovsky, Samuel Wanamaker, Martin Wulfson and Frank Bartelern. Dr. Shitlovski, Dr. Joseph Rosen, the representative of the *Agrojoint* in the Soviet Union, the well-known writer Waldo Frank, and the representative of the all-American rabbi's office Joseph Lockstein also spoke. The speeches conveyed the will to help the Soviet Union. More than two hundred respected representatives from the arts, literature, science, and social organizations signed the message from American Jews to Soviet Jews. Signatories included the world-famous scientist Albert Einstein, the well-known Yiddish writers Shalom Ash and Leon Kobrin, the respected Jewish-German writer Lion Feuchtwanger, as well as Leon Moissejew, the

designer of the Brooklyn Bridge, the artist B. Aronson, movie actors, Paul Muni, John Garfield, and others.

More than 20,000 people showed up at mass rally held in December 1941 in the largest hall in the world, Madison Square Garden in New York. The Senator from New York, Abraham Kaplan, was chairman. Shalom Ash, an author, expressed the feelings of the whole congregation when he said: "I bow gratefully before the Russian people, who give my people such great possibility." Those words gave rise to ovations. Every mention of the Soviet Union or comrade Stalin was enthusiastically received. The congregation gave representatives of the Soviet consulate a standing ovation. The mention of President Roosevelt's name as well as Mrs. Roosevelt's opening speech was greeted with enthusiasm and ovations. Other speakers included the foreign minister of Czechoslovakia, Jan Masaryk, Senators Albert Tomas and Robert Wagner, congressional representative Sol Blum and Rabbi Mordechai Kaplan.

Vice President Henry Wallace, Charles Edison, the governor of New Jersey, Albert Einstein, Philipp Marey, representative to the industrial union and many others, sent messages to the meeting. Comrade Litvinov's message met with standing ovations and chants of: "Long live the Soviet Union!" and "Long live the Red Army!"

In January 1942 a committee was established in the United States to create a federation of all committees working to assist the Soviet Union.

The call of our second meeting, our appeal to Jews throughout the world to collect money for a thousand tanks and five hundred airplanes for the Red Army, gave the Jewish Anti-Fascist Committee new and greater responsibilities and goals.

### *Eynikeyt's* Changing Function

On the one hand this newspaper served as a platform for the committee's leadership, and on the other it helped connect Jews who were fighting on every front throughout the Soviet Union. Missing person announcements, therefore, were appearing regularly.

The editor received dozens of letters and reports daily, some of which were published. Regular columns—"Our heroes," "Our sons and daughters," "Our scientists," etc.—told the story of the great participation of Jews in the battle against National Socialism, especially in the armaments industry, thereby countering anti-Semitic rumors attacking Jewish shirkers. Committee members often used material from the Bible, the Talmud or drew from history in their articles. For example, Lina Stern compared the heroic frontline soldier to the revolutionaries in ancient Palestine, the Maccabees and Bar Kokhba.

Up to 300 correspondents reported for the JAFC from all fronts of the war. They traveled into regions liberated by the Red Army, searched for Jewish survivors, gathered information about Jewish resistance and the mass murders of the Jews. The JAFC also established its own press agency, the ISPA, which provided articles for hundreds of foreign newspapers. Radio shows were broadcast from Moscow and Kuibyshev featuring soldiers and partisans, as well as poets and writers, speaking in Russian, Yiddish and English.

The last edition of *Eynikeyt*, issue 140/701, was published on November 20, 1948. Not a single article was concerned with Jewish issues; all were copied from the official Soviet press. The lead article "Holiday for the Soviet artillery" began with: "A great welcome to the Soviet artillery and the workers in the artillery industry! Long live the creator of the powerful Soviet artillery—the great Stalin!" This was followed by the usual reports detailing great successes in Soviet industry and agriculture as well as a report about a change in nature initiated by Stalin, honoring him as a great ecologist.

On November 28, the Politburo decided to dissolve the JAFC. The initial decision was that no one would be arrested. The newspaper was closed down the following day, totally surprising the JAFC and the *Eynikeyt* editorial staff.

## 17. THE JAFC IN AMERICA—FUNDRAISING AND "TREACHEROUS" CONTACTS

### Jewish Anti-Hitler Initiatives in the United States

Soviet party and government agencies had years of experience organizing friendship movements that appeared to be neutral but were, in reality, under their tight control. In America they were called Front Organizations; their members—fellow travelers, idealistic and energetic sympathizers—acted for the benefit of the Soviet Union. These organizations included the Yiddish Cultural Union (*Yidisher Kultur Farband*— YKUF)—based in New York. The organization's monthly magazine Jewish Culture (*Yidishe kultur*) was founded in 1938 and is still published as of this writing. Between 1941 and 1947 most of the editorial material was written in the Soviet Union. From 1941 to 1947, the YKUF publishing house printed many books and almanacs by Soviet Yiddish writers. Many contributions that appeared in the *Yidishe kultur* came from them. YKUF was the first organization to embrace and energetically spread the JAFC's ideas in America. The Jewish Council for Russian War Relief (JCRWR), founded in 1942, collected 10 million dollars for the Soviet Union, in the United States, during the war. The Yiddish daily newspapers *The Day, Morning Journal,* and *Freedom Morning (Der Tog, Morgn Journal,* and *Morgn Freiheit)* also strengthened the pro-Soviet propaganda front.

The American Committee of Jewish Writers, Artists, and Scientists (ACJWAS) became the most influential committee. Within a few weeks it had the support of over 200 prominent persons. The ACJWAS's executive committee was formed in mid-October, 1942. Albert Einstein became the honorary president and Ben Zion Goldberg its chairman. The well-known journalist and writer, Sholem Aleichem's son-in-law, served as the committee's workhorse. Other members included Pesakh Novik, publisher of the communist daily paper *Freedom Tomorrow (Morgn Freiheit),* Lion Feuchtwanger and the Yiddish writer Shalom Ash.

As early as December 1941 the committee organized a mass meeting of 20,000 Jewish backers in support of the Soviet Union. It distributed JAFC propaganda in the United States and founded two magazines: *Eynikeyt,* printed in Yiddish and *New Currents,* printed in English. *New Currents* is still being published today. Goldberg was able to get support from the World Jewish Congress, headed by Rabbi Stephen Wise and Dr. Nahum Goldmann, both conservatives. Goldberg and Novik stayed in constant contact with Soviet diplomats. They supported Soviet interests so efficiently that the FBI ordered them to be registered as official agents of a foreign power. Goldberg was even threatened with having his American citizenship revoked.

## Mikhoels and Fefer in America

During a conversation with Soviet ambassador Litvinov, Albert Einstein suggested that a JAFC delegation visit the United States. Litvinov was dismissed in March 1943, but he did pass the idea on to the JAFC. There were many reasons to intensify the JAFC's work in America. Following the murder of Alter and Erlich's suicide, and after Stalin broke diplomatic relations with the Polish government in exile because it had accused the Soviet Union of murdering more than 14,000 Polish officers at Katyn and Starobielsk, an anti-Soviet mood had developed, especially among Americans of Polish descent. Then, too, the Soviet Union desperately needed material help for the future, and the second front in Europe, demanded by Stalin, was nowhere in sight. The JAFC had the opportunity to demonstrate that its creation was not a mistake, despite the subsequent appearance of ideologically undesirable Jewish national feelings.

The visit was planned at the highest level, but instead of the original six-man delegation, only Mikhoels and Fefer were to go. Soviet president Kalinin received them before their flight departed. The October edition of *Yidishe kultur* reported—probably incorrectly—that Stalin had personally seen the two delegates off.[13]

The American organizers had prepared an impressive program. Mikhoels and Fefer visited Albert Einstein in Princeton. They met with the president of the Zionist World Organization and with the future first president of Israel, Chaim Weizmann. Mikhoels and Fefer also met with many mayors of America's largest cities. At the grave of Sholem Aleichem they met his family.

Dr. Nahum Goldmann, one of the leaders of the Jewish World Congress and the Zionist World Organization, did not allow American Jewish labor leaders to protest Alter and Erlich's murders. Mikhoels and Fefer gave innumerable press and broadcast interviews. Before having any meetings with former ideological opponents like Wise, Goldmann, and Weizmann, Mikhoels and Fefer had to ask for permission from the Kremlin via Soviet diplomats.

James Rosenberg, leader of the *Joint* in Europe since 1921, offered the JAFC delegates help for the many refugees in the Soviet Union. In Hollywood, Mikhoels and Fefer met Thomas Mann, Lion Feuchtwanger, Upton Sinclair, Charlie Chaplin, and Edward G. Robinson. Thousands of people came to the meetings in New York, Chicago, Boston, Detroit,

Los Angeles, San Francisco, and ten other cities in America. The largest demonstration was on July 8, 1943, at the Polo Grounds, a New York sports stadium. There, in addition to the honored Soviet guests, Goldmann, Wise and naturally also Goldberg spoke to an audience of 50,000. The famous singer Paul Robeson sang Yiddish and Russian folk songs.

On such occasions Fefer always wore his Red Army colonel's uniform. At several events, a Jewish soldier's coat, which had been perforated by bullets, was cut into little pieces and distributed like a relic. The July 16, 1943 edition of *Pravda* published a detailed account of one such meeting. The Society for Jewish Aid, which collected money for 1,000 ambulances for the Red Cross, was established during these events.

During the seven-month tour, Mikhoels and Fefer also visited Mexico, Canada, and England. A half million people, including many non-Jews, attended mass demonstrations in forty-six cities. Organizations to raise funds for the Soviet Union were formed everywhere after the two men spoke.

Lozovsky wrote this in his report about their journey:

> Comrades Mikhoels and Fefer were able to bring together all levels of the Jewish population and isolate hostile Menshevik Trotskyite fascist groups. The visit of the Jewish Anti-Fascist Committee's emissaries also found an echo in important circles of the non-Jewish public. The foreign press has judged this journey as a great historical event in the lives of the Jews of these countries, and a turning point in the battle against fascism by the alliance of Jewish masses.[14]

## Under the Control of the "Organs"

The NKVD and Kremlin leadership were fully informed about any of the delegation's activities. Immediately after arriving in the United States, Fefer was contacted by the NKVD Resident in the U.S., General Zarubin, and forced to become a secret agent. He was told to use the code name "Zorin," and had to constantly report to Zarubin. Fefer also had to chronicle the activities of his comrade, Mikhoels, and copies of these reports were sent to Molotov, Beria, and others.

Fefer discussed this at 8:50 p.m. on June 6, 1952, during a secret meeting of the court in the JAFC trial. None of the other accused was present during the trial and Fefer admitted to betraying many people's trust in the Soviet Union during his stay in the United States and England. During the proceedings of June 28, 1952, Fefer used the word *ispol'zovat'* (to take advantage of) and began listing names: Chaim Weizmann, Albert Einstein, Stephen Wise, and Shalom Ash. Also included were Sir Montague (owner of the fashion store chain "Marks & Spencer"), who sent 200 bolts of cloth to the Soviet Union, and Mr. Thelms, who had two million articles of clothing shipped.[15]

Mikhoels and Fefer were deeply impressed by the Jewish enthusiasm for the Soviet Union. Their speeches were full of hope for brotherly relations between Soviet Jews and other Jews around the world, after the destruction of Nazism. During an event in London organized by the Jewish Fund for Soviet Russia, Dr. Joseph Hertz (Chief Rabbi of the British Empire) greeted them as "ambassadors of the lost voices of Israel." He also expressed his trust in their return to Judaism after the demise of Nazi fascism. Further details of the visit to England can be found in an extensive pamphlet published by the Jewish Fund for Soviet Russia entitled "Calling All Jews to Action."[16]

At the beginning of December 1943, Mikhoels and Fefer returned to the Soviet Union. They had become famous abroad and had received many gifts, including expensive fur coats created by Jewish furriers, for them and for Stalin. On December 27, 1943, the Soviet Consulate General opened an exhibit in New York, which documented their visit to the United States, Canada, and Mexico. Out of a bibliography of 260 articles and news clippings only thirty contained negative comments about the trip—almost all of them were critical reports in *Forward* (*Forverts*) written mainly by Abe Cahan, the editor in chief. Seven Jewish poets even expressed their feelings in verse.[17]

## 18. ANTI-SEMITISM REAPPEARS IN THE SOVIET UNION AND ITS EFFECT ON THE JAFC

### Jews Are Not Welcome Here

Government agencies recognized that the growth of patriotism and pride among Soviet Jews was due to their contact with "Western Jews" (a term used to describe Jews from the annexed areas in eastern Poland, the Baltics, Bessarabia, and Bukovina). The threat of mass extermination had increased the sense of community. The government watched the rebirth of Jewish interest closely, blamed the JAFC, and secretly began to create new anti-Jewish measures.

Quotas for Jews, introduced in 1939, were based on verbal orders. The government shied away from documenting its break with old internationalist rhetoric. But by 1942 high-ranking party members were openly demanding anti-Semitic measures. Georgi Aleksandrov wrote such a memorandum on August 17, 1942. Aleksandrov was one of the leading party ideologists and a member of the Academy of Sciences. He was also head of the Central Committee's "Agitprop" division from 1940 to 1947. His opinion not only played an important role in the tragic history of the JAFC, but also in the persecution of non-Jewish authors, including Anna Akhmatova and composers like Shostakovich and Prokofiev. Aleksandrov, the Marxist philosopher, was finally attacked himself. He co-edited a volume on the history of philosophy that now presented a too favorable opinion of the reactionary attitudes of Hegel, Fichte, and other German philosophers. As a result of this, in 1944, his texts on the history of the USSR were accused of being too "tsar-friendly."[18]

His memorandum from 1942, addressed to central committee secretaries Malenkov, Shcherbakov, and Andreyev, carried the neutral title of "Selection and Advancement of Cadres in the Arts," in which he primarily complained about the presence of "non-Russian persons" (mainly Jews) in Soviet cultural institutions. The document also included a list of employees in important cultural facilities. The list began with the Bolshoi Theater, led by ten Jews, an Armenian and a Russian. Then he listed the conservatories in Moscow and Leningrad. Soviet publications became similar to pamphlets, such as those published by Alfred Rosenberg in 1941 for the German ministry of the occupied Eastern areas. Aleksandrov also criticized the fact that mostly "non-Russian music critics" praised only Jews and ignored Russian artists. The cultural editorial staff in party newspapers such as *Pravda* and *Izvestiia* published these lists. At the end of the list, there was a suggestion to promote Russian employees, and "in part renew the staff." This could only have been viewed as a call to fire all Jews.[19]

There was plenty of anti-Semitism within the Soviet administration in 1942. Boris Shimeliovich, one of the accused, explained the case against the JAFC:

> I never personally experienced anti-Semitism. I had never even heard anyone mention anti-Semitism. Then, around 1942, several

Jewish doctors that I knew told me that anti-Semitism existed among the higher-ups in the public health service. Former people's commissar for public health services, Miterev, had indeed made a big political mistake. Within two and a half months he fired all the Jews from the medical magazines' editorial staffs. There were also cases of anti-Semitism at the Academy of Health Sciences. I wrote about this in a letter to G. M. Malenkov and was immediately summoned to the central committee.[20]

At her trial, Lina Stern told a similar story. She had never heard of any differences being made between Jews and non-Jews until 1943. Nonetheless, her co-worker Shtor was advised to resign his position as head of the laboratory, but keep his job and salary. The university director declared that it would be inappropriate to have a Jewish department head at the Lomonosov Institute. Many others had already been fired for the same reason. Lina Stern, who opposed Shtor's resignation, did not want to believe that such an implicit declaration existed. Then two secretaries with "non-Russian" names were to be fired in response to a resolution calling for the reduction of Jews on the editorial staff. They worked on the staff of a self-published medical journal. This resolution was passed as a countermeasure to German leaflet propaganda. Like Lina Stern, Sergeyev was a member of the Academy of Sciences. He stated that 90% of the Jewish medical staff would have to be dismissed. Only prominent members (such as himself) were not let go. When Yemelyan Yaroslavsky, an official of the party cadre, the Academy, and the author of several studies of the Soviet communist party, denied the existence of such resolutions, Lina Stern wrote to Stalin. She was called in to see the central committee's office by order of the Generalissimo Malenkov and Shatalin spoke to her for two hours. Malenkov intimated that maybe members of the central committee were issuing such hostile directives; this could be happening because a large number of spies and saboteurs (*diversanty*) were being smuggled into the USSR. His criticism of Sergeyev and praise of Stern struck her as hypocritical.[21] The party leadership had not previously risked aggravating prominent and loyal Jews. This was especially true if they were still useful scientists.

## First Attacks on the JAFC

Peretz Markish may have had an inkling of the new anti-Semitic wave as early as August 1941 as the editor, Pospelov, explained that *Pravda* would not print his anti-fascist poem for political reasons.[22] In his memoirs, Ehrenburg wrote about his meeting with Shcherbakov, which occurred in 1943. Shcherbakov did not deny the existence of anti-Semitism:

> In the summer the *Sovinformburo* asked me to write an appeal to American Jews about Hitler's heinous acts and the necessity of destroying the Third Reich as soon as possible. Kondakov, who was Shcherbakov's co-worker, repudiated my text. He said that explicitly mentioning the heroic deeds of Jewish soldiers in the Red Army would be redundant and boastful. I wrote to Shcherbakov and he invited me to the office of Political Administration. Our discussion was unpleasant and lasted a long time. Shcherbakov said that Kondakov had overreacted, but it would still be necessary to remove certain passages from my text. I disagreed. Shcherbakov got angry and changed the subject. He praised and criticized my text at the same time: "Soldiers want to hear about Suvorov and you're quoting Heine."[23]

Nikolai Kondakov was one of the first *Sovinformburo* workers to openly attack the JAFC. Non-Jewish comrades believed that Kondarov found the committee redundant.[24] He shared the same views that Epstein expressed in a letter to Shcherbakov in 1943. During the JAFC court case Lozovsky called Kondakov a "creature of Aleksandrov" (Kondakov was his acting representative). Kondakov wrote several reports denouncing Lozovsky and other committee members. He diligently noted any growth of Jewish nationalism. Kondakov was fired from the *Sovinformburo* in 1944 for embezzlement. Then he became the chief editor for the publishing company of pedagogical sciences of the RSFSR. The head of the military court noted that Kondakov did not write reports "to cover up his crime, but rather to present information about the nationalistic activity of the Jewish Anti-Fascist Committee."[25]

Testifying in court, Yuzefovich stated that Volkov, a *Sovinformburo* employee, yelled at a New Year's party that all "Yiddish" people were traders and scoundrels. Volkov claimed that Lozovsky was one of these scoundrels, that he was a Trotskyite, Menshevik and "Yid." Volkov was immediately fired.[26]

It would be too simple to reduce attacks on the committee by calling them the intrigues of unscrupulous apparatchiks, who felt justified by the ever-growing patriotic course of Russian chauvinism. Jewish employees of the JAFC were also highly critical. For instance, at the beginning of 1945, Solomon Bregman* attacked Markish, a member of the presidium because in September 1944, Markish disapproved of the position Soviet agencies had taken regarding the return of Jews to liberated areas.[27] During the case against the JAFC, Bregman stated that Markish was appalled by the renaming of "Stalindorf" (Yiddish) to Stalin-Rayon (Russian): "...the Stalinist constitution is falling apart; the Stalinist foundation is falling apart! Why was Stalindorf renamed? We will have to go to Stalin about this." Even in 1946 and 1947, Markish continued to make such denunciations to the central committee.[28]

## Resurgence of Anti-Semitism in the Population

After 1941 people became noticeably more anti-Semitic. Partisans refused to house Jews. They would even rob groups of Jews who had fled into the woods. In 1943 partisans reclaimed several cities, behind German lines, in Galicia, but they did very little to save any Jews imprisoned in the ghettos.[29] Shmuel Ettinger, a historian, gave the following account: Jews in the countryside were slandered as being too cowardly to fight. All they wanted was to do business. Even Jewish war veterans were humiliated on the streets. They were accused of buying their medals on the black market in Asia, far from the front. Even the author and future Nobel laureate Sholokhov participated.[30]

The JAFC registered continual anti-Semitic occurrences in areas liberated from German rule. The protection of Shoah survivors became one of the most important and, for the government, undesirable tasks.[31]

Moscow received horrendous news, especially from the Ukraine. Bureaucrats often denied Jews right of passage, preventing them from returning to liberated zones. Local authorities refused to help if the new populace refused to allow Jews back into their homes. In September 1944, Ilya Ehrenburg wrote that the chairman of the (former Jewish) district of Kalinindorf told returnees: "Why did you return? Nobody needs you here. Nobody called you."[32]

This is but one of many such testimonials. In May 1944, Mikhoels and Epstein wrote Molotov about similar incidents. He in turn passed the letter on to Khrushchev in Kiev. Although during the 1920s anti-Semitism and its repercussions were important themes in propaganda campaigns in the Ukraine, these campaigns were not reinitiated from 1944 on, even though Jews had become scapegoats again. They were even blamed for shortages of food and living space. Anti-Semitism of the 1920s had not resulted in much bloodshed; after the end of the civil war however, in 1944, lives were lost during a pogrom in Kiev. Hundreds of Jews were beaten in riots after the war; there were even deaths reported.[33]

In August 1944 the Ukrainian state security agency wrote a letter to Khrushchev, concluding that anti-Semitism was partially caused by German and allied Ukrainian nationalist propaganda. They stated that another cause was the small percentage of Jews in the Red Army. This widespread prejudice was simply accepted as fact, without any objective proof. The letter stated that Jews were spreading the rumor that Ukrainians were being punished for collaborating, and that they refused to serve in the army or do physical labor. Apart from Nazi propaganda, therefore, according to the Ukrainian Chekists, anti-Semitism resulted from Jewish behavior. "Jewish nationalism" especially inflamed anti-Semitism. Simply acting against anti-Semitism was seen as Jewish nationalism (David Hofstein, a poet, was an example). Jews were encouraged to emigrate, told about better standards of living in the United States, and Zionism. Rumors spread that the Soviet Union would supposedly set aside a separate territory for Jews. It was also considered "nationalistic" when Jews asked the government to counter anti-Semitism. They were also "nationalistic" if they called Khrushchev and other leading politicians anti-Semitic. Consequently, the Ukrainian memorandum contained more suggestions for battling Zionism and "Jewish nationalism" than for fighting anti-Semitism.[34]

## The Third Meeting

At the third and final wartime session of the JAFC—it was the largest in its history—the anti-Semitism had been generally assailed. Three thousand people congregated at the headquarters of the labor unions in a prestigious and pillared union hall, beneath a large portrait of Stalin. The meeting occurred shortly after the Soviet spring offensive began. The entire Ukrainian territory was liberated, except for the Crimea. At the time death camps in Poland were running at full capacity; the size of the mass murder of the Jews was already well known. Despite this horrific news, there was still hope of rejuvenating Jewish life in the Soviet Union under the JAFC's leadership.

Officially, the JAFC still recognized only Stalin's role as "wise ruler of the people," and he was mentioned at the very beginning of every speech and salutation. Mikhoels expressed the necessary praise for the "ingenious Stalin" as well as national sentiments in all of his speeches. Just as Mikhoels had spoken to the "brothers and sisters, the sons and daughters of the Jewish people," he reminded his listeners of the Jewish tragedy and the heroism of Jewish people. "Within a few years 4 million of our brothers, one quarter of our population, have been assassinated in Europe," he said. "But we note with pride that Jews who have been decorated for military achievements on the battle front rank fourth among all Soviet nationalities."[35]

Fefer, who did not miss the opportunity to pay homage to the "older brother, the great Russian people," said, "The ashes of Babi Yar burn in our hearts and in our eyes; they cover our wounds and give us no peace. We are proud of our Soviet people and call upon all Jews to take part in the active fight against the Hamans. Follow the example of the Soviet people, the Soviet Jews, and the heroes of the Warsaw ghetto, so that we may proudly call you our brothers-in-arms."

Shortly before the meeting, Abraham Sutzkever,* a Yiddish poet and partisan, flew into Moscow by courier plane from a partisan camp. He spoke of Jews murdered in Vilna and of the battles that Jewish partisans fought. The head rabbi of Moscow, Shlomo Shliffer, praised "our best sons and daughters who were taking part in the holy war to destroy our enemy."

Those who spoke included Guards Colonel Rafael Milner and Guards Major Leonid Buber (both "Heroes of the Soviet Union"); Frigate Captain G. Goldberg, commander of a submarine flotilla in the Baltic Sea; Partisan Major Meir Blekhman; 70-year-old partisan Chaim Aron Khazanov; the mother of the fallen "Hero of the Soviet Union" Lazar Papernik; Boris Shimeliovich, and many others.

## The Third Plenum

During the JAFC's 3rd plenary assembly (April 8-11, 1944) Epstein only touched upon growing anti-Semitism. He warned people not to exaggerate or to generalize occasional incidents. Nourishing grounds for anti-Semitism did not exist in the Soviet Union. Instead, the JAFC should fight against unhealthy nationalist sentiment within its own ranks. During the JAFC presidium discussion in October 1944, Epstein warned Shimeliovich and Mikhoels about creating something that resembled a "commissariat for Jewish affairs."

Small groups discussed the JAFC's future duties before the meeting started. The connection to Western Jewish communities was a part of the discussion. It was unknown whether Kremlin leaders would tolerate continued contact with the World Jewish Congress. The WJC was scheduling a conference for November 11, 1944. The main topic was to discuss plans for aiding and rebuilding destroyed European communities after the war. JAFC leaders asked central committee member Shcherbakov to allow a ten-member delegation to attend this meeting. Members of the delegation were to include Generals Kreizer (head of the delegation) and Katz, Submarine Captain I. Fissanovich, Guards Captain Emma Wolf, Partisan Commander A. Zorin, Chairman of the Soviets of Birobidzan M. Silberstein, the scientist Frumkin, Shakhne Epstein, David Bergelson, and L. Gonor. Shcherbakov was in favor of a four-man delegation. In the end, no JAFC members were allowed to attend the conference.[36]

## Outcome of the JAFC

As Germany surrendered the JAFC had every reason to be proud of its participation in the victory. The Yiddish newspaper *Yidishe kultur* was the mouthpiece for *YKUF* in New York. Its May 1945 issue contained the following message to American Jews and the Jews of the world from the JAFC on the occasion of the Allied victory:

Forward to a new life!
Dear brothers and sisters!
The Jewish Anti-Fascist Committee of the Soviet Union greets you wholeheartedly on the occasion of the end of the war of liberation against Hitler's Germany, which resulted in Germany's complete defeat by the heroic Red Army and the Allied armies.
We are glad that the multicultural Soviet Union under the leadership of Marshal Stalin played such a decisive role in the largest battle in history for freedom and the happiness of all humanity. We are glad

that the sons and daughters of our Jewish people shared their part in this great victory.

It is with reverence that we commemorate on this historic day the heroic fighters of all nations who spilled their blood defending humanity's honor and the freedom from fascist vandalism and cannibalism. We bow our heads to the uncounted innocent victims. The fascists have covered the much-wounded Europe with their graves. Humanity will never forget the fascist infamy in Majdanek, Treblinka, Auschwitz, Buchenwald, Dachau, Babi Yar, Ponary, and dozens of other death factories.

Never in the course of our long history have the often persecuted Jewish people experienced such a bloody nightmare as in the murderous reign of Hitler's dark minions.

Despite the tremendous number of victims and losses, our people step out of the ring of death after a fight with the brown hangmen with a stronger, harder and more combative spirit; although reduced in number, we are full of hope and faith in the dawning of a new epoch for all people of the world.

The fascist military gangs have been reduced to dust on the battlefield, but every freedom-loving person must know that as long as fascism has not been politically and morally eradicated, no one can be sure that the long-awaited and costly peace will last.

For the sake of the happiness and freedom of future generations it is everyone's duty to work on the eradication and uprooting of fascism in all of its forms, everywhere, even if it is hidden behind a mask.

In a postwar world, fascist crimes and misanthropic racial hatred must be seen as standing outside of the law and be severely punished. The Jewish people have their own bill to present to Hitler's Germany. We should not lose any time in bringing forth our charges against these warmongers and exterminators before the courts of the United Nations.

The friendship between our nations has increased during these hard years of war. Mutual understanding among Jews of all nations has increased, and a foundation for stronger solidarity in our fight for the survival, welfare, and culture of our people has been formed.

The great victory requires us to strengthen our friendship even more in our fight against all forms of reaction within the Jewish community, and to fight open or hidden defenders of fascism.

Forward into the bright future of humanity! Forward to a new life that will be built on the principles of freedom, equality, brotherhood, and friendship among all nations!

JAFC documents held in the "Central State Archive of the October Revolution" have only been recently opened to the public. These documents allow the committee's activities during the war to be seen for the first time. As a direct result of Mikhoels' and Fefer's travels, hundreds of committees to provide aid for the Soviet Union were founded in America, England, and Palestine; 45 million dollars were collected in the West for the Red Army. This was an enormous sum, considering that the money came from private contributions only. More than 700 articles were printed in the countries visited. ISPA, the committee's press agency, distributed about 23,000 articles and books, and more than 3,000 photos to the foreign press, which were published by eight press agencies in 264 periodicals in 12 countries.

Considering such a small staff, working out of a modest building at 10 Kropotkin Street in Moscow, one wonders how they managed to achieve such important results. Most of the work was done without pay by a multitude of volunteers, war correspondents, translators, writers and journalists. Among the 1,273 volumes of the JAFC file archives one can also find indexes, listing all the people who worked for the daily *Eynikeyt*, the ISPA press agency, as well as for other war correspondents and branch offices in the provinces. The files also contain a list of 64 paid workers and another 349 volunteers. Thirty indexes of people active in the JAFC and in contact with foreign countries for this purpose are also included. These indexes lowered the life expectancy of these people during the secret trials. Finally there is an index with 4,015 writers who provided articles for the committee's publications.

In order to understand how the JAFC worked during the war, one more fact needs to be discussed. The central office in Moscow became a lively meeting place for Jews, where frequent "literary evenings" were held. They seemed to be replacing many of the destroyed facilities that existed prior to the war.[37] However, such activities as well as the committee's protest against the increasing tolerance of anti-Semitism fueled the dictator's hatred. The initiative that went into history as the "Crimea project," however, brought darkening clouds over the JAFC.

## 19. Jewish "Heroes of the Soviet Union,"
## Jewish War Heroes, JAFC Members and Their Part in the
## Victory Over Germany

In 1939 three million Jews lived in the Soviet Union, making them the sixth largest ethnic group after the Russians, Ukrainians, Belorussians, Uzbeks, and Tatars. By 1941, one third of all Soviet Jews had already been killed by the Germans. Yet 500,000 Jewish soldiers (including 30,000 Jewish partisans) served in every branch of the Red Army during the German-Soviet war. This was a very high percentage of the total population.

After the Bolshevik Revolution, many Jews joined the military to start a career and thousands received decorations and high marks. Between 1919 and 1945, 305 Jewish generals and admirals served in the Soviet military; statistics issued later on indicated that 160,772 decorations were awarded.

From 1937 to 1945, 40,000 officers were executed during the Red Army purges, including 169 Jewish generals. They included commanders of 1st rank (Lieutenant General) Yona Yakir and Yan Gamarnik, commanders of 2nd rank (Major General) Lazar Aronstam, Boris Ippo, Mikhail Landa, Joseph Slavin, Aleksandr Schifres, army corps commanders Leonid Vainer, Semyon Turovsky, Semyon Uritsky, Boris Feldman, Yakob Avinovitsky, Isaac Grinberg, Lazar Gruber, Lev Maier-Sakharov, Chaim Orlov, Israel Rasgon, Benedict Troyanker, and Mordechai Khorosh.

Many other Jewish generals took over some of the highest commands, such as General Yakov Kreizer and General Grigori Stern. They each commanded an Army Group. Yakov Smushkevich was the Supreme Commander of the Soviet Air Force and Yan Gamarnik headed the political administration of the Red Army. Nine Jewish generals commanded an army. Jewish generals were in charge of the medical and veterinary corps, the quartermaster's and paymaster's office, military justice, engineering and armored groups as well as other weapons classes. Twenty-three generals were chiefs of staff of Army Groups and army corps; twelve generals commanded an army corps and thirty-four generals commanded a division.

Three hundred five Jewish generals survived the purges, most of them fought in World War II. Their short biographies were compiled by the Russian military historian Fyodor Vassilyevich Sverdlov, in *Jewish Generals of the Armed Forces of the USSR (Yevrei-Generaly vooruzhennykh sil SSSR).*[38]

General Grigori Stern held the highest rank of any Soviet military officer in the Spanish Civil War. During the short Japanese-Soviet War of 1939, he won the battle of Khalkhin Gol and became a "Hero of the Soviet Union." He was executed in 1941 before the German invasion. General Yakov Smushkevich, air force commander during the Spanish Civil War, supreme commander of the Soviet air force after 1939 and recipient of two "Hero of the Soviet Union" awards, was also executed. General Manfred Stern, the founder of the International Brigade and defender of Madrid, was sent to a Gulag in 1938 and died there in 1954.

The distinguished service by Jews during the war was far greater than the numbers show. Between 1942 and 1945, Jewish soldiers received 160,772 medals and awards, ranking them fourth among all nationalities. This was kept secret in the Soviet Union after 1942. Jews were listed in last place, by percentage of nationality, in the party newspaper *Bolshevik,* after the Avarians, Kumyks, Yakuts, and six other Asian peoples. The number of medals earned was not mentioned. The Soviet populace was not supposed to find out that (by the middle of 1943) after the Russians and Ukrainians, Jews had earned the most honors. One hundred forty-six Jewish soldiers received the highest military honor, "Hero of the Soviet Union."

Several hundred Jewish generals and colonels fought for victory against Germany; they included Captain Mikhail Plotkin, who was the first Soviet pilot to bomb Berlin on August 7, 1941. He also took part in the bombing of Danzig, Königsberg, and Stettin. His airplane was placed on exhibit in the War Museum in Leningrad.

Eighteen soldiers were members of the JAFC, including the partisans Blekhman, Sutzkever, and Emma Wolf. JAFC member Yakov Kreizer was the highest-ranking Jewish general in the Red Army. (Lieutenant Generals and "Heroes of the Soviet Union" Yakov Smushkevich and Gregori Stern were executed in 1941, a few weeks before the beginning of the war. They would have automatically reached the rank of marshal.)

**Yakov Kreizer** was born on November 4, 1905, in Voronezh, outside the Jewish settlement area. At the age of twelve, Jakob's grandfather was forced into continuous military service for twenty-five years. This made Kreizer a soldier of the reserve and gave him the right to live anywhere in Russia. At 15 he lost both of his parents and had to earn a living for himself. Shortly before his 16th birthday he enlisted as a cadet in the Voronezh infantry school and became an officer with the 48th Moscow Division and, at the age of 37, Commander of the First Motorized Infantry Division, an elite unit.

When war broke out, his division defended the Minsk-Moscow highway for twelve days, thus stopping the advance of General Guderian's Second Armored Army. Even though he was injured, Kreizer never left the battlefield. His brave leadership prevented an earlier fall of Moscow he and received the medal of "Hero of the Soviet Union" one month after the war broke out. He was the first soldier to receive this award; then he was promoted to major general and commander of the Third Army. In October 1941 his troops, marching 60 kilometers at night, broke through the siege surrounding Moscow. By December 4, 1941, the battle for the capital had been decided. The 13th Army and Kreizer's 3rd Army played a major role in that victory. The German XXXIV Army Corps was almost completely annihilated during the offensive that followed.

In 1942, when Kreizer was voted in as a member of the JAFC's presidium, he published his thanks in the first issue of *Eynikeyt* and sent greetings to the first congress of the Jewish-Palestinian Victory League, which took place in Jerusalem in August 1942.

During a meeting of the JAFC in Moscow on August 31, 1942, he stated:

> My nation, which gave the world so many famous wise men and brilliant thinkers, is also the nation that fights for its freedom. Jewish history deals with the glorious victory of the Jews over the Romans, the ancestors of the modern-day Italian fascists. Bar Kochba was a shining example for many Jews...I am proud of the hundreds of thousands of Jews who fought on the front. As a general of the Red Army and son of the Jewish people, I swear that I will not lay down my arms until the last fascist has disappeared from the earth's surface.

In 1943, after heavy fighting on the southern front, Kreizer was promoted to lieutenant general and commander of the Second Guards Army, led by Marshal Malinovsky. His Fifty-first Army had recaptured the Crimean peninsula in May 1944. Then he fought in the Baltic battles as part of the First Baltic Army Group. This Jewish general accepted the capitulation of German armed forces in Kurland.

After the war he was named commander of the Far Eastern army, headquartered in Vladivostok. Here he was promoted to General of the Army, the highest rank before marshal. He received five Lenin medals, four Red Banner medals, Suvorov and Kutuzov medals as well as other awards. In his work, Shapiro lists more than twelve books about Kreizer, who died in Moscow after a long illness on November 29, 1969.

JAFC member **Wolf Vilensky** was born in Kovno, the capital of Lithuania, in 1919. His great-grandfather was forced to serve in the tsarist army for 25 years. Wolf visited a Jewish grammar school and joined the left-wing Zionist youth organization *Hashomer Hatsair.*

He served in the Lithuanian army in 1939 and then in the Soviet army in Vilna after 1940. After Germany invaded the Soviet Union, his unit received an order to hold the bridge over the Vileyka River until the main army retreated. The 22-year-old officer showed initiative and an unusual amount of courage during this action.

So many Jewish volunteers reported when the Lithuanian Division was formed on the Volga River in 1942 that 80% of the division was Jewish. Vilensky was promoted to captain, then to major of a battalion in the 249th Infantry Regiment. Despite the most difficult conditions and high losses, the division was able to withstand the attacks and was victorious at the Battle of Tula on February 24, 1942. Vilensky led his unit to decisive victories in the Battle of Kursk. He also led several exceptional commando operations.

In the fall of 1944 the division liberated all of Lithuania. The Wehrmacht fought to the bitter end to hold the Memel-Tilsit railway and road connection. On October 13, 1944, Vilensky's battalion repulsed attacks by two German regiments with tanks and artillery. When the last machine gun position on the front line fell, Major Vilensky ran to the machine gun and saved his troops through accurate firing.

Vilensky was made a "Hero of the Soviet Union" by decree by the chairman of the Supreme Soviet on March 24, 1945. He fought at the front of his battalion to the last day of the war. He spoke Yiddish and sang Yiddish folk songs with his troops and after the war he graduated with honors from the Frunze Military Academy. Later he became commanding general in Kovno, his place of birth. Many works were written about Vilensky's war heroism. The *Eynikeyt* wrote about him four times between 1943 and 1945. For twelve years Vilensky was denied an exit permit to Israel, where a large part of his family lived since 1971. He was finally able to leave twelve years later. When his El-Al plane landed in

September 1983, several of his brothers-in-arms (decorated with jackets and medals) greeted their former commander. Vilensky died a few years later, still serving as reserve general in the Israeli army.

JAFC member **Aron Katz** was born in 1901 in a village near Mogilev and already served as a volunteer in the civil war. After completing his education in engineering, he joined the army as a career officer. Katz was one of the best tank specialists in the Red Army and contributed to their construction, production, and maintenance. He also was a professor of armored weapons at the military academy. Because he was more available than the frontline officers, he often received foreign guests for the JAFC. According to an official statement, he had to retire with the rank of major general in 1947, due to health problems. He died in 1971.

JAFC member **Leonid Buber** was born in 1916 in Nikolayev in the Ukraine. He worked as a metal worker on a wharf and became a career officer after completing military school. During the Soviet-Finnish war he was awarded the "Hero of the Soviet Union" for personal bravery. Buber served as regimental commander in the Battles of Kursk and Oriol where he even led his soldiers in hand-to-hand combat. Although wounded, he stayed on the front. The April 6, 1944 edition of *Eynikeyt* quoted from his speech during the third meeting of the JAFC: "Victory is near, and then we will even the score for Babi Yar. We will avenge our victims for everything."

**Polina Gelman** was one of the most famous and popular military members of the JAFC. She was born in October 1919 in Berdichev. Both of her parents took part in the civil war. White army guards murdered her father. Her mother resettled in Gomel, where Polina went to school and became a member of the aviation sport club; after high school she attended Moscow University.

After the invasion by the Wehrmacht, Polina wanted to become a paratrooper and partisan. When she was turned down she took a course to become a nurse. Shortly thereafter, volunteers were needed for a female air force regiment; Polina was accepted and at first was folding parachutes. She trained to be a pilot and a navigator in Engels on the Volga, and then she was assigned to the 588th Female Night-Bombing Regiment under the command of Colonel Katarina Bershanskaya. Because the light P-2 bi-winged bombers of the women's regiment operated from airfields near the front, the women could fly six to eight sorties a night. They also transported supplies for the partisan camps. Polina fought near Donetsk, in the Caucasus, in Belorussia, and in Poland, and flew a total of 869 missions. Captain Polina Gelman was awarded the medal "Hero of the Soviet Union" on May 15, 1946.

Jewish female pilots Sima Hofman, Rachel Slotina and "Hero of the Soviet Union" Raissa Aronova flew in the same unit. As a popular member of the committee, Polina Gelman took part in receiving foreign guests for the JAFC. After the war she was a professor at the Institute for Social Sciences at Moscow University, until she became professor emeritus. In 1976 Polina traveled to Israel where she met with former comrades-in-arms. When she returned to Israel in 1998, she was an honored guest of the commander in chief of the Israeli air force, General Eitan Ben Eliyahu, who showed her the newest airplanes.

JAFC member **Israel Fissanovich** was born in 1914 in Yelisavetgrad, the son of an accountant. He became a toolmaker, but since childhood his dream was to become a submarine officer. In 1935 he completed the Frunze Naval Academy and served on a submarine. At the end of July 1941, Captain Fissanovich became commander of submarine M-172, which operated very successfully in the northern region. On April 3, 1942, he was decorated with the medal of "Hero of the Soviet Union." *Eynikeyt* reported about his life and the maneuvers of the M-172, one of the most famous ships in the navy; the entire crew was mentioned in a book. Captain Fissanovich declared his willingness to join the JAFC by cable from the submarine.

In the summer of 1944 the Soviet navy received four confiscated Italian submarines from the Western Allies. The hand-over and delivery of the ships from England to Murmansk was entrusted to the best submarine commanders of the Soviet navy: Captains Tripolski, Yoseliani, Kabo (a Jewish officer as well) and Fissanovich. During the mission, Fissanovich's submarine sank. No sign of him or his crew has ever been found.

Another high ranking naval officer, **Pavel Trainin**, also worked with the JAFC. He was born in 1895 in Pinsk and studied at the polytechnic. In 1917 he entered the Military Academy, which had been recently founded by the Kerensky Government, as a volunteer. By 1920 he was an officer in the naval artillery and later became captain of several battleships. In November 1940 he was promoted to rear admiral and commander of several flotillas, including the navy's minesweeping commandos. He received many honors, among them the Lenin Medal and the Medal of the Red Star. After the war he became vice chairman of the Allied Control Commission in Hungary and later a professor at the naval engineering academy. He died in June 1956 in Leningrad.

JAFC member **Rafael Milner** was born in the shtetl of Monastarishehe near Kiev in 1910. His father transported heavy materials and was a factory security guard. Milner worked as a blacksmith during his early youth and continued his on-the-job training as well as his political education. In 1932 he became a member of the party and then a career soldier. On June 23, 1934, he entered the Lenin Academy for political and military education and was immediately sent to the front as commissar of the 22nd Infantry Regiment. He saw action outside Moscow, near Kaluga and Oriol. In September 1943 his regiment captured and held a bridgehead, allowing the 61st Army to cross the Dniepr. On January 1, 1944, Milner was awarded the "Hero of the Soviet Union" medal. Lieutenant Colonel Milner's 37th Guards Regiment fought in Latvia and Poland, liberating Stettin and Altruppin near Berlin. *Eynikeyt* published articles about his battles and decorations several times.

After the war Milner was commander of the Kiev Military Region and later commander of several military academies. He published 25 books and articles on military science.

JAFC member **Pinkhas Turyan** was born in 1895 in Lebeda near Kiev. He served as a volunteer in the civil war until 1920 and took part in the annexation of eastern Poland in 1939 as a reserve officer. After the outbreak of the German-Soviet war he became an engineering officer and fought on the Bryansk front. Turyan's unit crossed the Dniepr in September 1943 and held the bridgehead for several days and nights despite continued heavy attacks.

On March 19, 1944, he was awarded the "Hero of the Soviet Union" medal; his son was also a frontline soldier. On August 3, 1944, *Eynikeyt* published a detailed article about his entire family. Pinkhas Turyan died in 1978.

## 20. THE WAR ON THE INVISIBLE FRONT

### The "Rote Kapelle"

The "Rote Kapelle" (the "Red Orchestra"—the code name given by the German counterintelligence organs) and the often extremely dangerous activities of its members have been chronicled in numerous documentaries, books, memoirs, and films. In this chapter we will present a short biography of the *Grand Chef* Trepper and a list of the Jewish members of this most successful and active espionage organization during the Second World War. These people were not paid agents or adventurers, they were communist idealists who wanted to hinder Hitler's victory and prevent the eradication of European Jews.

Leopold Leib Trepper was born in 1904 in the southern Polish town of Nowy Targ when it was part of Austria-Hungary. In 1914, when war broke out, Vladimir Ilych Lenin was arrested in this same village and accused of being a Russian spy. In 1921, Trepper's family resettled in Dombrowa in the Upper-Silesian coal mining area of Poland. Leopold worked near Bedzin, in a soap factory belonging to the Lustiger family. He was already the leader of the leftist Zionist youth organization *Hashomer Hatsair* and was conspiring with the communist youth group. In 1924 he and a group of comrades set off to Palestine. In 1925 he became a member of the Communist Party of Palestine, a branch of the party acknowledged by Moscow a year earlier. He lived with twenty other male and female comrades in a city commune in Tel Aviv. Sophie Posnanska, Hillel Katz, Leo Grossvogel, and Yekheskel Schreiber were members of that commune. Almost 20 years later they would become his brothers- and sisters-in-arms in Europe, losing their lives in the process.

Luba Brojde from Lemberg soon joined their commune. She had to flee from Poland because she supported the 17-year-old Jewish revolutionary Naftali Botwin. Botwin had assassinated a police chief who had sent many of Botwin's companions to the gallows. Botwin was executed and the Jewish unit that fought in the Spanish Civil War of 1937 was named after him. The British police arrested his and Luba's companions-in-arms for their communist activities many times.

In 1929 Trepper went to France where he hoped to earn a ticket to the land of his dreams, the Soviet Union, by working with the Jewish communist workers' movement. In Paris he founded the Yiddish newspaper *Der Morgn* and was active in the leftist Yiddish *Kultur-lige*. After his companion Alter Strom was arrested for espionage in the Soviet Union, he was ordered to Moscow in 1932. His family—his son was born in Paris—was supposed to follow. He became a student at the Markhlevsky University in Moscow, which educated the communist cadre from the West. His education also included full military training.

Trepper lived through the Stalin cult of personality, the Moscow trials and the liquidation of top leaders of several foreign communist parties. Almost all of the leading comrades of the Palestinian communist party were ordered to Moscow and executed. Most of them were Jews; there were hardly any Arabs.

After completing his studies, Trepper was assigned to become an editor at *Emes,* run by editor-in-chief Moshe Litvakov. Over time, many of his well-known companions disappeared after being summoned to the Lubyanka. They included Esther Frumkin, head of Markhlevsky University, an early member of the Bund and later a fanatical Bolshevik. She was executed in 1937.

The head of foreign espionage, General Yan Bersin, who led the Soviet espionage agency during the Spanish Civil War, ordered Trepper to build an espionage ring in France and Belgium. In this capacity he was able to serve the Soviet Union and, at the same time, avoid liquidation. The "Rote Kapelle" delivered numerous extremely valuable military secrets to the Soviet Union, which in turn were not systematically evaluated. Many members of the group had to pay for Moscow's mistakes with their lives. Miraculously, Trepper survived to the end of the Second World War. Upon returning to Moscow in January 1945 he was ordered to the Lubyanka and arrested. It wasn't until 1947 that he was sentenced to 15 years in jail and held in Lefortovo, Butyrki, and other prisons. In 1952 his sentence was reduced to 10 years.

In May 1954, more than one year after Stalin's death, Trepper was freed and rehabilitated. In 1957 he was allowed to return to Poland where he became chairman of the Jewish cultural organization and head of the publishing company *Yidish bukh.* Due to the Polish government's and the communist party's continuing anti-Semitic instigations, he applied for permission to immigrate to Israel in 1970, the country he had left more than forty years before as a glowing communist. His exit application was denied. Hundreds of public personalities, American senators, British parliamentarians, heads of labor unions from seven countries, government ministers, resistance fighters, and even the Archbishop of Paris, Cardinal Marty, sent letters of protest to the Polish government. In order to evade public pressure, the Polish government allowed his wife and three sons to emigrate in 1972. His family tried unsuccessfully to force the authorities to let Trepper leave by going on hunger strike in Copenhagen. In March 1973 representatives of the Trepper Committee in France, England, Denmark, Holland, and Switzerland met to show Poland that the world had not forgotten the heroes of the resistance. It took a serious illness for the Polish political "organs" to allow Trepper to go to London for medical treatment. The family was reunited in 1973 and moved to Jerusalem.

Were the battles and victims of communism for naught? Trepper felt that way.

> The revolution has degenerated and we have accompanied it during its demise…we wanted to change people, and failed. This century gave birth to two monsters, fascism and Stalinism. In this apocalypse our ideals have been destroyed. The absolute idea that gave meaning to our lives has taken on another face whose features we no longer recognize. Our defeat forbids us to pass judgment, but because world history is so full of the belief that it never repeats itself, it is allowed to nurture hope.[39]

## The Jewish Fighters of the "Rote Kapelle"

Leopold Trepper combined his knowledge with precise research to compile a list of his French, Belgian, Palestinian, and German companions to prevent them from being forgotten.[40] The following Jews were members:

Leo Grossvogel, Trepper's friend from Palestine, was arrested in 1942 and executed in 1944.

Hillel Katz, also from Palestine, disappeared without a trace in 1943.

Hermann Izbutsky was arrested in 1942 and beheaded in 1944 in Berlin.

David Kamy from Palestine was an officer of the International Brigades in Spain. His brother, Ben Yosef, was killed in Spain during his first encounter with the enemy. Kamy was arrested in 1941 and managed to fool the Gestapo for two years by impersonating a Russian officer until he was executed in Breendonk in 1943.[41]

Hersch Sokol was arrested in 1942 and tortured to death in 1943. His wife Mira suffered the same fate in Germany.

Sofia Posnanska from Palestine committed suicide in her cell in Brussels.

Isidore Springer, fighter in Spain, was arrested in Lyon and committed suicide in 1942.

Modeste Ehrlich died in a concentration camp.

Joseph Katz also died in a concentration camp.

Henri Rauch was arrested in 1942 in Belgium and died in 1944 at Mauthausen concentration camp.

Yekheskel Schreiber from Palestine was arrested in 1942 and died in a concentration camp.

Sarah Goldberg was arrested in 1943 and deported to Auschwitz. She survived the death march of 1945.

Abraham Raichman bought his own survival in 1943 through his treachery.

Dolly and Jacques Gunzig, both fighters in Spain, survived in the underground.

Vera Akkerman, a decoder and nurse in the International Brigades, survived. Her husband Israel and his brother Emiel died in action during the Spanish Civil War.

## 21. THE CRIMEA UNDER GERMAN RULE

In 1939, 85,000 Jews lived in the Crimea, including 7,000 Krimchaks. These were Jews who spoke their own language, related to the Tatar language. There were also 5,000 Karaites, members of a Jewish sect, whom the Germans later declared were not Jewish and, therefore, were not persecuted. After German troops invaded, *Einsatzgruppe D* murdered almost all the Jews. On April 16, 1942, the Crimea was declared "Jew free."

In July 1942, the German military government issued guidelines stating that the indigenous population—not the Jews but the Tatars—were allies of Germany. This was a propaganda lie of the invaders. In reality they wanted to settle the Crimea with Germans from Romania and south Tyrol and declare it "Gotenland." They wanted to create a "German Gibraltar" to control the Black Sea and build a "large German vacation resort." Hitler dreamt of an *Autobahn*, through which the Crimea could be reached in two days. Despite these plans, the occupiers' newspaper was published in the Tatar and Russian languages. The German governing body even allowed local Muslim committees to participate. Out of these committees a central committee was created that resembled a representative governing body. This political structure was far different from the earlier plans of the German government's minister for the east, Alfred Rosenberg. He wanted to create new states out of non-Russian nationalities that formed the core of the population. The Tatars sided with Germany partially because of anti-Russian sentiment. This position would become their death sentence under Stalin's rule.[42]

The most famous soldier of the JAFC, General Yakov Kreizer, achieved his greatest honor during the liberation of the Crimea. His 51st Army landed on the peninsula in March 1944. They were able to fight back twenty attacks on the bridgeheads by Zivash. On April 8, 1944, they began to attack the area defended by 200,000 German and Romanian soldiers. Five days later Simferopol and Yevpatoriya were liberated. The Sevastopol offensive resulted in the entire peninsula being liberated on May 7, 1944.

Two other Jewish "Heroes of the Soviet Union" distinguished themselves during these battles. Lieutenant Israel Yakubovsky's company in the Second Guards Infantry Division was almost wiped out; only five soldiers survived a German panzer attack outside Sevastopol. The injured company commander stayed in position with his troops. He died that same year in Poland. Major Jacob Chapitchev came from a Krimchak family. He was a career officer in the mountain artillery and also a talented poet. He died in 1945 during the liberation of Breslau.

By March 1944, Stalin had ordered the deportation of 180,000 Crimean Tatars as well as 33,000 Bulgarians, Greeks, and Armenians due to their alleged collaboration with the Germans. Two months later, within a few days, more than 200,000 people, including 40,000 children, were deported to Kazakhstan. The official reason given was that 20,000 Tatars had deserted, many of whom fought as volunteers in the Tatar Legion of the Wehrmacht.[43]

In reality no more than one-tenth of the Tatar population cooperated actively with the Germans. Even though there were also Russian and Ukrainian collaborators under German rule, none of these nationalities was generally persecuted.

## A Soviet California with U.S. Aid?

The Crimea project was discussed inside the JAFC circle long before the liberation of the peninsula. During the visit to the United States of Mikhoels and Fefer in the summer of 1943, James Rosenberg and the president of the Jewish Russian War Relief suggested reviving the Crimea project to philanthropist Louis Levine. Rosenberg complained that the millions of American dollars used for aid during the 1920s and 1930s had not yet brought satisfactory results.

There was hope that the Soviet leadership would not categorically deny the resettlement of the Jews and the founding of an autonomous Jewish territory. These hopes were based on the existential misery of the Jewish populace and demobilized war veterans in the liberated territories, the destruction of the Jewish colonies, as well as the self-sacrificing fight on part of the Jewish partisans and soldiers for the liberation of their Soviet homeland and the prospect of massive financial and material aid from abroad.

In his memoirs Pavel Sudoplatov, a high-ranking KGB general, stated that Stalin dusted off the Crimea idea himself in order to entice Jewish capital from the United States into the war-ravaged Soviet Union. He supposedly declared long before the end of the war that monies had to be freed up for the Jewish republic in the Crimea. He stated this during a meeting of the Atomic Energy Committee to Borisov, assistant director of the State Planning Office. Mikhoels had supposedly been named president of the Jewish Crimea Republic by the Kremlin.[44]

## The Crimea Memorandum

A few months prior to the awaited liberation of the Crimea, the issue gained momentum because of the thousands of homeless Jews. The thinking in the committee was that the resettlement of Jews in the Crimea, geographically close to the Jewish centers of the Ukraine, was a unique opportunity not to be missed. However, the members also discussed Peretz Markish's suggestion that Jews be resettled in the former German area of the Volga Republic, whose population had been deported as well.

How closely related these discussions about the Jewish territory were with Soviet deportation plans is uncertain. The JAFC archives contain several versions of petitions to government agencies, which were rejected because they seemed too Jewish-nationalistic. There were also several versions of the Crimea memorandum that had been sent to Stalin and were also found in the archives. Mikhoels, Epstein, and Fefer consulted Foreign Minister Molotov. It is possible that JAFC members had informed Polina Zhemchuzhina about the Crimea plans and requested her to arrange a meeting with Molotov. Nonetheless, this information comes from the interrogations of 1949. During the interrogations, those being interrogated had to admit to having knowledge of such discussions in order to incriminate Molotov's Jewish wife. There is no proof that Polina Zhemchuzhina was a "key figure" in the Crimea idea.[45]

In 1952 Fefer declared in court that Molotov meant that idea sounded good from a demographic standpoint, but it was not worth creating a Jewish republic in the Crimea because the Jews were city people that one could not put on tractors.[46]

A draft of the letter to Stalin dated February 15 contains a passage connecting Jewish nationalistic goals with Zionism. The authors naturally distanced themselves from the letter, contending that their aim was to suggest their intentions as a form of counter-project.[47] This passage is not included in the draft signed by Mikhoels, Epstein, and Fefer, which had to be considered as the final version. This document bears the same date and was given to Molotov to personally hand over to Stalin.

During the same court session, Lozovsky explained the history of the letter. He said that Mikhoels and Fefer returned from the United States with news that the *Joint* organization would give financial help for the resettlement of the Jews in the Crimea. During the meeting with Mikhoels and Fefer, Molotov said "We'll see." According to Lozovsky, in hindsight this statement did not mean that the resettlement issue was settled. Mikhoels and Fefer had interpreted Molotov's words in front of other JAFC members to be an agreement. Lozovsky further stated that support for certain projects through capitalist donations actually was not Soviet-hostile, as several examples in 1917 showed. He had been skeptical of the Crimean plan and told Mikhoels and Fefer that they could not draft the letter to the government leaders in the name of the committee. Shortly thereafter Fefer revealed during the court hearings that Epstein had requested him and Mikhoels to go see Kaganovich in mid-1944. He criticized the Crimea letter with the remark that the Jews did not want to move to the Crimea but would rather return to their former living areas. Poets and actors only could have created such a project.[48]

The Crimea memorandum was registered at Molotov's office on February 24, 1944. He sent copies to Malenkov, Mikoyan, Shcherbakov, Voznesensky, Litvinov, and Voroshilov. Molotov didn't inform Stalin's closest colleague, Kaganovich, or Beria and Khrushchev.[49]

The agreement with Molotov, the signature of Epstein (who kept his NKVD bosses of security informed), and the clarity of Lozovsky's text seemed good premises to expect a positive response from the Kremlin. In 1944 the JAFC assigned Kvitko, who knew the area, to travel to the

Crimea and scout out the situation for the creation of a Jewish autonomous territory or even a Jewish republic. His report was added to the
Crimea memorandum. The report about the murder of the population
of the Jewish colony of Dzhankoi was published in the *Black Book*.[50]

This subject dominated Jewish literary and cultural circles up until
1946. In 1945 and 1946 a series of articles appeared in *Eynikeyt* about the
Jewish settlement of the Crimea. Similar articles also appeared in the
American newspaper carrying the same name, and even expressing the
similar political ideas published by the American Committee of Jewish
Writers, Artists, and Scientists. The leading circles of the JAFC awaited
daily a positive response because implementing the project would have
solved many of the Soviet Jews' pressing problems. Markish considered
the memorandum a provocation and therefore refused to sign it. With
his knowledge of Stalinist anti-Semitism, the general political situation,
and his keen instinct, Ilya Ehrenburg warned against the Crimea plan.[51]

The project when considered dispassionately had to seem illusory
from the very beginning. Forced resettlement in the Jewish Autonomous Region of Birobidzan (which the JAFC propagated) would also
have stood in the way.[52] Still, it can in no way be seen as treason, after so
many of the highest Soviet personalities gave their seal of approval.
Was it the despair of the Jews after the war, wishful thinking, or simply a
sympathetic naiveté that allowed the leadership of the JAFC to believe in
the project's chances of success? During the JAFC court hearings, the
accused Yuzefovich stated:

> Mikhoels told me that there were instructions from Molotov
> about this. Because of his words I found it absolutely possible and
> never doubted for one second. I thought if a Jewish Autonomous
> Territory of Birobidzan already existed, then why couldn't a republic
> in the Crimea also exist? Jews were running away from Birobidzan
> because of bad conditions, and besides, the border to Japan was not
> far away, but in the Crimea one can establish oneself. I never saw
> anything unusual about that.[53]

They had already secretly distributed the government positions:
Mikhoels was to be the republic's president, Epstein the head of state,
Shimeliovich minister of health, Kvitko minister of education, Trainin
minister of justice, Yuzefovich head of the labor unions, and Markish
chair of the literary organization. In his memoirs, Khrushchev reports

that the Crimea project was a death sentence for more than those people just listed:

> Stalin saw in this suggestion the hand of American Zionists, which would serve themselves from the *Sovinformburo* offices. He exclaimed that the members of the committee were agents of American Zionism. They were trying to create a Jewish state in the Crimea in order to tear the Crimea away from the Soviet Union and to erect an outpost of American imperialism on our soil. This would pose an immediate threat to the security of the Soviet Union. Stalin allowed his imagination to roam freely in that direction.[54]

If Stalin saw the project as a starting point for a possible American invasion with the support of the Zionists, then why didn't he refuse it immediately? Why did he wait for years in order to finally have everybody involved executed? Vaksberg proposed a theory that Stalin himself instigated the whole idea as a provocation in 1944, in order to have the authors of the project liquidated.[55] It is still impossible to understand why a politician who blindly trusted the peace treaty with Hitler and ignored all warnings of a German invasion could be so amazingly visionary on such an unimportant question. Then too, Stalin did not need any complicated schemes in order to eliminate his enemies or to make it look legitimate.

In March 1948 the Crimea project provided security minister Abakumov with evidence of the JAFC's[56] nationalistic tendencies. The project served as the central basis of accusation when committee members were arrested in early 1949. The case against them was opened more than eight years after the memorandum. This alone is obvious proof that neither the investigating officials in the Lubyanka nor the military judges believed the fantastic accusations that state security and territorial existence were ever threatened. The Soviet leadership that waited so long without initiating military-judicial consequences had, according to the accusations themselves, committed treason.

Surely, Stalin and the highest leaders knew of the Crimea project ahead of time, otherwise they would not have kept any high-ranking government or party officials (and most definitely not the devoted Molotov) busy with this issue. The three signatories of the memorandum did not draft it as private individuals, but rather as leaders of the JAFC. The memorandum to Stalin contained the following text:

To: Comrade J. V. Stalin, Head of the Council of the People's Commissars of the USSR

Dear Joseph Vissarionovich!

During the course of the war for the homeland a few questions regarding the life and organization of the Jewish population within the Soviet Union arose.

Before the war more than 5 million Jews lived in the USSR; about one and a half million of them originated from the western territories of the Ukraine, Belorussia, the Baltics, Bessarabia, Bukovina, as well as Poland. In these temporarily occupied territories, not less than 1.5 million Jews were murdered.

Apart from the hundreds of thousands of soldiers who joined the Red Army, the Jewish population of the USSR was dispensed across Central Asian republics, Siberia, on the banks of the Volga, and in certain areas of the RSFSR.

The primary question that arises for the displaced Jewish population, as well as for other population groups, concerns the return to their homelands. Considering the tragedy that this war caused for the Jewish people, even this step would not be a definitive solution to the organization of Jewish society within the USSR.

First, the extreme fascist cruelty, under which the Jewish population had to suffer, and their total elimination in the temporarily occupied Soviet territories has led many displaced Jews to feel that their homeland has lost any initial ideal and material meaning. Not only were many houses destroyed, but the fascists turned the places of their past into cemeteries that will never again be able to be brought back to life—their families and friends are lying there. For Polish and Romanian Jews who became Russian citizens, the question of returning to their homelands is now a wrong question, since the entire Jewish population in their home countries has been eliminated and any evidence of Jewish culture has been erased.

Secondly, due to the increasing influence of many national cadres from friendly nations (of the USSR) who followed their own interests, there is little room left for Jewish intellectuals. Positions in various fields of employment that they formerly filled were no longer available to them, and there was no appropriate work available for the majority of the intellectuals.

Theoretically, they could have paid their share for the further development of Jewish society within the Soviet Union, due to the cultural successes and qualities developed over the centuries. The displacement of the Jewish population, of which only a minority still lives in the individual republics, made the realization of this project impossible.

The fact is that there is no political upbringing and cultural work such as education using (Yiddish) mother tongue among the Jewish masses anymore. Only a few cultural centers exist (some theaters, a publishing company and a single weekly newspaper), which nevertheless cannot fill the cultural aspirations or needs of a Jewish population of over 3 million.

If one were to leave the mass of this population group in a scattered state, without political or cultural education in the mother tongue, one subjects them to intrigues and foreign and enemy influence.

During the war certain capitalist influences became stronger in certain population groups, including the intellectuals. Rising anti-Semitic outbreaks are one of the most obvious signs of this development. These are instigated by fascist agents and foreign spies whose goal is to undermine one of the most important achievements of the Soviet regime: friendship among all peoples.

For the Jewish population, these unhappy developments represent a painful step backward—for them as true patriots of our country, whose sons and daughters fought heroically in the Patriotic War on the front and behind the lines. Anti-Semitic tendencies cause strong reactions among Soviet Jews without exceptions, because the entire Jewish people have experienced the largest tragedy in their history through this rampage of fascist barbarism. In Europe Jews have lost 4 million people, more than one-quarter of its total population. The Soviet Union is the only country in which almost half of the Jewish population survived. Otherwise anti-Semitic occurrences and fascist brutality have led to a rise in nationalistic and chauvinistic tendencies among certain circles within the Jewish population.

In order to normalize the economic situation of Jewish co-citizens, to support and develop Soviet Jewish culture, in order to institute all powers for the well-being of the Soviet homeland, to create equality among Jewish masses and the brotherly people, and to solve the problems of the post-war times, it is, in our opinion, urgently necessary to bring the question of the creation of a socialist Jewish Soviet republic to discussion.

An Autonomous Jewish Region was created in Birobidzan with the goal of creating a Jewish Soviet republic and an obvious state and judicial form for the Jewish population. For various reasons the experiment in Birobidzan did not yield the desired results. Existing power and possibilities were not fully used, and Birobidzan was too far away from the centers where Jews live and work.

Despite all these difficulties, the Autonomous Jewish Region became one of the most advanced regions in the Far East. This proves the capabilities of the Jewish population to create their own form of government within the Soviet Union. These capabilities were even more obvious with regard to the establishment of Jewish regions in the Crimea.

We consider the creation of a Jewish Soviet Republic in one of the above-named areas under specific political requirements certainly realizable. The Crimea seems to be one of the best-suited regions, as there is enough space for new relocation, and experiences have already been gathered in the creation of Jewish regions here.

The creation of a Jewish Soviet republic would once and for all solve, in the direction of Bolshevism, the state and judicial questions of the Jewish people in the spirit of the Leninist-Stalinist population policies. This question, to which no answer has been given for centuries, can only be solved in our great socialist nation.

The model of a Jewish Soviet republic enjoys large popularity among wide circles of the Jewish populace in the Soviet Union and among the most competent representatives of our brother peoples.

In the creation of a Jewish Soviet republic we could count on the support of the Jewish people around the world, no matter where they live.

On the basis of our above-mentioned points we suggest the following:

1. The creation of a Jewish Socialist Soviet Republic in the area of the Crimea.

2. The timely creation—before the liberation of the Crimea—of a government commission that will deal with the realization thereof.

We hope you will dedicate the proper attention to our suggestion; the fate of an entire people hangs on its realization.

S. Mikhoels
S. Epstein
I. Fefer[57]

The naiveté of the leaders of the JAFC, which was dictated by the suffering of the Jews, is to be admired; did they seriously believe that the creation of a Jewish Republic would be allowed? In the propaganda for Jewish land settlement in the Soviet Union, Yiddish slogans were used— The plow brings luck and blessings (*In der sokhe ligt masl un brokhe*). The agricultural projects in Birobidzan and in the Crimea brought the Soviet Jews bad luck and their demise.

*above*

Demonstration of Jewish revolutionaries, probably the Bund,
in Russia on May 1, 1917. The slogans on the banner read:
Long live the democratic republic./Long live national autonomy./
Long live international socialism./Long live the Jewish
socialist labor party.

*below*

Congress of Jewish Zionist soldiers on the Minsk front,
December 17, 1917.

*right*

Mastheads of military publications: *Red Army; The Free Soldier; Bulletin of the Executive Committee of the Jewish Soldiers of the 12th Army.*

*below*

It all started so fraternally: the coat of arms of the state of Belorussia with the watchword "proletarians of all countries..." in Belorussian, Yiddish, Polish, and Russian.

*above*

Poster of the Gezerd, in Russian Ozet. The Yiddish text
at the right says: "Become a member of the Gezerd."

*below*

The JAFC's first meeting; sitting, from left to right: Marshak, Markish, Bergelson, Ehrenburg;
standing: Yofan, Gilels, Flier, Oistrakh, Nussinov, Mikhoels, Sek, Zuskin, Tishler.

*above*
Four leaders of the JAFC; from right to left: Markish, Bergelson, Mikhoels, Ehrenburg.

*right*
The letterhead of
the JAFC in English,
Russian and Yiddish.

Jewish Antifascist Committee in the USSR
Moscow, ulitsa Kropotkina, 10. Telephone: Г-6-71-00, Г-6-47-07

Еврейский Антифашистский
Комитет в СССР
Москва, улица Кропоткина, № 10
Телефон: Г-6-71-00, Г-6-47-07

_____ 19V_year.

*below*
Mikhoels *(right)* and Fefer during a visit to Albert Einstein in Princeton, New Jersey.

*above*
Ilya Ehrenburg with Jewish partisans in Vilna
shortly after the liberation of their city.

*below*
Leopold and Luba Trepper

Jewish members of the
"Rote Kappelle."

*above*

Members of a Yiddish kolkhoz near
Larindorf in the Crimea on their way
to an election gathering in 1938.

*below*

JAFC reception in honor of Ben Zion
Goldberg's visit to Moscow in 1946: from left
to right, standing: Kvitko and Bergelson;
sitting: Fefer, Yusefovich, Markish, Goldberg,
Mikhoels, Bregman, Kushnirov, Halkin.

*Black Book* special edition of the New York Yiddish newspaper *Eynikeyt* in April 1946. The headline reads: "Special edition, dedicated in remembrance of the 6 million martyrs."

*above*
The last photo of Solomon
Mikhoels before his murder.

*left*
Polina Zhemchuzhina-Molotov

*below*
Miron Vovsi, one of the
senior Kremlin doctors,
a cousin of Mikhoels.

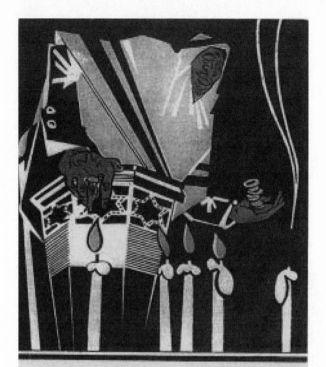

ІУДАЇЗМ
без прикрас

*right*
Ida Nudel

*below*
Refusenik, Colonel Efim
Davidovich with his wife.

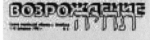

Jewish magazines after perestroika:
1. *Renesans*
2. *Czernovitzer bleter*
3. *Vozrozhdenie*
4. *Unser kol*
5. *Evreiskaia gazeta*
6. *Evreiskii istoricheskii al'manakh*
7. *Nasha zhizn'*
8. *Shalom*
9. *Evreiskii Mir*
10. *Einikait,* organ of the Jewish Cultural and Social Association in Kiev.
11. *Birobidzhaner Stern,* newspaper of the Communist Party and the Soviets of the Jewish Autonomous Region.

*above*
Martov and Dan with
their families in exile
in Berlin.

*below left*
Vladimir Kossovsky

*below*
Rafael Abramovich

*left*
Mark Liber

*below*
Mikhail Gots

Lazar Kaganovich

Leon Trotsky

# Part V

# THE FATE OF THE JAFC AFTER THE WAR

## 22. THE HISTORY OF THE *BLACK BOOK*

The *Black Book* was one of the most important JAFC projects and became part of the tragic history of the Soviet Jews. There is probably no other book for which the Latin saying *Habent sua fata libelli* (books have their own fates) is more appropriate. Jews from all occupied European territories documented their experiences under very dangerous conditions during the Shoah, the most famous of which is the Ringblum Archive. Established in the Warsaw ghetto, the archive was then hidden and almost completely exhumed after the war. The CDJC in Paris (which still exists today) dates back to an illegal documentation center founded by French Jews in 1943 in Grenoble. Italian Jews established the archive CDEC. Even Jewish members of the special commandos in the crematoriums of Auschwitz, sentenced to death, wrote reports for posterity. Some of the reports were found in the ruins of the death camps. One of the most important documentation centers in the world, the archive of the JAFC was kept under lock and key for nearly half a century. Two hundred fifty-seven war and non-war correspondents, Jewish and non-Jewish witnesses, sent their material to the committee and its newspaper *Eynikeyt*. An NKVD file contains data on 4,015 authors who had written articles, reports, and letters. Most of the articles dealt with the Shoah in the Soviet Union, the Jewish resistance, and the Jewish role in the victory over Germany.[1]

*Arno Lustiger*

## The Beginnings of the *Black Book*

The idea of publishing documents about the annihilation of Jews in occupied European countries originated with Albert Einstein. At the end of 1942 he suggested to Shalom Ash and Ben Zion Goldberg (both of the ACJWAS and JAFC) that material be collected for a *Black Book*. The plan was discussed during the committee's plenary meeting in February 1943, and later presented to Shcherbakov for approval.

The members (at a meeting of the JAFC in 1946, according to Fefer) were initially unsure of whether to "create such a *Black Book*, dedicated solely to the German atrocities against the Jews." In the summer of 1943, while visiting the United States, Mikhoels and Fefer agreed with Einstein's suggestion, after conferring with Moscow.

They agreed, even before the JAFC could formally draft a resolution, to publish a *Black Book* and other publications chronicling the Soviet Jews' suffering and resistance. They agreed that all organizations involved, i.e., the World Jewish Congress, the national council of the Jews of Palestine *Vaad Leumi*, and the ACJWAS, should collect material.

The ACJWAS, in which Moscow had total trust, was to coordinate the editing of the book. By July 27, 1943, *Eynikeyt* already publicized the *Black Book*, its contents, and size of approximately 1,000 pages. They also requested that their readership send them documents. *Eynikeyt* listed the names of the editors: Mikhoels, Fefer, Markish, Kvitko, Halkin, Shimeliovich, and Falkovich. Falkovich was the only one to survive, probably because he was a member of the Red Army.

Considering conditions in the Soviet Union, the *Black Book* was a very ambitious project. The secretary general of the JAFC, Shakhne Epstein, said that it would not only be published in Russian, but also in Yiddish, English, Hebrew, Spanish and German.[2] This explains the large donations received by the *Black Book* committee, which took up collections in various cities in the United States.

## Competing Concepts

In the spring of 1944, the JAFC's prestige rose when Ehrenburg was promoted to head the literary commission. The commission's prestige continued to increase when Grossman was accepted into the publisher's council of the *Black Book* in September 1944. Apart from the committee's discussions, Ehrenburg had been gathering material about atrocities committed by the Nazis (especially those against the Jews). He gathered a great deal of information working as a correspondent for the army newspaper *Red Star* (*Krasnaya zvezda*).

In September 1944 the author drafted a document to "government organizations" describing the project in detail:

> The book will contain reports from Jews that were saved, from witnesses to the atrocities, German orders, diaries, and confessions of the executioners, as well as memoirs and diaries of the Jews who were able to remain hidden.

Neither criminal charges nor protocols were necessary; real life reports should show the full extent of the tragedy. It was extremely important to show the solidarity of the Soviet people, the rescue of individual Jews by the Russians, Belorussians, Ukrainians, and Poles. Such accounts would help heal terrible wounds and set the ideal of friendship among nations even higher. It is necessary to prove that Jews went to their deaths bravely and to document every case of their resistance.[3]

Jewish Lubyanka agents and representatives of the Kremlin in the JAFC remarked that the book's publication would be allowed, "if it's good." Ehrenburg angrily rebuked that remark during a meeting of the commission on October 13, 1944: "...it is not we who are the authors of this book, but rather the Germans...after all this is not just some sort of work of fiction whose content is unknown."

Shcherbakov allowed material to be gathered and let the JAFC cooperate with an American publisher, but whether a Russian version would be allowed was still not certain. After endless debates two editorships were formed. The JAFC prepared the materials for the publication of the *Black Book* in foreign countries (especially the United States) and Ehrenburg's literary commission put all its energies into the publication of a Russian edition (*Chornaya Kniga*) in the Soviet Union.[4] During the JAFC trial, Lozovsky stated that he did not approve Ehrenburg's plan to publish a Russian version of the *Black Book* in the Soviet Union as well as a Yiddish version in the United States. The book, he said, was influenced by serious nationalistic tendencies. It was, however, useful in the fight against fascism, especially when taking into account that nationalism was not always reactionary, as exemplified by the national freedom fighters in the colonies and their support of Lenin. Nationalism in the USSR was without a doubt counterrevolutionary; therefore the book should not have been published, according to Lozovsky in 1952.[5]

The JAFC remained in contact with the three foreign project partners. In 1944, the People's Commission for Foreign Affairs sent 552 pages of documents for the *Black Book* to the United States. Fefer defended this in court in 1952 claiming that he had received a telegram from Ambassador Gromyko stating that the *Black Book* would appear in the United States without JAFC material.[6]

Ehrenburg had not allowed this, which caused greater tension between him and the JAFC. There were discrepancies within the Literary Commission as well: Ehrenburg wanted to shorten the eyewitness accounts slightly. Grossman wanted a much more liberal use of the documents; he wanted to speak on behalf of those murdered.[7] A special commission led by Solomon Bregman, in its expert analysis of February 26, 1945, validated both options. They nonetheless criticized both the adaptations of the texts as well as the Literary Commission (in other words, those of Ehrenburg and Grossman): "The sketches at hand contain an overbearing amount of detail in the reports of the scandalous activities among the Ukrainians, Lithuanians, etc. This weakens the strength of the main point of the indictment that is aimed at the Germans..."[8] The selections of the JAFC were criticized because there was too little about the Jewish resistance. The commission suggested that both variations be published only after they had been "revised and confirmed" by "competent political editorship." Lozovsky also suggested this to Ehrenburg in March 1945,[9] but continued controversies and further criticism of his work caused him to resign his chairmanship. At the end of 1945 a new editorial staff was put together and Vassily Grossman became the chief editor.

In June 1945 a special consultant (probably the journalist Subotsky) sharply criticized the already edited text. He was of the opinion that the "role of the local anti-Soviet elements in the elimination of the Jewish population" was described correctly. The Russian chauvinistic "government offices" criticized the representation of the Jewish councils.[10] On July 9, 1945, the editors' council accepted these critiques and decided to revise the final text. They decided to supplement the text with documents and photos from the State Commission for the Investigation of Nazi Crimes. The material was to be sorted according to Soviet republics, and published in a volume with a political and judicial introduction. The latter part was written by Trainin as planned, and the former by Grossman, after Lozovsky refused the assignment. The *Eynikeyt* published material and reports from the *Black Book* on many occasions.

## Material for Foreign Countries Only?

The *Black Book* was to be used as evidence by Soviet prosecutors during the Nuremberg War Crimes Trials, so it had to be completed quickly. The manuscript, expanded and censored in accordance with the new guidelines, was distributed to Soviet-friendly organizations in Bulgaria, England, France, Italy, Mexico, Austria, Poland, Romania, Czechoslovakia, Hungary, Palestine, and the United States. In 1980 an issue based on the distributed texts was published in Israel. This issue, however, was not the same as the edition handed to the *Emes* publishing company by Vassily Grossman's publishing collective in April 1946. The printing process was stopped in the fall, although some galley proofs already existed. In November 1946 Mikhoels, Fefer, Grossman, and Ehrenburg turned to the Secretary of the Central Committee, Andrei Zhdanov (1896-1948), for help. The Central Committee's Head Department for Agitation and Propaganda, led by Aleksandrov (1908-1961), ordered the book to be examined immediately.

At the end of 1946 Zhdanov, chief ideologist for the past year, unleashed a hysterical campaign against all tendencies in art or literature that supposedly undermined Russian chauvinistic dogmas of Soviet patriotism. *Eynikeyt* also published attacks against Jewish nationalism. The JAFC was placed under the direct control of the Central Committee and the opportunity for setting the printing passed by. In February 1947 Aleksandrov accused the JAFC of sending manuscripts to foreign countries without the permission of the Central Committee. His main complaint was that the *Black Book* gave a completely false impression of German fascism:

> The idea that the Germans robbed and murdered only the Jews goes through the entire book. The reader gets the impression that the Germans went to war against the USSR with the sole purpose of annihilating the Jews. One gets the impression that the Germans simply treated the Russians, Ukrainians, Belorussians, Lithuanians,

Latvians, and other nationalities condescendingly. Many reports stressed that in order to avoid death, one simply had to acquire a "Russian passport" so as not to look like a Jew, etc.[11]

In June 1947 the *Emes* publishing company was given the assignment to typeset the book and publish 50,000 copies. This assignment came despite Aleksandrov's conclusion that publication within the Soviet Union was not advisable. At the end of August 1947, the central censoring office *Glavlit* stopped all work on the book again, even though three-quarters of the copies were printed. Mikhoels asked Zhdanov to rescind this decision. His petition was processed by Aleksandrov's successors Mikhail Suslov (1902–1982) and Dmitri Shepilov, who finished the last act. On October 7, 1947, Morozov, the head of the publisher's department within the Head Department for Propaganda, informed the JAFC that the book could under no circumstances be published. He stated that the book contained severe political mistakes. In the end, Stalin himself forbade publication of the *Black Book*. His reasoning was that the Jews were not the only ones to suffer under German occupation, and that it would be wrong to emphasize their fate.

### The *Black Book*

Meanwhile in the United States the *Black Book* project grew into almost gigantic dimensions. On December 27, 1944, New York hosted an international *Black Book* Conference. Representatives from Morocco, Tunisia, Uruguay, Cuba, Argentina, Australia, England, and France, as well as several writers and members of American Jewish organizations, such as the ACJWAS and WJC, took part in the conference. The Head of the Jewish Council for Russian War Relief, Levine, declared that his organization had transferred 2 million dollars to the Soviet Union in 1944. Representatives of *Black Book* Committees in American cities reported that they had collected thousands of dollars.

Honorary members of the *Black Book* Committee were elected, including Albert Einstein, Thomas Mann, Eleanor Roosevelt, and Stephen Wise. Maurice Perlzweig, head of the political department of the WJC, spoke. His colleague, Dr. Goldmann, executive member of the *Black Book* Committee, sharply rebuked attacks made by the socialist newspaper *Forverts* regarding "Soviet-devoted" committee members. The pre-

sidium of the JAFC sent a comprehensive greeting, signed by all sixteen members.

On March 27, 1945, a mass meeting took place in Madison Square
Garden in New York to which all four partners of the *Black Book* project
had sent invitations: the JAFC, the WJC, the ACJWAS, and the *Vaad
Leumi* from Palestine. The slogans on the large placards read: "Justice for
6 million slain Jews. A historical demonstration. The Jewish indictment."
The New York *Eynikeyt* printed a special edition. Soviet Consul General
Yevgeni Kisselov and other high-ranking officials, including Ira Hirshman
and representatives of President Roosevelt, took part in a benefit ban-
quet for the *Black Book* at the War Refugee Board. Almost the entire
September issue of the New York *Eynikeyt* was dedicated to the *Black
Book*. Several full-page articles presented information about the project.
This was also how the ten-member publishing staff was also introduced.
Albert Einstein wrote the preface in German and all four members received a copy in their mother language. The JAFC, as well as the American branch of the ACJWAS, turned the preface down, because Einstein
indeed demanded the protection of national minorities and the abandon-
ment of the principle of non-intervention in internal affairs when human rights were being abused. The persecution and forced relocation of
entire peoples ordered by Stalin stood in stark contrast to these demands.
Einstein's energetic support for the national rights of Jews and a Jewish
state in Palestine must have hit the sublime resistance of anti-Zionist
Jewish Bolsheviks.

A draft of the letter to Ben Zion Goldberg signed by Mikhoels,
Grossman and Fefer, which was sent to Lozovsky on October 16, 1945,
is in the archives. The letter reminds the American partner again of the
decision in principle to accept only facts about fascist crimes:

> This is why we find the parts of the book redundant that deal with
> the history and further successes of our people. As people of vari-
> ous beliefs take part in the *Black Book*, all disputed sections must be
> removed. Only the pages containing facts that are irrefutable for us
> all should remain. Concerning a foreword about the persecution of
> the Jews, we believe that such a listing weakens our indictment against
> fascism.[12]

The American edition was to be published in coordination with the
JAFC, since they supplied the material. The manuscript was sent to Mos-

cow, but despite repeated pleas, the publishers' collective did not respond until January 23, 1946. Once again, Einstein's preface was criticized. When the revised version of the preface was still not accepted by the representatives of the JAFC in March 1946, Goldberg told them that the American version of the *Black Book* would appear without Einstein's preface.[13]

On July 26, 1946, in an official ceremony in the main hall of Congress in Washington, the first copies of *Black Book: The Nazi Crime Against the Jewish People* were presented to senators and congressmen. All the important news agencies took part in the subsequent press conference. The publishers received many letters in honor of this occasion. Many of the *Black Book* committees continued to collect money vigorously, even after the *Black Book*'s publication. One must ask for what purpose.

In 1947 the Romanian edition of the *Black Book*, *Cartea Negra,* appeared in Bucharest. It took 35 years, until 1980, for Yad Vashem in Jerusalem to release a Russian version of the *Black Book*, based on the incomplete manuscripts sent to Palestine. The English edition of this version was released in 1981 in New York, a Yiddish one in 1984 in Jerusalem, and one in Hebrew in 1991 in Tel Aviv. The 100-page chapter "Lithuania," written by Abraham Sutzkever, is missing completely in the first three editions. The Yiddish poet Abraham Sutzkever was one of the most important collaborators on the *Black Book*. He was part of the United Partisan Organization in the Vilna ghetto and joined the Jewish partisan group in the Narocz Forests in September 1942. Sutzkever told me that on orders from Ehrenburg he was flown in a courier plane from the partisan camp to Moscow in March 1944 so he could write the chapter about Lithuania. Ehrenburg and Sutzkever worked day and night on the manuscript in a Moscow hotel. In the corrected galleys, Sutzkever's name was erased by hand because he left the Soviet Union in 1947 to emigrate to Palestine. This, however, saved his life.

## The First Complete Edition

Ilya Ehrenburg's daughter Irina did not receive a copy of the galleys of the forbidden, destroyed, and previously unheard of book—dated July 14, 1947—until January 1992. In the same year, she asked me to find a German publishing company for the book and to act as its editor. The translation of the book, which was supposed to be published by Rowohlt, was very advanced when the original uncensored manuscript was found in the KGB archives. The book was printed in Vilna in 1993 and, until today, remained largely unnoticed in Russia. I had the censored texts printed in italics inserted into the translated text. The book contains, in addition to my preface, four essays and the epilogue by Irina Ehrenburg. The German edition of the *Black Book* is the first complete and uncensored edition in a Western language. Einstein's foreword to the American edition is also published for the first time in this edition. After tedious research I found the handwritten original German text in the Einstein Archive of the Hebrew University in Jerusalem.

Some critics called the book the "*Black Book* of the Century." We still know relatively little about the mass murder of Soviet Jews and their resistance. Most of this information comes mainly from the files of the perpetrators—this despite a large quantity of works written about the Shoah. Therefore, the *Black Book* is one of the most important primary sources regarding this topic.

Collaboration on the *Black Book* was one of the most important indictments against members of the JAFC during the secret trials, although the chief editors, Ehrenburg and Grossman, were never openly accused of this. The indicting institution would have made fools of themselves in front of millions of Soviet soldiers had they even suggested the nonsense that two famous and courageous war correspondents were spies. Many interrogations, court cases and two paragraphs of the court decision are dedicated to the *Black Book*. As with all other points of indictment they are typical bold constructs and fabrications of the NKVD. It is therefore not coincidental that Gorbachev was the first to release what happened at the rehabilitation hearings in the newspaper of the Central Committee in December 1989, 37 years after the secret murders.

Ilya Ehrenburg and Vassily Grossman are considered two of the most important writers of the Soviet Union. Both left behind their literary, political and moral testaments—Ehrenburg with his memoirs and Grossman with his novel *Life and Fate*. Thanks to the Rowohlt publishing company, the *Black Book*, compiled and in part edited by Ehrenburg and Grossman, could finally be released in its uncensored version in Germany in 1994, after a delay of almost 50 years. A French version was also published in the meantime, as well as an Italian and American version, some of them based on my German edition of 1994.

## What the *Black Book* Was Not to Contain

The comparison of the original manuscript (compiled under the conditions and circumstances described) with the censored, then allowed, set and finally forbidden and destroyed version, gives a thrilling visual example of the development of the reception of news about the Shoah in the Soviet Union. The forbidden texts give us an exact view of the changes in thinking of the Soviet leaders after the victory over Germany.

The editor had already had censored one passage of the preface by Vassily Grossman where he emphasized the importance of Jewish ideological and spiritual resistance as a primary step toward the armed struggle. Obviously Grossman's emphasis on the "use of culture" as "ideological protest" did not fit with the intentions of the Soviet leadership that was challenging Jewish cultural institutions. The first chapter of the *Black Book* was a report on the massacre at Babi Yar (one of the best-known crimes against the Soviet Jews), which was reduced by half. Indications that non-Jewish landlords and others betrayed the Jews to the Germans, as well as examples of people saving some Jews, especially when the savior was an Orthodox priest, were eliminated. The description of the condition of the execution camps *after* their liberation was also removed. Had the book been published in the Soviet Union, the reader would not have been allowed to find out that "dark criminal elements gained material advantage from the great misfortune, and were willing to enrich themselves in a greedy and profit-oriented way at the expense of the Germans' victims." Similar texts in other reports about the collaboration of the Soviet population in the extermination of the Jews were also censored. In one report from Khmelnik, the description of German atrocities as well as the heroic fight of the surviving Jews in the liberation of their city was cut. References to Jewish traditions such as the month and year of the Jewish calendar were also excised. Reports that one lived because of prayers to God, as well as salvation because of the "Russian passport" or the statement that one was circumcised because he was a Tatar were all removed. Readers of the censored version would not find out about the murder of Jewish women and children who were brought out to the Black Sea in boats outside Odessa and thrown overboard to drown. The entire report of the crimes committed by the German and Romanian occupiers against Jews in Czernowitz was cut. Even a short note about the desperate attempt of Jews in Lvov to break through to the partisans was not allowed by the

# Stalin and the Jews

censors. The same applied to the report from the Minsk ghetto. Reports of Ukrainian Bandera partisans who ruthlessly recruited people but who fought against the Germans was removed. The statement that Soviet power showed "little interest" in the survivors after their liberation was also removed.

The report from a young girl out of Bialystok about the burning of Jews in the synagogue was completely eliminated. In another report from that city, the following passage fell victim to the censors:

> Anyone who experienced the horrifying conditions the Jewish population lived in under Hitler's yoke, and how heroically they fought against the German executioners, understands what a meaningful contribution the Jews achieved towards the shattering of German fascism.[14]

In the archives of the JAFC, which have only been accessible a few years ago, numerous materials were found that could not be published in the *Black Book* simply because there was no space. These papers contained more than 6,000 pages. Ninety-three reports were selected by members of the Archives of the Russian Federation and by historians from Yad Vashem in Jerusalem, and were published in a 463-page book entitled *The Unknown Black Book* (*Niezvestnaya chorniya kniga*) in 1993. These newly published texts were also ignored because the cooperation of the local population in the murder of the Jews was depicted. More than half of the reports documented the events in cities and towns that were not mentioned in the *Black Book*. In the preface, it states: "In the reports, very often betrayal and heroism, desperation and hope, malice and self-sacrifice go hand in hand."[15]

## The Foreword by Albert Einstein

> This book is a collection of materials based on documentary evidence about the systematic work of destruction with which the German government murdered a great part of the Jewish people.

> The Jewish organizations that labored together to produce the work at hand and present it to the public now carry the responsibility for the truth of the facts communicated here.

*167*

The goal of this publication is obvious. It should convince the reader that an international organization for the security of existence can only effectively fulfill its purpose if it is not limited to protect countries only under military attack, but rather allows its protection to help the national minorities within individual countries. It is, after all, the single individual who should be protected against destruction and inhumane treatment.

It is true that this goal can only be attained when the principle of non-intervention, which has played such a fatal role in the last decades, is thrown overboard. No one today can doubt the necessity of this grave step. Even someone whose goal is simply to offer protection against military attacks obviously has to see that the development of the catastrophes of war are prepared within the individual countries and not only through military and war-technical preparations.

Only when humane conditions of existence for all people are created and secured, as well as the global obligation of all countries and people are acknowledged, will we be able to speak rightfully of a civilized mankind.

The Jewish people have lost more than all other afflicted peoples through the catastrophe of the last few years. Therefore, if we truly want to strive for a righteous redress, the Jewish people have to be given special consideration in the reorganization of peace. The fact that the Jews cannot be considered a nation in formal political terms, because they do not have a country or a government, should not be a hindrance. The Jews should be dealt with as a unified group, as if they were a country. Their status as a unified political group has been proven to be a fact by the actions of their enemies. Therefore, they should also be considered in the aspiration of stable international relations as if they were a nation in the usual sense of the word.

Something else also needs to be emphasized in this context. The existence of the Jews in parts of Europe would be impossible for years to come. The Jews have made it possible to settle in Palestinian soil through decades of hard work and voluntary financial aid by other peoples. All of these sacrifices were taken with the understanding that the official promises made by the governments involved after the last war would be kept. This was the promise that a safe haven be created for the Jewish people in the old homeland of Palestine. This promise—to put it mildly—has been fulfilled only slowly and partially. Therefore, after the Jews—especially the Palestinian Jews—

honorably earned a name for themselves, one must emphatically call attention to that promise. Palestine has to be opened to Jewish immigration within its economic capabilities. Should, however, international institutions want to gain the trust of the people, which must be the most important foundation, then it must be made clear that those who trusted these institutions and suffered the greatest sacrifices have not been betrayed.

## 23. ASSISTING IN THE BIRTH OF
## ISRAEL AND WORSENING OF ANTI-ZIONISM

### Soviet-Palestine Policy During the War

Winning support of the world's Jews during the war was one of the JAFC's priorities. Of course Zionists could not be overlooked. The *Yishuv* enthusiastically welcomed the Soviet Jews' appeal. The Jewish community of Palestine rejected it, seeing the mass murder of the European Jews, because during the Arab uprising in Palestine from 1936 until 1939, where hundreds of Jews were killed and injured, Moscow supported the Arabs and also those Jewish communists of the Palestinian Communist Party (PKP) who sanctioned anti-Jewish riots as justifiable anti-Zionist, anti-imperialist protest. Already in September 1941, the radio station, "The Voice of Jerusalem," broadcast a message of the official representation of the Jews, the Jewish Agency. In it, the political and cultural elite of the *Yishuv* campaigned for stronger support for the Soviet Union. The powerful federation of trade unions, *Histadrut*, started a big fundraising campaign, and the crypto-communist journalist Shlomo Tsyrulnikov founded with Arnold Zweig and other left-wing liberal personalities in the fall of 1941 a public action committee, which later became the Victory League.

In the summer of 1942, 250 delegates gathered in Jerusalem for the Congress of the V League (*V Liga*). For the first time the Soviet leadership sent two low ranking representatives, the diplomats Mikhailov and Petrenko from Ankara, to the Zionist enemy in Palestine. Even Weizmann, Ben Gurion, and Goldmann, leaders of the Zionist world organization, were interested in contact with and support from the Soviet Union, because the survival of the Jews and the foundation of the Jewish state depended on victory over Germany. Ben Gurion and Weizmann met Ivan Maisky, the Soviet ambassador, several times in 1941 and 1942, in Turkey and Great Britain. Maisky even visited Palestine in 1943, and spoke to, among others, Golda Meir.[16]

Contact between the Jewish and the communist anti-Zionists of the Soviet Union and the Jews of Palestine turned out to be extremely complicated. The Soviet press censured activities of the *V Liga* and the auxiliary work of the Jews of Palestine. Returning from America, Mikhoels and Fefer stopped over in Palestine. They were instructed by Moscow not to leave the Lod airport, even though Weizmann had officially invited them in New York.[17] In 1944 the JAFC justified this break with a telegram of untrue claims stating that *Liga* had changed its initial goals and activities.

Differences between pro-Israel foreign-policy propaganda and internal policy campaigning against Jewish nationalism sometimes came to light in text. Shakhne Epstein brushed off hopes of emigrating to Palestine, when he wrote in the November 8, 1944 issue of *Eynikeyt* that Palestine could only be a worthy goal for foreign Jews and that the problems of the Soviet Jews were solved exclusively by their own government. The headline of the article—"Rebirth of a Nation"—signaled, however, that the Soviet Union certainly did not completely disapprove of the founding of a Jewish state.[18]

Contradictions between domestic and foreign policy suddenly surfaced with the terror unleashed against the Soviet Jews in 1947. These included measures against the leadership of the JAFC, the murder of Mikhoels, and the intention to liquidate the JAFC and other Jewish organizations, especially in the field of culture. These actions coincided with the energetic support of the partition plan for Palestine.

## Support for the Founding of Israel

Without the intervention of the Soviet Union, the state of Israel would not have been founded, at least not in 1948. The Soviet Union supported the founding of the state obliquely because it would not hinder the emigration or flight of hundreds of thousands of Jews from the Eastern bloc into the DP camps in the Western occupied zones, Austria, France, and Italy. The distress of the Displaced Persons and their determination to get to Palestine, by any means, even illegally, put tremendous pressure on the UN, so much pressure that the partition of the country was decided on at the plenary assembly at the end of November 1947.

Stalin's Near Eastern policy, however, was not motivated by humanitarian considerations or a changed view on Zionism. He would stop at nothing to sap the energy of the British positions in the strategically important Near East. They were close to the southern frontier of the Soviet Union, an area rich in oil. Stalin hoped that the leaders of Palestine and a leftist-socialist government of Israel would support Soviet attempts out of gratitude, particularly since communists, left-wing socialists, and other groups there traditionally sympathized with Moscow. But these parties did not have much influence in policy-making decisions. In 1948, the Soviet-friendly party *Hashomer Hatsair* merged with the *Akhdut Haavodah* to form the *Mapam* party. During elections for the first parliament of Israel on January 25, 1949, the communists were able to gain 3.5 percent of the vote and four seats, while the *Mapam* gathered only 14.7 percent and won 19 of 120 seats. The *Mapam* was not involved in the formation of the first government either.

To improve the Soviet Union's image among Jews, above all in the U.S., Radio Moscow doubled the number of Yiddish broadcasts in 1947. The main issue was anti-Semitism in the western countries, which was the real cause behind a yearning for Palestine among the Jews. The radio station argued that the founding of a Jewish state would also solve the problem of Displaced Persons living in camps in Western Europe. These included many Jews from Eastern Europe, who fled virulent anti-Semitism in countries like Poland, as well as the communist dictatorships.[19] In May 1947, Andrei Gromyko, ambassador to the United Nations, had already supported a motion that the Jewish Agency take part in the UN special session on Palestine. That same month, he made his first speech about the Palestine issue, addressing the great suffering of the Jews under the Nazis. The struggle of the Jews for their own state was understandable, because the Western European states had not protected the "Jewish people" (which did not exist, according to internal Soviet ideology!). It was clear that this state did not have to exist for Soviet Jews, because, according to official accounts, their government protected them from the Nazis. Out of consideration for Arab interests, Gromyko pleaded for the partition of Palestine.

In his historic "Zionist" speech of November 26, 1947, at the UN in New York, Gromyko finally laid out principles for the formation of the state of Israel. Along with the Balfour declaration of 1917, when Britain declared solidarity with the Zionists' national claims, Gromyko's speech became the decisive statement for the international recognition of a Jewish state in Palestine. Ben Gurion himself could not have argued better for the formation of Israel. Here an abridged text of his speech:

> The USSR has, as everyone knows, no direct material or other interest in Palestine; it is interested in the Palestine question only because it is a member of the UN and because it represents a world power, which, like every other world power, has taken responsibility for the preservation of international peace.
>
> When the question of the future of Palestine was discussed at the special session of the general assembly, the government of the USSR pointed to the two most acceptable solutions of this question. One was the formation of one single Arab-Jewish state, in which Arabs and Jews would enjoy the same rights. In the event such a solution turned out to be unworkable because of worsening Arab-Jewish relations, the government of the USSR had indicated a second solution, namely the partition of Palestine into two separate, independent, democratic states—one Arab and one Jewish.
>
> Opponents of dividing Palestine into two separate, independent, democratic states normally point to the fact that such a decision is directed against the Arabs, against the Arab population of Palestine, and against the Arab states in general. Arab countries, for immediately obvious reasons, particularly emphasize this point of view. But the USSR delegation cannot agree with such a position. Neither the suggestion to divide Palestine into two separate, independent states, nor the decision of the "ad hoc" committee, which was formed at that session and which approved the suggestion now under discussion, is directed against the Arabs. This decision is not directed against any of the national groups living in Palestine. The USSR delegation takes the view that, on the contrary, this decision corresponds with the fundamental interests of both nations, i.e., with the interests of the Arabs as well as with those of the Jews.
>
> Representatives of the Arab state claim that the partition of Palestine is an historical injustice. But this point of view is unacceptable, even if only because the Jewish nation was very much tied to Palestine for a considerable period of time. Aside from this, we mustn't turn a blind eye to this position—and the USSR delegation pointed to this for the first time at the general assembly; we also mustn't turn a blind eye to the position in which the Jewish nation was placed as a result of the last world war. I won't repeat what the

USSR delegation said on this point at the special session of the general assembly. But it is important, my listeners, to remember once again that Jews have suffered more than any other nation as a result of a war brought on by Hitler's Germany. You know that there was no country in Western Europe that succeeded in protecting the Jewish nation from the arbitrary acts and violent measures of the Nazis.

The solution to the Palestine problem, based on a partition of Palestine into two separate states, will be of fundamental historical importance, because such a decision takes into account the legitimate rights of the Jewish nation. As you know, hundreds of thousands of Jews are still without a country, without a home, or have found accommodation for a short time in special camps in some countries in Western Europe.

The assembly makes a great effort to find the fairest, most practicable, most feasible and at the same time most radical solution to the Palestine problem.

Before these discussions began, a whole string of delegations, primarily the delegations of the Arab states, tried to convince us that this question exceeds the competence of the United Nations. As expected, they weren't able to come up with convincing arguments, only general and unsubstantiated statements and declarations.

The general assembly, as well as the entire United Nations, not only has the right to review this matter, but they have the duty, in light of the situation in Palestine, to make the necessary decision. From the perspective of the USSR delegation, the intention—as it was described by the "ad hoc" committee, as well as the necessary measures of the Security Council for a practicable realization—is in absolute agreement with the interest of keeping and enforcing international peace, and the interest leading to increased cooperation between states. Unlike most other delegations, that of the USSR was from the beginning of a clear, determined, and unambiguous opinion in this matter. The delegation does not have the intention of having an effect on or manipulating the vote, as is unfortunately attempted in the assembly, particularly in connection with the Palestine question. For these reasons, the USSR delegation supports the recommendation to divide Palestine.

Gromyko voted with all delegates from the Soviet bloc for the partition of Palestine. Even behind the scenes, Soviet UN representatives spoke in favor of the partition plan.

In addition, Stalin gave the Czechoslovak government the assignment of breaking the Western embargo against the newborn state of Israel and delivering arms, ammunition, and military equipment. Between May and September of 1948, Jewish pilots and paratroopers were trained in Czechoslovakia. A Czech brigade of Jewish volunteers took part in the fighting from December 1948 until the end of the war of independence in 1949.[20]

Holocaust survivors from Eastern Europe, immigrating illegally into Palestine via the DP camps, and the supply of arms enabled the new state to withstand the assault of five Arab armies.

## Israel Enthusiasm Among the Soviet Jews

On May 15, 1948, the state of Israel was proclaimed. On the same day, countless Jewish Soviet citizens wrote letters to the JAFC and to the editors of *Eynikeyt*, their only "Jewish" addresses, and many called and visited the office of the JAFC. Many had the intention to volunteer for the war of independence. The supreme attendant of the Lubyanka in the committee, Grigori Kheifets, registered names, addresses and occupations of these visitors and handed them over to the "organs" for future use. Shits, the editor in chief of *Eynikeyt*, asked the propaganda department if he should print pro-Israeli letters and statements. Later on, he denounced the senders to Stalin's crown prince, Malenkov.[21] One must indeed be a cruel Machiavellian to understand that the Soviet Union's public statements, particularly Gromyko's heartrending argument in favor of the Jews at the UN, were day-to-day political maneuvers.

The Soviet Union was the second state to recognize Israel diplomatically, after Czechoslovakia. Ilya Ehrenburg sent its citizens a message entitled: "The Soviet nation is with you." Generals, students and factory workers sent individual and collective letters and declarations.

On June 8, 1948, JAFC members Fefer, Shimeliovich, and Sheinin applied for a radio meeting on the events in Palestine to Suslov, where Anglo-American imperialism and its Arab accomplices were to be attacked. The broadcast was to make the USSR's position in the UN clear again to the "democratic" and "progressive" forces of the world, and to mobilize the Jewish masses of the world for the fight against reactionary forces and unmask the warmongers. Fefer, Zaslavsky, Bergelson, Ehrenburg, Shimeliovich, Kvitko, the Jewish war hero Polina Gelman, a

Jewish "Stakhanovite worker," as well as the Academy members Volgin and Tarle and the (non-Jewish) author Konstantin Simonov were recommended to be the speakers for the two-hour broadcast. The event, planned for June 15, was not allowed—the concept sounded too much like a sympathy rally for Israel.[22]

When the first ambassador from Israel, Golda Meir, arrived in Moscow at the beginning of September 1948, Soviet Jews' euphoria for Israel reached its climax. Golda Meir was born fifty years before, the daughter of a carpenter named Mabovich who lived in Kiev. Thousands accompanied her when she went from the Hotel Metropol to the Sabbath service in the Moscow synagogue on September 11. The same thing happened on September 16, when she went to the Yiddish theater. The apparatchiks watched in astonishment this un-Soviet activity, this tribute to a foreign diplomat.

### Ehrenburg and the Anti-Zionist About-Face

The regime had to notice that more than three decades of communist agitation were not enough to erase Jewish sympathy for Zionism. An explosive situation arose, which made the regime look foolish and threatened the existence of the Soviet Jews. Ehrenburg had orders from above to put out the fire. He wrote an article that filled an entire page of the September 21, 1948 issue of *Pravda*. The article, in the form of an open letter, was designed to answer a fabricated letter by a German Jew named Alexander R., who allegedly fought in the French resistance after his flight from Germany and returned after the war, the only survivor of his family, to study medicine in Munich. Anti-Semitic students at the university had verbally accosted him: Get out—Go to Palestine.

The letter writer admitted to never having been a Zionist, but to getting used to the idea of a Jewish state. He asked Ehrenburg, the famous author, in whom he always believed, to answer how a repetition of the Nazi crimes could be prevented. At the JAFC trial, Markish revealed, referring to an indiscretion by Fefer, "that nobody sent the letter to Ehrenburg; this was a political step."[23]

Ehrenburg's answer is a stylistic masterpiece of cleverly formulated casuistry. First, he reminded the reader that the Soviet Union was the first member of the UN to recognize the state of Israel. Alexander R. could possibly overcome his personal dilemma in Israel, but this state couldn't solve the problems of the Jews who were oppressed in many countries by the capitalists, or through lies and superstition because these problems do not depend on military victories in Palestine, but on the triumph of socialism over capitalism, on the victory of the working class over nationalism, fascism, and racism. This happened in the Soviet Union, where Jews lived in freedom and equality, regardless of whether they spoke Yiddish or Russian. Ehrenburg attacked Jewish nationalists and mystics, calling them the real authors of the Zionist program. At the same time, he stirred up strong sympathy for the Jews and contradicted the "dark men": strictly speaking, there is no worldwide association of Jews, only the solidarity of the oppressed victims of anti-Semitism.

> A Tunisian Jew and a Jew who lives in Chicago, who speaks English and thinks like an American, hardly have anything in common. If there are ties, however, they are definitely not mystical. On the contrary, anti-Semitism forges them. The unprecedented cruelties of the German fascists, the genocide of the Jewish population announced and realized in many countries, the racist propaganda, first the insults, then the ovens of Maidanek—all stirred in the Jews of extremely different countries the sense of fervent solidarity. It is the solidarity of the degraded and the insulted.[24]

According to his daughter, Ehrenburg expressed his real convictions[25] in this text. Certainly he declared that there was no anti-Semitism in the Soviet Union and as a result there was no reason for the Jews to leave the country, but in the quoted passage he expressed thoughts that were still forbidden to him in the *Black Book*. According to Fefer's testimony at the trial, Ehrenburg had even made it a condition to be allowed to condemn anti-Semitism in an article on the occasion of the arrival of Golda Meir.[26]

There is little doubt that Stalin edited, or at least approved, the printed version in *Pravda*. This article was an unmistakable warning shot, but the pro-Israeli euphoria continued. Golda Meir walked again to the Moscow synagogue on October 4, 1948, on the Jewish New Year's Day. This time between 15 and 20 thousand enthusiastic Jews walked there and back along with her.[27] All those who stood up for Israel, be it by their presence, their letters, phone calls, or in any other way were prosecuted.

The committee dealt with Israel in detail only at its last presidium session on October 21, 1948. Shits reported on articles that appeared in *Eynikeyt* on the occasion of the formation of Israel. Readers reacted coolly;

hardly any letters concerning this subject were received. Texts emphasized that the Soviet Union supported the formation of the state against the opposition of the U.S. and Great Britain, but Israel was not a socialist state and the masses had first to fight against imperialist forces and for the real democracy. The newspaper presented the population of Palestine, not Zionism and its leaders, in a positive light. To counteract sympathy among Soviet Jews for the state of Israel, more was written about Birobidzan and Soviet nationality policy and Soviet patriotism. "Each Soviet Jew answers the question, 'What has Soviet power given the Jewish nation?' with pride: 'The homeland.'" To continue working in this direction, articles about the "fight of Lenin and Stalin against nationalism and national separation" were written. When Bregman declared that the question of Israel's statehood would not be central for the committee, Fefer objected: "That's the least of all our concerns." He stressed that the work had been much harder before the formation of Israel, when one was inundated with questions. One had to continue to provide information about Israel's real character; a pamphlet should be written about it.[28] These intentions to make the committee an obedient tool of Stalin in dealing with Israel failed—the JAFC was staring disaster right in the face.

## 24. BARRAGE OF THE EXPERTS—THE JAFC IN THE INVESTIGATORS' SIGHTS

Changes in Soviet Middle East policy strengthened the "identity crisis" at the JAFC. Right after the end of the Second World War, there were serious differences of opinion about other goals and the scope of the committee's activity within Soviet Judaism. Conflict existed between advocates, like Lozovsky, who wanted to maintain absolute loyalty to Stalin and Mikhoels and others, who wanted to look after the interests of Jews even after the war. Mikhoels and his group didn't want to think of themselves simply as Stalin's propagandists—needed only during the war. In the territories liberated by the army, many survivors of the Shoah had to fear the collaborators who occupied their apartments during the war. Anyone in the JAFC who helped those uprooted with the procurement of accommodations, work, and with the search for relatives, also abroad, was strongly criticized and hindered by the organization's government-loyal members.

## Isolating the JAFC

In early 1945, Solomon Spiegelglas, who played no role in Jewish affairs, succeeded Shakhne, the Lubyanka agent and general secretary. When Epstein died in 1945, Grigori Kheifets, former secretary of Lenin's widow Nadezhda Krupskaya and a high-ranking agent of the NKVD in the U.S., was chosen to effectively head the JAFC. Without his signature, no document could leave the JAFC office. He remained in his position until the organization was shut down.

At the Zionist Congress in December 1946 in Basel, at which many left-wing socialist Zionists took part, a world conference was discussed with the participation of the JAFC. Numerous Jewish anti-fascist committees working in the U.S., England, Mexico, and above all, Palestine, wanted to continue operating even after the war by founding an international Jewish progressive (i.e., left-wing), pro-Soviet movement. The applications by Mikhoels and Fefer to the Central Committee to be allowed to visit appropriate assemblies in Europe or the United States were always denied.

The World Jewish Congress (WJC) also tried to include Soviet Jews in the reconstruction of the destroyed Jewish communities in Europe. Although delegates from Jewish organizations in communist countries took part in the WJC conference in April 1947 in Prague, the JAFC was prohibited from participating. Instead, more and more articles came out in *Eynikeyt*, attacking the WJC for its neutralism. The WJC was still attacked internally by Kheifets as an anti-Soviet "espionage organization."[29]

## Monopoly for Russian Nationalism

Toward the end of the war, the nationalist content in propaganda had been reduced a bit. But Russian-Slavic patriotism lived on after victory day, while the other "nationalisms," which had been promoted because of the war since 1941, were suddenly "forgotten" and, to help them into oblivion, eliminated. By 1946, at the latest, when the Iron Curtain closed down and the opinion of the Western world no longer mattered, Stalin was able to continue the Russification of the Soviet Union that had begun before the war. Many nationalities and their cultural institutions found out what it was like, but the Jews were the most affected because now official anti-Semitism from above, in addition to the latent one from below, could take its course.

The strongest Russian-nationalist announcement came from Stalin, who proposed the following toast on the occasion of the victory celebration:

> I'd like to propose a toast to the health of our Soviet nation and above all to the Russian nation (stormy, continuous applause, cries of "hooray"). I drink above all to the health of the Russian nation, because it's the most outstanding nation among all of the nations belonging to the Soviet Union. I propose a toast to the health of the Russian nation, because it deserves public credit in this war as the leading power of the Soviet Union among all nations of our country. I propose a toast to the health of the Russian nation, not only because it's the leading nation, but also because it has a clear head, steady character, and patience, too.[30]

If one were to replace the word "Russian" in this text by "Jewish," one would have a manifest of "Jewish nationalism" which brought everyone who spread it, as well as the JAFC leadership in 1952, before the guns of an execution squad. But double standards were applied. Russian chauvinism continued to be allowed; the national consciousness of other nations was forbidden. Even anti-fascist, anti-German comments were forbidden, mainly for foreign policy reasons.

On April 14, 1945, three weeks before the end of the war, Georgi Aleksandrov attacked Ilya Ehrenburg in *Pravda* for his animosity toward Germany. Ehrenburg—the recipient of the Lenin and Stalin awards, the most famous Soviet war correspondent, called a "marshal of our literature" by soldiers, author of more than 2,000 reports from the front, which came out in 1944 as a three-volume edition in Moscow—was addressed in this article simply as "Comrade Ehrenburg" and accused of not having differentiated between the Nazis and the German people.[31] Ehrenburg, who had offered four years of his life in continuous service to the victory over Nazi Germany, was not allowed to attend the German surrender in Berlin.

In October 1945, Aleksandrov proposed that the *Sovinformburo* be disbanded. He didn't neglect to express his criticism by decorating the employees of the office with a list of Jewish authors. But Stalin rejected the proposal.[32] On June 21, 1946, Mikhoels and Fefer provided Suslov, the aspiring party ideologist, with a detailed history of the committee's work and personnel. The committee leadership also corresponded with Beria, Molotov, and Malenkov—always in an apologetic and defensive tone.

Before the court, Fefer explained how he and Mikhoels were called to the CC. They were asked if they considered closing down the anti-fascist committee effective. Mikhoels felt that it was too early, since fascism had not disappeared and still had to be fought. Subsequently, a five-man CC commission had the complete JAFC archives removed on a truck. After examining those archives for almost three months the JAFC was informed that the disbanding of the committee would be delayed. At the end of 1946, the archives were confiscated a second time and returned in February 1947. The committee was told to continue working as it had in the past.

After additional examination, the CC commission concluded in July 1946 that the JAFC had an "inadmissible conception of Jews." On October 12, 1946, the MGB (Ministry of State Security)—the new name for all institutions that had been part of the "NKVD" until 1945—prepared material about the "nationalist indications among some officials of the Jewish Anti-Fascist Committee" for the CC cabinet. In August 1946 the JAFC was transferred out of the *Sovinformburo* and placed under the direct command of the CC Foreign Policy Division. During this period more and more Jews were informally dismissed from the *Sovinformburo*.

## The Inquisitors Begin Their Work

Suslov always guarded the purity of party doctrine and gradually became the chief ideologist, a role he didn't lose until the late Brezhnev era. On November 19, 1946, he sent an extensive memorandum of denunciation about the JAFC to Stalin, Molotov, Beria, Malenkov, Mikoyan, Voznesensky, Andreyev, Voroshilov, Kaganovich, Bulganin, Shvernik, Zhdanov, Kuznetsov, Patolichev, Popov, and Kosygin—the entire Soviet leadership. In this memorandum he stated that the JAFC's tendency to praise the role of Jews in world history and the Soviet Union was petty bourgeois, nationalist, and a Zionist exaggeration. Referring to Lenin's and Stalin's approach to the "Jewish question," he accused the committee of taking a "position of bourgeois Jewish Zionism and Bundism." National-Jewish positions were welcomed during the war; they were used to spur Soviet and Western Jews to greater feats for the Soviet Union. Now these views were labeled nationalistic, a chauvinistic Jewish deviation, although the very different positions of the Bund, Zionism, and "bourgeois" Jews were all being lumped together.

On January 7, 1947, Aleksandrov and Suslov issued a report addressed to Molotov and Kuznetsov, proposing that the JAFC be closed because it had done its job. They felt that the committee had taken on a "nationalist and Zionist" character, was overly instigating Soviet Jews against their state, and had joined with foreign bourgeois-reactionary Jewish circles. The draft of the resolution, to be signed by Mikhoels, mentioned only that the committee was no longer necessary and thanked its members.[33]

In an expert's opinion of April 1947, Aleksandrov praised the texts of the Jewish wartime authors as "optimistic and patriotic." He reacted with it to a reproach from Shcherbakov in October 1946, who had criticized that "nationalistic and mystic-religious" moods were expressed in the texts of Soviet Yiddish authors between 1941 and 1945. Of course, Aleksandrov didn't want to protect the JAFC members, but only to defend himself—after all, it was he who was responsible for the ideological observation of the committee, and retroactive accusations would be self-incriminating. After a new commission became busy with the *Sovinformburo*, Lozovsky was dismissed as leader on June 25, 1947, and a few days later the entire archives of the JAFC were again confiscated. The examination concluded that the JAFC had changed in fact to a Commissariat for Jewish Affairs (*Komissariat po Evreiskim delam*) and showed sympathies for Zionist ideas.[34]

The next blow, though not yet a lethal blow, occurred a few weeks later. Baranov and Grigoryan, two high CC officials, recommended in a report commissioned by Zhdanov and dated July 19, 1947, that the assignments of the committee be modified. The committee was credited for promoting "friendship between nations" in the Soviet Union in its earliest articles meant for publication abroad. This could only mean that it was benevolently recognized that these articles spoke less of the Jews and more positively about Russians. However, the committee did not use foreign relations for the procurement of useful scientific, technical, and political information. The quality of *Eynikeyt* was criticized as well. Above all, the JAFC should no longer act as a representative of the Soviet Jews. The most important assignments after re-orientation were the fight against Zionism, the propagation of the Soviet system and the extraction of information from abroad. *Eynikeyt* would be published monthly and current contributors would be partially replaced by qualified, politically reliable journalists.[35]

A final proposal to "heal" the JAFC and change it into an organ that would influence the "democratic" (i.e. pro-Soviet) Jews of the world, was submitted in April 1948 by the foreign policy department of the CC. An opinion, written again by Baranov, recommended that the presidium be reformed. Fefer, Frumkin, Halkin, Stein, Bregman, Briker, Bergelson, Sheinin, Shits, Yuzefovich, and Kvitko should be removed; Kreizer, Gubelman, Shimeliovich, Zuskin, Markish, Gonor, and Khaifets, on the other hand, should retain their positions. Marshak, Kreizer, Iofan, or Zbarsky should take over the chairmanship. New members should be appointed; these would include the famous artists David Oistrakh, Emil Gilels, I. Dunayevsky, and the prima ballerina Maya Plisetskaya, as well as General Dragunsky, twice decorated "Hero of the Soviet Union."

## State Security Pronounces the Death Sentence of the JAFC

On March 26, 1948, a 15-page report was sent to Stalin, Molotov, Zhdanov, and Kuznetsov from a person in a high position of power, minister of security Abakumov. His conclusions were blunt:

> The Ministry of State Security determined by methods used by the Bolshevik secret police that the leaders of the Jewish Anti-Fascist Committee are active nationalists who have fallen in with the Americans and carry out essentially anti-Soviet nationalistic work. A particularly conspicuous American influence in the committee's work began to show itself after Mikhoels and Fefer had journeyed to the United States. The committee's two leaders made contact with important Jewish activists, some of whom were connected with the American secret service. The former chairman of the committee, S. M. Mikhoels, was known as an active nationalist long before the war and to a certain extent was the showpiece of nationalistically leaning circles. He brought kindred spirits from the ranks of Jewish nationalist leaders into the committee.

Abakumov mentioned the leaders and their followers: Fefer, Markish, Bergelson, Kvitko, Dobrushin, Stern, Yuzefovich, Halkin, Shimeliovich, Zuskin, and Frumkin, the JAFC members who were later accused and executed. This group had used the committee as a cover for its "anti-Soviet activities." In the Ukraine and Belorussia, state security organs had unmasked similar "groups," misused by the JAFC to contact foreign Jewish nationalists. In this light, the trip to the U.S. by Mikhoels and Fefer furthered these hostile objectives. The people they had spoken with were all declared to be enemies of the Soviet state. Stephen Wise, Chaim Weizman, James Rosenberg, Nahum Goldmann, Archibald Silverman, Fritz Hollaender, and Selig Brodetsky, all of whom had supported the Soviet Union with material and propaganda during the war, were now accused of having ties with Trotsky or the American or British secret service. Mikhoels and Fefer had told all these enemies about the discrimination of the Jews in the Soviet Union. In 1944, under the direction of Mikhoels and Fefer, the JAFC began dealing with the Crimea question. Lozovsky took part in the meetings and had also helped draft the letter. The letter mentioned increasing (according to Abakumov, "alleged") anti-Semitism after 1944 and was viewed as further evidence of the committee's hostile actions. In reports for abroad, the committee had only written about Jews and had not opposed anti-Soviet propaganda. The visits of benevolent guests of the U.S. (Goldberg and Novick) were declared to be spies, and an American journalist, Robert Magidoff, was "unmasked" as an important contact. Abakumov's memorandum ends with the claim: "The ministry for state security has unmasked a number of American or British spies among recently arrested Jewish nationalists. These persons are enemies of the Soviet Union and were active subversively."

The absurd accusation of espionage demonstrates that after the war mere "contact" with Western countries was interpreted by Soviet ideologists as dangerous. The fight against fascism had to be followed by a consolidation of the Soviet sphere of influence, and this could only define itself as a counterbalance to America and Western Europe. Not only was the work of the JAFC no longer convenient to this new political and ideological policy, but the committee had to be re-judged based upon these premises. The national claims of the Jews were subordinated to the Palestine policy and its foreign-policy interests. With victory over Germany, the anti-fascist merits of the committee were a thing of the past. All that remained were contacts between Jewish anti-fascists from different countries and they were unable, or did not like, to separate national claims, anti-fascist resistance and socialistic convictions the way Soviet authorities wanted. The JAFC was undermined and presented as an agency serving the interests of the Jews, whereas the letters received by the committee since 1943 had again served as proof. MGB collaborators, raised in the spirit of Stalinism, could probably only imagine the letter writing or other reactions of the population as measures organized "from above."

Abakumov's memorandum contained no recommendation for further steps but it did anticipate the trial and even the judgment against the members of the JAFC in 1952. The highest leadership of the Soviet Union wasted a great deal of time and effort pursuing some harmless poets, authors, and scientists, even though they bravely fulfilled their duty to their Soviet homeland. Thousands of less prominent Jews— labeled "spies" or "nationalists"—were pursued, incarcerated and executed without trial.

## The End of the JAFC

The 25-page transcript of the session of the presidium of the JAFC on October 21, 1948, one month before its liquidation, is a highly informative and shocking document. The participants of the session were:

— Grigori Khaifets, secretary of the JAFC, condemned in 1952 to 25 years in the Gulag and released after Stalin's death;

— Grigori Shits, editor in chief of the *Eynikeyt*, arrested in 1949, died in prison in October 1954;

— Aron Katz, general of armored divisions in the general staff, died in 1971 in Moscow;

— Lev Alexandrovich Sheinin (not to be confused with the author and investigator Lev Romanovich Sheinin), high-ranking state official whose titles include principal of the technical academies, condemned in 1949 to ten years' imprisonment;

— Moisei Gubelman, long-standing party official, died in 1968 in Moscow;

— Abraham Gontar, Yiddish poet, survived imprisonment and died in 1981;

— Solomon Khaikin and Slepak, Yiddish journalists, survived their persecution;

— Aleksandr Belenky, historian and essayist, survived his persecution and died in Moscow in 1991;

— Aron Vergelis, editor of *Sovietish Heymland*, later founder of the Jewish Anti-Zionist Committee of the Soviet Union, was never pursued and lives in Moscow;

— Fefer, Kvitko, and Bergelson were executed, and Bregman died in prison.

No biographical particulars are known about Yeserskaya, Sislin, and Novik, who also participated.

After Slepak's report about Israel's development and the ensuing debate, committee participants decided to strengthen their stance against Zionism. Near the end, Fefer filed an application asking to be released from the committee. For three years he had wanted to return to literary work. Fefer's colleagues, perhaps suspecting that he just wanted to wiggle out of the slowly tightening noose, did not accept it.[36]

In spite of Abakumov's devastating memorandum, the committee remained virtually undisturbed for almost six months. I suspect this can only be explained by the Soviet Union's policy toward Israel, which suddenly shifted in the fall of 1948. Then the committee's deathblow came with the sullen abruptness of an administrative stroke of the pen. This last document regarding the JAFC is simultaneously the shortest and the most important. Labeled "Top Secret," it is an extract of protocol No. 66 from the CC Politburo session of November 20, submitted to Comrades Malenkov, Abakumov, and Smirtyukov. Point 81 commented on the JAFC:

> The cabinet of the USSR instructs the ministry for state security to immediately liquidate the JAFC, because the committee, as facts prove, is a center of anti-Soviet propaganda and regularly supplies foreign secret services with anti-Soviet information. Combined with that, the press organs of the committee are to be closed and the files of the committee to be confiscated. For the moment, no one should be arrested.[37]

### 25. THE ATTEMPT TO DECAPITATE
### SOVIET JUDAISM—THE MURDER OF SOLOMON MIKHOELS

The deadly logic of Stalinism deduced that anyone with a dissenting opinion was a criminal. This logic was evident in Abakumov's report of March 1948. It changed the initially purely ideological accusations by Suslov and Aleksandrov against the JAFC into "espionage" and similar political crimes. The opinions of Aleksandrov, Baranov, and Grigoryan show how ideological criticism turned the JAFC's deliverance of too much material about Jews to foreign countries into accusations that the committee had spied against the Soviet Union. The material from which Abakumov derived these absurd accusations was "produced" during investigations of individuals surrounding Mikhoels and mixed in with the ideological expert's opinions. What was originally meant to compromise some persons not even connected to the JAFC and Mikhoels, developed over time into a thick file of supposed "crimes" committed by the JAFC. Eleven months before these "crimes" were used to liquidate the JAFC, the state murdered Solomon Mikhoels in cold blood.

## Mikhoels as the Target

In 1940 investigators linked Mikhoels to Babel and a writers' conspiracy. From that moment on, the famous actor expected—as his daughters reported to journalist Louis Rapoport—to share Babel's fate.[38] In 1941 he triumphed with the JAFC and after the war he remained the unofficial representative of the Soviet Jews. In the history of the Soviet Union, no other Jewish personality was as popular, deserving and charismatic. This was also because of his independence—Mikhoels was an artist who refused to be used as a henchman for socialist realism. Legends circulated about him; some thought he was a kind of personal court actor for Stalin. This particular belief was the basis for Gastone Salvatore's play *Stalin*, produced in the 1980s, in which the dictator and Mikhoels engage in dialogue; all this, of course, has no historical basis because the two never met.[39]

After the war, Mikhoels produced some important plays, including *The Uprising in the Ghetto* by Markish and *The Forests Hum* by Brat and Lynkov. Bergelson's *Prince Reubeni* was rehearsed but no longer performed. Mikhoels' most brilliant production was *Something Happy* (*Freylekhs*); the production featured music and dance, a Jewish wedding and traditional jokes. Thousands, including many non-Jews, saw it and every performance was always sold out, showing the vitality of the Jewish people in spite of all the attempts at extermination. In 1946, the main characters—Mikhoels, Zuskin, Tishler, and others—were presented with the Stalin award. This was a masterly disguise of the Kremlin's already planned anti-Semitic activities. While Mikhoels was being officially celebrated, Zhdanov and Suslov, the party's chief ideologists, searched for reasons to liquidate his committee, which was no longer required for war propaganda. Mikhoels had urged that the committee be allowed to survive. In several letters he had referred to its merits, including the purpose it served during the war.[40]

In November 1947 the Soviet Union voted for the partition of Palestine. Stalin knew from informers in the Lubyanka how enthusiastic Soviet Jews were about the formation of a Jewish state. On the 30th anniversary of the death of the great Yiddish poet Mendele Mojcher Sforim, Mikhoels was met with frenetic applause when he pointed to Eretz Israel as a goal of Jews and in doing this he referred to Gromyko.[41] This development made it absolutely necessary that he be stopped. An official persecution of Mikhoels was not expedient because it had become clear that the engagement of the Soviet Union for the Jewish state in Palestine was only meant to weaken the British position in the Middle East. Stalin could not count on a 1930s-style show trial either, because Mikhoels was not like Zinoviev or Radek who, due to party discipline, had memorized the most absurd self-accusations. Stalin also dreaded that his own family affairs would become subject to investigation if Mikhoels went on trial.

## Stalin's Terror Against His Own Family

The first victims of Stalin's war against the Soviet Jews after 1945 were, strangely enough, not Jews but Stalin's non-Jewish family members—namely most of the relatives of his second and last wife, Nadezhda Alliluyeva, for whose death Stalin was at least indirectly responsible.[42] Nadezhda Alliluyeva, Svetlana Stalin's mother, supposedly committed suicide in 1932 at the age of 31. For years her family was persecuted and some of her relatives were murdered. Early in December 1947, American newspapers published details of Stalin's private life. He wanted to punish the informers, whom he assumed were the Alliluyevs and had several members of the family arrested and brutally interrogated. During her interrogation, Yevgenia Alliluyeva, the wife of Nadezhda Alliluyeva's brother Pavel, who had been arrested for "defamation of the head of the government," mentioned that Isaak Goldstein, a member of the Academy of Sciences and a family friend, was interested in Svetlana. Goldstein was arrested on December 19, 1947, and state security started to thread together the events at the JAFC with the Alliluyev affair. This was the secret police recipe. Something true was mixed in with something revealed under torture and something invented. When he fell from power after Stalin's death, Ryumin, who was to investigate the JAFC and the "doctor's plot," explained the mentality of the MGB officials and their chief, Abakumov, at the time of Goldstein's arrest:

By the end of 1947, in investigations of especially important matters, a new tendency was introduced. Starting with Abakumov and implemented by Leonov, Likhachev, and Komarov, the attitude was to look upon people of Jewish nationality as potential enemies of the Soviet state. This view led to the unfounded arrest of Jews who were accused of anti-Soviet activity and espionage for America.[43]

In 1946 Mikhoels found out that Isaak Goldstein, a well-known economist, was a close friend of the Alliluyev family. Nadezhda Alliluyeva had been his colleague and had worked with him at the official Soviet trade delegation in Berlin since 1929. Goldstein was well acquainted with other Alliluyevs and Svetlana Stalin and her Jewish husband, Grigori Morozov. It appears that Mikhoels requested that Goldstein speak to the Morozovs. He had naïvely and uselessly hoped that Svetlana could persuade her father to be friendlier toward the Jews. Under interrogation Goldstein confessed that in January 1948 Mikhoels had asked him to speak to Morozov who would speak to Svetlana[44] and she in turn would appeal to her father.

Morozov was already Svetlana's second "Jewish" love. In 1942 Stalin ended her short romance with Aleksei Kapler, the Jewish film writer, by sending Kapler to the Gulag because of his alleged espionage for England.[45] Svetlana later recalled that her father told her, "He can't even write decently in Russian! You could at least have chosen a Russian." She suspected that Stalin was mostly angry about Kapler being a Jew.[46] Svetlana married Grigori Morozov, a Jewish student, in 1944, also against her father's wishes. She had to leave the Kremlin. Stalin never met Morozov. He had chosen Andrei Zhdanov to be his son-in-law. Svetlana married him after Stalin forced her to separate from Morozov in 1947. In her letters she remembers the following conversation with her father, a dialogue shedding better light than many of the newly released documents on what Mikhoels and other members of the JAFC were experiencing:

"The Zionists foisted your wretched first husband on you as well," said Father a while later to me. "Papa, the youth are indifferent to everything; what should they want with Zionism?" I tried to object. "You don't understand this," he answered gruffly. "Zionism has infected the whole older generation, and it's handing it over to the youth as well."[47]

Stalin knew that a percentage of Jews—those Soviet citizens who had been too caught up in anti-Semitic prejudices, which became especially pronounced during the last year of the war—would not be infected with "Zionism." Stalin could only have meant that his immediate environment was being depraved by "Zionism." He suspected that top Jewish politicians like Kaganovich or Mekhlis, still surrounding him, as well as the Jewish wives of his Politburo comrades, had "nationalist" tendencies. If anyone around him made contact with a "representative" of the Soviet Jews, like Mikhoels, who had been in the now hostile America for several months, Stalin's paranoia had to interpret these actions as conspiratorial invasions of his personal privacy. They were part of a conspiracy directed against him and a capital crime. The question of real espionage was unimportant; the key factor was that there was a weak spot that could only be removed by the liquidation of the "traitors."

## The Anti-Semitic Interrogations Begin

Goldstein confessed that Mikhoel's interest in Morozov was based on a huge spy conspiracy that also involved the JAFC. Komarov conceded later that the "interrogation" methods were extremely primitive:

After interrogating Goldstein, Abakumov declared that:

> Goldstein's interest in Stalin and the Soviet government was based on providing information to a foreign secret service. We had no proof, but we continued to interrogate Goldstein on this basis. At first, he did not give any credence to these accusations, but after Abakumov had him beaten, Goldstein began to talk. Abakumov made no comment regarding Goldstein's testimony, saying only that he couldn't withhold Goldstein's statement and that he was obliged to inform the higher authorities.[48]

So Goldstein "confessed" what the investigators wanted to hear and signed a statement that included a note stating that his friend, Zorakh Grinberg, a researcher at the Institute for World Literature and a member of the JAFC's historical committee, told him that the JAFC pursued anti-Soviet, nationalist propaganda and maintained close relations with bourgeois and Zionist circles in America. It also stated that the JAFC wanted to form a Jewish republic and wanted to use Svetlana Morozov to influence Stalin. Goldstein's testimony, obtained under torture, resulted in the arrest, imprisonment and torture of the JAFC leadership. Goldstein was sentenced to 25 years in the Gulag on October 29, 1949. He was convicted without trial of being a dangerous spy and died in prison in October 1953.

On December 28, 1947, Abakumov arrested Zorakh Grinberg to have him confirm these senseless accusations. The torturers promised to release him if he did, but he died on December 22, 1949. When members of the JAFC were tried, the judge from Grinberg's "testimony" stated, "In the pursuit of this goal (nationalist activities), Mikhoels gathered kindred spirits in the Jewish Anti-Fascist Committee." In 1942 Grinberg felt "that this committee represents an organization that is hostile toward the Soviet Union."[49]

Lydia Shatunovskaya's recollections provide information about the methods used to obtain this testimony. She was of Jewish origin, an actress and a drama theorist and because of close relations with an old Bolshevik family Shatunovskaya lived in the Kremlin before the Second World War. Since she knew the Alliluyevs as well as Mikhoels, she was arrested and labeled as an additional "contact person" for the supposed anti-Stalinist Zionist conspiracy. Her interrogator was the compulsively anti-Semitic Komarov, who "taught" her on "quiet" nights when "he felt the need to open up and speak" about the relationship between the Communist Party and the Jews. Shatunovskaya witnessed such undisguised Soviet anti-Semitism for the first time. After ranting about the Yiddish press, which dared mention the heroic deeds of Jewish soldiers during the war, Komarov declared: "The rumors going around during the war, that the Jews ran away from the front and hid in the deepest hinterland, or that, at best, they hung around at headquarters and directors' offices, that not only were they incompetent soldiers, they were profiteers—we circulated those rumors ourselves." When Shatunovskaya objected and said that these rumors were considered to be a relapse into tsarist anti-Semitism and a result of Nazi propaganda, Komarov replied: "And I still considered you to be an intelligent woman. That, however, was the policy of the party and the government. We will drive all Jews into prisons and camps. We'll destroy the whole so-called Jewish culture and we'll exterminate all you Zionists. All of you!" Komarov's behavior was meant to frighten and provoke the arrested, but finally he outlined the aims of the state leadership with great precision. Referring to Stalin he went so far as to benevolently mention the achievements of Jewish physicians in state service, but they were only needed in the absence of Russian personnel. The old Jewish scientists would die and young ones would not be employed, "and in this way we gradually remove Jews from Soviet science."[50]

## Killers on Behalf of the Government

In January 1948, Abakumov personally presented the transcripts of the Goldstein and Grinberg interrogations to Stalin. This was to lead directly to a death sentence for Mikhoels. Stalin instructed Abakumov and his delegate Ogoltsov to organize the murder. It is not surprising that no written instructions were found in the archives, but there is Stalin's daughter's testimony:

> At one of the now very rare meetings with Father at his dacha, I came into the room while he was on the telephone. I waited. Someone was reporting to him and he listened. Then he said, summarizing, "Well, a car accident." I remember the intonation exactly. He was not questioning, he was stating. He didn't ask, but proposed something—a car accident, to be precise. After he was finished, he welcomed me in and then, after a while, said: "Mikhoels died in a car accident."[51]

Mikhoels was invited to Minsk to examine plays for the Stalin award along with theater critic Golubov-Potapov. He stayed at the house of his friend, General Sergei Trofimenko. On January 12, after speaking with some actors, Mikhoels and Golubov ate in the hotel. That evening they received a phone call inviting them to a meeting. In fact, they were taken to Tsanava's dacha. Tsanava, the minister of Belorussian State Security, had them murdered. Then they were run over by a truck several times to fake a traffic accident. Finally, their bodies were placed on a quiet side street in Minsk. Golubov-Potapov was also murdered because he was a troublesome witness.

After Stalin's death, Abakumov confessed to the murder and described the details. His testimony was passed from Beria to Malenkov, both of whom were interested in fully incriminating Abakumov in order to whitewash themselves. Abakumov's testimony confirmed Svetlana's recollections:

Beria's former deputy stated that Stalin directly ordered him to quietly liquidate Mikhoels. It was a rush job. When Stalin knew that Mikhoels had arrived in Minsk, he ordered Ogoltsov, Tsanava, and Shubnayakov to cause a car accident. In addition to professional killers, leading politicians of the Soviet Union contributed to the murder of a loyal, meritorious actor. Ogoltsov specified—also after Stalin's death—at his interrogation that it had been decided to fake a car accident after the murder of the victims, in order not to endanger their own collaborators with a provoked "real" accident. After the liquidation, Stalin was delighted and ordered that the culprits receive awards.[52]

### State Funeral for the Victim of a State Murder

Mikhoels' remains were brought to Moscow by train. At the Belorussian train station thousands gathered to welcome the dead man. Professor Boris Zbarsky, who had already embalmed Lenin, was given the order to prepare Mikhoels for public viewing in his theater. In front of the theater people waited in the sharp cold, in rows stretching for miles, to say goodbye. Mikhoels' wife, Asya, his daughters Natalia (nineteen) and Nina (fifteen) stood by the casket, along with members of the theatre troupe.

On January 14, 1948, *Pravda* printed an in-depth obituary, which was signed by fifty-eight Soviet artists, poets, and authors. Mikhoels was called one of the greatest actors of all time and his Soviet patriotism was emphasized. His Lenin and Stalin awards were also mentioned.

The niece of Lazar Kaganovich, daughter of his brother Mikhail, who had also been one of Stalin's victims, delivered her uncle's condolences to Mikhoels' daughters and his warning to never ask about the circumstances of their father's death.[53]

At the funeral service, Peretz Markish read the poem "S. Mikhoels— An Eternal Light at the Coffin." Markish wrote the poem the day before; he spoke about the "murder of Mikhoels." This poem could have been the reason for his arrest and execution. In court in 1952, Markish was asked and he writhed:

On the day of his death, the situation was quite confused, and a member of the committee for artistic affairs said that Mikhoels has been murdered. One could also be murdered by misfortune. For two days, I wasn't able to get rid of the notion that he was the victim of a crime. Then it was said that he had been drunk, but it turned out that he wasn't drunk. No one was clear that first day about how he died. It must be mentioned that he had a friend, the commander of the Belorussian military district Trofimenko—their wives were friends—and even this family didn't knew any details about his death. A situation where even the relatives didn't know how he died made me uncertain. I always thought that I might be wrong, and I wrote this poem under the sway of these feelings. But I didn't publish this poem; I only made a rough draft.[54]

Mikhoels was buried on January 16, 1948. In addition to many others, Itsik Fefer, representing the JAFC, gave a graveside speech. It is not possible to reconstruct what he said; apparently the tape recording was manipulated.[55]

Even during the funeral the rumors didn't stop. In court, in 1952, Zuskin declared that Professor Zbarsky confirmed that Mikhoels' death was undoubtedly caused by a car accident. Because of this, Zuskin did not want to believe or spread the rumors about a murder. Attending the funeral was a "person" known to the judge: Molotov's wife Polina Zhemchuzhina, who asked Zuskin at the open grave, "Say, can you believe that all this went so smoothly?!" At the pre-trial hearings, Zuskin said this "person" had at that time declared that Mikhoels had been killed by the authorities, but retracted his statement in court.

Zuskin said that Mikhoels had let him understand in the weeks before his death that he would become his successor. He had asked Zuskin to come into his study "and indicated his armchair with the stage gesture of King Lear: 'Soon you will sit in this place.' I said to him that I wanted to sit there least of all. Then Mikhoels took an anonymous letter out of his bag and read it to me. 'You ugly Yiddish mug, you climbed terribly high; don't lose your head now.'"[56]

Stalin tried very cleverly to counter these rumors about Mikhoels' murder and that anti-Semitism was ordered from above. He honored forty Jews among the 190 Stalin Award recipients, including Ilya Ehrenburg. Large obituary posters for Mikhoels were hung all over Moscow, and the theater was renamed after him. But a large funeral service was not held at the Yiddish Theatre until May 24, 1948. Ilya Ehrenburg characterized

Mikhoels as a great Soviet patriot, a fighter for world social justice and a good Jew. He also described Mikhoels as a good comrade of the soldiers fallen at the front, which was a delicate allusion to the murder. Mikhoels' closest friend and future successor Benjamin Zuskin was even clearer when he said that Mikhoels would be irreplaceable, but "we know in what times and in what country we live."

# Part VI

# OPEN WAR AGAINST THE JEWS—THE LAST YEARS OF STALIN'S DICTATORSHIP

## 26. THE CAMPAIGN AGAINST THE "ROOTLESS COSMOPOLITANS" AND THE WAVES OF ANTI-JEWISH PURGES

The liquidation of the JAFC and the murder of Mikhoels were the first critical stages of the anti-Zionist about-face in Stalin's domestic policies after the Second World War. This annihilation of Yiddish culture and the systematic elimination of Jews from different areas of public life was part of a large new purge, which covered the economy, science, medicine, the army, the secret services, art, and culture. Remnants of Jewish culture that had been tolerated were now subject to aggressive anti-Semitism—especially from the official side. Renowned representatives of Soviet Judaism, even Ilya Ehrenburg, became toys for Stalin and the ideological interests of his secret services. The postwar era has to be called the "black years" of Soviet Judaism.[1]

### Open Jew-Phobia: The Attack on the Theater Critics

At first it remained a secret that nearly all the leading JAFC members were in prison by the end of January 1949. On January 28, 1949, *Pravda* started a massive attack against the so-called cosmopolitans, which had a clear anti-Semitic impetus. In the article *Concerning an anti-patriotic group of theater critics*, in addition to the Russian dramatist Leonid Malyugin and the Armenian Grigori Boyadshiyev, five authors of Jewish origin were slandered as "parasites"— Aleksandr Borshchagovsky, Yefim Kholodov, Abram Gurvich, Joseph Yusovsky, and Yakov Varshavsky. All of them wrote for the Russian-language press and were not indebted to the Jewish national culture. Furthermore, they were accused of "gambling away their responsibility to the people" and being "bearers of a rootless cosmopolitanism, deeply repulsive to the Soviet human being and hostile toward it. [...] Who is A. Gurvich to even have an idea of the national character of the Russian Soviet person?"[2]

How did it come to be that the columns of the party press used unheard of tones, fed by the deepest reservoir of anti-Semitic phobias? Why did the theater critics, of all people, become the first victims of a renewed tightening of the anti-Jewish policy? The answer can be found in the intrigues of the Soviet cultural bureaucracy. Relations between the association of theater critics and the association of authors of the USSR and its secretary general, Alexander Fadeyev, had been strained for a long time. The critics' reviews allegedly favored foreign plays—Borshchagovsky, for example, had spoken very highly in *Izvestiia* in November 1948 of a play by Arthur Miller. That same month, the Agitprop division of the CC met with some of the soon-to-be-reviled critics, still on the side of the aggressors. Fadeyev, who in the 1920s had popularized the character of the loyal, tough Jewish Communist with his novel *The Nineteen*, was now criticized, along with the classic writers Ilf and Petrov, who were deemed to be "anti-Soviet."

Fadeyev prepared to retaliate. CC secretary Malenkov, chief of the cadre administration, and Beria, mainstay of Stalin's empire, stood by Fadeyev. A written denunciation by an *Izvestiia* journalist addressed to Stalin was used to focus his attention on the theater critics. It contained all Jewish names, which were later published in *Pravda*, and it anticipated the reproaches against the "cosmopolitans and profiteers": "They have no national pride, no ideas or principles, they are driven only by their personal careers and for the corroboration of the Euro-American view that there is no Soviet art." It is possible that Stalin himself had given instructions for this letter concerning Malenkov. In any event, he made it quickly plain as to where he stood. Dmitri Shepilov, member of the Agitprop division of the CC, had already very quickly proven himself worthy of the new anti-Semitic spirit of the time by demanding that Zhdanov stop publication of the *Moscow News,* a weekly paper whose editorial staff consisted of one Russian, one Armenian, and twenty-three Jews. In January, Stalin ordered the paper shut down and Shepilov immediately sacrificed the critics that he had protected. After he had pointed out the predominance of the non-Russians (85%) in the association of the theater critics to Malenkov, the bureau for organization of the CC decided to publicly ridicule the critics on January 24, 1949. Several drafts of articles were discussed, and Stalin edited the printed version, which caused a great deal of misery for many people.[3]

One of the climactic articles was published in the February 12, 1949 issue of *Literary Gazette (Literaturnaya gazeta).* The headline was entitled "Rootless cosmopolitans" in which it stated: "The cynical, fresh action of B. Yakovlev (Holzmann), who tried to publish a scandalous, anti-party article in *New World (Novy mir),* evokes deep outrage. B. Holzmann slanders all of our literature's achievements."[4] So the alleged Yakovlev was really Holzmann! The "uncovering" of Russian-sounding pseudonyms as "code names" for Jewish enemies aggravated the theater critic baiting. Even more relevant was that the article related to a piece published in advance about Jewish literature for the new edition of the *Great Soviet Encyclopedia* and unmasked "Jewish nationalism": it put forth the idea that all Jews belonged together, and were therefore cosmopolitans and not patriots. A few days earlier the writers' association had criticized the encyclopedia for allowing "tenth-rate" Jewish authors to be taken into consideration.[5]

The cosmopolitanism reproach was only used on theater critics and other culture-creating people who wrote in Russian and were assimilated Jews. A decree, dated March 28, 1949, signed by Konstantin Simonov, Fadeyev's delegate, and Anatoly Sofronov, secretary of the management, enabled the writers' association to exclude the "anti-patriotic critics." They lost all possibilities for being published, as well as their income and status in society. In contrast to leading authors and poets, however, the critics were not arrested until Stalin's death in March 1953.

In the fight against the assimilated Jews, cosmopolitanism as a propaganda slogan was easily changed to read Jewish nationalism, because it was hard to imagine that under Russian chauvinism the Jews should not have a fatherland. On the other hand, the "nationalists" could not easily be called "cosmopolitans," because the labels are contradictory. This is the reason that the court did not protest when the accused Fefer, Lina Stern, and Vatenberg brusquely rejected the accusations of being guilty of both deviations.

Stalinist strategy used very different methods towards assimilated Jews and those who expressed feelings of nationalism. The latter were secretly arrested and later murdered. The public—Soviet as well as international, where the Yiddish poets were well known—should not be able to figure this out. In addition, the closing of Yiddish theaters, the liquidating of Yiddish writers' associations and other attacks on "Jewish nationalism" were not publicized. On the other hand, Stalin chose the assimilated Jews in Russian cultural life to be the protagonists of a public ritual, in which the internationalist spirit was to be eradicated from the empire. Those affected did not have to be liquidated—it was enough to remove them from their jobs and to farm these jobs out to "real Russians."

The revealing of pseudonyms of the Jews had suddenly stopped in April 1950, but *Komsomolskaya Pravda* resumed this disgraceful practice once again in February 1951. In March, *Literaturnaya gazeta* published an article by Konstantin Simonov, who defended pseudonyms, saying they were a private matter to be decided by the author. Simonov later said that, in 1952, even Stalin became angry about the anti-Semitic practice of unmasking. For example, he had asked his colleagues at a meeting about a novel by Maltsev:

> Why Maltsev? And in parentheses it says Rovinsky? What does that mean? For how long should this go on? We already debated this last year. Nothing should be proposed with two names. Why? Why two names? If someone has chosen a literary pseudonym for himself, that's not a problem. We're speaking about one thing here, simple manners. Everyone has the right to write under a pseudonym. But there are those who obviously like to show that if one uses a pseudonym, he must be Jewish. Why underline that? Why? Why sow anti-Semitism? Who profits by it? Just publish it with the author's chosen name. Some like to use a pseudonym. It makes them feel comfortable. Why press him, tug at him?[6]

In his memoirs Ehrenburg says that Stalin had declared that this practice seemed like anti-Semitism in 1949 and arranged for the unmasking of pseudonyms to be stopped. Yet the following comment only appears in the posthumous edition of Ehrenburg's memoirs: the American communist publication, *Daily Worker,* asked Ehrenburg to refute the use of pseudonym revelation as anti-Semitism. Ehrenburg didn't even dare answer this request.[7]

Stalin's protest against name decoding and its anti-Semitism struck some as bizarre. Simonov had the feeling of being present at a theatrical performance. He understood that Stalin had been behind the campaign. Ehrenburg also learned this from Fadeyev. Did Stalin, whose pseudonym covered up his non-Russian origin, fear that the Russian chauvinistic avalanche, which he had launched, would snowball over him one day? Even while his security agencies gathered information about a supposed Jewish conspiracy, Stalin wanted to rein in open anti-Semitism so as not to put the party's reputation with the international left at risk.

### The Extermination of "Cosmopolitanism"

The expression "cosmopolitanism" was not considered negative at the beginning of the thirties or during the patriotic about-face of 1937.[8] Only when the CC of the CPSU presented Andrei Zhdanov's new thesis did *Zhdanovshchina* begin, and with it the flourishing of "anti-cosmopolitanism." Zhdanov was the main speaker at the foundation of the *Cominform* in the fall of 1946. The *Cominform* replaced the *Comintern*, liquidated by Stalin in 1943, and set forth the party's guidelines for artists. Any deviation from the canon of socialist realism as the only accepted artistic method was considered to be "formalism" and "estheticism." Acceptable examples were the magazines *Zvezda* and *Leningrad*, as well as the work of Anna Akhmatova and Mikhail Zoshchenko, both of whom were not Jews. The whole campaign focused on the West, certain to be the new opponent, and cultural politics were to be used to weld the people together against the enemy. Anything Western was suspicious, and any acknowledgement of the West was branded "subservience." To belittle Western achievements, the media reported about inventions that were made first by Russians. Marriages with foreigners were forbidden for Soviet citizens from 1947 until 1953. This was typical of the prevailing hysteria.

The anti-Jewish inference of the campaign was soon revealed. In 1946 the Jewish critic Isaak Nussinov was ridiculed in the magazine *Kultura i zhizn'* as a "vagabond without passport" who "Westernized" the national poet Pushkin and robbed him of his "Russian soul" like a vampire.[9] Thus the old anti-Semitic stereotypes of the eternally wandering Jew without a homeland merged with anti-Jewish and anti-Western resentments, a typical Russian combination. Under Ivan the Terrible, the Jews were considered to be the henchmen of the hostile Poles. During the First World War they were deported as supposedly being pro-German. Now their aversion to all "real Russian things" was building a fifth column of the West, led by the Americans.

After the January 1949 article condemning theater critics brought the "cosmopolitan campaign" and anti-Semitism out into the open, all scientific and cultural institutions held conferences at which supposed cosmopolitans were unmasked. Among the first were Jews. They were blamed for scientific "faults," e.g., overestimating Western research. They were too tolerant of "bourgeois objectivism," meaning enrichment, accumulation of power and nepotistic personnel policy—the reproach "Jews employ only Jews" was often heard. Periodicals published special issues about cosmopolitanism with lists of the practice's defenders. These lists were pages long and contained—as in *Voprosy istorii* (Questions of History)—more or less only Jewish names.[10]

## Mass Dismissal of Jews

Jewish pedagogues, journalists, artists and scientists, even those who never dealt with Jewish affairs, were dismissed and persecuted. The wave of purges included even middle and high army ranks. Between 1949 and 1953, 63 Jewish generals and 270 colonels and lieutenant colonels were prematurely suspended from active service. They had fought bravely during the war, and received thousands of decorations for bravery, but this was ignored. In 1950, out of 1,316 delegates in both chambers of the Supreme Soviet, there were only five Jews, among them Lazar Kaganovich and Ilya Ehrenburg. The dismissed citizens' only offense was that in the "fifth rubric" of their personal documents, their nationality was registered with the word *Evrei* (Jew).

In the state planning authority alone, 300 Jewish employees were dismissed. The editors of *Pravda* held ongoing conferences, unmasking four Jewish and one Russian member. Now even David Zaslavsky, the most loyal Stalinist Jew in the press, had to plead guilty because he had contact with Mikhoels and Shimeliovich, was a member of the JAFC, and had season tickets to the Yiddish Theater. When additional Jewish journalists were dismissed from *Pravda*, he had to resign the journalism chair at the party academy of the CC. Between 1950-51, the labor newspaper *Trud* gave forty employees notice, reducing the number of Jews on the editorial staff from 50 to 20 percent. The navy newspaper *Krasny flot* attacked people personally, calling them "the Jew Rudny," or "the Jew Ivich." The rest of the press did not venture into using this nearly Nazi-like tone.[11]

Persecution of Jews in industry assumed largely unknown dimensions and became tragic. After the Soviet Union was founded, Jews were among the pioneers of technology and leaders of the armaments industry. Vladimir Englard, an engineer, constructed the first Soviet tank in Petrograd. In 1920 Solomon Broide constructed the first tank with a gun and a machine gun, the MS-1. In 1930 Anatoly Stelfman led the first tank-construction group of the USSR. In the automobile and tractor industry, numerous Jews had been employed as researchers, designers, directors and skilled workers. When Israel's very existence was threatened after the Arab invasion and numerous Jewish employees in the Stalin automobile factories in Moscow demanded in a letter that the JAFC support the newly founded state, the investigators became active. They uncovered a "Jewish nationalist underground," followed by arrests, testimonies and accusations of spying. Ten of those arrested were executed and the others sentenced to lengthy imprisonment. Similar occurrences took place in many other industries, including ball-bearing factories and aircraft industries. Khrushchev remembered Stalin's reaction to this news:

> I still remember what Stalin said after he had heard through party channels and the state security service informed him about difficulties in the thirtieth aircraft factory. While we were sitting around and exchanging opinions at a meeting, Stalin turned to me and said: "Sticks should be given to the good workers in the factory, so they can really beat those Jews after work."[12]

Khrushchev believed that Stalin considered the Jewish group in the Stalin automobile factories to be a "conspiracy of U.S. imperialism." This case resulted in dismissals in the ministry for the automotive and tractor industry; even acting minister Kogan had to leave. In May 1950 the Politburo passed a resolution outlining the political problems in that ministry. The directives, compiled by Suslov, indicated the anti-Jewish character of the purge. However, Stalin preferred an ethnically "neutral" version. In June 1950, instructions to deliver yearly reports about their cadres were issued to all ministries. The historian Kostyrchenko interpreted this as bureaucratic preparation for the new purge (*chistka*), which later culminated in the "doctors' conspiracy."

Only Soviet nuclear scientists were spared from the hunt for "cosmopolitans" and persecution of the Jews, because Beria shielded them from Abakumov. In 1945 Stalin entrusted Beria, head of the NKVD, with the construction of enormous new military-industrial complexes, and nuclear research had priority. Because he was working on the A-bomb, Sandler, a physicist, had his life spared, even though he was automatically guilty since his cousin was one of the "Zionist leaders" at the Stalin car factory.

Other than nuclear researchers, physicists were not taboo. In 1943 an assistant professor of physics, Nosdryov Shcherbakov, pointed out that in 1938 only half as many Jews as Russians graduated from the study of physics while in 1942 the number of Russian and Jewish graduates was the same. Because of the "big danger of monopoly," Nosdryov demanded national quotas. He was divested of his authority in 1946 for, among other things, his too openly anti-Semitic attitude, but that same year an "abnormal personnel situation" was recorded, because among 765 scientists at the state university of Moscow (MGU) there were 208 Jews. In 1950, when Malenkov was told that a "monopoly group" had support from "representatives of the Jewish nationality" among the theoretical physicists of the MGU, he ordered purges.[13]

## 27. THE DESTRUCTION
### OF THE LAST REMNANTS OF JEWISH CULTURE

The *Great Soviet Encyclopedia* provides a measure of the relative importance the Soviet government conceded to the Jews. The first edition (1926-1936) consisted of 65 volumes and under the heading "Jews" in volume 24 are 55 pages of Jewish history, culture and literature. Ninety-three references are given, the texts of which could fill an entire book. The volume was published in 1932, before Stalinism had infected the country; many victims of the later purges, some of whom worked for the *Encyclopedia*, were still held in high esteem. In the second edition of 51 volumes (1949–1957), the heading "Jews" appears in volume 15. This volume, published in 1952, has two pages on "Jews" and only 16 references. The central thesis stated that the Jews are not a people. Thanks to the nationality policy of Lenin and Stalin, there no longer existed a Jewish problem in the Soviet Union. Jews have intermarried with the general population. Yiddish was once spoken in the Soviet Union, but only the Jewish petty bourgeoisie in the capitalist countries stick to Jewish traditions.[14]

## The Fight Against "Bourgeois Nationalism"

As the dictator and his party saw it, the Yiddish culture had two vices: (1) it was unnecessary, since the Jews would be assimilated anyway, and (2) it was dangerous, because it brought along with it "Zionist," "bourgeois nationalist" content, which could weaken the assimilation to socialist culture. After the murder of Solomon Mikhoels and the liquidation of the JAFC, Yiddish literature and the entire body of Jewish culture was ruthlessly attacked by the party and state agencies.

Other nationalities were also victimized by the campaign against "bourgeois nationalism." In 1944 Tatar historians and journalists (in 1945 it was the Bashkiri's turn, then the Ukrainians in 1946) were accused of not placing enough importance on joining in brotherhood with the Russians. They were told that they underestimated the progressive tsarist influence in the history of their countries, and that they did not report enough about the hostility from Iran and Turkey. A positive relation to their own national history was allowed only with the Russians. The "older brother" Russian had just set the other nationalities of the empire free.

In September, Fefer started attacking Jewish nationalism in *Eynikeyt*. Regardless of his own nationalistic stance during the war, the poet now attacked his friends and colleagues who wrote in Yiddish for not being flexible and shedding their beliefs of a lifetime quickly enough. An obscure Yiddish author, Aron Vergelis, who later became the brave keeper of the particular party line as editor of the journal *Sovietish Heymland*, joined the new line as well. Reports about the Holocaust or histories of Jewish personalities were no longer desired. Writing too much about the past and too little about class affiliation was considered to be an offense; "Hebrewisms" were condemned as signs of Jewish national feeling. It was even demanded that Jews not publish about Jews anymore. Jews were particularly singled out in this regard, since, for instance, Ukrainians still retained the right to write about Ukrainians.[15]

In the last two years of its existence, the newspaper *Eynikeyt* fought against everything that smacked of a Jewish interest. Kheifets reported in detail to his superiors at the Lubyanka that the JAFC was under the complete control of informers and executors of the MGB. But in spite of painstaking loyalty to the party line and the severest leading example, the days of Yiddish culture in the Soviet Union were numbered. Only five days after the liquidation of the committee, the Politburo ordered the *Emes* publishing house to close. The newspaper by the same name had been suppressed ten years earlier. On February 8, 1949, the Politburo ordered the liquidation of the Yiddish writers' association in Moscow, Kiev and Minsk. Nearly all Yiddish authors lost their jobs and the protection of their professional association. At the same time, the Yiddish journals *Heymland* in Moscow and *Der stern* in Kiev were forbidden. These actions were justified by economic loss on the one hand, and, on the other, by nationalist tendencies and "Zionist" deviations in the works published by them.

## Elimination of Jewish Cultural Institutions

Jewish cultural institutions were liquidated everywhere. Anyone who cooperated with these institutions was arrested. The local heritage museum in Birobidzan was closed, as were the Jewish museums in Vilnius and Tbilisi. In the middle of February 1949, Radio Moscow International stopped Yiddish broadcasts.

Yiddish theaters, which were once presented to foreign countries by the Soviet Union as a glorious chapter in their cultural policy, were hit particularly hard. In 1939 ten Yiddish theaters and two theater schools existed. In March 1948 and February 1949, the cabinet instructed that state promotional funds be reduced for all stages, yet these resolutions were only implemented for Yiddish theaters. Theaters of other small nationalities received even higher fund allocations.

In February 1949 the first secretary of the Belorussian CC, Gusarov, demanded that the Jewish writers' association be shut down and the Yiddish theater in Minsk be closed. He attributed the ideologically erroneous repertoire of the stage to the influence of the nationalist Fefer, who in the meantime had been unmasked, and to Mikhoels. One month later it was liquidated as the first of the Yiddish stages.[16]

Attendance at Yiddish theaters fell from 45 to 20 percent between 1948 and 1949 because visitors were afraid to reveal themselves as "Jewish nationalists," thereby attracting the interest of the "organs." Thus, it was easy to cite the theaters' lack of profitability. The Agitprop division of the CC also criticized Yiddish theaters for not performing enough of the great Russian authors' works. It was pointed out that only 4 actors out of 55 were communists. In Moscow, GOSSET initially received a reprieve from the CC. It was not closed down until 1950, after the CC committee for matters of art took the theater over, citing unprofitability. They closed the Mikhoels theater school as well.[17] Beginning in January 1949, when JAFC members were being arrested, GOSSET no longer bore Mikhoels' name.[18]

The Kaganovich Theater in Birobidzan was also closed down during this period. Attacks on "Jewish nationalism" were particularly heavy in the Autonomous Jewish region. The first secretary of the Birobidzan district committee, Bakhmutsky, still demanded that the district become a republic in December 1945. It was rejected in Moscow in 1946, but there was a resolution of the Soviet government to give stronger material support to Birobidzan. Because of this, the reach and circulation of the *Birobidzaner Stern* increased. Yet in June 1949, security minister Abakumov started investigating the "nationalist" Bakhmutsky. The inquisitors wanted to uncover a nationalist organization that included, among others, I. Emiot and J. Kerler, Birobidzan authors from Poland and the Ukraine. Both survived persecution and wrote about it later in their memoirs.[19] The arrests took place while the JAFC was being investigated. They were accused of belonging to this organization's spy network. Bakhmutsky was blamed for his contacts with the JAFC leadership as well, but in his defense he pointed to their "anti-Birobidzan" attitude. Bakhmutsky was accused of stirring up pro-American attitudes in the population in connection with U.S. aid deliveries. This was the reason for his dismissal and expulsion from the party in the summer of 1949. He was arrested in January 1951, and at his trial in February 1952 he was accused of having collaborated with traitors in the JAFC. He was sentenced to death, but this was changed to 25 years in prison. A Russian, who became the new first party secretary of the district committee and demanded that the Jewish theater be reopened, was dismissed again in 1952. The Russification of the leadership of Birobidzan shattered the last illusion that this district was to be the home of the Jews. In the bloody purges of the thirties, the Soviet leadership at least paid attention to the fact that the "followers" were again Jews.[20]

The wave of arrests and purges extended beyond Birobidzan, where many thousands of Yiddish books were destroyed in the state library. The persecutions affected Jews in the Baltic countries and Bessarabia in the same manner. Even if they did not belong to the official associations, nearly all Yiddish authors were arrested, a unique occurrence in the history of world literature.

## 28. Pursuing the "Zionist Conspiracy"

Suddenly after the liquidation order of November 21, 1948, the archives of the JAFC and *Eynikeyt* were loaded onto many trucks parked in a long row on Kropotkin Street. This was completed by midnight. The files were brought to the Lubyanka, where they were used as evidence against members of the JAFC. They were to remain secret for nearly 50 years.

After Mikhoels, Fefer was, understandably, the main suspect since he had also been in the U.S. An inveterate Stalinist, he had been an informer for the secret police for six years. He seemed to be a perfect witness for the "organs" and the prosecution at the planned secret trial. Fefer and Zuskin were arrested on December 24, 1948; Hofstein had already been arrested in the middle of September. It was revealed during the rehabilitation trial of 1955 that Fefer was not subjected to either solitary confinement or to torture but was accused after short references to the usual investigation methods of the murdered Mikhoels and other JAFC members. From the beginning, the strategy of the main investigators was to confront JAFC members and others accused with Fefer's denunciation and his self-accusation. This was meant to break their resistance and seemed to be successful.

### American "Agents"

When Fefer was forced to name Ben Zion Goldberg a spy, the investigators rejected all of his objections. Because there were no documents or tangible proof, a concoction of inventions and true facts was assembled. American journalists and publicists Goldberg and Novick were extremely well suited to be the purported agents because they had been in very close contact with the JAFC during the war. They received a great deal of propaganda from the Soviet Union, and had also hosted Mikhoels and Fefer during their stay in the United States. Most importantly, Goldberg and Novick spent a few months in the Soviet Union and had contact with all the leading JAFC members. Based on these visits, the accusations proposed a fantastic scenario of American agents wanting to create a spy network inside the Soviet Union. These ridiculous accusations would collapse during a public trial and were to be used only in a secret trial, because the supposed "spies" lived in the U.S. and could easily refute public accusations. This way, however, everyone who had any contact with Goldberg and Novick could be suspected and arrested for having been drawn to anti-Soviet activities. This was also true of James N. Rosenberg and the organization he headed, the *Joint*.

## Zhemchuzhina: Political VIPs in the Dock

Stalin, Malenkov, and Abakumov were interested not only in finding supposed espionage or the settling scores with "Jewish nationalism," but also in examining people in Stalin's immediate vicinity, especially people who were Jews or related to Jews. Fefer reported: "Abakumov demanded that I speak about L. M. Kaganovich and his attention to the Crimea question. Regarding Mekhlis, he asked if it was true that the Americans had invited him to America." Stalin was obviously behind these questions posed by Abakumov. Stalin wanted to know if these two Jews in his entourage had also been a part of the "Zionist" conspiracy. Molotov was doubly under suspicion because of his Jewish wife, Zhemchuzhina. Her name was the Russified version of her Yiddish name, "Perl." Fefer was supposed to have stated that he had seen her in the synagogue and that she had complained about Stalin's negative attitude toward the Jews. Fefer said this in court in 1952, but it is also possible that Abakumov wanted him to make false statements. It could be that Fefer lied at this point in the trial since Zhemchuzhina's presence at the synagogue was vouched for by Hofstein in court.[21] Fefer also knew that Abakumov had been dismissed and that he could pin the blame on him to exonerate himself. But he did not know that Zhemchuzhina was already in a camp. Fefer's only possible strategy in court would be to testify as negatively as possible about Abakumov and as positively as possible about Zhemchuzhina and thus about Molotov. In the declarations of others accused, truth was mixed with lies and ridiculous confessions. When reading the interrogation protocol and the trial documents, it is necessary to understand that these sources did not always speak the pure truth. The accusations were a conglomeration of lies and an act of political arbitrariness; they served a plan sanctioned by the highest authority for the annihilation of Jewish culture. The compliant investigators put some of the unjustly accused defendants through inhuman tortures. Some of the accused had to lie in order to save their lives, but in the end they were still found guilty.

The investigators tried to establish a relationship between the supposed "espionage center" of the JAFC and the wife of the still acting minister of foreign affairs. Zhemchuzhina had already incurred Stalin's anger several times. As a friend of Stalin's second wife, she knew "too much" about the dictator's private life. In 1941 she was deprived of her candidate status for the CC, but she retained her leading position in industry. In 1948, when general suspicion was directed at all Jews, Molotov separated from her under pressure from Stalin. When Golda Meir arrived in Moscow, they became even more suspicious of Zhemchuzhina—particularly since the two women spoke in Yiddish[22] for a while.

Two days after Fefer's arrest, Abakumov organized a confrontation that included Zhemchuzhina. Fefer said that he saw her at a memorial event, a *Kaddish* for murdered Jews, next to other Jewish Soviet VIPs[23] in 1945. Such an event took place then and in 1946; by 1947 it was already forbidden. In the presence of Fefer, Zhemchuzhina denied that she was there, maintaining that it was her sister. At the next confrontation she also denied Zuskin's repetition of the synagogue story and that she had spoken of murder at Mikhoels' grave. Although Zuskin was coerced with threats as well as promises of a lighter prison sentence into confirming all of Fefer's testimony,[24] his statements probably contained a kernel of truth. Why shouldn't Zhemchuzhina have taken part in a *Kaddish*? In 1945, future anti-Semitism could not be foreseen, but by the end of 1948 it was clear that confessing to visiting a synagogue at that time would be interpreted as proof of "Jewish nationalism."

Zhemchuzhina's denial of the allegations did not help, and at the end of December 1948 she was expelled from the party. Molotov abstained from the Central Committee's vote, as also did on the status of his wife. On January 20, 1949, however, Molotov wrote a secret letter to Stalin, stating that he was wrong to abstain and welcomed the party's exclusion of his now ex-wife. Molotov even admitted his "fault" to Stalin "for not having kept a person close to me away from taking the wrong steps and from keeping contacts with anti-Soviet nationalists like Mikhoels.'[25] When Molotov wrote this letter, Zhemchuzhina had already been arrested. New accusations against her stated that, in 1943, Mikhoels had met her brother, who had emigrated to the U.S. Mikhoels had given her a letter in 1944, containing allegations about discrimination against the Jews in liberated Ukraine. Abakumov forced Lozovsky to inform against Zhemchuzhina at another confrontation. Lozovsky stated that she was a contact person for the "nationalist" work of the JAFC. Its member Yuzefovich, who was arrested together with Boris Shimeliovich on January 13, stated that Zhemchuzhina had been considered in the committee as its "benefactor" and had promised to support the Crimea project. In addition to these accusations that ran parallel to the investigation of the JAFC, Zhemchuzhina was reproached in a most impertinent and despicable manner about her supposed love-life—again with "revealing" confrontations.[26] Zhemchuzhina didn't waver. She refused to confess to any contact with "Jewish nationalists," and therefore she also had to deny visiting the synagogue. She eventually confessed only to having defended some arrested "public enemies."

It cannot be ruled out that Zhemchuzhina's fate would have been much worse if she had confessed in 1952. Since she did not, she was sentenced to "only" five years of camp internment. Molotov said later: "She was in exile for more than three years and in prison for more than a year when Beria passed me at a Politburo session. He said, rather he whispered, into my ear: 'Polina's alive!' She was in the Lubyanka prison and I didn't know it."[27] Molotov had to suspect that he too was in danger. He was involved in the Crimea letter, and he must have known how the Committee would perceive this. Stalin was suspicious of him because he was married to a Jewess and, in his growing paranoia, the dictator suspected that Molotov had cooperated with the American secret service when he traveled throughout the U.S. in a private railroad car.[28] At the beginning of March 1949, Molotov was dismissed from his foreign minister post, but he was able to last in the center of power.

## The Head of the JAFC Disappears

It became clear that Abakumov, supported by Beria and Stalin, wanted to link Molotov's wife's case with the JAFC within a week after Zhemchuzhina's arrest, because at that point the vast majority of the future dissidents of the JAFC had also been arrested. This included the poets Peretz Markish, Leib Kvitko and David Bergelson; translators and editorial employees Emilia Teumin, Ilya Vatenberg and Chaika Vatenberg-Ostrovskaya and the famous physiologist Lina Stern. Hofstein had already been arrested two months before the committee was closed. Fefer and Zuskin were arrested in December, Yuzefovich and Shimeliovich in January. The last arrested, Leon Talmi, joined them in July 1949. Shortly before Peretz Markish's arrest on January 28, he entrusted a relative with what he considered his most important manuscripts. Markish was arrested by seven state security officers, as well as additional officers led by a lieutenant colonel. They searched the whole apartment. Markish was the only accused who had the "honor" of being arrested by so many henchmen.[29]

Along with the future dissidents, many others were arrested in connection with their work for the JAFC and *Eynikeyt*. They were always accused of anti-Soviet nationalist activities or espionage. For example, Professors Emdin and Svonov—correspondents for *Eynikeyt* in Leningrad—were sentenced to 20 and 25 years of camp imprisonment, respectively.[30] Those sentences were simply justified by the fact that the accused had complained about the liquidation of the committee.

When many Yiddish poets and authors stopped answering letters and no more Yiddish newspaper and books were printed, numerous Jewish and non-Jewish authors and artists, especially in the U.S., made inquiries. They tried to get information from Soviet authorities and from the Soviet writers' association, without success. Mary McCarthy was one such author. On the other hand, Jewish authors such as Norman Mailer and Arthur Miller showed no interest in the fate of their Yiddish-writing colleagues in the Soviet Union. Nearly all Soviet visitors in Europe and the U.S. lied knowingly about the authors' fates.

The singer Paul Robeson was particularly persistent with the Soviet authorities in trying to get information about his friend Fefer. He supported Fefer personally during his concert tours in the Soviet Union and when he stayed in Moscow for a longer period of time. This popular American artist was important for Soviet propaganda. Because they did not want to annoy or lose him, the secret police arranged a meeting between Robeson and Fefer. In 1949 Fefer was put back on his feet and properly dressed beforehand. The two met in a bugged room at the Hotel Metropol. Robeson understood that Fefer's despairing gestures did not match his words and he realized that Fefer was lost. With tears in their eyes, the two friends hugged and said goodbye. Robeson kept the details of this meeting secret until his death. He did not want to harm the reputation of his beloved Soviet Union. His son, Paul Robeson Jr., was allowed to reveal the truth to *Jewish Currents*,[31] a leftist New York newspaper, only after Robeson's death.

## In the Torture Chamber of the MGB

The MGB, which had already gathered the testimonies of Fefer incriminating the JAFC members, now tried as quickly as possible to extract matching confessions from the arrested. Altogether 35 investigators took part in the procedure—some as the persons pulling the levers, others as real torturers. Markish, for example, was subjected to prolonged interrogations lasting up to 17 hours. Often a nocturnal interrogation began at midnight and continued until the morning hours, a treatment applied to Markish until April 29. Altogether he was held in darkness for 16 days under the worst conditions, when Lina Stern had to accompany a civilian MGB cooperator to see Abakumov on January 28, the latter shouted immediately: "We know everything! Give up! You're a Zionist. You wanted to separate the Crimea from Russia to create a Jewish state there." When she disputed this, he screamed at her: "Why are you lying, you old whore?"[32] Then Lina Stern was taken into custody in the prisons of Lefortovo and Lubyanka and interrogated for months. The lead investigator, Rassypinsky, interrogated her ninety-seven times, yet he came away with nothing tangible and incriminating. That is why the examining magistrate tried to interpret Lina Stern's international scientific contacts and the visits of American scientists to the Soviet Union as espionage for the nuclear and bacteriological strategy of the U.S.

Bergelson later revealed in court how the investigation protocols were compiled. When, for example, the district attorney declared Goldberg to be an American spy, Bergelson threw in a surprised "Yes?" In the protocol, the question mark was simply omitted; Bergelson's protests against that practice were rejected and he was urged to sign. Vatenberg also described in court this technique of constructing protocols. His investigator immediately made clear to him that he was not his "secretary." Thus he wrote down the protocols not according to the wording but filtered or changed accordingly to fit the indictment. When Vatenberg was asked, for example, if a commission he was working for was busy gathering *espionage* information, he declared that the commission had really gathered information. But in the protocol it was written that the accused did not deny gathering espionage information by the commission.

Aside from the enormous physical pressure—beatings, sleep deprivation for months, nightly interrogations for hours and solitary confinement in bitterly cold cells or dark custody—those arrested were exposed to continuous indoctrination. The lawyer Vatenberg described this in court:

> One could fight, of course, reject everything, and so on—the only weapon that remained. I tell you quite frankly, I'm physically and morally no coward. But it's another thing altogether: against whom is one going to fight? How I envied the revolutionaries who faced the tsarist Okhrana or the American police. […] There's no abstract truth; the truth is tied in to the classes, and once the truth is tied in with the classes, one thinks that the investigator perhaps really is right. […] For a Soviet human the fact of having talked with an agent is enough, having given him any information, the most harmless, and even if he didn't know that it was an agent and even if he hadn't the intention of handing over espionage information, the mere fact to have only talked with an agent makes the Soviet human guilty of a crime, to which paragraph 58-1 [counter revolutionary crime] applies. Because it happened just like this, I confessed (it was on the night of February 6, 1949) to having engaged in espionage, and then everything started to go smoothly. Because I already confessed to the heaviest crime, that of treason, all the others were no longer important to me and I signed the protocols.[33]

This was—aside from all forms of torture and the insidious remarks to the family still living in freedom—the pattern according to which the candidates at the show trials of the thirties were treated. In this connection, an appeal was made to perform a service to the party and confess. The procedure was even more simple as it also was put to the test in the 1930s, to present the forced testimony of the one accused to the next one in line to be accused in order to "convince" him with it.

With this mixture of pressure and inner attrition, confessions were wrung from nearly all those indicted, incriminating themselves or others. At the center of all this were the accusations against their former leader, Lozovsky, head of the *Sovinformburo*, who was exposed to particularly aggressive treatment. Komarov interrogated him during eight nights, when he vented his hatred for the Jews, declaring them a despicable and dirty nation, undignified dirty pigs, etc. Moreover, he attributed all opposition endeavors in the party to having been the initiative of Jews; all Jews in the entire Soviet Union "hissed" against Soviet power; the Jews wanted to wipe out the Russians, and so on. Komarov threatened to let Lozovsky rot in jail and to beat him with rubber truncheons in such a way that he would not be able to sit any more. In his testimony in 1952 at court, Lozovsky said: "I then explained to them, better death than such tortures; they answered that they wouldn't let me die quickly, but that I'd die slowly." After these threats, Komarov had asked which high-ranking politicians in Moscow had Jews as wives and stated, "that there are no authorities in our state; because it was necessary, we arrested Polina Semyonovna Molotova... Then he started to demand that I testify about my supposed relations to Kaganovich and Mikhoels."[34]

The more adamantly the accused refused to make such confessions, the crueler the interrogations became. Shimeliovich, who was the least of all prepared for "confessions," felt this the hardest. In court he reported that in just one month—January 1949—he received 2000 blows. In a personal note to the judge he provided further details about the pervasive anti-Semitism during the interrogations. He was asked who the highest-ranking Jew in the Soviet Union was and named Kaganovich. Shimeliovich was now supposed to testify about him as his "high-ranking leader" and about Zhemchuzhina as his "deputy leader." During this interrogation he was beaten as well and heard for the first time statements from his tormentors that "all Jews are spies" and "all Jews are enemies of the Soviet Union."[35]

In March 1950 all of the accused were informed that the investigations were over. Abakumov must have realized that he did not get very much despite the signed protocols. A 1930s-style show trial couldn't possibly take place with these types of suspects. The closing report on March 25, 1950, showed that Stalin and his assistants dreamed of a much bigger procedure than the thin "confessions" seemed to permit. Lozovsky, Yuzefovich, and Zuskin retracted their confessions. Shimeliovich declared his complete innocence. The procedure was practically put on hold. The accused remained in custody without further explanations, but were no longer interrogated.

Sentences were meanwhile reached in many parallel procedures against others who collaborated with the JAFC. The security organs had not only arrested the group of those later accused in January 1949, but the authors Der Nister, Samuil Halkin, Dmitri Stonov, Noakh Lurye, the critics Dobrushin and Nussinov and many others who had been arrested even earlier. They were sentenced in 1950 to long camp sentences, which many of them did not survive. The most famous example of that is Der Nister. Death sentences by firing squad were handed down against Miriam Eisenstadt-Zheleznova and Nakhum Levin by the judge, Aleksandr Cheptsov, in the big JAFC trial. The indictments against them were the same as those against their colleagues who went on trial in 1950, namely of having handed over materials to the alleged U.S. spy Goldberg. The total count of all procedures was summed up in the rehabilitation document of 1989:

> From 1948 to 1952, in relation to the case of the "Jewish Anti-Fascist Committee," many other persons of Jewish nationality, among them party and state officials, scientists, authors, poets, journalists, artists, employees of state institutions and industrial concerns—altogether 110 persons—were accused of having acted as spies and having been active anti-Soviet nationalists, arrested and called to account under criminal law. Ten persons were condemned to maximum penalty, 20 sentenced to 25 years in a labor camp, three to 20 years, eleven to 15 years, fifty to 10 years, two to 8 years, one sentenced to 7 years and two sentenced to 5 years in a labor camp. One accused was also sent into exile for 10 years. Five persons died during the investigations; the proceeding was suspended against five other persons after their arrest.[36]

All these victims were rehabilitated in 1989. They were as innocent as the accused at the 1952 trial. Why was sentencing passed on some relatively quickly, while others were interrogated for such a long time, tortured and then completely "forgotten"? The reason is that those named last were supposed to serve as willing witnesses in a marathon trial, in which a conspiracy at the highest levels of government, all the way up to Molotov's wife, was to have been uncovered. When Abakumov failed, in spite of all the tortures and tricks, it didn't mean—according to Stalinist logic—that this conspiracy did not exist. On the contrary, it meant that even Abakumov was a potential traitor. This resulted—before the investigations moved on to the JAFC—in a major purge in the ministry for state security.

### The Downfall of Abakumov and the "Jewish Conspirators" in the MGB

On July 2, 1951, Ryumin, until then an inconspicuous employee of the MGB, informed on Abakumov in a letter addressed to Stalin. When he himself was accused, he declared that he wanted to preempt the uncovering of some shady sides of his biography. (His father has been a wealthy merchant; his father-in-law had even served in the White Army of Kolchak.) Ryumin accused Abakumov of having downplayed a "conspiracy" among high school pupils. A group of mostly Jewish pupils and students had founded an alliance for the sake of revolution," which Abakumov had brushed aside as harmless fooling around.[37]

Following this letter, Stalin signed a document about "injustices at the ministry for state security" on July 11, 1951. Abakumov, who was also accused of embezzlement of stolen art, was arrested. But Ryumin did not stop there. He maintained that a "Zionist" conspiracy within the ministry had prevented the establishment of conclusive evidence against the JAFC. Abakumov's colleague Shvartsman was arrested on July 15, 1951, followed in October by the arrests of Reikhman and Eitingon, specialists in bloody covert missions like the one that resulted in Trotsky's murder. Lev Sheinin, an author and an examining magistrate, and Andrei Sverdlov, the son of the first state president, were also apprehended in this anti-Jewish purge. Ryumin alleged that they all had feared that their nationalist anti-Soviet activities would be revealed during the JAFC trial. That's why they did everything they could to prolong and hush up that case.

According to the recollections of the secret policeman Pavel Sudoplatov, Malenkov and Beria, who wanted to get Abakumov out of the way, supposedly manipulated Ryumin. Sudoplatov's sister-in-law, who worked as a secretary in Malenkov's office, had been a witness as this denunciatory letter sent to Stalin was written.[38]

Astonishingly, not only the "Zionist" conspirators were arrested, but also Abakumov, the worst Jew-hater, was suspended from service and arrested as their alleged ringleader. In fact, some of the Jewish MGB cooperators began, while still under Abakumov, to criticize the hostile activities of their colleagues towards Jews.[39] The biggest anti-Semite, Komarov, complained in February 1953 in a letter to Stalin about having dismissed such an outstanding Chekist like him. Naturally, he especially praised those things that would meet with particular approval with Stalin:

> The arrested enemies knew and felt my hatred against them. They saw in me an investigator who followed a cruel punitive course against them, and so they tried in every single way, as the investigators reported to me, to avoid meetings with me and not to face me in an interrogation.... I especially hated the Jewish nationalists, toward whom I showed no mercy and in whom I saw the most dangerous and most malicious enemies. Because of my hate toward them, not only the arrested but also the former MGB cooperators of Jewish nationality considered me to be an anti-Semite.[40]

Komarov wanted to come under Ryumin's spell in his letter to Stalin and present himself as a "victim" of the Jewish conspirators within the MGB. Because non-Jews like Komarov could not be accused of cooperation in a Jewish secret organization, Ryumin accused them of planning to capture power jointly with Abakumov. New confessions, meanwhile, were forced from the arrested Jewish MGB employees during interrogations conducted in the usual style. The goal of the new social climbers around Ryumin was to prove the existence of a Jewish bourgeois nationalist secret group inside state security.

## Ryumin Takes Control

Ryumin was rewarded for his "unmaskings" by being promoted to the position of deputy minister for state security and becoming the investigator in particularly important cases. Ignatiev became the new minister, leader of the party, trade union and Komsomol division of the CC. At first he was inconspicuous as a colorless *apparatchik*, but in August 1951 he demanded the immediate arrest of the chairman of the Moscow Jewish community, Schliffer. The CC didn't approve of this suggestion because, as a JAFC member, Schliffer was still needed for propaganda purposes. Soon after taking office, Ignatiev discovered there were no protocols of the confessions of the JAFC prisoners. He reported this to Malenkov and Beria in a letter dated August 24, 1951, and announced an expansion of the investigation into this case.

Ryumin called upon experts to "prove," using the confiscated materials that the JAFC had been an "anti-Soviet nationalist center" since its founding. Before the "analysis" of the JAFC archive, Ignatiev and Ryumin boasted in a letter to Stalin that their insistence on examining and sorting out the documents made it necessary to resume the investigations. In so doing, they put themselves under pressure: if the investigation again produced no results, they must be failures—or traitors—in Stalin's eyes, just like Abakumov. To avoid this, the experts were manipulated and given only a selection from the huge files and publications of the accused (countless were in Yiddish, which most of the experts didn't speak anyway), and told what to look for.

On January 19, 1952, the proceedings were reopened and on March 5 it was decided to indict the fifteen main defendants from the many arrested in connection with the JAFC in a separate trial. Ryumin rejected the suggestion of some investigators not to interrogate the actor Zuskin and the translators Ostrovskaya and Teumin in the group proceedings, because they had no relation at all to the leadership of the JAFC.[41] And since Zhemchuzhina was already in a camp, she was no longer among the main conspirators.

Ignatiev, the minister for security, played almost no role at this stage. Stalin trusted Ryumin, who had proved himself to be particularly "vigilant" with his denunciations of Abakumov. He chaired the interrogations of the fifteen accused. As Shimeliovich testified later in court, they were not tortured anymore. But for the brave Shimeliovich, it was more difficult to accuse an investigator still holding office than the already disappeared Abakumov.

Ryumin declared, after he lost power, that he received a list from Stalin containing questions concerning the supposed relations of the interrogated with foreign secret services. It is difficult to say which was the stronger driving force for Ryumin: the ambition to present conspiracies to his great ruler Stalin, or—possibly an assignment already existing from the beginning—to "find" what Stalin, in his delusions, was already convinced of. In any case, the thrust was plain: there was a Jewish conspiracy to which all "Jewish nationalists," who had been arrested since the destruction of the Jewish cultural institutions, belonged.

One testimony pushed the next like a stack of dominoes. Under pressure of torture, the accused incriminated additional persons, who were also arrested and also "confessed" to taking part in the conspiracy. Sheinin was accused of nationalism; although he didn't deal with Jewish subjects in his plays, he recalled the nationalistic statements by other authors and fabricated a "nationalist group," among which he finally included even Ehrenburg and Grossman. Kaganovich, and Molotov were mentioned again and again in the interrogations as well.

The highest-ranking Jewish politicians were taboo for Ryumin and Ignatiev: Stalin therefore did not give them the green light, but out of the names heard in the interrogations, the MGB made a list of 213 persons against whom new investigations were ordered on March 13, 1952. The list included Ehrenburg, Grossman, Marshak, Kheifets, the doctor Zbarsky, and countless other Jewish VIPs. Had Stalin lived longer, these people would undoubtedly have faced trial in connection with the "doctor's conspiracy" uncovered in January 1953.

### First Signs of a "Doctor's Conspiracy"

The accusation that he shielded the JAFC leadership from being completely unmasked brought about Abakumov's downfall. But he committed—as Ryumin "found out"—a second crime that was much worse in Stalin's eyes. This intrigue was linked to the last act of the tragedy of the Stalinist persecution of the Jews, the so-called "doctor's conspiracy."

After 1949, purges also raged among the Soviet doctors to stop the supposed bad Jewish influence. Abakumov reported to Malenkov in July 1950 that the clinic for healing nutrition of the Academy of Sciences had been investigated, and that of 43 leaders and scientific cooperators 36 were of Jewish nationality. The minister for security wrote down the words "Jewish nationality" by hand in his report, so that this state secret remained secret even to the secretary who typed the rest. According to Abakumov, there was compromising material against 10 doctors. For example, the telephone number of one of the Jewish doctors was found in the notebook of an American tourist in 1939. The institute in question had to be purged of such individuals, meaning dismissals and later arrests and verdicts.[42]

In the fall of 1949, Yakov Etinger, one of the senior Soviet doctors, had already been dismissed in such a purge. He had been in regular contact with the JAFC since 1944. Fefer had incriminated Etinger during an interrogation on April 22, 1949, as a leader of the "bourgeois Jewish nationalists" among the doctors and declared that he had demanded Soviet support for Israel as well. Thereafter a bugging system was installed in Etinger's apartment and a conversation with his son that was critical of the government was recorded. Etinger was arrested on November 18, 1950, but evidently Abakumov soon realized that the indictments against him—concerning "criminal mistreatments"—were also untenable. On January 5, 1951, Etinger, who did not give a forced confession, was moved into the Lefortovo prison. Ryumin, who investigated his case, forwarded a list to Abakumov containing the name of Miron Vovsi, Mikhoels' cousin, with Etinger's "like-minded" Jewish doctors. As a result, many of these doctors were dismissed, and some arrested. Etinger died on March 2, 1951, from the effects of his imprisonment.[43]

In his letter to Stalin dated July 2, 1951, Ryumin maintained that Etinger had confessed to Abakumov of having willfully applied wrong procedures in the treatment of members of the government. As a result, he maintained that Abakumov had murdered Etinger and that he himself was involved in the plan to murder the party leadership with the support of the Kremlin doctors. To hush this up, he maintained that Abakumov had let Etinger be moved into the Lefortovo prison beforehand.

This completely fabricated informing led—together with the reproach of "forbearance" toward the JAFC—to Abakumov's downfall. The new leadership of the MGB under Ignatiev was immediately assigned by the CC to investigate the conspirators among the doctors. In April 1952 Ryumin finally found his "proof." The MGB collaborator Likhachev, one of the torturers of the JAFC members who was arrested along with Abakumov, "remembered," after lengthy interrogation, that Etinger confessed to Abakumov that Shcherbakov had been willfully mistreated out of hatred and, as a result, died before his time.

The accusation that the most important doctors maltreated the leaders of the state had its roots in a denunciation dating to 1948. This admittedly had a kernel of truth to it. In August 1948, the doctor and MGB informant Lydia Timashuk had sent an expert's opinion to the head of Stalin's bodyguards, Vlasik, in which she criticized the treatment methods used by the top doctors in the case of Zhdanov as insufficient. The doctors—among them Vinogradov and Etinger—had actually overlooked the symptoms of a heart attack. At this time, the secret police ignored

Timashuk's accusations; she was even dismissed from the Kremlin hospital. Her report—in which there was neither talk of crimes of the Jews nor of willful mistreatment—was seen as nothing less than an attempt to advance her career. But her document was still in Ryumin's drawer and belonged to the collection of material he intended to use against his former head Abakumov. But before Ryumin could make use of the complete potential of his new "findings" in 1952, the trial against the JAFC was set.

Lev Kamenev

Grigori Zinoviev

Yakov Sverdlov

Karl Radek

General Yan Gamarnik

*left*
Matvei Vainrub

*below*
General David Dragunsky
in the circle of the "Heroes
of the Soviet Union," who
distinguished themselves
during the capture of Berlin,
Vienna and Prague.

General Yevsei Vainrub

Henryk Erlich before and
during detention.

Viktor Alter before and
during detention.

Ilya Ehrenburg with Marshal Rokossovsky and other officers at the front.

Ilya Ehrenburg

Vassily Grossman (with glasses)

Abraham Sutskever

David Bergelson before
and during detention.

Itzik Fefer before and
during detention.

David Hofstein

Leib Kvitko before and during detention.

Peretz Markish before
and during detention.

Zelik Axelrod

Der Nister
(Pinchas Kahanovich)
before and during
detention.

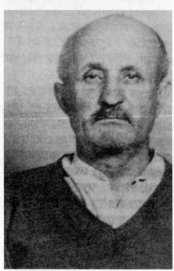

# Part VII

# THE TRIAL

## 29. THE INDICTMENT

### Verdict Before the Trial

On March 22, 1952, the MGB and military prosecutor declared the investigation closed. The documents, consisting primarily of the interrogation minutes of the last three years, filled a total of 42 extensive folders. These were then handed out to the accused shortly before the trial. Even though exhausted and with little time, they still managed to find numerous lies, contradictions, and stereotyped phrases in the documents.

On March 31, 1952, Ryumin gave his blessing to the indictments against the JAFC. The purported evidence of an even larger conspiracy, of which the JAFC was to be the center, was not considered. On April 3 Ignatiev gave Stalin the indictments against the "Jewish nationalist American spies Lozovsky, Fefer and others." Copies were also sent to Malenkov and Beria with an accompanying letter containing a suggestion of the sentences to be passed: all of the accused should be executed, with the exception of Lina Stern, who was to be exiled for ten years. One day later the MGB received information from the Politburo that the indictment was approved, as well as the suggested sentence of the firing squad; only Lina Stern was exiled for five years rather than ten.

In April the Soviet Supreme Court appointed a judge to preside over the trial. Their choice was the Lieutenant General of Justice, Aleksandr

Cheptsov. On April 21 Cheptsov, in a meeting with the senior prosecutor of the Red Army, was informed about the case. Cheptsov was an experienced lawyer and had been ceaselessly active in the Military Board of the Supreme Court since 1926. He had, in fact, passed death sentences on other members of the JAFC in 1949 and 1950, always with the justification as to how the charges were formulated. It was also ordered that neither representatives of the prosecutor nor the defense were to take part in the trial.

As he would later explain, Ignatiev had already informed Cheptsov as to what verdicts to issue.

### The Indictment

Kumin, the MGB investigator for especially important cases, was handling the composition of the documents,[1] which Ryumin confirmed. It stated that charges were filed against Lozovsky, Fefer, Bregman, Yuzefovich, Shimeliovich, Kvitko, Markish, Bergelson, Hofstein, Zuskin, Stern, Talmi, Vatenberg, Teumin, and Vatenberg-Ostrovskaya, for crimes according to paragraph 58-la, 58-10, part 2 and 58-11. These paragraphs applied to the accusations of "attempt to topple, undermine, or weaken the Soviet Union," as well as agitation, propaganda or organized action to that effect. For these "counterrevolutionary crimes," the death sentence was a possible consequence.

The charges were justified by the result of the investigation that the accused had transformed the JAFC into an espionage and nationalist ring, directly controlled by reactionary forces in the United States. Those held chiefly responsible were Fefer, Lozovsky, and the deceased Mikhoels and Epstein; all others were said to be accomplices. The main offense was the demand for a Jewish republic in the Crimea as a "bridgehead" for the Americans.

The indictment explained in great detail the "nationalistic" activities of the accused—which were referred to as belonging to "foreign classes"—prior to the founding of the JAFC. Special emphasis was paid to their activities in parties that, during the revolution, were enemies or competitors of the Bolsheviks, as well as the defendants' time spent in foreign countries. It was established that all of the accused were already enemies of the state at the time of the founding of the JAFC, and they were simply waiting for the opportunity to carry out their subversive activities and intensify them as soon as Mikhoels and Epstein could be recruited.

The strategy of maintaining contact with foreign Jewish organizations as allies was said to have come from Lozovsky, who for this reason numbered among the prime suspects still alive. The purpose for Mikhoels' and Fefer's trip to America, made possible by Lozovsky, was to ensure American assistance for their subversive activities. In return, they were to guarantee to the Americans that the infiltration by Jews of the Crimea would be carried out, and that Mikhoels and Fefer were to pass government secrets on to the United States.

Upon returning from the United States, their first collaborative act was to write the Crimea letter to the government, under the direction of Lozovsky. The basic idea of the Crimea letter was said to be "Zionist-nationalist" and in direct conflict to the Leninist viewpoint on Jewish issues. It was also said that the accused, in order to collect espionage information, had set up an elaborate communication network. Even harsher, however, were the accusations against the visits of the Americans Goldberg and Novick, in whose defense Lozovsky and Fefer had spoken in 1945-1946. As with Mikhoels' and Fefer's contacts in America, it was suggested that the government knew absolutely nothing of their contacts with Americans and that the "Jewish nationalists" had literally forced them. This was naturally to weaken the possible counter accusation that the Agitprop branch of the CC actually supervised and supported every step taken by the JAFC.

To further support the espionage theory regarding Novick, Goldberg and the JAFC, the indictment cited such harmless testimonies of Lozovsky that he had, while traveling, given Goldberg contacts and information about the daily life of Soviet citizens. The way this was written made every contact or conversation with Goldberg by any of the accused defendants (which all had had at some point), an exchange of espionage information and secrets. Lina Stern's contact with foreign scientists was interpreted in the same way.

The defendants were not only accused of espionage but also of nationalist propaganda. They were resisting—so it was said—the natural growing assimilation trend and were promoting the Jews' alienation from the rest of society. The nationalistic cooperation with the Jewish reactionaries from the United States was said to be especially obvious in the *Black Book*, which promoted the idea that Hitlerism was only a warning and endangering factor for the Jews, but not for world civilization as a whole. No less nationalistic was the work of the Moscow Jewish Theater. The accused had changed the JAFC into a center that had acted with complete hostility toward the friendship of the Soviet nation and also toward the interests of the USSR's working Jews.

The defendants had been convicted of all this through "confessions" (these were extensively quoted in the indictment) and also by the documents. In the last part of the indictment, separately listed, are all the accusations pertaining to and concerning every single defendant—every single one of them was burdened and loaded with crimes according to the already documented penal code paragraphs. It "smelled like blood," as Lozovsky would say later during the course of the proceedings.

## 30. THE TRIAL

The trial against the 15 JAFC members began around noon on May 8, 1952, in the auditorium of the Dzerzhinsky Club of the MGB. The court convened under Cheptsov. Assessors to the judge were Dmitriev and Saryanov; both had military ranks corresponding to those of the secretary, Afanasiev. After the 15 accused defendants had introduced themselves with their biographies and had called special attention to their numerous awards and medals, they proposed to bring more written material for inspection and observation. The accused poets tried to document with their works their pro-Soviet inclination. Lozovsky and Yuzefovich tried to prove that the materials they had given to foreign nations held no secrets. It was immediately clear to the judges who would show the strongest resistance: Shimeliovich insisted that he himself had never confessed or stated his guilt, and Lina Stern resisted and denied seeing espionage in the exchange of scientific thoughts or issues.

While Fefer and the editorial staff employee Teumin pleaded guilty after a reading of the indictment, Markish, Lozovsky, Bregman and Shimeliovich protested their innocence. Yuzefovich, Kvitko, Bergelson, Hofstein, Vatenberg, Zuskin, Talmi and Vatenberg-Ostrovskaya admitted to being "partially guilty." Stern explained that their guilt was because they were ranking members of the JAFC and, as party members, they did not concern themselves enough with the actual duties of the committee.

## Fefer—Witness for the Prosecution

The first of the accused to be interrogated was Fefer. He was, in fact, with the exception of Hofstein, who was considered politically less important, also the first to be arrested. As an MGB informant, he was simultaneously defendant and witness against the accused. Through his statements, the other defendants should have been, analogous to the preliminary hearings, put immediately on the defensive. Fefer gave his biography, confirmed having joined the Bund in 1917 for one and a half years, and to having met in 1920 the "Jewish nationalists" Bergelson, Hofstein, and Kvitko, whose opinions should have been obvious through their nationalistic writings.

Fefer began, as was expected of him, with immediate accusations—of which he too was a part and that included himself. Even with all his mistakes, he claimed never to have been an enemy of the state. He claimed his nationalistic tendencies first emerged during the mass liquidations of Jewish schools, newspapers, and other institutions in the 1930s, the so-called progressing "assimilation." He viewed the national holidays of the Uzbek culture with great jealousy. If he went to the synagogue a few times himself, it was not out of religious reasons but rather out of tradition for Jewish culture. And, above all, his work in cooperation with *Eynikeyt* was nationalistic, because the distribution of literature to glorify the heroism of the Jews was in direct conflict with the heroism of the Soviet people. The fact that he did this under orders of the Central Committee was, of course, not mentioned.

He came now to the committee's next crime—the Crimean question—bringing them into deadly territory. According to the indictment, the Crimean plan was hatched under orders from Rosenberg, the American, who with the support of the *Joint*, as had been discussed, described America's interest in the Crimean region due to the fact that it bordered on the Black Sea, Turkey, and the Baltic. The conversion of the Crimea into an American bridgehead was never explicitly discussed; however, he probably did not understand the true scope of American intentions.

Fefer was also asked about the *Black Book*, which was published in the U.S. even though it was banned. His response was that the People's Commissariat for Foreign Affairs had exported materials for the *Black Book* in 1944, prior to the book's banning. His interrogation, like that of all the other accused, jumped constantly between the issues of nationalism and espionage. The Jewish Theater—as explained by Fefer—was also a platform for Jewish nationalism and propaganda because it glorified and idealized the Jewish past. At that point the prosecution attempted to hang something on the already deceased Mikhoels, but Fefer defended Mikhoels adamantly, saying that while Mikhoels took a Bible with him to the U.S. for agitation purposes, the Bible nevertheless was one of the great treasures of Jewish culture. He quickly countered the accusation that he himself used biblical motifs by pointing out the valuable cultural inheritance of every people, and in that respect there was no reason to renounce Solomon.

As a further nationalist act, Fefer cited his poem "I am a Jew." His defiant self-accusation went so far as to name Stalin, otherwise heard only rarely during the trial:

> I said I love my people. But who does not love his people? I wanted to view my people the same as any other people. But when I saw how everything was closed, liquidated, I turned against Soviet power. It was this that motivated my interest in the Crimea and Birobidzan. It seemed to me that only Stalin could correct this great historical injustice committed by the Roman emperors. It seemed to me that only the government of the Soviet Union could correct this injustice by founding a Jewish nation. I didn't have anything against the Soviet state. I am the son of a poor teacher. The Soviets made a man of me as well as a fairly prominent writer. I have written that we "have drunk from Stalin's cup and been strengthened, that the Slavs are our friends." The target of my writing was that we would dance on Hitler's grave. You will find no other people that suffered as much as that of the Jewish people. Six million of 18 million Jews were exterminated; that is a third. This is a great sacrifice—and we had a right to our tears, and we fought against fascism."

With comments like these, Fefer quickly attracted criticism from the judges: during the preliminary hearing, he called the committee a nationalistic center. Fefer quickly cooperated and attacked Shimeliovich, formerly the closest advisor to Mikhoels, as one of the most aggressive nationalists.

Stern had also spoken often of the discrimination of the Jews in the Soviet Union and demanded to talk about it publicly, "like the Belorussians helped the Germans to destroy the Jews." Hofstein, who had devoted himself to the fostering and cultivation of the Hebrew language, could find similar nationalistic tendencies. He had always complained about the committee's lack of support for Palestine, but the committee did not want to have anything to do with Palestine because of the "Jewish fascists." That is why he had refused in the name of the committee, also according to the wish of some Jews, to place and send troops to Palestine.

Even though Fefer made some efforts to defend and justify himself during both days of the hearing by the judge (on May 8 and 9, 1952) he did not take back his damaging statements from the preliminary hearings. Now the other defendants began to place their questions. Lozovsky confronted him right away with questions about political competence and dependencies of the committee. Naturally, Fefer had to admit that the Central Committee now directed the committee and that *Eynikeyt* was placed under its press division. He had to admit also that Shimeliovich had written neither for *Eynikeyt,* nor had known anything about the *Black Book*. Shimeliovich wanted to ask Fefer further questions to correct his conflicting declarations from the preliminary investigations, but Fefer had only one answer: He could not remember.

After that, Kvitko tried to turn Fefer the denouncer into Fefer the delinquent. Fefer should have informed the committee about the mailing and transfer of the *Black Book* materials to the U.S. As the defendants revealed more and more absurdities in Fefer's denunciations, even the judge seemed to be irritated. To the supposedly pro-American statements by the translator Khaya Vatenberg-Ostrovskaya, the judge asked Fefer almost cynically if the accused criticized the constitution of the USSR, or if he just had preferred American clothing.

Still on the evening of the second day of the trial, the defendant Emilia Teumin was questioned. She had, as the only one besides Fefer, confessed her supposed guilt. At first she declared that Mikhoels had once stated his "nationalist tendencies." He had spoken about discrimination against Jews in the USSR and about the government not fighting anti-Semitism enough. "Instead of answering him, I remained silent. That was my fault." She was not a nationalist; she was rather the opposite. Too many Jews worked in the *Sovinformburo*. Concerning another accusation, that is, the editing of articles, she was really not responsible.

## Markish Counterattacks

Since it became quickly evident that Teumin—who had only worked once for the JAFC—knew really very little and had ended up in the prisoners' dock only because of some transfer of material to the alleged spy B. Z. Goldberg, the hearing of Markish began on May 10 and lasted three days. Markish declared the writers sitting next to him in the prisoners' dock to be his opponents. He especially attacked Fefer's poem "I am a Jew." This poem was "not only nationalistic but also tasteless." His second attack was aimed at Mikhoels: "Mikhoels was certain that nobody would do him wrong because…this would be seen and observed as anti-Semitism and as protest against the nationality policy of the party. Mikhoels and I were ideologically foreign to each other." Bergelson and Epstein were also nationalists and thus opponents. He backed off, though, from the declarations against Lina Stern that he had made during the preliminary inquiry.

Markish behaved much more carefully when judging the allegations to be espionage than during the harmless questions about nationalism. He found the assertion that the committee had transferred "espionage material" to be "objectively correct." He had not found out about it until the inquiries, though. He also did not know that Goldberg was supposed to have been a spy and the MGB supposedly did not notice this either. After this sharp final statement, it was the defendants' turn to question Markish. As with Fefer, they were able to discover discrepancies in his accusations. Fefer was able to confront Markish, for example, with the fact that he had really been close friends with Mikhoels.

When the chairman asked why Markish had accused himself at the preliminary hearing, Markish at first vaguely indicated his "abnormal" condition during the investigation. He declared later, though, that the minutes of the trial had been taken without his consent. In spite of this, Markish stuck to his main theme of accusation against the JAFC, namely, that it had developed into a nationalist center instead of pursuing the course planned by the government. He emphasized and extrapolated this with a personal attack against Fefer—maybe even out of revenge for his denunciation. Fefer, who wanted to give the Americans the Crimea as a bridgehead, had no right to look a Soviet judge in the eyes. In similar fashion he attacked Lozovsky. He declared then that Hofstein, Kvitko and Bergelson—whom he despised as poets and humans—certainly had not been spies at all, only nationalists.

Bergelson was next to be questioned. His biography contained such "suspicious moments" as his Talmud studies during childhood and his activities for the Cultural League during the period between the October Revolution and the Bolshevik conquest of the Ukraine. He did not attempt to hide the fact that his denial of the Bolsheviks was the motive for his flight from the Soviet Union in 1921. When the judge pointed out that, according to his confession, he was still fighting against Soviet power, he denied all accusations, saying that he had signed the confession against his own free will.

For Bergelson it must have been a personal liberation to openly declare that the hymn to the biblical characters was no more a crime than Fefer's poem "I am a Jew." He admitted, though, in various places his previous nationalist tendencies but argued strongly that the interrogation protocols of other arrested Jewish authors, such as Gordon, Dobrushin and Der Nister, were cited against him. Bergelson also retracted his own statement against the others accused.

## Forced Confessions

On May 15 the poet Leib Kvitko was interrogated. He declared himself guilty in front of the party and the Soviet nation for having worked at the committee that had greatly damaged his homeland but claimed that he had never been a nationalist. As with all the others, various details of his biography and long visits abroad were held against him. Shortly thereafter, Kvitko spoke about the methods of the preliminary investigation. His confessions were made under pressure by the interrogators, who had created the protocols at their own discretion. After the statements, the court was adjourned for a whole week. The minutes of the trial records contain no hint as to the cause for this adjournment until May 22, 1952. It was most likely not the fact of the forced confessions but rather the reaction to Kvitko's revelation of the interrogation methods during the preliminary investigation and hearing that shocked the judges. They had most likely assumed that the accused would play this farce out to the end, but things turned out differently. Not only did Kvitko refer to the reprisals but the defendants before him had also retracted their confessions.

When the trial reconvened, Kvitko repeated his statements of the previous week, which meant that the accused were not exposed to further extreme torment during the proceedings—not as in the show trial of 1938, in which the defendant Krestinsky was tormented and tortured after retracting his confession and was interrogated with methods of physical terror to the point that on the very next day he restated his original confession. Nonetheless, Kvitko stuck to his statement that the JAFC had been active in the nationalist sense. He said he wrote Yiddish to steer the Jewish people toward assimilation. Lozovsky undermined this through his personnel policies, in that he pulled assimilated individuals, such as Bregman, as "Jews" into the committee. Kvitko, a Yiddish poet of world renown, whose words one remembers, broken by years of imprisonment, closed this confusing accusations by pointing out that the JAFC and its "affiliate," Mikhoels' theater, had worked "against assimilation."

## "Jewish Nationalism" or Assimilation?

Fefer, who questioned Kvitko's pro-assimilation stance, countered that Lenin and Stalin had always supported the Jewish language as a part of Soviet culture. The assimilation of the Jews was not a political goal of the party, or else there would be no Birobidzan. Kvitko was obviously attempting to present himself as a perfectly pure anti-nationalist with support for the assimilation of the Jews; it was an attempt to placate more than any party announcement had ever been. By this he tried to get himself out of the line of fire. He went very far now to accept his own guilt in the use of Yiddish: "The use of a language that the masses had given up, that already had its history behind it, that not only isolates us from the life of the Soviet Union but also from the general mass of the Jewish people that had already assimilated, is in my opinion a special form of nationalism. Beyond that I do not feel guilty."

Next to retract his confession regarding nationalist beliefs was Hofstein. It was revealed that he had first heard of the Crimea letter during the procedure against him. Cheptsov's impatience grew even more when Hofstein allowed none of his confessions to be considered true and explained that the prosecution had forced all statements as well.

Yuzefovich also denied the accusation of treason against him. When, for example, he gave B.Z. Goldberg material for a book against English imperialism he forgot to get written permission from the Foreign Policy Branch of the Central Committee. He claimed that his self-destructive confession against the committee was only made under the stipulation that he later be allowed to appeal directly to Stalin and Molotov. After the grueling interrogations he would have admitted to being the nephew of the Pope and acting in his name. He now simply pointed out that the committee had always acted with approval "from the top." In the following questioning, in which Yuzefovich withdrew further accusations, Fefer accused him of nationalist tendencies that were evident in the fact that he had demanded a memorial for the Jewish victims in Maidanek.

## The Main Defendant

Lozovsky's hearing began on the evening of May 27. He was the highest ranking defendant and the only former representative of the center of power among them. The trial proceedings had already lasted about three weeks and it was evident that everything was supposed to be concentrating on Lozovsky. The testimony against him had been shown to be without support. He claimed himself to be innocent. Lozovsky stated his biography in great detail in order to weaken the prosecution's accusations. It is true that Lozovsky had been excluded from the party because he protested the state nationalization of the unions in 1917. After his reacceptance, he had never been an enemy of Soviet power.

Lozovsky now proved the absurd accusations against him to be totally unfounded and without evidence. How could he have avoided employing foreign persons for translations into foreign languages? Why was he especially accused in regard to the Jewish Anti-Fascist Committee and not for all five committees? (He had to repeat this criticism of anti-Semitic tendencies again toward the end of the interrogations against him.) Why should the meeting with Rosenberg have been criminal, but the meeting with the Polish politician Mikolajczyk, which was organized with permission of the Slavic Committee, not? The committee's members—meaning all the accused nationalist criminals—had been checked out by Alexandrov and were confirmed by Shcherbakov.

He then retracted in general all statements about confronting Fefer and accused him of "stepping forward as witness for the prosecution." Fefer—obviously attacked—defended himself by saying that he could not even know if Lozovsky had had knowledge about the nationalist goals of the committee. The commission collecting money from rich Jews in the U.S. had come from Shcherbakov and not from Lozovsky, whom he had clearly slandered during the court inquiry. Following this,

Bergelson, Kvitko, Bregman and Markish also retracted all their statements against Lozovsky.

One of the committee's tasks, according to Lozovsky, was to appear in the largest and most important bourgeois papers like the *New York Times*. If under "information" was understood in principle "espionage information," the entire *Sovinformburo*'s work would have been espionage.

No less extraordinary was the Crimea issue with which Lozovsky was burdened and heavily accused during the pre-examination because he supposedly had assisted Fefer and Mikhoels in the organization and completion of their pro-American commission. Lozovsky described how the wording of the letter took place and that he saw it only as a private declaration of individual Soviet citizens and not as the committee's activity. The demand for a Jewish territory—that he had not supported—was not a "sale of the Crimea." All the statements Fefer made regarding the talk between the *Joint* chief, Rosenberg and himself concerning important plans were dismissed by Lozovsky as political nonsense. His reactions became much more sarcastic. He made Fefer's declarations and statements sound laughable as "works of literature" and described himself with biting irony as an "enemy since 1919." This gallows humor approach was for him the only possible way to deal with the absurd accusations. The entire trial was a farce and it was questionable if there was even a way out of it.

This is the reason he did not use tactics and diplomacy but instead pointed to the fact that the interrogators themselves could only have produced the identical wording of isolated persons in the 42 volumes of indictment. Lozovsky strongly attacked the self-accusation of Yiddish authors who admitted to acting out of nationalism simply because of their language. It wasn't nationalism if one wanted to write and publish Yiddish because everybody should be allowed to write in any language. To this the presiding judge offered his spontaneous agreement. Regarding the question whether the materials handed to B.Z. Goldberg about English politics really had been secret, Lozovsky was able to get the judge to deny it.

Close to the end of his trial and hearing, which had taken six days, he retracted all statements against the three persons he had accused—against himself, Lina Stern and Polina Molotova. After that he offered a clever explanation as to why Fefer had denounced everyone else. Fefer really was a nationalist and thus the more individuals he involved in this indictment, the greater the uproar among the diplomatic representatives of

Israel would be. Fefer had wanted to start an international Soviet campaign against the closing of Jewish institutions. Lozovsky, on the other hand, had only wanted to direct the attention of politically responsible persons to the trial proceedings through the signing of totally absurd statements, which the anti-Semitic inquisitor Komarov decreed. Someone like Molotov would have to laugh if he only read that Lozovsky had "used" Zhemchuzhina to transmit letters to him, since Lozovsky had access and could see Molotov as deputy foreign minister. While in prison he was not allowed to write to Stalin or any other CC member. That is why he had signed the confession, to finally have an opportunity to tell the truth at the indictment.

## Torture and Testimony

Following a long interrogation of Lozovsky, which had developed into a debacle due to the absent plaintiffs, the medical doctor Shimeliovich was cross-examined on June 2. He reported methods at the preliminary inquest not known in detail before. He was beaten two thousand times, especially during the early phase of the inquiry. When Ryumin took over the inquiries after Abakumov's removal from power, psychological not physical torture methods were employed.

Shimeliovich insisted and stuck to his testimony that Markish had nationalist tendencies but was not a nationalist. Fefer, on the other hand, caught his attention because of his speeches in court, but actually since 1949 as being a convinced nationalist. All statements and testimony about nationalist "crime" in the record of the proceedings had definitely been created by Ryumin, except one: he had declared one time, it is true, that it was an honor for the Jewish people to be selected by Hitler for elimination. The judge branded this thought, originating with Ehrenburg, as evil nationalism.

The name Ehrenburg was barely mentioned during the trial. Bregman attributed the disagreements about the *Black Book* to Ehrenburg and Grossman, disagreements which were supposedly mainly about the State's royalties. After this blow below the belt, which had to do with Bregman's open dislike of the writers in the committee, there followed a detail from the *Black Book's* history that made readers of the protocol wonder. Bregman said that the commission under his leadership had found out that the material gathered by Ehrenburg and Grossman was much better than the

JAFC's. The JAFC's materials wrongly showed the Ukrainians and Belorussians to be the culprits in the Jews' extermination, while Grossman's material shows how they saved the Jews. Bregman used this to turn the facts upside down. In the judgment of February 24, 1945, the Ehrenburg material was criticized because it pushed the crimes of the native domestic population too strongly ahead of the rest. Why did Bregman turn this around at the Court of Justice? Possibly it could have been as a result of three years of grinding imprisonment, but a potential forgery of the facts would allow a certain logic: it seemed inadvisable to Bregman to criticize or taint Ehrenburg, who so far was being spared by the regime—otherwise he would have been among the indicted defendants.

Ehrenburg's special role in all the attacks on the JAFC later led to the myth that he himself was a witness for the prosecution in the trial. This is totally wrong. Lozovsky revealed that even in the preliminary inquiry records of the proceedings there had been statements by Fefer against Ehrenburg. The experts explained in a secret meeting at the end of the trial, though, that they were made for the purpose of assessing an article by Ehrenburg, "Because of a letter," together with the classics of Marxism-Leninism about the Jewish question. Ehrenburg was therefore used as an example of what still looked appropriate.

## An Agent Reveals Himself

Bregman's lie remains an unsolved puzzle, a warning to read the trial records with care. This pertains especially to the declarations which Fefer made on June 6, 1952, after Bregman's hearing at a secret meeting of the Court of Justice from which his JAFC comrades had been excluded.[2] Fefer withdrew his answers and revealed himself as an agent of the Ministry for State Security under the cover name "Zorin." What had led him to do that? It wasn't difficult to guess.

He had recognized that after almost one month into the trial the game in which he was supposed to play the main part was miserably lost. His declarations had originally had the effect of bringing forward more confessions. Obviously, Fefer had hoped to emerge from this proceeding with a lesser verdict for "nationalism" if he cooperated as chief witness. But all his testimony against the other defendants was proven to be false and he remained stuck in his own self-accusations. In this situation he must have decided to use his MGB bonus to give his countermands credibility. He explained openly to the court that the indictments were totally built on sand because, due to espionage material that had been sent to America, "It could not be different because all this did not exist in reality. I have nothing to add to my statements."

This followed another self-disclosure during a secret hearing of the Court of Justice immediately thereafter. Yuzefovich said that he had forced himself in 1938 to cooperate with the state security organs. Since he could not fulfill his task, because the Jewish writers he was allegedly to have spied on began to suspect him, he had asked to be relieved from the commission that same year. Then he explained to the jurisdiction that he had made these untrue statements against Lozovsky only because he was afraid of Abakumov's threats of torture. It is also true that he was beaten with a rubber cudgel and kicked. That was why he had decided to sign anything only to have his day in court.

## The Accused: A Language

On June 7, when the trial continued, Talmi was the next to declare his innocence. In spite of this, he showed his willingness to consider participating in the activities on behalf of *Icor*, the American partner organization of *Gezerd*.

At the end of July 1950, after fourteen months of nightly hearings, the inquisitors gave him quotations by Stalin and Lenin to read pertaining to the nationality question. This cleared his nebulous mind and he saw that all the work in the area of Jewish culture was in reality wrong and that a group of Jewish nationalists was misleading the government and party. "For the Jewish people to develop their culture, it was not necessary that everything had to be in Yiddish."

Talmi was not the last one on trial who started to deny the Yiddish language. One should see the reason not in a real change of mind, even if the dislike toward Yiddish as a dialect had a long tradition. The defendants recognized that their mother language also stood before justice. Talmi, who was arrested last, had witnessed the assaults on "Jewish nationalism," the closing of theaters and dissolution of the literary organizations while he was still free. Distancing himself from Yiddish helped to vindicate himself and should convince the court that the defendants did not fight the new anti-Jewish and anti-Yiddish tendencies in the cultural policy of the state— and that they really should be left alone and they could be spared.

At this point in time it seemed clear to the judge that all declarations and statements and testimony from the pre-examinations were pure fiction. When the defendant Vatenberg mentioned a forged protocol in which he supposedly confessed to espionage activities, Cheptsov did not even react anymore, although he had always inquired vigorously in similar situations with the other defendants. The defendants Vatenberg-Ostrovskaya and Zuskin also revoked their statements from their preliminary hearings, as did Lina Stern, who described the prison as the "front yard to hell," vegetating in a cell with a cement floor which was almost unheated in February. After this heartbreaking declaration the prosecution recessed for fourteen days.

## The Experts Disgrace Themselves

The proceedings continued on June 26, 1952, with testimony from the experts. The defendants were excluded. First the experts spoke to issues about treason regarding secrets. They complained that during the preliminary inquiry they had never had the JAFC's original records and files, only copies without detailed and precise information. They were also not told which materials had been sent to foreign countries and how. They were influenced, though, by suggestions that the materials had been smuggled through censorship. If they had known that the material had been correctly censored, they would have judged differently.

It also became evident that judging the reliability of the scattered information was assessed according to a list from 1945 that was no longer valid in 1948. The nature of the JAFC's informational espionage had been revealed because they were certain "that foreign countries would be only interested in, and ask for material that was, a state secret."

In closing, the experts admitted that their judgment was incomplete and insufficient. The result of the interrogated persons from the literary-minded judge was no less revealing on the following day. It became evident that the "nationalist" passages in Talmi's book about Birobidzan consisted of his stating that one Russian village was "not as pretty" as a Korean one. The literature expert responsible for the opinion claimed weakly that she had only studied the book superficially, but stubbornly insisted on treason pertaining to some alleged state secrets like the descriptions of gold mines.

The next hearing focused on a book concerning the policies of England, highlighting a trial already so rich in absurdities. This supposedly secret document was exclusively based on information from British newspapers and broadcasts. The transfer of these materials to B.Z. Goldberg was still branded as uttermost treason because the document was put together and created in a secret institute. Finally, the literary experts testified after they had researched the JAFC's ideology for a month. They had also been given only manipulated material for research with the indication that the JAFC had been supposedly liquidated as a nationalist center.

After this almost tragicomic interlude, which eliminated even the last spark of the proceeding's legitimacy, the defendants' hearings continued on July 2, 1952. Motions to allow more documents to be introduced were denied. After the experts' hearings the situation was clear to everyone: thus far no well-founded conclusion existed as to the legality of the prosecution.

## Last Declarations and Final Words

Once again the defendants were given permission to make additional statements. Fefer took this opportunity to accuse the experts of espionage-mania and of misleading a Soviet Court of Justice; he also withdrew his statements against Emilia Teumin. Markish—still an outsider—was outraged by several negative declarations about Yiddish that other defendants had made during the proceedings. He hoped that "Soviet culture allowed a history of Yiddish, a language that worked like an unschooled laborer for the masses, giving them songs and lamentations. Yiddish gave the people everything during the heavy and difficult years, when they lived in the settlement regions cut off from Russia..." Also ambivalent, Bergelson spoke about how Yiddish was the reason for his unmanageable nationalism. He was jealous of the Russian writers and their far richer language.

The penultimate day of the proceedings, July 11, 1952, began with a closed hearing for Fefer's secret statements. The previous day Shimeliovich had harshly attacked him for his behavior in court. Fefer—at the last second—abandoned his role as a special witness. He had spoken about his own nationalism and that of Markish and other writers, but he had no knowledge of nationalism as a crime. Part of his statements during the inquiries was true but other parts were not. The inquisitors had falsified his declarations about the nationalist inclination of others.

Fefer also started to discuss the physician Etinger, whose name had not come up once during the trial. Etinger had been arrested during the early phase of the supposed doctors' plot and at the time of the trial was already dead. Ryumin had tried to connect the alleged doctors' conspiracy with the JAFC, and along these lines Fefer must have been asked about physicians prosecuted later. Fefer declared now before justice that Etinger was very much interested in Israel and had criticized the Soviet government for supporting Lysenko's teachings.

On the following day the defendants delivered their final statements. Fefer pointed out that he had always been a communist. All the accomplishments of the Jews were thanks to Stalin's teaching and the example of the Russian people. Teumin said she had transferred informational material in the belief of doing something useful. Markish again rejected any accusation of nationalism on his part. In the future he wanted to "write conscientiously in the language of Lenin and Stalin." If he had made a mistake through his connections with the JAFC, he regretted this during the three and a half years he spent in prison; he was supposed to be released soon. Yuzefovich emphasized that he had never committed espionage, and for his mistake he was responsible only to the party. Lozovsky declared succinctly that he considered this proved that the accusations against him were unsubstantiated and unfounded. Kvitko said he still didn't understand why he was accused of such crimes and demanded to see proof.

Bergelson agreed that he had not yet reached the level of a pure Soviet person, although he was the only one from the generation of Bialik and Ash who had embraced the ideas of Lenin and Stalin. Hofstein had nothing more to say. Vatenberg stated that all the material directly proved his innocence. Shimeliovich, the bravest of the defendants, attacked the inquisitors anew with force and fury. To prove his loyalty he said that he had agreed at the time to release 18 Jewish editors of medical magazines. He alone demanded that physical punishment and torture in prison be forbidden and he tried to convince "a few MGB coworkers" that it was not their investigation section but the party's that was most holy. This may sound naive today because we know that Stalin and the party stood behind the criminal inquisitors, but in 1952 Shimeliovich was the only one who had dared to speak directly about this torture. Much more restrained were Zuskin, who spoke about his life, and Talmi, who placed the fate of his family up front. (His son was also arrested in 1947 because of connections with foreigners.) Khaika Vatenberg-Ostrovskaya expressed her hope that the court understood that she had nothing to do with the JAFC. As during the whole trial, Lina Stern was the last. She declared bravely and proudly that her arrest had done much more harm to the Soviet Union than all the activities of the JAFC combined. That was why she would again return to her medical research work.

If one were to summarize the mood of the "last words," it seems that the defendants were hopeful of emerging from this situation at least partially intact and unhurt. It was obvious in the course of two months that the charges were brought by the inquisitors in a very transparent way. Real proof had never existed and the combined retractions of the testimony robbed Stalinist justice of its most important elements: self-accusation and spontaneous confessions, which had been the centerpiece of the great show trials of the 1930s. When at 5:50 p.m. on the evening of July 11, 1952, the court recessed and stepped back into the consultation chambers, the defendants probably did not expect the worst.

## 31. The Sentence

### A Judge Doubts

Judge Cheptsov must have also been convinced that the indictment was unfounded. In a letter dated August 15, 1957, to General Shukov and the members of the CC Presidium of the CPSU—Khrushchev, Bulganin, Suslov, Brezhnev, Voroshilov, Shvernik, and Mikoyan—he expressed his doubts. Beginning with the case's prehistory, the letter describes the judicial inquiries against the JAFC's "nationalism," and also the arrests of Goldstein and Grinberg. Even though the Politburo believed serious inquiries had taken place, in the course of the proceedings so many curious details struck him that he wanted to conduct new inquiries. Even if the experts had ascertained that the defendants represented in their works the idea of a Jewish unity across all classes, it had been done openly and with official agreement. Moreover, Ryumin would have been unable to reveal that the contact persons from the U.S. were spies.

Suspecting that Ryumin had falsified the entire case, Cheptsov went to Ignatiev but the security secretary no longer enjoyed Stalin's trust. His attempts to stall the proceedings had come to nothing and he had turned directly to Malenkov.

Malenkov listened to him in the presence of Ignatiev and Ryumin, whereupon the latter immediately attacked the judge as a "liberal." After his arrest and shortly after Stalin's death, Ryumin confessed that he not only concealed the revoked confessions of the prisoners, but also—against the Court of Justice's wish to conduct additional inquests—had insisted that the judgment must be based on the existing "inquiry results."[3] Malenkov refused to change anything as the proceedings had been checked over three times by the Politburo and its judgment would be "appropriated by the nation." Cheptsov wrote in 1957 that he agreed to this—and that Ryumin immediately started to collect incriminating material about him.[4] In typically remarkable fashion, Cheptsov did not write this letter until Malenkov was finally and permanently out of power. His disclosures are supported by the rehabilitation document of 1989, which states:

> Cheptsov pointed out in […] explanations to the Party Control Commission of the CPSU's CC, that the Court of Justice had doubts about the completeness and objectivity of the inquiries in this case and thus should have denied its closing verdict at that time without additional inquiries; this, however, did not happen.
>
> Because of Cheptsov's explanations, A.A. Vohn, chief justice of the Soviet Supreme Court, had to report to G.N. Safonov, the USSR's attorney general, N.M. Shvernik, the chair of the presidium of the Supreme Soviet of the USSR, P.K. Ponomarenko, the secretary of the CPSU(B) and M.F. Shkiryatov, the chair of the Party Commission of the CC of the CPSU(B), that it was necessary to conduct additional inquiries but he had not received any support from them. They all advised him to consult Malenkov on this issue […]
>
> Cheptsov's explanations were confirmed. Ryumin, who had been involved and was present at the inquiries and interrogations in the case of Solomon Lozovsky and the others on July 24, 1953, during his judicial examination as defendant, confessed: "When the court in this case tried to reject a subsequent proceeding, I insisted that the verdict should be given based on the material present."
>
> P. Grishayev, former assistant to Ryumin, said: "I know from Ryumin that General Cheptsov turned for help during the judicial proceeding in the case of the 'Jewish Anti-Fascist Committee' to the court of judicature (probably meaning the CC) where he complained

about the deficiencies and blunders in these trial proceedings. But as Ryumin told me, General Cheptsov criticized this case not because he found the procedures questionable but because the indicted persons were not revealed and the roots of the crimes not yet discovered."

The final explanation quoted above could be interpreted to mean that Cheptsov was not at all as critical as he presented himself in 1957. Much more, though, it also appeared that he wanted to uncover a much larger conspiracy through further interrogations and gathering of more circumstantial evidence. One has to consider, however, that Cheptsov had to conform to the paranoid jargon used around him if he wanted to stall the prosecution—open criticism would not have been advisable. The criticism of the Secretary of State for Security, Ignatiev, and the Stalin loyalist Malenkov was already risky; it didn't matter in what kind of rhetoric the criticism was clothed. If Cheptsov's confrontation deserves respect, he still acted as an opportunist. After his one-week intervention, he announced on July 18, 1952—that is, one week after the last hearing—the verdict of the military collegium at 12 o'clock noon.

## Legalized Murder

Against his better knowledge, Cheptsov announced a verdict that meant the execution and death of thirteen innocent persons—a murder in the name of justice. He then advised the condemned victims of their right to submit a request for pardon to the Presidium of the Supreme Soviet of the USSR. According to Cheptsov's own declaration, he wanted to give the condemned a last hopeless chance.

The reason for the judgment could not be supported or justified; it could not fall back on proof of guilt or be supported by findings that had come to light and evidence presented during the past three-month-long prosecution. So the indictment was simply more or less paraphrased.[5] The course of proceedings was reconstructed this way: Lozovsky, a disguised enemy of the CPSU, supposedly had turned to Mikhoels and Epstein. As convinced long-time Jewish nationalists, they recruited, again supposedly with the knowledge of Lozovsky, the well-known Jewish nationalists Fefer, a former Bundist, along with Kvitko, Markish, and Bergelson. These last three were writers who were completely hostile to the October Revolution and had fled to foreign countries in the early

1930s. Next came Lina Stern from a "class-hostile" social milieu who had come from abroad to the USSR; Shimeliovich, a former Bundist; Yuzefovich, in the years 1917-1919 a leader of the "internationalists," who criticized the Bolsheviks; and finally Zuskin, the famous actor. The other committee members had no less suspicious and criminal biographies: Hofstein was a Zionist who had written in the reactionary Palestinian press; Talmi, initially a worker at the Jewish nationalist organization in the Ukraine, fled to the United States in 1921; Vatenberg was a member of the *Poale Zion*.

As in the indictment, the "trading" by the defendants with Jewish reactionaries of the United States was described: in exchange for "national activity" within the Soviet Union the Americans were supposed to provide material help for the Crimea. Under the direction of Rosenberg, the *Joint* chief, Mikhoels, Fefer, Epstein and Shimeliovich were supposed to have written, with the knowledge and agreement of their accomplices, a letter to the Soviet government in which they would explain and describe their plan to settle Jews in the Crimea and develop a Jewish republic there. This letter was to have been edited by Lozovsky before being mailed. (Lozovsky was still named by the prosecution as the sender of the letter.)

Contrary to the experts' affidavits, the indictment insisted that the materials mailed by the committee contained state secrets. In addition, the committee had participated in nationalist propaganda on behalf of American Jews in *Eynikeyt* and other Yiddish publications that spoke of the Jews' heroism and their successes in science.

Stronger than the indictment, the verdict indicated that the defendants praised biblical characters—this seemed to offend Cheptsov personally. Another newly added accusation was that the anti-Soviet work of Lozovsky, Fefer and their co-defendants had encouraged other nationalist Jews to turn to the JAFC, pleading to send them to Palestine to form volunteer units there for Israel. Like the indictment, the verdict stated that the committee's work had furthered the suspicion of discrimination against Jews in the Soviet Union and that the publication of the *Black Book* was to take place in cooperation between the JAFC and Jewish nationalists in the United States and Palestine with Lozovsky's agreement.

The court of justice had therefore come to the conclusion that all the "criminal anti-Soviet acts of the JAFC's leaders" bore witness to the fact that the JAFC had become an espionage and nationalist center. The indicted persons had known about it and actively participated in it.

As in the indictment, the individual offenses of the accused were cited once again. Because there was no evidence of any major criminal acts as proof to justify the verdict, greater attention was given to their background and social class as well as to their questionable biographies. All this was a cheap and poorly executed deception to wrap up the verdict, which had already been decided long in advance.

All the sentenced defendants, with the exception of Lina Stern, received the ultimate sentence—death by firing squad—with confiscation of all their belongings and property. Lina Stern received three and a half years imprisonment in a work-improvement camp and the suspension of her citizen's rights for three years without confiscation of property. Upon completion of her sentence, she was to be exiled to a distant region for five years and her pre-inquiry time of imprisonment since January 28, 1949, was to be counted toward her sentence. The length of imprisonment was exactly computed, though, so that Lina Stern could be immediately exiled. The reason to exile her and therefore save her life was that to her persecutors—the Politburo or the judges—she was no less "guilty" than the others but "more important." They still expected results from her research that she could complete and carry out in exile, for example, something that could prolong Stalin's life.

All the other defendants were stripped of their medals of honor. These were all awards "For heroic work during the Great Fatherland War" or "For Victory over Germany." Lozovsky even had an Order of Lenin and an Order of the Fatherland War First Class; Markish was also a recipient of the Lenin Medal. The verdict was final and without the possibility of appeal. Bregman was not sentenced; his prosecution ended July 9 after he collapsed due to his brutal imprisonment. He died on January 23, 1953.

The sentence was carried out on August 12, 1952 when the thirteen sentenced victims were shot to death.

Joseph Kerler*
Twelfth of August, 1952

O this day, this day, this day!
Sorrow and agony—grief and helpless lament,
Sorrow in the heart, soundless numb a woeful tone:

---

* Joseph Kerler was among the Soviet-Yiddish poets who survived Stalin's persecutions.

Markish...
Hofstein...
Kvitko...
Bergelson...

Nobody was there who could comfort them this night,
As they all were murdered.
The Light they saw in the bloody night:
Murderous lightning! The salvo roars!
O this day, this day, this day,
Blood soiled—like a gravestone
Now carry my song. And my heart must as light
Burn alone, for there is no grave:
Nothing, not a stone and not a light and not a sound
Markish...
Hofstein...
Kvitko...
Bergelson...

## 32. THE REHABILITATION OF THE JAFC

After the execution of the JAFC members, the fate and death of the defendants was kept secret. No government office or jurisdiction wanted to give any information to the surviving defendants who had also been arrested or exposed to repression. The Soviet leadership denied this unbelievable crime. Questions from foreign friends of those who had disappeared were answered with lies. Not until many years after the executions did the only living survivor of the secret proceedings, Lina Stern, tell the victims' widows and children details about the imprisonment and trial.

On April 4, 1956, five weeks after Khrushchev's secret report at the CPSU's Twentieth Party Conference (where the JAFC was not mentioned) the Yiddish newspaper, *Voice of the People* (*Folksshtime*) published in Warsaw an obituary under the title "Our pain and our comfort." The *New York Times* printed the column on April 12, 1956. There was obviously no interest anywhere in this tragic event. I have no knowledge of any intervention by the PEN Club in favor of their Yiddish-writing colleagues.

For many years the "Congress for Jewish Culture" in New York investigated the fate of the disappeared Jewish artists and intellectuals and came up with a list of 450 names—238 writers, 106 actors, 19 musicians, 87 painters and sculptors.[6] It does not include the names of state and party functionaries who were also among the victims. The executed of August 1952 had not been the first Jewish victims of Stalin, not even counting the many deaths during the 1930s show trials.

During these "black years" Soviet Jews destroyed millions of Yiddish books because possession alone could have led to the loss of freedom, if not worse. As if this were not enough, in July 1949 Glavlit. the Office for Censorship, ordered the removal of all the arrested authors' books from libraries, and other unsuitable works, such as the disturbing works by Lev Deich about the part the Jews played in the Russian Revolution.[7]

## The Secret Proceedings of 1955

On November 22, 1955, more than three years after the executions, preliminary proceedings by the military collegium of the Soviet Supreme Court of Justice were initiated once again against the JAFC. In the rehabilitation proceeding it had been discovered that Goldstein had been tortured into making accusations against Mikhoels and the committee. This led again to further arrests and it was established that Fefer was an agent of the MGB services.

The MGB methods of coercing signatures on falsified protocols, through torture and sleep deprivation, were openly displayed. Soviet representatives had actually approved Fefer's meetings in the U.S. This was just as clear to the inquisitors as the true ideological position of the alleged agents Goldberg and Novick. But even in 1955 the JAFC could not be exonerated of every criticism. Supposedly it became obvious in the judicial inquiries that some of the defendants thought they filled functions they did not have. They had supposedly interfered in issues about work placement in favor of the Jews or had attempted to achieve a release of Jews in the camps. Nationalist phrases could actually be found in some of their literary work. However, in 1955, counterrevolutionary state crimes could not be inferred from those accusations. Therefore it was decided to cancel the verdicts posthumously and halt all ongoing trials.[8]

Even high-ranking functionaries in the Soviet Writers' Association lied to their foreign colleagues about details pertaining to the disappear-

ance of Jewish poets and authors. The few publications in the West dealing with this topic did not receive appropriate attention. Even if, in the
1950s, erroneous ideas about the number of persons prosecuted and
tried still existed (e.g., Hofstein had not been shot because he had lost his
mind), important facts were also known, for example, about Fefer's role
as the only witness for the prosecution.[9]

Most of the surviving committee members emigrated to Israel in the
1970s, where the JAFC was reported sporadically in the press. A few
cities named streets after the executed of August 12, 1952. In Jerusalem,
on the initiative of Joseph Kerler, a memorial for the 24 victims of Stalin
was inaugurated on August 1977 to commemorate the 25-year anniversary of the execution of the JAFC members.

### The Public Rehabilitation of 1989

It was only in 1988 under Mikhail Gorbachev that the Central Committee of the Communist Party decided to reopen the judicial inquest of
the JAFC trial, begun in 1955 under Khrushchev, but not made public by
either him or his successor Leonid Brezhnev. A rehabilitation commission with high-ranking members took up its work and presented the results in a six-page report published in *Izvestiia CC* (the Central Committee
organ), number 12, in 1989. Incidentally, in addition to liberals like Yakovlev
and Medvedev, several members who had plotted in August 1991 against
Gorbachev also belonged to the commission.

In January 1989 *Pravda* announced the rehabilitation of the indicted
persons. The weekly supplement of *Izvestiia* published an interview with
a participant of the rehabilitation commission, Petukhov, who disclosed
the basic nature of the case. Shortly thereafter *Literary Gazette* printed a
contribution from Arkadi Vaksberg in which Cheptsov's 1957 letter to
Zhukov is quoted in detail. Vaksberg also reported about the last living
inquisitor against the JAFC, Pavel Grishayev, whose colleagues had been
executed after Stalin's death. He made a career as a law professor and
published, among other things, on the subject of "Repression in capitalist countries." This man, who could speak precisely and with great detail
about his deeds in the war, suddenly when asked by Vaksberg was unable
to recall events from that phase of his life.[10] David and Simon Markish
subsequently tried to initiate legal proceedings against Grishayev for the
murder of their father.[11]

The official document regarding the rehabilitation of the JAFC members did not provide much in the way of news for the public. The main responsibility was pinned on Malenkov, who was still in power in 1955. While the methods of torture were clearly described in the unpublished document from 1955, the 1989 document stated only "that the investigation and the trial were conducted with severe violations of justice and the methods to obtain confessions were conducted with impermissible practices." Cheptsov's explanations from 1957 state that "the indictment of innocent persons and the signing of the unjust sentence through him was decided by subordinate leadership beforehand." From Cheptsov's writing it can be also concluded that in 1955 Lozovsky, Fefer, Yuzefovich, Kvitko, Markish, Teumin, Bregman and Lina Stern had been admitted posthumously into the party. In 1988 this "honor" was extended to Shimeliovich and Hofstein. Not one word can be found about Fefer's membership in the MGB—even during the *glasnost* years the working procedures of state security remained taboo.[12]

On February 12, 1989, the Jewish Mikhoels Cultural Center was inaugurated on Taganka Place in Moscow. Nobel Prize recipient Elie Wiesel spoke, and musicians from Israel gave a concert. The director of the center, Mikhail Glus, also invited this author. My full-page essay in the *Frankfurter Allgemeine Zeitung* on August 14, 1991, with the Yiddish title "Zu unsere brider un schwester ojf die ganze welt" ("To Our Brothers and Sisters in the Whole World") summarized the tragic fate of the JAFC for the first time in the German media. The article was broadcast over Russian radio and several other stations in several different languages.

# Part VIII

# AFTER THE TRIAL

### 33. A CATASTROPHE AVERTED—STALIN'S LAST MONTHS

#### "Conspiracy of the Kremlin Doctors"

At the beginning of 1952, Stalin's physician Vinogradov fell into disfavor because he had advised the dictator to withdraw from political life to save his health. The paranoid Stalin saw this as an attempt to deprive him of power. He also warned Minister of Security Ignatiev that he would meet the same fate as Abakumov if he did not reveal who was behind the doctors' conspiracy. Stalin had been "informed," through Ryumin's denunciations, about allegedly intentional maltreatment methods since the summer of 1951. Based on these files, Stalin ordered the arrest of a group of physicians in September 1952. Ryumin found further "proof" that the physicians Vinogradov, Yegorov, Vasilenko, Busalov (none of them Jews), Etinger, Sofia Karnai, and others had been responsible for the death of Shcherbakov and Zhdanov. Vinogradov, Vovsi, Vasilenko, and Kogan were arrested in November 1952, with further arrests in December.

Stalin no longer trusted even Ryumin, whom he himself had appointed to this powerful position, and arranged that the JAFC's executioner be removed and transferred, on November 14, 1952, to a position at the Ministry for State Control. The new inquisitor against the physicians, S. Golidze, was especially interested in their "connections" to foreign secret services. Miron Vovsi was repeatedly accused of being—by way of his cousin Mikhoels—an important contact person to the Americans, and even an agent of the CIA and of the Israeli Secret Service. Stalin demanded daily reports about the interrogations and the prosecution proceedings. Just as in the 1930s show trials, the indicted persons were offered a deal. If they agreed to denounce other persons and furnish as many additional conspirators as possible and reveal their foreign co-conspirators, they would save their own lives and their families.

. Soon Stalin received letters of indictment in which Vovsi and Kogan confessed that in July 1952 they had resolved to murder Stalin, Beria and Malenkov. Because the medical methods didn't work, they had even planned assaults on the government's automobiles, but the security organs (who praised and glorified themselves with ever more fantastic and wilder fabrications) had prevented these from taking place.

An open trial against the physicians was planned. Even though not only Jews would have sat in the prison docks, this would have been the exact opposite of the secret sentence of the JAFC leadership. The Slansky trial, begun on November 20, 1952, in Prague, seemed to be, in retrospect, the final rehearsal for a Soviet anti-Semitic tribunal. In 1949 and 1950 leading Jewish functionaries of the communist parties of Hungary, Czechoslovakia, Poland and the GDR were already being confronted with repression. In the GDR a trial was even prepared against the non-Jew Paul Merker, who, among other things, worked for reparations.[1]

This parallel points to the different procedures in Stalin's persecution of his Jewish victims. Why had the JAFC members been murdered secretly in August 1952, while others found their death through show trials? Stalin's paranoia and anti-Semitism in the last years of his life cannot be the only explanation. Writer Borshchagovsky and historians Kostyrchenko and Redlich, while each making different points, showed that the dictator had organized a secret trial of the JAFC leadership. Leonid Luks assumes that Stalin thought a show trial of little known Yiddish writers by the broad population wasn't spectacular enough. The Jewish Kremlin physicians, the "murderers in white smocks," were much better suited to bring the nation's soul to boil than the little group of JAFC intellectuals.[2]

Stalin became more and more suspicious during his last months—he called Molotov, Mikoyan, Voroshilov and Beria agents of foreign secret services. Starting in October 1952, Molotov and Mikoyan were denied access to the office of the Presidium (the new name of the Politburo).

Khrushchev described in his speech at the Twentieth Party Congress what was going on in those days within the inner circles of power:

> The former Minister of State Security, Comrade Ignatiev, was at the Party Congress as a delegate. Stalin told him frankly, "If you cannot get a confession from the doctors, we will make you one head shorter."
> (Commotion in the hall)
> Stalin summoned the investigating judge, issued instructions and gave orders regarding the methods to be used in the examinations; these methods were very simple: beat, beat and beat again.
> Shortly after the arrest of the doctors, we members of the Politburo received the statements with the confessions. After the reports were handed out, Stalin explained to us, "You are all like young kittens; what will you do without me? Our country would come to an end because you don't understand how to recognize enemies."[3]

The number of arrests increased rapidly and did not even spare Stalin's closest colleagues. On December 15, 1952, the chief of the bodyguards, Vlasik, was arrested for passing Lydia Timashuk's letter on to the archives. Stalin's personal secretary, Aleksandr Poskrebyshev, who, at the 19th Party Congress had demanded a hard line to counter the "capitalistic encirclement" because of the Jews, was fired.

On January 9, 1953, the Politburo discussed the imminent declaration by TASS. Stalin read the letter from Lydia Timashuk to his comrades, but left the meeting early. The press campaign that followed, under the leadership of Suslov, Shepilov, Mikhailov (the new Agitprop leader of the CC), and the party philosopher, Chesnokov, had very deep anti-Semitic tendencies.

On January 13, 1953, a front page article was published by *Pravda* about the "murdering doctors" of whom the majority was supposedly connected to the "Jewish bourgeois-nationalist organization *Joint*," and that supposedly received the order from Moscow doctor Shimeliovich and the well-known nationalist, Mikhoels, to "exterminate the leading cadre of the USSR." This was all supposedly corroborated by Vovsi's confession. "The murdering physicians, monsters in human form, trampled on the holy banner of science and were paid agents of foreign espionage." Three of the accused physicians were Russians; six were Jews. On the same day the Office for Censorship, Glavlit, confiscated a book about Mikhoels in all libraries; it just happened to be the fifth anniversary of his murder. One week later Lydia Timashuk received the Order of Lenin and was celebrated by the press as an example of the vigilant Soviet citizen.

On February 9, 1953, members of the Zionist-nationalist underground exploded a bomb in front of the Soviet embassy in Tel Aviv in protest against the anti-Jewish measures in the USSR. Three days later the Kremlin broke off diplomatic relations with Israel, but reinstated them in July 1953, four months after Stalin's death. Even though the culprits were sentenced to long terms of imprisonment, the anti-Semitic incitement became even stronger in the Soviet Union.

In the course of a regular media campaign, articles appeared condemning "the national and racist chauvinism as a leftover of the morality from the times of cannibalism." Attacks against the Jews, as purported spies and economic criminals, were a daily occurrence. Thirty-seven persons were arrested in February, including more physicians and their relatives. Mass hysteria ensued as a result of the press campaign. People refused to take medications from Jewish physicians because they were afraid of being poisoned. Jews were insulted and affronted on the streets, in shops and in public transportation; many lost their jobs.

On February 13, 1953, Lev Mekhlis died. He was born in 1889 in Odessa and was the loyal Jewish vassal of Stalin. In 1950 he was relieved of his last position, Minister for State Control. Now his ceremonial funeral signaled that there were also "good Jews" in the system and all the harassment against Jewish physicians did not indicate the desire for an open display of anti-Semitism.


Were the Soviet Jews Going To Be Deported?


In those seven weeks—fateful for the Soviet Jews—from January 13 until Stalin's death at the beginning of March 1953, many events took place, leading to many legends. Until recently they could not be completely solved because of a lack of documentary evidence. The general pogrom atmosphere showed the Jews how strongly officials were manipulating the deep-seated anti-Semitic prejudice of the population. In their despair, the Jews were isolated and found no advocates or friends to speak for or defend them, like Tolstoy, Korolenko, or Gorky during the tsar's reign.

Many historians and authors have written detailed accounts of anti-Jewish scenarios planned by Stalin, which relied more on oral reports from witnesses than documented proof. Israeli historian Yehoshua Gilboa described the planned proceedings of anti-Jewish measures without being able to indicate any evidence.[4] The American-Israeli journalist and writer Louis Rapoport entitled one chapter of his book *Hammer, Sickle, Star of David* "The Jews before the deportation: Stalin pushes his final solution." I find this to be an unacceptable relativization of the mass murders during the Nazi regime.[5] For support, he cites a book by Anton Antonov-Ovseenko—a son of Vladimir Antonov-Ovseenko, one of Lenin's fighting comrades in October 1917, later ambassador to Czechoslovakia and Poland and subsequently murdered. This particular book to this day has been ignored in research.[6]

According to these publications, the massive propaganda campaign against the Jews should have reached its peak in a show trial against the Kremlin physicians and the accused were to have been hanged publicly in Red Square in Moscow. The idea was that, after the angry raging masses of the people had lynched the delinquents, in spite of resistance from the security guards, this would have been the signal for countrywide anti-Jewish pogroms.

The idea for the most important aspect of the murderous anti-Jewish scenario—the deportation of thousands of Soviet Jews—supposedly originated with Stalin's protégé Dmitri Chesnokov. He had been editor in chief of the magazine *Questions of Philosophy* (*Voprosy filosofii*) since 1948 and was a known anti-Semite. The party philosopher had been unexpectedly elected into the presidium of the CC at the Nineteenth Party Convention in October 1952. His article, *Why the Jews Must be Resettled from the Industrial Regions*, which supposedly had been published by the Ministry for Internal Affairs in a mass edition and should have been distributed shortly before the beginning of the deportations, is used as Marxist-Leninist rectification of Stalin's "historically necessary measures" against the Jews. To this day no one has ever found such a pamphlet or article in the open archives.

It is further stated in the reports that the show trial had been planned for March. By the end of February thousands of primitive barracks had supposedly been erected in Birobidzan and other regions in Siberia. At the same time, many freight and cattle cars were supposedly concentrated on reserve railroad tracks around Moscow to transport the Jews to their places of exile. The trains were to be attacked on the way by angry masses.

It was expected that at least half of the exiled would perish from exposure to the cold and starvation during the long journey. Aleksei Rybin, one of Stalin's bodyguards, later reported that the addresses of the Jews to be arrested had already been distributed.[7]

The deportation camps were described very precisely in a book by Zinovi Sheinis, published in Moscow in 1992, in which the journalist reports the confession of CC functionary N. Polyakov:

> In the late forties, early fifties the total deportation of the Jews was decided. The implementation of this action was given to a newly established commission under Stalin's direct supervision. M. Suslov was elected as representative and head of the commission. I myself was elected secretary. To accommodate those deported, barracks complexes—a kind of concentration camp—were quickly erected, among other places also in Birobidzan. At the same time lists...of all persons of Jewish descent were compiled. The deportations were to proceed in two steps. First the racially pure Jews had to be deported, followed by the half-Jews. The action was to have been conducted during the second half of February. There were delays ...The lists weren't ready in time. Stalin, though, had set very strict timetables. The trials of the physicians were to take place from the 5th until the 7th and their execution on March 11-12.[8]

### The Planned Letter of Jewish Personalities to *Pravda*

Letters to *Pravda* have a long tradition in the Soviet Union. Many changes in the government's policies have been signaled through them. Readers were supposed to be deceived by false promises that freedom of opinion and the possibility to influence political and governmental affairs in the Soviet Union existed for everybody, even from the bottom of society. But every Soviet citizen knew that the texts, down to the smallest detail, were composed in the Kremlin, and very often by Stalin himself. A letter from prominent Jews to the editor of *Pravda* could be used to justify the rekindled anti-Jewish hysteria as a necessary reaction to the crimes of other Jews. Journalists David Zaslavsky and Yakob Khavinson, historian Isaak Mints and scientist Mark Mitin, were chosen to sign such a "Jewish" letter of submission, addressed to Stalin, to include the condemnation of the "murdering physicians." They had all survived the campaign against the "cosmopolitans" with great difficulty. In 1949 Mints had been relieved from the leadership of the publication "History of the Civil War" and fired along with the editorial staff of the magazine, *Voprosy istorii*. He had no illusions about the character of the impending purges.

The letter from prominent Jewish figures of the USSR was drafted in the offices of *Pravda* and sent to the persons who were to sign by courier. This was not a "private initiative" by worried Jews hoping to save as many lives as possible by kowtowing, nor was it an act by obedient servants rushing to preempt the Kremlin "paranoids," but an initiative ordered from high up. The signatories did not receive a copy of the letter. Therefore the text could be only reconstructed from memory. Louis Rapoport gives the following text:

> We request that the government of the USSR, and Comrade Stalin personally, protect the Jewish population against possible violence and persecution against it following revelations about the physicians and poisoners as well as the involvement of Soviet citizens of Jewish origin caught red-handed in an American-Zionist conspiracy meant to destabilize the Soviet government and who have been arrested. Together with all nations of the Soviet Union we welcome the punishment of the murder-hungry physicians, whose crimes deserve the highest degree of punishment. The Soviet nation is most enraged by the steady growth of treason and disloyalty, and about the fact that to our sorrow many Jews helped the enemy to develop a fifth column. Misled ordinary citizens could be influenced and driven to attack and assault Jewish citizens indiscriminately. This is the reason why we beg you to protect the Jews and have them relocated into the developing regions in the East, where they could do useful work and also at the same time avoid the understandable rage that has been stirred up by the treacherous physicians...[9]

The undated text[10] of this letter was unknown until now and is published here for the first time in translation. It was obviously created and written during the second half of February 1953, since the bombing attack in Tel Aviv is mentioned. Because of Stalin's unexpected death, the text was not published.

The letter is a nationalistic hymn in praise of the Russian *people*. The Jews, on the other hand, are defined with such expressions as "Jewish population" or "Jewish workforce." Only the phrase "progressive powers of the Jewish people" (*Evreiskogo naroda*) in the final part of the letter can be considered an acknowledgement of the existence of a Jewish people. The text reflects the demagogical debates of the time about such concepts as nationality and people and the spirit of the absurd ideas expressed at the Slansky trial about the danger of war coming from Israel and America.

On April 3, 1953, one month after Stalin's death, the accused professors and physicians Vovsi, Vinogradov, M. and B. Kogan, Yegorov, Feldman, Etinger, Vasilenko, Grinstein, Selenin, Preobrazhensky, Popova, Sakusov, Shereshevsky, and Mayorov were rehabilitated. The "Eighty-Two Days of Fear" of the Soviet Jews had passed.

Khrushchev, Kaganovich, and Bulganin, who was at that time deputy head of the government, had all been informed and later discussed Stalin's plans against the Jews. Their statements cannot be given much historical credence, because they wanted to cleanse themselves from any guilt or burden for participating in crimes of the regime by blaming everything on Stalin alone.

Whether or not the purpose of the letter was to prepare the Soviet population to a planned wave of arrests of supposedly pro-Israel Jews remains unsolved. The text of the letter doesn't match with Rapoport's published reconstruction. Since no documented evidence exists thus far of a planned mass deportation of all Soviet Jews, which, according to many declarations was planned for the beginning of 1953, such statements have to remain and must be taken, as rumor and legend until evidence to the contrary is discovered.

Gennadi Kostyrchenko is the Russian historian who has researched most of the available documents in the Soviet archives. His opinion is that the thesis of a mass deportation of Soviet Jews cannot be proved. At the end of his book he poses the question: "Did Stalin really want to drag the physicians to the Court of Justice, or was he planning to abstain in the end? What would have been the consequences of such a trial—the mass deportation of the Jews, as some researchers insist? Or would the leader have punished his comrades through a political decree, as others again suspect? Maybe both things could have happened. Let us hope to find a clear answer to these and other questions someday."[11]

*Arno Lustiger*

Letter to the Editorial Office of *Pravda*

In this letter we feel that it is our responsibility to voice our disturbing thoughts and feelings regarding the international situation. We would like to appeal to the Jewish workers everywhere in the world, to think with us together about some questions concerning the vital interests of the Jews.

There are individuals who act as "friends" and even as representatives of the entire Jewish people and thus declare that uniform and common interests exist among all Jews. All Jews are supposed to be united by a single universal goal. These persons—the Zionists—are supporters and helpers of the rich Jews and the worst enemy of the Jewish working classes. Every working human understands that a Jew does not necessarily equal another Jew, and there is no common ground between persons who work for their daily bread with their own two hands and the financial magnates.

According to this, two camps exist among the Jews—the camp of the working laborer and the camp of the exploiting profiteers. The Jewish working people are most interested in strengthening the cause of freedom, peace and democracy, together with all progressive powers. We know that in the camp of the fighters against the arsonists of war, the representatives of the Jewish worker also play an active part.

The Jewish industrial and banking magnates, however, go another way, the way of international adventure and provocation, kindling a new world war. The Jewish millionaires and multimillionaires need this war, as do the rich of other nations, because for them war is a source of enormous profits. The politics practiced by the rich Jews are most harmful to the Jewish worker. These politics are full of deadly consequences for the Jewish worker.

Where is there a common path, where is there any "unity"[12] and common interest of all Jews, as they conjure the false "friend" of the Jews—the Zionist? Hiding behind hypocritical words like a "common path," a "common interest" of all Jews, the leaders of Israel declare that they represent the interests of all Jews. But let us examine whom the leaders of the state of Israel represent and whom they serve. Isn't it a fact that in Israel only the gang of the rich enjoys the wealth, while at the same time the majority of the Jewish and Arab population suffers and endures great poverty and deprivation, and half live in misery? Is it not a fact that the rulers of Israel doubly enslave the working people through Jewish and American capitalism?

That means now that the state of Israel—like every other bourgeois state everywhere else in the world—is an empire for the exploitation of the masses, an empire of easy profits for the clan of the rich. That means that the governing clique in Israel does not represent the Jewish people, who consist mostly of workers, but the Jewish millionaires, who are united and connected to the American monopolists.

That also determines the policy of the present leaders of Israel. They have changed Israel into a weapon to unleash a new war, into an outpost of arsonists. The state of Israel has become indeed the exercise ground for American aggression against the Soviet Union and all peace-loving nations.

Not long ago honorable people around the world were shocked by the news of the explosion of a bomb at the representation of the USSR to Israel.[13] The actual organizers and instigators of this explosion are the leaders of Israel today. With their game of playing with fire, they sharpen the already tense world situation that the Anglo-American war incendiaries have created.

And further: which interests is the international Zionist organization *Joint*, a branch of the American Secret Service, defending? We know that not long ago an espionage group of murdering physicians was discovered in the USSR. The criminals, mostly bourgeois Jewish nationalists who had been recruited by the *Joint*—M. Vovsi, M. Kogan, A. Feldman, J. Etinger, A. Grinstein—had made it their responsibility, using harmful medical methods, to shorten the life of the Soviet Union's politically active citizens, to eliminate the leading cadre of the Soviet army and to thereby undermine the state's defense. Only persons without honor and conscience, who have sold themselves body and soul to imperialism, could invent such horrible crimes.

It is absolutely certain that the leaders of the state of Israel, the leaders of the *Joint* and of other Zionist organizations, enforce and carry out the will of the important Jewish imperialists and those who are their real masters. And it is no secret that these gentlemen are the American and English millionaires and multimillionaires, those who thirst after the blood of nations in the name of new profits.

We, the signatories, refuse the ridiculous requests of the Ben Gurions, Sharetts[14] and the other incendiaries who make these requests in the name of the Jewish people whose interests they claim to represent. We are convinced that even these Jewish workers, who had believed even until now in the supposed unification of all Jews, will reflect and follow our assessment of the true character of the policies of the Jewish rich and their accomplices.

Israel has been changed by its leaders into a hereditary fief of the Americans, and now they say that imperialist America is a "friend" of the Jews. Toward the Soviet Union, though—against the protecting power of peace and equality among nations—they lead a campaign of lies and hate. The reason for this can be explained.

Who wouldn't know that in reality the Jewish workers in the United States must live like forced laborers and are persecuted by the most gruesome machinery of capitalist exploitation? Who wouldn't know that the most unrestrained racism and anti-Semitism exist in that country? Who wouldn't know that anti-Semitism is characteristic of the fascist cliques that are totally supported by the imperialists in the United States?

At the same time it is known throughout the world that the nations of the Soviet Union, and above all the Russian nation, has saved humanity in their self-sacrificing fight against the onslaught of Hitlerism—and the Jews before their total liquidation and death. Today the Soviet people are in the front lines with the peace fighters and defend with determination the cause of peace in the interest of all humanity.

In the Soviet Union, true brotherhood among nations, both large and small, is a reality. For the first time in history the Jewish working people, together with all workers of the Soviet Union, have reached a free and happy existence. Is it not clearly evident that the legend about the imperialist America as a "friend" of the Jews is only a willful forgery of reality? Is it not clearly obvious that only notorious calumniators can deny the strong and lasting friendship between the peoples of the USSR?

The enemy of freedom and friendship among nationalities that is tightly anchored to the Soviet Union, wants to repress among the Jews their highly developed feeling of social responsibility as Soviet citizens. They want to turn the Russian Jews into spies and the enemy of the Russian people, and thereby prepare the ground to revive anti-Semitism, that horrible leftover from the past. The Russian people understand, though, that the vast majority of the USSR's Jewish population is friendly to the Russian people. It will be impossible for the enemy to undermine the trust by tricking the Jewish people against the Russian people; it will be impossible to separate us from the great Russian people.

The Jewish workers in the world have one common enemy. These are the imperialist oppressors served by the reactionary ringleaders of Israel, as well as the spies and delinquents—all the Vovsis, Kogans, Feldmans, etc. All Jewish workers of the world unite for the common task: to defend and strengthen the nature of peace and freedom with all peace-loving people. It is impossible, in the course of this struggle, to protect and defend the Jewish workers' right to live in the lands of capitalism, impossible to be a fighter for freedom of nations and peace if one does not also lead the battle against the Jewish millionaires and multimillionaires and their Zionist agency.[15]

The most important interest of the Jewish workers is to confirm the friendship with workers of all nationalities. The tighter the union of working people of all nationalities, the more stable the nature of peace and democracy will be.

All Jewish workers who hold dear and important the cause of peace and democracy must unite in their efforts and step forward in a broad front against the adventurous politics of the Jewish millionaires and multimillionaires, against the ringleaders of Israel and international Zionism.

Faced with the importance of unity of all progressive Jews, but also for correct information about the situation of the working Jews in different countries and the battle of nations for security and peace, we find it necessary to publish a newspaper in the Soviet Union that will reach the broad levels of the USSR's Jewish population and those living abroad.

We are convinced that our initiative will find passionate support among all working Jews in the Soviet Union and in the entire world.[16]

Yakov Marinin (Khavinson)[17] and David Saslavsky[18] collected signatures for the letter. Numerous personalities signed it but others refused. Ilya Ehrenburg asked for time to think. He knew that he played a key role in the regime's operations abroad—as living witness and alibi for the non-existence of anti-Semitism in the Soviet Union. On December 20, 1952, he received the International Stalin Peace Award, which was usually given only to foreigners. In his acceptance speech for the award, on January 27, 1953, he avoided the request to condemn the "murdering physicians" and declared:

Whatever the national origin of one Soviet person or another may be, he is first of all a patriot to his fatherland and a true internationalist, an opponent of any racial and national discrimination, a fighter in the front ranks, a champion of brotherhood, a fearless and courageous defender of peace.

After this brief criticism of the Stalinist Jewish persecution, Ehrenburg switched to open accusation:

At this celebration in the festive White Hall of the Kremlin, I want to commemorate those partisans of peace who have been persecuted, tormented and hunted down. I want to mention the night of the prisons, the inquisitions and the proceedings at the Court of Justice: the courage of so many.

The following day the Soviet press manipulated this commentary on the happenings in their own country. The "persecuted" was turned into "persecuted by the reactionary powers."[19]

Ilya Ehrenburg gambled with his own life when he decided to write the following letter to Stalin:

Dear Joseph Vissarionovich,

I have only decided to bother you because I have a question that seems extraordinarily important but which I alone cannot solve.

Comrades Mints and Marinin have informed me today about the text of a letter to the editorial office of *Pravda*, and they have proposed that I should sign it. I feel it to be my responsibility to exchange with you my doubts and ask you for advice. It seems to me that the only radical solution to the Jewish question in our socialist system of the state is the total assimilation, the melting of the people of Jewish descent with the other peoples among which they live. I am afraid that a collective effort by a group of representatives of Soviet culture, whose only common characteristic is their origin, could strengthen nationalist tendencies. In the text of the letter appears the definition "Jewish nation"; this could encourage the nationalists but also people who have not understood yet that a Jewish nation does not exist.

I am especially worried about the influence of such a "Letter to the Editorial Office" upon the peace movement. Whenever the question was posed to me at the various commissions at press conferences as to why there are no Yiddish schools or newspapers in the Soviet Union, I have answered always in the same way: that after the war no reminders of former "settlement regions" remained, and that the new generations of Soviet citizens of Jewish heritage did not want to separate themselves from the nations and peoples among whom they live. The publication of a letter that is signed by scientists, writers and composers, who speak about unity and united characteristics of the Soviet Jews, could lead to a blowing up and magnification of the nasty anti-Soviet propaganda, which at the time was propagated and spread by the Zionists, Bundists, and other enemies of our fatherland.

From the viewpoint of the progressive French, Italian, English people, etc., the concept of the "Jew" as representative of a defined nationality does not exist. In these countries the concept of "Jew" is one of religious confession, and calumniators could use this "Letter to the Editor" for their low purposes.

I am convinced that every effort should be made to fight even the smallest attempt to revive Jewish nationalism; this would without a doubt lead to treason. I thought that, on one hand, enlightening articles (also from people of Jewish heritage) are needed, and on the other hand clarification from *Pravda* itself, as it is already stated in this letter: namely that a large majority of the workforce of Jewish descent is deeply devoted to the Soviet fatherland and to Russian culture.

It seems to me that such articles would disturb the foreign calumniators very much and would give our friends who fight for peace very good arguments.

You understand, dear Joseph Vissarionovich, that I myself cannot solve these questions alone, and that is why I have dared to write to you. This concerns an important political step, and I decided to ask you to commission somebody who will tell me your decision, if it is wished for me to sign such a document. If leading comrades convey to me that the publishing of the document and my signature is useful for the defense and peace movement of our fatherland, I will sign the "Letter to the Editor" right away.

Sincerely,
Ilya Ehrenburg[20]

Ehrenburg chose a tactic similar to the accused defendants from the JAFC before justice: to avoid the worst, he acknowledged total assimilation. Ehrenburg believed this in any case, but he wanted to fight Stalin with Stalin's own tactics and weapons. If a Jewish nationality did not exist, as the "great leader" had already declared in 1913, then no representative could place such a demand on Stalin—and also could not be punished collectively. Ehrenburg suspected, obviously, that Stalin had already known about the letter from the prominent Jews for a long time, and also had at least approved it; and maybe that he even initiated it. Unfortunately, it is not known how Stalin reacted to Ehrenburg's letter.

Only the death of the dictator on March 5, 1953—the circumstances of which are the subject of various hypotheses and rumors—saved the lives of thousands more Jews and led to the release of the physicians. At the end of January 1953, Stalin had ordered the transfer of Polina Zhemchuzhina—Molotov's divorced wife—from exile to Moscow, because the physicians had described her as a "bourgeois nationalist." She was interrogated until March 2, 1953 but shortly after the tyrant's death was readmitted into the party.

Ryumin, who had already been demoted at this point, was arrested on March 16, 1953. On April 6 he was pilloried in *Pravda* as a "leading impostor of the government," and sentenced to death on July 7, 1954. Abakumov's execution followed in December 1954. Ignatiev was thrown out of the CC but admitted again after Beria's fall from power. Suslov and other ideological initiators of the destruction of Jewish culture in the Soviet Union remained unharmed and managed the transfer into the post-Stalin era without losing power.

## 34. DEVELOPMENTS IN EASTERN EUROPE

With his speech to an "election gathering" on February 9, 1946, in Moscow, Stalin ended the cooperation with the West, made necessary by the war, and declared a *Cold War*. At the invitation of President Truman, Winston Churchill spoke in Fulton on March 4, 1946:

> From Stettin on the Baltic Sea to Trieste on the Adriatic an iron curtain has descended across the Continent. Behind that line lie all the capitals of the ancient states of Central and Eastern Europe. Warsaw, Berlin, Prague, Vienna, Budapest, Bucharest, Belgrade and

Sofia; all these famous cities and the populations around them lie in what I must call the Soviet sphere, and all are subject to one form or another, not only to Soviet influence but to a very high and, in many cases, increasing measure of control from Moscow.

America reacted to the Soviet predominance in Eastern Europe, which was to be secured through manipulated elections and terror from the Soviet security organs, with the policy of containment. Highlights in this bloodless war were the Truman Doctrine of March 1947 and the Marshall Plan of June of that same year, as well as the Berlin Blockade from June 24, 1948, to May 12, 1949.

## Stalinist Persecutions and Trials in Eastern Europe

In September 1947 the Cominform, the information office of the communist parties of the Eastern Bloc, France, and Italy, was established. It signaled that Stalin had given up the imperial paradigm and indicated the Kremlin wanted to swear in the communists to the global confrontation with the United States. The division of Germany, prepared since 1948, and the establishment of further satellite states in Eastern Europe, cemented this situation. In June of the same year, President Truman advised and ordered the newly established American intelligence service, the Central Intelligence Agency, to organize secret operations in the states of the Eastern Bloc. Propaganda, economic warfare and subversion through the support of resistance movements against the communist regime enlarged and increased Stalin's paranoid fears. The politically and economically besieged Soviet Union no longer felt the need to come to terms with the West and tried to stabilize its empire by terror and show trials against its own comrades.

Tito's rebellion against the nationalist-communist movements and his control of Yugoslavia confirmed Stalin's mistrust toward foreign communist leaders. On June 24, 1948, the Cominform passed a resolution in which the Yugoslav communists were accused of nationalism. In Albania the first trial started in May 1949, against the pro-Tito faction. This secret trial, which ended with the execution by shooting of the secretary for internal affairs, Koci Xoxe, in June 1949, was followed by further secret proceedings, during which several hundred alleged or real partisans of Tito were executed.[21]

On May 11, 1949, the American Noel Field, the leader of the Unitarian Service Committee (USC), the aid committee of the Quakers, was arrested near Prague. This man had organized and supervised the aid actions for refugees, anti-fascists and veterans of the Civil War in Spain from Geneva and was very pro-Soviet. Field was delivered to Budapest, where he was a witness in the indictment against the former Spanish veteran, CC member and secretary for internal affairs, Laszlo Rajk, and seven other defendants. As an American with many contacts to anti-fascists in many nations, Field was, for the plotters at the trial in Moscow, a quickly chosen candidate to prove alleged connections between American spies and communist functionaries.

Only six days after the opening of the Xoxe trial and the arrest of Field, the Soviet "councilors" unleashed a wave of arrests in Hungary, and more arrests also followed in Bulgaria after May 18, 1949. In October 1949 the communist leaders of Hungary, Rajk and comrades, were executed after their "confessions." Secret trials against hundreds of Rajkists and the show trial against Traicho Kostov and ten other accused, in December 1949 in Sofia, created more victims.

## The Slansky Trial

The show trials in Budapest and Sofia set the pattern for more such trials in Eastern Europe. The Soviet "councilors," experienced NKVD officers who came to Prague for the preparation of the Slansky trial, were to repeat the drama of the Moscow trials of the 1930s with great success.

The Slansky trial was the first and historically most important anti-Semitic trial in an Eastern Bloc country. Preceding this trial, there were many persecutions and numerous show trials against non-communist politicians and Catholic priests in the CSR. On November 11, 1951, Anastas Mikoyan appeared unexpectedly in Prague on Stalin's personal orders to arrest the general secretary of the party, Rudolf Slansky. This took place on November 24. Slansky was coerced into confessing under torture that he harbored tendencies hostile to the regime. In February 1952 he tried, unsuccessfully, to commit suicide. In January and February 1952 more than fifty functionaries of the party, army, police, and other government officials were arrested.

In August 1952 the preliminary inquiries started under the supervision of the Soviet "councilors" and Chief Prosecutor Urvalek. The accusations were full of vulgar anti-Semitism, anti-Zionist and anti-Israeli inferences. One of the three trial survivors, Eugen Löbl, remembered the following words from the NKVD Colonel Mikhail Likhachev, who had received special praise and commendations during the inquiries of the JAFC members, two years before: "You are neither a communist nor a Czech. You are a dirty Jew; Israel is your only true fatherland. You have sold socialism to your bosses, the Zionist-imperialist leaders of world Judaism, but the time will come soon, to exterminate everyone of your kind."[22]

The accused were forced to memorize, on the orders of the inquisitors and the Soviet "councilors," during their long months in prison in Ruin near Prague, a complete written scenario that included a detailed script of the proceedings during the trial.

The "Trial against the leadership of the center of the plot hostile to the state" began on November 20, 1952. The Jewish and bourgeois origins of eleven of the fourteen accused defendants in the main trials were pointed out and very strongly emphasized. Several had fought with the French resistance, in Spain, in Allied armies, and as partisans against fascism.

Rudolf Slansky, party chief until 1951 and also vice prime minister, born in 1901, had already been a communist functionary in his youth and since 1929 was a member of the CPCS's CC. He had lived in Moscow during the war and in 1944 participated in the uprising in Slovakia. Otto Sling, CC member since 1949, was a member of the International Brigades. Bedrich Reicin, vice minister of defense, a pre-war communist, had fought in the Czech divisions formed in the Soviet Union until 1945. Ludvik Frejka, CP functionary for almost 20 years, in exile in London from 1939 until 1945, was responsible for the economy as a CC member. Bedrich Geminder, chief of the CPCS's International Branch, had worked at the Lenin Institute in Moscow. The journalist Andre Simone (Otto Katz), leading propagandist of world communism in France, Spain, and Mexico, had been relieved in 1946 as editor in chief of the party's organ *Rude Pravo* and since then was writing his commentaries under a pseudonym.

They were all accused of high treason, espionage, sabotage, military espionage, insufficient alertness and education about Trotskyite and Titoist centers. They were even accused of former Zionist youth organizations' membership, even though they already belonged to the leadership of the CPCS for years and were decidedly anti-Zionist. But the accused who were not Jews, like Foreign Minister Clementis, Deputy Defense Minister Svab and deputy General Secretary of the CPCS Frank, were also branded as "Zionists" and sentenced. Mordechai Oren and Shimon Orenstein, members of the Israeli pro-Soviet party Mapam, were arrested in Prague and forced as witnesses for the prosecution through torture to reject the state of Israel and Zionism. They were also sentenced to long-term imprisonment.

The indictment stated: "Ben Gurion's government changed Israel into an American property…and supported without restriction the criminal plans of the American war incendiaries, who wanted to develop Israel into a military base against the USSR."[23] One of the prosecution's points was based on Stalin's military support for the state of Israel, which had been established with Soviet support.

The sentence was announced on November 27, 1952. Hajdu, Löbl and London were sentenced to life imprisonment. Slansky and ten other defendants received the death sentence and were executed on December 3, 1952. Altogether thousands of state and party functionaries were accused and 178 persons were executed. More than 50,000 people were imprisoned or put in camps without sentencing.

Artur London, who had worked in Moscow at the Lenin Institute, and had later fought in Spain and France in the resistance, must be credited and thanked for the fact that an exact description of the criminal Soviet legal murder apparatus is available.[24] As former deputy foreign minister, he was accused of collaboration with the American and French Secret Service, and also with the Gestapo, the Trotskyites and Titoists. He confessed to having filled diplomatic positions with "Zionists, Trotskyites and bourgeois nationalists." His life was spared only by a massive protest from the French Communist Labor Union CGT and the personal intervention of his French wife and Spanish veteran, Lise.[25]

For months following Stalin's death in March 1953, the legal murder machine continued to function in Prague and Bratislava. In Romania, the Hungarian minority and the Jews were also persecuted, tortured and sentenced for cosmopolitanism, nationalism and Zionism. The accused in the Slansky trial were not rehabilitated until December 1963—more than eleven years after their sentencing.

## The Planned Trials in Poland

Like Boleslaw Bierut, Poland's first president after World War II, CCP chief Wladyslaw Gomulka had survived the Moscow massacres only because he had been in prison in Poland in 1939. During the Tito crisis in

June 1949, Gomulka called for a Polish, meaning a patriotic path to socialism, without a one-party dictatorship or the collectivization of agriculture. On Moscow's orders he had to revise his plans and was removed, together with his partisans, from all party positions.

In the Rajk trial the accused had also confessed under torture to alleged treacherous connections to the Polish communists. Several members of the Espionage Defense Section of State Security, *Urzad Bezpieczenstwa*, known by the abbreviation *Bezpieka*, were arrested shortly after that. They had contacts with Noel Field, had fought in Spain, and were Jews. After *Bezpieka* colonel Jozef Swiatlo had collected and gathered incriminating material against the Polish "Fieldists," in Budapest, General Spychalski was arrested and gruesomely tortured. He was supposed to play the part of the main accused in the planned public show trial. After that more arrests of officers of the army, counterintelligence, and State Security followed. Most of those arrested were of Jewish origin. The commander of the army units of the ministry for internal affairs, General Waclaw Komar, also of Jewish descent who had been founder and commander of the 129th International Brigade during the Spanish Civil War, was said to be the head of the alleged conspiracy center within the security organs.[26]

Komar not only confessed under torture to all the alleged espionage and sabotage activities, but also accused the entire leadership of Poland of being accomplices. This unbelievable accusation led to a delay of the planned show trial, because the Polish Stalinists used Komar's absurd accusations as grounds to conduct further inquiries. They were willing to sacrifice their Jewish comrades, who had fought and suffered for communism, to save Gomulka's life. This was the only way they could withstand Soviet pressure and delay the opening of the trial for two years. Gomulka was arrested in 1951.

After Stalin's death the "organs" staged a show trial to cover their tracks. Many of those arrested were released, and reinstalled in their former positions. Marshal Spychalski became chairman of the Senate of the People's Republic of Poland from 1968 until 1970. Gomulka, who was not released until 1955, was first secretary of the party from 1956 until 1970.

The situation of the surviving Jewish victims of Stalinism in Poland was totally different. Shortly after the Six-Day War ended, many high-ranking Jewish officers were relieved from their positions—including Colonels Dodik, Heinstein, Sadykiewicz and Asman. In 1968 all Jewish officers, from cadets to generals, had been removed from the army; all state officials were also discharged. Within the framework of state-sponsored anti-Semitic harassment, about 66,000 Jews had been forced to leave the country by 1969. They were stripped of their citizenship and retirement claims; these measures have not been revoked to this day.

## German-Jewish Communists

Herman Weber lists the names of 242 German communists murdered or missing in the Soviet Union. Forty of them were Jews, including Hans Bloch, Kurt Cahn, Marie Fischmann, Dorothea and Leo Friedländer, Hilde Hauschild, Max Katzenellenbogen, Max Levien, Alfred Levy, Jack Nawrey, Heinz Neumann, Kathe Pohl, David Scheel, and Fritz Sturm. The survivors include August Kleine, Edith and Nathan Steinberger.[27] Leo Flieg and Heinrich Süsskind, who had leading positions in the German Communist Party (KPD) during the Weimar Republic, were among Stalin's early victims. Aleksandr Fomin, David Fritz, and Aleksandr Emel had been called by the chief prosecutor, Vyshinsky, during the first Moscow show trial of August 1936, clowns, pygmies, pugs, barkers, murderers, criminals, thieves, and mad dogs. The sentence issued was death. The KPD waited fifty years before rehabilitating the comrades who had been executed.

After the signing of the Hitler-Stalin Pact [August 23, 1939], hundreds of German and Austrian communists had been sent to Germany in February 1940, some directly out of the Gulag, into the claws of the Gestapo, thereby assuring their death. Among the approximately 1,000 persons who were deported to Germany between 1937 and 1941,[28] many were Jews. Hanns-Walther David, Ernst Fabisch, Kathe Rosenbaum and Julius Simon died. The physicist Aleksandr Weisberg Cybulski, who survived, described his odyssey in detail.[29] Miraculously, the German communist Margarete Buber-Neumann, daughter-in-law of Martin Buber and widow of the KPD functionary Heinz Neumann, who was executed in the Soviet Union in 1937, also survived. She lived through several labor camps and the women's concentration camp at Ravensbrück. In Frankfurt in 1951, during the trial of communist functionary Emil Carlebach, who claimed that the deported woman was a "fifth columnist" and Gestapo agent, Mrs. Buber-Neumann had to defend the honor of the wretched, unfortunate communists deported from the Soviet Union from these Stalinist defamations. At an organized "anti-fascist" proclamation of the KPD in March 1951, in Munich, she was insulted with names like "agent," "war instigator" and "liar." During many unforgettable conversations in Frankfurt she told this author of the deep chasm between ideals of "her" communism and Soviet reality.

## The Jews in the GDR

About eight thousand German Jews of the Soviet-occupied zone survived persecution by the Nazi regime: in the concentration camps, in hiding, mainly in Berlin, as emigrants to the West, as volunteers in the Allied forces and as spouses of non-Jews. Among them, only the surviving "fighting" communists, who were not many, were recognized as "victims of fascism." Those who suffered racial persecution were excluded, with the explanation that "they did not fight but endured without resistance." The "Red Kapos" from Buchenwald, whose survival chances had been much higher than those of a young Buchenwald prisoner like me, were considered fighters. Only through the influence of the Western Allies in Greater Berlin and all of Germany was this screaming injustice later softened somewhat. The "Muscovites" like Walter Ulbricht, along with former concentration camp prisoners in the KPD or SED leadership, viewed the Shoah either as a class problem or from a Manichean viewpoint. The Jews were either heroic fighters like Herbert Baum and his resistance group in Berlin, or were viewed as cowardly victims. The result is that the SED leadership, in contrast to the Bonn government, denied restitution and reparation for the Jewish victims of Nazism. Despite this shameful practice, many left-wing Jews who had survived the Third Reich through emigration to Western countries and who wanted to rebuild a better Germany returned to the GDR. When, in 1948, both Christian churches were reinstituted and given their property back in the GDR, the Jewish communities were given almost nothing. However, despite this "special treatment," they had to be loyal to the state, because otherwise it was impossible for them to survive without the help and support of the party and state agencies. Measures to counter anti-Jewish sentiments within the population were seriously delayed; since 1948 most Eastern Bloc countries initiated repression against the Jews, encouraged by the Kremlin and disguised as anti-Zionism. The pro-Moscow elements in the SED leadership also suspected Jewish communists of ideological disloyalty. The chairman of the Jewish community in Berlin, Erich

Nehlhans, was sentenced to 25 years' forced labor. The deputy president of the police in Berlin, Fritz Katten, was arrested.

In August 1950 the hysterical "Fieldist" fever also erupted in the GDR. The reason for it was that the non-Jew Paul Merker, who was, besides Dahlem, the only Western emigrant in the SED's CC, was relieved of his functions, as an alleged "Zionist" and later arrested. Paul Merker had been involved with the fate of the Jews in 1942, while he was in exile in Mexico, by publishing the article "Hitler's Anti-Semitism and Us," emphasizing the moral responsibility of the Germans for reparations and calling for Jewish immigration to Palestine. Merker was to play the part of the "German Slansky" in the future public show trial in East Berlin.

The overture to the systematic repression of Jews in the GDR came as a conversation—though more likely it was an interrogation lasting several hours—between the Information chief in the Soviet Military Administration, Colonel Tyulpanov, and the chairman of the GDR's Union of Jewish Communities, Julius Meyer, who was also a member of the People's Chamber, the "Parliament."

The Soviet occupiers ordered the SED leadership in January 1952 to register all the Jews in the GDR. Erich Mielke,who described the Jewish comrades as "petty bourgeois cowards,"[30] was commissioned to set up a Jew's card index. At the beginning of January 1953 the Jewish communities' representatives were to have issued a statement in which they justified the Slansky trial because the defendants had to be punished as traitors. On January 8, 1953, Meyer was ordered to make a list of the recipients of the "CARE packages" from the Jewish-American aid organization, *Joint*. He was also to certify that the *Joint* had been exposed as an American espionage organization. The Stalinists did not want to admit that the support measures for the Jewish brothers and sisters in the GDR were the result of humanitarian motivation only and without any expected reward.

With the excuse of preparing the desired declaration, Meyer asked all community representatives to report to the office of the West Berlin congregation in Fasanenstrasse, on January 13, 1953. On the same day *Pravda* published the story of the Jewish Kremlin physicians' plot to murder the Kremlin leadership. *New Germany* (*Neues Deutschland*), the official organ of the party, reproduced the article the next day. Meyer and his colleagues had decided not to sign the requested declaration under any circumstances but to flee because of the threatening arrests.

The purge had disastrous results: within a few weeks the GDR lost more than half its loyal Jewish citizens. The first to flee was Leo Zuckermann, chief of Wilhelm Pieck's Presidential Chancellery, together with Julius Meyer followed by the congregation chairmen from Leipzig, Halle, Erfurt and Schwerin. Schwerin's community chairman, Dr. Franz Unikower, a former Auschwitz prisoner, who later became my colleague at the Frankfurt Community Council, described the situation that led to the flight in detail. The chairmen of the Jewish communities of Magdeburg, Eisenach, and Oschersleben had to leave the country a short time later. The members of the East Berlin community of the temporary board also followed soon thereafter.

My camp comrade from Blechhammer, Dr. Bernhard Littwak,[31] was also driven away. He was the commanding officer of Military Hospital No. 1 of the International Brigades in Albacete, Spain. His wife Eva worked there as head nurse, and their four-year-old daughter Carmen had been placed in the custody of foster parents in Switzerland. After imprisonment in several internment camps in France and concentration camps in Germany, the Social Democrat, Spain veteran, physician and Jew had begun a new life as a doctor in 1945 in Eisleben. A friend warned him by telephone about the planned arrest. With a small suitcase he fled from the land of the Stalinist "anti-fascists" to Frankfurt am Main.[32]

On the other hand, thousands of former Nazis and military officers had been guaranteed by decree, in October 1952, that they would have full citizenship and equality. They could ignore their past as servants of the Nazi regime and again be placed in official state positions. The Association for the Persecuted of the Nazi Regime (VVN) was dissolved in February 1953 because the GDR felt it had already fulfilled all responsibilities toward those who had been persecuted by the Nazi regime.

## The Planned Show Trial in East Berlin

All these anti-Jewish campaigns were directly connected to the Slansky trial. In addition to Paul Merker, many more comrades had been arrested who at some point had had contact with Noel Field or his relief organization. Among these were Leo Bauer, editor in chief of the German Radio Station (*Deutschlandsender*); Bruno Goldhammer from Berlin Broadcasting (*Berliner Rundfunk*); State Secretary Paul Baender and the editor in chief of *Leipzig People's Newspaper* (*Leipziger Volkszeitung*), Hans-Heinrich

Schrecker; Jürgen Kuczynski, president of the Society for German-Soviet Friendship; Aleksandr Abusch, general secretary of the GDR's Culture Union; and Gerhart Eisler, head of the Government Information Office. Other communists of Jewish descent, as well as emigrants from the West, were relieved from their functions. Lex Ende, editor-in-chief of the party newspaper *New Germany*, died while working in a uranium mine at forced labor. When Rudolf Feistmann, foreign editor of *New Germany*, committed suicide, the cause given in the obituary notice in his newspaper was food poisoning from eating meat. Functionaries from the middle and lower levels of the party and state apparatus were also arrested or discharged, as Helmut Eschwege has ascertained.[33]

On January 4, 1953, the "lessons from the trial against the center of the conspiracy, Slansky" were published in *New Germany* (*Neues Deutschland*). This had been decided already by the end of December 1952. It stated:

> Sailing under the Jewish-nationalist banner, disguised as a Zionist organization and as diplomats of the American vassal government of Israel, these American agents undertake their work. In the "Morgenthau-Acheson Plan," revealed in the Prague trial, it became clearly evident that American imperialism has organized and carried out its espionage and sabotage activities, through the state of Israel and with help of Zionist organizations, in the people's democratic countries.[34]

Long passages were dedicated to Paul Merker. His demands for reparations for the Jewish Nazi victims had inspired the authors of the paper to the most outrageous insults.

The preparations for an East German show trial were underway since 1949. As a precaution, other potential defendants like Ibolya Steinberger and Bernd Steinberger and others, who had contact with Noel Field during the war, had been arrested, tortured and interrogated. Several communists were lured or kidnapped out of West Germany into the GDR, like Fritz Sperling and Erika Wallach, the German-Jewish foster daughter of Noel Field, and Kurt Müller. Those arrested were personally tortured by Soviet MVD officers and interrogated. Erich Mielke announced to them that a show trial would take place in the very near future.

The scenario had been already planned. The non-Jew Merker was to be accused of being the chief of a Zionist group of agents. Franz Dahlem, political commissar of the International Brigades in Spain and a prisoner at the Mauthausen concentration camp, and other VVN Jewish chairmen were also selected to be defendants. Many communists with suspicious connections in the West were arrested.

In the end, the show trial in East Berlin was canceled, because the regime was afraid of being too damaging to the Soviet Union. How could it be explained to the communists living in West Germany and Western Europe, or to the numerous sympathizers of the Soviet Union, that their heroic friends from Spain, from the resistance and the West who had escaped the Nazi terror, were common criminals and the enemies of the Soviets? Besides that, the future of Germany was still undecided. Maybe the Western Allies would agree to Stalin's proposal of a neutral, unarmed Germany. Initially, those imprisoned were transferred to the MVD, where military tribunals sentenced them, in several secret trials in the summer of 1952, to death or long-term imprisonment. Leo Bauer, Communist Party State Chairman in Hesse after the war, was sentenced to death on December 28, 1952, by such a Soviet military tribunal. Afterwards he was brought to the Soviet Union and sentenced to 25 years in the Gulag. Not until his class enemy Adenauer stepped in was he allowed, along with German prisoners of war, to return home in 1955.

After Stalin's death on March 5, 1953, all claims of crimes by Zionist agents disappeared into thin air. The GDR leadership did not speak up until 1956—in vague, veiled tones through the party newspapers—of unjustly accused comrades and of corrections to the "abuse of power by the security organs." Georg Hermann Hodos[35] reported about the repression in East Germany:

> Officially, the talk was of 11,896 prisoners who were released from the prisons and forced labor camps while appeals were proceeding. Most of them were political prisoners. How many of them had formerly been party members is unknown. The number of people caught in the net of the "Field Affair" and purged was thought to be more than 300. For many communists "arrested by mistake," the "corrections" came too late. Their careers and their family lives were destroyed, and some of them died in prison.

Paul Merker was sentenced in a secret trial in 1955, as a "servant of the Jews," to eight years in prison. An absurd misanthropic anachronism took place possible only in communist dictatorships: in other Eastern Bloc countries trials like these were no longer held two years after Stalin's death. The process described should shame every East and West German who feels any nostalgia for the GDR. The scandalous occurrences have not been sufficiently analyzed, despite essays by Olaf Groehler, Mario Kessler, and Jeffrey Herf. The disturbing facts about the planned proceedings, persecution and expulsion of the Jews from the GDR are described in books by Angelika Timm, Wolfgang Kiessling and Michael Wolffsohn.[36] Ulrike Offenberg has described the events in greater detail in the chapter "The anti-Jewish policies of 1948–1953" of her publication concerning the Jewish communities in the SOZ and the GDR.[37]

## 35. STATE-SPONSORED ANTI-SEMITISM AFTER STALIN

### No Thaw Under Khrushchev

After Stalin's death, anti-Semitism did not disappear from the arsenal of Soviet government policy. On the contrary, the state enforced and promoted systematic anti-Semitic agitation into the 1980s. Even during the worst Jewish persecutions under Stalin, some Jews held powerful positions. After 1957, though, only a very few Jewish high officials were working in the government. Informal access restrictions for Jews existed in key security, army, and economic installations.

Under Khrushchev, and later Brezhnev, anti-Semitism was a general reason to attack the Jews—and not just individual Jewish "conspirators" like the "bourgeois nationalists"—and a much more important element of politics than under Stalin. Khrushchev at times expressed himself much more disparagingly toward the Jews than Stalin had ever done. Under his aegis, a wave of "economic trials" took place against alleged speculators after 1958. Every year over a hundred proceedings were logged. In almost every one the press pointed to involvement with Israeli citizens and uncovered synagogues as places for the black marketers and similar activities. Between 1961 and 1967, in trials against alleged black marketers, 163 death penalties were handed down against Jews and only five against non-Jews. Anyone who sees Khrushchev as a liberal ignores the fact that, until his overthrow by Brezhnev, he instigated anti-Jewish economic trials. Anti-Semitism also flourished among the population. Every year between 1959 and 1962 a synagogue was burned down. The subsequent criminal proceedings were held secret from the Soviet public, even though Ehrenburg had recommended a public trial.[38] The culprits were from the Komsomol, the Young Communists League.

## Anti-Semitism Disguised as "Anti-Zionism"

The Brezhnev years brought an unbelievable heightening of the anti-Semitic campaign under the guise of anti-Zionism. From 1967 until 1980, 1700 anti-Zionist cartoons stylistically resembling the Nazi *Stürmer* cartoons, appeared in the Soviet press. More than half these cartoons suggested plans by the Zionists to take over the world. Books and pamphlets recalling the worst anti-Semitic traditions flooded the Soviet market. A bibliography compiled by N. Bibichkova of anti-Semitic books published in the Soviet Union during the period from 1960-1981 lists more than 200 titles—some of them true bestsellers—with editions of more than a hundred thousand copies each. Their anti-Semitic authors left out any connection to historical truth. They stated coarse lies as proven facts, which were then quoted and repeated in the popular literature in many pamphlets and booklets.

That "Zionists" meant all Jews (and their "helpers' helpers"), was evidenced, for example, in an article in *Komsomol Truth* (*Komsomol'skaya Pravda*) of October 1967, where it was clearly stated that 20 to 25 million Zionists were living in the U.S. and that 69 percent of the physicists in the armaments industry, as well as 43 percent of all industrialists in America, were Zionists. The statistics, cited in the time-honored anti-Semitic tradition, suggested that Jews were behind the most hostile U.S. institutions—the military and the banks.

A clique of professional Jew-baiters published numerous books and magazines, spreading their crazy ideas through lecture tours around the Soviet Union. A few classics of racist Jewish harassment should be mentioned here. Trofim Kishko wrote the first extensive anti-Semitic book, *Iudaizm bez prikras* (Judaism without make-up), full of lies and clichés about the Jewish religion and the Jewish people. The many cartoons it reproduced resembled those from the *Stürmer*. After its publication in 1963 by the Ukrainian Academy of Sciences in Kiev created a storm of worldwide protests, the volume was removed. Nevertheless, Kishko published another such work in 1968, *Judaism and Zionism* (*Iudaizm i tsionizm*), in which he again served up the old lies about Jewish plans for world conquest. In *Caution: Zionism!* (*Ostorozhno: Tsionism!*), of which 70,000 copies were printed in 1969, Yuri Ivanov stated that Zionism was supposed to be over two thousand years old. Other classics of anti-Semitism are Lev Korneyev's *Class Character of Zionism* (*Klassovaya sushchnost' tsionizma*) and *By a Course of Aggression and Racism* (*Kursom agressii i rasizma*), with a printing of 100,000 copies each.

The most bizarre character among the Soviet writers was the Arabist Valery Yemelyanov, an obviously demented man. In his book *De-Zionization*, which was published by the PLO publishing house in Paris, he even surpassed Jewish harassment in the Soviet Union. For this he was excluded from the party. In April 1980 he murdered his wife, dismembered her corpse, and threw it in a garbage container. He was not sentenced to death for this crime, but placed in a psychiatric institution. When the national fascist *Pamyat* movement was created in Moscow in 1987, Yemelyanov stepped forward as their most important speaker and agitator.

*Izvestiia, Literaturnaya gazeta, Sovetskaya kul'tura* and almost all other official press organs praised the anti-Semitic works. Only a few journalists dared to criticize this scandalous campaign. One of them was Lieutenant General N. Makeyev, editor in chief of the central organ of the Red Army, *Red Star (Krasnaya zvezda)*. The poet Martynov demanded in a letter to party chief Andropov punishment of the "pseudoscientific anti-Semite Korneyev, who dishonors our nation under the pretext of fighting Zionism and works together with the neo-Nazis in the West." This would have consequences. Thanks to Korneyev's intervention, Martynov was exposed to constant terror and in June 1985 was locked up in a psychiatric institution.

## 36. Reaction of the Jews to State-Sponsored Anti-Semitism

### International Conferences for Soviet Jews

State-sponsored anti-Semitism in the Soviet Union, only a few years after the Holocaust, upset the Jewish community in the West. Many communists, including leading comrades, were also shocked. More than a few who had been active in favor of the Soviet Union for decades left their respective parties.

At first there was no consensus as to the kind of response. Some wanted to meet this discrimination only through quiet, behind-the-scenes diplomacy. Others, such as Daniel Mayer, a cabinet minister in several French governments, called an international conference of the Jewish World Congress to Paris in 1960, where the Jews' situation in the Eastern Bloc countries was to be discussed. The large Jewish organizations in the U.S. did not acknowledge the extent of the new Jewish persecutions until after the Six-Day War, even though many single groups that fought very effectively for the protection of the Soviet Jews were created in the West.

They organized congresses where the only theme was the dilemma of the Soviet Jews, and gave worldwide recognition through their publications to the fate of the refuseniks. In South Florida alone, Jews organized several international conferences and published 15 books with hundreds of life stories by refuseniks. Barbara Stern published a three-volume documentation series in Canada, both in English and French about them.[39] *Refusenik* (an American-Russian word) was the name given to Jews who had been turned down in their application to emigrate from the Soviet Union. In the Soviet Union, the Jews who had been refused permission to leave the country called themselves *Otkazniki*, from the Russian *otkazat'*—to refuse.

In February 1971, 830 delegates from 38 countries met in Brussels. A parallel conference assembled in New York. Both resonated outside the Jewish circle as well. At the Second Brussels Conference in February 1976, 1,320 delegates from the Soviet Union demanded to uphold the international Helsinki agreement, that the Jews' right of emigration be acknowledged, the Jewish harassment stop, and the Jews' right to education, culture and religious practices not be restricted. The "Brussels Manifesto" closed with the words: "We will not rest until the Jews in the Soviet Union are free and can decide their own fate. Let my people go!"[40]

The members of the support groups kept in constant contact with their chosen "godchildren" in the Soviet Union, mostly by telephone. This was an effective way for protection against sudden arrest and later disappearance in the Gulag. On April 30, 1972, designated as the "Day of Solidarity with the Soviet Jews" in the U.S., ceremonies were held in 100 cities, where many senators, state governors and mayors were present. One million Americans signed a petition to the leadership of the Soviet Union. At the same time, relatives and sympathizers of the Soviet Jews in London, Rome, Paris, Stockholm and Bern organized hunger strikes and demonstrations. In October 1977 delegates from 35 states came together in Belgrade, and at a conference in Madrid, in November 1980 delegates from 34 countries accused the Soviet government anew of offenses against the Helsinki Manifesto.

Many non-Jews in the Western world also took part in these activities, while in West Germany only the penniless Union of Jewish Students in Aachen and a few personalities, like the film producer Artur Brauner in Berlin, stepped forward in support of the Soviet Jews. The Central Council of Jews in Germany never participated in the campaign for the Soviet Jews.

*Arno Lustiger*

# The Jewish National and
# Emigration Movement in the Soviet Union

The many years of discrimination and malicious campaigns, the destruction of their national culture and the murder of their intellectual leaders couldn't destroy the national awareness of the Soviet Jews. In fact, the result was exactly the opposite; many publicly stated their attachment to Judaism, wanted to learn the long-repressed Hebrew language, embrace their culture and history, build up their community life and have contact with Jews around the world.

In the 1960s a Jewish national, partially Zionist-oriented dissident movement was formed in the Soviet Union. It fought for the rights of the Jews to live as a full-fledged nationality with its own culture, language, history and tradition—religious or secular. In 1966 the police forcibly broke up a peaceful demonstration of several thousand Jews in Riga that was held because of a concert by artists from Israel. In October 1967, in front of the synagogue in Moscow, 20,000 Jews congregated for the Simkhath Torah celebration and to protest quietly against official policy.

Much more important for the majority of Soviet Jews was the right to free emigration to Israel. In August 1969 the heads of eighteen Georgian families addressed the Human Rights Committee of the UN, asking to go to Israel.[41] With that began a new Aliyah.

Jewish activist groups, which supported themselves in the uneven fight against the officials, formed in many cities and regions. Anatoly Shcharansky and Yuli Edelstein, Jewish dissident leaders, were among the founders of the Soviet Committee for Maintaining the Helsinki Manifesto. Other Jews participated in the activities of the general human rights groups.

The "organs" reacted to these impertinent acts of insubordination, unknown until then in the Soviet Union, in the usual manner. Between 1970 and 1972 hundreds of activists were arrested and sentenced to severe punishment in numerous trials in Moscow, Leningrad, Riga, Kishinev, Kiev, Chernovtsy, Kharkov, Odessa, Sverdlovsk, and Ryazan. The "Prisoners of Zion," as they called themselves, went into the Gulags. In May 1971 the founders of the Soviet Human Rights Committee, professors Andrei Sakharov, Valery Khalidze and Andrei Tvardovsky, protested against the newest persecutions of the Jews in an appeal to the Supreme Soviet.

The Russian Orthodox Christian and dissident Andrei Sinyavsky, who published his works out of protest under the Jewish pseudonym Abram Terts, became involved very early in the rights of Soviet Jews. The most important and influential Russian dissident, though, was Andrei Sakharov, who severely criticized state-sponsored anti-Semitism in worldwide appeals, in letters and discussions with foreign correspondents. At every opportunity he condemned the shameful anti-Israeli policies of the Soviet power mongers during the Yom Kippur War in 1973. Sakharov was in close contact with Jewish activists like Anatoly Shcharansky, whom he strongly supported. The officials considered these activities and the struggle for the Jews' emigration rights as pro-Zionist activities.

In contrast to the general Soviet dissident movement, which wanted a reorganization and transformation of the system, most Jewish activists just wanted their right for a self-governed Jewish life and cultural activities in the context of existing laws and an observance of human rights.

Some groups, though, had lost hope of fair and just treatment for the Jews in the Soviet Union. They believed that the officials would never allow legal emigration, and prepared to hijack an airplane in 1970 in Leningrad. The KGB knew about these plans and foiled them shortly beforehand. The potential hijackers, including Mark Dymshits, a fighter pilot in the Second World War, and Eduard Kuznetsov, were severely punished for their actions, designed to wake up foreign countries and inform them about the situation of the Soviet Jews. Both were sentenced to death, later commuted to long-term harsh Gulag sentences. Kuznetsov was exchanged in 1979 for a Soviet spy, and, like Dymshits prematurely, who was released, emigrated to Israel.

The trials, with their disproportionately high sentences—two death penalties and imprisonment sentences of 10 to 15 years—unleashed a wave of protests abroad. Through pressure from the world public, more than 13,000 Jews were allowed to emigrate in 1971, while in 1970 only 1,027 Jews were allowed to leave the country. Between 1971 and 1977, a total of 155,000 Jews were able to leave the Soviet Union.

The repression caused a national awakening of the Soviet Jews. It was like a renaissance of their long repressed feelings of dignity, and self-esteem that could be viewed, due to the magnitude and effect it had on the non-Jewish population, as a kind of cultural revolution.

The government's efforts at assimilation ended in a failure, including Russified Jewish Bolsheviks who had followed the then-governing anti-Jewish party directives, sometimes even up to self-denial and negation of their Jewish heritage.

Beginning with 1970, Jewish samizdats (self-publishing houses) issued hundreds of periodicals and occasional publications. These contained original contributions, copies from old or unavailable books and translations. One of the first samizdat publications carried the title of Leon Uris' historical novel *Exodus (Iskhod)*, which David Bergelson's niece had translated into Russian. These few hundred copies, produced under great effort and danger, gave a whole generation of Russian Jews knowledge of their people's culture, literature and history.

In 1973 the collection edited by Aleksandr Voronel and Viktor Yakhot, *I am a Jew: Essays in Jewish Identity in the Soviet Union,* was published in New York. This volume was almost like a revolution by the illegal self-publishing houses. For the first time samizdat authors, who were among the scientific and historical elite of the Soviet Union, were identified by their full names. A list of Jewish activists was even printed at the end.

The documentation and bibliographies in illegal Jewish publications in the Soviet Union, which appeared at universities in Israel and other places, are evidence of the unbelievable daring and will to personal dignity and self-image by the Soviet Jews, worthy of the greatest admiration.[42]

Daniela Bland-Spitz has described in detail in her 500-page dissertation[43] the Jewish dissidents' letters, telephone calls, petitions and appeals to the Soviet government and the international community; interviews with foreign press and television correspondents; legal action against Soviet offices and officials; return of Soviet medals of honor; denial of Soviet citizenship and petitions for Israeli citizenship; and many other initiatives. Many Jewish citizens from different levels of society, who had once been loyal to the system or were even completely convinced of its correctness, also participated in sit-ins, demonstrations and hunger strikes as the *ultima ratio.* Before President Richard Nixon visited Moscow on June 17, 1972, Jewish groups organized hunger strikes in Moscow, Leningrad, Riga, Kovno, and Vilnius to get the world media to focus on the desperate situation of the Jews. Many participants were arrested before they came in contact with the president's entourage.

Scholars like the physicist Aleksandr Voronel organized scientific seminars and symposia about Jewish history and culture. The Hebrew language was taught in intensive courses in preparation for the Aliyah to Israel, and also to bring Jewish culture closer through the content of its original writings. The learning tools had to be created by the lecturers themselves and also duplicated. These clandestine arrangements could only take place in private locations that endangered all those participating.

The Fight for the Right to Emigrate—The Refuseniks

Petitions for emigration were denied with varying but always vague reasons. This was in strict contrast to the Helsinki and other pacts the Soviet Union had signed in 1975 as a result of pressure from the international community. The authorities always came up with new ways of harassment. For example, the Jews were burdened with an emigration tax as compensation for their state-financed academic education, or were called up for military service before the normal time. Thousands lost their jobs and could only make ends meet with occasional work. They were also treated like pariahs by the government, their neighbors and former co-workers and constantly lived in fear of arrest.

In several secret and public trials, the most active refuseniks and leaders of the Aliyah were sentenced to harsh Gulag punishment. The security agencies hoped, though without success, to weaken the movement that was influencing the Armenians, Germans, and other nationalities through all these infamous measures. On the contrary, the "prisoners of Zion" motivated the Jews even more to seek emancipation.

In 1987 the Anti-Defamation League, a Jewish-American organization in New York, published lists with the names of Jewish prisoners, exiles and dissidents.[44] The British historian Martin Gilbert, who had met many refuseniks during his stay in Russia, described their tragic situation in a book.[45]

His biography of Anatoly Shcharansky, the most famous refusenik who was also active in the dissident movement, gave Gilbert the subtitle "A hero of our time."[46] Shcharansky, born in 1948 in Moscow, was a mathematician. After the authorities had denied him an emigration visa in June 1973, he was arrested again in March 1977. In a spectacular trial in July 1978, he was convicted of espionage for the United States and for anti-Soviet activities. He was threatened with capital punishment, but the court of justice sentenced him to "only" thirteen years' imprisonment in the Gulag. His last words at the reading of his sentence were, "I turn to my people and my wife, Avital, and say, "Next year in Jerusalem!" And to you, you from the court of justice, who have issued the predetermined sentence, I have nothing to say."[47] Even though a massive international campaign was started, Shcharansky was not released until February 1986, when he was exchanged for a high-ranking Soviet agent imprisoned in the United States, on the Glienicke Bridge near Potsdam. His activities, suffering, and the fight for his liberation were told in a dozen books and a movie. After his arrival in Israel, Shcharansky, who "came in from the cold," was enthusiastically celebrated. At a mass demonstration in Tel Aviv, the popular song *Gesher tsar meod* was sung, which was intoned later at all events for the Soviet Jews. The simple but moving chorus say,: "The whole world is a very narrow bridge, but the most important thing is not to be afraid." For many years, thousands of "Prisoners of Zion" and refuseniks displayed this fearlessness in the face of the brutal regime.

The American best-selling author Chaim Potok created a literary monument for Vladimir Slepak and his family.[48] Solomon Slepak, the father of this famous refusenik, Aliyah activist and "Prisoner of Zion," had returned in 1918 from the United States to Russia, fought as a brigade commander and had become a leading Bolshevik. In April 1970 Vladimir Slepak applied for emigration and was arrested five times. The electronic engineer could not be kept down, not even with the threat that he would never receive an emigration visa. In April 1975 his family went on a three-week hunger strike, and in October 1986 they were finally allowed to emigrate to Israel.

The most popular personality among the refuseniks was undoubtedly Ida Nudel. For many years "the angel of the prisoners of Zion" had visited her brothers and sisters in the most remote exiles in far-away corners of the country and had organized help for them. When she placed a poster in her window, where she pledged to be united with her sister living in Israel, she was herself exiled for four years.

In April 1987 the U.S. Secretary of State, George Schultz (not a Jew), invited Ida Nudel and several other well-known refuseniks, to a Seder celebration at the U.S. embassy in Moscow. The presidents Nixon, Ford, Carter, Reagan and Bush Sr. also earned themselves merits for helping the Soviet Jews. Hollywood actress Jane Fonda led an international campaign for the Committee I-WIN (Israeli Women for Ida Nudel). Israel's President Shamir, Foreign Minister Peres, Jane Fonda and 200 world media reporters came to the Lod airport to welcome Ida Nudel. In October 1987, she arrived triumphantly in a private jet belonging to the American oil millionaire Armand Hammer, who had been a personal friend of Lenin and one of the first persons to engage in commercial relations with the Soviet Union. At a demonstration in Tel Aviv before 5,000 people, Ida Nudel thanked the governments of Israel, the U.S., France, Norway, Sweden, Australia and West Germany for not forgetting the Soviet Jews and for working for the liberation and emigration of those imprisoned. The I-WIN organization published a document about her and other "Prisoners of Zion" and refuseniks.[49]

*Stalin and the Jews*

## The Refusenik Colonels

Half a million Jewish soldiers and officers fought in the Second World War. Thousands were rewarded for their bravery, many of them with the golden star as "Hero of the Soviet Union." After the war they disappeared from the lists of awards for bravery, which were organized according to nationality. Anti-Semitic propaganda made them out to be service dodgers who had bought their awards on the black market in Tashkent. For this reason alone, many veterans, soldiers and officers applied very early for emigration visas.

In addition to General Wolf Vilensky, the pilot Lieutenant Colonel Lev Ovzisher was among the best known. Ovzisher, who had received a total of 17 awards for bravery and had been shot down over Stalingrad, applied several times for emigration papers after 1971. He was demoted, stripped of his insignia and had his pension reduced. Not until *perestroika* was he allowed to resettle in Israel.

Less fortunate was his friend Colonel Yefim Davidovich from Minsk. Wounded five times, he had received 15 awards for bravery. He too applied for emigration in 1971. When he again survived a heart attack—he had already had numerous attacks—he sent his thirteenth letter to Brezhnev, after which he was also demoted, stripped of his rank and honors, and denied his pension. He died in Minsk in 1975.

## *Perestroika*, Gorbachev, and the Jews

When Gorbachev came to power in March 1985, the Jews could again, in the course of *perestroika* and *glasnost*, freely embrace and spread their national culture after decades of repression. Cultural organizations, schools and press organs were established. It was possible, without fear of persecution, to learn Hebrew again and to participate in religious services in the synagogue and travel to Israel. After 1985, more than a hundred Jewish newspapers and other periodicals were established in Russia and other regions of the CIS states. Russian Judaism had reached the point it was in between the February and October Revolutions of 1917.

From 1971 to 1977, 155,000 Soviet Jews emigrated to Israel, followed by another 30,000 in the decade from 1978 to 1988. While only 796 Jews were allowed to emigrate in 1984 (as few as in 1965), their number climbed steadily during the Gorbachev era and reached its peak in

1990 with 181,140 emigrations to the U.S., Europe, and Israel. This was 50,000 more than between 1980 and 1989. Close to a million Jews emigrated, most of them to Israel.

The old Stalinist structures and its functionaries remained in the most important power centers of the Soviet Union—the party, economy, army and secret service. Nationalists, Nazis, and religious fanatics of all stripes used their newfound freedom of speech to make the Jews scapegoats once again for all economic and social problems. The polarization of society was intensified by nationality conflicts, which led to actual clashes.

The revived chauvinism, racism and anti-Semitism had taken on dimensions that were impossible even during tsarist times. This presented the Jews who remained with the question: to be or not to be. Chauvinist Russian intellectuals and writers, who formed the *Pamyat* movement, an iron front of antagonism towards the Jews, played a sorry role in all this. For example, such extreme forms as "zoological anti-Semitism" was spreading open, shameless and pure Hitler-style racism. The cover of the magazine *Russian Resurrection* (*Russkoe voskresenie*) always featured a swastika with a photo of Hitler and a quotation from *Mein Kampf* about the destruction of the Jews being a godly mission.

Wolf Oschlies defines the extremist anti-Semitic movement as follows:

> Post-communist anti-Semitism integrates all prior forms of the game—the traditional enmity toward Jews plus national socialist hatred of Jews, classic propaganda clichés plus provocative negation of the Holocaust, "anti-Zionist" disguise plus trendy "progressive" criticism of Israel—and instrumentalizes them.[50]

In their extensive works, Walter Laqueur and Mathias Messmer have thoroughly researched the confused history and complicated problem of the anti-Semitic Russian right wing.[51]

Some non-Jewish personalities and writers supported the umbrella organization of the Russian Jews, VAAD (Committee), established at the end of 1989 to fight against unrestricted anti-Semitism.

### The Anti-Zionist Committee of the Soviet Public

The anti-Zionist campaigns in the declining Soviet Union were outgrowths of political ignorance, arrogance, and misanthropy. To complete this chapter we want to recall briefly in the following section the wretched events of this period. In 1975 the Soviet Union voted for UN Resolution No. 3379, which stigmatized Zionism as racism. One hundred eleven Eastern Bloc states, Muslim, and Third World countries had voted in favor of this impertinent decree; only 25 spoke against it and 17 withheld their vote. The UN did not rescind it until 1992.

On secret orders of the Central Committee of the Communist Party, the Anti-Zionist Committee of the Soviet Public—ACSP (*Antitsionistkii komitet sovietskoi obshchestvennosti*) was established on April 21, 1983, in Moscow, followed by similar committees throughout the Soviet republics. This organization was a creation of the KGB and the Central Committee. Its mission was to fight the provocations of the alleged Zionists who, "under the guise of fighting for the Soviet Jews' rights," pursued damaging anti-Soviet propaganda. The April 1, 1983 issue of *Pravda* opened with a large anti-Zionist article, starting a campaign by the Soviet press against world Zionism, which was placed on an equal footing with fascism and racism. Bolsheviks also participated in this impudent agitation against their fellow Jewish citizens in Russia and their brothers and sisters in Israel and in the West.

General David Dragunsky was elected president of the committee. The presidium included 37 persons, most of them Jewish "Quislings" who followed any anti-Jewish directive that came from the top. The true leaders were historian Isaak Mints and the writer Aron Vergelis.

Isaak Mints was one of the Soviet regime's most loyal representatives, even though he was partially released from government service. He was born in 1896 in Krinichiki, near Yekaterinoslav. In April 1917 he joined the RSDRP(B). After the October Revolution he was among the Red Army's first volunteers. As commissar of the Second Ukrainian Division in the Red Cossacks' Corps, he fought in the Civil War on many fronts, including Poltava.

In 1922 he returned to civilian life and in 1924 began his studies at the Institute of the Red Professors, which researched the history of the communist party. He published, in addition to the *History of Diplomacy* and the *History of Soviet Foreign Policy*, more than 600 historical works, for which he received the Lenin Award once and the Soviet State Award three times. He was a professor at Moscow University and director of the Institute for Soviet History at the Party School for the CC, as well as in the relevant sections of the Soviet Academy of Sciences. All these functions were connected, naturally, with the editorial offices of such scholarly journals as *Voprosy istorii*. When in 1949 Stalin's vassals gathered materials against the Jewish professor, they found out, for example, that in an article about Lenin he had not shown sufficient esteem to Stalin's *Short Course of Instruction about the CPSU's History*. In April 1949 Mints and many of his closest co-workers, amid the fervor of the hysterical campaign against "rootless cosmopolitans," were dismissed from all academic positions. After Stalin's death, the historian was restored to all his duties. The leaders could be totally assured of his loyalty to the Kremlin regime.

Aron Vergelis was the only Yiddish writer who had never been exposed to the Soviet organs' persecution of Yiddish authors. He was born in 1918 in Lubary in Volynia. In 1930 his family resettled to Birobidzan. In the mid-1930s he published his first literary texts in the *Birobidzan Star*. In 1940 Vergelis ended his studies at the Teachers' College in Moscow and became the youngest member of the Soviet Literary Union. In the war his assignments as a parachutist took him to Berlin. He was wounded three times. Vergelis was one of the Yiddish speakers of Radio Moscow; after the war he supervised the station's Jewish branch. From 1947 to 1948 he was deputy editor in chief of the Yiddish almanac *Homeland* (*Heymland*). When the officials again allowed a Yiddish publication, Vergelis founded the monthly journal *Soviet Homeland* (*Sovietish Heymland*) in 1961. He wrote numerous literary reviews and several theater pieces and during his life remained loyal and true to the Communist Party. For thirty years he functioned as a Yiddish literary oracle and had the monopoly of the Soviet Union's publication of Yiddish-language texts, serving the state with great dedication as the regime's tireless propagandist in the Soviet Union and in foreign countries. Numerous offensive articles about Israel and those Jews who did not sympathize with the Soviet Union were published in *Soviet Homeland*. Memorial articles about persecuted and murdered Yiddish poets, whom Vergelis had known personally, and who were more or less his true teachers, were not printed until the late 1960s.

## Epilogue to the Refusenik Story

Is it not an irony of history that in Jerusalem, of all places, the Soviet flag was raised and the Soviet anthem played worldwide for the last time in December 1991? Shortly before the downfall of the Soviet state, the Kremlin had established diplomatic contact with its former deadly enemy Israel. When the designated Soviet ambassador, Alexandr Bovin, presented Israeli state president Chaim Herzog with his credentials, the Soviet Union no longer existed. Bovin automatically became the Russian ambassador.

Between 1989 and 1997, 723,453 Jews emigrated from the Soviet Union to Israel. Several hundred thousand emigrated to the U.S., and more than 50,000 resettled in West Germany. In Israel the Soviet Jews are contributing greatly to the development of the economy, science and culture, but they do not entirely give up their own cultural traditions. Several Russian daily newspapers, illustrated weekly and monthly periodicals and publishing houses have been established, and a Russian symphonic orchestra can be found in almost every Israeli town. Jewish-Russian soloists give concerts throughout the world.

In 1995 the Russian Jews founded their own party—*Israel Ba'aliyah*—that at the parliamentary elections one year later gained seven seats. The former refuseniks Anatoly Shcharansky and Yuli Edelstein became ministers in Netanyahu's cabinet.

Mikhail Gorbachev was warmly welcomed in 1993 in Israel for ending the decades-long absurd and irrational fight of the Soviet communists and organs against the Jews, Zionism and the state of Israel. He had also allowed hundreds of thousands of Jews to emigrate. At a benefit event for Israel in Berlin on March 2, 1998, to commemorate the fiftieth anniversary of the founding of the Jewish state, he said:

> A people that has tried for hundreds of years to create and restore its own homeland; a people that—under the most difficult environmental conditions and no less difficult external circumstances—has had to mourn so many victims on its way to its goal; and a people that has done so much for its land that one has to say today, it is a "blooming, thriving land"; such a people deserves respect and admiration.

# Part IX

## 37. In the Balance:
### Russian Jews Between Hitler and Stalin

Looking at the history of the Jews under the Soviet dictatorship as a whole, a few major episodes stand out. Following the apparent improvement in Jewish life came a phase when old prejudices and enmities were mixed to new revolutionary tendencies, and the places where Jewish existence traditionally sought refuge disappeared or were destroyed.

The Russian Marxists never accepted the fact that they were practically indebted to Jewish revolutionaries. Jews belonged, on the one hand, to the movement's avant-garde and, on the other, the "Jewish element" of the revolution would be phased out at every available opportunity. By abandoning the "Jewish" internationalist "cosmopolitan" heritage, Bolshevism or Soviet communism was transformed into a Russian imperialist ideology. The assaults by Lenin and Stalin against the Bund were proof enough, no less than the anti-Jewish harassment campaigns against Trotskyism surfaced as "anti-cosmopolitanism" and "anti-Zionism."

Soviet power never accepted autonomous Jewish interests. Even the periods of great liberty (as the 1920s) can only be viewed as "repressed tolerance," allowing some free space to exist. The roots are to be found in the ambitions of the state and the party, which were largely opposed to the vital interests of the Jews. The manipulation of the Jews is evident in the failed development of a Jewish region of Birobidzan and also in the initially very successful JAFC.

One could argue that this government control technique was intended for every region within the Soviet dictatorship. Certainly it did not only concern the Jews, but the hostile relations between Russian and Jewish revolutionaries since the establishment of Russian social democracy must be borne in mind. These clashes by no means only originated in deep-rooted prejudices and anti-Semitism in Russian society, but also from the special role the Jewish labor movement played and the self-confidence of the Jewish Bolsheviks.

Jews helped determine Russia's fate in the first half of the twentieth century. At the Second Party Congress of the RSDRP in 1903, the Bund delegates Kosovsky and Liber could not prevent the splitting of Russian Social Democracy, agitated by Lenin, which resulted in the forming of the Bolshevik faction. The dream of thousands of revolutionaries, a dream of a free socialist state in Russia, was over. For a short time after the February Revolution, all government discrimination against the Jews was lifted. Many Jewish revolutionaries, most of them Mensheviks, social revolutionaries, Bundists or left wing Zionists, participated in political life. Only a few of them supported the October putsch instigated by the Bolsheviks. Zinoviev and Kamenev, the original opponents of armed resistance and revolution, later joined Stalin to form a troika against Trotsky, who had played the decisive role in the breakthrough of Bolshevik ideology in the RSDRP. Adolf Ioffe refused to sign the treacherous "peace pact" dictated by the German general staff at Brest-Litovsk, which Lenin anyhow carried through.

The Bolsheviks, under the guise of emancipation, destroyed traditional religious and political structures that had been part of Jewish life in the waning years of the tsarist reign. During the civil war the Jews were driven into the arms of the Bolsheviks because the victory of the White Guards would have meant their elimination.

The pressure of assimilation was softened in the 1920s through the establishment of secular Jewish institutions and a blossoming of Jewish—and especially Yiddish—culture that conformed to the system. On one hand, the Jews were subjected to the proletarization process—about half were robbed as non-proletarians of their most basic rights and had to live their unhappy existence as *Lischenzy*; on the other hand, new opportunities opened up in Soviet society. In the 1930s the true meaning of Stalin's nationality policies became obvious. All gains achieved during the initial period were sacrificed to the growing Russification of the Soviet Union. The persecution of "nationalist deviation" not only destroyed the predominantly loyal Jewish culture and its institutions, but in the purge and the Great Terror many former comrades and loyal communists, many of them of Jewish origin, were imprisoned and executed or driven out of the country.

The German assault forced the Soviet Union into a struggle for life and death. To mobilize all energies against the enemy, the Kremlin leadership allowed limited freedom to the Soviet Jews. They could embrace their national culture and be in contact with their brothers and sisters abroad. Under the Jewish Anti-Fascist Committee's banner, a Jewish illusion was created, only to be hunted down later in a bloody persecution as "bourgeois nationalism." The anti-Jewish campaigns of Stalin's last years—with the liquidation of the JAFC leadership the major incident—were followed after the dictator's death by only a very short period of relaxation. The hope for a rebirth of the Jewish community was not fulfilled; rather, official anti-Semitism continued to gather strength until the downfall of the Soviet Union. Change came only with *perestroika*, but freedom for Jewish culture was now (and will be) accompanied by equally unlimited freedom for anti-Semitic activities.

Under tsarism and Stalinism specific suspicion was directed against the Jews as being disloyal. This included the "Elders of Zion" and the secret *Kahal* that developed, allegedly along with the *Joint* organization, a Zionist world plot. To the rulers and the organs of both regimes, the Yiddish national culture, the feeling for unity among a population that did not have its own territory, was most suspicious because this group of people could easily withdraw from any simple control and surveillance. Jews, though, were not the only victims of the Stalinist terror regime, nor was anti-Semitism the only motive for the persecutions: the paranoia of treason—and with that various inner-party intrigues that suddenly appeared regarding Stalin's succession—led to the destruction of party cadres in Leningrad in 1950 Jews or the hatred for Jews played no part in this.

The mounting anti-Jewish fever during the late Stalin dictatorship can only be understood as a combination of an all-out attack on society and the reactivation of anti-Semitic traditions in Russian history. It is not easy to know if the judges—and their employer, Stalin—really believed in a Jewish plot, even a worldwide plot as an anti-Semitic obsession. It certainly did work for some of the inquisitors; many of them, though, were unprincipled characters who wanted to eliminate every "enemy," whether a Jew or member of another nationality.

In the late 1940s, Jews began to be suspected more often than members of other nationalities. According to totalitarian logic, trials should have also been initiated against the representatives of other anti-fascist committees. At any time another committee, like the Slavic or Anti-Fascist Women's Committee, could be unmasked as the hidden cell of an ideology hostile to the Soviets—this wouldn't have been more absurd than the real accusations leveled at the JAFC. Under the rehabilitated Russian chauvinism, with all its Judeo-phobic elements, Jews were the main targets of investigation because they were particularly suspected of being sympathetic toward the West. The members of the JAFC were especially suspect and were accused of wanting to leave the country to go to Palestine. Because of this, the inquisitors and judges were especially harsh and eager to condemn their travel abroad.

In the last years of Stalinism the Jews became the enemy par excellence in yet another way. As the only nationality in Stalin's empire, all their activities were suspect and attacked as being mistakes: they were criminals if they participated or agitated in "nationalist" activities; they were criminals if they "smuggled" themselves into Russian culture using a pseudonym—like the theater critics did. A Jew was suspect if he or she spoke Yiddish; a Jew was suspect if he became a Russian; a Jew was an enemy if he declared to be or viewed himself as part of the worldwide Jewish community and if he saw Israel as his home country. The Jews were to assimilate themselves in the country they lived as quickly as possible, but on their passport, as with all Soviet citizens, there was the written indication of their nationality: *Jew* (*Yevrei*). The Jews were to disregard their shtetl mentality and become useful Soviet citizens, but because they were successful and made careers in scientific institutes, in the economy, in government positions and in the military they were accused of being too eager and ambitious and therefore accused of pushing back the Russians and thereby damaging the all-Soviet national harmony.

Did Stalin become a second Hitler in the end? In fact, some historians have compared Stalin's anti-Semitic policies with the crimes of National Socialist Germany, but not only did they compare the Shoah; they put both at the same level. One example is the title under which Borshchagovsky's book appeared in France, *L'Holocauste inachevé*. This suggests an unfinished Holocaust, the attempt by Stalin to eliminate all the Soviet Jews like Hitler did.

As a survivor of the Holocaust, I feel no urge to comment upon such easy and recently stated similarities between the mass murder of the Jews and the crimes of communism; this led to a relativization of the

Holocaust if not worse. Gerd Koenen defines the extraordinary nature of the Shoah as follows:

> The Jewish murder was singular because it was the most radical genocide experiment that had ever been tried. It was the attempt—with quasi-scientific, race-biological arguments, plus the resources of a modern bureaucracy, plus the technical possibilities for mass killing—to achieve something like a perfect, complete genocide. This undertaking is absolutely unique in the history of mankind. It was an extreme, an uttermost dehumanization of human society in its entirety. And it will remain an extreme example as such in memory.

Remarkable differences between Hitler's tasks and Stalin's crimes against the Jews cannot be overlooked: Hitler proclaimed anti-Semitism openly, while Stalin never dared to detach himself from the traditional international programs of socialism and communism. Even in the worst times of the Stalinist harassment of the Jews, rhetorical distances from anti-Semitism still existed. Only by baptizing Jews—including very many loyal Soviet citizens and opponents of the Jewish state, Palestine—as "Zionist," could he persecute them in an ideologically acceptable manner.

It could be inferred that this did not help the victims. In reality, this difference contributed to saving many. In contrast to Hitler's all-encompassing racial craze, which saw in everyone with one drop of Jewish blood an enemy who had to be eliminated, Stalin wanted to eliminate Jewish nationalism and cosmopolitism. Stalin wanted to destroy Jewish culture and the national feelings of the Jews; Hitler was after the Jews as a people. If the latter worked towards the genocide, the former remained on the level of a "cultural genocide," which he pursued with murderous effectiveness.

We have no proof that Stalin planned gas chambers, shooting commandos, extermination through labor or other crimes for the Jews, as had already become the reality under the German dictatorship. The last straw under Stalin was brutal mass deportation that had been practiced on the Volga Germans, the Tatars and other ethnic groups. These measures had cost thousands their lives and would have cost, in the case of the Jews, many more thousands of lives, but they do not stand for a Soviet Auschwitz or Maidanek. That does not make the terror any better at any point, and it will remain an unbelievable crime against humanity.

Recently, attempts have been made to rewrite the history of the Soviet Union through sensational revelations about communism's crimes. True, many archives and KGB files now available have been the subject of research, along with documents from regional administrations reconstructed by historians. The details available now offer a deeper and better understanding of the Soviet Union's dictatorship, but much of what is now celebrated as new discovery had been known for decades. The difference is that the actual reports, Jewish newspapers and authors were not read or no one wished to draw any conclusion from these sources. Arthur Koestler in *Darkness at Noon* and *The Yogi and the Commissar*, and Vassily Grossman in *Life and Fate* have described in their novels the inhuman policies of Stalinism very effectively. The latter-day former communists and Maoist apostates have no fear to equate their ideas about the most horrible crimes in human history—which they drafted on their laptops (Wolfgang Wippermann) on the same level as any other group of victims.

The statement by Stéphane Courtois, that "the uniqueness of the genocide of the Jews hinders the concept of acknowledging comparable circumstances in the communist world," makes me particularly angry. Who has hindered whom? The rhetoric of his statements very much resembles the well-known Agitprop jargon. For total *chutzpah* I find the following sentence equating "racial genocide" on the same scale as "class genocide": "The death of a Ukrainian *kulak* child, whom the Stalinist regime forces with determination into starvation, weighs exactly as much as the death of a Jewish child in the Warsaw ghetto, who fell victim to starvation brought by the Nazi regime." The overwhelming majority of the 1,500,000 Jewish children that were murdered during the Shoah did not starve to death; they were murdered together with their parents in the gas chambers, in the ghettos or in the ravines as Babi Yar and Ponary.

If Stalin had been a second Hitler, the fight of the JAFC on Stalin's side would have been an absurdity. But the historical truth—and I am concerned only about this in my research and its description of the history and the story of the Jewish Anti-Fascist Committee—was a different one. In spite of the tragedy of the committee members' destruction by the secret police, their fight *with* the Soviet regime *against* Hitler was an absolute necessity for which there was no other alternative, not just for the Soviet Jews.

After having thoroughly examined in this book crimes against the Soviet Jews perpetrated by Stalin and his successors, how can we fail not to remember the millions of Soviet soldiers who died or fell prisoner in the fight against Hitler's Germany? Without their sacrifice the world would be lost; they saved us from the murderous dictatorship of Nazism. We owe our survival to the heroes of the Red Army as well as to the Western Allies.

# THE PEOPLE

The history of the Soviet Union and the Soviet Jews must be rewritten. We have to consider more intensive oral history and get a solid grounding in biographies in historical research. The life and fate of individuals presents a different perspective on the crimes of the 20th century than theoretical writings and ideology or party-line presentations. Therefore, the people in this book, as well as in my other books *Schalom Libertad!* and *Zum Kampf auf Leben und Tod,* are offered as objects and subjects of the historical events who need to be rescued from oblivion.

> Do not read works of history, only biographies, for that is life without theory.
>
> *Benjamin Disraeli*

## MENSHEVIKS AND BUNDISTS

### Vladimir Kosovsky

Vladimir Kosovsky (Nahum Mendel Levinsohn) was born in Daugavpils, Latvia, into a wealthy, educated family. He was already close to the Narodniki while attending high school in Kaunas and was very much involved with the Jewish workers in Vilnius after 1895. As one of the cofounders of the Bund (1897), he was part of the first CC and started the first Bundist newspaper, *Yiddish Worker (Der yidisher arbeter)* that was printed abroad and smuggled illegally into Russia. After the CC headquarters moved to Minsk because of many arrests, Kosovsky published the newspaper, *Workers' Voice (Arbetershtime)* there. He wrote many propaganda brochures and was arrested in 1898. As the train with the prominent prisoner arrived in Moscow, the leading officials of the tsarist regime had gathered, including the Moscow army commander, Minister of Justice Muravyov and Subatov, the notorious chief of the *Okhrana*. In April 1900 Kosovsky was released with Arkadi Kremer, also a CC member. Shortly after that, he fled to Geneva where he ran the foreign office of the Bund, founded by John Mill in 1898, and published their newspaper, *Last News (Poslednie novosti)*, as well as numerous program writings. His request to organize the RSDRP as a union of national parties elicited repeated attacks of the PPS and the Leninist *Spark (Iskra)*. Kosovsky's sharp debates with Lenin at the Second Party Congress of the RSDRP in 1903 not only impressed the Bundists, but the members of the friendly socialist parties as well. In 1904 Kosovsky was elected as the Bund representative to be a member of the Socialist International in Amsterdam. During the revolution of 1905, he and Vladimir Medem returned to Russia with forged passports. On instructions of the CC, Kosovsky and Mark Liber were to publish a legal newspaper, *The Jewish Worker (Yevreiski Rabochi)*. However, officials soon shut down the printing house. The daily newspaper that Kosovsky founded in Vilnius, *The Worker (Der wecker)*, was forbidden after 33 issues. The successor publication, *People's Newspaper (Folkstsaytung)*, was published up to 1907. When the editorial staff of the newspaper, *The Hope (Die hofnung)*, was arrested, Kosovsky gave up the fight against the police and wrote for various other papers, some of them printed abroad, such as *The New Time (Die Naya Tsayt)*, *Questions of the Time (Tsaytfragn)*, *Questions of Life (Fragen fun lebn)*, *New Voices (Die Naya shtime)*, and the Russian-language *Otkliki Bunda (Echo of the Bund)*. Between 1911 and 1931 he wrote hundreds of articles for *Future (Zukunft)*, the New York paper of the Bund.

In April 1917, six weeks after the February Revolution, the Tenth Congress of the Bund was held in Petrograd, which elected an enlarged central committee led by Kosovsky. He couldn't take part because he hadn't applied for a German transit visa, like Lenin did, but remained in very close contact with his comrades. It is worth reading his 74-page pamphlet, *The Bolshevik Regime in Russia*, written in November 1918 and published in Olten, Switzerland, as one of the first unsparing criticisms of the Leninist state. In the final chapter Kosovsky discussed how Russia could be liberated from the Bolshevik yoke and the duties of democracy.

In 1920, Kosovsky lived in Berlin where he wrote numerous articles for the daily Bund paper *Folkstseytung*, published in Warsaw. After 1930 he lived permanently in the Polish capital. At one of the last conferences of the party council of the Bund in April 1939, he predicted: "The Nazis will destroy all the Jews, everywhere they march in." In September 1939 he managed to escape to Pinsk, which was occupied by Soviet forces. Because the NKVD, with the help of Jewish communists, was looking for leaders of the Bund, Kosovsky first went underground in Vilnius, but had to register with the public commissar's office of the Interior, because the American federation of Labor (AFL) had been able to get some union leaders entry visas for the U.S. With a passport under the name of Moshe Kamenstein, he came to New York in April 1941 via Moscow, Vladivostok and Tokyo. In New York he worked for the Bund magazine *Naya Tsayt*. He died on October 19, 1941. His appeal to support the invaded Soviet Union did not appear until after his death.

## Yuli Martov

Yuli Martov (Tsederbaum), born in 1873 in Constantinople, was one of the leaders of the Mensheviks. His father owned the representation of a Russian shipping company in Constantinople; his grandfather Aleksandr Tsederbaum founded several Yiddish, Hebrew, and Russian-language newspapers, including *Hamelits* and *Dawn* (*Rassvet*). Martov began his political career as a 19-year-old student in St. Petersburg. In 1895 he was one of the co-founders of the "Liberation of Labor Group" in St. Petersburg and he appealed in Vilnius for the formation of an independent social democratic workers' organization. Eight years later he was one of the main opponents of Kosovsky (who demanded a federalist structure) and resigned from the Bund, because, like Trotsky, he felt the struggle of the Bundists for national autonomy to be a drawback. Martov was arrested twice and exiled to Vilnius. From 1901 to 1905 he lived in exile. He was one of the co-founders and collaborators of *Iskra*; during the revolution of 1905 he was one of the leaders of the St. Petersburg workers' council. In 1907 he emigrated again. An assimilated Jew, he considered the universal values to be more important than Yiddish culture. That's why everyone held him in high esteem as a leader of the Mensheviks. In the First World War he was prominent within the pacifist Zimmerwald Movement. In May 1917 Martov returned to Russia. After the October putsch he strived for the formation of a socialist government and fought against the despotism of Lenin and his "professional revolutionaries." Shortly before the assassination attempt on Lenin, Martov published in August 1918 an urgent appeal against the death penalty. All his life he continued to be a sharp critic of Bolshevik terror—Lenin gave him his exit permit in 1920—and led the Russian exiled opposition against the Soviet dictatorship from Berlin. This courageous, honest and honored exponent of Russian and European socialism died in 1923 in Germany. His unfinished work, *Geschichte der russischen Sozialdemokratie (History of Russian Social Democracy)*, was published in Berlin in 1926.

### Fyodor Dan

Fyodor Dan (Gurvich), a medical doctor, was Martov's closest collaborator. He was born in St. Petersburg in 1871. In 1895 he was, in addition to Martov and Lenin, one the co-founders of the St. Petersburg of the "Liberations of Labor Group." Because of his revolutionary activities, he was exiled to Siberia for three years. After 1901 he headed the *Iskra* group in Berlin and organized the Second Party Congress of the RSDRP. After the split in the party he sided with the Menshevik leadership and was their secretary general at various times and edited the party paper, *Voice of the Social Democrat (Golos sotsialdemokrata)* in Paris with Martov. When war broke out in 1914, Dan was exiled to Siberia and drafted as a medical officer in Irkutsk. In March 1917 he returned to Petrograd. He was elected vice chairman of the central executive committee of the Soviets, the highest committee of the revolution, and became editor in chief of *Izvestiia*.

Together with Yuli Martov, whose sister he had married, he led the semi-legal Menshevik party after the October putsch until 1921. Abram Gots, Mark Liber and he were labeled counterrevolutionaries and traitors by the Bolsheviks with the slogan "Gotsliberdan," for speaking out against the death penalty in the army. Dan supported Jewish self-defense groups against the pogroms and fought against Zionism. In 1921 he was arrested, deported abroad and managed to escape to the U.S. in 1940. There he broke with Menshevism because he was still under an illusion about humanizing and democratizing the Soviet regime. He died in 1947, isolated in New York.

### Rafael Abramovich

Rafael Abramovich (Rein) was born in 1880 in Dvinsk, Latvia. During his studies in Riga he worked in illegal revolutionary circles and became a member of the Bund in 1901. Later he followed the Bund student groups in Liège and Zurich. In 1905 he returned from Switzerland to Russia as a Bund candidate for the second Duma. He was arrested several times and sent into exile in Siberia. In 1911 he managed to escape abroad where his activities in the Bund brought him into contact with Lenin and other future Soviet rulers in Zurich. When he returned to Russia he was welcomed at the Finland station by his parents, as well as numerous Bundists and Mensheviks, including Henryk Erlich and Mark Liber. He became a member of the Soviet central executive committee. In August 1917 he took part in the conference of the Ukrainian Bund in Kiev. After the October putsch, Bolsheviks and left social revolutionaries formed the government. The Constitutional Assembly, in which the social revolutionaries had a strong majority, was dissolved in January 1918. Abramovich and his comrades got a taste of the Red terror, but the Bolsheviks did not yet dare to openly subject former members to physical repression. In May 1918 the leadership of the Bundists and the Mensheviks moved to Moscow, where the government was still located.

In the summer of 1918 the libel case of Stalin versus Martov was held at the supreme tribunal in Moscow. Martov had described in a newspaper article the role played by the Commissar for Nationalities Stalin in the armed robbery of the National Bank of Tiflis, when 250,000 rubles were added to the party funds of the Bolsheviks. During this "expropriation," several soldiers were killed and this was the reason, he wrote, Stalin was expelled from the Bolshevik party. Martov's lawyer, Abramovich, immediately wanted to submit to the court proof of Stalin's participation, but the motion was denied. Stalin exacted revenge nearly 20 years later when his agents kidnapped and murdered the son of Abramovich, Marc Rein, who lived in Paris and had moved in 1937 to Barcelona to fight for the Spanish republic. The Spanish government and its secret service tried in vain to pick up the murderers' trail.

In 1920 Abramovich, along with Martov, was granted an exit permit by resolution of the central committee of the CPR, and moved to Berlin, where he co-founded the party paper *Socialist Messenger* (*Sotsialisticheskiii vestnik*). After Martov's death, Abramovich and Dan took over the direction of the Mensheviks in exile. From 1923 to 1929 he was executive member of the Socialist International. From exile in Berlin and Paris he tried to inform the international public about the communist terror. In 1930 his pamphlet, *The Political Prisoners in the Soviet Union (Die politischen Gefangenen in der Sowjetunion)*, was published in Berlin, ending with the following words:

"Systematic extermination" of all dissenters, insofar as they openly risked their opinion—this is one of the most important elements of the Bolshevik "five-year plan" for the realization of integral socialism in the "first working-class state in the world." Anyone who doesn't understand this understands nothing of the essence of the Bolshevik dictatorship in Russia. Will the conscience of the socialist proletariat of the world ever be able to reconcile with such a system?

In 1940, Abramovich escaped to the United States, where he continued to be active in the publishing world. His two volume memoirs were published in 1944, and in 1956 the Jewish Socialist Association of America published his work *Di farbrekhens fun Stalin, die farbrekhens fun sovietishn rezhim.* He died ten years later, highly respected and loved by many comrades in New York.

## Mark Liber

One of the most active leaders of Jewish Socialism, first within the RSDRP as an opponent to Lenin, and later as a member of the board of the Bund party, was Mark Liber (Michal Goldman). He was born in Vilnius in 1880, the son of a Yiddish poet, Yitskhak Goldman. His older brothers, Boris and Leon Goldman, had been working in Social Democratic circles in Vilnius and St. Petersburg since 1890. Boris defended his friend and comrade Martov after his arrest. Leon represented the RSDRP at the Socialist Congress in Paris in 1900. In high school, Michal Goldman was already considered, along with his schoolmate Felix Dzerzhinsky, one of the most active in revolutionary circles. Thanks to his education and rhetoric, he created an image for himself under the party name of Mark Liber very early on as a striking representative of the interests of the Jewish proletariat. As an indefatigable organizer and ideologist, he represented the Vilnius Bund at the 4th Bund Convention in 1900 in Geneva, and was part of the five-man delegation from the Bund at the Second Party Congress of the RSDRP in 1903 in Brussels and London, where after Lenin and Trotsky, he gave the greatest number of speeches. His explanation regarding the withdrawal of the Bund from the united party led to the creation of the Bolshevik faction. In 1904 he took part in the International Socialist Congress in Paris.

During the Revolution of 1905, Liber and Trotsky were members of the Workers' Council of St. Petersburg, and avoided arrest purely by accident. In 1906 the American Bundists invited him to a lecture tour and fundraising campaign in the United States. Exhausted by the endless arguments between the different factions of the revolutionary parties, he decided in 1908 to give up underground work. At first, Liber lived with his family in Vilnius and then in St. Petersburg. Due to his involvement in *The Free Economic Society*, which combined liberal and radical circles, he was arrested in 1915 in Odessa and exiled to Buzuluk, Siberia, where he lived until the outbreak of the revolution in February 1917.

Liber was appointed, along with Henryk Erlich, as a representative of the Bund to the executive council of the workers' and soldiers' councils of Petrograd, and supported close cooperation between the socialist parties and the Social Revolutionaries. Besides Tseretelli, Cheidze, Dan, and Gots, he was one of the most popular leaders of the democratic February Revolution. Because he fought *against* the Bolsheviks and *in favor of* the Provisional Government, he incurred the hatred of both Lenin and Trotsky. Liber rejected a ministerial position he was offered by the head of government, Kerensky. At the Bund Congress in November 1917 in Petrograd, shortly after the October putsch, he declared: "There cannot be compromises with the counterrevolutionary Bolsheviks. We have to recognize the right of the people to revolt against the Bolsheviks and we should be their spokesmen." He was elected to the central committee of the Mensheviks in 1918. Until 1920 Liber lived in the Ukraine. Bolshevik propaganda slandered him, Fyodor Dan and Abram Gots with the slogan "Gotsliberdan," as counterrevolutionaries and traitors, because they spoke out against the death penalty in the army.

Liber criticized the pro-communist attitude of Bundist comrades like Moshe Rafes and Esther Frumkin, who not only reconciled themselves to Soviet power, but became leading *Yevseki*. He probably survived persecution only because he was the brother-in-law of Dzerzhinsky, chief of the Cheka. During the Great Terror he was taken to Alma Ata and placed into custody there with approximately 10,000 mostly political prisoners. It wasn't known until 1947 that he had been shot and killed, together with Abram Gots and other revolutionaries in 1937. Today Liber's name has fallen into oblivion.

ZIONISTS

## Yekhiel Chlenov

The leader of the Russian Zionists, Yekhiel Chlenov, was born in 1863 into a wealthy family in Kremenchug. After obtaining his degree in medicine in Moscow, he was a practicing physician after 1888. Because of the pogroms of 1881, he became a Jewish nationalist and Zionist and was a delegate at several Zionist conventions. In 1902 he became president of the Russian Zionist Congress in Minsk. After a journey to Palestine in 1907 he founded the Migdal settlement on the Sea of Galilee. In 1911 he was elected vice president of the Zionist World Organization (whose president was Otto Warburg), and moved to Berlin, where the head office was located. In 1912 he was among the cofounders of the Technion in Haifa and the Hadassah hospital in Tel Aviv. In 1915, as a Russian citizen, he had to leave Berlin and return to Moscow where he was in charge of aiding Jewish refugees who were deported by the tsarist army out of Poland. He was president of the All-Russian Zionist Congress of June 6, 1917, in Petrograd and later went to London, where he supported, together with professor Chaim Weizmann, the passing of the Balfour declaration in November 1917. He died in London one year later.

## Ber Borokhov

Ber Borokhov is considered to be the theorist, ideologist and founder of the socialist-Zionist labor movement (*Poale Zion*). He was born in 1881 in Solotonosha in the Ukraine. The family later lived in Poltava, where he attended Russian schools. As a Jew he did not obtain a place at the university, but as an autodidact he acquired a rich knowledge in philosophy, economics, Jewish philology, statistics, and several languages. In 1901 in Yekaterinoslav he founded a circle of the *Poale Zion*, which participated in all Zionist conventions. In his study, *Class Struggle and the National Question* (1905) and in the programmatically scripted *Our Platform* (1906) he elaborated a synthesis of academic Marxist socialism and Zionism. In 1907 Borokhov left Russia, worked as a journalist in Western and Central Europe and founded the world association of the *Poale Zion* in The Hague that had national organizations in numerous countries. In 1914 he led the American *Poale Zionists* in New York and edited the Yiddish party organ *The Truth* (*Di Varhayt*). After the First World War began, Borokhov continued party work in Russia. At the *Poale Zionist* convention in August 1917, he talked about building settlements and the class struggle in Palestine. He died at the age of 36 during a lecture tour in the Ukraine. Borokhov wrote numerous papers and essays, which were translated after his death into several languages. The anthologies, *Class and Nation—On the Theory and Practice of Jewish Nationalism* and *Socialism and Zionism, a Synthesis. Selected*, were published in German in 1932. A bibliography of his works was published in Yiddish, Hebrew, German, and English.

## SOCIAL REVOLUTIONARIES

### Grigori Gershuni

The legendary Grigori Gershuni (1870-1908) was cofounder of the Social Revolutionary Party (SRP). He founded the terrorist department of the SRP, the *Boyevaya organisatsiya*, which carried out numerous assassinations of leading representatives of the Tsarist regime. The attacks on the hated Minister Plehve and on the governor of Moscow, Grand Prince Sergei Alexandrovich, made the party popular among the people.

In 1904, Gershuni was arrested and condemned to death by a military tribunal, although the sentence was reduced to life imprisonment in Siberia. In court, he accused the regime of persecuting the Jews. He was able to flee and reached Western Europe via China, Japan, and the United States. When he died in 1908 as a result of the imprisonment and escape, friends buried him in the Parisian cemetery Montparnasse, next to other famous Russian revolutionaries.

### Mikhail Gots

Mikhail Gots was one of the most important leaders of the social revolutionaries. He was born in Moscow in 1866, the son of a rich family of tea importers. As a student, he was a member of the *Narodnaya volya*, arrested in 1886, and wounded during the mutiny against the 3,000 kilometer-long death march to Siberia in 1889. After a campaign launched in the British press, he was amnestied and deported in 1901. In exile, he financed and edited many party organs. Gots was the leading ideologist of the SR. His arrest in Italy and extradition to the tsarist police caused a diplomatic crisis. He died in 1906 in Berlin at the age of 40, and was buried in Geneva.

### Abram Gots

Abram Gots, the brother of Mikhail Gots, was born in Moscow in 1882. After his studies, he joined the fighting organization of the SR. He was involved in numerous assassinations, including of the governor of Moscow, Count Shauvalov. In 1906 he was exiled to Siberia. In 1917 he led the strong SR faction in the Soviet in Petrograd, and was elected as the first chairman of an all-Russian executive committee. In 1918 he joined other SR comrades against the inhuman Bolshevist dictatorship. When the regime consolidated in 1922, 47 of its enemies were brought to court in one of the first great Soviet show trials. Due to the intense protests of all three Socialist Internationals, the number of accused was reduced to 32, of whom 22 were SR members. The secret police started demonstrations by thousands of factory workers who spontaneously turned on the "traitors" of the revolution; absurd accusations were raised at the trial. Leading personalities of the Socialist International, like Vandervelde and Liebknecht came to Moscow to defend the accused, but soon realized they were being manipulated by the secret police as an alibi to show that the country was under the rule of law. Gots was condemned to death with eleven other SR comrades. The sentence was reduced to five years in prison, which he served in Alma Ata. There are differing reports as to his fate. According to official documents, he was active in the economy until 1937. Viktor Sensinov and Viktor Chernov admitted that he had been shot along with other prisoners of Alma Ata in 1937.

### Osip Minor

Osip Minor belongs to the distinguished but less known leaders of the SR. He was born in Minsk in 1861, the son of Salomon, a liberal scholar and rabbi working for the state, who taught Lev Tolstoi Hebrew. During his studies in Moscow, he joined the *Narodnaya volya*, was arrested many times and banned to Northern Siberia for ten years in 1887. After his release in 1896, he continued his revolutionary activities, was cofounder of the SR, member of the CC, and Chief of the Department for Organization. In 1909 Asev, the SR member and a tsarist spy, informed on him. This time he was sentenced to eight years in jail. The Revolution in 1917 brought him his freedom. He wrote articles for the newspaper, *Days (Dni)* and was elected to Mayor of Moscow, the city from which his family had been expelled. In 1919 he emigrated to France where he founded the Aid Society for Political Prisoners in Russia. Minor died in Paris in 1932. His memoirs, *This Was Long Ago* (*Eto bylo davno*), were published one year later.

## Isaak Steinberg

Isaak Steinberg, born in Dvinsk in 1888, came from a wealthy, educated family. At 18 he was arrested as a member of the SR following revolutionary activities, sentenced to a term in prison, and expelled from Moscow University. He continued his law studies in Heidelberg, where he received his degree in 1910. Later he practiced as a lawyer in Moscow. After the split of the SR, Steinberg joined the left wing of the party, the one that cooperated with the Bolsheviks. The Sovnarkom, the first and last coalition government in Soviet history, was formed in 1917; it included seven members of the left socialist revolutionaries. Dr. Isaak Steinberg was elected Commissar of Justice. Out of protest against the unlawful activities of the Cheka under Felix Dzerzhinsky, he stepped down from office after only three months. When the leftist SR broke from the Bolsheviks, he was arrested numerous times.

Steinberg left Russia; from 1923 on he represented the SR in Berlin, where he worked together with Anarcho-Syndicalists like Rudolf Rocker and Franz Pfemfert. He also supported aid for political prisoners in the Soviet Union. From 1933 to 1939, he lived in London, and from 1943 on in New York. From 1943 to 1956 he was editor of a monthly magazine *Oyfn shvel*, the organ of Freiland-Liga, which aided the Jewish settlement projects outside of Palestine. As a Jew who believed in God and a left wing socialist who also was politically active in inner-Jewish questions, he was the most colorful among the Jewish revolutionaries. The ideas he advocated, the synthesis of humanistic socialism, the ideal of human solidarity and Jewish ethics, remained a vision.

In his published works in Russian, Yiddish, and German, he criticized the inhumane Soviet regime. The following were published in Germany: *Ten Years of the October Revolution* (*Zehn Jahre Oktoberrevolution*) (Berlin 1927), *When I was the People's Commissar* (*Als ich Volkskommissar war*) (Munich 1929, followed by an English and Yiddish edition in 1931), *Violence and Terror in the Revolution—The Fate of the Humiliated and Offended in the Russian* (*Revolution Gewalt und Terror in der Revolution—Das Schicksal der Erniedrigten und Beleidigten in der russischen Revolution*) (Berlin 1931, Reprint Berlin 1981). The play *The Way of Thorns* (*Der Dornenweg*) (1929) was performed in Germany and translated into Yiddish.

*Arno Lustiger*

## ANARCHISTS

### Vsevolod Volin

Vsevolod Volin (Eichenbaum) was among the leadership of the Russian anarchists. He was born in 1882 near Voronezh into a physician's family and educated by French and German governesses. As a Social Revolutionary, he took part in the revolution of 1905 and was sent into exile in Siberia. In 1907 he managed to escape to Paris, where he was active among exiled Russians. As leader of the pacifist propaganda division of the SR abroad, he was arrested in Paris in 1915. Before being deported he managed to flee to the United States, where he edited the anarcho-syndicalist newspaper *The Voice of Labor* (*Golos truda*). He belonged to the leadership of the anarchist Union of Russian Workers, which had more than 10,000 members. The multilingual eloquent revolutionary was a welcome reinforcement the ranks of the American anarchists.

In 1917 he returned to Russia and took command of the anarchists in Petrograd and later in the Ukraine. In Bobrov he saw his wife and children again for the first time since his flight from Russia. Until the Bolsheviks began hounding the anarchists, he edited the newspaper *Ringing the Alarm Bell* (*Nabat*). Volin fought during the civil war on the side of Machno and became chairman of Machno's military council in 1919.

While he was ill with typhoid in January 1920, he was arrested by the 14th Red Army and handed over to the Cheka. Trotsky wanted him executed, but after the intervention of Aleksandr Berkman and Viktor Serge, Volin was taken to the Butyrki prison and released after the armistice in October 1920. On the eve of a congress that he organized, which was to have opened on December 25, 1920, the Bolsheviks arrested him and the entire leadership. He was again brought to the Butyrki and later to the Lefortovo prison in Moscow. After a hunger strike and the intervention of Profintern leaders, he was released and deported on the instructions of Lenin. During his stay in Germany Rudolf Rocker supported him and he edited the paper *Anarchist Messenger* (*Anarkhisticheskii vestnik*). In 1924 he moved to France, where he founded the weekly newspaper, *L'Ouvrier Anarchiste* and drafted a pamphlet about the persecution of anarchism in the Soviet Union. During the Spanish Civil War he was editor of the newspaper of the Spanish anarchists, *L'Espagne Rouge*. He described Lenin's terror state in detail in his memoirs. Volin died in Paris in 1945. His book, *La Révolution Inconnue*, published there, is a standard work on the history of the anarchist revolution in Russia.

## BOLSHEVIKS

### Leon Trotsky

There are scores of books by and about Trotsky (Bronstein). Although Trotsky's Jewish background is a well-known fact, his attitude toward Judaism is examined only in one treatise (Joseph Nevada: *Trotsky and the Jews*. Philadelphia 1972). This is why some episodes of Trotsky's life should be mentioned here in order to understand his attitude as a "non-Jewish Jew."

In 1903 Trotsky declared to the Bundists that he was neither Russian nor a Jew, but a social democrat, though in fact he considered himself as more Russian than Jewish. In his autobiography he reported with hidden pride that the Red Cossacks had declared, "Trotsky isn't a Yid; Trotsky is a fighter! He is ours...a Russian...Lenin, yes, the communist...a Yid!" He used this completely nonsensical anecdote to show that the anti-Semitic propaganda of the White Guards hadn't caught on inside the Red Army.

When Lenin ordered him to lead the fight against the counterrevolution as Interior Commissar, Trotsky answered that nobody should place a weapon such as his Judaism into the hands of the enemy. The Second Soviet Congress elected Trotsky as Peoples' Commissar for Foreign Affairs; in March 1918 he became Peoples' Commissar for the Army and Navy and, after September, chairman of the Revolutionary War Conference. He belonged to the executive committee of the Socialist International until 1924.

In April 1919, Trotsky explained the chauvinist slogans of the Red Army to the fact that Latvians and Jews made up a disproportionate number within the Cheka, in the executive committees and in central Soviet councils, while they were fewer in number among the soldiers. He demanded a recasting of the Politburo, so that the ratio of all nationalities on the front lines and on the home front would be better balanced. In slightly exaggerated terms it can be said that Trotsky anticipated the dismissal of the Jews from the political and cultural organizations, which became Stalinist policy after 1942.

Trotsky refused to accept that anti-Trotskyite sentiment also carried an anti-Semitic smear campaign with it until the mid-1920s. In a 1926 letter to Bukharin he described how party speakers in the factories stirred up hatred against the opposition by calling them "Yids." As this subject was too controversial for him, he wrote the letter by hand rather than dictating it to a secretary. In the 1930s he gave interviews to American Yiddish newspapers, in which he referred to the anti-Semitic accusations against him as being "Judas-like." He forbade the publication of an essay about Stalinist anti-Semitism, written in 1937—the subject seemed to be unpleasant to him. He didn't want to remind others of his Jewish background or to be reminded of it himself.

As long as he was in power, he had no contact at all with the Jewish institutions of Soviet power. There were no relations with the *Yevsektsiia* or the *Gezerd.* Concerning the settlement of Birobidzan, he made a generally empty statement that each nationality had to have its own schools, press and so forth. But if a nationality was in downfall, it should happen naturally and not by administrative discrimination. In the end he did not care about the fate of Jewish national culture and the Yiddish language, which he did not command very well, if at all.

### Lazar Kaganovich

Lazar Kaganovich held high positions in the central committee or in the government from 1924 to 1957, meaning that among all the Jews in the Soviet Union he was a member of the center of power for the longest period. He was born in 1893 in the village of Kabany in the district of Chernobyl, where Ukrainian peasants and Jewish workers lived together. He was the leading Jewish Bolshevik who knew what life was like in the shtetl. At the age of 18 he joined the Bolsheviks in Kiev, where he worked in a leather factory. In 1924 he became a member of the organizational office of the Central Committee, and in 1925 Stalin appointed him secretary general of the Ukrainian CP, because he expected a Jew to smash Ukrainian nationalism. From 1930 to 1935 Kaganovich was party leader of Moscow, where he pushed through an ambitious and ruthless program of modernization. He destroyed historic buildings and forced the construction of the Moscow subway system at which 70,000 workers toiled around the clock. He was directly involved in the enforced collectivization and the party purges in the 1930s, the worst violence of Stalinism. He put his signature on a list of thousands of "public enemies" to be shot, which he had been compiling since the mid-1920s. As Peoples' Commissar for Transportation (1935-1937 and 1938-1942) and Heavy Industry (1937-1939 and 1943-1944), as well as assistant chairman of the cabinet of the USSR, he achieved remarkable power.

Kaganovich did not comment during public appearances on Jewish affairs; however, he privately reprimanded Mikhoels for portraying Jews negatively in his theater.

From March to December 1947, Kaganovich was appointed party leader of the Ukraine. From 1947 until Stalin's death he did not hold government offices, but remained the only Jew in the Politburo. He did not object to the anti-Semitic policies of the late Stalin years, even though his brother was killed during the purges. Assertions that he protested quite openly in 1953 against Stalin's intentions to deport Jews cannot be verified. In 1957, in the process of Khrushchev's struggle against the old Stalinist guards, Kaganovich was released from all functions and in 1961 even expelled from the party, which troubled him very deeply. He spent his long retirement (he lived to nearly 100), busy writing his memoirs, published in 2001, five years after his death in 1996. Neither there nor in conversations with the journalist Chuyev, which were published as *Confession of a Stalinist Apostle*, did Kaganovich have any regrets or remorse about his role in the Stalinist crimes.

### Yakov Sverdlov

Lenin's closest friend and collaborator, Yakov Sverdlov was born in 1885 in Nizhni Novgorod, where as a youth he founded a revolutionary council. As a member of the district committee of the Urals (after 1906), he was arrested several times and exiled to Siberia in 1910. In 1912 he became a member of the Central Committee of the RSDRP. He spent time in prison for many years from 1903 to 1917. In April 1917 he went to Petrograd and became a member of the Bolshevik Central Committee. Because of his organizing genius, he managed to build a tight network of loyal representatives and revolutionaries throughout the country in a very short time. On his instructions, the Bolshevik party cadre could be mobilized at any time. He founded newspapers in different districts of the province as well. Because he played a decisive role in the success of the October Revolution, he was appointed by Lenin on November 8, 1917, to be chairman of the All-Russian Executive Committee and, as a result, became a nominal head of state of the Soviet Union. Lenin considered Sverdlov to be irreplaceable and Trotsky described him as secretary general of the revolution. Sverdlov died in 1919, his health his ruined by his enormous workload.

## Adolf Yoffe

Adolf Yoffe was born 1883 in Simferopol in the Crimea, the son of a wealthy Karaite family. The Karaite belonged to a Jewish sect that had broken away from rabbinical Judaism more than a thousand years before. Already at the age of 16 Yoffe was active in revolutionary circles. In 1902 he became a member of the RSDRP. Because he was expelled from Russian universities, he studied law and medicine in Zurich, Vienna and Berlin. He took part in the revolution of 1905 and after 1908 edited *Pravda* in Vienna with his friend Trotsky. Yoffe was arrested in 1912 and sent into exile in Siberia. In 1917 he and Trotsky joined the Bolshevik Central Committee. During the peace negotiations at Brest-Litovsk in December 1917, Lenin entrusted him with directing the Soviet delegation. Yoffe did not want to bow to the diktat of the German generals and refused to sign. Trotsky, Dzerzhinsky, and Krestinsky signed the document instead.

Yoffe was only able to work at the embassy in Berlin from April to November 1918, because the mission was used as a base for German revolutionaries and diplomats who were deported. Between 1920 and 1922 Yoffe led delegations that signed peace agreements with Poland and the Baltic countries, and the Treaty of Rapallo with Germany. He later served as ambassador to Peking, Vienna, London, and Tokyo. Because he was a friend of Trotsky, he was shuffled aside and appointed professor at the University of the Orient in Moscow.

After 1925 Yoffe tried to establish an opposition to Stalin, because he saw the peaceful and humane development of the Soviet Union to be in grave danger. When Trotsky and Zinoviev were expelled from the party on November 14, 1927, he abandoned any belief in reforms. Three days later he committed suicide. His widow survived twenty years of the Gulag and later emigrated to Israel.

## Grigori Zinoviev

Grigori Zinoviev (Ovsei-Gerschen Radomyselski-Apfelbaum) was born in 1883 in Yelisavetgrad in the Ukraine, the son of a Jewish farmer. As an assimilated Russian Marxist, he joined the RSDRP in 1901. Because of his theoretical knowledge and brilliant rhetorical and journalistic talents, he already was at an early age part of the bigwigs of the Bolsheviks and worked in the editorial offices of the most important legal and illegal party papers and magazines (*Proletarii, Sotsialdemokrat, Rabochaya gazeta, Zvezda, Pravda, Mysl'*). From 1908 to 1917 he served the party in St. Petersburg and outside Russia. Following the Fifth Party Congress of the RSDRP, he became a member of the Central Committee (1907) and the Bolshevik Center (1907-1910).

On October 9, 1917, he and Kamenev were the only members of the Central Committee of the RSDRP(B) who disapproved of the armed revolt. Both resigned from the Central Committee because they supported the participation of non-Bolsheviks in the first Soviet government. At the end of 1917, Zinoviev was elected chairman of the Soviet of Petrograd, which he led until January 1926. In March 1919 he founded the Comintern. The climax of his life, however, was the triumvirate with Stalin and Kamenev in 1923-24, which was to assume power after Lenin's death. When Stalin stripped the left opposition and Trotsky of political power in 1925, Zinoviev's turn had come. He was expelled from the Politburo and the Comintern in October 1926, and from the party in 1927, but reinstated after a remorseful declaration in 1928. In 1932 he was again expelled in connection with the "Association of the Marxists-Leninists" trial and again reinstated in 1933. Another arrest and third party expulsion followed Kirov's murder on December 1, 1934. In January 1935 he and 15 other defendants were sentenced to ten years' prison in the first Moscow show trial. In August 1936 the High Military Committee heard the case of the "Trotskyite-Zinovievist terrorist center," in which Zinoviev and others were charged with having organized terrorist groups on Trotsky's instructions, of having murdered Kirov and planning Stalin's murder. He received the maximum penalty and was executed on August 25, 1936. Several books and writings of Zinoviev were published by the Comintern publishing house, among them his *History of the CPSU (b)* in 1923.

### Lev Kamenev

Lev Kamenev (Rosenfeld) was born in Moscow in 1883. Already as a student he belonged to Russian revolutionary circles and was arrested several times. After 1908 he lived abroad, where he edited the party newspapers *Proletarii* and *Sotsialdemokrat*. In 1914 Lenin ordered him to Moscow to head the Bolshevik faction of the Fourth Imperial Duma, but shortly thereafter all communist members of parliament were sent into exile in Siberia. After the revolution in February 1917, he spoke out in favor of the Provisional Government and of cooperation with the Mensheviks. Like Zinoviev, he dissociated himself from the violent putsch of the October revolution. As chairman of the Moscow Soviet (1918-1924) and as a member of the five-man Politburo (1919-1926), he was at the zenith of his power. Membership in the anti-Trotskyite triumvirate with Stalin and Zinoviev signaled his decline. In 1926 he lost all functions and was expelled from the party in 1927. In the "Kremlin trial" of July 1935 he received a ten-year prison sentence. The Military Committee of the High Court of the USSR charged him with participation in Kirov's murder and with plotting Stalin's murder. The sentence—his execution—was carried out on August 25, 1936.

## Karl Radek

Karl Radek (birth name Sobelsohn), who was among the leading Bolsheviks, was born in 1885 in Lvov (Lemberg), a subject of the Austro-Hungarian Empire. After 1902 he was active in the Polish social democratic party *PPS* and *SDKPiL*. Between 1908 and 1913 he was involved in social democracy in Germany. During the First World War he worked with Lenin in Switzerland and accompanied him to Russia in April 1917. He was one of the co-founders of the KPD (German Communist Party), was arrested in February 1919 and deported from Germany at the end of 1919. From 1919 to 1924 he was a member of the Executive Committee of the Comintern and at the same time a member of the Central Committee of the CPR(B). He tried in vain to get the left *Poale Zion* admitted into the Comintern. Because he joined the Trotsky opposition in 1924, he was expelled from the party in 1927 and sent into exile behind the Urals. When he admitted his "guilt" in 1930, he was reinstated into the party and wrote numerous articles for *Pravda* and *Izvestiia* as a hard-working propagandist for Stalin. In January 1937, in the second Moscow show trial against 17 members of the fictitious "parallel anti-Soviet Trotskyite center," he was the only one sentenced not to death, but to ten years in the Gulag—perhaps because he wrote the self-accusation that was to be memorized by the co-defendants. He was probably shot in 1939.

## Yevseki and other Jewish Bolsheviks

### Semyon Dimanstein

Semyon (Shimen) Dimanstein was one of the few old Bolsheviks and Lenin co-fighters who had a Jewish education and a firsthand knowledge of the Jewish background, having become involved in the affairs of communism in the *yidisher gass* (*Jewish street*). From the beginning until the bitter end, Dimanstein was a founder and official of different Jewish institutions of the party and the state.

He was born in 1888 in Zebesh near Vitebsk, the son of a poor plumber, and grew up in a strict religious environment. At the age of 12 he went to a Talmudic college and graduated as a rabbi. In Vilnius he came in contact with revolutionary Bundist circles. After the split of the RSDRP in 1903, he joined the Bolshevik faction and translated its program into Yiddish and Hebrew. He was arrested in 1906, and in 1908 in Rzhev he was exiled to Siberia. He managed to flee to Paris in 1908, where he worked as a factory mechanic and was an activist with the Bolsheviks.

After the February Revolution he returned to Russia, where he contributed to a northern front newspaper in Riga and was chairman of the communist soldiers' organization. In 1918 he became—under the commissar for nationalities, Stalin—leader of the *Yevkom*, the commissariat for Jewish affairs. He also founded the official Yiddish party newspaper, which was first called *The Truth* (*Die Varheyt*), and later on, in Yiddish, *Der Emes*, a party newspaper directed against the Jewish religion, Zionism and, above all, against the Bund.

On July 23, 1919 he signed circular no. 1367 of the commissariat for Jewish affairs, *Yevkom,* which announced, in addition to the already liquidated religious communities, the end of Jewish middle-class and Zionist organizations like *Tarbut* and *Hekhaluts*. After the dissolution of the commissariat for minorities in 1924, Dimanstein founded the Jewish sections in the party, *Yevsektsii*. He was active as a member of the Central Committee of the CP in Byelorussia and Latvia and as commissar for education in Turkmenistan.

He returned in 1927 to "Jewish work" as All-Union Chairman of the organization Society for the Organization of Jewish Farmers in the Soviet Union (*Gezerd—Geselschaft far einordenung af erd arbetndike yidn in ratfarbend*). At the same time he was head of the department of minorities in the Central Committee. As one of the Bolshevik intellectuals, he wrote many books and pamphlets, published articles and was editor of the journals *Revolution and Nationality (Revolutsiia i natsional'nost')* and *Tribune of Jewish Society (Tribuna Evr. Obshchestvennosti)*. In 1935 in Birobidzan he edited the book, *Jews in the USSR (Evrei v SSSR)* and the Yiddish publication, *Forpost.* The party rebuked him because of his vote against the forced collectivization of agriculture. During the liquidation of the *Gezerd* in 1937, he was arrested, together with the last chairman of the organization, Mereshin, and the leaders of the "Jewish work"—Litvakov, Chemerisky, Liberberg and many others—and sent to a penal camp. He is thought to have died in 1937.

### Moshe Litvakov

Moshe Litvakov was one of the most important officials of the *Yevsektsii* and a sort of Yiddish cultural tsar. He was born in 1875 in Cherkassy in the Ukraine. At the age of 17 he interrupted his studies of the Talmud at a yeshiva, passed an external school exam, and studied philosophy, history and literature at the Sorbonne in Paris from 1902 to 1905. In 1904 he became a member of the Central Committee of the party of the Russian Zionist-Socialists, later of the *Fareinikte* party, and edited Yiddish newspapers in Vilnius. As a brilliant literary critic, he published numerous articles in Russian and Yiddish journals. After 1917 he became a member of the *Kombund,* in 1919 a member of the CP and after 1921 a leading member of the *Yevsektsiia* of Moscow. As a leading Yvsek and editor in chief of the official Yiddish party newspaper *Der Emes* (since 1924), he shared responsibility for the destruction of the Jewish religion, its structures and institutions, the persecution of rabbis and the liquidation of Hebrew culture and Zionist organizations, including its publishing houses.

From 1924 to 1928 he managed the Yiddish schoolbook publisher *Shul un Bukh* and the magazine *Emes zhurnal.* Litvakov was also professor of Jewish literature at the Second University of Moscow. Hundreds of students went to his lectures. He kept a relentless eye on compliance with the particular party line in all newspapers, books and other publications. For those Yiddish authors, poets or officials criticized or praised by Litvakov, his opinion meant their existence. He edited, together with Esther Frumkin, the eight-volume edition of Lenin's complete works in the Yiddish language. Because of his good tactics, and his informing on his colleagues, and because of his own contrition, he remained editor in chief of *Emes* until 1937. In the April 18, 1937 issue, Litvakov published a long and extremely critical article, *The Class Struggle for the Foundation of the Jewish Autonomous District,* followed by the arrest of the whole leadership of Birobidzan, starting with Professor Liberberg. A few months later Litvakov was arrested. He died in the Gulag, probably in 1939.

### Yuri Larin

The Soviet economist and local politician, Yuri Larin (birth name Mikhail Lurye) was born in 1882 in Simferopol in the Crimea, the son of a Hebrew and Zionist author and rabbi Solomon Salman Lurye. He belonged to the RSDRP since 1901 and was sent into exile in Siberia in 1902, from whence he escaped abroad. From 1905 to 1913 he was active for the revolution in the Crimea, the Ukraine and Georgia, where he was once more arrested and sent into exile. In July 1917 Larin switched allegiance from the Mensheviks to the Bolsheviks. Because of his economic knowledge, he became chief of state planning for the Russian Federal Soviet Republic.

As chairman of the *Ozet* and member of the management of the *Komzet*, he supported the agricultural settlement of the Jews in the Crimea, for which he, along with Abraham Bragin, also laid the ideological foundations. He was the only leading Jewish communist who supported the foundation of a Jewish republic in the Crimea, and also the only Soviet official who showed interest in the problems of the Jews. His daughter Anna had married Nikolai Bukharin, and therefore he belonged as father-in-law of the "darling of the party" to the top thousand of the Soviet *nomenklatura* and was protected from various purges. He died in 1932. The Jewish village Larindorf in the Crimea was named for him.

### Joseph Liberberg

The future chairman of the Soviet of the Jewish Autonomous District of Birobidzan, Joseph Liberberg, was born in 1899 in Volynia. Before the revolution of 1917, he belonged to the *Fareinikte* party, then became a Bolshevik and fought on different fronts of the civil war. From an early age he wrote numerous articles on current themes in Yiddish, Ukrainian and Russian. He later devoted himself to history and literature and became a professor at the age of 25. He was deeply committed to the Jewish labor movement and to Yiddish as the language of the Jewish masses. In 1924 he furthered his historical and philological studies in Germany. When Kiev became the center of the officially promoted Yiddish literature, Liberberg founded in 1926 the division for Jewish culture at the Ukrainian Academy of Sciences, which subsequently became the Institute for Proletarian Jewish Culture. For years he was the principal of this institute with 100 academics and candidates, and established a Judaica library. He was co-founder of the Jewish historical-ethnographic institute in Leningrad as well. Liberberg wrote numerous historical works, for example, about the French Revolution and *The year 1848 in Germany.*

His work *Jews in the USSR* was published in 1935. In the same year he became chairman of the Soviet of the Jewish Autonomous Region of Birobidzan, where he supported, in particular, the structure of cultural and educational institutions. He was unable to participate in the Birobidzan congress on September 19, 1936, because he was arrested along with the entire leadership of Birobidzan. He was accused of being a "Trotskyite nationalist"—an absurd combination—and then of trying to bring all Jewish cultural institutions of the Soviet Union to Birobidzan to create a Jewish state, a second "Palestine." Such ridiculous accusations were not unusual during the Great Terror. On March 9, 1937, the military court in Khabarovsk sentenced Liberberg to death and he was executed at the age of 38. Only in March 1955, 18 years later, was the sentence rescinded. One year later the territorial committee of the party declared his exclusion null and void and rehabilitated him.

## GENERALS OF THE RED ARMY

### Yona Yakir

Yona Yakir was born in 1896 in Kishinev. In 1917 he joined the communist party and the Bessarabian government committee. In 1918 he organized the Red Guards to fight against the Romanian troops heading toward Kishinev. Yakir was one of the founders of the Red Army; during the civil war he initially commanded the 45th Division of the Red Army and later an Army Group (called in Russian "Front"). He was a member of the Revolutionary Military Conference of the Soviet Union, a member of the Central Committee and the Politburo after 1934, as well as commander of several military districts, including that of the Ukraine in Kiev. As a leading military figure, he was a guest of the Reichswehr on several occasions. On June 12, 1937, Yakir was executed, along with Marshal Tukhachevsky, following a secret trial in a military court. His rehabilitation took place in 1945.

## Yan Gamarnik

Yan Gamarnik was born in 1894 near Zhitomir and joined the party after 1916. He studied law in Kiev from 1915 to 1917, was a member of the revolutionary committee there in 1918 and led covert units in the German-occupied zones in the Ukraine. In 1919 he commanded the communist rebellion against the Ukrainian leadership and led the committee for the defense of Odessa. In 1920 he was political commissar of the 58th Infantry Division. In 1928 he became secretary of the Central Committee of Beloussia and in 1929 chief of the political administration of the Red Army and editor in chief of the army newspaper, *Krasnaya zvezda.* After 1930 he was deputy commissar for the defense of the USSR as well. He took his own life in 1937, shortly before he was to be executed.

Neither Yakir nor Garmarnik had any involvement in Jewish affairs, although Garmarnik's wife was the sister-in-law of the Hebrew poet Chaim Nachman Bialik.

## Yakov Smushkevich

Yakov Smushkevich was born in April 1902 in the shtetl of Rakishki in Latvia. There he worked with his father as a carrier and coachman to support their large family. During the First World War the family was deported to Arkangelsk, where the then 13-year-old Yakov worked as a baker in a lumberjack camp. In 1918 the family returned to Rakishki. Yakov went to Minsk and volunteered in the Red Army. He soon became commissar of the 36th Infantry Regiment. In 1922 Smushkevich was detached to Minsk as commissar of the Fourth Air Squadron, which was being formed, and where the best pilots in the country were instructors. He was soon considered one of the Soviet Union's top flyers.

In 1936, under the pseudonym General Douglas, he commanded Soviet and Spanish airmen in the Spanish Civil War, fighting for the defense of the Spanish republic, until April 1939. With his chief engineer, Colonel Zelik Yoffe, another Jewish-Soviet officer, he set up numerous field airstrips and flight-training schools. During the Sino-Japanese war Smushkevich's airmen defeated the Japanese decisively in the battle of

Khalkhin Gol in September 1939. Smushkevich was gloriously celebrated, and nominated as a candidate for the Central Committee and promoted to Chief of Staff of the Soviet Air Force and member of the general staff of the Red Army. For his battles in Spain and Manchuria he was twice decorated with his country's highest honor, "Hero of the Soviet Union."

He continuously warned his colleagues and Stalin about a German attack. Perhaps for this reason he was arrested from his sickbed on June 7, 1941, and shot on October 28, 1941.

### Grigori Stern

Grigori Stern was one of the generals executed on the eve of the German attack on the Soviet Union. He was born in 1900 in Smela near Cherkassy, the son of a doctor. As a high-school student he moved in revolutionary circles and was arrested several times. In the civil war from 1919 to 1921 he fought as commissar of the 46th Infantry Division. At the age of 23 he was regimental commissar. After graduating from the Frunze military academy, he first became a high-ranking officer in the ministry of defense and in 1934 the people's commissar for defense. In 1937 Stern was posted to Spain. As General Grigorevich, he was the highest Soviet commander-in-chief in the Spanish Civil War and helped decisively in establishing the International Brigades and the Spanish army.

Grigori Stern is often confused with another Jewish general, Manfred Stern, who founded International Brigades under the pseudonym General Kléber and ended his life in 1954 in the Gulag. In 1938 Grigori Stern became chief of staff of the Soviet Far Eastern army and led the Soviet army in the war against Japan in 1939. As winner of the battle of Khalkhin Gol, he was decorated "Hero of the Soviet Union." Stern was a delegate to the Supreme Soviet and a member of the Central Committee. Like his brother-in-arms in the war against the fascists in Spain and against the Japanese, General Smushkevich, Grigori Stern was executed on October 28, 1941. He was rehabilitated in August 1954.

### Semyon Krivoshein

Semyon Krivoshein was one of the few generals of the Red Army who survived the Stalinist purges as both Spanish fighter and Jew. He was born in 1899 in Voronezh, the son of a watchmaker, and graduated from high school in Ostrogorsk. He volunteered in 1918, joined the civil war in Budyonny's First Cavalry Army and later became a professional officer. In 1931 he graduated from the Frunze military academy, became chief of staff of a mechanized regiment and later commander of an armored regiment as well as of an armored brigade. When the Spanish Civil War broke out, Colonel Krivoshein was one of the first military advisors to the republican army. In October 1936 Soviet tanks went into action under his command in the battle for Madrid to prevent the capture of the city in November 1936 and, with it, an early Franco victory. In 1939 Krivoshein commanded tank units in Manchuria in the war against the Japanese. As general, he commanded the tank units that rolled into Eastern Poland on September 17, 1939, following the Hitler-Stalin Pact. Together with German General Guderian, Krivoshein was at the German-Soviet troop parade on September 21, 1939, in Brest-Litovsk.

At the outbreak of the German-Soviet war, Krivoshein commanded the 25th Mechanized Army Corps. In the course of the war he commanded an elite unit, the Second Guard Armored Corps. In the summer of 1944 he took over the First Red Guards Armored Corps of the White Russian as part of Army Group. In the battle for Belgorod, Krivoshein soldiers destroyed one hundred German Tiger tanks. On April 22, 1945, Krivoshein was the first to reach Berlin with three Soviet tanks. On May 29, 1945, General Krivoshein was decorated "Hero of the Soviet Union." He was decorated with the medals of Lenin, Kutuzov, Suvorov, and the Red Star.

Semyon Krivoshein described his battles in the Russian civil war, in Spain and in the Second World War in a book trilogy. He died in September 1978 in Moscow.

### Yevsei and Matvei Vainrub

The brothers Yevsei and Matvei Vainrub played a considerable role in the victory over Germany as generals of the Red Army armored units. Yevsei and Matvei were born in 1909 and 1910, respectively, in Novy Borisov in White Russia, sons of a poor sawmill worker.

Yevsei Vainrub studied forestry after his high-school diploma; later he became a professional officer of the armored troops and graduated from the Frunze military academy. From the first day of war he commanded the 219th Armored Brigade in stock of the First Red Banner Corps under the command of the Jewish general, Semyon Krivoshein. After August 1944, it belonged to the First White Russian Army Group

(Front) under Marshal Zhukov and covered 1,000 km fighting between mid-January and mid-March 1945. His armored unit captured several extermination camps in Poland. Yevsei Vainrub was wounded several times. On April 22, 1945, after violent battles, his armored soldiers captured the Weissensee district of Berlin. The 219th Armored Brigade was called the Berlin Brigade because of its considerable role in the capture of the German capital, and received the Lenin decoration. After the war, Yevsei Vainrub worked as an engineer in a tractor company in Minsk. He emigrated to Israel in May 1995, where he again met many of his former fellow combatants.

His brother Matvei Vainrub served as an officer of a cavalry regiment in his home area of Borisov for many years. Later, he graduated from the Orlov tank school and in May 1941, like his brother Yevsei, from the Frunze military academy. Shortly after the war broke out, his armored unit was involved in fierce fighting in which he was wounded. Without waiting to recover, he returned to the front as assistant commander of an armored brigade of the Seventh Army in Stalingrad, which later went down in history as the 62nd Army under Marshal Zhukov. Vainrub's armored brigade was decimated by the superior German troops to such an extent that only one single tank remained in working order. His soldiers later fought in Stalingrad until the capitulation of the Sixth German Army under Field Marshal General Paulus on January 31, 1943. The famous 62nd Army was renamed the Eighth Guards Army. When General Pushkin, chief of the armored corps of the Eighth Army, was killed, Vainrub became Major General and commander of the unit of the Third Ukrainian Army Group (Front). His tanks captured Odessa in April 1944 and Lublin in July. Early in January 1945, Marshal Zhukov transferred the command as an autonomous mobile tank unit to his brave fellow combatant at Stalingrad. Near Lodz, Vainrub was wounded for the fourth time and was in battles up to Küstrin. On April 30, 1945, the tanks of the Jewish general reached the Reichstag. General Vainrub participated in surrender talks between General Krebs and Marshal Zhukov. On April 6, 1945, the title "Hero of the Soviet Union" was conferred on Matvei Vainrub. After the end of the war, he was commander of the military district of Kiev. The sister of the Vainrub generals served as a military doctor on the Leningrad front. None of the Vainrub family survived at home at Borisov.

Marshal Zhukov mentioned the brothers Vainrub several times in his memoirs, and *Pravda* and *Krasnaya zvezda* reported on them as well.

The Yiddish newspapers, *Eynikeyt* and *Sovietish Heymland*, published comprehensive reports on the two "Heroes of the Soviet Union," their lives and their battles.

### David Dragunsky

David Dragunsky was born in 1910 near Bryansk. The son of a poor tailor, he had to work hard from the age of 13. In 1930 he joined the Communist party and began his military career in 1933. As an officer of the armored troops, he fought against the Japanese in 1938. After the battle of Lake Khazan, he was decorated with the first Red Banner decoration. In the war against Germany he was one of the most successful commanders of the armored troops. In November 1941 he became chief of operations of the northern Caucasian Army Group. First he commanded the 55th Armored Brigade that captured Gorodok and Lvov, as colonel and then as general. For his battles in Poland he was decorated "Hero of the Soviet Union" in September 1944. On April 23, 1945, Dragunsky received the order to cross the Teltow channel in Berlin. Three days later, he captured the Reichssportfeld. On May 5, Dragunsky's unit was sent to Prague. He was one of the few commanders to capture *two* capitals. On May 31, 1945, he was decorated "Hero of the Soviet Union" for the second time. His unit as part of the First Ukrainian Army Group was honored in the victory parade in June 1945 in Moscow. In addition, he received the Lenin Order, four Red Banner decorations, the Suvorov decoration, two Red Star decorations and numerous foreign decorations. General Dragunsky led the elite military academy *Vystrel* for 15 years. Later he was chairman of the war veterans' committee and was sent abroad on countless missions to Austria, Belgium, France and the U.S., where he tried to counter the international community's criticism of Soviet anti-Semitism and treatment of Soviet Jews. These efforts were just as unsuccessful as those of the "anti-Zionist committee," of which he was one of the founders.

### Boris Levin

Boris Levin was born in 1922 near Smolensk. As a guards first lieutenant and commander of a combat bomber squadron of the 230th Guard Bomber Division, he contributed greatly to the liberation of the Kerch peninsula by shooting down several enemy aircraft and knocking out 15 tanks, several trains and many cannon. For these feats, the 22-year-old officer was decorated on October 26, 1944 as "Hero of the Soviet Union."

### Liliana Litvak, the "White Rose of Stalingrad"

Liliana Litvak was the best-known female fighter pilot of the Soviet Air Force. She served in the 586th Women's Fighter-Pilot Regiment, which, along with the 587th Women's Bomber Regiment under the command of "Hero of the Soviet Union" Klavdia Fumeshova, and the 588th Women's Night-Bomber Regiment, was one of three all-female formations. Because she had a white rose painted on the nose of her airplane after each downing of a German airplane, and because she was successful in numerous dogfights, she was called in the Soviet press the "white rose of Stalingrad." A memorial was erected in her honor in Krasny Luch in the Donets Basin, where she was shot down in 1943.

### Miriam Eisenstadt-Zheleznova,
biographer of the Jewish war heroes

Miriam Solomonovna Eisenstadt (pseudonym Zheleznova) was born in 1909 in Kiev to Jewish parents. In 1932 she graduated with a degree in philosophy and literature in Leningrad. Until the outbreak of the war, published several essays in *Literaturnaya gazeta* and in *Komsomolskaya pravda*. Like Shmuel Persov, she collected all available testimony of the important contribution the Jews to the war effort. She requested to look through the materials of Mikhoels about Jewish "Heroes of the Soviet Union". Because her husband, Lieutenant Colonel Eisenstadt, editor of the illustrated journal of the ministry of defense, recommended her at the division of war decorations of the ministry of defense, she was able to write essays on 85 Jewish war heroes. She wanted to support Ehrenburg's idea to publish a "Red Book" about the battles of Jewish soldiers. Later she sent these texts to B.Z. Goldberg in New York for publication in the U.S. Although nearly all of her sources were already censored and published in official press organs, she was arrested on April 4, 1949, for spying and tortured into making absurd self-accusations. The high court military committee under General Cheptsov condemned her to death on November 22, 1950. She was executed shortly thereafter.

Miriam Eisenstadt was rehabilitated on December 28, 1955, but her fate remained unknown until the newspaper, *Evening Moscow (Vechernaya Moskva)* printed a short notice about her, complete with photo. She was buried in the Donskoy cemetery in Moscow. Her name can be found on the monument for the victims of August 1952 in Jerusalem.

## THE PRECURSORS OF THE JAFC

### Henryk Erlich

Henryk Erlich was born in 1882, the son of a wealthy miller in Lublin. After 1903 he studied law in Warsaw. As member of the illegal Bund, he was jailed several times and expelled from university. In 1904 he went to Berlin to study economics and political science. In 1906 he registered as a law student at the University of St. Petersburg. In 1908 he finished his studies and moved again to Warsaw, where he was sentenced to imprisonment and subsequent exile because of Bundist activity. In the Bundist university group he met Sofia, the daughter of the important Jewish historian Simon Dubnov, and married her in 1911 in St. Petersburg. In 1911-1912 both studied in Munich, until Erlich was sent to Russia by the Bund CC to be the parliamentary secretary of the Menshevik faction in the Duma. In 1913 the young lawyer became CC member of the Bund and editor of the socialist newspaper *Den'* (Day), the Yiddish Bund organ, *Our Time (Unzer Tsayt)* and the magazine, *Jewish News (Yevreiskie vesti)*.

At the start of the February Revolution in 1917, Erlich was elected as a member of the workers' council of the capital to the all-Russian central executive committee of the workers' and soldiers' councils (TsIK). Later, Stalin publicized his opinion of Erlich's remarks throughout Russia: *The Only Reasonable Speech in the Committee was the One by Henryk Erlich (V ispolkome samaya tolkovaya rech', eto Genryka Erlicha)*. He was a delegate of the Bund in the CC of the Mensheviks, the center of power of the revolution as well. At his suggestion, a peace conference among socialists of the nations at war was held in Stockholm, where he was one of the five delegates. The solution was a peace treaty without annexations and reparations. The conference was doomed to failure. In August 1917, Erlich became member of the Provisional Council of the Russian Republic, which was liquidated after Lenin's putsch in October. As a close friend and collaborator of Yuli Martov, he belonged to the CC of the Mensheviks and worked for its organ, *Working Newspaper* (*Rabochaya gazeta*).

When the Bolsheviks turned more and more against their former socialist comrades, Erlich brought his family in October 1918 to safety in Poland. He himself wanted to return to Russia, but the leader of the Bund, Vladimir Medem, asked him to lead the Bund in the newly independent Poland. In November 1918 he condemned Lenin's political terror in *Unzer Shtime.*

Erlich was active for 20 years as Bund leader in Poland, which was simultaneously a political party, a trade federation, and an educational and social association with numerous institutions, schools, sanitariums, and cultural and cooperative organizations. He represented the Bund at conferences of the Socialist International, including those in Hamburg, Marseille and Vienna and was a member of the executive committee. In all elections for the Polish parliament in which the Bund participated, he was the leading candidate. Until 1939 he held office at the Warsaw municipal council as well. With his moral integrity and his intellectual abilities, he tried to prevent the fratricidal battles between communists, Zionists and Bundists among the Jewish workers from further escalating. Erlich wrote many books and hundreds of articles and essays that were published in the Bundist newspaper he edited, *The People's Newspaper* (*Die Folkstsaytung*), and in other papers. He was a personal friend of numerous leaders of the socialists and the labor unions, such as Léon Blum in France and David Dubinsky in the United States.

## Viktor Alter

Viktor Alter was born in 1890 in Mlawa in Western Poland, the son of a lumber merchant and woods owner. Alter attended high school in Warsaw after the family moved there. In 1905 he organized the famous pupils' strike for the establishment of the Polish language in the schools in tsarist-ruled Poland. The result was a ban for all schools. As a member of the "technical" division of the Bund's fighting organization, he and his brothers and sisters hid weapons in the family's cellar. He was reported, and the Warsaw police chief personally wanted to arrest him, but shortly before that a bomb planted by Polish socialists killed the chief.

In 1906, Alter had to leave Poland and went to Belgium to take a high-school exam. He finished his studies in electrical and mechanical engineering at the College of Advanced Technology in Liège with an engineering diploma. Even there he continued his work as a Bund activist and was in contact with the foreign leadership in Geneva. In 1912 he returned to Warsaw, was arrested by the tsarist police for revolutionary activities and sent into exile to Siberia. Alter managed to escape to Belgium and fought as a volunteer in the war, but was later evacuated to England, where he became a member of the English Bund organization and the Marxist British Socialist Party.

When the February Revolution broke out in 1917, he went with Jewish and Russian comrades to the Ukraine, the center of the Jewish workers' movement at that time. In August he was elected in Moscow into the CC of the Bund, and co-opted into the management of the internationalist faction of the RSDRP. During the conference of Russian socialists in July 1918, the Cheka arrested him. After his release, he returned to Poland and resumed his Bundist activity.

Like numerous socialist parties, the Bund was also under the illusion of potential cooperation with the communists. In June 1921 Alter traveled illegally to Moscow as a member of the Bundist delegation to the Third Congress of the Comintern. He met many leaders whom he knew from way back, like Karl Radek. He was arrested and taken to Butyrki prison because he was supposed to have smuggled a letter from England and began an eleven-day hunger strike. Because his Bund comrades threatened heavy consequences, and Lenin at that time still shied away from international scandal, Alter was released.

After that, Alter concentrated on trade union work and on the defense of the interests of Jewish workers and the thousands of home workers who were practically deprived of their rights. He represented the 100,000 members of the Bund trade unions at the central commission of the Polish Federation of Trade Unions in 1939. As a forceful and highly respected colleague, he frequently drafted binding documents for the entire Polish workers' movement. He joined the Warsaw municipal authorities from 1919 to 1939 as a Bundist. His efforts on behalf of the poor and weak brought him great recognition and gratitude. To point out to the Polish public the problems of Jewish workers, he founded the Bundist daily newspaper, *Daily Letter* (*Pismo codzienne*) and the weekly paper, *New Letter* (*Nowe pismo*). The censors sealed the printers or banned distribution on several occasions.

Following the Moscow trials in 1937 against Zinoviev, Kamenev and others, he wrote in the Yiddish *Folkstzaytung*:

The shots from Moscow not only hit the convicted men. They also heavily wounded the revolution. That's the reason for the deep sorrow that fills all of us. Each Bundist, and probably each communist as well, feels a burning shame because of the trial and its effects, because the shame of the Russian Revolution is also the shame of all of us. Comrade communists! Watch over your dignity! Look at what happened to your leaders of yesterday!

From his manner of speaking, he was clearly bitter about Jewish and other social democrats being attacked and hurt at that time by the communists as "social fascists."

During the Spanish Civil War, Alter and his Polish comrade Zdanowski visited the numerous Polish and Jewish volunteers at the front. The reactionary Polish press threatened that each Pole who took part in the civil war would be denaturalized. Alter was tirelessly active for the Bund and the Jewish workers until the war started in September 1939.

## THE PRESIDENT OF THE JAFC

### Solomon Mikhoels

Mikhoels was born Solomon Vovsi in March 1890, with his twin brother, Chaim, in Dvinsk. Both boys went to the Kheyder, the traditional children's Bible school. Already at the age of nine, Mikhoels wrote and staged a Yiddish play called *Youthful Sins*. As twelve-year-old boys, the brothers founded the Zionist youth group *Hanoar*, where practicing the Hebrew language played an important part. Mikhoels wrote several articles and poems for the group's magazine. The brothers later went to a high school in Riga and tutored many pupils. Mikhoels particularly distinguished himself by being well grounded in the Russian language. In 1915 he continued his law studies in St. Petersburg, where the family had moved.

In the cold and half-starved Petrograd of 1918, Aleksandr Granovsky risked creating an experimental theater, Yiddish Studio. Granovsky, who came from a wealthy family, received his education in Germany and was a teacher's pet of Max Reinhardt. Mikhoels, at that time a student in the last semester, wrote his school qualification thesis and studied at the same time at Granovsky's studio. Leon Trotsky's sister led the theater division, founded in 1918 at the commissariat for education. After 1919 all theaters in Russia formed a central theater committee. Granovsky was ordered to found in Moscow the Yiddish state theater, *Gosudarstvenny Yevreiskii Teatr*, GOSSET. Thus the days when poor Yiddish actors roved from shtetl to shtetl were a thing of the past. For the first time, a state was sponsoring a Yiddish theater. In Granovsky's productions, the language of the shtetl was combined with European art finesse and rich fantasy. The sets and costumes by Marc Chagall, at that time commissar for art in Vitebsk, also prevented unimaginative stage realism. Mikhoels moved to Moscow and became the first GOSSET actor.

In January 1920, the house in Chernyshevsky Street solemnly opened with the production of *Three Jewish Raisins*, after themes of Sholem Aleichem. Chagall had painted all the walls of the little theater with phantasmagoric pictures of the shtetl and expressionist-revolutionary motifs. The big canvases disappeared until 1990; they were found in a cellar in Moscow and shown at the Schirn art gallery in Frankfurt in August 1991.

In addition to productions of Mendele Mokher Sforim, Sholem Aleichem and Yitskhak Leib Peretz, the three great classical writers of Yiddish literature, the GOSSET performed plays by famous contemporary authors (Dobrushin, Wiewiorka, and Oyslender) and younger Soviet-Jewish authors (Markish, Bergelson, Halkin, and Resnik). World literature productions by Maeterlinck, for example, were also staged. The company, consisting of young singles, lived in a commune in the theater building. The actor Benjamin Zuskin, who enjoyed a close lifelong friendship with Mikhoels, soon became part of the group. Granovsky produced *Sulamit* and *The Witch*, with Mikhoels as the hawker Hotsmakh, and other plays by the great Yiddish artist Abraham. In 1925 Mikhoels played the main part in the silent movie *Yidishe Glikn* (based on themes of Sholem Aleichem), which was also shown abroad.

After a few years, the theater gained considerable standing among the avant-garde theaters and was thought to be the most important and most famous Jewish institution in the Soviet Union. The Jewish "cultural tsar," Moshe Litvakov, wrote a book to celebrate the fifth anniversary of the establishment of the theater. After a long tour through Germany, Austria, France, Belgium and Holland, the GOSSET returned without Granovsky. He produced in 1930 in Berlin the first performance of Arnold Zweig's play *The Quarrel Over Sergeant Grischa* (*Der Streit um den Sergeanten Grischa*) and went to Hollywood in 1932. He died there in 1937.

The spectacular successes of the GOSSET in the capitalist foreign countries and the "desertion" of Granovsky stirred up the mistrust of the authorities. Mikhoels, who defended Granovsky's decision, took over the supervision of the theater until he was executed.

After the proclamation of the first Five-Year Plan in 1928, culture and art were officially declared an instrument of the working class. Eighty thousand party censors supervised the mobilization of literature and theater for economic development. The fight against "public enemies" was the most sought after subject. In *Pravda* of October 6, 1928, cultural commissar Lunacharsky criticized the shortage of Soviet subjects and ideology in the performances of the GOSSET. Nevertheless the theater was until 1941 considered a cultural institution of triumphant socialism in the Yiddish language. Mikhoels set up a drama school connected to the theater. The graduates founded twenty Yiddish theater companies, eleven of them in the Ukraine. Of course, they had to perform the plays in conformity with the rules of socialist realism in a realistic esthetic. In 1935, Mikhoels created with Shakespeare's *King Lear* one of the most famous performances of the Yiddish theater in the world. He played the main role and Zuskin played the court jester. Mikhoels was now a celebrated star.

During the great purges of the 1930s, many actors, producers and other theater people were forced into the Gulag. Still, the glorious GOSSET was an advertisement for the regime and guarded Mikhoels against repression, although he officially spoke up for Mandelstam, Meyerhold, and other victims of persecution. For the solemn 20th anniversary of the theater in 1938, state institutions heaped honors on Mikhoels: he became a "People's Artist" of the Russian Federation and the USSR and Lenin prizewinner. That year he protested in a speech against the November pogroms in Germany and appeared in the movie *Oppermann Brothers*, based on the novel of Lion Feuchtwanger, filmed in Moscow. In 1941 he was appointed professor. He was a member of the Moscow municipal Soviet and of many other institutions. The entire cultural elite of the capital were regular visitors at his house. In May 1941, the play *Roaming Stars* was the last production of the theater before the German-Soviet war. The GOSSET was evacuated. Later, the actors played at front theaters. Mikhoels, who had to move to Tashkent with his family, went often to the seat of government in Kuibyshev. During the war years, his friendship grew with the authors Aleksei Tolstoy and Ilya Ehrenburg, as well as several generals and scientists. Many non-Jews rightly considered Mikhoels as the unofficial representative of the Soviet Jews. From that point of view, his vocation as chairman of the JAFC comes as no surprise. His reputation and prestige in the Soviet Union, as well as abroad, were positive for the purposes of the committee. He earned the Stalin prize for the production of *Freylekhs* after the reopening of the GOSSET.

Mikhoels was murdered on January 12, 1948. Armed sentries guarded his apartment day and night for five years—until March 17, 1953, two weeks after Stalin's death. His second wife and their two daughters, Nina and Natalia, made a living selling books from their 5,000-volume library. Nina studied for several years at the school of theater and had to repeat the graduation exam five times because of minor discrepancies. Afterwards she was able to go on tour in the Soviet Union with a theater company for three years. In 1972 the daughters were given permission to emigrate to Israel. Natalia wrote a biography of her father and asked Marc Chagall for the illustrations. Chagall rejected her request with the explanation that he did not like to support projects critical of the USSR.

The murder of the JAFC president signaled the end of the committee and shattered the hopes, nurtured since the war, of a regular representation for the Soviet Jews. By edict of the Supreme Soviet of April 30, 1953, Mikhoels was re-awarded the Lenin medal and the title "People's Artist of the USSR." However, the document bore the comment, "No press publication."

Peretz Markish

An Eternal Light at the Coffin
(A Memorial to Solomon Mikhoels)

Your last appearance to the public
Surrounded by chunks of ice and thick snow
However—your word is missing, your mouth remains silent
Only your cool breath makes us tremble

It seems to us that we still softly hear
On eagle's wings the trusted beating
With which the people once thought of you
You are a comfort to them, echoing their sorrow.

The curtain here will never fall again
In the hall, the light still burns in the chandelier
Your royal head now sleeps in an open grave
Where silhouettes, timeless, whisper your words

## Arno Lustiger

We say farewell to you and may you rest in peace
You carried in you the agony of a hundred years
You allowed Sholem Aleichem's tears
Shine as dear as gems

Today we don't miss your wig
It is still necessary that the purple billows
To recognize you are King Lear
Who exchanged his crown for wisdom

The wounds in your face have been snowed in
So it won't be touched by black shadows
But in the dead eyes the suffering burns
Screams from the heart that they stepped on

So near I come to your threshold, eternity,
Marked by murder and slanderous talk
As they, in five sixths of the world's face
Attack my old people with lashes and hate

Read these signs, do not pass them by
You should hold them in your memory forever
For each scratch in your face
A woman with her child escaped a thug

You were not made deaf by the murderer's hand
The snow covers not the smallest sign
The pain in the beaten eyes warns
Equal to the mountains that reach high to the heavens

A train of people; the next one follows
The streams flow softly into one another
To honor you, six million rise up
Persecuted, hanged—killed

As did you in your last fall honor them
In the snow of Minsk, in the middle of ruins
Deep in the night, alone, torn by pain
Surrounded only by storm and cold white dunes.

As if you wanted to stand up for them even in death
For their peace, their suffering and their honor
You teach the eyes of the world to see—
A bloody reproach, ice-covered emptiness

We let our mourning run free
A tear will be ripped across the heart of the people
From the graves, six million stand up
Whom you honored, in your fall, upon the paths in Minsk.

The heavens light a new light for you
The stars take you happily into their rounds
You, distorter of disgrace and pain—don't ever be ashamed!
Only eternity itself has to be ashamed!
(1948)


## THE (TRUE) CHIEFS OF THE JAFC

### Shakhne Epstein

The secretary general of the JAFC, Shakhne Epstein, was born in 1883 in the shtetl of Ivye near Vilnius, the son of a rabbi. Instead of studying the Talmud like his father, he learned Hebrew and wrote his first prose texts in this language. At the age of 16 he went to Warsaw and became involved in the Jewish trade union movement. At first he sympathized with Zionism, but became a Bundist in 1903 and worked as a Yiddish journalist. Because of his participation in the May Day demonstration in 1905 and other revolutionary activities, he was arrested and taken to the infamous citadel of Warsaw. In 1907 he managed to escape to Vilnius, where he became a contributor to the Bundist *Folkstsaytung*. After his second arrest, he was exiled to Vologda. From there he was able to escape abroad. In Geneva he worked as secretary of the international organization of the *Bund* and in 1909 he went to New York in the same capacity. He worked as an official of Jewish trade unions and editor of the Bundist paper *Tsukunft*, for the organ of the Jewish clothing union "*Gleykhheyt*," and for the Russian socialist paper, *New World* (*Novy mir*). Later, he lived in Chicago and wrote for the *Yidishe Arbeter Velt*. He wrote several plays using a pen name.

After the February Revolution in 1917, Epstein returned to Russia with his wife and son, who was born in America, to continue his political activities as an official of the Bund and of the Kombund. In 1919 he broke with his political background and became a member of the CP as well as of the *Yevsektsiia*, whose duties included the liquidation of bourgeois Jewish culture and all non-communist Jewish organizations. He led the section of Jewish authors as well and edited the semi-official Yiddish paper *Der Emes* after 1920. From 1920 to 1929, Epstein worked again in Jewish-communist circles in the U.S. where he founded Soviet-friendly press organs like *Freedom* (*Frayhayt*). After his return to the Soviet Union, he became editor of the magazine, *Red World* (*Royte Velt*) in Kharkov, contributor to *Pravda* and wrote numerous articles for the Yiddish-communist press in America. Throughout the 1930s he repeatedly carried out assignments for the Soviet secret service as a loyal party soldier in Germany, France, Switzerland and elsewhere. The famous American communist Juliet Pointz, known to Epstein before 1917, wrote an account of the criminal methods of the Soviet state security following her visit to the Soviet Union. Before she could publish the account, she was kidnapped with Epstein's connivance in New York, in June 1937. [Pointz disappeared and was murdered by the NKVD. NDT]

His political reliability and his knowledge of languages qualified Epstein for the position as JAFC secretary general and editor in chief of *Eynikeyt*. As a co-signatory of the Crimea memorandum, he would certainly have been arrested along with all the other leading personalities, but he died in July 1945 in Moscow of a sudden hemorrhage.

In September 1945, a funeral service was held at the city hall in New York with the pro-Soviet VIPs of America. Of course, Ben Zion Goldberg was chairing the event. The poet Weinper read an ode to the deceased. P. Novik, L. Levine from Russian War Relief, I. Budish from Ambidjan and L. Olkin from Icor acknowledged the merits of their longstanding friend and fellow combatant. At the end, a long telegram from the JAFC in Moscow was read—signed by Mikhoels and Fefer.

### Solomon Spiegelglas

After the sudden death of Shakhne Epstein, there was no qualified successor having the Lubyanka's confidence, with inside knowledge of the Jewish milieu, and the required knowledge of languages. For lack of a better alternative, Solomon Spiegelglas was appointed secretary general.

Spiegelglas was born in Warsaw in 1900. In the revolutionary year 1917, a Jewish fellow student got him interested in Bolshevism. Until then he had been a politically uninvolved student at Moscow State University. During the civil war he led a sanitary unit against the typhoid epidemic in the Red Army. Lenin became aware of the young man, who meanwhile had become a member of the party, and appointed him political commissar in the railroad administration—an extremely important job during the civil war. In this function, he organized the secret transport, ordered by Lenin, of the tsarist gold treasure from Siberia to Moscow.

After the civil war, Spiegelglas studied journalism and became editor of *Pravda*, was a trade union official in Moscow, and later a high-ranking party official of the CC in Moscow and Kiev. He informed Goldberg, whom he accompanied on his journeys to the Soviet Union, of these biographical details.

Although he had an insufficient command of the Yiddish language, and never had contact with Yiddish authors from foreign countries, he was able to lead the administration of the JAFC and prepare the committee's Yiddish publications. Spiegelglas died in 1946; he left no publications after his death.

### Grigori Khaifets

Grigori Khaifets, born in 1899, was one of the most effective agents of Soviet foreign espionage. He had a good general and technical education, spoke many languages fluently, and was already, as a young man, a convinced communist. After Lenin's death, he became the secretary of his widow, Nadezhda Krupskaya. For several years he was active in the foreign service of the Comintern, then moved to the secret service of the GPU and founded espionage cells in Germany, including one at the University of Jena in the 1930s. For a while, he was the GPU representative in fascist Italy.

When the U.S. resumed diplomatic relations with the Soviet Union in 1934, Khaifets, who had already played his part in the founding of the American CP, was the only candidate for the most important post (*rezidentura*) of the secret service in California. In San Francisco he officially had the title of vice consul. He soon obtained important military-technical information and made contact with nuclear scientists like Robert Oppenheimer, which became invaluable for nuclear espionage. Through Bruno Pontecorvo he also became acquainted with other nuclear physicists, such as Frédéric Joliot-Curie and Enrico Fermi. Khaifets was the first agent to report to Moscow about frantic American efforts regarding the atom bomb, in an encoded telegram in 1941. Among others, he gained the sympathies of Bertolt Brecht, Lion Feuchtwanger, and Heinrich Mann for his pro-Soviet activities.

In 1944 he was recalled to Moscow, where he was entrusted with important assignments in the NKVD. In 1947 the "organs" infiltrated him as acting secretary general and as a member of the chairmanship committee of the JAFC. He informed about all visitors and all activities of the JAFC, especially about any indications of a nationalist character and contacts to foreign countries. No document left the JAFC without his signature. Until the committee was dissolved, he sent as its actual chief many reports and documents to national security.

After the foundation of the state of Israel in May 1948, many Jews who wanted to defend their "historical home" against the Arabs or to organize donations and aid, volunteered with the JAFC. Khaifets took note of their personal data and addresses and handed these lists over to the NKVD, party and state organs, which had these people shadowed and arrested. In the fall of 1948, Khaifets himself was arrested for alleged involvement in a Zionist plot. In August 1952 he was sentenced in a second trial with other defendants to 25 years in the Gulag. He was probably released after Stalin's death. Khaifets died in 1967.

## THE AMERICANS

### Ben Zion Goldberg

Ben Zion Goldberg was born in 1895 in Golszany near Vilnius, the son of a rabbi. When he was twelve, the family emigrated to the U.S. Shortly thereafter he wrote for Yiddish and English newspapers and met Sholem Aleichem (Shalom Rabinowitsch, 1859-1916), the great author of Yiddish literature. Goldberg had married Aleichem's youngest daughter in 1917, and thus belonged to the Yiddish aristocracy. In the Soviet Union the works of Sholem Aleichem came out in the Yiddish original as well as in nearly all national languages in editions of several million copies—even at a time when no books by other Yiddish authors were being printed. The family, who lived in New York, received considerable royalties in foreign currencies for decades. Goldberg also benefited from this.

In 1920 he finished his studies at Columbia University and became a doctor of psychology and started to work at New York's liberal Yiddish newspaper, *The Day (Der tog)*, where he became editor in chief from 1924 to 1940. He traveled around the world and wrote hundreds of reports describing the life of Jewish communities. Articles extolling the Soviet Union caused intense discussions with other bourgeois and socialist Yiddish newspapers like the *Forverts*. For years Goldberg belonged to the management of the YIVO Institute for the Study of Yiddish Literature in New York.

In 1934 he was invited by the Soviet government to visit the Jewish centers of Kiev and Minsk and the Jewish colonies in the Crimea. He spent quite some time in Birobidzan, the newly founded Jewish Autonomous Region. After his return, he founded the Ambidjan Committee, which publicized and supported the colonization of Birobidzan, and in 1937 he created the *Ykuf—Yidisher kultur farband*. Goldberg was considered to be the unofficial branch office of the JAFC and Soviet war propaganda; he organized the American journey of Mikhoels and Fefer as well. The FBI shadowed the *spiritus rector* of all pro-Soviet initiatives in the U.S. and ordered him to register as an agent of a foreign power.

After the war Goldberg was invited on a second official visit to the Soviet Union. He dedicated 50 pages of his book, *The Jewish Problem in the Soviet Union*, published in 1961, to this journey of several months, which he began in January 1946. Accompanied by Solomon Spiegelglas, Goldberg visited numerous towns, but he was not allowed to travel to Birobidzan, for which he personally obtained millions of dollars of donations in the U.S.

Goldberg was for the third and last time in the Soviet Union in 1959. His friends of the JAFC were still missing without any official explanation three years after Khrushchev's speech at the Twentieth Congress of the CPSU. There was only one Jewish institution—the Moscow synagogue—in this gigantic country at the time. Goldberg called his encounters with the few survivors of the Yiddish cultural scene a parade of shadows. He considered Birobidzan to be an illusion and saw the only hope for the Jews in the Zionist state of Israel, which he had resisted for years. Until his death in 1972 in Tel Aviv, he wrote for the left-socialist party paper *Al-hamishmar* and Yiddish newspapers in other countries.

## Pesakh Novik

Pesakh Novik was one of the most active pro-Soviet Jewish propagandists in the United States. He was born in Brest-Litovsk in 1891 and was already a member of the Bund at the age of 16. From 1910 to 1912 he lived in Zurich, then became active in New York as secretary of the Jewish Socialist Federation and editor of the Yiddish magazine, *The New World* (*Die naye velt*). During the February Revolution in 1917, he returned to Moscow as an official of the Bund. In 1919 he went to Poland to edit the Vilnius newspaper *Der tog*. After 1920, he wrote in New York for Yiddish socialist newspapers. When Novik became a member of the CP of the United States, he broke with his Bundist comrades and the newspaper, *Forwerts*. Together with Moshe Olgin, he founded in 1921 the communist Jewish daily newspaper *Freiheit*, which merged later with the paper *Morgn* and was published until 1988 as *Morgn Freiheit*. Over the course of decades he wrote thousands of articles as editor, and since Olgin's death in 1939 as editor-in-chief. He turned his paper into the platform of left wing pro-Soviet-minded Jews of America. During the war his pro-Soviet articles caused heated disputes with other Yiddish newspapers, which could not forgive the Soviets for the execution of Alter and Erlich. In 1935 his book about four decades of the workers' movement in the U.S., *The Socialist Party: Its History and Its Record* (*Die sotsialistishe partey, ir geshikhte un ir rekord*), was published in New York.

Like Goldberg, he was always in contact with all Soviet authorities that received his aid packages. Novik was also a member of the management of the Ambidjan association in support of Birobidzan. From September 1946 until the spring of 1947 he visited the USSR, his ideological home. He regularly reported in his paper about meetings with important members of the JAFC, and also visited Europe and Palestine. In the last issue he called *Morgn Freiheit* a fighting paper of the factory workers for a better life and against the plague of assimilation. Novik died in New York in August 1989, the patriarch of an ideology whose working model, the socialist bloc, imploded that same year.

## James N. Rosenberg and the *Joint*

James N. Rosenberg, an American, was described in the secret trial as the power broker of the Crimea affair. Without being present, he was one of the main defendants of the trial.

Rosenberg was born in 1874 in Allegheny City, Pennsylvania. Despite his professional duties as a lawyer, he supported persecuted Jews around the world throughout his life. In 1921 he asked for time off from his legal office and became chairman of the *Joint* in Europe. The biggest non-state-controlled aid agency in the world, the American-Jewish *Joint* Distribution Committee, called AJDC or *Joint*, was founded in November 1914 in New York by wealthy Jewish-American bankers, Orthodox congregations and trade unions, to alleviate the misery of the European and Palestinian Jews in the war zone. After the First World War, the *Joint* sent a large team of its staff members to Poland, Russia, and the Ukraine, where thousands of victims of the pogroms needed care. Between 1921 and 1924, over $24 million was spent with the approval of the Soviet government to set up hospitals, vocational schools, and craft and agricultural cooperatives. The *Agrojoint* was to support, according to the agreement with the Soviet government, the settlement of Jews in the Ukraine and the Crimea with more millions of dollars. James Rosenberg supported the cause of the Soviet Jews for decades among the financial backers and managers of the *Joint*. Therefore, he led, in close cooperation with the appropriate Soviet party and government organs, settlement projects of 30,000 settlers in Birobidzan and the Crimea. On the instructions of Foreign Minister Molotov, it was at a meeting with Mikhoels, Fefer, and Rosenberg in New York that settlement projects of the *Joint* were discussed. Their conversations were held, as Consul General Kiselov had ordered, in the presence of an official Soviet interpreter. On that occasion the Jewish settlements in the Crimea that were being destroyed by the German army were also discussed. The *Joint* and *Agrojoint* had donated millions of dollars, to secure their reestablishment after the Nazis had killed the Jews living there.

At the trial, the government-ordered meetings with the representative of an organization that had provided immense aid for the Soviet Union over two decades were portrayed as a political crime. James Rosenberg died in 1970 and, in addition to legal texts, he wrote his memoirs, which were published under the title *Unfinished Business*.

*Arno Lustiger*

## THE EDITORS OF THE *BLACK BOOK*

### Ilya Ehrenburg

The author Ilya Ehrenburg struggled in his immense literary and journalistic life's work with the contradictions and aberrations of this century. He was born in Kiev on January 27, 1891, the son of a wealthy assimilated Jew who managed a brewery in Moscow. His mother, Hanna, née Arnstein, grew up in a respected Jewish family. The acquaintance with Nikolai Bukharin—who was his high school classmate—and his hatred for the anti-Semitism of Russian society and of the tsarist regime, led him to join the revolutionary movement and later the Bolsheviks. The 14-year-old Ilya participated in the revolution of 1905 and was arrested in 1908. After his release, he left Russia and lived mainly in Paris, where his first volume of poetry was published in 1910, until 1917. Ehrenburg felt a close bond with the French language, literature, and culture; his favorite poet was François Villon, with whom he shared the extreme libertarian, anarchist way of life and opinion and whose ballads he translated into Russian.

In 1917 Ehrenburg returned for several years to Russia, where he became a friend of Mayakovsky and Pasternak, but spent the next twenty years, from 1921 until 1941, mainly in France. His picaresque novel *The Remarkable Adventures of Julio Jurenito and His Followers*, published in 1922, a satire on modern civilization, made him famous. The satirical novel *The Eventful Life of Lasik Roitschwants* (1927) must be read as a pastiche on the hard life of a Jewish Schweik-type character. Ehrenburg associated with the leading intellectuals and artists of France in the cafés of Montparnasse and his friendships with world-famous writers protected him against persecution. He was a delegate of the Soviet writers' congress in 1934 in Moscow and the congress for defense of culture in 1935 in Paris and in 1937 in Madrid. He is considered the best-known intellectual fighter on the European anti-fascist cultural front up to 1939. Shortly before Germany's invasion of the Soviet Union, he traveled to Moscow via Berlin, where he wrote *The Fall of Paris*, which amazingly won Stalin's approval and was published.

Shortly after the outbreak of the war, Ilya Ehrenburg became a war correspondent under the editor in chief of the Red Army newspaper *Red Star* (*Krasnaya zvezda*), General David Ortenberg-Vadimov. He was one of the most important correspondents of the Second World War, writing more than two thousand articles at that time, which were read and examined before they went to press by Stalin himself. His articles about fighting Jewish partisans and the death of Jewish war heroes were re-printed in numerous front and home front newspapers, anthologies and pamphlets. Soldiers and civilians wrote him thousands of letters about their front experiences and the genocide of the Soviet Jews. Ehrenburg sifted through and sorted out the letters and thus created the core of an archive for the *Black Book*. A selection of these letters was published in 1945 in Paris under the title *Cent Lettres*. After the liberation of Poland and the discovery of the extermination camps, he wrote the pamphlet *Merder fun felker*, which was never published in the Russian original, but only in Yiddish.

In his proclamation of January 1, 1945, Hitler called Ehrenburg, Morgenthau and de Gaulle the most dangerous enemies of Germany. The accusation that Ehrenburg had called for the rape of German women and other atrocities in his leaflet was an invention of anti-Soviet propaganda. In fact, the opposite was true. When Ehrenburg witnessed the plundering and rapes by the Red Army in East Prussia, he protested vehemently to the appropriate army headquarters. As a result, Viktor Abakumov, the head of counterespionage *Smersh* (*Smert' shpionam*—Death to Spies) and later minister of national security, informed on him in a secret letter to Stalin, dated March 29, 1945, which read:

> I consider it necessary to report to you that lately the author I. Ehrenburg, who makes public appearances in talks about his impressions after a trip to East Prussia, is slandering the Red Army. On March 21 of this year, Ehrenburg claimed in the presence of leading cadres of the Frunze military academy, where approximately 150 soldiers were present, that the cultural level of our troops, who are advancing in East Prussia, was supposedly very low and that they were badly prepared in political terms. They were not capable of maintaining order, and that's why members of the armed forces are committing arbitrary acts.

Ehrenburg was dismissed as a war correspondent and not allowed to participate in the ceremonies for the surrender of the German armed forces in May 1945 in Berlin.

Even Ehrenburg was deceived by Stalin's sincerity concerning the foundation of the state of Israel. On May 19, 1948, he stated his outrage at England's armed support of the Arabs in this fight for the existence of Israel's Jews in a telegram to Albert Einstein:

Only thanks to the Soviet people, who, wading in bloodshed, brought an end to the power of racism, did Jews remain alive after the horrible years of fascism in Europe. The Soviet government immediately recognized the state of Israel. This action will mobilize the heroes who defend Israel today against the mercenaries.

Five days later, on May 24, 1948, Ehrenburg dedicated a part of the funeral oration for Mikhoels to the state of Israel, then just nine days old:

Today, as we remember the great Soviet tragedian Mikhoels, far away from here bombs and grenades are falling—Jews of a still young state defend their towns and villages against English mercenaries... [Meaning the Arab Legion founded and commanded by the British in Transjordan. A.L.] I am convinced that the picture of Mikhoels— this great Soviet citizen, great artist and great man—that his picture will inspire the people in the old city of Jerusalem, in the catacombs, where the fight is now taking place to heroic deeds.

When Stalin suddenly ended the Israeli-friendly policies in the fall of 1948, Ehrenburg had to publish on September 21, 1948 a full-page article in the form of an open letter in *Pravda*, to explain to the Soviet Jews that Israel must not be the object of their hopes. Later, Ehrenburg was one of the few brave persons who refused to sign an open letter to Stalin. Instead, he addressed his own letter to Stalin, in which he carefully stated his reservations about the planned anti-Jewish measures.

In his book *The Thaw*, published in 1954, that announced the era by the same name, Ehrenburg expressed the hopes of Soviet citizens after the horrible Stalin era ended. His memoir, *People, Years, Life*, printed in the magazine *Novy mir*, was later published worldwide. Not without good reason, this and other books by Ehrenburg provoked the rage of literary hardliners like Mikhail Sholokhov, because the passages about his cooperation in the *Black Book* and the stories about Jewish VIPs and friends made the text an important document of Soviet history. Many of his thoughts on the fate of the Jews and Stalinism were to appear only in posthumous addendums to his memoirs in the *glasnost* years.

In the extensive, well-organized "Jewish" Ehrenburg archive are not only the letters of the frontline soldiers, but those of numerous Soviet Jews, because he was the only addressee for complaints, requests for help and expressions of opinion after the liquidation of the JAFC. While he was still alive—as Yad Vashem announced in December 1987—he had arranged for the transport of the archive to Jerusalem, where it is being carefully worked on in the Yad Vashem archive. In 1993, the book *Soviet Jews Write to Ilya Ehrenburg* (*Sovetskie Yevrei pishut Ilye Erenburgu*) was published with a selection of letters that document Jewish life during and after the war and the painful experiences with Soviet bureaucracy and non-Jewish neighbors.

The letters of nonconformists like Anna Akhmatova and Nadezhda Mandelstam prove that Ehrenburg cannot easily be called an opportunist. His critics say that an indication of his Stalinist attitude was that he was not exposed to repression and survived the hard times. But what protected him was his international popularity and his merits as a war correspondent. Ehrenburg died on August 31, 1967 in Moscow. Thousands tried in vain to attend his burial.

### Vassily Grossman

Vassily Grossman was born on December 12, 1905, in Berdichev in the Ukraine, into a wealthy family. His father was a chemical engineer, and his mother a teacher of French. After he finished his chemical studies in Moscow, he worked, beginning in 1929, in the laboratory of a coal mine in the Donets area and later at the Institute for Pathology and Hygiene in the Workplace, where he contracted tuberculosis. He came to Moscow in 1933 and started his literary career with a story about the civil war, *In the Town of Berdichev*, which was adapted for the screen thirty years later by Aleksandr Askoldov under the title *The Female Commissar*. The movie fell victim to censors and was not released until 1987, twenty years later. Because of his novel *Glückauf* (1934), Maxim Gorky became his promoter. By 1941 many stories and several novels had been published.

Grossman was, from the first until the last day of the war, a frontline reporter of the army newspaper *Krasnaya zvezda* with the rank of lieutenant colonel. He particularly distinguished himself in the battle of Stalingrad, where he shared for five months the struggles and sufferings of the frontline soldiers. His oldest son was killed during the training of recruits, and the Germans murdered his mother in Berdichev. In his novel *The People are Immortal,* he wrote about the defeats of the year 1941, which he experienced with the Red Army. In 1943 his story *The Old Teacher* (*Stary utchitel'*), the first work of world literature about the Holocaust, was published. That same year he began his Stalingrad novel

*The Change at the Volga* (*Za pravoye delo*) which still showed his attachment to the Soviet Fatherland. In 1944 *The Ukraine Without Jews* (*Ukraina bez evreyev*) was published.

Grossman was one of the first to see the Treblinka extermination camp. His authentic report *The Hell of Treblinka* (*Treblinski ad*), published in 1945 in Moscow, was reprinted in the *Black Book*. Grossman's cooperation was positive for the *Black Book* project. Together with Ehrenburg, he ranked among the few competent authors who could work largely unhindered by the secret police because of their experiences and merit in the war. Grossman wrote some articles himself and edited most of the reports.

Approximately one month after the disclosure of the alleged Kremlin Jewish doctors' plot, a devastating criticism of Grossman's works appeared in *Pravda* on February 13, 1953. A similar judgment followed in the magazine *Kommunist* in March 1953. Stalin's death a few days later may have saved Grossman's life. His negative experiences, even with the publication of the *Black Book*, turned a regime loyalist and communist proletarian author into a top critic of the cruel Soviet reality. The violent collectivization of agriculture and Stalin's terror before the war, as well as the war experiences and mass murder of the Jews radically changed the life and work of Grossman in the extreme. His story *Everything Flows* (*Wsyo tetchot*) is not just the story of a prisoner who returns from the Gulag, but rather a general settlement of accounts with the Soviet system, from Lenin and Stalin to the present. In 1960 Grossman had completed the manuscript of *Life and Fate* (*Zhizn' I sud'ba*) his great work, but handed it over only two years later to the publisher Znamya for publication. The editor in chief informed on the author immediately at state security. All copies and even the typewriter ribbons were confiscated. The sheer terror in Grossman's novel brings to light the horrible truth about Soviet society—despite the "thaw" and Khrushchev's secret speech at the Twentieth Party Congress. A Central Committee official predicted to Grossman that his novel could be published in two hundred years at the earliest. In February 1962, two years after the confiscation of the manuscript, Grossman tried, in a personal letter to Khrushchev, to have the prohibition lifted. As a result, a three-hour conversation with the chief ideologist Suslov took place in July 1962. It was unsuccessful. On September 14, 1964, Vassily Grossman died of lung cancer.

Thanks to fortunate coincidences, the manuscript was preserved. Urged by his closest friend Semyon Lipkin, Andrei Sakharov secretly allowed the thick manuscript to be copied onto microfilm in his institute.

Not until 1980, twenty years later, did the book come out in Lausanne; additional versions followed (Paris 1983 and Berlin 1987, edited by Simon Markish and Yefim Etkind). It was finally published in the Soviet Union in 1988, but not without censorship. A short chapter with theoretical reflections on anti-Semitism was omitted.

### Abraham Sutskever

Abraham Sutskever was born in 1913 in Smorgon near Vilnius. After 1922 the family lived in Vilnius. He studied literature and literary criticism there and founded the Jewish literature group *Yung Vilne*. In 1933 he published his first poems and in 1937 the first book of poems. Joseph Roth, whom he met before the war, praised the power of his poetry. By the age of 24, Sutskever was a leading figure of Jewish literature. From June 1941 until September 1943 he lived in the Vilnius ghetto and saved many priceless books and manuscripts of the YIVO institute from destruction and seizure by the Nazis. He left behind more than 80 poems about life in the ghetto. Some were set to music and are among the best-known ghetto and partisan songs. In 1945-46, his books *Die Festung, Lider fun Geto* and *Fun Vilner Geto* were published.

After his escape from the ghetto, he fought as a partisan and wrote a chronicle of the partisan movement—he was an active member of the United Partisan Organization, FPO. In March 1944, Ilya Ehrenburg had him fly with a courier plane from the partisan camp to Moscow, where together they planned the chapter "Lithuania" for the *Black Book*. Sutskever spoke at a plenary congress of the JAFC and took part as a witness for the Soviet prosecution in the Nuremberg trial in 1946. Emigration to Palestine in 1947 probably saved his life. There he founded the most important Yiddish literary journal, *Die goldene keyt*, of which he is still editor in chief today. His works formed a unique contribution to Yiddish literature. The bibliography with works by and about Sutskever comprises 2,496 titles. One year after his emigration to Israel, Sutskever composed the elegiac poem *Yiddish*—an irate declaration of love to his mother tongue.

Yiddish

Must I begin from the beginning?
Should I, who am no Abraham
For the sake of the brotherhood, knock down all the idols?

Must I, living, be translated to the netherworld?
Should we bury our tongues in the ground
And wait til they change,
As in the old tradition,
Into grapes and almonds?
What bad jokes
Are these
My brother poet with the sideburns, when you preach
That my mother tongue must soon die out?
Surely, a hundred years from now we will still be sitting
Arguing by the Jordan
Because a question nags and pesters:
Does he know exactly where
Berdischever's prayer
Jehova's song
And Kulbak's word
Will meet their end?
And there would still be the problem
Of where, then, the language will go to die,
Maybe to the wailing wall in Jerusalem?
And if it did and if it wanted to fall silent
Then I would come and I would open my mouth
Like a lion and
Licked by flicks of fire
Would gulp down the language that is dying,
Gulp it down, and wake all living things with
 My soft growl.

(From the anthology *Der Fiedler vom Ghetto, Röderberg-Verlag, Frankfurt 1985, translated by Hubert Witt; English translation by Catherine Dop.*)

## THE ACCUSED

**Solomon Lozovsky** (Drisdo) was born on March 29, 1878, into a poor family in the village of Danilovka near Yekaterinoslav. In the Kheyder, he learned Hebrew and read the Bible, but had to contribute to the family income as early as eight years old. He worked as a market seller, butcher and blacksmith. During his high school education, he volunteered in the

236th Battalion in Kazan, because in military service he could prepare for the high-school exam. In 1901 he passed the exam and moved to Lozovaya (thus his party pseudonym Lozovsky). There he founded social democratic railwayman circles. In 1903 he continued his revolutionary activity in St. Petersburg, was arrested that same year in October, and after one year in prison was exiled to Kazan. In May 1905 he joined the committee of the Bolsheviks of Kazan, and in June he was again arrested but set free by factory workers. In October 1905 he distributed weapons among the students that had been seized from policemen during a demonstration. Three days later, army units overpowered the revolutionaries; Lozovsky was free again after three weeks' imprisonment.

In December 1905 he took part in the party congress of the Bolsheviks in Tammerfors, Finland. Afterward he went to St. Petersburg, where he was arrested in January 1906, released on bail, but immediately re-arrested. Until 1908 he sat in several prisons and was to be exiled to Siberia but managed to escape during the trip, and in January 1909 reached Paris via Geneva. There he joined the Bolsheviks and was secretary of the bureau of Russian emigrants, as well as secretary general for two years of the French hat makers' union, whose members were mostly Jewish. He passed an exam as chauffeur and worked as a blacksmith, turner and auto mechanic. In 1911 he established within the General Federation of Trade, CGT, a Jewish commission and edited its organ, *Der yidisher arbeter*. After 1912 he was editor of several party newspapers, leader of a Bolshevik group and a leading member of the CGT, whose internationalist group he co-organized after 1914. In May 1917 he received a visa from the French authorities and went via England, Sweden, Norway and Finland to Petrograd. At the 3rd All-Russian Trade Union Congress in June 1917 in Moscow, the delegates of 976 unions elected him secretary of the All-Russian Central Council of the Unions with 1.4 million members. Because of his opposition to Lenin's totalitarian policies before and after the October Revolution, and because he had been chairman of the CC of the international faction of the RSDRP and editor of its organ, the RKP(B) expelled him in 1918. Since the young Soviet state could not do without the service of the internationally known official, he became secretary general of the All-Russian Textile Workers' Union in February 1918, and in July 1918 secretary general of the powerful All-Russian Union Council of Railwaymen. In these positions Lozovsky opposed the suppression of freedom of the press and the duty of the trade unions, postulated by Lenin, to take over state functions, which amounted to a betrayal of the rights of the working class. In December 1919, however, he gave up and merged his internationalist group into the party. With that, the independence of the trade unions from the state, as demanded by the Mensheviks, was finally eliminated in the Soviet Union, but with the infiltration and enforced conformity of the workers' organizations in foreign countries, which was one of the most important goals of the Comintern, Lenin's tactics were fruitless:

> If it must be, we must make use of all sorts of tricks, ruses, and illegal methods; we have to hide and to keep the truth quiet, just to enter the trade unions…and at any price do communist work inside them, come what may.

The attempt to infiltrate Western trade unions by the Red Trade Union International, called Profintern, founded in July 1920 at the Second Congress of the Comintern in Moscow, also came to nothing. Communist trade unions from different countries belonged to the Profintern. Organizationally it was under the executive committee of the Communist International. Lozovsky was elected secretary general and traveled to Western Europe in August 1920 to campaign for the Profintern. After his appearance in a Berlin beer hall was stormily celebrated, the government of the Reich had him expelled because he violated the prohibition against political agitation. At the Fourth Congress of the Profintern in July 1924, delegates demanded unification with the social-democratic oriented International Federation of Trade Unions, founded in 1919 in Amsterdam, but the Western union leaders continually rejected Lozovsky's suggestions. Lozovsky belonged, *ex officio*, to the highest committees of the Comintern, and at their conventions he made impressive but completely ineffective speeches. In 1943 the Comintern was formally dissolved, and all its organs ceased their activities.

From 1937 to 1939 Lozovsky was manager of State Literary Publishing House (Goslitizdat) and professor of international relations at the college of the CC. After 1927 he ran for election to the CC of the CPSU, and in 1939 he became a member and acting people's commissar, deputy minister for foreign affairs of the USSR. As acting manager of the *Sovinformburo* (1941-1948) and director of this authority (1945-1948), Lozovsky was responsible for the JAFC.

Lozovsky, a well-educated man, wrote a large number of books, magazines and studies about the trade unions. He edited a multi-volume ency-

clopedia of the international trade union movement, as well as the encyclopedic dictionary of diplomacy, and he was one of the main editors of
the *Great Soviet Encyclopedia*. He never wanted to have anything to do with
Judaism, and was always anxious to hide his Jewish roots. Until his activity in the JAFC, he never took a stand on Jewish affairs. Only the genocide of the Soviet Jews brought the Jewish identity of the loyal party
soldier back to mind, not least because he always believed to be acting in
the Soviet interest. Whatever he did happened on behalf, and with the
consent of, the Kremlin. On January 26, 1949, he was arrested. He was
the oldest defendant and was executed on August 12, 1952.

  With the murder of **David Bergelson**, Jewish literature lost, in the
opinion of several literary critics, besides Sholem Aleichem, Mendele
Mokher Sforim and Yitskhak Leib Peretz, its youngest major author.
Bergelson was born on August 12, 1884, in Okhrimovo near Uman in the
Ukraine, the son of an educated and well-to-do wood and grain merchant. In his youth he already read Yiddish, Hebrew and Russian literature. After the death of his parents, Bergelson lived with his older brothers in Kiev. At the age of fourteen he wrote novels in Russian and Hebrew, for which no publisher was found. In the novel *At the Railway Station (Arum vokzal)*, praised by the literary critics, and which came out in
1909 in Warsaw in Yiddish, Bergelson tells about the decline of a shtetl.
The poet secured his fame with the novel *Nokh alemen*, which was published in 1913 in Yiddish and Hebrew (published by *Ha-olam* in Odessa)
and in 1923 under the title *Das Ende vom Lied* in German. He described
very sensitively, from the perspective of a young Jewish girl, the existential crisis of the middle classes in the shtetl and the tragic fate of Jewish
intellectuals who were confronted with a radical upheaval of traditional
values. Until the civil war, he wrote additional novels and stories. Bergelson
cooperated with literary magazines, founded the *Folkfarlag* of Kiev in
October 1918, and was one of the co-founders of the *Kultur-lige*, which
supported leftist Jewish culture all over the world.
  After living in Moscow for two years, the poet went to Berlin in
1921, where he became a member of the strong Jewish-Russian colony
and a close friend of Max Reinhardt and other members of the cultural
elite of the Weimar Republic. He wrote for the socialist newspaper
*Forwerts*, for the communist *Morgn Freiheit*—both published in New
York—and for *Emes*, in which he mostly discussed revolutionary subjects. Like Der Nister, he was editor of the literary part of the *Pomegran-*

*ate (Milgroym)*, a large-format magazine with many original illustrations and pictures. The *Breadmill (Brotmühle)* and other plays were performed in several countries. Extensive travel took him to Romania, Poland, France and America. In 1933 he visited the Jewish Autonomous Region of Birobidzan and returned to the Soviet Union. He was convinced that Yiddish culture could only survive and prosper there. With his two-volume autobiographical social novel *At the Dnieper (Bam Dnepr*, 1933-1940), Bergelson established himself once and for all as a leading Yiddish author in the Soviet Union. In this epic he tried to combine elements of Marxist messianism and socialist realism with his lyrical-emotional style. Through an analysis of socialist and Zionist ideas, the main character developed into a combative atheist and convinced communist who detested the Jewish tradition and its religious values.

Bergelson was one of the earliest JAFC members. His appeal to the Jews of the world in August 1941 was transmitted by Radio Moscow and communicated through Poland and France in the underground press in the Yiddish original. The newspaper *Eynikeyt*, where he was a member of the editorial staff, printed many of his contributions and narrations. The title of his play *We Will Live (Mir veln lebn)*, written in 1941, is a quote from Psalm 118:17. The main protagonist, an old Jew and proud Soviet citizen, loses his first-born son in the First World War; his younger son falls in the first days of war as a brigade commander of the Red Army. The play was performed only in the U.S. and in Palestine. For his drama *Prince Re'ubeni*, Bergelson drew inspiration from an adventurer and usurper of the 16th century who raised messianic hopes for the re-foundation of the Jewish state in Palestine—a subject that had interested other authors, Max Brod, for example, to write historical novels. The GOSSET started with rehearsals before the murder of Mikhoels, but the play was never performed in the Soviet Union.

After Germany's surrender, several narrations were written—including *In the Mountains, The Witness* and *The Memorial Candles*—in which the patriotism of Soviet Jews during the war becomes a subject of discussion. Bergelson was arrested on January 24, 1949, and executed on August 12, 1952, his 68th birthday.

There is little biographic information in official Jewish or Soviet sources concerning **Solomon Bregman**, because he dealt with Jewish affairs only as a JAFC member and was only in the middle ranks of the *nomenklatura.* He was born in 1895 in Slynka near Bryansk, the son of a merchant. He testified before the court:

> I have a middle-school education, have belonged to the party since 1912, was never expelled from the party and never received a party rebuke. My last function was deputy minister for state control of the RSFSR. I'm married and have a son. I was decorated with the medals "For the defense of Moscow," "In honor of the 800th anniversary of the founding of Moscow," and "For heroic work during the Great Patriotic War 1941-1945."

In July 1944, Bregman was appointed to the JAFC presidium on advice of CC member Shcherbakov. The loyal party official and obedient civil servant was to dedicate the committee again towards its initial aims, intensify war propaganda and prevent an enlargement of its authority as the representative of the Soviet Jews. Bregman's knowledge of Yiddish was scant; he could read *Eynikeyt* only with great difficulty. He played a larger role in the *Black Book* commission by criticizing the many ostensible political mistakes of the authors and editors.

Bregman was arrested on January 28, 1949. In the course of the long inquiry, under torture, he accused himself and other defendants. He later revoked part of his evidence. During imprisonment, he collapsed, unconscious, and had to be admitted to the ward of the Butyrki prison. At the hearing of July 9, 1952, his trial was separated from the main trial. Because at that time he was continually unconscious, the suit against him was suspended. He died on January 23, 1953, in Butyrki prison.

**Itsik Fefer** was born on September 23, 1900, in Shpola in the Ukraine, into a cultured family. His father—a teacher and casual poet—was murdered in 1941; Fefer's mother-in-law was among the victims of Babi Yar. At the age of twelve Fefer worked for a printer as a typesetter. From 1917 to 1919 he belonged to the Bund and was secretary of the local trade union. In 1919 he became a member of the communist party of the Ukraine and party secretary in Shpola. Shortly thereafter he volunteered in the Red Army and fought in the civil war. During the occupation of Kiev by the White Guardist General Denikin, he worked in the communist underground, was arrested along with the Yiddish literary critic Nussinov, and imprisoned. Once free, he was appointed to the CC of the Ukrainian CP as secretary of the cultural trade union.

Fefer's articles, reviews and poems were published in several newspapers and journals, such as *Yugnt, Folktsaytung, Die royte velt, Oyf barikadn, Literarishe bleter, Komunistishe fon*. The poet David Hofstein, who was eleven years older, strongly supported him. In 1922 Fefer founded the literary group *Wiederwuchs* and the publishing company by the same name. In 1924 his poetry anthology *About Me and Like Me* was published. He also made his mark as a speaker; he spoke often in front of thousands of workers in factories and took part in literary discussions. He gave the main speech at the inaugural meeting of the Jewish section of the Proletarian Writers' Union of the Ukraine in 1927 in Kharkov and headed the section in the 1930s.

On behalf of the commissar for popular education of the Ukraine, Fefer traveled in 1928 with Oyslender and Liberberg through Poland, Czechoslovakia, France and Germany to promote proletarian poetry and literature. His criticism of Jewish authors who did not sufficiently praise the achievements of the Soviet Union caused intense reactions among Yiddish writers. He wrote several odes to Stalin. When General Yakir, a loyal Jewish communist and full member of the CC of the CPSU, accused the chief of staff Marshal Tukhachevsky and other also Jewish generals of conspiracy with the Nazis, who were then executed in 1937, Fefer supported the judgment and polemicized against the alleged traitors. In October 1937 he came under the gunsight of state security himself for befriending the important Ukrainian poet Ivan Kulik, who became a victim of *Yezhovshchina.* He was investigated, but not arrested. According to Borshchagovsky (p. 350), that hearing was not part of the investigating records of the JAFC trial. It is uncertain whether or not he cooperated already at that time with the "organs."

In the 1930s Fefer was part of the editorial staff of *Prolit* and *Farmest*, as well as other journals, and belonged to the presidium of the Soviet writers' union. By 1939 he had published thirty poetry anthologies and several textbooks. A bibliography of his works would take up many pages. His style reminded one of the simple folktale style of the poems of Heinrich Heine. He responded to Jewish bourgeois culture and its religious traditions with scorn and contempt. In his politically motivated Jewish self-hatred, he exceeded at times the anti-Semitism of his non-

---

* That is, the period characterized by the methods of Nicolai I. Yezhov, head of the NKVD from 1936 to 1938, the main instigator of Stalin's purges.

Jewish compatriots. In 1939 and 1940 Fefer repeatedly visited the annexed Polish territories, where he traveled for pro-Soviet propaganda among the Eastern Polish Jews. He was assigned to the political administration authority of the Red Army with the rank of colonel. In 1940 he received the Order of Lenin.

Fefer became secretary of the JAFC and deputy editor in chief of *Eynikeyt*. In view of the mass murder of the Jews, as well as the crimes against his family and against Jewish compatriots in the Ukraine, he suddenly changed his attitude toward Judaism and the values it promoted. The Soviet government also underwent such a policy change, halting atheistic propaganda and allowing all Soviet citizens to practice their religion, because nationalist and religious arguments motivated people for the war.

Fefer's famous poem *Ikh bin a yid* proves this change and is the most Jewish of his works. In line with the nationalist movement, tolerated by the regime because of the disastrous war situation, Fefer sings the hymn of the Jewish nation and religion, invokes the enemies of the Jews, the pharaohs Haman and Titus, praises ancient Jewish heroes Bar Kochba, the biblical figures Samson, King Solomon and the prophet Isaiah, Rabbi Akiba, the Jewish poets and thinkers Halevi, Mendele and Heine, Marx, and Spinoza, the Jewish "heroes of the Soviet Union" and, last but not least, Stalin. The poem was first published on December 27, 1944, in *Eynikeyt* and was reprinted and set to music many times after that. In each later version, other stanzas are missing, aside from the eleventh stanza, which is always left out, because it speaks very exuberantly of Stalin. I'm convinced that Fefer expressed his real feelings and thoughts on the Jews in this poem for the first and last time; it is his creed, which appears again in his play *The Sun Does Not Set*, performed in the Jewish state theater.

Fefer's fame in the Jewish world increased considerably when he was able to travel to the West with Mikhoels. He became close friends with Paul Robeson, who sang Russian and Yiddish folksongs at an event in the United States. Immediately after his arrival in America, Fefer was obliged by General Zarubin, the head of Soviet espionage, to report all meetings, people and appearances.

After his return from the U.S., Fefer threw himself into his literary and organizational work for the JAFC. He took part in all conferences of the committee and in all public events. In New York in 1944, Fefer's cycle of poems *Heymland* appeared with illustrations by Marc Chagall, and in 1946, the pro-Soviet Yiddish publisher *Ykuf* printed his great canto *Shadows of the Warsaw Ghetto*. This stirring epic of more than one hundred multi-lined stanzas was included in a selection of his works published in 1967 in Moscow. There is no mention of Fefer's condemnation and execution in the foreword.

Fefer, along with Mikhoels and Epstein, had signed the Crimea memorandum of February 1944, which had been worked on by Lozovsky and his bosses Molotov and Shcherbakov. He could not foresee at that time, not quite 15 months before victory over Germany, that this affair would be a cause of the tragedy of the members of the JAFC. Fefer must have been informed about the resolution of November 20, 1948 to liquidate the JAFC, because shortly before he helped Abakumov and the NKVD seize numerous files in Mikhoels's apartment and in the Jewish State Theater. When the JAFC was liquidated in a coup-like manner on November 21, 1948, the offices of the JAFC and the newspaper *Eynikeyt* were closed and the immense file holdings were loaded onto trucks. Fefer assisted the "organs" in filing, sorting and removing the materials into the cellars of the NKVD.

Fefer was arrested one month later, on December 24, 1948. He pled guilty and incriminated the co-defendants with his testimonies. Toward the end of the trial, Fefer revealed himself as an agent and corrected most of his testimony or recanted completely. With that, he was lost as a witness for the prosecution, but the court nevertheless imposed the death penalty on all defendants except Lina Stern. In his closing words, Fefer said:

> My whole life, my whole work, was tied to the communist party. My works were always published in communist newspapers and magazines of different capitalist countries... For thirty years, I had the good fortune of singing the praise of the heroic work of the Soviet nation, and I wrote more about Russia and the Ukraine than about the Jews, for which I was even criticized by quite a few people. I request that the court take into consideration what I said here and not deprive me of the possibility of serving the Soviet nation until my last breath.

The same court that had proclaimed the death sentence rehabilitated Fefer and the other defendants on November 22, 1955. The CC lifted the party expulsions for most of them, but neither resolution was announced in the official gazette until December 1989.

Itsik Fefer

**I Am A Jew**
**(Ikh bin a yid)**

The heady wine of generations
Hasa strengthened me upon my road,
The evil knife of gloom and pain
Could not destroy my treasured load—
My faith, my people, nor my striving—
My spirit always rose anew
From under swords my cry was heard:
I am a Jew!

Eternity forever bears the pride
That's mine upon her hands.
It would not break! It did not yield
To tyrants of whatever lands.
No Haman ever stilled my soul!
Through pyre flames of every hue
From Spain's auto-da-fe I called:
I am a Jew!

In forty years of Nomad's trek,
Through searing storms I did not tire.
The winds that forged and steeled my heart—
They fanned Bar Kochba's sacred fire.
My grandfather has left with me
A heritage—his stiff-necked view.
I stand with him:
I am a Jew!

I gathered gold? Yes, when I could—
I had no hearth, I had no home.
It did not sate my spirit, no.
But lay upon my grief like foam.
No precious metals quenched my thirst—
My wealth increased, it grew and grew—
Through all my grief:
I am a Jew!

Rabbi Akiba lives in me
And Isaiah's lofty song.
I am nourished by their wisdom still;
And more than hate—my love runs strong.
And always I have paid with blood—
As now again this day I do.
Yet my outcry will not cease:
I am a Jew!

The Maccabbean rebel blood
Still courses through my every vein:
Solomon's wisdom rests with me
And Heine's smile of bitter pain.
Halevi's song is in my heart;
Spinoza's depth and outcry: Do—
Do what you will and still
I am a Jew!

Spinoza's spirit knew no dam,
It soared out above the din,
The market roar of Amsterdam,
And the light of Marx, that too,
Reached deep into my ancient blood,
My never-ending flame:
I am a Jew!

My eyes reflect the silent mood
Of evenings when the sun is low—
Expressed so well by Levitan*—
Of Russian bayonets aglow
And scythes swinging in the blue,
I am of Soviet land a son—
I am a Jew!

I left the centuries behind,
But not my ancient will to be.
No fading smoke, no wilting flame,
My love of life burns bright in me.

———

* Isaac Levitan (1861-1909), famous Russian-Jewish painter.

## Stalin and the Jews

Mendele is still my guide
And Sholem Aleichem's humor too—
Through tears and laughter we are heard:
I am a Jew!

The busy sounds of Haifa's harbor
Echo in my song and speech;
From Buenos Aires and New York—
Like unseen telegrams they reach
My pulse, my heartbeat and renew
My pledge, my call:
I am a Jew!

I am one of fortune favored
To drink of Stalin's wonder-cup,
And those who in their wishes savored
Moscow's ruin—their time is up!
To those I call: Not now! Not ever!
The Russians are my brothers, too—
With all the peoples of the East:
I am a Jew!

Twofold is my ship of glory:
My blood lights up in a timeless road—
My pride is Yankov Sverdlov's story
And Kaganovich—Stalin's friend!
A youth of snow, of storms and blizzards,
My sturdy heart survived, broke through;
My fortunes flutter over trenches:
I am a Jew!

Not I alone! My strength is mounting!
Today the battle is my bread—
I bless the flame in my accounting,
The storm that sweeps upon the fascists' death!
Papernik's * and Gorelik's ** voices—

---

\* Lazar Papernik (1918-1942), Jewish soldier in a ski unit of the Red Army, who died in the battle for Moscow; "Hero of Soviet Union."
\*\* Solomon Gorelik (1913-1941), Jewish officer of the 1st Armored Brigade in the Red Army, who fell in the battle for Belgorod; "Hero of the Soviet Union."

Voices that we loved and knew—
I hear them rising from our earth:
I am a Jew!

No matter what my foes prepare—
What harsh, what cruel, what deadly fate—
What Torquemada could not kill
Will not be killed by all their hate—
And I will yet my vineyards plant!
From out of flames I will come through!
On Hitler's grave I will yet dance;
I am a Jew!

The poem *Ikh bin a yid* was reprinted in August 1990, on the 38th anniversary of Fefer's execution, in the Yiddish original in the *Sovietish heymland*, but without stanzas 11 and 12, where Stalin is mentioned. The English translation reproduced here is a free translation by Martin Birnbaum published in *Jewish Currents* July-August 1980.

With the execution of **David Hofstein**, Yiddish literature lost one of its most important, most erudite and most prominent representatives. He was born on June 24, 1889, in the shtetl of Korostyshev near Kiev. After attending the traditional Kheyder children's Bible school, he learned Russian and Hebrew with private teachers. In Kiev, he passed an external high school exam, did his military service and became a student at a commercial college.

Already as a nine-year-old boy, Hofstein wrote Russian, Hebrew, and Ukrainian poems; after the October Revolution, which he welcomed with enthusiasm, he wrote only in Yiddish. In 1917 his first poems were published in the newspaper *Naye Tsayt* in Kiev, in the Yiddish military newspaper *Die royte armey* and in the workers' newspaper *Di komunistishe fon.* Hofstein was also in the Yiddish literary almanacs *Eygns, Ojfgang,* and *Baginen.* Together with Kvitko and Markish, he formed the famous Yiddish poetic triumvirate. He was also editor of the newspaper *Der junge kemfer,* of the literary almanac *Shtrom* and co-founder of the *Kultur-lige.* He then moved to Moscow, where he gave lectures on Yiddish literature at the university. Without being a member of the party, he was responsible as editor for literary publications of the communist youth association. In 1919 he created with *Oktiabr* one of the most important Yiddish poetries about the revolution in Russia. Marc Chagall illustrated his elegies, published in 1922, for the Jews murdered during the pogroms in the Ukraine and for the destroyed shtetls.

When the Yevsektsiia began to liquidate Hebrew literature, their publishing houses and printers, and persecute Hebrew writers, Hofstein signed a protest resolution, drawn up by the Association of Jewish Authors. Attacks by the Yevseki forced him to go abroad. Before he moved to Palestine in 1925, he lived in Berlin. *Saul, the Last King of Israel, Messiah's Times* and other verse of his were published in the socialist newspaper *Tsukunft* in New York. He translated several of Pushkin's works into Yiddish.

Hofstein couldn't accustom himself to Palestine, neither privately nor as an author. His poems, narrations, and theater and literature reviews were published in Palestine's leading Hebrew newspapers, but Yiddish, the original language of his poetry, was not respected in the country, and Yiddish authors were rather hindered. He missed not only both his sons and his mother, who remained in Russia, but also Yiddish.

In 1926 he published a letter showing his remorse in the semi-official newspaper *Der Emes*, returned to Moscow and criticized himself because of his support for the protest resolution of 1923. In Kiev he founded, together with Itsik Fefer, the magazine *Communist Youth-Guard (Komyugishe guardye)* and the Jewish section of the Proletarian Writers' Union of the Ukraine. In their organ *Prolit*, which he headed, he condemned the Jewish symbolism and nationalism of his colleagues, like Der Nister. When his friend Leib Kvitko was heavily criticized because of supposed nationalist deviation, he staunchly protected him and was expelled from the association. His productivity did not suffer from these difficulties. In addition to several volumes of poetry, he wrote schoolbooks for Yiddish schools, poems for children and adaptations from Russian and German. He translated Shakespeare's *The Merchant of Venice*, Ibsen's *Nora*, and other works of world literature into Yiddish; together with F. Schames he wrote the book *A Theory of Yiddish Literature and Poetry*, and began an autobiographical novel. He praised the great achievements of the Soviet Union untiringly and in several articles and poems spoke very highly of the colonists of the Jewish autonomous district of Birobidzan. Eventually, he felt limited by the principles of socialist realism. During the war he wrote to a friend: "Don't judge us too harshly. Nobody knows what we had to go through. It's a miracle that we somehow kept our human mentality."

Hofstein was an active member of the JAFC since its foundation. *Eynikeyt*, the *Kiewer Stern* and *Heymland* published many of his articles. In 1948 a one-volume selection of his poems was published in Moscow.

The Soviet Union's support of the partition of Palestine and the foundation of a Jewish state at the United Nations in 1947 filled Hofstein with enthusiasm. On the day the state of Israel was founded, he suggested in a telegram to the Ukrainian Academy of Sciences in Kiev establishing a chair of Hebrew language. Had the fulfillment of the centuries-old dream of a state obscured his sense of political reality and reduced his caution toward possible consequences? Several poems expressed his deep pride and his solidarity with the Jews of Palestine and of the world, in view of this historical event. Thus, it was not merely by chance that Hofstein was arrested on September 16, 1948, four months before the arrest of most of the defendants in the JAFC trial.

For more than four years, the poet's family was told in response to their inquiries that he was still in Lefertovo prison. In January 1953— Hoftstein had already been dead for five months—seven officials informed the family, as relatives of a public enemy, that they were being threatened with eviction. To the objection that there still was no judgment, an official read out the necessary document. The relatives of the other defendants were not informed about the sentence, either in writing or verbally. Hofstein's family was arrested and sentenced to ten years of exile in the Siberian village of Yeniseysk near Krasnoyarsk. There they had to register with the police once a month, like the other exiles.

David Hofstein

## In the Yiddish Language (1929)

In the Yiddish language that is so wild, so mild and dear
A living strength hiding within, a rebellious fire,
Even winds that impetuously chase across the plains
Cannot take away its burning breath;
Ashes from a hundred years haven't darkened the embers,
That, when it's still, break out and fire up anew.

In the Yiddish language, that, having just escaped its bonds,
Roams the steppe and fields to find itself,
Lies the secure peace and width to bind epic poems.
Not from the high priests of verse—in the sounds of the
shepherd's song,
In the reaper's gentleness and pride, their simple songs,

Swings a cheerful tone high over the threshing floor and the barn,
In the Yiddish language so mild and dear.

**Joseph Yuzefovich** was born in 1890 in Warsaw, the son of a tanner. As a fifteen-year-old he joined the youth organization of the Bund and took part in the revolution of 1905 in his hometown. In 1912 he was arrested because of illegal activities in the Polish social democratic party and sentenced to four years in prison, which he served in Warsaw and Lomza in Poland. After his release, he traveled to Moscow, where he was active in the underground. He became a member of the RSDRP(B) and of the central bureau of the trade unions of Moscow in May 1917. He founded the tanners' union of Moscow and its organ, *Tanners' Voice* (*Golos kozhevnika*). After 1918 he cooperated in the internationalist faction of the RSDRP, headed by Solomon Lozovsky, and joined the party of Lenin in 1919. After the constitution of the Profintern, he worked closely together with Lozovsky. In 1921, 1923 and 1925, Yuzefovich took part as a Soviet delegate in the international tanners' unions congresses in Vienna, Dresden and Oslo and in the congress of Amsterdam's Trade Unions International. In 1923, he campaigned in Berlin for the affiliation of the German unions with the Profintern. Until 1927 he was a member of the CC of the Soviet tanners' unions. He spent the years 1931-1933 on a secret mission in the United States. His detailed knowledge about the powerful American trade union alliances, which would be useful to the JAFC ten years later, dates from this time.

Yuzefovich declared in a secret conference of the court, in the absence of the other co-defendants on June 6, 1952, that he had committed himself temporarily in 1938 to report to state security about possible anti-Soviet sentiments among Jewish journalists and intellectuals. After 1939 he was an academic assistant at the institute for history of the Soviet Academy of Sciences and belonged to a working group, led by Lozovsky, which edited the anthology *Against Right Socialists*. When the *Sovinformburo* was founded in 1941, Yusefovich ranked among the most important collaborators because of his contacts with leftist circles and unions throughout the world and his knowledge of languages, and also became a member of the presidium of the JAFC. He could no longer obtain a doctorate for his already completed dissertation about the coup by Marshal Pilsudski of Poland in 1926.

Yuzefovich, who was to act as union leader of a future Jewish Crimean Republic, was arrested on January 13, 1949, and executed on

August 12, 1952. His wife Maria and his daughter Marina were arrested as well and taken into custody in Kazakhstan, together with the Markish family.

**Leib Kvitko** was born on November 11, 1890, in Olesko in the Ukraine, the son of a teacher. He was orphaned at an early age when his whole family died of tuberculosis. At the age of 10 he began working as an apprentice to a shoemaker, and later, in Nikolayev, Kherson, and Odessa, at a tannery as a freight carrier and groom. At the age of 12 he was writing poems. In 1915 in Uman he met the already famous David Bergelson, who saw his talent and encouraged him to write. His first poem was published in May 1917 in the Kiev newspaper, *The Free World* (*Dos fraye vort*). In 1918 he moved to Kiev with his wife, where he formed, along with Hofstein and Markish, the famous Yiddish poetic triumvirate. The poems *Tritt* and *Red Storm* (*Royter shturm*), the first Yiddish work about the October Revolution, are very emotional. Kvitko was an official of the *Kultur-lige* and worked in a children's home and wrote children's poems as well. His poetry was published in journals such as *Eygns, Baginen* and *Komunistishe fon*. Later he moved to Berlin, where he contributed to the journals *Milgrojm* and *Zukunft*. In 1922 his cycles of poems *Grin groz* and *1919*, a jeremiad to the pogroms in the Ukraine, were published.

Kvitko went from Berlin to Hamburg, where he was active as an employee of the Soviet trade delegation in the harbor. Der Nister and he contributed to the secret loading of Soviet arms to China. Kvitko became a member of the KPD (Communist Party of Germany). The novella *Riogrander fell* (1928) is based on his experiences in Hamburg. In 1925 he was expelled from Germany and lived in Kharkov until 1936. He was a member of the Jewish section of the proletarian writers' union of the Ukraine and led the editorial office of the *Red World* (*Royte Velt*), in which many of his poems were published, as well as the children's newspaper *Zay greyt*. In 1929, Kvitko, with his criticism of the official "Yevseki" Yiddish press, headed by the feared Moshe Litvakov, started a dispute in the *Royte Velt* that shook the foundations of his life. Jewish party officials declared that Kvitko's objections were a right-wing attack on the party. Because of the "Kvitko affair," several Yiddish authors had to write repentant letters. He himself was dismissed as editor and had to work at the Kharkov tractor factory. In 1933 the first volume of his complete works, which contained works written between 1916 and 1927, was published. In 1935 he became editor of the *Kindershafung*.

Kvitko led the section of children's and juvenile literature of the Soviet writers' union. His poems, fables, and prose texts were printed in Yiddish and Russian editions, as well as in schoolbooks for other nationalities. The children's poems alone reached an edition of 11 million and many of them were set to music. In 1939 he was decorated with the Order of the Red Labor Banner.

Before the war Kvitko became a member of the CPSU. Lozovsky and Epstein invited him by telegram to come to Kuibyshev from Alma-Ata (where he had been evacuated) and work with the JAFC. He was one of the editors of the *Eynikeyt*, for which he wrote many articles and whose monthly children's page he edited. In addition, he published several pamphlets, the prose volume *The Blood Calls for Revenge (Dos blut ruft tsu nekome)*, a collection of children's poems, *Children's Hearts (Kinder herzer)* (1943) and the poetry volume *Enemies (Feier oyf sonim)*. In 1947 his cycle *The Singing of My Soul (Gesang vun mayn gemit)*, written from 1941 to 1946, was published in Moscow. In these articles and poems Kvitko expressed his solidarity with the persecuted Jews and his pride in the Jewish heroes of the war. After the war he was secretary of Moscow's bureau of the association of Yiddish authors and planned the founding of a hostel for homeless authors. He was arrested on January 29, 1949, and executed on August 12, 1952. At the trial against the JAFC he was accused of having nationalist tendencies.

**Peretz Markish** was one of the most original and productive representatives of Yiddish literature. His use of pathos mirrors the tragedy of the Jewish nation in the monumental epic in verse *War (Milkhome)* written under the shock of the Shoah and difficult to translate because of the stylistic variations. His other works were mostly translated only into Russian. No less than 42 translators worked on a volume of selected works that appeared in 1957 in Russia. Charles Dobrzinski translated some of his poems into French.

Markish was born on December 7, 1895, into a poor family in Polonoye in Volynia. His father was a tailor and private tutor, and his mother sold herring at markets. In the Kheyder he learned Hebrew and read the Bible. He soon left his parents and was already, at the age of thirteen, assistant choirmaster in Berdichev. At fifteen he began writing poetry in Russian. He earned his living as a day laborer, private teacher and bank employee. Soon he passed an external high school exam.

The nineteen-year-old Markish was drafted in 1914 as a tsarist front soldier and served until February 1917. Then he went to Yekaterinoslav.

His first published poem, *The Fighter* (*Der kemfer*), came out in the Yiddish newspaper of the town with the same name. His poetry, *Volynia*, was published in 1918; later in Kiev further poems appeared in the Yiddish almanac *Eygns*. Already in 1920 he had a solid reputation as an avant-garde poet. He was the youngest member of the Yiddish poetical triumvirate of Kiev, which included David Hofstein and Leib Kvitko. When, during the pogroms in the Ukraine, rumors about his execution started, his obituary was printed in the Yiddish press. On behalf of the Jewish section of the CC of the Ukrainian CP, he moved to Poland in 1921 to do pro-Soviet work among Jewish authors. There his famous poem *The Pile* (*Die kupe*), whose title referred to the corpses of the victims of the pogroms, appeared. Together with other poets, he founded the literary magazine *The Gang* (*Khaliastre*), illustrated by Marc Chagall. Between 1922 and 1923 Markish visited the centers of Yiddish literature in Paris, London, and Berlin, and also traveled to Palestine. There he said that two events justified the creation of the world: the communist revolution in Russia and the rebuilding of Palestine by the Zionists. In Warsaw in 1924 he founded the magazine *Literarishe bleter*, in which he published many reviews, poems and essays of literary criticism. During this time he wrote experimental poems about the city and perfectly shaped sonnets about his home. He was often invited to readings and lectures in Poland, Berlin and Paris. In Paris the handsome, vivacious man was the Bohemian prince of Montparnasse, friend of all well-known artists, Yiddish or French poets. He often sat in the famous Cafés Dôme or La Rotonde and discussed politics and literature. With Chagall, whom he met in Russia, he was bound by deep friendship, not least because Chagall was a Yiddish poet too.

His return to the Soviet Union in 1926 sparked a creative and human crisis. How narrow, petty and bureaucratic Russia must have seemed to him after Berlin, Warsaw and Paris, and how limited were the possibilities and chances for development of a modern Jewish cultural and literary center. Litvakov—the "tsar" of Yiddish language and culture in the Soviet Union—made a disastrous impression on Markish. When the *Literarishe bleter* in Warsaw published a poem of his in 1928, he had to criticize himself, because a Soviet poet was forbidden to be printed in capitalist foreign countries. His works were often branded by the official critics as nationalist and narrow-minded. In spite of his revolutionary zeal, Markish could not deny his roots in the Jewish and secular tradition. He did not forget the deep wounds caused to him and to Russia's Jews, nor the mediocrity and dogmatism of the bureaucratic literature officials, who accused him of being too tolerant in his descriptions of Jewish life before the revolution and opposed his spontaneity toward the traditional Jews. In his poetic work *Don't Worry* (*Nit gedayget*), published in 1931, which he later dramatized, he describes the life of the Jews in the new colonies in the Crimea and Dzhanskoy. The Jewish farmers always inspired his hopes for a normalization of the basis of life of the Jews in Russia. The play *The Fifth Horizon* deals with the life of the mineworkers in the Donets Basin and was staged by Vakhtangov.

Markish was allowed to move into a newly built house together with his wife Esther and his son Simon (the second son David was born in 1938). Neighbors of the family included Boris Pasternak, Osip Mandelstam, Mikhail Bulgakov, Ilya Ilf, Viktor Shklovsky, the poet Shmuel Halkin and the professor of Yiddish literature, Isaak Nussinov. Markish soon developed a close friendship with Boris Pasternak and Osip Mandelstam and was elected chairman of the Jewish section of the Soviet authors' union at the first authors' congress in 1934. Maxim Gorky chaired the congress and the guests included André Malraux and Rafael Alberti. Karl Radek and Nikolai Bukharin gave theoretical lectures.

Markish was spared the purges of 1937, which took a heavy toll on numerous poets and authors and even the fanatical communist Litvakov. He was the only Yiddish poet to receive an award in 1937, with the Lenin Order. He then had to join the party. After the Red Army's invasion of Poland in September 1937, he went to the annexed regions of Vilnius and Bialystok, where he was able to help Alter Katsyzne, Rachel Korn, and Chaim Grade and other Yiddish authors.

Markish, along with Mikhoels, was one of the founders of the JAFC. He did not care much about organizational matters, but his prestige and glory served the common goal. His enemy in the committee was Itsik Fefer, who envied the success of his brilliant colleague and criticized him on every occasion. Markish was considered tainted because he had lived abroad in the West, among the class enemies, and thus soon lost his position as head of the Yiddish-speaking program of Radio Moscow.

On behalf of the JAFC, Markish sent several works, poems and articles to the U.S., including *Göring's Green Portfolio, A Half-Century* and *On the Threshold of the Year 1948*. They appeared in the Yiddish pro-Soviet newspapers and magazines *Morgn freiheit, Der tog, Yidishe kultur* and *Neilebn*. The leading Yiddish poets in the America such as Opatoshu, Meisel, and Glattstein, celebrated Markish in their reviews as one of the greatest poets alive.

Markish's greatest work was *War (Mikhome)*. The four sections, "In the Beginning," "Moscow," "Stalingrad," and "In the West" contain a total of 1,276 sixteen-line poems. The main figures are the young Jew Gur-Arye ("young lion" in Hebrew) and his Russian comrade and officer Aleksei Sadovsky. Both visit Babi Yar. The confrontation with the crimes committed here forces them to tackle their identity. While Aleksei exudes self-confidence and optimism, Gur-Arye is dogged by self-reproach and racked with doubts about his existence as a citizen and a Jew. Markish applies numerous poetical and biblical metaphors, like Ezekiel's vision of dry bones and Daniel in the lions' den. But the work also glorifies Stalin and the Soviet nation, its soldiers and its leadership. And it criticizes the tolerant attitude of the West toward Hitler.

During the war, several plays by Markish were performed in Yiddish and other theaters, including *Kol nidre* (the name of the prayer on Yom Kippur day), *Uprising in the Ghetto* and *Forest Brothers*. One of his famous poems has the title *The Dancer from the Ghetto*. In 1948 Markish finished his last work, *March of the Generations (Dor oys, dor ayn)*, in which he described the suffering of the Jews from the beginning of the war until the uprising in the Warsaw ghetto and especially the fights of his Yiddish-writing colleagues. The novel was to have been published by *Emes*, which in the meantime had been liquidated. The manuscript did not turn up until 1956. The Jewish magazines, *Writings (Shriftn)* and *Folksshtime* in Warsaw, *Sovietish heymland* in Moscow, *Pariser Tsaytshrift* in Paris and *Yidishe kultur* in New York printed fragments.

After Markish's arrest on January 28, 1949, his family was without any income and lived off the sale of their furniture. They were sentenced in December 1952 as traitors to the Fatherland to ten years of exile in Kazakhstan—the then thirteen-year-old David reported on this time later in his autobiographical novel *From One Who Moved Away*. The questions of his wife Esther about the fate of her husband were never answered. The family was not allowed to leave Kazakhstan until August 1954, without knowing anything about the fate of Peretz Markish. For many years she fought to emigrate to Israel. In August 1971, on the 19th anniversary of the murder, the Markishes demonstrated on the street for their right to emigrate. Not until November 3, 1972, were they informed that they had to leave the country within 72 hours. Two years later the report, *Le long retour*, by the literary scholar Esther Markish appeared in Paris, followed by many editions in several languages. Simon Markish is a professor in Geneva. David Markish, a respected journalist and author, lives in Tel Aviv.

The poem about the murder of Mikhoels, which unmasks the official version as a lie that Mikhoels died in a traffic accident, was the subject of the secret trial. Markish paid for this courageous poem with his life.

**Boris Shimeliovich** was born in Riga on December 3, 1902, the son of a *Shemes*, a synagogue beadle. As a seven-year-old child he distributed, on behalf of his older brother Julius, revolutionary appeals in his father's synagogue, where weapons and illegal literature were also hidden. His brother was arrested several times and the police interrogated Boris as well. The Yiddish Theater performed a play in 1934 about the last months of Julius, murdered in 1919 by White Guardsmen. Boris passed an external high-school exam as an autodidact. After a five-month membership in the Bund, he joined the Bolshevik party in 1920. He was immediately ordered to work on hunger aid, which was supported, among others, by the *Joint*. Later, Shimeliovich studied medicine in Voronezh, became a doctor and led the public health authority of the town, where he rendered outstanding service in the fight against the typhoid epidemic.

On March 1, 1931, he was appointed chief of the administration of the biggest medical center of the Soviet Union, the Botkin clinic, which was decorated with the "Red Banner" in the same year as the best hospital. More than 700 doctors worked under his leadership. He founded post-university medical training schools and other medical institutions, which were attended by 8,000 doctors. He was decorated for his decades of self-sacrificing activities in the public health system of the Soviet Union with many awards, including "Outstanding doctor of the Soviet Union."

Shimeliovich was arrested on January 13, 1949, and did not make a false confession despite very heavy torture. He was executed on August 12, 1952.

**Lina Stern** was born in Liepaia (Libau) in Latvia into a wealthy trader family. Her parents lived in Königsberg/Eastern Prussia. The father exported Russian grain to Germany. Lina spent some of her childhood years with very religious grandparents, until she returned to the home of her assimilated parents. After the high-school exam, she started studying medicine and chemistry in Geneva in 1898. During this time she met Chaim Weizmann, the future president of the Zionist world organization and the state of Israel, and the Plekhanov family. After completing her doctorate in 1903, she worked in Geneva as a professor of physiological chemistry.

In 1917 she was appointed the first female full professor at the University of Geneva. After 1923 she received, as a famous scientist and because of her support for communism, several invitations to Moscow from the Soviet government. At the beginning of 1925 she moved to Moscow to take part in building the Soviet Union. In the even she returned, the University of Geneva kept her chair open for several years.

From 1929 until 1948 she was chair and director of the physiological institute at the Academy of Sciences in Moscow, where 60 employees worked and did research. She headed the institute for the physiology of aging and pediatrics. In 1926 she founded the section for biochemistry at the institute for infectious diseases. From 1935 to the moment of her arrest she was chief editor of the *Bulletins for Experimental and Biological Medicine*. It wasn't until 1938, 13 years after her emigration to the Soviet Union, that she joined the party. She was the only woman who was both a member of the Academy of Sciences of the Soviet Union and the Soviet Medical Academy, and wrote more than 400 scientific papers in biochemistry and physiology.

She was jokingly called the "Soviet Einstein in a lady's skirt." She was decorated with the Red Star and the Red Work Banner, as well as with the medal "For heroic work during the Great Patriotic War 1941-1945." She received the Stalin award in 1943 for her work, *The Haematoencephalic Barrier*.

Lina Stern never married. She devoted her life and her energy to science and research in her socialist fatherland. She educated two generations of Soviet scientists and never considered leaving the Soviet Union.

She was a member of the JAFC from its beginning. In the spring of 1944 she was appointed to the presidium. She was also active in three other anti-fascist committees—women, youth, and scientists. After the war she joined the "international fighting committee for peace and freedom" and took part in many events with foreign visitors. As a member of the board of the "Soviet society for foreign states," she made speeches in English, French and German.

In 1943 Lina Stern already protested against the dismissal of Jews. She also became a victim of unbridled anti-Semitic attacks during interrogations by Abakumov. During the trials in 1952, Lina Stern insisted on giving her own detailed account of her life and work in the Soviet Union. The court did not grant this request until July 2, 1952. Her speech of one and a half hours, in which she presented the truth uncompromisingly, took up the whole session of the court in the morning.

She was the only main defendant not condemned to death, but to three years of the Gulag and subsequently five years of exile. Because the pre-trial detention was taken into account, she was sent directly into exile, to Dzhambul in Kazakhstan. Three months after Stalin's death she was released and reinstated into the academy. Rumor had it that she was not executed because, in addition to her other qualifications, she was a specialist in the research for the extension of life—a subject that always interested Stalin.

From 1953 to 1968 she led the physiology section of the institute for biophysics of the Academy of Sciences. On November 22, 1955, the military collegium of the Supreme Court of the Soviet Union reversed the sentence against her and shortly thereafter her membership in the party was restored by resolution of the committee for party control in the CC. In 1960 she was given an honorary doctorate by her alma mater, the University of Geneva. The grand dame of Soviet science died in Moscow on March 7, 1968, at the age of 90.

**Benjamin Zuskin** was born in 1899, the son of a tailor, in the Jewish shtetl of Ponieviez in Latvia, the seat of a Hassidic rabbinical dynasty and a Talmud academy. When his parents once took him along to a performance of a Yiddish touring theater, little Benjamin learned by heart all the songs of the play *The Witch* by Abraham Goldfaden and performed several scenes in front of friends and members of the family. He was to play this role many years later as a celebrated star of the Yiddish theater in Moscow to sold-out audiences. Already as a youth he was active as a comedian (*Bodkhen*) at weddings and other happy family parties. Although the family was very poor, they made it possible for their son to attend junior high school. Shortly after the outbreak of the First World War, the family moved to Pentsa. After secondary school qualification from the military junior high school in 1915, Zuskin began his studies at the mining academy in Yekaterinburg, the future Sverdlovsk. In 1920 he attended the mining institute of Moscow.

In March 1921 he was engaged by Aleksandr Granovsky as a member of the company of the GOSSET theater in Moscow. Thus started his nearly three-decade-long theatrical career in which he played many roles of both the Yiddish and world theater literature. Unforgotten and unequalled remained his interpretations of the jester in Shakespeare's *King Lear* in 1935, the witch in Goldfaden's play and the farmhand Senderl in Mendele Mokher Sforim's play, *The Journeys of Benjamin the Third*. In addition, he worked as producer and actor in several films, teacher at the stage school connected with the GOSSET and as assistant professor at the theater academy in Moscow. Although he was not a member of the party, after 1932 he was twice representative of a district Soviet of Moscow.

When the war began, he was evacuated to Tashkent in October 1941, together with the theater company and his wife and daughters, Tamara and Ala. He lived and worked there until October 1943. After the third convention of the JAFC in July 1944, he took an active part in the work of the committee. In 1946 he was given the Stalin award and decorated with the Red Banner and the medal "For heroic work during the Great Patriotic War 1941-1945." He received the title "National artist of the RSFSR" and "National artist of the Uzbek SSR." He enjoyed a lifelong close personal and artistic friendship with Mikhoels. When Mikhoels was murdered, Zuskin was appointed artistic manager of the state theater. He was supported by the manager of the theater academy and dramaturge in chief of the Moisey Belenki Theater.

Zuskin had his appendix removed in the summer of 1948. The permanent shadowing by secret agents had resulted in stress and chronic insomnia. During a sleep-therapy session in the Botkin clinic in Moscow—managed by Shimeliovich, his colleague at the JAFC—he was arrested on December 24, 1948, and taken to prison on a stretcher. He had to submit to the first interrogation while still in a semiconscious state. Even the minister of Soviet state security Abakumov was present at some interrogations of the apolitical artist. In horrible fear for his life, he incriminated some persons who were no longer alive and denied even his closest friend Mikhoels. Toward the end of the trial he retracted, like the other accused, all accusations and disputed every single recrimination.

His wife and daughters were banished. In the fall of 1953, half a year after Stalin's death, the family was sent to Karaganda and freed only much later. They weren't told about the arrest, trial and execution of Benjamin Zuskin for many years. In 1975 the family was allowed to emigrate to Israel.

**Leon Talmi** was born as Lezer Talminowiecki in 1893 in the Jewish shtetl of Lachowicze, near Baranowicze in eastern Poland. His father died very early and the young widow, who owned a small hardware store, had to raise her two sons, Isaak and Leon, on her own. In 1912 the two brothers emigrated to the United States. In July 1917 Talmi went to Petrograd to take part in the revolution. He became a member of the Socialists-Zionist who united with the Jewish Socialist party. The new party, called United Socialist Workers' Party (*Fareinikte*), sent him to Kiev shortly thereafter where he edited the Yiddish party newspaper, *New Time* (*Naye Tsayt*) and wrote numerous articles and essays. When the Bund split under pressure from the communists, Talmi joined the Bolshevik-oriented Kombund. After the Polish-Soviet war, Talmi returned first to Kiev, then went on to Moscow. In 1921 the Comintern sent him to the United States where he was to disseminate communist propaganda among Jewish workers and intellectuals, and edit the newspaper *Oyfboy*. In New York, Talmi worked for the Russian communist newspaper, *Spark* (*Iskra*) and the English-speaking *The Nation*. He set up the YIDGEZKOM office in the U.S., which organized aid packages for the hungry Jews of Russia, supported the Soviet organizations OZET and Komzet and became secretary general of the aid agency *Icor*, founded by communists and other sympathizers of the Soviet Union. In 1929 he accompanied, along with Ilya Vatenberg, an *Icor* delegation of American agricultural experts to the Soviet Union and Birobidzan. The delegation later published a detailed report about the journey and the colonies in the autonomous region. Talmi wrote a book about the Jewish colonists, published in 1931 in New York and in the New York Yiddish newspaper, *Morning Freedom* (*Morgn Freiheit*), edited by the CC of the CPUSA.

He returned to the Soviet Union in 1943 and became editor in chief of the state publishing house for foreign-language literature, *Foreign Literature* (*Inostrannaya literature*), that until 1939 published editions of Marx, Engels, the twelve volumes of Lenin's works, the writings of Stalin, and many others in the English language. As an untiring fighter on the propaganda front, he translated many books himself.

When the war started, Talmi volunteered for the army, although he was already 48 years old. Lozovsky gave him the assignment to organize a translation bureau for English-speaking war propaganda. After the war, he translated many important political texts and declarations that were part of official publications into English.

Talmi was active with the JAFC after 1942. Until then he had shown no interest in Yiddish literature or in Jewish affairs. He looked upon the work at the JAFC as a temporary assignment. His arrest, like the other accused who had lived occasionally in the U.S., was used to present the JAFC as an anti-Soviet American spy headquarters. Talmi's son, who was an officer in the Soviet military administration in Germany, was arrested in 1947 because a book by the Soviet deserter Kravchenko was found in his possession. He testified against his father under the threat of torture and informed on him as being a secret Zionist and Bundist. Talmi was arrested among the last of the accused on July 3, 1949, half a year after the others, and murdered with them on August 12, 1952.

**Emilia Teumin** was born in 1905 in Bern to Jewish revolutionaries from Russia. Her mother was arrested because of her participation in a May demonstration and contracted tuberculosis in a tsarist prison. During a stay at a health spa in Switzerland, she met Emilia's father, who had left Russia as a member of the CC because of the threat of imminent arrest by the tsarist police. After Emilia's birth, the Teumins returned to Russia. The father joined the CP in 1920. All members of the family were Soviet citizens, loyal to the regime, and did not much care about Jewish affairs.

Because of her knowledge of languages, Emilia Teumin was employed at the international section of the *Sovinformburo*, founded after the war began. Solomon Lozovsky, the acting head of the bureau, was her supervisor; she had hardly anything to do with the JAFC. As a translator and typist, she had no conceptual assignments and did not carry any political responsibility for the content of the texts either written or translated by her. She was arrested, together with the active members of the JAFC, for espionage.

During one of the visits of Ben Zion Goldberg, the most committed Soviet sympathizer in America, a Soviet propaganda journey into the Baltic republics was planned. Goldberg was to write a major texts about the Baltic republics for the Soviet Union. Emilia Teumin, who was always interested in the Baltic states, was ordered to compile relevant material for Goldberg. It was material already known abroad: articles from semi-official party newspapers of the three Baltic Soviet republics and reports from the extraordinary state commissions for the investigation of Nazi atrocities in the Soviet Union. All documents and sources were already censored and, like all Soviet printed matter, supplied with a detailed censorship certificate. Teumin's other duties at the *Sovinformburo* included looking after all anti-fascist committees, the Slavic committee, the youth, women and scientist committees as well as the JAFC, making hotel reservations for the members and guests of the different committees, and similar organizational duties. After the war she worked on editing the *Dictionary for Diplomacy*, which was written and edited by Lozovsky.

During the three years of confinement and torture, the examining magistrates got Emilia Teumin to testify about the work for the *Black Book* and other affairs of the JAFC with which she was never involved.

Emilia Teumin, the most innocent of all innocent victims of the JAFC trial, was arrested on January 28, 1949, and executed at the age of 47 on August 12, 1952.

**Khaya Vatenberg-Ostrovskaya** (diminutive Khaika or Chaika), Ilya Vatenberg's wife, was born in 1901 in the shtetl of Svenigorodka near Kiev. Her father was a Jewish butcher and died shortly before her birth. She emigrated to America in 1914 with the rest of the family, graduated from junior high school in New York, began studies at a university and worked at the Yiddish-socialist trade union *Jewish Workers' Union*. She also typed manuscripts for the Yiddish workers' theater and worked in Yiddish, editing the *Jewish Telegraph Agency*.

Under the influence of Ilya Vatenberg, whom she married in 1922, she became a dedicated communist, organizing party conventions, distributing leaflets and finding subscribers for the party paper. She accompanied her husband in 1926 on his journey to the Soviet Union and moved there with him in 1933. Because of her knowledge of English and Russian, she immediately found work as a typist in the office of the scientists' association. Later, like her husband, she worked at the state publishing house for foreign-language literature and after the founding of the JAFC as a typist and translator for English, Yiddish and Russian. She accompanied and acted as interpreter for American, Soviet and JAFC sympathizers and officials, such as Novik and Goldberg, during official visits to the Soviet Union. The prosecution and the investigators knew perfectly well that she had no political authority and was only a skilled office worker, and therefore bore no responsibility at all for the activities of the JAFC. Her arrest and confession, obtained by torture, were to compensate for the absence of any documentary proof of betrayal and espionage and thereby merge the mix of false accusations and invented incidents into a reasonably plausible indictment. Her long stay in America was enough to substantiate the theory of an American-Zionist conspiracy and espionage against the Soviet Union. With Emilia Teumin, Khaya Vatenberg-Ostrovskaya was one of the most arbitrary victims of the Stalinist executioners. Both women were murdered on August 12, 1952.

**Ilya Vatenberg** was born in 1887 in Stanislawow in Poland, the son of a poor Jewish lumberjack. Vatenberg finished high school in his hometown, studied in Lvov and Vienna and obtained his doctorate in economics and law. He had a law office in Stanislawow until 1914, after which he lived in Vienna until 1920.

Since his youth, Vatenberg was active in the workers' movement in Poland and in Austria, particularly as member of the Socialist-Zionist workers' party *Poale Zion*. After the split in the party, he joined the communist-oriented wing, the *Left Poale Zion*. He emigrated to America in 1920, where his whole family was still living—his father, who worked in a clothing store, his brother, who later became a lawyer as well, and his sister. He continued his political activities in the U.S. In 1921, he wrote *The History of the Socialist Idea* in Yiddish. In the U.S. he became a CC member of the *Left Paole Zion*, which accepted all of the 21 restrictive terms for admission set forth by Lenin at the Second Comintern Congress in Moscow in 1921. He agitated for the party during several journeys through the U.S. He wrote for communist newspapers and tried to bring as many members as possible into the CPUSA, which he succeeded in doing in 1924. After that, he was officially viewed as a brave communist. He suggested, following the example of the Yevsektsiia in the Soviet Union, the founding of Jewish sections in Western communist parties that had many members with Jewish origin in the U.S., France and England. At the same time he translated left-wing political literature from English, German and other languages into Yiddish and wrote many articles for the communist press. In 1925 he wrote a textbook about the October Revolution for the numerous Yiddish socialist schools.

In 1924 he was co-founder of the American Association for Jewish Colonization in the Soviet Union (*Icor*), which pursued propaganda for the Soviet Union as well as fund-raising campaigns for Birobidzan in the U.S. In 1929 he organized the journey of a delegation of American agriculture and colonization experts to travel to the Jewish autonomous region of Birobidzan. These activities were undertaken under assignment by the Soviet Union and in coordination with the Soviet state agencies. As an *Icor* official, Vatenberg visited the Soviet Union in 1926 at Moscow's request, but he did not finally move there until after he opposed the negative press about Birobidzan, that was then reaching its peak in America, with his own propaganda pamphlets. After emigrating to the Soviet Union in 1933, Vatenberg became a control editor, a sort of pre-censor, at the state publishing house for foreign-language literature, *Inostrannaya literatura*, in Moscow. Because of his political credentials, his contacts abroad (especially in America), and his knowledge of languages, Vatenberg was an ideal JAFC official. He wrote many articles, which were published in *Eynikeyt*.

Over the decades, Vatenberg wrote countless political, literary and economic publications, which were widely distributed. The December 21, 1944 issue of *Eynikeyt* published his article *Who Will Judge the Nazi War Criminals?* Although Vatenberg was always a party stalwart, a soldier and propagandist, he was arrested on January 24, 1949, and murdered on August 12, 1952.

## THE OTHER PERSECUTED AND VICTIMS

**Zelik Axelrod**, born in 1904 in Minsk, was the first Jewish-Soviet journalist and poet to be murdered by the Soviet "organs" after the outbreak of the Second World War. His poems on the subjects of Jewish history and the ethical values of Judaism appeared in journals, literary almanacs and Yiddish newspapers, including the *Red World* (*Royte Velt*), *Minsk Star* (*Minsker Stern*) and the *Minsker vecker*, whose editorial staff he later joined. They were read with enthusiasm, but the literary critics objected to the missing reference to the proletariat.

After the annexation of the eastern Polish districts and the Baltic states, including a large part of Latvia, by the Soviet Union in September 1939, Axelrod visited the Jewish centers in Bialystok and Vilnius, where he met the poet and future partisan Shmerke Kacherginsky and other Yiddish authors. He protested to the authorities, along with the poet Elia Kahan, about the liquidation of the *Vilnius Truth* (*Wilner emes*), the only semi-official Yiddish newspaper. Both received at first a rebuke, but were then sentenced to prison in Minsk in 1940 because of "nationalistic machinations." His guards executed Axelrod on May 26, 1941 in the prison courtyard. Kahan was considered to be an ordinary criminal and was released with other non-political prisoners. He later died in the war.

**Der Nister** (Yiddish "the hidden," pseudonym of Pinchas Kahanovich) was one of the most important authors of Yiddish-Soviet, even world, literature. He was born on November 1, 1884, in Berdichev in the Ukraine, the son of a Hassidic fish wholesaler. In his childhood and youth, he studied in the Kheyder and later in the Yeshiva, a Talmud academy. His older brother Aron—a Bratslav's Hassid and author of mystical Hassidic stories—had a strong influence on him. Kahanovich was close to the Socialist-Zionist movement *Poale Zion*, whose leader Ber Borochow he made into the protagonist of his novel *Fun finftn yor*. To escape tsarist military service, he left his hometown in 1905 and earned his livelihood as a teacher in Zhitomir under a false name. He was an extremely productive author; his early works were published in Yiddish literary journals. He published the first book of poems, *Thoughts and Motifs* (*Gedanken un motivn*), in 1907 under the pseudonym Der Nister, which he used until his death. In 1910 the book of poems *Hekher fun der erd*, appeared in Warsaw; the book commemorates his meeting with Itshak Leib Peretz, a great artist of Yiddish literature, in the Polish capital. *Song and Prayer* (*Gesang un gebet*), the third book, was published in 1912 in Kiev with the support of Bergelson. The almanacs published in Kiev, *Eygns* and *Oyfgang*, which could be called cornerstones of Yiddish-Soviet literature, printed further texts in 1919. Der Nister translated numerous works of world literature into Yiddish, and, like his friend Kvitko, wrote children's books as well.

He left the Soviet Union in 1921 and went via Kovno to Berlin, where a selection of two volumes of his fantastic and visionary narrations was published under the title *Fictitious* (*Oysgedakht*). During his stay, he edited, together with Bergelson, the literary part of the journal *Milgroym*. From 1922 to 1925, Der Nister worked with Kvitko at the Soviet trade mission in Hamburg. Like many Jewish emigrants, he saw himself as a dissident and kept in contact with the Jewish literary journals in Russia, mainly with the almanac, *Stream* (*Shtrom*).

He returned to the Soviet Union in 1926 and lived in Kharkov. In 1928 his book of poems *Of My Goods* (*Fun mayne giter*) and narrations in the journal *Royte Velt* appeared. Influenced by Russian symbolism, Der Nister developed an original style, which can be called a synthesis of mystic visions and fantastic elements. After 1929 he had to embrace socialist realism, but did not give up his style of representation, as the travel impressions *Three Capitals* (*Dray Hoyptshtet*, 1934), demonstrate. In the 1930s he began to write his major work, a large-scale family saga entitled *Di mishpokhe Mashber* ("Maschber" means "crisis" in Yiddish-Hebrew), about the fate of a Jewish family in Eastern Europe from the 1870s until his time. Although the party-conforming Yiddish-proletarian literature had presented this subject thus far with biting satire and contempt, the critics praised the first volume, published in Moscow in 1939. His writings were a monument to the Hassidim of Bratslav, whom he highly respected.

When the war began, the author lived in Tashkent, where he wrote the second volume of the Mashber saga. His daughter Odel, a Yiddish poet, starved to death during the siege of Leningrad. Der Nister came to

Moscow in 1942 as an active collaborator of the JAFC. Because he did not yet belong to the Bolshevik literary elite, his presence gave the committee considerable prestige. He published several accounts about the fate of the Polish Jews under German occupation: *Heshls Ausheles, Der Seyde mitn eynikl, Meir Landshaft, Meyn bakanter* and others. In an article published in 1944 in the *Eynikeyt*, Der Nister predicted that a Jewish state in Palestine would ensure the survival of the Jews. In the summer of 1947 he spent two months with Jewish colonists in Birobidzan and described his extremely positive experiences in reports that were published in *Eynikeyt* and in *Heymland*. After his arrest, he was accused of having described the life of the Jewish colonists with biblical metaphors.

Despite repeated promises, *Der Emes* did not publish the second volume of the *Mishpokhe Mashber* before it was liquidated like all Yiddish publishing houses and newspapers. The *Ykuf* publishing house in New York published the first volume in 1943 and the second volume in 1948. Further editions, as well as Hebrew, French, and English editions, followed. In 1995 a German translation appeared under the title *Die Brüder Maschber*. A chapter of the third volume was printed in 1967 in the journal *Sovietish heymland*. Khone Szmeruk pointed out that the Yiddish-Soviet journalists manipulated the Maschber text. To this day there are various legends about the fate of the missing manuscript of the third volume.

Der Nister was arrested and tortured at the end of January with many other members of the JAFC. The accusation of having written nationalistic texts would more likely have been true of him than of the socialist-proletarian realists like Fefer. According to an entry in *The Small Soviet Encyclopedia* of 1960, the poet died on June 4, 1950, in prison or the Gulag. His mastery of language and stylistics had influenced Yiddish-Soviet literature, while the public recognized his extraordinary talent only in his last years. He should have been a candidate for the Nobel Prize.

**Yekheskel Dobrushin** was born in 1883 in the Ukraine. After his studies at the Sorbonne, he lived in Kiev from 1909 to 1920, where he taught at the Jewish teacher training college. Later he worked at different academic institutes in Moscow. Before the Revolution, Dobrushin wrote Hebrew and Yiddish prose. He was one of the founders of the Yiddish literary group *Shtrom* and of the almanac of the same name in Moscow. As a dramatist, theater historian, author and literary scholar, he displayed numerous talents. He wrote many articles for the *Eynikeyt* and participated as a top-ranking member of the JAFC in all initiatives of the committee. Dobrushin dramatized and produced plays by the great Yiddish authors Goldfaden, Sholem Aleichem, Mendele and Peretz for the state theater. He also published monographs about Zuskin and Mikhoels. He was arrested at the beginning of January 1949, and died in August 1953 in the Gulag.

**Shmuel Halkin**, along with Der Nister, was one of the few Yiddish-Soviet authors who denied neither their traditions nor the universal and ethical values of Judaism and Hassidism. He was born on December 5, 1897, in Rogachev in Belorussia, the ninth child of a poor family, and was raised by his older brother. He attended an art academy and took Russian lessons with a private tutor. His career as one of the most talented Yiddish poets began in Kiev in 1917. In 1922 he moved to Moscow, where his poems were published in the almanacs *Vidervukhs, Shtrom,* and *Barg aroyf* and in the newspapers *Der Emes, Stern* and *Royte Velt.* He wrote Hebrew poems as well and considered emigrating to Palestine. His anthology, published in 1929, *Vey un mut,* was violently criticized by the proletarian authors as a product of a petty bourgeois Zionist. He had to renounce such differences in order to be able to continue to exist as a poet. His translations of Shakespeare, Longfellow, Pushkin, Gorky, Yesenin, Blok, and Mayakovsky into Yiddish identified him as a very expressive master of the Yiddish language. In 1939 he wrote the play *Umshterblekhkeyt,* which was first performed by Mikhoels's state theater in 1941.

After the war started, he became a member of the JAFC and editor of the *Eynikeyt,* which published many of his poems. He used the fact that the "organs" gave the Jews a certain freedom during the war to describe characters of Jewish history in his works, which had been impossible until then. Thus he wrote dramas like *Sulamit* and *Bar Kochba*; his play *Getograd—Oyf toyt un of lebn* was about the uprising of the Warsaw ghetto. It was to be performed in Moscow, but the closing of the theater and the JAFC preempted the performance. He was a candidate as minister of education of the planned republic in the Crimea.

Halkin was arrested at the end of January 1949. Was it his service to Russian literature that got his judges to separate his trial, even though he was one of the editors in chief of the *Eynikeyt* and a member of the presidium of the JAFC? Halkin was sentenced on January 5, 1950, to ten years of the Gulag. Seriously ill, he was released in 1955 and died five years later.

**Aron Kushnirov** was born on January 7, 1890, in Boyerka near Kiev—the shtetl of Boyberik, made famous by Sholem Aleichem. As an orphan, he had to work hard at the early age of 13 and educate himself. During the First World War he was a tsarist soldier and volunteered for the Red Army in 1920. His first poems appeared in a Yiddish front newspaper and in the newspaper *Der komunist*. The later ones were published in the Yiddish literary almanacs *Shtrom* and *Oktiabr*. The critics praised them as an example of true proletarian literature. In addition to his poems, combining classic and expressionist stylistic elements, he wrote many stories, several plays, and translated works of Russian literature into Yiddish.

In 1941 the 51-year-old author volunteered at the front, where he received several decorations as an officer and was seriously wounded. Not until 1942 did he become a party member and editor of the *Eynikeyt*. At the end of May 1945, as a veteran with an amputated leg, he delivered the keynote speech at the meeting of Yiddish authors. By 1947 a selection of his earlier works had been published and in 1948 the anthology of his war narratives, *Foter Komandant*, was also published.

When in mid-1949 the Soviet writers' union ordered him to announce the liquidation of Yiddish literature and publishing houses at a meeting, he collapsed on the stage, lost his voice, and died shortly thereafter on September 7, 1949.

**Nakhum Levin**, born in 1908, was a communist Yiddish journalist and author. As editor in chief of the newspaper *Eynikeyt*, he was a top-ranking member of the JAFC. In November 1946 he became acting secretary of the JAFC. In 1949 he was arrested, together with all top-ranking officials of the JAFC, and accused of leading an anti-Soviet nationalist underground. He was sentenced to death and executed on November 23, 1950.

**Isaak Nussinov** was born in 1889 in Chernigov in Volynia. He studied art history and literature in Switzerland and Italy. In 1917 he returned to Russia. Nussinov is considered to be one of the most important Russian literary scholars. He was a professor of literature at the University of Moscow (since 1925) and at the Moscow Lenin Institute for Education; he was also employed at the Institute for Jewish Proletarian Literature at the Ukrainian Academy of Sciences.

He was the author of many scientific studies, essays, reviews, articles and reports in the *Great Soviet Encyclopedia*, as well as in the literary encyclopedia. In 1932 his book, *Problemen fun der proletarisher yidisher literature*, was published, followed in 1941 by *Pushkin and World Literature*, which sparked violent criticism of his entire lifework. He was arrested in 1948 because of his active collaboration with the JAFC and because he had sent 15 articles about the committee to be published in the U.S. After two years of confinement and torture, he died on October 31, 1950, in Lefortovo prison in Moscow.

**Zorakh (Sakhari) Grinberg** was born in Belaya Tserkov in the Ukraine on March 13, 1889, the son of a Kheyder teacher. He studied agriculture and taught history and geography at a Jewish high school in Minsk. He had been a member of the Bund since 1906, and in 1917 he joined the CP. One year later he argued against the Zionists in a pamphlet of the commissariat for Jewish affairs. In 1920 he edited the Yiddish popular-science newspaper *Di velt*, the communist political magazines *Die freie welt*, *Die freie shtime*, *Di kommune*, *Kamf un lebn*, and edited the almanac *Kultur-fragen*. He worked on Jewish ethnic studies as well, and taught Jewish history at the pedagogical institute of the University of Moscow.

In 1921 he worked as a high-ranking official in the commissariat for popular education and later served three years as a member of the official Soviet trade delegation in Berlin. During this time he met Nadezhda Alliluyeva, the future wife of Stalin, and the entire Alliluyev clan. After his return to the Soviet Union, he was in the administration of the historical museum and the armaments museum in the Kremlin. From 1927 to 1945 he taught and did research at the Gorky Institute for World Literature in Moscow.

After the founding of the JAFC, he was chairman of the historical section of the committee. He was arrested on December 28, 1947. Because of his relation to the Alliluyev clan and to Mikhoels, he was an ideal character in the invented scenario that led to the arrest of the top-ranking JAFC members. He was tortured into making the most absurd accusations. He died in prison on December 22, 1949, without being sentenced—or was murdered, after his testimony had been transcribed and his life had no further value to his Lubyanka executioners.

**Grigori Shits** was born in 1903. A talented journalist, he worked for several Yiddish newspapers—including the *Stern* in Kharkov and the *Minsker Stern*—before being appointed to the editorial staff of *Eynikeyt*.

After Epstein's death, he became a member of the presidium of the JAFC and editor in chief of the *Eynikeyt*, which he headed until its closing. He was arrested in 1949 and given a long sentence in 1950. He died in prison on October 8, 1954.

**Eliyahu Spivak**, one of the most respected Soviet philologists, was born in the Ukraine in 1890 and taught at Jewish schools for many years. He was a member of the Ukrainian Academy of Sciences after 1938 and led the institute for Jewish culture there. Spivak was arrested as a member of the JAFC in January 1949 and died on April 4, 1950, in a NKVD prison without being sentenced.

**Joseph Kerler** was born in the Ukraine in 1918; he spent his youth in the Crimea. His first Yiddish poems were published at that time. He fought on the front lines after 1941 and was wounded several times. After the war Kerler wanted to move to Birobidzan, but returned to Moscow instead. As a collaborator of the JAFC and a Yiddish poet, he was arrested in 1950 and sentenced to ten years in the Gulag. After five years of camp imprisonment in Vorkuta, he obtained his freedom. Kerler worked in the Zionist underground until he could emigrate to Israel in 1971, where he has lived since then. There he founded the Yiddish magazine *Yerushalaimer Almanakh* and initiated a monument to the victims of August 1952. His book *Zwelfter August 1952*, published in 1978 by *Eygns*, also pays homage to his murdered friends and to the Yiddish language. The name of the publishing house refers to the Yiddish literary journal whose authors were murdered 30 years later.

## AUTHORS AND EDITORS OF THE *BLACK BOOK*

**Margarita Aliger** was born in 1915 in Odessa. She studied literature from 1934 to 1939; her first poems appeared in 1933. During the Second World War she was at the front lines and in besieged Leningrad as a war correspondent. During this time she wrote the verse-epic *Zoya* about the young partisan Zoya Kosmodemyanskaya. Her poetry *Your Victory*, published in 1945 in the magazine, *Banner (Znamya)*, takes the genocide of the Soviet Jews and the Jewish resistance as its themes. She later published several anthologies of poems. Stalin put her on the list for the Stalin award. She died in 1992 in Moscow.

**Moshe Altschuler** (1887-1969), journalist, wrote articles in Yiddish and Russian.

**Pavel Antokolsky** (1896 St. Petersburg-1978 Moscow), poet and translator, studied law at the University of Moscow. His first poems were published in 1921. Until 1934 he worked as a producer at the Vakhtangov Theater in Moscow. He was a war correspondent and led a frontline theater. His verse narrative *The Son*, published in 1943, is one of the most important works of Soviet war poetry. In the poems *The Extermination Camp* and *The Uprising in Sobibor* (together with V. Kaverin), written in 1945, he describes the extermination and the resistance of the Jews. In 1946 he wrote the poem *No Eternal Memory*.

**Vagram Apresyan** was a frontline correspondent during the war. The author and essayist collected material about the Treblinka death camp. His report about the tragedy of Jewish children in this camp, "The children of the black way," was incorporated in the *Black Book*.

**L. Basarov**, worked on the *Black Book*.

**Abraham Derman** (1880-1952), literary scholar and author, wrote several works about Chekhov, Korolenko and other authors.

**Abraham Efros** (1888-1954), translator, literary and theater critic, and assistant professor of the theory of drama.

**Shakhne Epstein** (see biography)

**Itsik Fefer** (see biography)

**Ruvim Freierman** (1891 Mogilev-1972 Moscow), studied at the technical university in Kharkov, and worked first in various jobs and later as a journalist. He wrote narratives, primarily for children. His first literary works were published in 1924. In 1941 he joined the ranks of the public military; during the war he was a frontline correspondent for army newspapers.

**Valeria Gerasimova** (1903 Saratov-1970 Moscow), author and literary critic. She studied until 1925 at the educational college of the University of Moscow, and was later a teacher and active in the Komsomol. Her narratives and novellas began to appear in 1923. During the war she worked as a frontline correspondent.

**Leib Goldberg** (1892-1955), Yiddish author. He translated the works of Sholem Aleichem into Russian and wrote for the newspaper *Eynikeyt*.

**Yefim Hekhtman,** journalist, a captain during the war, worked as a frontline correspondent for the army newspaper *Krasnaya zvezda*.

**Vassily Ilyenkov** (1897 Shilovo-Uspenskoye-1967 Moscow), after studying history and philosophy was active as an author after 1929. During the war he was also known as a journalist. He wrote the novels *The Father's House* (*Rodnoi dom*) and *To That Shore* (*Na tot bereg*).

**Vera Inber** (1890 Odessa-1972 Leningrad), poet, author and journalist. She studied in Odessa and Paris, where her first book of poems was published in 1914. In 1941 she went to Leningrad and lived in the besieged city until 1944. She describes her experiences during the siege in the book of poems *The Meridian of Pulkovo* (*Pulkovskii meridian*), and in the Leningrad diary *Nearly Three Years* (*Pochti tri goda*).

**Vsevolod Ivanov** (1895 Lebyashye-1963 Moscow), author and dramatist. He set, printed and published his first works himself in 1919. He was a correspondent for *Izvestiia* during the war, accompanied the army to Berlin and reported on the Nuremberg war crimes trials. He wrote many appeals, narratives and dramas. His complete works were published in Moscow in 1958-1960 and 1973-1980.

**Meir Yelin,** born in 1910, wrote prose in Yiddish and Latvian. He lived during the war in the ghetto of Kaunas (Kovno), where he took an active part in the Jewish resistance movement and kept a ghetto chronicle. He emigrated to Israel in 1973.

**Yakov Yossade,** born in 1911, Latvian author and dramatist. He fought as a volunteer in the 16th Latvian Division and wrote for frontline newspapers.

**Venyamin Kaverin** (Benjamin Silber) (1902 Pskov-1989 Moscow), author, studied Arabic in Moscow and St. Petersburg and did his doctorate in Russian philology. He was a war correspondent with the press agency TASS and *Izvestiia*. His book *Two Captains* (*Dva kapitana*) appeared in 1947, in which he described the battles and the sailor's death of the submarine captain and "Hero of the Soviet Union" Israel Fissanovich. Together with Pavel Antokolsky he wrote a book about the uprising in Sobibor and about the Jewish resistance. Kaverin was a member of the JAFC.

**Rachel Kovnator** worked as a journalist at the JAFC and wrote for the newspaper *Eynikeyt*. In 1943 *Emes* published her biography about the "Hero of the Soviet Union" Joseph Makovsky, who was seriously wounded several times as lieutenant colonel of the armored corps, in 1943.

**Leib Kvitko** (see biography)

**Vladimir Lidin** (V. Gomberg) (1894 Moscow-1979 Moscow) studied the Middle East and law and wrote novels and narrations after 1916. He was a frontline correspondent for *Izvestiia* and for army newspapers during the war.

**Bernard (Berl) Mark** (1908 Lomza-1966 Warsaw) was a Jewish-Polish historian, literary critic and journalist. He edited articles in the Jewish press and the two-volume *History of Social Movements in Poland* in Yiddish (1932 and 1939). He lived in the Soviet Union during the war, collaborated with the JAFC and the Union of Polish Patriots in the USSR. In 1944 he wrote the standard work on the uprising in the Warsaw ghetto, *Powstanie w getcie Warszawskim*, which came out in several editions and many languages, in Moscow. From 1947 until his death, Mark was director of the Jewish Historical Institute in Warsaw. He published many historical books, including *Die ungekumene shreibers fun getos un lagern un zeiere verk*, and edited the magazines, *Newsletter of the JHI* (*Bleter far geshikhte*) and *Biuletyn ZIH*).

**Solomon Mikhoels** (see biography)

**Georgi Munblit** was an author, critic and screenwriter. During the war he worked as a journalist.

**Hirsh Osherovich**, born in 1908, and wrote in Yiddish. He was a correspondent for the newspaper *Eynikeyt* and wrote several publications about the JAFC. After the liquidation of the committee, he was arrested in 1949 and released in 1956. He emigrated to Israel in 1971.

**Lev Oserov** (Lev Goldberg) (1914 Kiev-1996 Moscow) studied Russian and Ukrainian philology in Kiev, and history, philosophy, literature, Latin, and Greek in Moscow after 1934. He specialized in Russian literature of the 19th and 20th centuries and was also active as a poet, translator and critic. During the war he was a correspondent for an army newspaper. He was the first to describe the tragedy of Babi Yar based on eyewitness testimony. His report was selected as the opening article of the *Black Book*, but abridged to half by the censors and published in its entirety for the first time in the German version by this author. His poem *Babi Yar* was published in 1946, and a collection of his poetry—*Lirika 1931-1966*—in Moscow in 1966. Oserov died shortly after a visit to Paris, where the French edition of the *Black Book* was presented.

**Ovadi Savich** (1896 Warsaw-1967 Moscow) studied law in Moscow. As a TASS correspondent, he took part in the Spanish Civil War and wrote immediately after his return to Moscow in 1938 the book *People of the International Brigades* (*Liudi internatsional'nykh brigad*). The poet and journalist was a close friend of Ilya Ehrenburg. During the Second World War he worked as a frontline correspondent.

**Mikhail Shambadal** was active on the editorial staff of the *Black Book* as an editor and translator from Yiddish.

**M. Sheinman** (no biographical data known)

**Maria Shkapskaya-Andreyeva** (1891 Petersburg-1952 Moscow) studied philosophy in Toulouse. She published her first poems in 1910, and in 1921 a first book of poems. Later, she worked as a journalist at the Leningrad newspaper, *Red Evening Newspaper* (*Vechernaya Krasnaya gazeta*). In 1942 her book about the atrocities of the German occupiers in the Soviet Union appeared: *This Really Happened* (*Eto deistvitel'no sluchilos'*). The censors heavily abridged her report, "The Germans is Radziwillow," in the *Black Book*. An anthology of her poems was published in London in 1979.

**Viktor Shklovsky** (1893 St. Petersburg-1984 Moscow) published in 1923, after studying philosophy and literature, his first novel, *Senti-*

*mental Journey (Sentimental'noe puteshestvie)*, and worked after 1926 as a screenwriter and author of children's books. He was one of the most important literary scholars, authors and critics of Soviet literature, and analyzed in his theoretical works, among others, the works of Tolstoy, Gogol, and Mayakovsky. *Theory of Prose (Teoriia prozy)* (1984) is one of his main works.

**Lydia Seifulina** (1889 Varlamovo-1954 Moscow), author and playwright, Seifulina was a teacher by profession. In one of her first novels, *The Runaways (Pravonarushiteli)*, she devoted herself to the problem of the *Bezprizorniki*, the war orphans, who went to seed during the civil war. During the Second World War she wrote articles for newspapers and several narratives, including in 1942 *On One's Own Ground (Na svoei zemle)*. She was also active in broadcasting.

**Hirsh Smolar**, born in 1905 in Zambrow, Poland, in his youth was active in the illegal Polish CP. He fled to the Soviet Union and returned to Poland in 1929 to work in the communist underground. He was arrested and imprisoned for four years, managed to escape in 1939, and reached Bialystok via the USSR after the annexation of the Polish Eastern districts. There he was the editor of the Yiddish newspaper, *Bialystok Star (Bialystoker Stern)* until 1941. During the German occupation he was one of the leaders of the resistance movement in the ghetto of Minsk. At that time he wrote the narrative, *From the Minsk Ghetto (Fun minsker geto)*, which was published in Poland in 1946 and in Russian translation in 1947. After his escape from the ghetto, he commanded a Jewish partisan unit and helped to create additional partisan units. He returned to Poland in 1946, where he led the Jewish culture section at the CC of the Polish United Workers' Party and worked with the Yiddish-language newspaper *Folksshtime*. In 1968 he was discharged by the communist rulers and emigrated to Israel in 1971, where he was active in academic and literary fields. He is also the author of the play *The Soldier of Poshuty (Poshuter Selner)*.

**Leib Strongin** (1896-1968) worked from the age of thirteen as a typesetter for printers. He joined the CP in 1917 and printed illegal communist newspapers in Belorussia. Then he became press commissar and after 1924 chairman of the Belorussian state publishing house. In 1939 he took over the management of the official Yiddish newspaper and publishing house *Der Emes* in Moscow, as successor to the executed Moshe Litvakov. Strongin was a member of the JAFC and editor of the newspaper *Eynikeyt*. He was arrested in 1949 and released after Stalin's death.

**Abraham Sutskever** (see biography)

**Ilya Trainin** (1887–1949) was a lawyer and member of the Academy of Sciences in the USSR. As chairman of the Academy's institute of law, he collected documents and materials about fascist crimes in the occupied areas of the Soviet Union. He was a member of the JAFC as well as of the "extraordinary national commission for discovering and investigating the evil deeds of the fascist German invaders and their accomplices with regard to the immense crimes of the German government."

**Osip Czorny**, born in 1899, was an author, art theorist and director.

## MEMBERS OF THE JAFC IN MAY 1945

Mikhoels, Solomon, professor, folk artist, chairman
Epstein, Shakhne, secretary general, editor in chief of the newspaper *Eynikeyt*

Bakhmutsky, Aleksandr, secretary of the CP of Birobidzan
Bergelson, David, author
Blekhman, Meir, commander of a partisan unit, major, award recipient
Bregman, Solomon, acting minister of state control of the RSFR
Briker, V., chairman of the film and photographers' union of the USSR
Buber, Leonid, guards major, "Hero of the Soviet Union"
Dobrushin, Yekheskel, literary critic and dramatist
Dvorkin, M., kolkhoz chairman in the district of Moscow
Ehrenburg, Ilya, author
Ermler, Friedrich, film producer, recipient of the Stalin award
Falkovich, Elie, first lieutenant, philologist
Fefer, Itsik, poet
Flier, Jakob, pianist

Frumkin, Aleksandr G., chemical physicist, member of the academy, recipient of the Stalin award

Gelman, Polina, bomber pilot, "Heroine of the Soviet Union"

Gilels, Emil, pianist

Goldberg, G., captain, commander of the submarine fleet in the Baltic Sea

Goldmakher, I., acting chairman of the Soviet of Birobidzan, member of the Supreme Soviet of the USSR

Gonor, Lev, major general, "Hero of socialist work," manager of an armament factory

Grade, Khaim, poet

Grinberg, Zorakh, historian

Gross, I., actor in the Yiddish theater in Birobidzan

Grossman, Vassily, author

Gubelman, M., chairman of the factory workers' union of the USSR

Halkin, Shmuel, poet and dramatist

Hofstein, David, poet

Iofan, Boris, architect, recipient of the Stalin award

Kaganowski, Efraim, author

Khazanov, A., partisan

Korn, Rachel, author

Krein, Aleksandr, composer, folk artist of the USSR

Kreizer, Yakov, lieutenant general, "Hero of the Soviet Union"

Kushnirov, Aron, guards captain, poet and dramatist

Kvitko, Leib, poet

Levin, Khana, poet

Markish, Peretz, poet and dramatist

Marshak, Samuil, poet, recipient of the Stalin award

Milner, Rafael, guards lieutenant colonel, "Hero of the Soviet Union"

Nagler, S., manager of an armament factory

Nussinov, Isaak, professor, literary critic

Oistrakh, David, professor, violinist

Pulver, composer, folk artist of the USSR

Rabinovich, I., artist

Riklin, G., journalist

Zaslavsky, David, editor in chief of the newspaper *Pravda*

Schats-Anin, M., professor, lawyer

Sheinin, Lev A., director of the railroad engineer academy

Shimeliovich, Boris, director general of the "Botkin" medical center in Moscow

Shliffer, Shlomo, chief rabbi of Moscow
Silberstein, M., chairman of the executive committee of Birobidzan
Sobsoy, P., sculptor, recipient of the Stalin award
Spivak, Eliyahu, director of the medical department for Jewish culture of
    the Ukrainian Academy of Sciences
Stern, Lina, member of the Academy, recipient of the Stalin award
Strongin, Leib, manager of the Yiddish publishing house *Der Emes*
Sutskever, Abraham, poet, partisan
Tairov, Aleksandr, producer, folk artist of the USSR
Talmi, Leon, journalist
Tchaikov, Joseph, sculptor
Tishler, A., artist
Turyan, Pinkhas, captain of the guards, "Hero of the Soviet Union"
Vatenberg, Ilya, journalist
Vilenski, Wolf, major, "Hero of the Soviet Union"
Vovsi, Miron, major general of military medicine and chief physician of
    the Red Army
Yong, Klara, actress
Yuzefovich, Jossif, journalist, trade union official
Zuskin, Benjamin, actor, folk artist of the USSR

### MEMBERS OF THE PRESIDIUM OF THE JAFC IN MAY 1946

| | |
|---|---|
| Bergelson, David | Markish, Peretz |
| Bregman, Solomon | Mikhoels, Solomon |
| Fefer, Itsik | Sheinin, Lev A. |
| Frumkin, Aleksandr N. | Shits, Grigori (1903-1954) |
| Goldberg, Lev, journalist | Spiegelglas, Solomon |
| Halkin, Shmuel | Stern, Lina |
| Kreizer, Yakov | Yuzefovich, Joseph |
| Kushnirov, Aron | |

Seven of the 15 members of the presidium of 1946 were among the
accused in 1952.
**Source:**
Jidische Kultur, New York, June 1945

## MURDERED YIDDISH AUTHORS AND PUBLISHERS

| | |
|---|---|
| Abram, Leib 1896-1948 (?) | Kharik, Isi 1898-1937 |
| Abchuk, Avrom 1887-1937 | Khashin, Aleksandr 1886-1939 |
| Agursky, Shmuel, 1884-1937 | Kiper, Moh 1869-1938 |
| Alek, Sch. ?-1937 | Klitenik, Shmuel 1904-1940 |
| Aleksandrov, Hilel 1890-? | Koblenz, Baruch ?-1937 |
| Alter, Viktor 1890-1941 | Kopelevich, Benje 1891-1941 |
| Altschuler, Yehoshua ?-1934 | Kulbak, Moshe 1896-1940 |
| Averbuch, Shmuel ?-1937 | Kvitko, Leib 1890-1952 |
| Axelrod, Zelik 1904-1941 | Levin, Nakhum 1907-1950 |
| Baasow, Herts, 1904-1937 | Levin, Yankl 1882-1937 |
| Bergelson, David 1884-1952 | Levitan, Mikhel 1882-1937 |
| Bilov, Shlomo 1888-1949 | Liberberg, Joseph 1889-1937 |
| Brakhman, Aleksandr 1897-1942 | Litvakov, Moshe 1879-1937 |
| Bril, Hirsh 1901-1937 | Markish, Peretz 1895-1952 |
| Bronstein, Yasche 1906-1937 | Marshak, Daniel 1872-1952 |
| Damesek, Avrom 1893-1937 | Mats, David 1902-? |
| Der Nister 1884-1950 | Mereshin, Avrom 1880-1937 |
| Dimanstein, Shimen 1888-1937 | Nadel, Volf 1897-1939 |
| Dobrushin, Yekheskel 1882-1953 | Nussinov, Itzchak 1889-1950 |
| Dubrovitsky, Moshe | Osherovich, Elie 1879-1937 |
| Dunyets, Khaskel 1896-1937 | Persov, Shmuel 1889-1952 |
| Dushman, Leon 1886-? | Rafalski, Mikhael 1889-1937 |
| Erik, Maks 1898-1937 | Ratner, Salman 1884-1938 |
| Erlich, Henryk 1882-1938 | Ravin, Joseph 1890-1937 |
| Fefer, Itsik 1900-1952 | Ravin, Shloyme-Itshe 1892-1937 |
| Fridland, Zvi 1897-1936 | Rivkin, Herts 1908-1951 |
| Frumkin, Esther 1880-1938 | Rosental, Anna |
| Gelfand, Kleopatra | Rubinstein, Nachum 1902-1938 |
| Gildin, Chaim 1884-1944 | Segalovich, Volf-Hirsh 1890-1937 |
| Grinberg, Sorak 1887-1949 | Shayevich, Chaim ?-1937 |
| Gutyansky, Benjamin 1906-? | Shemerinski, Aleksandr 1880-1936 |
| Hofstein, David 1889-1952 | Shits, Herschl 1896-1953 |
| Holmstok, Feivel 1880-? | Shneier-Okun, Salman ?-1952 |
| Kabanov, Noah | Siskind, Lev 1896-1937 |
| Kadishkevitsch, Menachem 1895-1937 | Soloveichik, Henech ?-1936 |
| Kamenstein, Moshe | Spivak, Elie 1890-1952 |
| | Sprakh, Efraim 1890-1937 |

| | |
|---|---|
| Stelmakh, Anna 1900-1950 | Volobrinsky, Aron 1900-1937 |
| Strelits, Oskar 1892-1937 | Yakinson, I 1887-1937 |
| Tsart, Leon | Yankelevitch, Yankl 1904-1938 |
| Tsinberg, Israel 1873-1939 | Yawetz, Chaim 1906-? |
| Vatenberg-Ostrovskaja, Khajka 1901-1952 | Yudelson, Aron 1907-1937 |
| | Zuskin, Benjamin 1899-1952 |
| Veinstein, Aron 1877-1938 | |

### YIDDISH AUTHORS KILLED IN ACTION AS SOVIET SOLDIERS

| | |
|---|---|
| Altman, Pesach ?-1941 | Kofstein, A. ?-1939 |
| Aronsky, Moshe 1898-1944 | Koifman, Khenoch 1916-194? |
| Barsuk, Sakharia | Kurland, David |
| Borodyansky, Aron 1915-1941 | Leltschuk, Shimon 1918-1941 |
| Chernis, Nakhum 1902-1941 | Levin , Moshe 1927-1942 |
| Dechtyar, Mote | Lopatin, Shlomo 1902-1943 |
| Diamant, Hirsh | Lozik, Israel, Itsik |
| Dubilet, Moche 1897-1941 | Olerski, Busi 1908-1941 |
| Dushatsky, Chaim ?-1942 | Redko, Velvel 1918-1941 |
| Eisenvarg, Shmuel 1920-1941 | Reisen, Reuben 1911-1942 |
| Eliovich, Joseph | Riminik, I. |
| Gershenson, Moche 1903-1944 | Rosin, Shmuel 1890–1941 |
| Godiner, Shmuel 1893-1941 | Shmein, Nechemia 1907-1943 |
| Goldenberg, Shimon 1908-1942 | Shokhat, Abraham 1891-1941 |
| Goldstein, Moche 1900-1943 | Shvedik, Khenokh 1914-1942 |
| Gorstein, Aron 1895-1941 | Seldin, Yasha 1901-1942 |
| Grinseid, Itsik 1905-1942 | Solovei, Nachum 1916-1942 |
| Hadas, M. | Talalei, Leib 1906-1943 |
| Hartsman, Motl | Tusman, Zadok 1906-1941 |
| Helmond, Shmuel 1905-1941 | Veinhaus, Note |
| Hofstein, Arale 1919-194? | Veinhus, N. |
| Kahan, Elia 1909-1944 | Viner Meir, 1893-1941 |
| Khashchevachsky, Moshe 1897-1943 | Vokhnovisky, Mendl |
| | Vorobeichik, Aron |
| Koroveinik, Berl | Yelin, Kh. |

## YIDDISH AUTHORS REPRESSED

Altman, Moshe
Arones, Feibish
Baliasne, Rive
Beregovsky, Moshe
Beretskin, Hirsh
Broderson, Moshe
Bronfman, Itsik
Buchbinder, Yosl
Dolgopolsky, Zadok
Druker Irma
Epelbojm, Mikhail
Feigin, David
Feldman, David
Frei, Sonya
Gontar, Abraham
Gordon, Shmuel
Gorochov, Gershon
Grubyan, Motl
Gutyansky, Benjamin
Halkin, Shmuel
Heler, Lipe
Hodes, Eser
Huberman, Baruch
Jo, Michael
Kahan, Abraham
Kahan, Elia
Kaminetsky, Herschl
Kantar, Yakob
Kipnis, Itsik
Lerner, Joseph
Levisky, Khaim

Lubimov, Saul
Lurye, Note
Lurye Noyakh
Maidansky, Moshe
Miler, Busi
Mindlin, Joseph
Mishritsky, Moshe
Moskhovich
Ogulnik, Menakhem
Pinchevsky, Moshe
Platner, Eisik
Polianker, Hersch
Rabin, Joseph
Rabinovich, Yekhiel
Rafes, Moshe
Rashkes, Itsik
Sabare, Natan
Shekhtman, Eli
Schulman, Zinovi
Sterberg, Yakob
Strongin, Leib
Sturman, Motl
Sudarsky, S.
Talalotsky, Motl
Teif, Moshe
Vasserman, Liuba
Veinerman, Khone
Veitsblit, I.
Velednisky, Abraham
Vendorf, Salman
Yakir, Yankl

## HEBREW AUTHORS MURDERED

| | |
|---|---|
| Alsarif, I. | Lutch, Shmuel |
| Anus G. | Mordekhayov, I. |
| Avronin | Novak, Shmuel |
| Bakhot, A. | Preigerson, Zvi |
| Borokhin, Jakob | Raisky, Pesakh |
| Borovich, Yitskhak | Reberbi, Yekhiel |
| Chiyug, Moshe | Rosenstein, Chaim-David |
| Elin, Aron | Rudin, Elisha |
| Fredkin, Ben Zion | Shvarts, Nakhum |
| Fried, Gershon | Tartakov-Khabone, Shimon |
| Friman, Abraham | Veiss, Shlomo |
| Grinberg, Israel | Zaftman, Joseph-Leib |
| Kahan, Izhak | Zborovsky, Joseph |
| Lansky, Chaim | |

## JEWISH GENERALS

305 Jewish generals and admirals served in the Red Army.
27 of them received the highest honors.

| "Heroes of the Soviet Union" | |
|---|---|
| Beskin, Israel, lieutenant general | Rybkin, Boris, major general |
| Bykhovsky, Abram, major general | Shevelyov, Mark, lieutenant general |
| Dragunsky, David, colonel general (twice) | Shmushkevich, Yakob, lieutenant general (twice) |
| Dyskin, Yefim, major general | Stern, Grigori, colonel general |
| Kontsevoy, Zinovi, major general | Vainrub, Matvey, lieutenant general |
| Kotlyar, Leonti, colonel general | Veitsman, Samuil, major general |
| Kreizer, Yakov, general of the army | Vernikov, Yakob, major general |
| Krivoshein, Semyon, lieutenant general | |
| Kremer, Simon, major general | |
| Lev, Boris, major general | |

| Jewish admirals | |
|---|---|
| Bogdanovich, Abram | Shindel, Daniil |
| Galitsky, Anatoly | Shteinberg, Genrikh |
| Genkin, Abram | Tsyrulnikov, Khaim |
| Kaidanov, Grigori | Vishnevsky, David, major general |
| Khanin, Nikolai | Volosatov, Boris |
| Konovalov, Vladimir | Yanovsky, Mikhail |
| Orlov, Aleksandr | Yurovsky. Aleksandr |
| Pilipovsky, Grigori | Zhukovsky, Oskar |

| "Heroes of socialist work" | |
|---|---|
| Gonor, Lev, major general | Rabinovich, Isaak, major general |
| Gurevich, Mikhail, major general | Sheslov, Mikhail, major general |
| Lavochkin, Semyon, major general (twice), son of a rabbi and chief architect of the Soviet air force | Slatsman, Isaak, major general |
| | Vannikov, Boris, colonel general (three times) |

| Fallen | |
|---|---|
| Berezinsky, Lev, major general 1943 | Orlov, Aleksandr, admiral 1945 |
| Borisov-Shister, Arkadi, major general 1942 | Shneider, Boris, major general 1945 |
| Broid, Yakob, major general 1942 | Stelmakh, Grigori, major general 1942 |
| Maloshitsky, Isaak, major general 1943 | Susmanovich, Grigori, major general 1944 |

**Sources:**
Leiser, Ran (pub.): *Mit der peretz-fohn. Credos-Antologye Yidish-Sovietisher Shreiber, gefaln mitn biks in hand.* New York 1982
*Yidishe Kultur,* New York, No. 7/8 and 9/10 1994
*Sovietish heymland,* No. 5, Moscow, 1975
*Shvut,* Tel Aviv, 2/1974

**General Manfred Stern**—Founder of Inter-Brigades, Defender of Madrid, Died in the Gulag

Among those Jewish generals intentionally forgotten by the Soviet historiographers is Manfred Stern. In no issue of the great Soviet encyclopedias is the name of one of the most famous generals of the Spanish Civil War mentioned.

Manfred Stern was born on January 20, 1896 in Woloka, near Czernowitz in Bukovina as the son of a Jewish small farmer. He was drafted in 1914 and was sent to the Russian front. He was a not quite twenty-year-old cadet of the Austrian army and, on August 31, 1916, he ended up as a Russian prisoner and was kept at the Tschita Camp near the Mongolian border.

After the October Revolution in 1917, Stern was involved in putting together revolutionary units in Siberia that were made up of former prisoners of war who had been freed and fought on the side of the Bolsheviks. His superiors quickly recognized the exceptional military and organizational capabilities of the young Austrian officer. He became commissar of a partisan unit that operated behind the White Guard troops of Admiral Kolchak. In the summer of 1921, he fought in the Transbaikal region against the troops of General Baron Ungern von Sternberg. In these battles, he was wounded many times. Shortly thereafter Stern was promoted to the Chief of Staff of the Far East Troops of the Red Army who fought against the Japanese Intervention Troops and Czech Legionaries.

From 1925 until 1926 he studied military science at the Frunse Military Academy in Moscow. Directly after that, he was Chief of Staff of a gunner regiment that was a part of the Moscow Proletarian Division, and later, he was an employee of the Frunse Military Academy. During this time he married Vera Krylowa and in 1926 his son, Vilmar, was born.

In 1931 Stern was accredited with the title of Soviet Commercial Attaché in New York. At that time, he managed to get the prototype of a new tank, including the construction documents that belonged with it, and had it smuggled into the Soviet Union with a ship's load of Cadillacs.

His next area of operations was China, where he often acted as the Chief Military Advisor of the Comintern at the Central Committee of the Chinese Communist Party. From Shanghai, the Communist Party directed the central Soviet region in South China in which Mao Ze-dong's Long March into North China began.

After the Civil War broke out, the Moscow leadership sent the military expert of the world revolution, Manfred Stern, to Spain. He arrived in Madrid on September 15, 1936. On the morning of November 7, the battle for Madrid began, which would decide the further destiny of the republic. The defenders of Madrid also received support from armored units, commanded by Soviet-Jewish Colonel Krivoschein, and from republican planes, commanded by General Jakob Smuschkewitsch (Douglas), which broke the air supremacy of the Fascists over Madrid. Although the XI Brigade was only made up of just 2,000 soldiers, it strengthened immensely the militia's and the people's will to defend.

As Stern arrived in Madrid with the first International Brigade that he founded, he sent an appeal to the people that said: "We have come to help you defend your capital with the same dedication as if it were the capital of every one of us."

On the night of November 9, the troops under the command of Generals Miaja and Stern, alias Kléber, succeeded in destroying the opponent at the Casa del Campo. It was clear at dawn on the morning of November 10 that Madrid had been saved. The XI Brigade conquered the entire park up to the hills of Garabitas, but had lost one third of its fighters.

General Kléber was celebrated as the Savior of Madrid by all those native to Madrid and by the foreign correspondents who had remained in the city during the fighting. The polyglot, pleasant, and dynamic forty-year-old general was a more interesting person to the media than his superior, General Miaja. Miaja was certainly bitter that Kléber harvested all the laurels, although the majority of Madrid's defenders were Spaniards.

Exactly one month later, Kléber was relieved of his command. It is not to rule out that, in the name of the Moscow "cleansing," the sword of Damocles already hung over this charismatic Comintern functionary with Jewish heritage, as his qualities were poor prerequisites to survive in the time of Stalin.

With the blink of an eye, the hero of the Spanish Civil War and defender of Madrid became an "unperson." In October 1937, Stern was ordered back to Moscow. Because he had an idea of what was before him, he divorced his wife to protect her and his son from repressions. On July 23, 1938 he was arrested and delivered to the Lefortovo prison in one step. He was immediately subjected to brutal interrogations with torture and no sleep. He confessed to spying for Germany and to belonging to an anti-Soviet, Trotskyist organization in Spain. At this time NKVD

General Jan Bersin was also called from Spain and arrested in Moscow. He accused Stern of being a Trotskyite and was later shot as a spy himself. In March 1939, Stern withdrew his self-accusations.

The Military Staff of the Supreme Court sentenced Stern to 15 years in the gulag for espionage on May 13, 1939. At the end of May 1939 he was brought by way of Vladivostok to Kolyma. It was the beginning of the tragedy lasting 15 years. Interventions and petitions by Manfred Stern's brothers, Wolf and Leo, as well as by numerous Comintern functionaries were never answered. In June 1944 Stern asked in a letter to Stalin that he be permitted to actively take part in the war. This letter also remained unanswered. On November 26, 1945 Stern was sentenced to further ten years in a special prison as a Trotskyite and spy for supposed anti-Soviet agitation among the prisoners, in other words as a dangerous criminal. The end of his imprisonment would have been on November 26, 1955.

In October 1952, Stern again wrote to Stalin. In twenty pages he described his life's path and his accomplishments as a loyal Soviet citizen and Communist, lamented his many years of undeserved imprisonment, and asked to be released. On January 24, 1954, ten months after Stalin's death, he turned to the government at the time with a request to be released, also without success. Less than one month later, on February 20, 1954, he supposedly died of cerebral hemorrhage.

## General Boris Vannikov

It is thanks to General Boris Vannikov, among others, that the Soviet Union ended the war victoriously. The Jewish general, however, counts as one of the least known and completely forgotten personalities of the Second World War today. He was born near Baku as the son of a Jewish working-class family. After he finished school, he worked as a petroleum workman and participated in the Civil War in the Caucasus as a volunteer. After his studies at the technical schools in Baku, Tbilisi and last, at the Moscow Institute of Technology, he became the leading engineer and later, director in the armaments industry. In 1937, he became Deputy Commissioner and in 1939 Commissioner for the Armaments Industry in the Soviet Union and member of the Central Committee (until 1961). Together with Lazar Kaganovich, he was the only Jewish member of the government at this time.

In 1941, a few months before the attack on the Soviet Union, as he discovered that Stalin, without his knowledge, had stopped the production of armor-piercing weapons, he protested strongly. As a punishment for this insubordination, he was arrested at the beginning of June 1941. Still in jail, he worked out the evacuation plan for the armament industry. Only three weeks later, he was released because Stalin realized that the war would be lost without his Minister of Armaments.

Vannikov received the order from Stalin to evacuate the entire heavy industry as well as the armaments industry behind the Ural Mountains, and, despite the heaviest bombardments from the German Luftwaffe, he managed to succeed completely. He was able to organize the forced production of tanks, artillery and airplanes, which made the later victory possible. He was made Lieutenant General in January 1944 and in November 1944 was promoted to General of Technical Services of the Red Army.

Stalin knew how to acknowledge Vannikov's achievements. Upon his personal order, he was made Minister and Chief of the Atom Bomb Project of the Soviet Union. He was the only one to receive the medal "Hero of Socialist Work" three times, in 1942, 1949, and 1954, which was of the same rank as the medal "Hero of the Soviet Union." He also received the Lenin-Decoration six times as well as the Suvorov and Kutuzov Decorations. In 1958, despite the highest achievements, he was released from the governing gerontocrats at only 61 years old. He died three years later and was buried at the wall of the Kremlin.

## NKVD General Alexander Orlov—Stalin's Long Arm in Spain

Among the more than 6,000 Jews who fought for the Spanish Republic, there were many antifascists who were persecuted by Stalin's thugs. There were, however, also a few offenders. The most powerful and the most important of them, NKVD General Alexander Orlov, was the supreme chief of the Soviet Secret Service in Spain. Orlov, whose civil name was Lev Feldbin, was born the son of a pious Jewish timber trader on August 21, 1895 in the White Russian Bobruisk. He was studying law in Moscow as he was summoned to the 104th Cavalry Regiment of the Tsarist army in 1916. In 1917 he became a cadet in one of the officers' schools founded by the Kerensky government, and he left it as a lieutenant. During the Civil War he was Commander of the Counter-Intelligence Service of the 12th Army, which fought against the Polish invasion in the Ukraine. He commanded a partisan unit. Later, on orders of the founder of the Cheka, Feliks Dzerzhinsky, he led the counter-espionage in Archangelsk. In 1924 he began to work for the secret service, and later became commander of the border troops in Caucasus, with its headquarters in Tissis.

In 1926, Orlov was able to succeed with several spectacular operations, disguised as a traveling salesman in France. From 1928, he coordinated and kept surveillance of secret weapons deals between the German army leadership and the Red Army. In April 1934, he traveled with an Austrian passport from Vienna to London, where he was successful with one of the greatest coups in the history of espionage; the recruitment and guiding of the agents Kim Philby, Donald Maclean, and Guy Burgess, who called themselves "The Three Musketeers." Orlov was Stalin's master spy.

A few days after the revolt, Franco agreed with the Politburo of the KpdSU to send Orlov to Spain as the Chief of the NKVD. Why was he chosen in particular? As the only Chekist in a high position, Orlov had not only had experience in counterespionage, partisan warfare, and operations abroad, he also spoke several languages. He arrived in Madrid on September 16, 1936 and was greeted with a military and political chaos. As the Spanish government left Madrid at the beginning of November, he remained as one of the few officials in his headquarters.

Spain would pay dearly for the Soviet aid that enabled the victory in the Battle of Madrid. Hundreds of Comintern agents and NKVD officers, on orders from Moscow and with Orlov in the lead, strove to take the republic, its organs, and the army under Soviet control. All real and potential political opponents were to be eliminated either by arrests or intimidation. The hunt for supposed deviants, Trotsyists, anarchists and other antifascists found its climax in May of 1937 as the FNT-FAI and the POUM were forbidden and the fighting regiments on the front were dissolved. Orlov smuggled NKVD officers into most units of the Spanish counterintelligence and into the "Military Investigation Service." His colleagues forged military documents to verify the supposed collaboration of the anarchists with the fascists. Because of these false accusations, many of those accused were kidnapped and killed. Among those was the leader of the POUM, Andres Nin. Orlov allowed his agents to act for themselves behind enemy lines.

Spain also had to pay in concrete terms for the Soviet aid: with gold. The Republic owned the fourth largest treasury of gold in the world, valued at $788 million, of which $155 million was used for purchases of weapons in the west. More than 510 tons were left over, valued at $633 million, or according to today's value $4.7 million or 10.4 million DM.

Because the Western powers practiced a strict embargo against the Republic in 1936, the Soviet Union was the only country in which the treasury of gold was securely kept and could serve as a deposit for the weapons deliveries.

Orlov received the order from Stalin himself to bring the treasury of gold, under the strictest secrecy and divided up onto four ships, to the Soviet Union. The plan was to transport the gold through partially mountainous terrain to the heavily bombed Marine base Cartagena, 500 km away. The gold was to be temporarily stored in a cave not far from the harbor, and loaded onto the ships. The almost impossible was successful. On November 9, 1936 the ships arrived in Odessa. The gold was transported immediately to Moscow, and the treasure was counted and weighed for the next year. Not until 1938 did the Spanish government receive a receipt for more than 510,079,243 grams of gold.

At the beginning of July 1938, General Orlov received the order from Moscow to drive immediately to Paris, and from there to Antwerp, where he was to take part in a conference on board the Soviet steamship "Svir." At this time, hundreds of NKVD officers were being arrested and shot under the *Yezhovshchina* (the period when Yezhov was the NKVD chief), and Orlov had a feeling that he, too, was to be liquidated on board the ship. His colleague in Spain, NKVD General Abram Slutzky, former Chief of Foreign Affairs, had been murdered in Moscow in February 1938. Instead of registering at the Soviet embassy in Paris, as he had been ordered to do, he was able to escape to Canada via Cherbourg with his wife and daughter. As Orlov disappeared, the Volkskommissar Yezhov sent a NKVD killer troop out to find him. Orlov wrote two sealed letters, addressed personally to Stalin and Yezhov, which an American relative delivered to the Soviet embassy in Paris. In the letters, Orlov threatened to reveal his secret knowledge of Stalin's and Yezhov's crimes should anything happen to him, his wife, and daughter, as well as his mother and mother-in-law still living in the Soviet Union. He surrendered to the FBI and, after twelve years of hiding, he published the book *The Secret History of Stalin's Crimes*. In reality however, he never revealed any significant secrets and only wrote that which was already known. His silence allowed the English spies he had recruited, Maclean and Burgess, to flee from England in May 1951.

On April 6, 1953, one month after Stalin's death, *Life* magazine published the first of four extracts from Orlov's book. A better time could not have been chosen; his book became a bestseller. Orlov's colleague,

NKDW General Walter Krivitsky, the Chief of Espionage for Europe, whose seat was in Holland, was also a "turncoat." He had already published his book *In Stalin's Secret Service* in 1940 at Albert de Lange, the Amsterdam publishing company in exile. On February 11, 1941 Krivitsky was found shot to death in his Washington, D.C. hotel. Orlov, however, died in April 1973 of natural causes in Cleveland, Ohio—the only one of all the high-ranking refugees of Soviet espionage.

## SIGNIFICANT PUBLICATIONS ABOUT THE JAFC

One of this book's main sources is the volume *Nepravedny sud. Posledni stalinski rasstrel* (Editor: Professor Vladimir P. Naumow. Moscow 1994), published by the committee president of the Russian Federation for the rehabilitation of the victims of political persecution, that contains— apart from secondary abbreviations—the complete transcripts of 1952 secret trail.

*The Black Years of Soviet Jewry* (Boston, Toronto 1971) by Yehoshua Gilboa is one of the early standard works about the history of the JAFC. Born in Poland, the author spent eight years in the Soviet gulag, then became an editor at the Israeli newspaper *Maariv* and, invited by professor Erich Goldhagen, worked in many American archives, where he analyzed with great accuracy the tragic destiny of the Soviet Jews between 1939 and 1953.

Professor Shimon Redlich of the Ben-Gurion-University in Beersheba wrote the first detailed history of the JAFC with his book *Propaganda and Nationalism in Wartime Russia. The Jewish Antifascist Committee in the USSR. 1941-1948* (Boulder, Colorado 1982). A native of Poland, he researched in over 20 archives and interviewed many contemporaries; only a few are still alive today. The bibliography of his book contains 150 titles.

The book, *Holocaust and Stalinism. A Documented Study of the Jewish Anti-Fascist Committee in the USSR* (Luxemburg 1995), published by Shimon Redlich, was compiled by Israeli and Russian researchers and published by the Ben-Gurion University in Beersheba, the State archives of the Russian Federation and the Yad Vashem Institute. The publication is over 500 pages and contains besides many other studies 181 official and very extensive documents from the former Soviet Union State archives, inaccessible until then, a critical apparatus and short biographies. This publication is the essential standard reference book on this subject.

Louis Rapoport's book, *Stalin's War Against the Jews. The Doctor's Plot and the Soviet Solution* (New York 1990), published 1992 in Berlin and titled *Hammer, Sichel, Davidstern. Judenverfolgung in der Sowietunion,* is based on English sources and on conversations with contemporaries. The Soviet archives were not yet accessible and the author born in Los Angeles in 1942 spoke neither Russian nor Yiddish. Beside some speculative chapters the book contents many new details about the persecution of the Jews in the USSR and about the history of the JAFC. These facts that were humiliating to the Soviet Union, were never discussed in the press nor in public. Rapoport was the publisher of the *Jerusalem Post* for 18 years. He died of a heart attack in 1991.

Gennadi Kostrychenko's book, *Imprisoned by the Red Pharaoh (V plenu n krasnowo faraona)* was published 1994 in Moscow, the English translation *Out of the Red Shadows. Anti-Semitism in Stalin's Russia* 1995, Amherst, New York. In this hitherto most thorough description of the persecution of the Jews during late Stalinism the 1954 born historian analyzes a multitude of archival material. Kostyrchenko was General Volkogonov's associate, publishing the several volumes with him including *History of World War II*; since 1992 he is the leading researcher at the former Central Party Archives in Moscow. He published several books on related topics.

Arkadi Vaksberg, born in 1939, is one of the best-known Russian journalists and vice president of the Russian Pen-club. His book *Hidden Secrets (Neraskrytyje tainy)* was published 1993 in Moscow and 1994 in New York, as *Stalin Against the Jews.* Vaksberg's Vyschinsky biography and the book *Soviet Mafia* were translated into several languages. In 1993 the Rowohlt Verlag published *Stalin's Persecutees. From the KGB's Dungeons (Die Verfolgten Stalins. Aus den Verliesen des KGB).*

Aleksandr Borshchgovsky is the only author, himself a victim of persecution of the Jews by Stalin. The well-known playwright and novelist was born 1913 in the Ukraine and is living in Moscow since 1938. He is one of the seven drama critics, who were denounced as anti-Soviet, rootless cosmopolitans in the *Pravda* of January 28, 1949. In his book *The Blood is Accused—A Documentary Novel (Obvinaetsia krov—Dokumentalnaia povest)* (Moscow 1994) Borsctschagovski analyses inquiry—and court files, which were first accessible in the nineties, as well as voluminous sources. Already in 1995 a French translation titled *L'Holocauste Inachevé, Ou comment Staline tenta d'éliminer les juifs d'URSS* exists, the German edition was titled *Orden für einen Mord (Decoration for a Murder). Stalin's Persecution of the Jews (Die Judenverfolgung unter Stalin)* was published in Berlin in 1997.

Khone Shmeruk, author of many essays and books about the history of the Soviet and East European Jews, is the most important historian and bibliographer of Jewish-Soviet literature and press. His unique reverence book *Jewish Publications in the Soviet Union (Pirsumim yehudiim bevrit hamoatsot 1917-1960)* includes 3,482 titles of Yiddish books and other publications, 400 newspapers and other periodical titles and 148 titles of publications in Russian language. Shmeruk also published the anthology, *A shpigl oyf a shteyn.* The anthology is more than 800 pages and includes the works of twelve murdered Jewish poets and authors: Axelrod, Bergelson, Charik, Der Nister, Fefer, Halkin, Hofstein, Kulbak, Kushnirov, Kvitko, Markish, and Persov. Piekarz Medel honors the life and work of the aforesaid—except Charik and Kulbak, who were already killed in 1937 and 1940. Professor Shmeruk died in July 1997 in Warsaw.

Under the leadership of the Israeli historian Benjamin Pinkus all Soviet press articles of the "black years" from 1948 to 1953 were published in seven large anthologies as a facsimile reprint: *The Jews and the Jewish People. 1948-1953. Anthology with Material from the Soviet Press (Evrei i evreiski narod. 1948-1953. Sbornik materialov sovietskoi pechati)*, Jerusalem 1973.

Matthias Vetter is one of the few German historians who researched the anti-Semitic attitudes of the Bolshevik party and of Stalin toward the Jews. His book, a doctoral thesis, *Antisemitismus und Bolschewiki. Zum Verhältnis von Sowjetsystem und Judenfeindschaft 1917-1939* (Berlin 1995), contains a wealth of material on the subject. I owe him the translation of many important and still unknown documents. Roman Brackman belongs to the group of Jewish historians and victims of Stalinist persecutions, like Aleksandr Borshchagovsky (see Brackman's biography at the end of the Introduction to the present book). In his book, *The Secret File of Joseph Stalin. A Hidden Life* (London 2002), he reveals unknown facts in the biography of Stalin as an informer and spy of the tsarist secret police, *Okhrana.* He attributes the role of Polish and Jewish officials in the uncovering of the secret files about him to the hatred for those groups which led to the Hitler-Stalin pact and World War II.

Beside the authors already mentioned several Israeli and Russian historians and scientists from other countries have written further studies that were partially published in historical magazines. To these belong Mordechai Altschuler, Avraham Greenbaum, Dov Levin, Matitjahu Mintz, Schmuel Spektor, Sima Ycikas from Israel as well as Ilya Altman, Brun-Zechowoi, Boris Chasanow, Vadim Dubson from Moscow. Andrei Sakharov supported this research during his lifetime.

ARCHIVES AND JOURNALS

Thanks to the Soviet bureaucracy millions of documents have been carefully archived and can be researched since the opening of the archives. The notes *Chranit vechno* and *Soverschenno sekretno*—"keep for ever" and "top secret"—are written or printed on the upper edge of most of the documents.

After the sudden liquidation of the JAFC in November 21, 1948 the large archives of the JAFC, of the newspaper *Ejnikeit,* of the ISPA press agency, especially material about their contacts with foreign countries and documents that were confiscated during the search of the JAFC-member's houses, were transported to the warehouses of the ministry of state security. There they were arranged for the secret trail and archived again. Because of this material besides the main indicted individuals, many other persons, amongst other things in the provinces, were arrested. In 1956 most of the material, amongst other things 1,294 volumes of files of the JAFC, was transported to the central archives of the October Revolution—today State Archives of the Russian Federation (*Gossudarstvenny archiv Rossiskoj Federazii*). More documents are at the *Rossiskoj zentr chranenija i isuchenia dokumentov noveishei istorii.* (Russian center for storage and study of documents of the recent history), the former archives of the institute for Marxism-Leninism at the ZK of the KPdSU. A 14-page-long and well-founded essay from Vadim Dubson in the magazine *JJTSU,* 16 (1991) 3 gives information about the size of the archives of the JAFC and about the broad spectrum of activities of the committee during the six years of its existence.

More than thousands of volumes of files concerning the history of the Soviet Jews as well as the confiscated archives of many Jewish organizations, among them the archives of 20 Jewish parishes, are stored at the Central Historical State Archives of the Ukraine (*Tsentralny Derzhavny Istoricheskii Arkhiv Ukrainy*) in Kiev. Other archives are, albeit not as large as in Moscow or Kiev, in the sate archives of other former Soviet republics.

Dr. Yitzhak Arad, the former director of Yad Vashem, and Dr. Schmuel Krakovski, chief archivist of this institute, have collected and researched material about the destiny of the Soviet Jews for centuries. Since the opening of the archives both traveled to the former Soviet Union for several times and sighted 1.5 million of file sheets. Thousands and thousands of copies concerning the persecution of the Jews in the

Soviet Union, the Jewish resistance and the JAFC, but also the Jewish archive of Ilya Ehrenburg, were catalogued in Jerusalem and can be researched now.

Yad Vashem also published an incomplete version of the *Schwarzbuch* in Russian, Yiddish, English and Hebraic language and a collection of hitherto unpublished subscriptions for the Russian original manuscript of the *The Unknown Black Book* (*Schwarzbuch: Neiswestnaja tschornaja kniga*), published by Arad, Pavlova, Altman, Krakovski, Spektor and others (Moscow and Jerusalem 1993). In the same year Yad Vashem published a selection of letters from Soviet Jews to Ilya Ehrenburg: Altschuler, Arad, Krakowsi (Publisher): *Soviet Jews Write to Ilya Ehrenburg* (*Sovetskije evrei pischut Ilje Erenburgu 1943-1965*).

Together with the archives of Yad Vashem this documentation builds a solid basis for serious, proceeding research that will correct many history books.

For several years scientific magazines have published studies about the Soviet Jews. *Soviet Jewish Affairs*, London, *Jews and Jewish Topics in the Soviet Union and Eastern Europe*, Jerusalem, which has been titled *Jews in Eastern Europe* since 1992, belong to it. Since 1973 *Shvut—Yahadut brit hamonatsot vemizrakh Europa* is published in Tel Aviv. The JWC publishes the magazine *Behinot Yehudey brit hamoatsot vemizrakh Europa* in Tel Aviv. In Jerusalem the yearbook *Yehudey brit hamoatsot—Alija wemetoak* is published. The 1961 founded official Yiddish-Soviet literary magazine *Sovietish heymland* is publishing many memorial articles about the murdered Yiddish writers since the sixties. In 1993 this flagship of the official Yiddish-Pro Soviet circles was stopped and substituted for the magazine *Die jidische gass*, whose 200 pages long edition from February 1993 was dedicated to the murdered writers.

# SELECTED BIBLIOGRAPHY

Ainsztein, Reuben: Der jüdische Widerstand im deutschbesetzten Osteuropa. Oldenburg 1993

Altshuler, Mordechai: Hayevsektsia bevrit hamoatsot. Tel Aviv 1980 (Hebrew)

Altshuler/Arad/Krakowski: Sovetskie evrei pishut Il'e Erenburgu 1943-1966. Jerusalem 1993

Altshuler, Mordechai/Ycikas, Sima: Were There Two *Black Books* About the Holocaust in the Soviet Union? In: JJTSU 17 (1992) l, p. 37-55

Arad/Pavlova/Altman/Krakovski/Spektor: Neizvestnaia chernaia kniga. Moscow/Jerusalem 1993

Aronson, Gregor: Russian Jewry 1917-1967. New York 1969

Aronson, Gregor: Die geshikhte fun Bund. 4 vols, New York 1960. (Yiddish)

Baron, Salow: The Russian Jews Under Tsars and Soviets. New York 1964

Berkman, Aleksandr: The Bolshevik Myth. London 1989

Black Book, The: The Nazi Crime Against the Jewish People. New York 1946

Borschtschagowski, Aleksandr: Orden für einen Mord. Die Judenverfolgung unter Stalin. Berlin 1997

Brackman, Roman: The Secret File of Joseph Stalin. A Hidden Life, London 2002

Bragin, Avraham/Ivolzov, Mikhail: Sud'ba evreiskikh mass v Sovetskom Soiuze. Moscow 1924

Brat'ia evrei vsego mira. Vystupleniia predstavitelei evreiskogo naroda na mitinge, sostoiavshchegosia v Moskve 24 avgusta 1941. Moscow 1941

Brider yidn fun der gantser veit. Reden vun vorstejer funem jidischn folk afn miting, vos is forgekumen in Moskve, dem 24 aprii 1941. Moscow 1941 (Yiddish)

Brod, Peter: Die Antizionismus- und Israelpolitik der UdSSR. Voraussetzungen und Entwicklungen bis 1956. Baden-Baden 1980

Chruschtschow erinnert sich. Introd. S. Talbott. Reinbek 1971 [Khrushev Remembers, ed. Strobe Talbott, Boston 1970]

Davies, Norman/Polonsky, Antony: Jews in Eastern Poland and the USSR 1939-1946. London 1991

Deich, Lev: Di yidn inder russisher revoluzye. Zikhroynes vegn yidn-revolutsionern. Berlin 1923 (Yiddish)

Dobroszycki, Lucjan/Gurock, Jeffrey S.: The Holocaust in the Soviet Union. Armonk, N.Y 1993

Dubson, Vadim: The Archive of the Jewish Antifascist Committee. In: JJTSU 16 (1991) 3

Ehrenburg, Ilja: Menschen, Jahre, Leben. 3 vols. Munich 1965

Ehrenburg, Ilja: Merder fun felker. Moscow 1944 (Yiddish)

Emjot, Israel: Der Birobidshaner inyen. Rochester, N.J. 1960 (Yiddish)

Evreiskii narod v bor'be protiv fashizma. Material III antifashistskogo mitinga predstavitelei evreiskogo naroda i III plenuma evreiskogo antifashistskogo komiteta v SSSR. Moscow 1945

Furier, Bernhard: Augen-Schein. Deutschsprachige Reportagen über Sowjetrußland 1917-1939. Frankfurt 1987

Garrard, John and Carol: The Bones of Berditchev. New York 1996 (Grossman-Biography)

Geizer, Matvei: Solomon Mikhoels. Moscow 1990 (Biography)

Gelbard, Arye: Der jüdische Arbeiter-Bund Rußlands im Revolutionsjahr 1917. Vienna 1982

Gilboa, Yehoshua: A Language Silenced. The Supression of Hebrew Literature and Culture in the Soviet Union. New York 1982

Gilboa, Yehoshua: The Black Years of Soviet Jewry 1939-1953. Boston, Toronto 1971

Gitelman, Zvi: Jewish Nationality and Soviet Politics. The Jewish Sections of the CPSU. 1917-1930. Princeton 1972

Goldberg, Ben Zion: Sovietnfarbend—feind oder fremd. New York 1948 (Yiddish)

Goldberg, Ben Zion: The Jewish Problem in the Soviet Union. New York 1961

Goldman, Emma: In Exile-From the Russian Revolution to the Spanish Civil War. Boston 1989

Goldman, Emma: My Disillusionment in Russia. Garden City, N.Y 1923

Grossman, Chajka (Ed.): Sefer hapartisanim heyehudiim. 2 vols. Jerusalem 1958 (Hebrew)

Grossman, Wassili/Ehrenburg, Ilja: Das Schwarzbuch. Der Genozid an den sowjetischen Juden. Ausgabe Lustiger, Arno. Reinbek 1994

Heer, Hannes/Naumann, Klaus (Ed.): Vernichtungskrieg. Verbrechen der Wehrmacht 1941 und 1944. Hamburg 1995

Heller, Otto: Der Untergang des Judentums. Die Judenfrage, ihre Kritik, ihre Lösung durch den Sozialismus. Berlin 1931

Henryk Erlich and Victor Alter, Two Heroes and Martyrs for Jewish Socialism. Hoboken 1990

Henryk Erlich un Wiktor Alter. (A gedenkbukh). New York 1951 (Yiddish)

Hertz J.S. (Ed.): Doyres bundistn. 3 vols. New York 1956-1968 (Yiddish) Hirszowicz, Lukasz: NKVD Documents Shed Light on Fate of Erlich and Alter. In: East European Jewish Affairs 22 (1992) 2, p. 65-85

Hodos, Georg Hermann: Schauprozesse.Stalinistische Säuberungen in Osteuropa 1948-1954 Frankfurt a.M. 1988

Jelen, Ch./Unger, L.: Le Grand retour. Paris 1977

Kaganovitsch, Mosche: Der yidisher onteyl in der partisaner-bavegung vun Sovietruslend. Rom T94S (Yiddish)

Katscherginski, Schmerl: Tsviscn hamer un serp. Paris 1949 (Yiddish)

Keiier, Joseph: Zwelfteraugust 1952. Jerusalem 1978 (Yiddish)

Kerler, Joseph: Beim onhejb funem sof, Samlbuch. Jerusalem 1974 (Yiddish)

Kochan, Lionel (Ed.): The Jews in Soviet Russia Since 1917. Oxford 1978

Kopelev, Lev: Im Willen zur Wahrheit. Analysen und Einsprüche. Frankfurt 1984

Kostyrchenko, Gennadi: Out of the Red Shadows. Anti-Semitism in Stalin's Russia. Amherst, N.Y 1995

Krakowski, Schmuel: Unveröffentlichte Materialien für das "Schwarzbuch" In: Grossman/Ehrenburg (Ed.): Das Schwarzbuch, p. 1085-1092

Larin, Iurii: Evrei i antisemitizm SSSR. Moscow 1929

Leneman, Leon: La Tragedie des Juifs en U.R.S.S. Paris 1959

Lenin, Vladimir I.: Werke. Berlin (DDR) 1955

Lenin, Vladimir I.: Über die Judenfrage. Moscow 1932

Levin, Nora: The Jews in the Soviet Union Since 1917. Paradox of Survival. 2 vols. New York, London 1988

Loyew, Moshe: Der sach-hakel. In: Yidishe Kultur Nr. 7/8 u. 9/10, New York 1994 (Yiddish)

Lustiger, Arno: Die Geschichte des Jüdischen Antifaschistischen Komitees der Sowjetunion. In: Grossman/Ehrenburg (Hg): Das Schwarzbuch, p. 1093-1101.

Lustiger, Arno: Schalom Libertad! Juden im spanischen Bürgerkrieg. Frankfurt 1989

Lustiger, Arno: Zum Kampf auf Leben und Tod! Vom Widerstand der Juden 1933-1945. Köln 1994

Maggs, Peter B.: The Mandelstam and Der Nister Files. An Introduction to Stalin-Era Prison and Labor Camp Records. Armonk, London 1996

Marcou, Lilly: Wir größten Akrobaten der Welt. Ilja Ehrenburg. Eine Biografie. Berlin 1996

Markish, Esther: The Long Return. New York 1978

Markish, Simon: Le Cas Grossman. Paris 1983

Meisel, Nachman (Ed.): Ykuf-Almanach. New York 1961 (Yiddish)

Messmer, Matthias: Sowjetischer und postkommunistischer Antisemitismus. Entwicklungen in Rußland, der Ukraine und Litauen. Konstanz 1997

Naumov, V. (Ed.): Nepravednii sud. Poslednii stanskii rasstrel. Stenogramma sudebnogo prozessa nad chlenami Evreiskogo Antifashistskogo Komiteta. Moscow 1994

Novick, E: Eyrope tsvishn milkhome un sholem. New York 1945 (Yiddish)

Oberländer, Erwin (Ed.): Sowjetpatriotismus und Geschichte. Dokumentation. Köln 1967

Panisch, Awigdor: In sturmishe jorn. New York 1977 (Yiddish)

Piekarz, Mendl: Biografies. In: Shmeruk, Khone (Ed.): A spiegl oyf a shtein. Jerusalem 1987 (Yiddish)

Pickhan, Gertrud: Das NKWD-Dossier über Henryk Erlich und Wiktor Alter. In: Berliner jahrbuch für osteuropäische Geschichte 1994/2, p. 155-186

Pietrow, Bianka: Stalinismus, Sicherheit, Offensive. Das Dritte Reich in der Konzeption der sowjetischen Außenpolitik 1933 and 1941. Melsungen 19S3

Pinkus, Benjamin: The Jews of the Soviet Union. The History of a National Minority. Cambridge 1988

Pinkus, Benjamin (Ed.): Shvut. Studies in Russian and East European Jewish History and Culture. Tel Aviv and Beersheba 1995

Pinkus, Benjamin, und Greenbaum, Albert A.: Russian Publications on Jews and Judaism in the Soviet Union. Jerusalem 1970

Podeh, A.: Nealmim venealamim, tsiyunim bio-bibliografiim. In: Shvut, Nr. 2., Tel Aviv 1974 (Hebrew)

Pomeranz, Aleksandr: Di sowjetishe harugey malchus. Zu seier 10-tn yortseit. Buenos Aires 1962

Porter, J.N. (Ed.): Jewish Partisans. A Documentary of Jewish Resistance in the Soviet Union. 2 vols. Washington 1982

Rafael-Tsentsiper, Arie: Bemaevak lege'ula. Sefer hazionut harussit. Tel Aviv 1956 (Hebrew)

Rapaport, Yakov: The Doctors' Plot. London 1991

Rapoport, Louis: Hammer, Sichel, Davidstern. Judenverfolgung in der Sowjetunion. Berlin 1992

Reabilitatsiia. Politicheskie protsessy 30-50-kh godov. Moscow 1991

Redlich, Shimon: Propaganda and Nationalism in Wartime Russia. The Jewish Anti-Fascist Committee in the USSR. Boulder, Colorado 1982

Redlich, Shimon (Ed.): War, Holocaust and Stalinism. A Documented History of the Jewish Anti-Fascist Committee in the USSR. Luxemburg 1995

Redlich, Shimon: The Crimean Affair. In: JJTSU 15 (1990) 2, p. 55-65

Rehabilitation of the Jewish Anti-Facist Committee, eingel. v. A. Greenbaum. In: Soviet Jewish Affairs 19 (1989) 2, p. 60-70

Ro'i, Yaacov (Ed.): Jews and Jewish Life in Russia and the Soviet Union. Ilford 1996

Ro'i, Yaacov: Soviet Decision Making in Practice. The USSR and Israel 1947-1954. New Brunswick, London 1980

Rubenstein, Joshua: Tangled Loyalties, The Life and Times of Ilya Ehrenburg. London 1996

Schapiro, Leonard: Die Geschichte der Kommunistischen Partei der Sowjetunion. Frankfurt 1962

Schapiro, Leonard: The Role of the Jews in the Russian Revolutionary Movement. In: Russian Studies. London 1986, p. 266-289

Shatunovskaia, Lidiia: Zhizn' v Kremle. New York 1982

Schauprozesse unter Stalin 1932-1952. Zustandekommen, Hintergründe, Opfer. Berlin 1990

Schein, Joseph: Arum moskver yidishn teater. Paris 1964 (Yiddish)

Shmeruk, Khone (Ed.): A shpigl oyf a stein. Jerusalem 1987 (Yiddish)

Schwarz, Solomon M.: The Jews in the Soviet Union. New York 1951

Schwarz, Schlomo: Di yidn in sovietn-farbend. Milkhome un nochmilkhomir-yorn 1933 and 1965. New York 1967 (Yiddish)

Shapiro, Gershon: Evrei—Geroi Sovetskogo Soiuza. Tel Aviv 1982

Silberner, Edmund: Kommunisten zur Judenfrage. Zur Theorie und Praxis des Kommunismus. Opladen 1983

Slowes, Chaim: Sovjetisch yidishe melukhishkeyt. Paris 1979 (Yiddish)

Sluzki, Jehuda/Kaplan, Mordechai (Ed.), Khayalim yehudiim betsvaot eyropa. Tel Aviv 1967 (Hebrew)

Smoliar, Hersch: Fun inveynik. Sikhroyna vegn Yevsektsie Tel Aviv 1978 (Yiddish)

Sudoplatov, Pavel/Sudoplatov, Anatoli: Die Handlanger der Macht. Enthüllungeneines KGB-Gerierals. Düsseldorf 1994

Spiegelglas auf Stein. Eine Anthologie unter Stalin ermordeter sowjet-jiddischer Literaten, hrsg. v. A. Jendrusch. Berlin 1992

Stalin, Jossif Wissarionowitsch: Werke. Hamburg 1971

Sto sorok besed s Molotovym. Iz dnevnika F. Chuieva. Moscow 1991

Sutzkewer, Avroin: Ilja Ehrenburg. A kapitl Zikhroynes fun die yorn 1944-1946. In: Die Goldene Kejt, Nr. 61, Tel Aviv 1967 (Yiddish)

Sverdlov, Fedor: Evrei - Generaly vooruzhonnykh sil SSSR. Moscow 1993

Tschornaja Kniga. Jerusalem 1980, Kiev 1991, Vilna 1993

Vaksberg, Arkady: Stalin Against the Jews. New York 1994

Vaksberg, Arkadi: Die Verfolgten Stalins. Aus den Verliesen des KGB. Reinbek 1993

Vetter, Matthias: Antisemiten und Bolschewiki. Zum Verhältnis von Sowjetsystem und Judenfeindschaft 1917 and 1939. Berlin 1995

Vovsi-Mikhoels, Natalia: Mon pere Salomon Mikhoels. Souvenirs sur sa vie et sa mort. Paris 1990

Wassiljewa, Larissa: Die Kreml-Frauen. Erinerungen, Dokumente, Legenden. Zürich 1994

Weber, Hermann: Weiße Flecken in der Geschichte. Frankfurt 1989

Wegner, Bernd (Ed.): Zwei Wege nach Moskau. Vom Hitler-Stalin-Pakt zum Unternehmen Barbarossa Munich 1991

Weinberg, Robert: Purge and Politics in the Periphery: Birobidzhan in 1937. In: Slavic Review 52 (1993), p. 13-28

Wiehn, Erhard Roy (Ed.): Die Schoah von Babij Jar. Das Massaker deutscher Sonderkommandos ander jüdischen Bevölkerung von Kiew, Fünfzig Jahre danach zum Gedenken. Konstanz 1991

Volkogonov, Dimitri: Lenin. Utopie und Terror. Düsseldorf 1994

Volkogonov, Dimitri: Stalin. Triumph und Tragödie. Ein politisches Porträt. Düsseldorf 1989

Zinberg, Israel: Die geshikhte fun literatur bei yidn. New York 1943 (Yiddish)

## ARTICLES AND JOURNALS ABOUT SOVIET JEWS

Bol'shaia Entsiklopediia. Moscow, 1. Vypusk. 1926-1936, 2. Vypusk 1949-1957

Branover, Gerraan (Ed.): Rossiiskaia Evreiskaia Entsiklopediia. Moscow 1994 and 1995

Buchbinder, N. A.: Materialy dlia istorii evreiskogo rabochego dvizheniia v Rossii. Materialy dlia biograficheskogo slovariia uchastnikov evreiskogo rabochego dvizheniia. Petrograd 1922

Deiateli SSSR i revoliutsionnogo dvizheniia Rossii - Entsiklopedicheskii slovar' Granat. Moscow 1989

Roth, Cecil (Ed.): Encyclopaedia Judaica. 16 vols. Jerusalem 1972

Fluk, Louise R.: Jews in the Soviet Union. An Annotated Bibliography. New York 1975

Gutman, Israel (Ed.): Enzyklopädie des Holocaust. 3 vols. Berlin 1993

Keiner, B.E./Eliashevich, D. A.: Literatura o evreiakh na russkom iazyke 1890-1947. St. Petersburg 1995

Korsch, Boris: Soviet Publications on Judaism, Zionism and the State of Israel.1984-1988. NewYork 1990

Krasnik, Vladimir: Jewish Periodicals in Russia 1960-1994. Tel Aviv 1994

Leksikon vun der neier jiddischer literatur 7 vols. New York 1956-1965 (Yiddish)

Orenstein, S.: Source Book on Soviet Jewry. An Annotated Bibliography. New York 1981

Lückert, Yelena: Soviet Jewish History. An Annotated Bibliography. New York, London 1992

Pinkus, Benjamin: Soviet Jewry 1917-1973, Bibliography. Jerusalem 1974

Pinkus, Benjamin (Ed.): Evrei i Evreiskii narod. 1948-1953. Sbornik materialov iz sovetskoi pechati. 7 vols. Jerusalem 1973

Rothenberg, Joshua: An Annotated Bibliography of Writings on Judaism, published in the Soviet Union 1960-1965. Waltham. Mss. USA 1969

Shmeruk, Khone: Pirsumim yehudiim bevrit hamoatsot. Jerusalem 1961 (Hebrew) Abkürzung: JJTSU—Jews and Jewish Topics in the Soviet Union and Eastern Europe

# NOTES

## Part 1: History of the Russian Jews

1. Around 1900, the Ashkenazi and Sephardic Jews were estimated to total 10.5 million persons, 3.9 million of whom in Russia, excluding Poland. See Hildermeier, M.: *Die jüdische Frage im Zarenreich. Zum Problem der unterbliebenen Emanzipation.* In: *Jahrbücher für Geschichte Osteuropas* 32(1984) 3p.322.

2. Hildermeier, M.: *Die jüdische Frage im Zarenreich. Zum Problem der unterbliebenen Emanzipation.* In: *Jahrbücher für Geschichte Osteuropas* 32(1984) 3p.322.

3. Ben-Sasson, Haim Hillel (Ed.): Ben-Sasson, Halm Hillel (Ed.): Geschichte des jüdischen Volkes. Von den Anfängen bis zur Gegenwart. München 1992, p. 999.

4. Polyakov, L.: Geschichte des Antisemitismus. Bd. 7. Frankfurt. 1989.Vol. 7. Frankfurt a. M. 1989.

5. See Ben-Itto, Hadassa: Die Protokolle der Weisen von Zion. Anatomie einer Fälschung. Berlin 1998.

6. Cohn, N.: Die Protokolle der Weisen von Zion. Der Mythos von der jüdischen Weltverschwörung. Köln, Berlin 1969. [*The Protocols of the Elders of Zion. The Myth of the Jewish World Conspiracy.*]

7. Löwe, H.-D.: Antisemitismus und reaktionäre Utopie. Russischer Konservatismus im Kampf gegen den Wandel von Staat und Gesellschaft 1890-1917. Hamburg 1978.

8. Deich, Lev: *Di yidn in der russischer revolutsije.* Zikhroynes vegn yiden-revolutsionern. Berlin 1923; Shapiro, L.: *The Role of the Jews in the Russian Revolutionary Movement.* In: Russian Studies. London 1986, pp. 266-289.

9. Hertz, J.S. (Ed.): *Dojres bundistn* (*Unionists*). Vol. 1. New York 1956, pp. 11-67.

10. Aronson, Gregor. (Ed.): Di geschihte fun Bund. Bd. 1. New York 1960 p. 109-122.

11. Lustiger, Arno: *Sog nit keymol* (*Don't Say Never*). Jewish Worker and Partisan Songs. Frankfurt 1990.

12. Aronson, G. (Ed.): Di geshikhte fun Bund. Bd. 2. New York 1962, p. 500,529.

13. Dubnow, S.: Dubnow, S.: Mein Leben. Berlin 1937; Grossman, Wassili/ Ehrenburg, Ilja (Ed.): Das Schwarzbuch. Der Genozid an den sowjetischen Juden. German ed. by Arno Lustiger, Reinbek 1994, p. 695.

14. Gitelman, Zvi: *Jewish Nationality and Soviet Politics. The Jewish Sections of the CPSU 1917-1930.* Princeton 1972, p. 238.

15. Stalin, Joseph Vissarionovich: Werke. Bd. 2. Hamburg 1971, p. 46.

16. Abramowitsch, R.: In zvey revolutsyes. New York 1944, S. 230.; Lustiger, Arno: Schalom Libertad! Juden im spanischen Bürgerkrieg. Köln 1991, S.218.

17. Tschernow, W.: Yidishe tu'er in der partei sozialistn revolutsionern. New York 1948, p. 219-245.

18. Volin, W.: Die unbekannte Revolution. 3 vols. Hamburg 1977.
19. Pinkus, Benjamin: *The Jews of the Soviet Union. The History of a National Minority.* Cambridge 1988, p. 77.
20. Angaben aus: Deiateii SSSR i Oktiabrskoi revoliutsii. Entsiklopediia Granat. Bd. 41, Moscow 1927-1929; siehe Vetter, Matthias: Antisemiten und Bolschewiki. Zum Verhältnis von Sowjetdiktatur und Judenfeindschaft. Berlin 1995, p. 69.
21. Lenin, Vladimir I.: Die Stellung des Bund in der Partei. In: ders.: Werke. Bd. 7. Berlin (DDR) 1956, p. 82-93, hier zitiert nach Fetscher, I. (Ed.): Marxisten gegen Antisemitismus. Hamburg 1974, p. 160.
22. Stalin, J.V: Marxismus und nationale Frage. In: Werke. vol. 2. Hamburg 1971, p. 266-333.
23. See Schiesser, Gerhard/Trautmann, Jochen: Russisches Roulette. Das deutsche Geld und die Oktoberrevolution. Berlin 1998.
24. Lenin, V.I.: Über die Judenfrage. Moscow 1932.
25. Aronson, Gregor: *Jewish Communal Life in 1917-1918.* In: Aronson, G. Russian Jewry 1917-1967. pp. 13-38.
26. Abramson, H.: *Jewish Representation in the Independent Ukrainian Governments of 1917-1920.* In: Slavic Review 50 (1991), pp. 542-550.

### Part 2: Janus-Faced Liberation:
### The Jewish Ascent After the October Revolution

1. Gorky, M.: Unzeitgemäße Gedanken über Kultur und Revolution. Frankfurt 1972, S. 57; see. Gelbard, Aiye: Der jüdische Arbeiter-Bund Rußlands im Revolutionsjahr 1917. Wien 1982, p.39 p. 173; Gitelman, Zvi: Jewish Nationality and Soviet Politics. The Jewish Sections of the CPSU 1917-1930. Princeton 1972, p. 92, p. 153, p. 170.
2. Gergel, N.: The Pogroms in the Ukraine in 1918-21. In: Yivo Annual 6 (1951), p. 237-252; Vetter, Matthias: Antisemiten und Bolschewiki. Zum Verhältnis von Sowjetsystem und Judenfeindschaft 1917-1939. Berlin 1995, p. 25.
3. Tscherikower, I.: Antisemitism un pogromen in Ukraine 1917-1918. Berlin 1923; in.: Die Ukrainer pogromen in yhr 1919. New York 1965.
4. Lenin, Vladimir I.: Werke. Vol. 29. Berlin (GDR) 1963, pp. 239, here according to Fletscher (Ed.): Marxisten gegen Antisemitismus. Hamburg 1974, p. 169.
5. Pipes, R.: Unpublished Lenin. In: Brovkin, V: The Bolsheviks in Russian Society. The Revolution and the Civil Wars. New Haven 1997, p. 201-211, hier p. 203.
6. Gitelman, Z.: Jewish Nationality and Soviet Politics; Altshuler, Mordechai: Hayevsektsia bevrit hamoatsot. Tel Aviv 1980; Smoliar, Hersch: Fun inveynik. Zikhroynes wegn Yevsektsje-. Tel Aviv 1978.

7. Glebov, V.: *Sovremennyi Antisemitizm i bor'ba s nim.* Moscow, Leningrad/Petersburg 1927, p. 6, quoted after Vetter, M.: Antisemiten und Bolschewiki. Berlin 1995

8. Shmeruk, Khone: *Pirsumim yehudim bevrit hamoatsot.* Jerusalem 1961, pp. 17-41, 406-409.

9. Gilboa, Yehoshua: *A Language Silenced. The Suppression of Hebrew Literature and Culture in the Soviet Union.* New York 1982, p. 151.

10. Larin, Iurii: *Evrei i Antisemitizm v SSSR.* Moscow 1929, p. 285.

11. Vovsi-Mikhoels, Natalia: Mon pere Salomon Mikhoels. Souvenirs sur sa vie et sa mort. Paris 1990.

12. Shmeruk, Ch.: *Pirsumim yehudiim bevrit hamatsot,* pp. 41-417; in.: Yiddish Literature in the U.S.S.R. In: Kochan, Lionel (Publ.); *The Jews in Soviet Russia since 1917.* Oxford 1978, pp. 242-280.

13. Heller, Otto: *Der Untergang des Judentums. Die Judenfrage, ihre Kritik, ihre Lösung durch den Sozialismus.* Berlin 1931, p. 192

14. Vetter, M.: *Antisemiten und Bolschewiki,* p. 165, p. 213; Larin, J.: *Jewrei i antisemitism w SSSR,* p.101., p. 238.

15. Rafaeli-Zenziper, Arie: *Bemaavak lege'ula. Sefer hazionut harussit mehamapekhat 1917 ad yamenu.* Tel Aviv 1956.

16. Heller, Otto: *Der Untergang des Judentums.* p. 190.

17. Bauer, Yehuda: *My Brother's Keeper. A History of the American Jewish Joint Distribution Committee 1929-1939.* Philadelphia 1974.

18. Gitelman, Zvi: *Jewish Nationality and Soviet Politics,* p. 431

19. Bauer, Y.: *My Brother's Keeper,* pp. 60ff.

20. Larin, Iu.: *Evrei i antisemitizm v SSSR* p. 308.

21. Quoted acc. to Heller, O.: *The Destruction of Judaism,* pp. 220f.

22. Larin, Iu.: *Evrei i antisemitizm v SSSR* p. 184.

23. Gitelman, Z.: *Jewish Nationality and Soviet Politics,* pp. 475ff.

24. *The Great Terror and the Jews.* In: *Soviet Jewish Affairs* 4 (1974) 2, pp. 80-86, Quotation pp. 82f.

25. *Sotsialisticheskii vestnik (Socialist Westerner/West),* Nr. 4-5/1939, pp. 63ff. I thank M. Vetter for the indication of this source.

26. Slowes, Chaim: *Sovietish yidishe melukhishkeyt.* Paris 1979; Emjot, Israel: *Der Birobidshaner in Jen.* Rochester, N.J. 1960.

27. Margolina, S.: *Das Ende der Lügen.* Berlin 1992.

28. The International Bundist, Zionist and general Jewish press, numerous Jewish journalists, but also authors, revolutionaries and travelers have negatively judged the Soviet system of injustice for decades. The following selected bibliography, in chronological order, gives an overview of these works.
   Lifschnitz, F.: *Die russische Revolution,* Bern 1917.
   Kossowsky, W.: *Das bolschewistische Regime in Rußland.* Ölten, Switzerland 1918.

Klibanski, H.: *Der Kommunismus in Rußland und die Diktatur des Proletariats.* Berlin 1919.

Hollitscher, A.: *Drei Monate in Sowjetrußland.* Berlin 1921.

Mirsky, B.: *Les Juifs et la Revolution* Russe. Paris 1921.

Rocker, R.: *Der Bankrott des russischen Staatskommunismus.* Berlin 1921.

Goldman, E.: *Die Ursachen des Niedergangs der russischen Revolution.* Berlin 1921.

Goldman, E.: *My Disillusionment in Russia.* Garden City, N.Y. 1923.

Berkman, A.: *Der Arbeiter in Sowjet-Rußland.* Stuttgart 1923.

Berkman, A.: *The Bolshevik Myth.* New York 1925.

Koigen, D.: *Apokalyptische Reiter* Berlin 1925.

Benjamin, W.: *Im Lande der roten Fahne* Berlin 1926.

Friedländer, O.: *Hammer, Sichel und Mütze* Berlin 1927.

Roth, J.: *Reise in Rußland* Frankfurt. 1927.

Rubiner, F.: *Für oder gegen Sowjetrußland.* Berlin 1928.

Chanin, N.: *Sowjet-Russland: wie ich hob ihr gesehn* New York 1929.

Frei, B.: *Im Land der Roten Macht. Ein sowjetrussischer Bilderbogen..* Berlin 1929.

Anonymous: *Memorandum der Zionistischen Arbeiterpartei Hitachduth in Russland an den XVI. Zionisten Kongress 1929* in Zurich.

Abramowitsch, R.: *Die politischen Gefangenen in der Sowjetunion.* Berlin 1930.

Solomon, G.: *Unter den roten Machthabern. Was ich im Dienste der Sowjets persönlich erlebte.* Berlin 1930.

Toller, E.: *Quer durch. Russische Reisebilder.* Berlin 1930.

Weichmann, H. and E.: *Alltag im Sowjetstaat. Macht und Mensch. Wollen und Wirklichkeit in Sowjet-Rußland.* Berlin 1931.

Steinberg, I.: *Gewalt und Terror in der Revolution* Berlin 1931.

Shvarts, S.: *Lénine et le mouvement syndical.* Paris 1935.

Abramowitsch, R.: *In zvey revolutsyes. Di geshikhte fun a dor.* New York 1944 (Yiddish).

Voline: *La Revolution Inconnue.* Paris 1947.

Katscherginski, S.: *Zwischn hamer un serp* Paris 1948 (Yiddish).

Koestler, A.: *Sowjetmythos und Wirklichkeit.* München 1948.

Abramowitsch, R.: *Di farbrekhns fun Stalin, di farbrekhns fon sowjetishn re-shim.* New York 1956 (Yiddish).

Weisman, B.: *Yoman ivri mivrit hamoazot.* Ramat Gan II 1973 (Hebrew).

Smoliar, H.: *Fun inveynik. zikhroynes vegn der »Evsektsje-*Tel Aviv 1978 (Yiddish).

Mendel, H.: *Erinnerungen eines jüdischen Revolutionärs.* Berlin 1979.

Axelrod, P., Martow, J., Dan, Th. In: *Sozialistische Revolution in einem unterentwickelten Land. Texte der Menschewiki* Hamburg 1981.

Rosental, E.: *Oyf vegn un umvegn* Tel Aviv 1982 (Yiddish).

Salzman, M.: *Menschn un geshehnishn* Tel Aviv 1988 (Yiddish).

*Arno Lustiger*

## Part 3: Prehistory and Foundation of the JAFC

1.  Stalin, Jossif Wissarionowitsch: *Werke.* Vol. 8. Hamburg 1971, p. 26.
2.  Molotov, Viacheslav: *Konstitutsiia sotsializma. Rech' na Chrezvychainom VII Vsesoiuznom s"ezde sovetov 29 noiabria 1936 g.* Moscow 1937, p. 21; quoted by Vetter, Matthias: *Antisemiten und Bolschewiki. Zum Verhältnis von Sowjetsystem und Judenfeindschaft 1917-1939* p. 346.
3.  Vetter, M.: *Antisemiten und Bolschewiki,* pp. 297
4.  Trocci, Lev: *Thermidor und Antisemitismus.* In: Fetscher, I. (Ed.): *Marxisten gegen Antisemitismus.* Hamburg 1974, pp. 179-188; Nevada, Joseph: *Trotsky and the Jews.* Philadelphia 1972, pp. 186.
5.  *Prozeßbericht über die Strafsache des trotzkistisch-sinowjewistischen terroristischen Zentrums* Moscow 1936, p. 39.
6.  *Leitartikel der Prawda vom 19. 3. 1935 und vom 15. 1. 1937.* In: Oberländer, Erwin (Ed.): *Sowjetpatriotismus und Geschichte. Dokumentation.* Cologne 1967, pp. 62.
7.  Markish, Esther: *The Long Return.* New York 1978, p. 78.
8.  *Sto sorok besed s Molotovym. Iz dnevnika F. Chuieva.* Moscow 1991, p. 274.
9.  Churchill, Winston S.: *The Second World War. Memoirs.* Vol. 1, *The Gathering Storm* Boston. 1948, pp. 366-367.
10. Gnedin, J.: *Das Labyrinth. Hafterinnerungen eines führenden Sowjetdiplomaten* Freiburg i.Br. 1987, pp. 71.
11. Lustiger, Arno: *Shalom Libertad! Juden im spanischen Bürgerkrieg* Frankfurt a.M. 1989, pp. 104.
12. Vaksberg, Arkadi: *Die Verfolgten Stalins. Aus den Verliesen des KGB* Reinbek 1993, pp. 43ff; Vaksberg Arkady: *Stalin Against the Jews.* New York 1994, p. 89.
13. Vaksberg, A.: *Die Verfolgten Stalins.,* pp. 58.; *Stalin Against the Jews,* p. 94.
14. Novyi mir, Nr. 9, September 1966, p. 24.
15. Gross, J.: *Die Sowjetisierung Ostpolens, 1939-1941.* In: Wegner, Bernd: (Ed.) *Zwei Wege nach Moskau. Vom Hitler-Stalin-Pakt zum »-Unternehmen Barbarossa«.* Munich 1991, pp. 56-74.
16. Sierkierski, M.: *The Jews in Soviet-Occupied Eastern Poland at the End of 1939. Numbers and Distributions.* In: Davies, Norman/Polonsky, Anthony: *Jews in Eastern Poland and in the USSR.* London 1991, pp. 110-117.
17. Grossman, M.: *In the Enchanted Land. My Seven Years in Soviet Russia.* Tel Aviv 1960, pp. 55f.
18. Shvarts, S.: *Evrei v Sovetskom Soiuze s nachala vtoroi mirovoi voiny (1939-1965).* New York 1966, pp. 30ff.
19. Wood, E.T./Jankowski, S.: *Jan Karski - Einer gegen den Holocaust. Als Kurier in geheimer Mission.* Gerlingen 1977.
20. Karski's Report in Davies, N./Polonsky, A.: *Jews in Eastern Poland and the USSR,* pp. 260-274, Quotation pp. 265f.
21. Sandkühler, T.: *Endlösung,, in Galizien. Der Judenmord in Ostpolen und die Rettungsinitiativen von Berthold Beitz 1941-1944.* Bonn 1996, p. 62.

22. Memorandum from Gross, J.: *Und wehe, du hoffst... Die Sowjetisierung Ostpolensnach dem Hitler-Stalin-Pakt 1939-1941*. Freiburg i.Br. 1988, pp. 179f.

23. Schocher, S.: *Polish Jewish Officers Who Were Killed in Katyn*. In: Dobroszycki, Lucjan/Gurock, Jeffrey S. (Ed.): *The Holocaust in the Soviet Union*. Armonk, N.Y. 1993, pp. 237-247.

24. Meirtchak, Benjamin: *Jewish Military Casualties in the Polish Armies in World War II. Jewish Officers, Prisoners of War Murdered in Katyn Crime*. Tel Aviv 1997.

25. Davies, N./Polonsky, A.: *Jews in Eastern Poland and the USSR*, pp. 276-300, Quotation pp. 282f. The document was originally written in German and is here translated back by the author. Where Kleinbaum speak of the GPU, the correct abbreviation would be NKVD.

26. Pinchuk, B.: *Soviet Media on the Fate of Jews in Nazi-Occupied Territory (1939-1941)*. In: Yad Vashem Studies 11 (1976), pp. 221-233, Quotation pp. 229f.

27. Stalin, J.: *Reden, Ansprachen, Tagesbefehle aus den Jahren 1939-1943* Celerina 1943, pp. 71ff.

28. Lustiger, A.: *Shalom Libertad!* p. 79.

29. Erlich and Alter: *A gedenkbukh*. New York 1951 (Yiddish).

30. Pickhan, Gertrud: *Das NKWD-Dossier über Henryk Erlich und Wiktor Alter*. In: *Berliner Jahrbuch für osteuropäische Geschichte 1994/2*, pp. 155-186.

31. Henryk Erlich and Viktor Alter. *Two Heroes and Martyrs for Jewish Socialism*. Hoboken 1990, pp. 71.

32. Pickhan, G.: *The NKWD Dossier*, p. 179.

33. Reprint by Henry Erlich and Viktor Alter. *Two Heroes*, pp. 184ff.

34. Erlich and Alter: *A gedenkbuch.*, pp. 188-199.

35. Kot, S.: *Listy z Rosji do Generala Sikorskiego*. London 1956, p. 204; quoted by Pinkus, Benjamin: *The Jews of the Soviet Union. The History of a National Minority*. Cambridge 1998, pp. 140, 340.

36. Reprinted by: Redlich, Shimon (Pub.): *War, Holocaust and Stalinism. A Documented History of the Jewish Anti-Fascist Committee in the USSR*. Boulder, Colorado, pp. 169f.

37. Leneman, Léon: *La Tragédie des Juifs en U.R.S.S* Paris 1959, p. 108.

38. Hirszowicz, Lukasz: *NKVD Documents Shed Light on Fate of Erlich and Alter*. In: East European Jewish Affairs 22 (1992) 2, pp. 65-85.

39. Erlich and Alter, *A gedenkbukh* pp. 200-229.

40. Schtschit i Metsch, 3 Sept. 1992, p. 13; Sudoplatov, Pavel and Anatolii: *Missions Spéciales*. Paris 1994, p. 360.

41. These and the following quotations in Unison, No. 1 of 7 June 1942; also in: *Brider yidn fon der gantser Welt*. Moscow 1941.

42. Naumov, Vladimir (Publ *Nepravedny sud. Poslednii stalinski rasstrel. Stenogramma sudebnogo protsessa nad chlenami Evreiskogo Antifashistskogo Komiteta* Moscow 1994, p. 147.

43. *Statement on the JAFC's Activities. Documents from the Private Archives of Lozovsky, Moscow*.

44. Aly, G.: *Endlösung—Volkerverschiebung und der Mord an den europäischen Juden.* Frankfurt a.M. 1995.

45. Förster, J.: *Das Unternehmen "Barbarossa« als Eroberungs- und Vernichtungskrieg* In: Boog. H. (Ed.): *Der Angriff auf die Sowjetunion.* Frankfurt a.M. 1991, pp. 498-538, Quotation p. 526.

46. Michaelis, M.: "Stalin, Ribbentrop, and the Jews." In: *Bulletin on Soviet and East European Jewish Affairs,* 5 (May 1970), pp. 91-93; Vetter, M.: *Antisemiten und Bolschewiki,* p. 352.

47. Longerich, P.: *Massenmord zur -Endlösung«. Die Erschießung von jüdischen Zivilisten in den ersten Monaten des Ostfeldzuges im Kontext des nationalsozialistischen Judenmords,* in: Wegner, B.: (Pub.): *Zwei Wege nach Moscow,* pp. 251-274.

48. Pinchuk, B.: "Was There a Soviet Policy for Evacuating the Jews? The Case of the Annexed Territories." In: *Slavic Review* 39 (1989), pp. 44-55.

49. Luks, Leonid: *Die Entstehung der kommunistischen Faschismustheorie.* Stuttgart 1984, pp. 200ff.

50. Saslavskii, D.: *Evrei v SSSR.* Moscow 1933, pp. 4.; Trainin, I. *Bespravie i proizvol v fashistskoi Germanii,* Moscow-St. Petersburg, 10ff.

51. Wiehn, Erhard Roy (Ed.): *Die Schoah von Babij Jar. Das Massaker deutscher Sonderkommandos an der jüdischen Bevölkerung von Kiew, fünfzig Jahre danach zum Gedenken.* Constance 1991.

52. Heer, Hannes: Killing Fields. *"Die Wehrmacht und der Holocaust."* In: Heer, Hannes/Naumann, Klaus (Pub.): *Vernichtungskrieg. Verbrechen der Wehrmacht 1941 bis 1944* Hamburg 1995, pp. 57-77.

53. Herzstein, R.: "Anti-Jewish Propaganda in the Orel Region of Great Russia 1942-1943. The German Army and Its Russian Collaborators." In: *Simon Wiesenthal Center Annual 6* (1989), pp. 33-56.

54. Förster, J.: *"Die Sicherung des -.Lebensraumes"* In: Boog, H. a.o. (Pub.): *The Attack on the Soviet Union.* Frankfurt a.M. 1991, pp. 1227-1287, Quotation pp. 1237.

55. Kirchner, K.: *Flugblätter aus Deutschland 1941* Bibliography/Catalog. Erlangen 1987, p. 85.

56. Laqueur, W. *Was niemand wissen wollte: Die Unterdrückung der Nachrichten über Hitlers "Endlösung"* Frankfurt a.M. 1981, pp. 88ff.

57. Fedorov, Ia.: *Antisemitizm, otravlennoe oruzhie fashizma.* Leningrad 1941.

58. Struve, V.: *Fashistskii antisemitizm perezhitok kannibalizma* Moscow, Leningrad 1941.

59. Kopelev, Lev: *Jüdischen Frage in der UdSSR«. In: ders.: Im Willen zur Wahrheit. Analysen und Einsprüche.* Frankfurt a.M. 1984, pp. 68-92, Quotation p. 72.

60. Grossman, Vassily/Ehrenburg, Ilya (Pub.): *Das Schwarzbuch. Der Genozid an den sowjetischen Juden* German Edition ed. by Lustiger, Arno. Reinbek 1994, pp. 884ff.

## Part 4: JAFC Activities Inside and Outside the Soviet Union

1.  *Evreiskii narod v bor'be protiv fashizma. Materialy III antifashistskogo mitinga predstavitelei evreiskogo naroda i III plenuma evreiskogo antifashistskogo komiteta v SSSR.* Moscow 1945, p. 67

2.  Collected in: *Soobshcheniia Sovetskogo Informbiuro* 8 Vol. Moscow 1944 to 1945; Soviet Government Statements on Nazi Atrocities. London, New York 1946.

3.  Bonwetsch, B.: *"Der »Große Vaterländische Krieg«: Vom deutschen Einfall bis zumsowjetischen Sieg."* In: *Handbuch der Geschichte Rußlands.* Vol. 3. 2. Stuttgart 1992, pp. 910-1008, here pp. 947ff.

4.  *Pravda,* 25 May 1942, quoted in Redlich, Shimon (Pub.): *War, Holocaust and Stalinism. A Documented History of the Jewish Anti-Fascist Committee in the USSR.* Luxembourg 1995, pp. 203ff.

5.  Redlich, S.: *War, Holocaust, and Stalinism,* pp. 207f.

6.  Accountability Report about the Activity of the JAFC, Document from the Private Archive of Lozovsky, Moscow.

7.  *Evreiskii narod v bor'be protiv fashizma. Materialy III antifashistskogo mitinga* Moscow 1945, p. 74.

8.  Unison, 15 March 1943.

9.  Redlich, S.: *War, Holocaust, and Stalinism,* pp. 214f.

10. Lustiger, Arno: *Zum Kampf auf Leben und Tod! Vom Widerstand der Juden 1933-1945.* Munich 1997, pp. 207-232.

11. Ibid., pp. 5f.

12. The author was able to work through publications of the Yiddish-Soviet Unison newspaper, *Eynikeyt*) and the magazine of the same name published in New York, in Jerusalem in the Archive of Yad Vashem.

13. Gilboa, Yehoshua: *The Black Years of Soviet Jewry. 1939-1953.* Boston, Toronto 1971, p. 52.

14. Accountability Report about the Activities of the JAFC. Document from the Private Archive of Lozowski, Moscow.

15. See Naumov, Vladimir (Pub) *Nepravedny sud. Poslednii stalinskii rasstrel. Stenogramma sudebnogo protsessa nad chlenami Evreiskogo Antifashistskogo Komiteta.* Moscow 1994, pp. 234f. and 334f.

16. *Calling all Jews to Action,* published by the Jewish Fund for Soviet Russia. London 1943.

17. "Yiddish Culture, January and February 1944," quoted in Gilboa, Y.: *The Black Years of Soviet Jewry,* p. 53.

18. Kostyrchenko, Gennadii: *V plenu u krasnogo faraona.* Moscow 1994, pp. 21f. Vaksberg, Arkady: *Stalin Against the Jews.* New York 1994, pp. 134f.

19. Ibid., pp. 9ff.

20. Naumov, V.: (Pub.): Nepravednyi sud, pp. 209.

21. Ibid., pp. 317f.

22. Markish, Simon: *Le Cas Grossman.* Paris 1983, p. 57.

23. Ehrenburg, Ilya: *Menschen Jahre, Leben, 1942-1965.* Vol. 3. Munich 1965, pp. 131f.
24. Redlich, S.: *War, Holocaust, and Stalinism,* p. 289.
25. Naumov, V.: (Ed.) *Nepravednyi sud,* pp.223f.
26. Ibid., pp. 130f.
27. Redlich, S.: *War, Holocaust, and Stalinism,* p. 67.
28. Naumov, V. (Ed.) *Nepravednyi sud,* pp. 223f.
29. See Ben-Sasson, Haim Hillel (Pub.): *Geschichte des jüdischen Volkes. Von den Anfängen bis zur Gegenwart* Munich 1992, p. 1274.
30. Rubenstein, Joshua: *Tangled Loyalties. The Life and Times of Ilya Ehrenburg.* London 1996, p. 205.
31. Redlich, S.: *War, Holocaust, and Stalinism,* pp. 38f.
32. Altshuler/Arad/Krakowski (Ed.) *Sovetskie evrei pishut Il'e Erenburgu 1943-1966.* Jerusalem 1993, p. 152.
33. Shvarts, S.: *Evrei v Sovetskom Soiuze s nachala vtoroi mirovoi voiny,* p. 160; Kostyrchenko, G.: *V plenu u krasnogo faraona,* pp. 52ff.
34. Altshuler, Mordechai: "Anti-Semitism in the Ukraine Toward the End of the Second World War." In: *Jews in Eastern Europe* 22 (1993) 3, pp. 40-81.
35. Quotations from *Eynikeyt,* No. 2.
36. Redlich, S.: *War, Holocaust, and Stalinism,* pp. 80f.
37. Ibid., p. 50.
38. Sverdlov, Feodor: *Evrei—Generaly vooruzhennykh sil SSSR.* Moscow 1993.
39. Trepper, Leopold: *Die Wahrheit. Ich war der Chef der Roten Kapelle..* Munich 1975, p. 345.
40. Ibid., pp. 369-378.
41. Biography of David Kamy, see: Lustiger, Arno: *Schalom Libertad! Juden im spanischen Bürgerkrieg.* Cologne 1991, pp. 371-373.
42. Dallin, A.: *Deutsche Herrschaft in Rußland, 1941-1945. Eine Studie über Besatzungspolitik.* Düsseldorf 1981.
43. Marie, Jean-Jacques: *Les peuples déportés d'Union Soviétique.* Paris 1995, pp. 93-96, 160-164.
44. Sudoplatov, Pavel and Anatolii: *Missions Spéciales. Mémoires du Maître-espion soviétique Pavel Soudoplatov.* Paris 1994, p. 362.
45. See Rapoport, Louis: *Hammer, Sickle, Star of David. Judenverfolgung m der Sowjetunion.* Berlin 1992, p. 132.
46. Naumov, V. (Ed.) *Nepravednyi sud,* p. 28.
47. Kostyrchenko, G. *V plenu u krasnogo faraona,* pp. 44ff.
48. Ibid., pp. 174ff.
49. Vaksberg, A.: *Stalin Against the Jews,* pp. 122ff.
50. Grossman, Vassily/Ehrenburg, Ilya (Publ.): *Der Genozid an den sowjetischen Juden* German Edition by Lustiger, Arno. Reinbek 1994, pp. 443ff.
51. Redlich, Shimon: *Propaganda and Nationalism in Wartime Russia. The Jewish Anti-Fascist Committee in the USSR.* Boulder, Colorado 1982, p. 56.

52. Gilboa, Y.: *The Black Years of Soviet Jewry*, p. 241f; Dubson, Vadim: The Archive of the Jewish Anti-Fascist Committee. In: JJTSU 16 (1991) 3, p. 73.
53. Naumov, V.: (Ed.) *Nepravednyi sud*, p. 136.
54. *Chruschtschow erinnert sich. (Khrushchev Remembers)*. Ed. by S. Talbot. Reinbek 1971, p. 264.
55. Vaksberg, A.: *Stalin Against the Jews*, p. 124.
56. Redlich, S.: *War, Holocaust, and Stalinism*, p. 459.
57. Redlich, S.: *War, Holocaust, and Stalinism*, pp. 264ff. Identical text of 21 Feb. 1944 to Molotov in Kostyrchenko, G.: *V plenu u krasnogo faraona*, pp. 44ff.

## Part 5: The Fate of the JAFC After the War

1. Dubson, Vadim: The Archive of the Jewish Antifascist Committee. In: JJTSU 16 (1991) 3, pp. 64-77.
2. *Evreiskii narod v bor'be protiv fashizma. Materialy III antifashistskogo mitinga predstavitelei evreiskogo naroda i III plenuma evreiskogo antifashistskogo komiteta SSSR.* Moscow 1945, pp. 89f.
3. Redlich, Shimon (Pub.): *War, Holocaust, and Stalinism. A Documented History of the Jewish Anti-Fascist Committee in the USSR.* Luxembourg 1995, p. 350.
4. Altshuler, Mordechai/Ycikas, Sima: *Were there two Black Books about the Holocaust in the Soviet Union?* In: JJTSU 17 (1992) 1, pp. 37-55.
5. Naumov, Vladimir (Pub.): *Nepravednyi sud. Poslednii stalinskii rasstrel. Stenogramma sudebnogo protsessa nad chlenami Evreiskogo Antifashistskogo Komiteta.* Moscow 1994, pp. 189f.
6. Ibid., p. 31.
7. Altman, L.: *Das Schicksal des "Schwarzbuchs"* In: Grossman, Vassily/Ehrenburg Ilya (Pub.): *Das Schwarzbuch*. German Edition ed. by Lustiger, Arno. Reinbek 1994. pp. 1063-1097, here p. 1069.
8. Ibid., p. 1069.
9. Redlich, S.: *War, Holocaust, and Stalinism*, pp. 355ff.
10. Altman, L.: *The Fate of the "Black Book."* In: Grossman, Vassily/Ehrenburg, Ilya (Pub.): *Das Schwarzbuch* p. 1073.
11. Ibid., p. 366.
12. Copy of the documents in the archives of Yad Vashem.
13. Altman, L.: *Das Schicksal des "Schwarzbuchs"* In: Grossman, W./Ehrenburg, I. (Pub.) : *Das Schwarzbuch* p. 1075.
14. Grossman, W./Ehrenburg, I. (Pub.): *Das Schwarzbuch*, pp. 35, 47ff., 768ff., 66, 77ff., 100, 114, 107, 739, (139), 149, 153ff., 180, 254f., 208ff., 366, 395.
15. Arad/Pavlova/Altman (Ed.): *Neizvestnaia Chernaia Kniga*. Moscow, Jerusalem 1994, p. 32.
16. Brod, Peter: *Die Antizionismus- und Israelpolitik der UdSSR. Voraussetzungenund Entwicklungen bis 1956*. Baden Baden 1980, pp. 43ff.

17. Gilboa, Yehoshua: *The Black Years of the Soviet Jewry 1939-1953*. Boston, Toronto 1971, p. 70.
18. Redlich, S.: *Propaganda and Nationalism*, p. 148.
19. Ro'i, Yaacov: *Soviet Decision Making in Practice. The USSR and Israel 1947–1954*. New Brunswick, London 1980, pp. 74, 112f.
20. Brod, P.: *Die Antizionismus- und Israelpolitik der UdSSR*., pp. 70f.
21. Redlich, S.: *War, Holocaust, and Stalinism*. pp. 122ff., 373ff.
22. Copy of the documents from the archives of Yad Vashem.
23. Naumov, V.: (Ed.) *Nepravednyi sud*, p. 63.
24. Quoted after Ehrenburg, Ilya: *Menschen, Jahre, Leben*. Munich 1965. Vol. 3, p. 358.
25. Mercou, Lilly: *Wir größten Akrobaten der Welt. Ilja Ehrenburg. Eine Biografie*. Berlin 1996, p. 257.
26. Kostyrchenko, Gennadii: *V plenu u krasnogo faraona*. Moscow 1994, p. 121.
27. Meir, G.: *Mein Leben*. Frankfurt a.M. 1983, pp. 255f.
28. Copy of the meeting minutes at the archive of Yad Vashem.
29. Redlich, S.: *War, Holocaust, and Stalinism*, pp. 79ff.
30. Oberländer, Erwin (Pub.): *Sowjetpatriotismus und Geschichte. Dokumentation*. Cologne 1967, p. 80.
31. Ehrenburg, I.: *Menschen, Jahre, Leben* Vol. 3, pp. 209f.
32. Kostyrchenko. G.: *V plenu u krasnogo faraona*, p. 60.
33. Redlich, S.: *War, Holocaust, and Stalinism*, pp. 425ff.
34. Kostyrchenko, G.: *V plenu u krasnogo faraona*, p. 62.
35. This and the following judgments are according to Redlich, S.: *War, Holocaust, and Stalinism*, pp. 436-464.
36. Copy of the records of October 21, 1948 in the archive of Yad Vashem.
37. Kostyrchenko, G.: *V plenu u krasnogo faraona*, p. 125.
38. Rapoport, Louis: *Judenverfolgung in der Sowjetunion* Berlin 1992, p. 98.
39. Vovsi-Mikhoels, Natalia: *Mon père Solomon Michoëls. Souvenirs sur sa vie et sa mort*. Paris 1990, p. 199.
40. Redlich, S.: *War, Holocaust, and Stalinism*, pp. 339ff.
41. Vovsi-Mikhoels, N.: *Mon père Solomon Michoëls*, p. 219.
42. Wassiljewa, Larissa: *Die Kreml-Frauen. Erinerungen, Dokumente, Legenden*.Zurich, pp. 108ff.
43. Kostyrchenko, G.: *V plenu u krasnogo faraona*, p. 95.
44. Ibid., p. 84ff.; Vaksberg, Arkady: *Stalin Against the Jews*. New York 1994, pp. 154ff.
45. Volkogonov, Dimitri: *Triumph und Tragödie. Ein politisches Porträt*. Düsseldorf 1989, pp. 232f.
46. Allilujewa, Svetlana: *Zwanzig Briefe an einen Freund*. Vienna 1967, p. 257.
47. Ibid., p. 276; Allilujewa, Svetlana: *Das erste Jahr*. Vienna 1969, p. 25.
48. Statements by Kamarov of 15 to 22 June 1953, quoted from the file about the cancellation of the proceedings of 1955, see Naumov, V.: (Ed.) *Nepravednyi sud*, pp. 389f.

49. Ibid., pp. 213f.
50. Shatunovskaia, Lidiia : Zhizn' v Kremle. New York 1982, pp. 332ff.
51. Allilujewa, S.: *Das erste Jahr*, pp. 141f.
52. Redlich, S.: *War, Holocaust, and Stalinism*, p. 449.
53. Vovsi-Mikhoels, N.: *Mon père Solomon Michoëls*, p. 223.
54. Naumov, V.: (Ed.) *Nepravednyi sud*, p. 62.
55. Vaksberg, A.: *Stalin Against the Jews*, p. 171.
56. Naumov, V.: (Ed.) *Nepravednyi sud*, p. 309.

### Part 6: Open War Against the Jews—The Last Years of Stalin's Dictatorship

1. From Israeli historian Yeoshua Gilboa in his most important work *The Black Years of Soviet Jewry, 1939-1953* (Boston, Toronto 1971).
2. Reprinted in: Pinkus, Benjamin (Ed.): *Evrei i evreiski narod. 1948-1953. Sbornik materialov iz sovetskoi pechati.* Jerusalem 1973, p. 1382.
3. Kostyrchenko, Gennadi: *V plenu u krasnowo faraona.* Moscow 1994, pp. 184ff.
4. Pinkus, B. (Ed.): *Evrei i evreiski narod*, pp. 1417ff.
5. See Borshchagovsky, Aleksandr: *Orden für einen Mord. Die Judenverfolgung unter Stalin* Berlin 1997, p. 299.
6. Simonow, K.: *Aus der Sicht meiner Generation, Gedanken über Stalin* Berlin 1990, pp. 207f.
7. Ehrenburg, Ilya: *Menschen, Jahre, Leben* Vol. 3, Munich 1965, p. 366; in: Ljudi, Gody, Shisn. Vol. 3. Moscow 1990, pp. 103f.
8. *Kosmopolitismus im Wandel der sowjetischen Interpretationen. In: Osteuropa-Info 55 (1984) 1 (Juden und Antisemitismus in Osteuropa)*, pp. 40f.
9. Rapoport, Louis: *Hammer, Sichel, Davidstern. Judenverfolgung in der Sowjetunion.* Berlin 1992, p. 103.
10. Nekritsch, Aleksandr: *Entsage der Angst. Erinnerungen eines Historikers.* Frankfurt 1983, pp. 54ff.
11. Kostyrchenko, G.: *V plenu u krasnogo faraona* pp. 210ff.
12. *Chruschtschow erinnert sich. (Khrushchev Remembers.)* Published by S. Talbot. Reinbek 1971, p. 267.
13. Kostyrchenko, G.: *V plenu u krasnogo faraona*, pp. 263ff.
14. *Bol'shaia Sovetskaia Entsiklopediia*, 1 Ed., Vol. 24 (1932), Col. 149ff; *Bol'shaia Sovetskaia Entsiklopediia*, 2 Ed., Vol. 15 (1952), p. 378.
15. Pinkus, Benjamin: *The Jews of the Soviet Union. The History of a National Minority.* Cambridge 1998, p. 149.
16. "The Agony and Liquidation of the Jewish State Theater of Byelorussia (1948-1949)." In: *Jews in Eastern Europe* 25 (1994) 3, pp. 64-72.
17. Kostyrchenko, G.: V plenu u krasnogo faraona, pp. 162ff.
18. Pinkus, Benjamin (Ed.) *Evrei i evreiskii narod*, p. 219.

19. Emjot, Israel: *Der Birobidshaner inyen* Rochester, N.J. 1960; Kerler Joseph: Twelfth August 1952. Jerusalem 1978.

20. Kostyrchenko, G.: *V plenu u krasnogo faraona*, pp. 168ff.

21. Naumov, Vladimir (Ed.) *Nepravednyi sud. Poslednii stalinskii rassrel. Stenogramma sudebnogo protsessa nad chlenami Evreiskogo Antifashistskogo Komiteta.* Moscow 1994, p. 116.

22. Meir, G.: *Mein Leben.* Frankfurt a.M. 1983, pp. 258f.

23. See the protocol in the interpretation filled with mistakes by Vassiljewa, Larissa: *Die Kreml-Frauen. Erinnerungen, Dokumente, Legenden* Zurich 1994.

24. Borshchagovsky, A.: *Orden für einen Mord*, pp. 196ff.

25. Radzinsky, E.: *Stalin.* New York 1996, p. 532.

26. Extracts from the Protocols by Vassilyjewa, L.: *Die Kreml-Frauen*, pp. 250ff.

27. Sto sorok besed s Molotovym. Iz dnevnika F. Chuyeva. Moscow 1991, p. 473.

28. *Chruschtschow erinnert sich (Khrushchev Remembers)*, p. 314.

29. Markish, Esther: *The Long Return.* New York 1978, pp. 154ff.

30. "The Liquidation of the Newspaper Eynikayt (Unison) and Repressions in Leningrad," in: *JJTSU* 16 (1991) 3, pp. 57-59.

31. Rapoport, L.: *Hammer, Sichel, Davidstern* pp. 138ff.; Robeson, P. Jr.: "How My Father Last Met Itsik Fefer." In: *Jewish Currents*, November 1981, p. 4.

32. Markish, E.: *The Long Return*, p. 240.

33. Naumov, V. (Ed.): Nepravednyi sud. p. 272.

34. Ibid., p. 194.

35. Borshchagovsky, A.: *Orden für einen Mord*, pp. 114ff.

36. Isvestija CC, Nr. 12, December 1989, quoted according to: *Schauprozesse unter Stalin1932-1952. Zustandekommen, Hintergründe, Opfer.* Berlin 1990, pp. 403-411.

37. Kostyrchenko, G.: *V plenu u krasnogo faraona*, pp. 139f.

38. Sudoplatov, Pavel/Sudoplatov, Anatoly: *Die Handlanger der Macht. Enthüllungen eines KGB-Generals.* Düsseldorf 1994, p. 359.

39. Borshchagovsky, A.: *Orden für einen Mord*, p. 122.

40. Introduction to: Naumov, V. (Ed.) Nepravednyi sud, p. 7.

41. Borshchagovsky, A.: *Orden für einen Mord*, pp. 183f.

42. Kostyrchenko, G.: *V plenu u krasnogo faraona*, pp. 298ff.

43. Etinger, I.: "The Doctors' Plot: Stalin's Solution to the Jewish Question." In: Ro'i, Yaacov (Pub.): *Jews and Jewish Life in Russia and the Soviet Union.* Ilford 1996, pp.103-124.

### Part 7: The Trial

1. In the draft of the indictment that had been given to me for examination by the Hamburger Institut für Sozialgeschichte. The verbatim quotations from the trial are from: Naumov, Vladimir (Ed.): *Nepravednyi sud. Poslednii stalinskii rasstrel. Stenogramma sudebnogo protsessa nad chlenami Evreiskogo Antifashistskogo Komiteta.* Moscow 1994, pp. 33, 48, 61, 111, 234, 249f, 323, 338, 364.

2. Naumov, V.: (Ed.): *Nepravednyi sud,* pp. 234f.

3. Borschtschagowski, Aleksandr: *Orden für einen Mord. Die Judenverfolgung unter Stalin.* Berlin 1997, p. 371; Vaksberg, Arkady: *Stalin Against the Jews.* New York 1994, pp. 228ff.

4. Izvestiia CC, Nr. 12, December 1989, quoted from: *Schauprozesse unter Stalin 1932-1952. Zustandekommen, Hintergründe, Opfer. Berlin* 1990, pp. 403-411.

5. Judgment by: Naumov, V.: (Ed.) *Nepravednyi sud,* pp. 375ff.

6. Leneman, Leon: *La Tragédie des Juifs en U. R. S. S.* Paris 1959, p. 67.

7. Kostyrchenko, Gennadi: *V plenu u krasnogo faraona,* p. 222.

8. Comp. to Naumov, V. (Ed.) *Nepravednyi sud,,* pp. 388ff.

9. Leneman, L.: *La Tragédie des Juifs en U. R. S. S.* pp. 92ff.

10. Vaksberg, Arkady: "Zasluzhennyi deiatel'." In:*Literaturnaia gazeta,* 15 March 1989, p. 13.

11. "Rehabilitation of the Jewish Anti-Fascist Committee," intr. b. A. Greenbaum. In: *Soviet Jewish Affairs* 19 (1989) 2, pp. 60-70.

12. Izvestiia CC, Nr. 12, December 1989, reprinted in: *Schauprozesse unter Stalin 1932-1952,* pp. 403-411.

### Part 8: After the Trial

1. Hodos, Georg Hermann: *Schauprozesse. Stalinistische Säuberungen in Osteuropa 1948-1954.* Frankfurt a.M. 1988; Herf, J.: *"Antisemitismus in der SED. Geheime Dokumente zum Fall Paul Merker aus SED- und MfS-Archiven."* In: *Vierteljahreshefte für Zeitgeschichte 42* (1994), pp. 635-667.

2. Luks, Leonid: *"Zum Stalinschen Antisemitismus - Brüche und Widersprüche."* In: *Jahrbuch für Historische Kommunismusforschung 1997.* Berlin 1997, p. 42.

3. "Khrushchev's Secret Speech." In: *Entstalimsierung. Der XX. Partei tag der KpdSU und seine Folgen* Frankfurt a.M. 1977, p. 524.

4. Gilboa, Yehoshua: *The Black Years of Soviet Jewry 1939-1953.* Boston, Toronto 1971.

5. Rapoport, Louis: *Hammer, Sichel, Davidstern. Judenverfolgung in der Sowjetunion.* Berlin 1992, p. 208.

6. Antonow-Owssejenko, A.: *Stalin. Porträt einer Tyrannei.* Munich, Zurich 1980.

7. Vaksberg, Arkady: *Stalin Against the Jews.* New York 1994, pp. 257-259.

8. Sheinis, Zinovii: *Provokatsiia veka.* Moscow 1992. I thank Professor Leonid Luks for this real find, which he had published in his essay *"Zum stalischen Antisemitismus"* im *Jahrbuch für Historische Kommunismus forschung* (Berlin 1997).

9. Rapoport, L.: *Hammer, Sichel, Davidstern* p. 208.

10. Typed draft of a letter without handwritten signature, deposited in the archive of the Russian Federation's president, reprinted in: Istochnik, Nr. 1/1997, pp. 143-146.

11. Kostyrchenko, Gennadi: *Out of the Red Shadows. Anti-Semitism in Stalin's Russia.* Amherst, N.J., p. 305.

12. In the original the word "Edinstvo" is also set in quotation marks. It is the Russian title of the JAFC's publication *Eynikeyt*, therefore a quotation from the newspaper whose publisher had been murdered six months before.

13. The bomb attack on the Soviet embassy in Tel Aviv on February 9, 1953, was the cause for the breaking off of diplomatic relations on February 12, 1953.

14. Moshe Scharett (1894-1965), first Israeli foreign minister.

15. Meaning the internationally acknowledged Jewish Agency as official representative of the Jews in Palestine and of the Zionist World Organization as determined by the League of Nations in 1922.

16. After the text of the letter a list follows with the names of the 58 Jewish personalities who should have signed the letter to Stalin:
    S. Volf'kovich, MAS, SPW, D. Dragunskii, Colonel, two-time HSU, I. Ehrenburg, Winner of the International Stalin Prize "For the Manifestation of Peace between the Nations," Y. Kreizer, Major-General, HSU, D. Kharitonskii, Pourer in the factory "Hammer and Sickle," L. Kaganovich, MCCPSU, M. Reisen, NASU, SPW, B. Vannikov, MCCPSU, HsW, L. Landau, MASc, SPW, S. Marshak, Writer, SPW, M. Romm, Movie Director, NASU, SPW, I. Mints, MASc, SPW, D. Reiser, Ministry of the SU, SPW, S. Lavotchkin, Constructor, HsW, A. Zirlin, Colonel-General, O. Zurlonskaia, Physician, I. Dunayevsky, Composer, NASU, SPW, M. Briskman, Kolkhoz Representative, D. Reichin, Principal, G. Landsberg, MASc, SPW, J.Feier, Conductor, NASU, SPW, W. Grossman, Writer, M. Gurevich, Constructor, SPW, S. Kremer, Major General in the Tank Force, HSU, M. Aliger, Writer, SPW, I. Trakhtenberg, MASc, N. Nosovskii, Factory Director, David Oistrakh Violin Virtouso, NASU, SPW, Mariia Kaganovich, Union Representative, M. Lipshits, MePhSU, B. Wul, MASc, SPW, S. Livshits, Factory Foreman, SPW, M. Prudkin, NASU, SPW, M. Smit-Fal'ker, MASc, M. Lantsman, Engineer, Factory Director, E. Gilels, Musician, NASU, SPW, M. Rozental', Philosphy Professor, M. Blanter, Composer SPW, D. Talmud, MASc, SPW, A. Iampol'skii, Railroad Worker, M. Rubinstein, Dr. of Science, S. Roginskii, MASc, SPW, L. Kassil', Writer, SPW, Y. Khavinson, Journalist, A. Leider, Chief Constructor, D. Shchishikov, MASc, SPW, W. Weiz, MASc, SPW, Fikhtengol'd, Musician, I. Koltunov, Engineer, Deputy Factory Director, A. Jerusalem, History Professor, SPW, A. Gel'fond, MASc, S. Messerer, National Artist of the SU (NASU), B. Shapiro, Factory Foreman, K. Solotar, National Educational Functionary, S. Bruk, MASc, M. Smirin, Historian, SPW, E. Lokshin, MASc, A. Shafran, Agricultural Specialist, HSL.
    Abbreviations:
    HSL—Hero of Socialist Labor
    HSU—Hero of the Soviet Union
    MASc—Member of the Academy of Sciences
    SPW—Stalin Prize Winner
    NASU—National Artist of the Soviet Union

MePHSU—Merit Physician of the Soviet Union
Titles are not completely accounted for; and locations were omitted.

17. Yakov Marinin (Khavinson), 1901-1992, was director of TASS from 1939 to 1943 and editor of *Pravda* from 1943 to 1946.

18. David Saslavskii, 1880-1965, was one of the Soviet Union's most famous journalists.

19. Ehrenburg, Ilya: *Menschen, Jahre, Leben* Vol. 3. Munich 1965, p. 551.

20. Altshuler/Arad/Krakovskii (Ed.) *Sovetskie evrei pishut Il'e Erenburgu 1943-1966,* Jerusalem 1993, pp. 79f.

21. See Hodos, G.H.: *Schauprozesse*

22. Cotic, Meir: *The Prague Trial. The First Anti-Zionist Trial in the Communist Bloc.* New York 1987, pp. 219ff.

23. Hodos, G.H.: *Schauprozesse*, p. 139.

24. London, Artur: *Ich gestehe. Der Prozeß um Rudolf Slänsky.* Hamburg 1970.

25. Lise London took part in the presentation ceremony of the French edition of my book *Shalom Libertad!* on September 1991 at the Senate of the Republic in Paris. In the film by Costa Gavras about the trial, based on London's book, Simone Signoret played Lise London in the struggle for the life of her husband and his fight for his comrades from the resistance.

26. London, A.: *Ich gestehe.* pp. 107-111.

27. Weber, Hermann: *Weiße Flecken in der Geschichte. Die KPD-Opfer der Stalinschen Säuberungen und ihre Rehabilitierung.* Frankfurt 1989.

28. See Schafranek, Hans: *Zwischen NKWD und Gestapo. Die Auslieferung deutscher und österreichischer Antifaschisten an Deutschland 1937-1941.* Frankfurt a.M. 1990.

29. Weisberg-Cybulski, Aleksandr: *Hexensabbat. Rußland im Schmelztigel der Säuberungen.* Frankfurt a.M. 1951.

30. Quoted in: Timm, A.: *Hammer, Zirkel, Davidstern. Das gestörte Verhältnis der DDR zu Zionismus und Staat Israel.* Bonn 1997, p. 113.

31. Biography of Dr. Littwak, see Lustiger, Arno: *Schalom Libertad! Juden im spanischen Bürgerkrieg* Frankfurt a.M. 1989, pp. 246-252.

32. A documentary film by the Hesse broadcasting company by Carmen Köper reveals the adventurous life of the Littwaks.

33. Eschwege, H.: *Fremd unter meinesgleichen.* Berlin 1991.

34. Quoted from: Kessler, M.: *Zwischen Repression und Toleranz. Die SED-Politik und die Juden 1949-1967,* p. 57.

35. Hodos, G.H.: *Schauprozesse*, pp. 196ff.

36. Timm, A.: Hammer, *Hammer, Zirkel, Davidstern;* Kiessling, W.: *Partner im 'Narrenparadies'. Der Freundeskreis um Noel Field und Paul Merker.* Berlin 1994; Wolffsohn, M.: *Die Akte Deutschland. Tatsachen und Legenden.* Munich 1995.

37. Offenberg, Ulrike: *"Seid vorsichtig gegen die Machhaber." Die jüdischen Gemeinden in der SBZ und der DDR 1945 bis 1990.* Berlin 1998, pp. 78-90.

38. Ehrenburg, Ilya: *Liudi, Gody, Zhizn'*, Vol. 3. Moscow 1990, p. 324.

39. Sanford, Margery (Pub.): *Belgrade. Breach or Breakthrough? Case History of Refuseniks*. Miami 1977; in. (Pub.): *Mission in Madrid: Monitoring Moscow. Case Histories of the Refuseniks*. Miami 1980; Stern, Barbara: *A Study of Jews Refused Their Right to Leave the Soviet Union*. Montreal 1981.

40. Schloss, Rolf W.: *Laß mein Volk ziehen. Die russischen Juden zwischen Sowjetstern und Davidstern*. Munich 1971, p. 307.

41. Bland-Spitz, Daniela: *Die Lage der Juden und die jüdische Opposition m der Sowjetunion 1967-1977*. Diessenhofen (CH) 1980, pp. 333-334.

42. *Evrei i Evreiskii narod. Sbornik materialov iz sovetskoi pechati*. Jerusalem 1973; *Evreiskii Samizdat. Evrei i Evreiskii narod Jerusalem*, Luckert, Yelena: *Soviet History 1917-1991. An Annotated Bibliography*. New York 1992; Korsch, Boris: *Soviet Publications on Judaism. Zionism and the State of Israel 1984-1988*. New York 1990; Fluk, Louise, R.: *Jews in the Soviet Union. An Annotated Bibliography*. New York 1975; Karasik, Vladimir: Jewish Periodicals in Russia 1960-1994. Tel Aviv 1994.

43. Bland-Spitz, D.: *Die Lage der Juden und die jüdische Opposition in der Sowjetunion 1967-1977*.

44. *A Uniquely Jewish List: The Refuseniks of Russia*. New York 1987.

45. Gilbert, Martin: *Jews of Hope*. London 1984.

46. Gilbert, Martin: *Scharanski. Hero of Our Times*. London 1986.

47. Ibid., p. 268.

48. Potok, Chaim: *Novembernächte. Die Geschichte der Familie Siepak.*. Vienna 1998.

49. Our Ida Nudel. *Testimonies of Former Prisoners and Refuseniks*. Tel Aviv 1980.

50. Quoted according to Messmer, Matthias: *Sowjetischer und postkommunistischer Antisemitismus. Entwicklungen in Russland, der Ukraine und Litauen*. Constance 1997, p. 331.

51. See Laqueur, Walter: Der Schoß ist fruchtbar noch. Der militante Nationalismusder russischen Rechten. Munich 1995; Messmer, M: Sowjetischer und postkommunistischer Antisemitismus.

# INDEX

| DATE | | | |
|---|---|---|---|
| | | | |
| | | | |
| | | | |
| | | | |
| | | | |
| | | | |
| | | | |
| | | | |
| | | | |
| | | | |
| | | | |
| | | | |
| | | | |